Hymes-Ind

Language Intervention Series
Volume IV

# NONSPEECH LANGUAGE AND COMMUNICATION

**NONSPEECH LANGUAGE AND COMMUNICATION Analysis and Intervention**, edited by Richard L. Schiefelbusch, Ph.D., is the fourth volume in the **Language Intervention Series**—Richard L. Schiefelbusch, series editor. Other volumes in this series include:

***Published:***

Volume I **BASES OF LANGUAGE INTERVENTION** edited by *Richard L. Schiefelbusch, Ph.D.*

Volume II **LANGUAGE INTERVENTION STRATEGIES** edited by *Richard L. Schiefelbusch, Ph.D.*

Volume III **LANGUAGE INTERVENTION FROM APE TO CHILD** edited by *Richard L. Schiefelbusch, Ph.D., and John H. Hollis, Ph.D.*

***In preparation:***

**EMERGING LANGUAGE IN AUTISTIC CHILDREN** edited by *Warren H. Fay, Ph.D., and Adriana Luce Schuler, M.A.*

**DEVELOPMENTAL LANGUAGE INTERVENTION Psycholinguistic Applications** edited by *Kenneth F. Ruder, Ph.D., and Michael D. Smith, Ph.D.*

**EARLY LANGUAGE INTERVENTION** edited by *Richard L. Schiefelbusch, Ph.D., and Diane D. Bricker, Ph.D.*

Language Intervention Series
Volume IV

# NONSPEECH LANGUAGE AND COMMUNICATION

## Analysis and Intervention

Edited by

**Richard L. Schiefelbusch, Ph.D.**

University Professor
and
Director, Bureau of Child Research
University of Kansas

Technical Editors

**Marilyn Barket**

**Robert Hoyt**

Bureau of Child Research
University of Kansas

**University Park Press**

Baltimore

UNIVERSITY PARK PRESS
International Publishers in Science, Medicine, and Education
233 East Redwood Street
Baltimore, Maryland 21202



Typeset by American Graphic Arts Corporation
Manufactured in the United States of America by
The Maple Press Company



Jacket illustration by Myron Sahlberg
Jacket design by Bob Christensen

**Library of Congress Cataloging in Publication Data**

Nonspeech Language Conference, Gulf Shores, Ala., 1977.
Nonspeech language and communication.

(Language intervention series; v. 4)
Bibliography: p.
Includes index.
1. Language disorders in children—Congresses.
2. Handicapped children—Language—Congresses.
3. Nonverbal communication—Congresses.
I. Schiefelbusch, Richard L. II. Title. III. Series.
RJ496.L35N66 1977 618.9'28'55 79-26190
ISBN 0-8391-1558-X

## contents

# participants


†**Cathy Alpert, M.A.**
Bureau of Child Research
University of Kansas
Lawrence, Kansas 66045

**Joseph K. Carrier, Jr., Ph.D.**
P.O. Box 21
Bellvue, Colorado 80512

***John B. Carroll, Ph.D.**
Kenan Professor of Psychology
Department of Psychology
University of North Carolina at Chapel Hill
Chapel Hill, North Carolina 27514

***Robin S. Chapman, Ph.D.**
Professor
Department of Communicative Disorders
University of Wisconsin
Madison, Wisconsin 53706

**Joseph B. Couch, Ph.D.**
Department of Psychology
University of Oklahoma
Norman, Oklahoma 73069

**Ruth E. Deich, Ph.D.**
Institute for Research in Human Growth
1737 Finecroft Drive
Claremont, California 91711

**Roger S. Fouts, Ph.D.**
Research Associate
Department of Psychology
University of Oklahoma
Norman, Oklahoma 73069

**Macalyne Fristoe, Ph.D.**
Director, Speech Clinic
Associate Professor
Department of Audiology and Speech Sciences
Purdue University
West Lafayette, Indiana 47907

**Timothy V. Gill, Ph.D.**
Georgia State University
Atlanta, Georgia 30303
and
Yerkes Regional Primate Research Center of Emory University
Atlanta, Georgia 30322

**Sam Glucksberg, Ph.D.**
Professor and Chairman
Department of Psychology
Princeton University
Princeton, New Jersey 08540

***Deberah Harris, Ph.D.**
Area Coordinator, Training and Communication Research
Trace Research and Development Center for the Severely Communicatively Handicapped
University of Wisconsin
Madison, Wisconsin 53706

**Patricia Hodges, Ph.D.**
Institute for Research in Human Growth
1737 Finecroft Drive
Claremont, California 91711
and
Department of Psychology
California State University
Los Angeles, California 90032

***John H. Hollis, Ed.D.**
Research Associate
Bureau of Child Research
University of Kansas
Lawrence, Kansas 66045
and
Kansas Neurological Institute
3107 West 21st Street
Topeka, Kansas 66604

†**Barbara Kates, M.A.**
Ottawa Crippled Children's Treatment Centre
395 Smythe Road
Ottawa, Ontario
Canada

**Robert M. Krauss, Ph.D.**
Professor and Chairman of Psychology
Columbia University
New York, New York 10027

**Lyle L. Lloyd, Ph.D.**
Chairman and Professor of Special Education
Professor of Audiology and Speech Sciences
Purdue University
West Lafayette, Indiana 47907

**Linda McCormick, Ph.D.**
Department of Special Education
School of Education
University of Alabama
Birmingham, Alabama 35294

***Eugene T. McDonald, Ed.D.**
Research Professor Emeritus
Division of Special Education
The Pennsylvania State University
University Park, Pennsylvania 16802

***Shirley McNaughton, B.A.**
Ontario Crippled Children's Centre
350 Rumsey Road
Toronto, Ontario
Canada M4G 1R8

†**Jon F. Miller, Ph.D.**
Professor and Section Head
Department of Communicative Disorders
Waisman Center on Mental Retardation and Human Development
2605 Marsh Lane
University of Wisconsin
Madison, Wisconsin 53706

***Donald F. Moores, Ph.D.**
Head, Division of Special Education and Communication Disorders
The Pennsylvania State University
University Park, Pennsylvania 16802

**D. Kimbrough Oller, Ph.D.**
P. O. Box 520006
Biscayne Annex
Mailman Center for Child Development
University of Miami
Miami, Florida 33152

**Charity R. O'Neil, M.S.**
Parsons Research Center
Parsons State Hospital and Training Center
Parsons, Kansas 67357

**Dorothy A. Parkel, Ph.D.**
Georgia Retardation Center
4770 North Peachtree Road
Atlanta, Georgia 30341
and
Georgia State University
Atlanta, Georgia 30303

**Duane M. Rumbaugh, Ph.D.**
Chairman and Professor
Department of Psychology
Georgia State University
Atlanta, Georgia 30303
and
Yerkes Regional Primate Research Center of Emory University
Atlanta, Georgia 30322

**E. Sue Savage-Rumbaugh, Ph.D.**
Georgia State University
Atlanta, Georgia 30303
and
Yerkes Regional Primate Research Center of Emory Univerity
Atlanta, Georgia 30303

***Benson Schaeffer, Ph.D.**
Associate Professor of Psychology
University of Oregon
Eugene, Oregon 97403

*Richard L. Schiefelbusch, Ph.D.
University Professor and Director, Bureau of Child Research
University of Kansas
Lawrence, Kansas 66045

†Howard C. Shane, Ph.D.
Development and Evaluation Clinic
and
Hearing and Speech Division
Children's Hospital Medical Center
300 Longwood Avenue
Boston, Massachusetts 20155

S. Tom Smith, Jr., M.A.
Georgia State University
Atlanta, Georgia 30303
and
Georgia Retardation Center
Atlanta, Georgia 30341

Herbert F. W. Stahlke, Ph.D.
Georgia State University
Atlanta, Georgia 30303
and
Yerkes Regional Primate Research Center of Emory University
Atlanta, Georgia 30322

*Paula Tallal, Ph.D.
Department of Psychiatry
University of California, San Diego
La Jolla, California 92093
and
Children's Hospital and Health Center
San Diego, California

*Gregg C. Vanderheiden, M.S.
Director
Trace Research and Development Center for the Severely Communicatively Handicapped
University of Wisconsin
Madison, Wisconsin 53706

Harold Warner, B.E.E.
Yerkes Regional Primate Research Center of Emory University
Atlanta, Georgia 30322

*Ronnie Bring Wilbur, Ph.D.
School of Education
Division of Reading and Language Development
Boston University
Boston, Massachusetts 02215

†Diann Hahn Woolman, M.S.
Language and Speech Specialist
Los Angeles County Superintendent of Schools
Los Angeles, California

*S. Vanost Wulz, M.A.
Bureau of Child Research
University of Kansas
Lawrence, Kansas 66045
and
Kansas Neurological Institute
3107 West 21st Street
Topeka, Kansas 66604

David E. Yoder, Ph.D.
Chairman
Department of Communicative Disorders
University of Wisconsin
Madison, Wisconsin 53706

* Contributing author to this volume and conference participant.

† Contributing author only.

# foreword

All children are expected to speak. Parents jot down and cherish the novel words that their children learn. Clinicians and teachers persist in attempts to teach speech even after their efforts fail or produce only limited success. Both parents and professionals know that society expects speech, responds easily and enthusiastically to speech, and designs speaking environments for children.

Alternative modes of communication are usually considered poor substitutes for speech. That is why we all want our children to speak and why we seek diligently to teach speaking skills. The field of speech and hearing is a testimonial to the importance of speaking. Our culture is shaped by the form and the content of our speech. Even our mental health, we are told, depends on our ability to communicate our thoughts, intentions, and needs. Although the dominant form of this communication is speech, the "nonspeech" designs in this volume represent a significant addition to the language literature. Likewise, the designs for analyzing and maintaining alternatives to speech may lead to facilitative symbol behavior for thousands of language-impaired individuals.

On the surface, the expectations of adults for speech behavior in children and our assertion that nonspeech alternatives are highly desirable are ostensibly incongruous. One of the purposes of this book is to resolve this apparent incongruity. In doing this we hope to provide an organized structure for analyzing language and communication, with and without speech modes of presentation. We are aware that we have been accustomed to thinking that language and speech are virtually synonymous. Human language after all is *spoken*, is *audible*, and is learned by *listening* to others. Parents eagerly await the first word and spend hours sorting through the child's babbling and echoic noisemaking for evidence of speech. Children who talk early and well are considered to be bright. Children with speech delays are viewed with mounting concern or even alarm.

Missing from this analysis of speech acquisition are functional designs for noting receptive language (in the absence of speech) and for estimating the extent of the child's unspoken understanding of symbol relationships. "Deaf and dumb" was used for many years to denote deaf children who do not speak. That label suggests that society generally has not perceived language and cognitive functions apart from speech.

The casual reader at this point might conclude that at all costs we must teach a given child to talk. If so, the reader is misled. Instead it should be assumed that nonspeech langauge is important, feasible, and situationally necessary. Perhaps it is easily forgotten that speech as used for transacting language is most feasible for individuals with functional, auditory-perceptual motor systems, who can manage complex cognitive processes and who also are comprehensible to, and able to comprehend, other speakers. Much is taken for granted as we perceive the simple, natural acts of speaking, and as we feel and observe the consequences of speaking.

The first thing we take for granted is that speech is an inherent ability that comes with growth and development. When we observe a nontalking child, we conclude that some developmental component is missing. The assumption may lead us to believe that we should provide for the missing component as quickly and as completely as possible and then proceed to teach speech. The ratonale for such restorative efforts has been taken for granted. The overwhelming desirability of the goal has served to predict the form of the program to be designed. For instance, in many locations one could predict that all deaf children would be taught orally, that all cerebral palsied children would be exhorted to phonate and articulate, and that mentally retarded children would be strongly reinforced for all noises produced with the mouth. In like manner autistic children would be steadfastly taught speech in an interface with the teacher even when the child's preoccupations are limited to drawings or pictures.

The purpose of this book is not to discourage the teaching of speech but rather to examine the range of issues relating to language and communication and to find alternatives for children who cannot speak. The book takes a broad look at language and communication functions. Possible functional models are presented, and strategies for developing alternatives for impaired individuals are considered.

Speech should be taught to all individuals for whom it is functionally feasible. For others we should design viable alternatives so that they may enjoy the benefits of communication, enhance cognitive development, extend social participation, and eventually strengthen their economic well-being.

For some individuals an alternative symbol system will facilitate the attainment of more complex or more standard forms of communication, including speech. For others, the alternative mode will provide an entré into a subculture, into a learning environment, into human fellowship, or into a new world of human dignity. There are many aspects of symbolic processing that we do not understand. Nevertheless, symbol systems permit new dimensions of communication. As we bring functional symbolization into the lives of impaired individuals we will learn important facts that apply to the well-being of everyone who has either a functional or an academic interest in communication.

Richard L. Schiefelbusch, Ph.D.

# preface

The Nonspeech Language Conference held at Gulf Shores, Alabama, in March, 1977, produced a wealth of very functional information for the rapidly expanding study of nonvocal communication. The participants in that conference presented several major papers relating to specific aspects of nonvocal communication, and during the conference they discussed literally dozens of additional issues relating to language and language intervention.

That most fruitful interchange in Alabama has resulted in a compendium of work that has been split into two volumes to make the information more manageable and more accessible to more persons who have an investment or interest in nonvocal communication.

The first volume, *Language Intervention from Ape to Child*, provided historical perspectives on language research with apes and discussed the relevance of that research to human children. It also presented language research that has come from clinical programs with deaf, cerebral palsied, mentally retarded, and autistic children.

That first volume provides a good frame of reference for the content of this second volume. The work in both volumes is synthesized under common models of language and communication. Both volumes assume that certain principles of language and communication are applicable to all children with a variety of handicapping conditions, children who will eventually use similar alternative modes of communication. Taken as a whole, these two volumes provide a model of language that encompasses research with apes and with children, and then extends the language model to include communication events.

Because the complex social events in which handicapped children must survive have such a great influence on their communication, there is an emphasis on social competence. Social demands are equally important for deaf children who cannot produce subtle vocal cues, for mentally retarded children who cannot comprehend subtle messages, and for autistic children who pay little attention to either cues or messages.

Because there has been such an increase in interest in nonvocal communication, these two volumes are of value to a much larger audience than would have been the case even two years ago, and we predict continued expansion of this interest. An even wider professional concern and interest in this area will be seen in the years just ahead.

Thus, our intent in this work is to present the best of what has been done in nonvocal communication so that the best workers in the field, no matter what their academic or professional affiliation, will be able to expand the theory and application of nonvocal communication to more and more handicapped children in a variety of training and living environments.

The fact that this work is now published is due largely to a number of persons other than the editor. Prominent among those persons is Dr. Donald Harrington, who advised, encouraged, guided, helped plan, and supported the funding for this project.

The logistics of the actual conference were handled without flaw by Linda McCormick and her helpers from the University of Alabama at Birmingham.

Extensive assistance in conceptualizing the nonspeech themes of the two books was done by Joe Carrier, Macalyne Fristoe, Roger Fouts, Lyle Lloyd, and Don Moores. Don was instrumental in planning this book and in designing the section on Perspectives on American Sign Language.

The editor proudly acknowledges his editorial colleagues Marilyn Barket and Robert Hoyt. Their intelligence, taste, style, and good sense are reflected in the mechanics of the book. We are also grateful for the quiet competence of Mary Beth Johnston and Thelma Dillon who monitored and prepared the manuscript that led to the completion of the project.

We are proud of the work and grateful for the assistance we received in getting it to print. And we are hopeful that our audience will benefit from reading it and using it to assist them in their work with those handicapped persons who are in dire need of functional communication systems.

R.L.S.

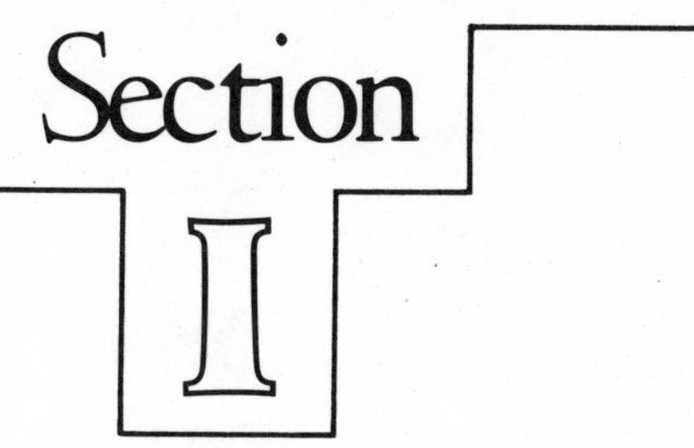


# Introduction

The chapter, "A General System for Language Analysis: Ape to Child," which appeared in the previous Language Intervention series volume, *Language Intervention from Ape to Child* (1979), emphasized the development of nonspeech language using the chimpanzee as a model or "drawing board." It stressed the functional analysis of language and provided a detailed overview in approaches to the development of basic language skills (i.e., receptive language, linguistic rules, and expressive language) in the chimpanzee. The chapter developed in detail a *general system for language* that contrasted a communication channels approach (operant analysis) with a psycholinguistic analysis. This general language system is compatible with language development in the chimpanzee and with speech and nonspeech modes in the human child. The chapter also dealt with functional issues in language development, including physical and psychological environment, social interaction, cognitive development, lexicon source, and communication modes.

The following introductory chapter, "A General System for Nonspeech Language," draws heavily on the chapter in the previous volume and, in addition, develops a language deficiencies model based on the communication channel model of the previous volume. The language deficiencies model provides for a psycholinguistic analysis in a reciprocal system. The chapter concludes with a discussion of communication with respect to functional transactions.

chapter

1

# A General System for Nonspeech Language

*Richard L. Schiefelbusch*

*Bureau of Child Research*
*University of Kansas*
*Lawrence, Kansas*

*John H. Hollis*

*Bureau of Child Research*
*University of Kansas*
*Lawrence, Kansas*
*and*
*Kansas Neurological Institute*
*Topeka, Kansas*

contents

Language and communication are learned rapidly by normal children in informal, casual contexts. Their listening and speaking behaviors combine at an early age to form skills that enable them to participate in a variety of communication contexts. On the way to these skill attainments, infants and preschool children develop their auditory-vocal systems and use speech as the dominant response mode. We correctly assume that individuals with efficient auditory-vocal processes are likely to have flexible communication at all stages of development.

Nevertheless, many children go through the important language acquisition years without learning to talk. Such children are often hearing impaired, severely mentally retarded, autistic, or cerebral palsied. Even at an early age a large proportion of these children seem to be *at risk* for expressive (auditory-vocal) communication. If children cannot vocalize efficiently, or if their auditory inputs are not correctly perceived or perceptually interpreted, they are not likely to acquire speech. Nevertheless, speech is the form of communication behavior that children are expected to produce. The perseveration of this expectancy often extends into the school years.

Unfortunately, as time is lost in the acquisition of a functional language system, the child's handicap may become more serious. The point is that children apparently need an active symbol system with which to map their world and to get appropriate responses from adults who help them learn conceptual relationships.

A child's initial understanding of the world is a product of sensory impressions that are combined into a cognitive/semantic map of the environment. However, given persistent sensory confusions, children may not develop concepts that increase their understanding of language behavior. Lags in acquiring perceptions and concepts may also lead to delayed cognitive development. The effects of these conditions multiply throughout their childhood.

Some children who do not acquire speech-delivered language systems early and quickly do acquire reasonably adequate speech skills later through training. However, others do not make appreciable progress even after years of persistent and skillful programming. Several assumptions justify continuing speech training for language-impaired children. First, speech is the dominant mode in the culture and the one that most persons use in social interactions. Second, the speech system is the most flexible, varied, and semantically complete language usage system available. Third, there are more professionals available to teach speech and to use speech in teaching other language-derived communication forms, such as reading, writing, and spelling. Fourth, specialists who

---

Preparation of this chapter was supported in part by grants HD 07339 and HD 00870 to the Bureau of Child Research, University of Kansas, from the National Institute of Child Health and Child Development.

develop or prescribe training for such children may be unskilled with other language and communication systems.

The last of these issues raises questions for parents and professionals who teach a first language system. This book is addressed to them. If speech usage is beyond the capabilities of many children, an alternative symbol system is necessary. The nature of the alternative system depends on the nature of the child's deficits and upon the characteristics of his impairment. Manual signs, plastic symbols, or lexical displays may be the only communication system the individual can develop. Often, however, the alternative system will be antecedent to the speech-oriented system or will be supplemented by a speech system. In either event, nonspeech alternatives may play an important role in language acquisition.

The orientation of this book is to functional intervention. The purpose is to provide strategies that can be used to teach language and communication.

Unfortunately, researchers and clinicians who study normal and impaired language functions do not have a common functional model. Although there is general agreement that language is a system and that the communication activities of persons who use language are systematic, these complex events are not perceived and studied by all professionals in a common systematic manner. Since language behavior is complex, individuals must determine which events they want to study and why they want to study them. An effective method is to construct a model (an arbitrary organization of events according to some rationale) and find effective ways to relate to a feasible, valid set of events.

If language interventionists have models that have been agreed upon within the research or service communities, there should be little controversy and little reason to develop new models. However, as pointed out in the previous volume (Schiefelbusch and Hollis, 1979), there is confusion about terms, procedures, and operational events across areas of language activity. Perhaps what is needed is a set of explanations covering a general system of language and communication. Given this common orientation, professionals from different backgrounds, using different response modes, could communicate about common issues and functions.

Nonspeech language may be even more difficult to communicate about at this stage than is more conventional language with an auditory-vocal mode of delivery. For instance, articulation, phonation, and inflection have well defined parameters that permit precise scientific analyses and rigorous designs for interpretation and explanation of the analyzed results. Indeed, the entire field of spoken language has progressed to the point where the rules for analysis and description have an accepted set of scientific descriptors that are agreed upon by a rapidly expanding group of related but diverse users. Fortunately, codified designs enable many interventionists to communicate with common terms about issues and results. We do not question the parameters that we listen for, that we record, that we teach, or that we evaluate. Language in this context is a system that is oral, audible, and rule governed.

However, the functions of language, as defined by Moores (Chapter 2, this volume), Harris and Vanderheiden (Chapters 11 and 12, this volume), McNaughton and Kates (Chapter 13, this volume), and Wulz and Hollis (1979), are not dependent on an auditory-vocal mode. Consequently, a common general system of language and communication is needed to encompass the functions that help in planning for nonvocal[1] language and communication.

## A GENERAL SYSTEM OF LANGUAGE

A general system for language is based on a functional analysis of communication channels and linguistic processes (Hollis and Carrier, 1978). Although the system may be viewed as a philosophical orientation, it includes operational definitions and exemplars for the acquisition of nonspeech alternatives in the development of language and communication (see Hollis and Carrier, 1978; Hollis and Schiefelbusch, 1979). In the previous volume (*Language Intervention from Ape to Child*, 1979) issues that bear upon language processing were considered. Included in that design was a language channel model and a psycholinguistic analysis model (see Hollis and Schiefelbusch, 1979).

The channel model involves sensory input, integrative and mediation functions, and response output. The modes of sensory input as displayed are visual, auditory, tactile, and olfactory. The integrative and mediation process levels are imitation, symbolization, construction, and transformation. The modes of output are gross motor actions, signing, writing, and speech (see Hollis and Schiefelbusch, 1979).

---

[1] Three terms frequently appear in discussions of children who do not have a functional speech system: *nonvocal*, *nonspeech*, and *nonverbal*. Unfortunately, none is entirely accurate. *Nonvocal* is used with increasing frequency as a generic designation. However, since most nonspeaking children have relatively intact vocal systems and do make unrefined vocal productions, the term is somewhat misleading. The term *nonspeech* is often inaccurate because many of the children respond to spoken language and may have a small repertoire of spoken words or word-like symbol responses. The term *nonverbal* is also misleading because it literally means that there is no symbol behavior. This condition seldom exists, even for the most impaired children.

In this book a combination of the *nonvocal* and *nonspeech* designations, where the choice depends on the meaning context, is used. The term *nonspeech* refers to children who cannot manage a productive system of spoken language, i.e., children who are nonfunctional in a reciprocal speech system.

The psycholinguistic analysis model includes receptive functions, both nonlinguistic and linguistic conceptualizations, linguistic rules, and expressive language.

In the general system for language, the two models (communication channel and psycholinguistic) are combined and illustrated in Figure 1. The general system for language is discussed in detail in *Language Intervention from Ape to Child*; however, it is reproduced here in order to emphasize the issue of alternative modes, i.e., input–sensory modes (receptive language) and output–response modes (expressive language).

Language intervention strategies are directed toward those individuals who are deficient in receptive language, mediation and integrative functions, and expressive language (Hollis and Carrier, 1978). The communication channel model and the psycholinguistic analysis model provide a convenient method for the assessment of language deficiencies; that is, the models can be set up in a different manner to form a communication and language deficiencies model. Figure 2 illustrates the communication and language deficiencies model.

In the deficiencies model (Figure 2) the channel concept appears on the left as overlapping circles. In the channel model the input-integration (S–O) interaction and the integration-output (O–R) interaction appear as areas of functional difficulty. The psycholinguistic analysis model is similarly displayed on the right of Figure 2. In the psycholinguistic analysis model the areas of functional difficulty are represented as the interaction between receptive language and linguistic rules (A–B) and the interaction between linguistic rules and expressive language (B–C). The possible failure points for both models with respect to class of language deficiency are illustrated in Table 1.

Table 1 lists and labels seven points in the communication and language model at which an impairment or deficiency could significantly affect the communication process. The deficiency model is based in part on the work of Osgood (1957); also see Hollis, Carrier, and Spradlin (1976) and Hollis and Carrier (1978). It should be noted that the language deficiencies model is a single-subject model; the dyadic communication situation is illustrated later in Figure 4.

In the communication and language deficiencies model (Figure 2 and Table 1), areas at which deficiencies may impinge upon the communication process are indicated. For example, a deaf child might be deficient in the following areas: 1) Input (S or A)—Auditory, 2) Output (R or C)—Speech, and 3) Feedback (R–S)—Auditory. If we assume that the child's integration, decoding, and encoding processes are functional, then the communicative deficiencies could be overcome by shifting to a visual input (S or A) and manual sign output (R or C). However, if the deficiencies also include problems of integration (e.g., as in mental retar-

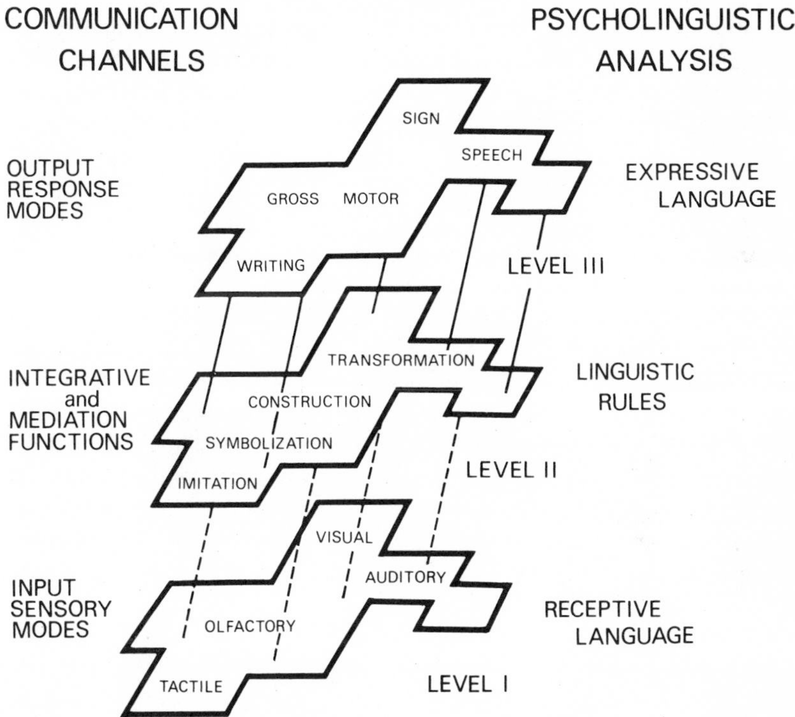


Figure 1. A general system for language. This schema presents a single-subject design contrasting a communication channel approach (operant analysis) with a psycholinguistic analysis.

dation), it may be necessary to institute remedial or prosthetic training procedures to overcome the deficiency.

## A SIMULATED COMMUNICATION PROBLEM

Up to this point the discussion of language and communication has primarily involved a single-subject design. However, communication involves a social transaction model (Figure 3). Therefore, to illustrate communication situations, the dyad is used in the following discussions.

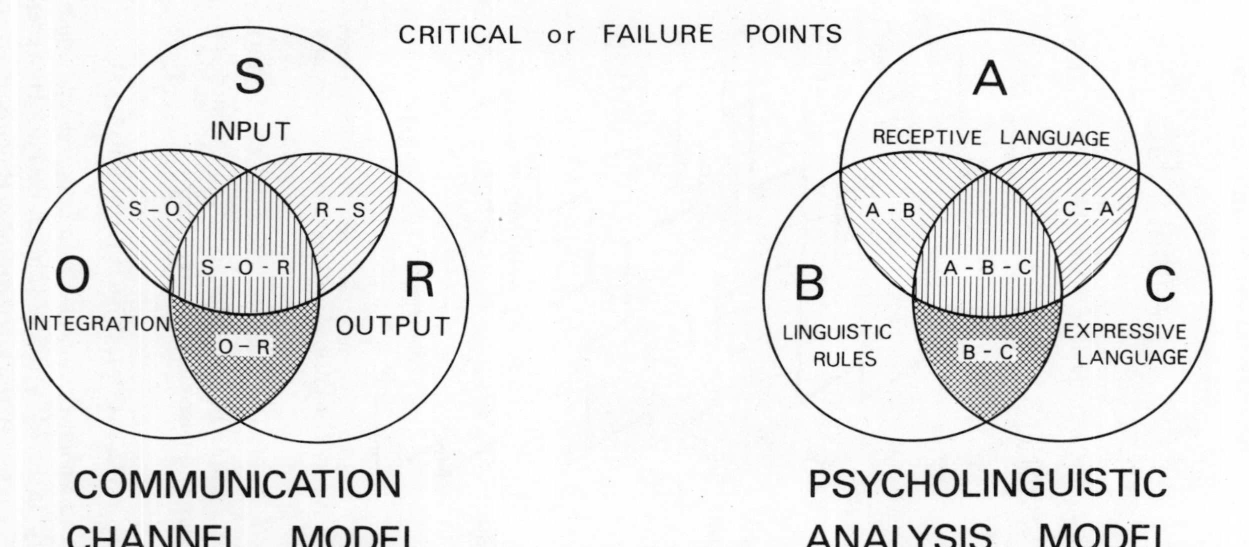


Figure 2. Communication and language deficiencies. This figure compares the communication channel model and the psycholinguistic analysis model with respect to critical or failure points. See text for discussion.

REFERENTIAL COMMUNICATION

Figure 3. Referential communication. The speaker (expressive) and the listener (receptive) have identical sets of blocks (marked with different symbols), but only the speaker knows the correct order for stacking. The speaker must describe the symbols to the listener so an identical stack can be produced (from Glucksberg, Krauss, and Weisberg, 1966).

An important attribute of communication is the process of reference, i.e., the use of symbol modes to designate objects or referents (Rosenburg and Cohen, 1966). A common dyadic situation is one in which a receiver (listener) must select a lever or an object, known as the referent, from a set of nonreferents on the basis of a message (manual signs, speech, and so forth) provided by another individual, the expressor (speaker).

The dyad has been used to study communication between nonhuman primates (Mason and Hollis, 1962) and severely mentally retarded children (Hollis, 1966). The results show that the members of the dyad can learn referential communication. That is, in a four-choice lever situation, the operator (receiver/listener) could select the correct lever (referent) from a group of four levers (referents) on the basis of the informant's (sender's/speaker's) message (symbol mode). Analysis of the data from the nonhuman primate and retardate dyads suggests that *encoding* (Table 1) is the most difficult to learn or reflects the greatest potential for deficiency in the communication system.

A method for studying referential communication in normal preschool children has been reported by Glucksberg, Krauss, and Weisberg (1966). The basic tasks developed by Krauss and Weinheimer (1964a, 1964b) require that visually separated individuals cooperate in a task that requires communication about novel graphic forms (Figure 3). Basically, the children were provided with six blocks, each with a different novel form on the four vertical faces. The task requires that one child (sender/speaker) communicate to the other (receiver/listener) which one of the blocks to stack next (Figure 3). It should be pointed out that the environmental event (novel forms) was the same for each member of the dyad. However, the name or description (symbols) for each novel form (referent) could be idiosyncratic rather than reciprocally shared in the communication situation. In the former case little success would be expected in stacking the blocks in a specific sequence. However, in the latter case there should be a high degree of correspondence between each child's sequence of blocks. In summarizing their research, Glucksberg, Krauss, and Weisberg (1966, p. 334) tentatively concluded:

1. Like adults, preschool children refer to novel forms in terms of object names when attempting to direct the discriminative behavior of a partner.
2. Unlike adults, pairs of preschool children were unable to converge upon a shared nomenclature for novel forms.
3. Preschool children perform reasonably well as listeners when given reference phrases formulated by adults.
4. The reference phrases formulated by preschool children function adequately when used as messages for the individual who formulated them.

**Communication Deficiencies: A Reciprocal System**

In a communication situation each member of a dyad modifies or modulates the other's behavior. This can be illustrated by a simple analysis of referential communication in which four aspects have been suggested by Glucksberg, Krauss, and Weisberg (1966, p. 334): 1) the initial verbal (symbol) message by sender/speaker, 2) the discriminative response of the receiver/listener, 3) verbal (symbol) feedback by receiver/listener, indicating to sender/speaker the nature of his discriminative response, and 4) the effect of the feedback upon sender/speaker, i.e. modification of the initial message by sender/speaker in response to the feedback.

Figure 4 illustrates communication as a reciprocal system and notes those areas where deficiencies can disrupt communication in a dyadic situation. Deficiencies can exist with the sender/speaker (communicant A), the receiver/listener (communicant B), or take the form of trans-

Table 1. The deficiency model

| Communication channel model (Notation) | Class of deficiency (Label) | Psycholinguistic analysis model (Notation) |
|---|---|---|
| S | Input | A |
| O | Integration | B |
| R | Output | C |
| S–O | Decoding | A–B |
| O–R | Encoding | B–C |
| R–S | Feedback | C–A |
| S–O–R | Compound | A–B–C |

mission distraction variables unrelated to the performance or behavior of communicants A and B. Even this simple analysis of communication within dyads suggests at least 15 points at which deficiencies can cause distortion, disruption, or failure in communication. It should be pointed out that, in therapy or language training, communicant A is usually the therapist or teacher.

## Classes of Communication Impairment and Developmental Deficiencies

Developmental deficiencies may adversely affect the acquisition of language and the development of functional communication. This introductory chapter has presented a general system for communication and language based on the assumption that its integral parts can be operationally defined and manipulated. The system also provides for the assessment of specific deficiencies (e.g., sensory input or response output) and a method of assessing points of communication breakdown in the dyadic situation (Figure 4). Thus, the general system is oriented toward those handicapping conditions that contribute to deficiencies in communication.

Table 2 relates classes of communication deficiencies to developmental deficiencies. The table is an extension of Figure 4 and shows the specific points in a reciprocal communication system at which a deficiency could cause the system to fail. In Table 2 the various types of developmental deficiencies are listed with respect to the labels used to denote the various classes within the population. For example, the blind or visually impaired child would fall in class S (impairment of sensory input–visual stimulus). A cerebral palsied child most likely would have impairments of class R (impairment of behavior–motor response) and R–S (impairment of response analysis–motor feedback).

From the standpoint of a communication system analysis (Figure 4 and Table 2), the remediation or prosthesis of the blind child's deficiency

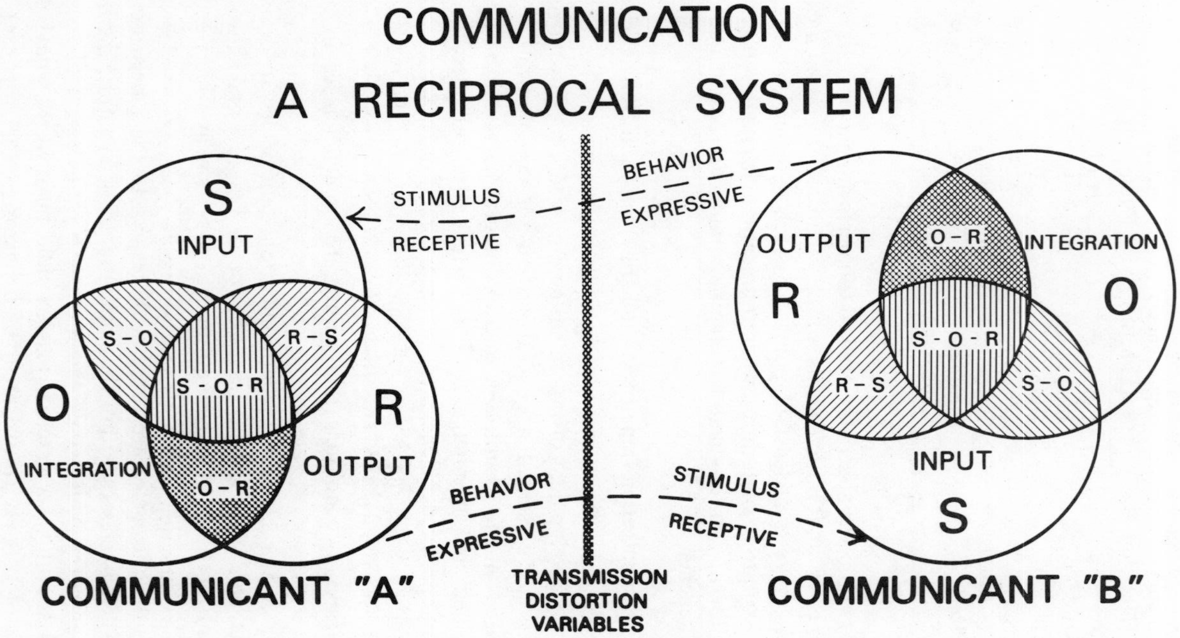

Figure 4. Communication, a reciprocal system. A social transaction analysis of communication. This figure extends the critical or failure points analysis (Figure 2) to a reciprocal system. See text for discussion.

Table 2. Communication deficiencies: A reciprocal system

| Notation | Class of impairment/deficiency | Developmental deficiencies: Type of deficiency | Developmental deficiencies: Population example Impairment labels |
|---|---|---|---|
| S | Impairment of sensory input | 1. Auditory<br>2. Visual<br>3. Tactile<br>4. Olfactory | Auditory impairment (Deaf)<br>Visual impairment (Blind)<br>Oral-kinesthetic<br>Neurological |
| O | Deficiencies in integration and mediation function | 1. Imitation<br>2. Symbolization<br>3. Construction<br>4. Transformation | Mental retardation<br>Aphasia<br>Specific learning disability<br>Autistic/Psychotic |
| R | Impairment of behavior–motor response | 1. Speech<br>2. Writing<br>3. Sign<br>4. Gross motor | Mental retardation<br>Cerebral palsy<br>Neurological<br>Apractic/Dysarthic |
| S–O | Deficiencies in stimulus analysis–decoding | 1. Representation<br>2. Selective attention<br>3. Displacement | Mental retardation<br>Aphasia<br>Neurological |
| O–R | Deficiencies in grammatico-semantico–encoding | 1. Semantics<br>2. Syntactics | Mental retardation<br>Aphasia<br>Neurological |
| R–S | Impairments of response analysis–feedback | 1. Response<br>a. Modulation<br>b. Modification | Auditory impairment<br>Visual impairment<br>Oral-kinesthetic<br>Cerebral palsy |
| S–O–R | Compounded deficiencies or impairments | 1. A totally nonfunctional communication system | Mental retardation—profound<br>Global aphasics<br>Autistic<br>Psychotic |

would involve, for example, shifting to the auditory and/or tactile sensory input class. However, in the case of the cerebral palsied child, where motor behavior deficiencies are significant, prosthetic devices may be employed, for example, touch or pressure switches that will operate communication boards (Harris and Vanderheiden, Chapter 12, this volume). For this type of child, impairments of response analysis–feedback may be shifted from the motor–kinesthetic to the visual and/or auditory mode using prosthetic devices.

At this point in the analysis of communication deficiencies it is essential that we analyze the discussion. The reader should reexamine Figure 2 and note that the communication channel model and the psycholinguistic analysis model are each displayed as a cluster of three overlapping circles. We should now turn to Figure 4 to see that only the communication channel model was used to display the reciprocal (communication) system. One must infer that when channel transactions (input and output) and integration issues are considered, discussions of rule functions pertaining to the syntactics, semantics, and pragmatics of communication are omitted.

We must infer, then, as Krauss (1979) does, that the simple referential system displayed in Figures 3 and 4 is not a fully functional model of language and communication. In the next section, functional dimensions are added to the model. However, a further cautionary note is essential at this point. Both Krauss (1979) and Glucksberg (1979) point out that referential language skills developed in the reciprocal paradigm indicated in Figure 3 do not necessarily generalize to other referential language tasks. This means that one should not assume that skills developed in prescribed contexts will generalize to contexts in other settings.

In summary, the communication channel model of language relates to the structure of language. The input sensory modes and the output response modes (Figure 1) emphasize that alternative language systems may have nonvocal forms of reception and response that serve the process of communication. In the real world this process may break down (Figure 4 and Tables 1 and 2). If nonvocal language is to be functional, it must serve the practical demands of a reciprocal system.

Integrative and mediation processes can also be included in the channel model of language. The rules that govern these features, however, are included in a psycholinguistic analysis of language.

## COMMUNICATION: FUNCTIONAL TRANSACTIONS

In Figure 2 a psycholinguistic analysis model and a communication channel model are presented in order to show the failure points of communication and language deficiencies. However, when the reciprocal nature of communication is displayed in Figure 4, only the channel model is employed. Thus, if the psycholinguistic model is to be used to explain reciprocal functions, additional explanations must be provided.

Perhaps, then, we should reexamine the psycholinguistic design to see what functions should be highlighted.

In the previous volume, Hollis and Schiefelbusch (1979) stated:

> The development of linguistic rules is predicated on the following assumptions: 1) that the child has learned some basic nonlinguistic conceptualizations of environmental events (imitation), 2) that the child has learned that "X" is the name of "Y" (symbolization), 3) that the child has learned to sequence symbols to form a sentence (construction), and 4) that the child's sentence forms demonstrate a knowledge of linguistic rules (transformation). . . . At an abstract level, linguistic rules are a symbolic map that overlays or corresponds to the critical elements within the nonlinguistic conceptualization of the environment (pp. 23–24).

This analysis of linguistic rules bears directly on the syntax of linguistic form. However, it does not explicitly acknowledge the social functions of language and does not project the rules of social discourse. Such rules are an essential part of a system of language and communication.

It is necessary to ask why a child needs a language system. What functions are served by language? Chapman and Miller (personal communication) list several major functions of language in communication.

1. To give information
   a. Reference
   b. Prediction
2. To get information
3. To describe an ongoing event
4. To get the listener to
   a. Do something
   b. Believe something
   c. Feel something
5. To express one's own
   a. Intention
   b. Beliefs
   c. Feelings
6. To indicate a readiness for further communication
7. To solve problems
8. To entertain

The first two functions, to *give* and to *get* information, are classic features of referential language. The third function, to describe an ongoing event, should also be regarded as essentially referential in nature.

However, such descriptions may serve a number of other social functions in certain contexts (to share, to be friendly, to open a conversation, and so on).

The fourth category is clearly indicative of control or influence functions. This is often considered to be an essential function for healthy social existence. The fifth category denotes personal features that are also essential to social transactions. These disclosures key the "other person" to the purposes or features that give meaning to utterances. Category 6 is highly important to the continuity of social exchange.

Category 7, to solve problems, implies both a referential function (to share information) and pragmatic functions (e.g., to influence the listener). The product of these transactions may go beyond the single individual's own capabilities.

The function of entertaining (category 8) may express a desire to be liked, to have fun, to escape boredom, and the like. It expresses a primary feature of gregarious, social activity.

Small children apparently first learn these functions in simple form in direct interactions with adults in the home. A number of simple communicative functions even precede the acquisition of formal language. This fact should have considerable bearing upon our planning for small children who are at risk for speech acquisition. Simply stated, it means that we should engage in social play with a child so that communication functions can be experienced and learned in natural contexts, and it means that we should provide some language symbols for the child to use in mapping these functions into a language system. It seems apparent that the language system need not be expressed in the modes of speech (vocally expressed and auditorially perceived), but can be transacted as sign language, Blissymbols, abstract plastic forms, or other codified features that the child and an adult can share. This sharing, of course, is primarily a beginning stage of the child's language experience that should soon include a range of other communicants. The status of the child as a language user will depend largely on the existence of a flexible, mutually acquired set of functional symbols that the child can use to control his environment, that is, to give and to get information, to describe, to influence, to express intentions, and to entertain. The feasibility of such functions for a nonspeaking child determines whether or not a child has a socially adequate language system.

Speech provides the optimal, flexible means by which transactional functions can be contextually displayed. In comparison, an alternative system may be less flexible. Nevertheless, signs and lexical systems can be used to convey the sheer joy of social expression, to tell a joke or a story, to suggest a plan, to express pleasure or sorrow, or to request information. Furthermore, the social utility of a communication mode depends largely on the social designs into which the system is placed and the skill with which the communicants exercise their pragmatic designs. It is likely that all modes provide the means for increasing skill and dexterity as a consequence of practice. The tragedy is that some children move through important stages of potential experience with no functional system for socializing. The consequences of such a deprived state are severe. The objective, then, should be to design a functional system of language for communication to fit each child. The challenge of that objective is considered in each section of this book.

## SUMMARY

The language model advanced by Hollis and Schiefelbusch is made up of several standard and nonstandard components for considering nonspeech strategies. The standard components include the communication channel analysis advanced by Osgood (1957). This analysis includes an input sensory mode, integrative and mediation process levels, and an output response mode (encoding).

The analysis of channels is subsequently shown to be essential for an alternative system to spoken language.

The input sensory modes include tactile, olfactory, visual, and auditory modes. The integrative and mediation functions include imitation, symbolization, construction, and transformation. The output response modes include gross motor actions, signing, writing, and speech.

In their analysis of alternative output forms, the authors suggest the possibility that linguistic conceptualization may be expressed through lexical, manual, or other systems. The full range of these possible systems is suggested throughout this book.

A general language system plots the essential process components of language as a researcher would organize them. However, it also provides several useful distinctions for clinicians.

1. Integration and mediation are divided into four functions: imitation, symbolization, construction, and transformation. These functions are roughly equivalent to the phases children go through during the intentional sensorimotor period (see Chapman and Miller, Chapter 9, this volume).
2. The *response mode* is broken down into several different classes, each of which can represent the mediation functions.
3. The response modes are also designated as *symbol modes* which can be examined independent of *linguistic rules*. However, when the two

dimensions are considered together, they comprise a dual structure model of language (Hollis and Carrier, 1978).

If one were to summarize what is useful about a general language system, one could say it highlights the issue of *channels*, *integrative functions*, and differential *input and output modes*. As evidenced by the material presented in this volume, each of these issues figures prominently in designs for alternative language systems.

## ACKNOWLEDGMENTS

The authors would like to express their appreciation to those individuals who contributed to the development of this chapter. Special thanks go to Barbara Horrocks and Susan Wulz who contributed substantially to discussion of the general language system and the organization of figures and tables.

## REFERENCES

Glucksberg, S. 1979. Language and communication models. *In* R. L. Schiefelbusch and J. H. Hollis (eds.), Language Intervention from Ape to Child, pp. 107–117. University Park Press, Baltimore.

Glucksberg, S., Krauss, R. M., and Weisberg, R. 1966. Referential communication in nursery school children: Method and some preliminary findings. J. Exp. Child Psychol. 3:333–342.

Hollis, J. H. 1966. Communication within dyads of severely retarded children. Am. J. Ment. Defic. 70:729–744.

Hollis, J. H., and Carrier, J. K., Jr. 1978. Intervention strategies for nonspeech children. *In* R. L. Schiefelbusch (ed.), Language Intervention Strategies, pp. 57–100. University Park Press, Baltimore.

Hollis, J. H., Carrier, J. K., Jr., and Spradlin, J. E. 1976. An approach to remediation of communication and learning deficiencies. *In* L. L. Lloyd (ed.), Communication Assessment and Intervention Strategies, pp. 265–294. University Park Press, Baltimore.

Hollis, J. H., and Schiefelbusch, R. L. 1979. A general system for language analysis. *In* R. L. Schiefelbusch and J. H. Hollis (eds.), Language Intervention from Ape to Child, pp. 3–42. University Park Press, Baltimore.

Krauss, R. M. 1979. Communication models and communicative behavior. *In* R. L. Schiefelbusch and J. H. Hollis (eds.), Language Intervention from Ape to Child, pp. 49–72. University Park Press, Baltimore.

Krauss, R. M., and Weinheimer, S. 1964a. Changes in the length of reference phrases as a function of social interaction: A preliminary study. Psychonom. Soc. 1:113–114.

Krauss, R. M., and Weinheimer, S. 1964b. The effect of feedback on changes in reference phrases. Paper read at the meetings of the Psychonomic Society, Niagara Falls, Ontario.

Mason, W. A., and Hollis, J. H. 1962. Communication between young rhesus monkeys. Animal Behav. 10:211–221.

Osgood, C. E. 1957. A behavioristic analysis of perception and language as cognitive phenomena. *In* J. S. Bruner et al. (eds.), Contemporary Approaches to Cognition. Harvard University Press, Cambridge, Mass.

Rosenberg, S., and Cohen, B. D. 1966. Referential processes of speakers and listeners. Psycholog. Rev. 73:208–231.

Schiefelbusch, R. L., and Hollis, J. H. (eds.). 1979. Language Intervention from Ape to Child. University Park Press, Baltimore.

Skinner, B. F. 1957. Verbal Behavior. Appleton-Century-Crofts, New York.

Wulz, S. V., and Hollis, J. H. 1979. Application of manual signing to the development of reading skills. *In* R. L. Schiefelbusch and J. H. Hollis (eds.), Language Intervention from Ape to Child, pp. 465–489. University Park Press, Baltimore.

# Section II

# Designs for Analyzing Language and Communication

chapter

2

# Alternative Communication Modes

## Visual-Motor Systems

*Donald F. Moores*

*Division of Special Education and Communication Disorders*
*The Pennsylvania State University*
*University Park, Pennsylvania*

contents

It is well known that language and communication functions are learned rapidly by children in informal contexts. By the beginning of elementary school most children have acquired integrated speaking and listening skills, which enable them to interact with and influence their environments. These skills include initiating communication, giving and following directions, narrating stories, and taking turns. Within a few years of school entrance, such skills provide the basis for the development of activities like reading, writing, group discussion, and hypothesizing.

The development of such behavior in most children is related to the auditory-vocal channel. The system works with great efficiency, well enough that there is reason to believe that human beings have evolved in such a way as to utilize language in an auditory-vocal manner. All societies have spoken languages. Human beings have undergone secondary adaptation of organs originally developed for other functions such as eating, breathing, and tasting. Also, it appears that very young children have a built-in sensitivity to the human voice and speech sounds. It is generally accepted that the endless diversity of human languages is more apparent than real. Despite superficial variation, all languages seem to be cut from the same cloth.

Even though there appear to be universal features of language and communication systems, there are individuals in all cultures who have not acquired language through the auditory-vocal channel. In order to help individuals who have not acquired language and communication skills in the usual manner, some very basic questions must first be addressed:

1. Is the basis of human language restricted to the auditory-vocal mode or is it related to unique characteristics of the human mind?
2. What is the relationship between speech and nonspeech systems? Can one facilitate the other or impede the other?
3. Can techniques and behaviors learned in a restricted (clinical) situation generalize to other situations?
4. When one moves away from an auditory-vocal mode, what constraints—linguistic or nonlinguistic—are placed on the communication system?

Most of the recent growth of interest in the use of nonspeech systems can be traced to evidence of the effectiveness of manual communication with deaf children of deaf parents and to the introduction of sign language as a pedagogical tool in most programs for the deaf in the United States. At the same time there has been widespread interest in the work conducted with chimps, including those using variants of American Sign Language, abstract plastic symbol systems, and computer displays.

Given the current enthusiasm for manual communication and other nonvocal symbols systems, it is appropriate to sound a cautionary note. American education has a history of enthusiastically embracing fads, expecting miracles, and then completely rejecting the ideas and techniques when miracles do not occur. At present manual communication and other nonvocal systems represent a fad. Although the evidence suggests their use is beneficial to at least some children, there is no evidence that such systems should be introduced without modification for all types of handicapping conditions.

There is a tendency to believe that if something is successful with one group of children it will be successful with all children. It cannot be overemphasized that, although many children may exhibit a common lack of verbal and vocal behavior, the causes and, by implication, the treatment may vary. Failure to achieve what appears to be an identifiable characteristic of the human species—language—may be attributable to one or more of a number of factors, including sensory deficits, such as deafness, mental retardation, or severe emotional-behavioral disturbance, and physical disabilities, such as those suffered by some cerebral palsied individuals.

In dealing with problems of fostering adequate development of severely handicapped children and adults, educators and psychologists have labored under the influence of many assumptions or implicit beliefs that to a large extent have determined goals and even specific diagnostic and remedial techniques. Two highly interrelated forces that in the past have militated against the use of nonvocal communication systems might be identified as the press toward "normalcy" and the concentration on output, or response modes, to the exclusion of careful consideration of the complete child within a particular environment.

The goal of normalcy is justifiable; the harm accrues when this goal is distorted or becomes the only objective established for a handicapped individual. The worst abuses of the present mainstreaming movement illustrate the extremes to which such a concept can be pushed. The concept of *least restrictive environment*, promulgated by federal judges, has been distorted in some cases to such an extent that it is believed that mere placement of severely retarded, deaf, and autistic children in "normal" environments, i.e., in physical contiguity in classrooms with nonhandicapped age peers, will tend to normalize handicapped children. Concentration only on output, in coordination with the push toward normalcy, predictably leads to a misperception of fundamental problems. For example, in the case of communication channels, for more than 200 years large numbers of educators of the deaf have perceived the major handicap of deafness as an inability to *speak*, not as an inability to *hear*. In looking at the behavior of deaf children this is a logical—but superficial and incorrect—conclusion. As a result, the greatest effort in education of the deaf traditionally has been directed to the teaching of speech at the expense of academic, social-emotional, and linguistic development. The concentration on speech as the major factor is not limited to educators, speech pathologists, and audiologists. Meadow (1966) has reported that most parents of deaf children tend to perceive the greatest problem as related to inadequacies in speech. Meadow's position is that, without counseling sensitive to their needs, most parents are unable to work through their grief to the extent that they understand that, regardless of speech ability, deafness is permanent and that deaf children grow up to be deaf adults.

It should also be noted that many deaf adults make similar distinctions. It is interesting that in American Sign Language the sign referring to a hearing person is not related to the sign for *hear*. Rather it is a sign that may be used interchangeably with *speak* or *say*.

It is becoming apparent to more and more people that normalizing the environment does not automatically ensure normal development for a handicapped child. For example, Rondal (1977) has shown that mothers of trainable mentally retarded (TMR) and normal children matched for mean length of utterance (MLU) interact verbally with their children in similar ways. In fact, a non-normal environment may be more effective at fostering development than a "normal" environment. The results of several investigations in which deaf children of deaf parents who used signs were compared to deaf children of hearing parents who relied only on speech indicate superiority for the children of deaf parents in social-emotional adjustment, academic achievement, and even English skills. The children who theoretically had a less normal environment in extent of exposure to spoken English somehow ended up functioning in a more normal manner in relation to standard norms.

The above results suggest a number of possibilities that must remain conjecture for the present but should be explored if intervention programs for handicapped children are to be improved. For example, it is possible that human evolution has predisposed us to naturally and automatically interact with children in ways that are beneficial to development. In relation to language acquisition, examples of this may be observed in turn-taking behavior, parental expansion of children's utterances, reinforcement of attending behavior, and parental modification of their rates of speech, tone, and grammatical complexity.

In opposition to a parental natural predisposition to act in certain ways is the evidence that for some children such natural parental behavior does not seem to facilitate optimal development. In fact, in some cases it may actually impede progress. If so, what is needed is intensive evaluation of the characteristics of various types of handicapped children with careful attention to their development under different environments. It is possible that some parents may have to be trained to unlearn, consciously or unconsciously, certain behaviors that would be used naturally and effectively with nonhandicapped children.

Because manual communication systems and sign language systems have been viewed as exotic and outside the realm of normal behavior, their use and potential effectiveness have been misunderstood by most educators. One of the greatest barriers to the utilization of such systems has been the assumption that one had to choose between a vocal system and a manual one. In other words, a belief has existed that use of manual communication detracts from oral skills, impedes the acquisition of English, and is restricted to only concrete situations. Its use was limited only to "failures," that is, to those children who had not acquired oral skills by a certain age and who were condemned to be different.

Beginning with the influence of the work of Stokoe (1960), linguists and educators have come to accept sign systems as true languages in every sense of the word, with complex syntactic, morphological, and semantic properties. In the past 10 years, evidence has accumulated to indicate that the use of manual communication with deaf children, beginning at very young ages, can have positive effects on linguistic, academic, and psychological development. Moores (1974, 1977) and Wilbur (1976) have reviewed the literature on this topic extensively.

Although the use of manual communication, usually in coordination with speech, has received growing acceptance among educators of the deaf, there has continued to be some reluctance to consider its possibilities with other types of handicapped children. The reasons for such reluctance may vary as a function of the handicap and severity of involvement. The uncertainty may also reflect the belief previously held by educators of the deaf that manual communication may impede the development of oral skills. Its use, then, may be seen as a last resort or an admission of failure.

Of equal concern is the previously noted fact that techniques and procedures that have been demonstrated as effective with deaf children suffering from no other handicaps cannot necessarily be applied effectively without modification to children who are severely retarded or who exhibit autistic-like behavior. For example, a deaf child with deaf parents may be exposed to a complete language system from birth and acquire mastery over language in a natural manner. Parents with normal hearing may learn a variant of sign language designed to approximate aspects of English grammar and then use it in coordination with speech with their deaf children in everyday home activities. It is doubtful that either system by itself would be of great benefit for a severely retarded or multihandicapped child.

The nature of the communication system must depend on the nature of the child's deficits and upon the characteristics of the impairment. An alternative nonvocal system might be introduced prior to, in coordination with, or independent of the vocal system, depending on the individual's characteristics and progress. There are several rationales upon which selection of a nonvocal communication system for use with a child or adult might be based:

1. An alternative system may be used as part of a diagnostic procedure to determine patterns of functioning. The introduction of the system may be the first step in a clinical program that may later be generalized to other systems or to other environments.
2. A system may be the most effective means for provision of factual information, for concept development, and for the understanding of a relationship.
3. A system may provide the individual with a mechanism for expressing needs.
4. A system may provide a basis for the establishment of functional language processes.
5. A system may be used to develop, supplement, and/or strengthen oral language skills.
6. An alternative system may enable an individual who understands spoken language but who is not able to speak intelligibly to have a means of expressive communication.
7. An alternative system may provide some individuals with their only effective means of communication.

Nonspeech communication systems include systems of manual communication, graphic systems, which themselves could be subcategorized into orthographic, syllabic, and logographic systems (Clark and Woodcock, 1976), and expressive communication aids for nonvocal, severely handicapped children (McDonald and Schulz, 1973; Vanderheiden and Harris-Vanderheiden, 1976). The present chapter's major concentration is on manual systems. For those readers in need of historical and linguistic information on manual communication, reviews by Moores (1974, 1977) and Wilbur (1976) are recommended.

## WRITTEN AND SYMBOL-SYSTEM MODES OF COMMUNICATION

The manual mode of communication involves the visual-motor channel as the primary means of communication (Moores, 1974). It may involve the use of gestures, fingerspelling, and/or a form of American Sign Language. The manual system may be used either independently or in coordination with the spoken word.

Although the purpose of this chapter is to examine the manual mode as an alternative or supplement to the vocal mode, it should be noted that other modes of communication are available and are being used. These are discussed in detail in Chapter 3 and throughout this book and are therefore mentioned only briefly here. For purposes of the present chapter, other alternative modes may be defined arbitrarily as the written and symbol-system modes.

**The Written Mode**

Aside from the inclusion of fingerspelling, which represents a one-to-one correspondence with the 26-letter written alphabet, the manual mode is distinct from the written mode, which has been used to some extent with handicapped individuals. Broadly defined, the written mode of communication involves the use of written words, phrases, and sentences to communicate. The basic elements of this mode would be the written letters of the alphabet. Many cerebral palsied children, because of severe motor disabilities, are unable to develop functional speech. Frequently they are denied the practice and experience necessary to develop communication and social skills. For the most basic communication a child might be provided cards with the words *yes* and *no* printed on them to convey basic agreement or disagreement. McDonald and Schulz (1973) enabled cerebral palsied children to express their needs by providing pictures and printed words on a language board and allowing the children to point to appropriate pictures and words. As a result of reducing the response demands placed on the children, they appeared more relaxed, and oral responses and vocalizations actually increased.

Using Peck's (1971) system of functional communication, Marshall and Hegrenes (1972) worked with an autistic boy by allowing him access to a typewriter. An investigator would provide the appropriate phoneme to match any letter he would type. He was led through the development of words and phrases and learned to point to correct cards on cue when the words were presented and to sequence them properly. By the final step of the program, the child was expected to write messages in his own words to express his needs.

The use of written, graphic systems, however, has apparently met with success with only a relatively small number of nonvocal children. The major failing seems to be a lack of generalizability to nonclinical environments. This lack of generalization relates to the use of cards. If a child could write, the written form of communication would be quite generalizable. But the problem with writing is that the development of sophisticated spelling and reading skills is mandatory. In other words, if a child does not reach the level of writing his own messages, the system is not generalizable. Thus, although writing is relatively generalizable, this generalization is very difficult to attain because it requires sophisticated spelling and reading skills.

### Symbol-System Mode

The symbol-system mode of communication refers to a nonspeech system that may use symbols varying in size, color, and other attributes, in order to provide the child with the means of receiving and/or expressing messages. Probably the best known example of such a program is the Non-speech Language Initiation Program (Non-SLIP) developed by Carrier and Peak (Carrier, 1974, 1976; Carrier and Peak, 1975), which is based on the work of Premack (1970, 1971; Premack and Premack, 1972, 1974).

Non-SLIP consists of a nonspeech symbol system in which plastic chips in abstract shapes are used as symbols. It is designed to teach the child a set of conceptual skills necessary to the acquisition of functional linguistic communication. Carrier and Peak operated under the assumption that for many children the complexity of the speech response system interferes with language acquisition (Schiefelbusch, Ruder, and Bricker, 1976). Using plastic forms as language constituents, the child may select and arrange units in ways to convey appropriate messages. Similarly, using training procedures based on Premack's work, McLean and McLean (McLean, 1973; McLean and McLean, 1974) trained two of three autistic children to a criteria of six three-element sentences using plastic chips. The investigators assumed that it was effective to reduce the response requirements placed on the children and provide them with the elements of communication (plastic chips) rather than requiring them to generate utterances, either vocal or nonvocal, on their own. Although Schiefelbusch, Ruder, and Bricker (1976) reported mixed success with such an approach, results to date suggest that many children who do not exhibit any language/communication ability when vocal responses are required can develop at least some demonstrable expressive and receptive skills when symbols are provided for them.

De Villiers and Naughton (1974) developed a nonspeech training program, which also was based on Premack's work. Reported success was minimal. This may have been attributable in part to limited amounts of time devoted to training, which averaged only 15 minutes per child per week.

The rebus system (Clark and Woodcock, 1976) uses ideographic symbols as a means of initiating reading instruction for a variety of children exhibiting a range of communication problems. It has also been used with nonhandicapped children as a mechanism for developing prereading skills while phasing into decoding of traditional orthography.

The Bliss system (Bliss, 1965; Clark and Woodcock, 1976), which employs ideographic symbols to represent concepts, has been used with nonvocal, physically handicapped children with some success (McNaughton and Kates, 1974).

Clark (1977) compared the ease of learning three logographic systems (Non-SLIP, Blissymbolics, and rebus) to that of acquiring traditional orthography. Traditional orthography was more difficult to learn than the logographic systems. The rebus system was easiest to learn, followed by Blissymbolics and Non-SLIP. In all cases, the differences were statistically significant ($p < 0.05$).

Language boards have been employed with symbol systems as well as with written modes. For example, Hagen, Porter, and Brink (1973) reported that children with cerebral palsy learned to respond to coded picture boards to signal distress or a desire for attention. There also has been some work with computers, which is discussed in later chapters in this volume.

**Combined Modes**

Although any mode of communication might be relied on separately, it is probable that much of the research in this area will focus upon combinations of modes. Certainly this is true of investigations into the effectiveness of simultaneous vocal/manual instruction used with deaf children. A program that offers great potential for use with nonvocal children is the Minnesota Early Language Development Sequence (MELDS) program (Clark, Moores, and Woodcock, 1975a, 1975b), which combines the vocal mode, a manual mode (American Sign Language), and a symbol mode (rebus). The program consists of 120 lessons for the classroom or clinic, coordinated with 120 home lessons. The parent or teacher points to, says, and signs each word. Meaning is demonstrated physically, with objects and with pictures. The experimental edition of MELDS has been field tested successfully with hearing-impaired and severely mentally retarded children, as well as with children with developmental language deficits.

It is necessary that the relative effectiveness of the various modes, in isolation and in combination, with handicapped individuals exhibiting various characteristics be investigated so that communication can be initiated as early and as efficiently as possible. The ideal outcome would be the ability to identify the most suitable intervention approach for a particular child at a particular stage of development.

## VISUAL-MOTOR SYSTEMS

### Sign Languages

It is apparent that the development of language in young children involves close integration between sensorimotor and auditory-vocal channels especially in the first two years of life. It is also apparent that adults incorporate visual-motor signals, at least on a paralinguistic basis, into their everyday communication. However, of even more importance is the evidence that human beings from a wide range of cultures can and do develop sophisticated systems of communication based completely on the visual-motor channel when some members of the culture are unable to communicate vocally. In Plato's *Cratylus* the following exchange between Socrates and Hermongenes is reported (Levinson, 1967):

> Socrates: And here I will ask you a question: Suppose that we had no voice or tongue, and wanted to indicate objects to one another, should we not, like the deaf and dumb, make signs with the hands, head and the rest of the body?
> Hermongenes: How could it be otherwise, Socrates? (p. 359).

In a similar vein St. Augustine argued (Fay, 1912):

> If a man and woman of this kind (deaf) were united in marriage and for any reason they were transferred to some solitary place where, however, they might be able to live, if they should have a son, who was not deaf, how would the latter speak to his parents? How can you think he would do otherwise than reply by gestures to the signs which his parents make to him? . . . for what does it matter, as he grows up whether he speaks or makes gestures, since both these pertain to the soul (p. 213).

When de l'Epée established the first school for the deaf in the eighteenth century he developed a program of instruction based on a manual communication system used by deaf people in Paris. Many of the original signs are part of the lexicography of the present American Sign Language (Moores, 1977).

Although the above references are to classical Rome and Greece and to modern Western cultures, it may be assumed that, even if written records are not available, the situation has been, and is, similar in societies outside of the Hellenic-Judaic tradition. For example, the Tasaday, until recently a completely isolated group in the Philippines, developed a sign language to accommodate deafness in the tribe (Nance, 1976).

Within the past 15 years, the results of several research studies suggest that deaf children of deaf parents appear to be superior in academic achievement, social-emotional adjustment, reading, and ability to express themselves in English compared to deaf children of hearing parents (Stevenson, 1964; Meadow, 1966; Stuckless and Birch, 1966; Vernon and Koh, 1970; Brasel and Quigley, 1975). Coupled with the apparent failure of oral-only preschool programs, which permitted no manual communication (Phillips, 1963; Craig, 1964; McCroskey, 1968), the studies provided the impetus for the introduction of manual communication in the home and classroom with deaf children. The dramatic nature of the change is documented by the results of a survey of communication modes in programs for the deaf reported by Jordan, Gustason, and Rosen (1976), which indicated that 64% of 796 programs for which responses to the survey were received used Total Communication (a combination of speech, sign, and fingerspelling). During the period 1968 to 1975, 302 programs had changed from an oral-only program at the preschool, elementary, junior high school, and high school levels and 335 programs had changed to Total Communication. On the other hand, only five programs had changed to oral-only methods during this period and only eight had changed from Total Communication (p. 530).

It is important to note that such a major revolution was accomplished in a short period of time on the basis of very little empirical data concerning the use of manual communication in the classroom. The change came about largely as a result of indications that deaf children of deaf parents had a language system that developed in a normal manner, in the face of widespread dissatisfaction with the results of oral-only techniques in the classroom. However, whether or not deaf parents use sign language, they may have a greater empathy for deafness, not be subject to major trauma when faced with deafness in a child, and may therefore be better able to foster normal development in a deaf child. This is a possibility which can and should be investigated empirically.

The only major research addressing the classroom use of Total Communication versus oral-only instruction has been longitudinal study of preschool programs (Moores, Weiss, and Goodwin, in press). However, the changes in classrooms reported by Jordan, Gustason, and Rosen (1976) occurred before the final results of this study were reported. Although the results suggest that programs using Total Communication may be more effective than oral-only programs, the use of the Rochester Method, i.e., fingerspelling plus speech—without signs—is just as effective and may produce superior academic achievement.

Related to the tendency of educators not to distinguish between the utilization of a language system by an identifiable group and its use for pedagogical purposes, the Soviet educator Zaitseva, in a review of American Sign Language research, stated (1976):

> . . . it is not clear how the problems of the roles of each of the methods of communication—vocal, dactylic and sign speech—is solved theoretically

> and practically in the total communication system. A unified opinion of how sign language should be used is lacking: as an accepted language of the deaf or, as signs, representing literary English. Evidently, our American colleagues do not yet have sufficient data available to solve this problem, and put before themselves the task of further research in this area (p. 84).

## Pedagogical Modifications

Conscious modification of sign languages for instructional purposes can be traced back to the work of de l'Epée, who added morphological elements to the sign language in use in Paris to reflect elements of French grammar such as verb tenses, number, gender, and so on. In the United States in the nineteenth century controversy existed over whether American Sign Language was a variant of English or a language in its own right and whether or not it should be modified to conform more closely with English morphology and word order. For instruction purposes, signs were developed for parts of the verb *to be* and for articles that were not used in everyday conversation by deaf adults (Moores, 1977). Following the elimination of manual communication from the classroom, many of these elements were dropped from American Sign Language.

At present there are two schools of thought on the issue. On one hand, some linguists argue that American Sign Language is separate from English and that deaf children might first learn this language and later acquire mastery of English as a second language (Stokoe, 1974). The second school holds that such an approach is unrealistic because most parents have normal hearing and therefore the question of the separateness of American Sign Language is irrelevant. Hearing parents of deaf children, according to this argument, can learn a sign language more easily if it is based on spoken language. Several systems, primarily based on the signs of American Sign Language, have been developed for classroom use that add morphological elements for adverbial markings, articles, verb tenses, parts of the verb *to be*, and so forth. The systems have been developed in recent years, coinciding with the renewed acceptance of manual communication in the classroom after decades of neglect. Apparently unaware of the work done in the nineteenth and twentieth centuries, the developers of the "new" systems have invented new signs in a manner highly similar to the process employed by de l'Epée and nineteenth century American educators.

In most instructional programs for the deaf, signs, when used, have been uttered in coordination with the spoken word. Thus the order of signed and spoken words is similar under classroom conditions but not necessarily in social situations among deaf people themselves where sign is not necessarily accompanied by speech. Teachers, then, have for the most part signed in English word order and resorted to fingerspelling elements not commonly used in American Sign Language or expressed in such a manner that they were not perceived by signers with normal hearing. Some examples of commonly spelled elements would be the articles *the* and *an*; prepositions *of* and *by*; parts of the verb *to be—is*, *are*, *was*, *were*, etc.; verb endings, *-s*, *-es*, *-ing*, *-ed*, *-en*, etc.; and the adverbial form *-ly*. For the sentence *The boys were walking quickly*, a teacher would spell *the*, sign *boy*, spell *s*, spell *were*, sign *walk*, spell *-ing*, sign *quick*, and spell *-ly*.

Although the process described may appear tedious, it can be done at the speed of normal conversational speech. The spelled words and affixes represent elements that supposedly are absent in American Sign Language.

Several attempts have been made in recent years to develop signs to represent morphemes of English. The first of this genre in the United States was the Seeing Essential English, or SEE 1, system developed by Anthony (1971), from which two variants, Signing Exact English, or SEE 2 (Gustason, Pfetzing, and Zawolkow, 1972), and Linguistics of Visual English, or LOVE (Wampler, 1971), have grown. Each system is based primarily on the signs of American Sign Language and has added components to convey function words of English, English verb tenses, and other bound morphemes. Reliance on fingerspelling is kept to a minimum. Although the systems vary somewhat, each of their originators claims a close approximation to English morphology has been attained. In terms of use of a particular sign, a two out of three rule is followed; if two words are identical in two of the three categories of pronunciation, spelling, or meaning, they are signed in the same way. In this manner the word "right" referring to *direction* and the word "right" meaning *correct* would be signed the same way in SEE 2 but signed differently in American Sign Language because the two differ conceptually. SEE 2 has become the most commonly utilized of the new systems. In fact, according to a study conducted by Jordan, Gustason, and Rosen (1976), the *Signing Exact English* manual was used as the primary resource in 384 programs from the preschool through high school level. The only other resource that approached its popularity was *A Basic Course in Manual Communication* (ABC), developed by O'Rourke (1973), which represents a system that relies more on fingerspelling and signs combined. ABC was the primary reference source in 334 programs. SEE 2 and ABC were used as the reference source more than all other resources combined.

Although the developers of the sign language modifications claim their systems are based on linguistic principles, the systems present a number of difficulties. SEE 2 is the most sophisticated of the three programs (SEE 1, SEE 2, and LOVE) but still suffers limitations. Wilbur (1976) has dicussed some of the inconsistencies in the newly developed pedagogical systems. For example an *-en* suffix is signed in the words REDDEN (RED+EN), LIGHTEN (LIGHT+EN) and WHITEN (WHITE+EN). Even though in two of the three cases the spelling would not be the same (RED+EN ≠ REDDEN; WHITE+EN ≠ WHITEN), the procedure does follow an English rule for deriving verbs from adjectives (*verb+en*). Unfortunately, the -EN sign is also used for grammatically unrelated items such that *chicken* is signed CHICK+EN; *mitten* as MITT+EN, and *mine* as MY+EN. To further complicate matters, the -EN sign is also used to signify the past participle.

Although no objective evidence exists, it has been the author's subjective opinion that the new systems have had some impact on the manual communication systems used by deaf children and, to some extent, by deaf adults. It is much more common to observe, especially in relatively formal situations, deaf adults utilizing some of the "new" signs to differentiate different parts of the verb *to be* and to express number and tense. The influence seems to be differential, however. For example, the author has noted that the sign IT, which is made in front of the chest, is used more frequently than the signs HE and SHE, which are made at head level. In addition to procedures that may be questioned on purely linguistic bases, it is possible that the developers of the systems were unaware of some physical constraints of visual-motor systems. As an example, in spoken languages, words used most frequently tend to be the shortest words, e.g., *the*, *a*, *of*, *in*, *she*, *he*, *no*, *yes*. This is an example of a natural tendency to conserve effort or to function efficiently. Since it requires greater muscular activity to sign, it is safe to assume that the most commonly used signs would require relatively little effort. It is possible that the invented sign for *it* will be accepted into American Sign Language because of its ease of utterance but that, for *he* and *she*, fingerspelling the short letters in front of the chest will be preferable to the effort of raising the hand to the head.

At present no research exists concerning the relative effectiveness of different types of pedagogical systems. Decisions about which program to use are being based on factors that do not include results of carefully conducted studies.

**Fingerspelling**

The use of fingerspelling, spelling each letter of a word or message, has been documented as a tool in educating deaf children as far back as the early seventeenth century (Bonet, 1620). In fact, the manual alphabet used by the Spanish educators was adopted by de l'Epée in France and is essentially the same alphabet presently in use in the United States (Moores, 1977). Some 300 years ago, the Scottish philosopher Dalgarno (1680) advocated the use of fingerspelling by all members of a family with a deaf child, arguing in this way that the child would grow up and acquire spelled languages as naturally as hearing children acquire spoken language. His position essentially is that of educators of the deaf in the Soviet Union, who begin training through fingerspelling with no signs.

The relatively minor influence of research on classroom methods employed with deaf children in America is best exemplified by the fact that investigators comparing fingerspelling with oral-only programs and with oral-manual programs consistently favor the use of fingerspelling with speech but without signs. However, a relatively small number of programs reserve a primary emphasis for finger spelling. In the Soviet Union, over a period of several years, more than 70 experiments were conducted comparing the effectiveness of fingerspelling alone and fingerspelling plus speech with the traditional Pure Oral Methods. On the basis of results, the Soviets reorganized educational programs for the deaf and instituted Neo-oralism, which has a heavy emphasis on fingerspelling (Moores, 1972). Hester (1963) reported that children in the United States in a preschool program using the Rochester Method (simultaneous speech plus fingerspelling) achieved at higher levels than children who had gone through the program previously when it employed oral-only methods. Quigley (1969) compared children, ages 3½ to 7½ years, taught in an oral-only program to children taught by the Rochester Method and reported that those taught by the Rochester Method were superior in written language, reading, and speechreading.

In a longitudinal study of seven preschool programs across the United States, Moores, Weiss, and Goodwin (in press) found that the children in the one program using the Rochester Method seemed to lag at early ages. By the last year of the study, at an average age of eight, the only difference in academic achievement was a significant superiority for children in the Rochester Method program over children in the one remaining oral-only program. Scores for children in the five total communication programs were intermediate between the two extremes.

Quigley (1969) compared over a five-year period students in three schools being instructed by the Rochester Method matched to students in three schools taught by speech signs and fingerspelling. In all six schools children had been taught exclusively by oral-only techniques until the beginning of the experiment and no differences existed in academic achievement at the beginning of the experiment. At the end of the five-year period, the students taught through the Rochester Method scored higher on all subtests of the Stanford Achievement Test and exhibited superior grammatical skills. The earlier the age that the Rochester Method was begun in the three schools, the greater the relative academic advantage over those using signs, fingerspelling, and speech.

Given the demonstrated effectiveness of the Rochester Method, it is somewhat surprising to note that it is now reportedly used in only six of

353 high school programs and ten of 624 preschool programs (Jordan, Gustason, and Rosen, 1976). In fact, some of the programs that used it experimentally in the research reported above have added signs to instruction. Perhaps fingerspelling is seen as more restrictive or less natural than signing. It would be intriguing to investigate reasons why such a system is so heartily embraced in the Soviet Union but not the United States (or Western Europe).

**Manual Communication with Severely Handicapped, Nonvocal Children**

Although it is reasonable to believe that the use of manual communication might help some children who have not developed adequate vocal skills, it is obvious that in many cases the manner in which manual communication is introduced and the goals established will vary. For example, it is unrealistic to believe that children with severe cognitive, physical, or emotional handicaps would benefit from exposure to the Rochester Method (with its demands on perceptual and motor integration), the complete, sophisticated American Sign Language, or one of ASL's variants.

Rather, the use of manual communication will tend to be on a more restricted basis, usually developed with specific, restricted goals in mind. In fact, signs per se may not even be used. Webster et al. (1973), for example, used a gesture approach to train a nonvocal, autistic boy to follow and give instructions. Rutter (1968) reported that many autistic children respond appropriately to gestures or demonstration but not to the spoken word. Churchill (1972) successfully used a simplified sign language to teach an autistic child association. Baumtrog (1976) achieved some success in teaching signs to three autistic children but reported that hearing was not generalized outside the clinical situation because signs were not used consistently throughout the day.

Miller and Miller (1973) have used American Sign Language, body awareness exercises, and language-training films to train 19 autistic children to use and understand signs related to designed activities or goals. Creedon (1973) has been involved in a program using Total Communication, simultaneous speech, and signing, with autistic children. Creedon reported improvement in socialization and play with resultant decreases in self-stimulation. Children's use of signs was first limited to teachers, and later expanded to include other adults and children. Like Miller and Miller, Creedon found that some of the children who first began to communicate by sign later attempted vocalization. The results suggest that, rather than impeding attempts to develop vocal communication, signs may be an initiator of speech for some children.

Bricker (1972) used sign training effectively with severely language-delayed children by first training children through imitation and later shaping appropriate responses when presented with specific stimuli. Hoffmeister and Farmer (1972) trained a group of institutionalized, deaf, retarded adults to develop a repertoire for functional signs to express needs related to everyday living.

An indication of the expansion of the use of manual communication with nonvocal handicapped individuals is provided by the results of a national survey of speech, hearing, and language services for the retarded (Fristoe, 1975), which reported that 10% of the respondents were using some form of nonvocal communication system. A large proportion of the respondents used vocabulary from American Sign Language, but not necessarily. Mayberry (1976) has discussed various types of manual communication systems and their appropriateness for use with nonverbal individuals of differing etiologies. She argues that success cannot be obtained simply by introducing a hitherto noncommunicating individual to signs.

## SUMMARY

It is clear that manual systems will be used with increasing frequency with nonvocal individuals; however, a precise pattern has not evolved, and thus there is some uncertainty over the forms such systems will take. Systems of manual communication would seem to be uniquely suited for many handicapped individuals. The vocabulary may be as large as the English language or may be limited to a small core of single utterances. Syntax and morphology may be directed or may correspond to the English language. The available evidence suggests that manual communication does not inhibit the development of speech or language skills but might, in fact, act as a facilitator. It is hoped that creative and productive procedures will be developed and evaluated in the near future. With this may come answers to the generalizability of techniques from the clinical situation and closer delineation of constraints inherent in a visual-motor communication mode.

## REFERENCES

Anthony, D. 1971. Seeing Essential English. Educational Services Division, Anaheim School District, Anaheim, Cal.

Baumtrog, C. 1976. The use of nonvocal symbol systems as a means of communication in autistic children. Unpublished master's thesis, University of Minnesota, Minneapolis.

Bellugi, U., and Fischer, S. 1972. A comparison of Sign Language and spoken language: Rate and grammatical mechanisms. Cognition 1:173–200.

Bliss, C. K. 1965. Semantography. Semantography Publications, Sydney, Australia.

Bonet, J. 1620. Redución de las Letras y Arte para Ensenar a Hablar los Mudos. Par Francisco Arbaco de Angelo, Madrid.

Bornstein, H. 1973. A description of some current sign systems designed to represent English. Am. Ann. Deaf 118:454–463.

Brasel, K., and Quigley, S. P. 1975. The Influence of Early Language Environments on the Development of Language in Deaf Children. Institute for Research on Exceptional Children, Urbana, Ill.

Bricker, D. D. 1972. Imitative sign training as a facilitator of word-object association with low functioning children. Am. J. Ment. Defic. 76:509–516.

Carrier, J. K., Jr. 1974. Application of functional analysis and a non-speech response mode to teaching language. ASHA Monogr. No. 18.

Carrier, J. K., Jr. 1976. Application of a nonspeech language system with the severely language handicapped. *In* L. L. Lloyd (ed.), Communication Assessment and Intervention Strategies, pp. 523–548. University Park Press, Baltimore.

Carrier, J. K., Jr., and Peak, T. 1975. Non-speech Language Initiation Program. H & H Enterprises, Lawrence, Kan.

Churchill, D. W. 1972. The relation of infantile early autism and early childhood schizophrenia to developmental language disorders of childhood. 2:182–197.

Clark, C. 1977. A comparative study of young children's ease of learning words represented in the graphic systems of rebus, Bliss, Carrier-Peak, and traditional orthography. Unpublished doctoral dissertation, University of Minnesota, Minneapolis.

Clark, C., Moores, D., and Woodcock, R. 1975a. The Minnesota Early Language Development Sequence: Teacher's Manual. Development Kit #1, University of Minnesota Research, Development and Demonstration Center in Education of Handicapped Children, Minneapolis.

Clark, C., Moores, D., and Woodcock, R. 1975b. The Minnesota Early Language Development Sequence: Parent's Manual. Development Kit #2, University of Minnesota Research, Development and Demonstration Center in Education of Handicapped Children, Minneapolis.

Clark, C., and Woodcock, R. 1976. Graphic systems of communication. *In* L. L. Lloyd (ed.), Communication Assessment and Intervention Strategies, pp. 549–606. University Park Press, Baltimore.

Craig, W. 1964. Effects of preschool training in the development of reading and lipreading skills of deaf children. Am. Ann. Deaf. 107:280–296.

Creedon, M. P. 1973. Language development in nonverbal autistic children using a simultaneous communication system. Paper presented at Society for Research in Child Development Meeting, March, Philadelphia.

Dalgarno, G. 1680. Didascopholus, or The Deaf and Dumbe Man's Tutor. Timothy Holton, Oxford. (Reprinted, 1857, Am. Ann. Deaf 9:16–64).

deVilliers, J., and Naughton, J. 1974. Teaching a symbol language to autistic children. J. Consult. Clin. Psychol. 42:111–117.

Fay, E. A. 1912. What did Lucretius say? Am. Ann. Deaf 57:213.

Friedman, L. 1975. On the semantics of space, time and person reference in the American Sign Language. Language 51:940–961.

Fristoe, M. 1975. Language Intervention Systems of the Retarded. Lurleen B. Wallace Development Center, Decatur, Ala.

Fulwiler, R., and Fouts, R. 1976. Acquisition of American Sign Language by a noncommunicating autistic child. J. Aut.Child. Schizo. 6:43–52.

Gustason, G., Pfetzing, D., and Zawolkow, E. 1972. Signing Exact English. Modern Signs Press, Rossmoor, Cal.

Hagen, C., Porter, W., and Brink, J. 1973. Nonverbal communication: An alternative mode of communication for the child with severe cerebral palsy. J. Speech Hear. Disord. pp. 448–455.

Hester, M. 1963. Manual communication. Proceedings, International Congress on Education of the Deaf, pp. 211–222. U.S. Government Printing Office, Washington, D.C.

Hoffmeister, R., and Farmer, A. 1972. The development of manual sign in mentally retarded deaf individuals. J. Rehabil. Deaf. 6:19–26.

Jordan, I. K., Gustason, G., and Rosen, R. 1976. Current communication trends at programs for the deaf. Am. Ann. Deaf 121:527–532.

Levinson, R. (ed). 1967. A Plato Reader. Houghton Mifflin Co., Boston.

McCroskey, R. 1968. Final progress report of four year home training program. Paper read at Alexander Graham Bell Annual Convention, June, San Francisco.

McDonald, E. T., and Schulz, A. R. 1973. Conversation boards for cerebral palsied children. J. Speech Hear. Disord. 38:73–88.

McLean, L. P. 1973. Acquisition of a nonverbal language form by developmentally delayed, nonverbal children. Unpublished doctoral dissertation, George Peabody College, Nashville.

McLean, L., and McLean, J. 1974. A language training program for nonverbal autistic children. 39:186–193.

McNaughton, S., and Kates, B. 1974. Visual symbols: Communication system for the prereading physically handicapped child. Paper presented at the annual meeting of the American Association on Mental Deficiency, June, Toronto.

Marshall, N., and Hegrenes, J. 1972. The use of written language as a communication system for an austistic child. J. Speech Disord. 37:258–261.

Mayberry, R. 1976. If a chimp can learn sign language, surely my nonverbal client can too. Asha 18:223–229.

Meadow, K. 1966. The effect of early manual communication and family climate in the deaf child's development. Unpublished doctoral dissertation, University of California. Berkeley.

Miller, A., and Miller, E. 1973. Cognitive developmental training with elevated boards and sign language. J. Aut. Child. Schizo. 3:65–85.

Moores, D. F. 1972. Neo-oralism and education of the deaf in the Soviet Union. Except. Child. 38:377–384.

Moores, D. F. 1974. Nonvocal systems of verbal behavior. *In* R. L. Schiefelbusch & L. L. Lloyd (eds.), Language Perspectives—Acquisition, Retardation, and Intervention, pp. 377–417. University Park Press, Baltimore.

Moores, D. F. 1977. Educating the Deaf: Psychology, Principles, and Practices. Houghton Mifflin Co., Boston.

Moores, D. F., Weiss, K., and Goodwin, M. Early intervention programs for hearing impaired children: A longitudinal assessment. ASHA Monogr. In press.

Nance, J. 1976. The Gentle Tasaday. 1976. Harcourt Brace Jovanovich, New York.

O'Rourke, T. J. 1973. A Basic Course in Manual Communication. National Association of the Deaf, Silver Spring, Md.

Peck, B. 1971. Compendium of patterned language. Asha 10:2–3.

Phillips, W. D. 1963. Influence of preschool training on language arts, arithmetic concepts and socialization of young deaf children. Unpublished doctoral dissertation, Teachers College, Columbia University, New York.

Premack, A. J., and Premack, D. 1972. Teaching language to an ape. Sci. Am. 227:92–99.

Premack, D. 1970. A functional analysis of language. J. Exp. Anal. Behav. 14:107–125.

Premack, D. 1971. Language in chimpanzees? Science 172:808–822.

Premack, D., Premack, A. 1974. Teaching visual language to apes and language-deficient persons. *In* R. L. Schiefelbusch and L. L. Lloyd (eds.), Language Perspectives—Acquisition, Retardation, and Intervention, pp. 347–375. University Park Press, Baltimore.

Quigley, S. P. 1969. The influence of fingerspelling on the development of language, communication and educational achievement of deaf children. University of Illinois Institute for Research on Exceptional Children, Champaign-Urbana.

Rondal, J. 1977. Maternal speech to normal and Down's syndrome children matched for mean length of utterance. Am. Assoc. Ment. Defic. Monogr. No. 3.

Rutter, M. 1968. Concepts of autism: A review of research. J. Child Psychol. Psychiatry 9:1–25.

Schiefelbusch, R. L., Ruder, K. F., and Bricker, W. D. 1976. Training strategies for language deficient children: An overview. *In* N. G. Haring and R. L. Schiefelbusch (eds.), Teaching Special Children. McGraw-Hill Book Co., New York.

Stevenson, E. 1964. A study of the educational achievement of deaf children of deaf parents. Cal. News 80:143.

Stokoe, W. C. 1960. Sign Language Structure: An Outline of the Visual Communication System of the American Deaf. Gallaudet College, Washington, D.C.

Stokoe, W. 1974. The use of sign language in teaching English. *In* J. Maestas y Moores (ed.), Educating the Deaf: Some Practical Considerations, pp. 62–85. University of Minnesota, Minneapolis.

Stuckless, E. R., and Birch, J. 1966. The influence of early manual communication on the linguistic development of deaf children. Am. Ann. Deaf 111:452–460, 499, 504.

Vanderheiden, G. C., and Harris-Vanderheiden, D. 1976. Communication techniques and aides for the nonvocal severely handicapped. *In* L. L. Lloyd (ed.), Communication Assessment and Intervention Strategies, pp. 423–500. University Park Press, Baltimore.

Vernon, M., and Koh, S. 1970. Effects of manual communication in deaf children's educational achievement, linguistic competence, oral skills and psychological development. Am. Ann. Deaf. 115:527–536.

Wampler, D. 1971. Linguistics of Visual English. Santa Rosa Public Schools, Santa Rosa, Cal.

Webster, C. D., McPherson, H., Sloman, H., Evans, M. A., and Kucher, E. 1973. Communicating with an autistic boy by gestures. J. Aut. Child. Schizo. 3/4:337–346.

Wilbur, R. B. 1976. The linguistics of manual systems and manual sign languages. *In* L. L. Lloyd (ed.), Communication Assessment and Intervention Strategies, pp. 423–500. University Park Press, Baltimore.

Zaitseva, G. 1976. Main aspects of sign language studies for the deaf in American surdopedagogy. Defectologia 82–85.

chapter

3

# Early Identification and Treatment of Children at Risk for Speech Development

*Eugene T. McDonald*

*Division of Special Education*
*The Pennsylvania State University*
*University Park, Pennsylvania*

contents

Some children can comprehend spoken language but cannot produce intelligible speech. Their competence in receiving and processing language can be demonstrated in many ways, but their expressive use of language is impaired. The effects of this impairment are tremendous. Language and speech have little intrinsic value except for communication.

The work *communicate* comes from a Latin root which means "to make common." It suggests the sharing of ideas and feelings and the asking of questions. Communication is more than the passive reception of what is expressed by others. Communication is a dynamic interpersonal process in which constant shifting of the receiver and expresser roles takes place. Because persons locked into the role of receiver with no expressive capabilities are likely to suffer stunted cognitive, social, and emotional development, it is important that they be identified early and taught how to express themselves by nonspeech means.

## PREEMINENCE OF *COMMUNICATION*

While teachers and speech pathologists have often concentrated on developing language and speech and neglected communication, this recognition of the super-importance of communication is not new. In one of the earliest books about speech problems, Seth and Guthrie (1935) quote Gardiner (1932), who criticized the "common definition in which speech is described as the use of articulate sound-symbols for the expression of thought." They note Gardiner's view that "such a definition overlooks the fundamentally cooperative character of speech which 'presupposes at every stage the mutual interaction of speaker and listener,' and it neglects the facts of its origin in the conditions of socialized or community life."

The views of Seth and Guthrie about speech, language, and communication, expressed in 1935, continue to provide direction for professionals who work with children whose speech is inadequate for communication:

> Speech finds its biological utility insofar as it enables human beings to *communicate* [emphasis supplied] with one another in order to secure cooperation in the accomplishment of ends which they cannot achieve unaided. If expression were the ultimate purpose of speech, it would be achieved when the speaker had succeeded in externalizing the mental process that was the occasion of the particular utterance. But invariably the ultimate purpose of the speaker is to produce some effect upon the persons at whom his speech is directed, to enlist their sympathy, or to influence their thought or behavior along a particular line. The act of speech most often comes full circle only when the speaker receives some indication in the response of his listener that his speech has had the intended effect. The nature of the process is not fundamentally altered when we consider the other form of applied language, namely written speech. The differences are differences of manner or method only, resulting from the lack of immediate contact

> between the writer and his audience. . . . *The life of a human society persists and develops in and through communication* (pp. 64–65; emphasis supplied).

It is impossible to exaggerate the importance of *communication*. As Gray and Wise (1959) point out, "If human beings had no method of communicating with one another, none of the human institutions—industry, religion, government, education—would be possible; there would not even be any human beings." Not only is communication important for society, but the ability to communicate has a powerful influence on a child's social, emotional, and cognitive development as well. Piaget (1926) says that the egocentric child seems to show a lack of concern with being understood, that is, with communicating. The sociocentric child "addresses his hearer, considers his point of view, tries to influence him or actually exchanges ideas with him."

Gray and Wise (1959) offer the observation that communication through language enables individuals to adjust themselves to their physical and social environment. In discussing the socializing function of language, Bram (1955) points out that the ability to speak is prerequisite to full participation in one's society. Clearly, when understandable speech cannot be produced, another mode of expression must be developed if the child is to function actively in even the most simple social setting.

It is not the author's intent to downplay professional efforts directed toward teaching language or developing speech. Rather, the aim here is to set a perspective in which language and speech are important but are not ends in themselves. In the evolution of civilization and in the development of an individual, the importance of language derives from *communication* between one generation and another generation and one individual and another individual (Korzybski, 1933; Hayakawa, 1948). Speech is one way of using language. Vygotsky (1962) says that "the primary function of speech, in both children and adults, is communication, social contact."

Two anecdotes support the view that the ability to *communicate* is more important than mature language competence or intelligible speech:

In Mexico I visited Indian villages, jungle areas, and other remote sections where little English was spoken. The guide for our group was able to get any information we requested, interpret menus, handle warranted and unwarranted complaints from group members—all in all an impressive demonstration of the social utility of language, speech, and communication. He even managed in a remote village to recover a stolen camera and binoculars. I was impressed by his successful communication in these situations and assumed that he possessed considerable linguistic competence. I became aware of how little language one must know in order to communicate effectively when he told me that, other than

English, his knowledge of language consisted only of a modest lexicon in Spanish and the ability to construct sentences in the present tense. Knowing that he intended to make a career of conducting tours in this Spanish-speaking area, I asked him about his plans for learning more Spanish. His answer has important implications for anyone who wants to help handicapped children communicate. He said, "All I need to do is expand my vocabulary." We must be careful that our scientific fascination with language does not result in a concentration on teaching language to the neglect of developing basic *communication* skills for handicapped persons. Obviously, the full use of intelligence and creativity requires a high level of language development; however, many of life's needs can be met and interpersonal relations can be developed with simple language.

The second anecdote demonstrates that emphasis on developing speech for a severely handicapped child can be a misplaced emphasis. David, the first child for whom my colleagues and I developed a communication aid more than 25 years ago, was an early teenage athetoid with good intelligence, but his speech was unintelligible except to his mother. For years, speech pathologists, including myself, had tried without success to teach David to speak. With David in the car, his mother was involved in a serious automobile accident and she was taken unconscious to the emergency room of the hospital. David was uninjured but ambulance and emergency room personnel, not recognizing cerebral palsy, assumed that his unintelligible speech and inability to walk were the result of the accident. It was some time before his difficulty was diagnosed properly. David was shaken by this experience, and his inability to communicate in this critical situation made us realize that our emphasis on speech and language training had very little practical significance. We made him a very simple communication aid consisting of simple statements typed on cards that were held together by a ring. On one card was typed, "My name is David Smith. I live at [such and such an address]." Another card carried the message, "I am cerebral palsied. I can understand but I can't speak." Other cards indicated needs and feelings. This simple communication aid did more than years of speech training to make David a participant in what Mysak (1968) refers to as his "communisphere." With it he was able to communicate to others about who he was, where he lived, the nature of his disorder, his capabilities (seeing, hearing, understanding), his limitations and needs, and his feelings. This simple device so increased his feelings of security that he kept it with him at all times.

One must wonder why, in the face of such strong evidence that children need to develop communication skills, professional workers and parents continue to emphasize speech and language training and hesitate to teach nonspeech methods of communication. Since it is often necessary to counteract these views in order to help a child develop an effective mode of communication, a brief discussion of why professionals and parents resist nonspeech methods of communication might be helpful.

The concerns of the early group of professionals, who are now known as speech/language pathologists, were concentrated on *correcting* defective speech. These early practitioners were known as *speech correctionists*. Their clinical activity was identified as *speech correction*. Their professional organization was called *The American Speech Correction Association*. While delayed speech development was recognized as a clinical problem, it was rarely diagnosed before the child was four or five years old. Treatment was then directed toward developing intelligible speech. For children unable to express themselves orally, development of another mode of expression was seldom attempted. In fact, it was discouraged in the mistaken belief that expression by any means other than speech would interfere with acquisition of speech. We know today that the use of a communication aid actually facilitates speech development (McDonald and Schultz, 1973; Vicker, Schurman, and Kladde, 1974). But until recently, many professionals believed that children should not be encouraged to use gestures, pantomime, or other nonspeech methods of self-expression. That is why many children who, for various reasons, could not (despite the best efforts of speech therapists) learn to talk intelligibly were doomed to passive and limited interpersonal relations.

A subgroup of children with delayed language and speech development, the hearing impaired, attracted the attention of another group of professionals—educators of the deaf. These teachers recognized the importance of early language training, but they could not agree on whether to develop speech, manual expression, or a combination of the two. The oral-manual controversy raged for years, with the oralists claiming—as had the speech correctionists—that the use of manual expression would discourage speech development.

As a result of their experiences with hearing-impaired servicemen during and after World War II, many speech pathologists developed an interest in speech reception. The special field of audiology was born, and the American Speech Correction Association became the American Speech and Hearing Association (ASHA), reflecting an interest in more than correcting defective speech. This broadening of interest has continued. Speech/language pathologists have turned their attention to language training largely in response to expanded educational programming in such areas as mental retardation and learning disabilities. An even broader interest is reflected in a statement published by ASHA to inform the public about the problems of speech-, hearing-, and language-defective persons. The statement proclaims, "Communication is the binding force in every human culture." The importance of this statement for children with unintelligible speech cannot be exaggerated. Children who can receive but who cannot express language develop only weak bonds to the culture. They are often doomed to exist outside the culture or to fumble around on the fringe of it. Professionals who teach only language and speech skills that do not help the child function in the culture may be doing the child a disservice. The objective should always be to develop *communication* skills. In a recent move, ASHA has changed its name to the American Speech-Language-Hearing Association to further underscore the importance of communication.

We have encountered speech pathologists who continue to work for oral expression even after it is apparent that the learner cannot acquire the central processing skills or the neuromuscular control necessary for producing understandable speech. Perhaps, in addition to the view that use of another mode of expression will inhibit speech development, speech pathologists subconsciously feel that teaching a nonspeech mode of expression is an admission of the inability to facilitate speech development and, hence, a professional failure.

There is another important reason why alternative expressive modes are not taught to many children who are unable to develop intelligible speech. It has often been said that speech is "uniquely human." As Denes and Pinson (1963) put it, "Speech, in fact, is one of those few, basic abilities—tool making is another—that set us apart from animals and are closely connected with our ability to think abstractly." Lieberman and Crelin (1971) suggest that "man is human because he can say so." Not to speak, it is claimed, represents a failure to develop an important human characteristic. Many parents insist that their nonspeaking children be taught to talk. They reject a nonspeech method of expression. Parents, therapists, and children of this persuasion must learn the importance of *communication* and realize that speech is but one mode of expression. Other channels for expression may be opened when the speech channel is irremediably disabled.

## FOUNDATION OF LANGUAGE DEVELOPMENT

To help parents understand how children develop language and speech and why some children can understand the speech of others, yet not express themselves, simple figures can be used. Figure 1 explains the foundations of language development, stressing the importance of interactions between the child and the environment (McDonald, 1964; McDonald and Chance, 1964). Using simple language, we explain that at the foundation is the *child* who must possess certain characteristics in order to develop language. First, the child must have a sensorium to

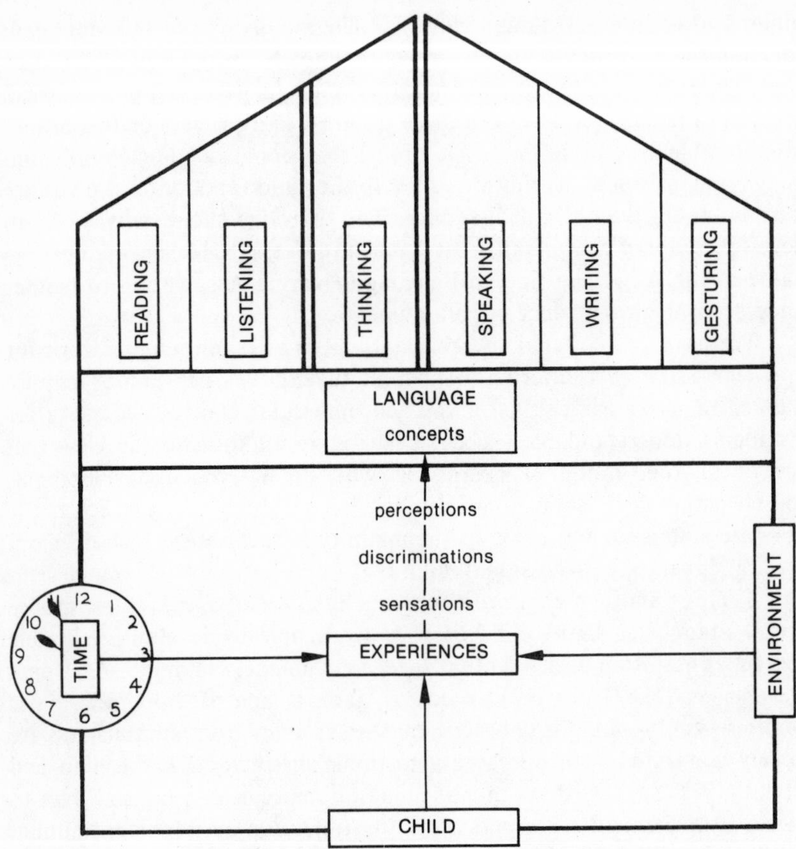


Figure 1. Foundations of language development.

detect stimuli arising in the environment. Second, the child must be able to process these stimuli (receive, interpret, store, retrieve, and so on). The second component of the foundation of language development is the *environment* in which the child exists. The environment includes mother, father, grandmother, grandfather, brothers, sisters, pets, and other signal or stimuli generators. The environment must provide stimuli that the child's sensorium detects, and the environment must reinforce selectively some of the child's reactions to this stimulation. The third component of the foundation of language development is *time* during which maturation and learning take place. The "model" proposes that the *child's* interaction with the *environment* in *time* gives rise to *experiences* that are the building blocks of *language*.

As the child interacts with his environment the first experience appears in the simple form of *sensations*. The stimulation either does or does not produce sensation; that is, either the child detects a change in the environment or the change goes undetected. Later the child notices that some stimuli arising from his environment are different from others. The child thus *discriminates* among stimuli, noting that some sounds are louder than others, some sounds have a different pitch, some visual sensations are different from other visual sensations, and so on. *Perception* occurs as the child adds meaning to these discriminations and generalizes these perceptions into *concepts*.

The diagram helps parents understand why some children can understand speech but cannot speak. It shows that language is used *receptively* for listening and reading; *centrally* for thinking; and *expressively* for speaking, writing, and gesturing. It is possible for children to develop receptive and central language functions, that is, to listen, read, and think without developing expressive functions. However, the reverse is not true. Children cannot develop the expressive functions of speaking, writing, or gesturing until they understand language.

By referring to the diagram, attention can be called to several points at which malfunction might interfere with learning the language. For example, if the child's sensorium does not allow him to detect stimuli arising in his environment, he will have difficulty developing language. If the child's central processing system cannot encode the sensory input, store it, attach symbols to it, and so on, there will be difficulty in developing language. There can be marked deficits in the environment. The severely involved cerebral palsied child might find himself in an environment that provides little or inadequate stimulation. Mother, when she talks with her child, expects to see the child smile or react and thus provide positive reinforcement for her own behavior. When she sees the child smile or his eyes brighten, or when the child makes a movement indicating that he is responding, the mother is inclined to continue her stimulating behavior. But what reinforcement does the mother of a severely handicapped child get? She may get no vocal response, or she may get bizarre responses such as the child grimacing instead of smiling. The child may make unpleasant sounds or grotesque movements that disturb the mother. When a mother's stimulating activities produce such responses in her child, it is natural for the mother to minimize or discontinue activities that enhance language development. For these reasons, many cerebral palsied children do not receive the stimulation they need for experiences that lead to language.

## THE PROCESS OF SPEECH PRODUCTION

Parents sometimes have difficulty understanding why a child can make sounds but cannot learn to speak clearly. Figure 2 can be used to explain

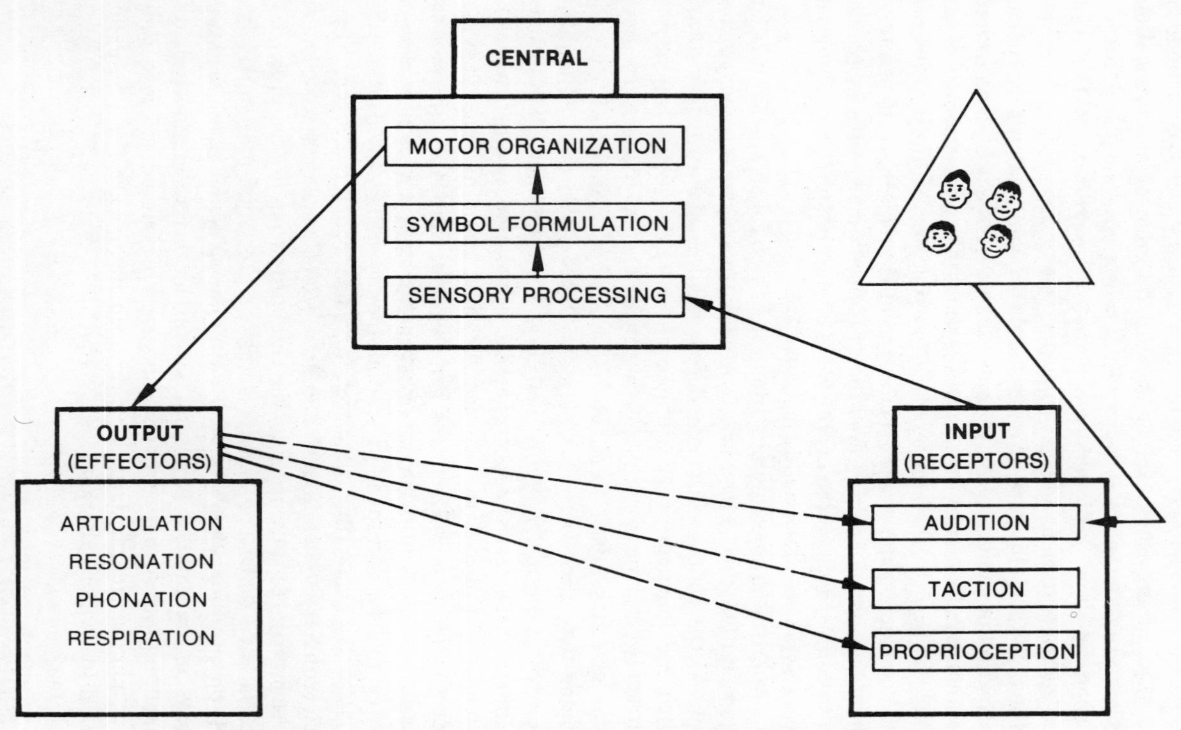


Figure 2. Sensory, central, and motor processes involved in speech production.

in simple language how speech is produced. This very simple model envisions a receptor unit consisting of auditory, tactile, and proprioceptive inputs, a central unit that processes the sensory data, formulates symbols, and issues motor commands, and an output system in which several processes are involved in the production of speech—respiration, phonation, resonation, and articulation.

The basic input for developing speech comes from speakers who provide auditory stimuli. This sensory input goes into a central unit for processing. With maturation and experience the child learns to associate symbols with this input. Later he learns to issue a motor command which directs the speech production mechanism in making noises we call "speech." As he performs these speech-producing functions he gives rise to tactile and proprioceptive sensations that, along with the auditory stimuli arising from his own speech, provide data for controlling the movements of speech. A brief analysis of the effector processes gives clues for interpreting success or failure in reaching milestones in the control of the speech-producing mechanism. The effector system consists of: 1) the respiratory mechanism which provides a source of power in the form of an airstream directed into the 2) larynx where phonation occurs and pitch and loudness changes are effected, and 3) the supralaryngeal vocal tract where the sounds of speech—vowels and consonants—are shaped.

The normal speaker modifies the vegetative respiratory pattern for speech production, changing from a pattern in which inspiration and expiration are about equal in duration to a pattern where inspiration is quicker and expiration is longer and more controlled (Bouhuys, 1974). The speech breathing pattern requires a higher level of neuromuscular integration than is required for rest breathing. Further modifications of the rest breathing pattern are required for producing the phrases and stress patterns for suprasegmental features of connected speech. Some children with neuromuscular dysfunction cannot develop the respiratory control necessary for intelligible speech (Westlake and Rutherford, 1961; McDonald and Chance, 1964; Darley, Aronson, and Brown, 1975).

In speech production, laryngeal function must be changed from the relatively simple valving to prevent aspiration of foreign materials to a more complicated valving in which the vocal folds are approximated with just the right amount of muscle tone to allow the variable horizontal and vertical displacement that produces phonation. Some cerebral palsied children may be observed to adduct the folds with such hypertonus that they are unable to initiate phonation. When such a child attempts to respond to a greeting or question, appropriate articulatory posturing may be observed but no sound is produced. In children who are unable to approximate the folds, their speech is produced with abducted folds and has a breathy quality. Some children have such poor control of laryngeal valving that the air is allowed to escape too rapidly to produce combinations of syllables. The laryngeal condition most incompatible with speech production is hypertonus which interferes with initiation of phonation (Palmer, 1949; McDonald and Chance, 1964; Mysak, 1971; Darley, Aronson, and Brown, 1975).

The vowels, and a few consonants, require only gross movements of oral structures. Production of other consonants requires precise and complex articulatory movements (Perkell, 1969). Malfunction in the supralaryngeal component is sometimes so severe that even the vegetative functions of swallowing and chewing do not develop normally. While speech movements do not evolve from sucking, swallowing, and chewing movements, it seems that a child must have the vegetative functions developed before he can develop the higher level functions necessary for speech production (Bosma, 1975). We have not seen a child with grossly defective chewing, sucking and swallowing who was able to produce intelligible speech. This is not to say that we can develop speech by working solely on chewing, sucking, and swallowing, but it appears that if a child cannot develop the patterns of neuromuscular activity required for the vegetative functions it is unlikely that he will develop the patterns required for intelligible speech (McDonald and Chance, 1964; Finnie, 1968).

## IDENTIFICATION OF CHILDREN AT RISK

Three types of information may indicate that a child will have difficulty developing intelligible speech: 1) history of pregnancy, birth, and neonatal period, 2) comparison of vocal output with expected output at each stage from birth to two years, and 3) examination findings.

### History

Conditions frequently associated with brain damage (e.g., maternal illnesses during pregnancy, difficult delivery, low Apgar scores, and atypical neonatal signs) should cue physicians to alert a specialist in early speech development to follow the infant. Of special concern are those infants with histories of anoxia, seizures, feeding difficulties, atypical cry, hyper- or hypoactivity and respiratory dysfunction (Denhoff and Robinault, 1960; Alderman, 1972).

### Developmental Lags

Increasingly complex neuromuscular control is required as the child's vocalizations progress from crying and reflexive sounds to words and sentences. Careful observation and analysis of vocal behavior at the following stages can reveal early signs of delayed or defective neuromuscular development. While the ages cited are approximate times when a vocal behavior appears, speech development progresses rapidly from birth through three years of age (Van Riper, 1939; Berry, 1969). If the history has been significant and abnormal oromotor signs are present, a developmental lag of a few weeks might be cause for concern.

**During First Two Weeks** Undifferentiated vocalizations consisting of frequent crying and reflexive sounds, such as grunts and hiccups, occur. Only simple neuromuscular control is required to sustain exhalation, approximate the vocal folds, and hold the articulators in simple postures. Failure to cry or crying of peculiar vocal quality may indicate abnormal tone in laryngeal musculature.

**About End of First Month** Vocalizations become more differentiated. One cry quality is associated with hunger, another with pain. Gurgling and cooing sounds are associated with contentment. To produce even this limited variety of noises the infant must exert a greater degree of control over his sound-producing mechanisms. Laryngeal and articulatory adjustments must be made to produce differentiated sounds. Failure to produce differentiated sounds may signal difficulty in obtaining and maintaining articulatory postures through action of the mandibular muscles and the extrinsic lingual musculature.

**About Two Months** Play with vocalization of a single vowel, varying pitch and loudness, emerges. Other vowels are added. The child vocalizes when stimulated and often laughs aloud. This behavior reflects the greater neuromuscular control needed for producing the physiological correlates of pitch and loudness. Production of different vowels requires increased control of lingual and mandibular musculature.

**About Four Months** Child produces consonant-vowel combinations, uttering one CV syllable per exhalation. In connected speech, several syllables are produced on an exhalation. At four months the infant has not yet developed a speech breathing pattern and utters only one syllable on the expiratory portion of a rest breathing cycle.

**About Five Months** Child vocalizes to attract attention. At this point the child is learning the social utility of language. Sufficient neuromuscular control has been achieved to permit simple vocalization on a more voluntary basis.

**About Six Months** Child produces several CV syllables on an exhalation. At this point a speech-supporting breathing pattern has been acquired. This is an important milestone. Some dysarthric children are unable to modify vegetative respiratory patterns to power production of continuous speech. They persist in producing one syllable per exhalation.

**Seven to Eight Months** Child practices inflections while producing several CV syllables on an exhalation. This vocal behavior requires a higher degree of neuromuscular control than the two-month-old infant's variation of pitch and loudness when vocalizing a single vowel.

**About Nine Months** Child initiates vocalization. As an indicator of developing neuromuscular control of the speech-producing mechanism, this is an important milestone. To imitate a sound the infant must detect the acoustic characteristics of the sound and then translate these into a motor command that will result in production of the same acoustic characteristics.

**About 12 Months** Child produces chains of syllables with various consonant-vowel combinations. His expressive vocabulary is comprised of two to three words. For an utterance to be recognized as a word, the same combination of sounds must be produced consistently in association with the referent. Consistency in producing the same articulatory movements for words like "Mama" and "Dada" requires considerable oromotor control. After the first year, speech development consists largely of learning increasingly complex articulatory maneuvers to and from target areas for the phonemes of speech as they occur in a variety of phonetic contexts. For the production of some consonants, fine control of the intrinsic lingual muscles is necessary, a level of control that some children cannot acquire. Even though their vocabulary growth and linguistic competence do progress, they remain incapable of articulating the phonological units called for by their language. Children whose level of oromotor control is adequate for only gross movements of the tongue may never learn to produce the consonants essential to intelligible speech.

### Examination Findings

Of particular interest are evidences of persistent primitive reflex patterns (Fiorentino, 1963; Mysak, 1963; Bobath, 1965), abnormal oral neuromotor signs (Gesell and Amatruda, 1949; Mueller, 1972), and indications of conditions often associated with difficulties in developing intelligible speech (Darley, Aronson, and Brown, 1975).

**Reflex Development** Persistence of tonic reflexes usually signals delayed or pathological development of the central nervous system. The resultant abnormal distribution of muscle tone can interfere with coordination of respiratory, phonatory, and articulatory processes. Retained strong suckling is often associated with inability to perform the complex movements of articulation.

**Abnormal Neuromotor Signs** Uncoordinated movements during sucking and swallowing are typical of the neonate. Early attempts at chewing are not well coordinated. Persistence of these and other immature oromotor functions beyond the age indicated below suggests pathology that might preclude development of intelligible speech:

| | Normal (to age specified) |
|---|---|
| Deficient sucking | 1–2 weeks |
| Choking on fluids | 1–2 weeks |
| Jaw clonus | 6 weeks |
| Choking on semi solids | 28 weeks |
| Excessive air swallowing | 40 weeks |
| Mouth open, drooling | 40 weeks |
| Failure to chew | 18 months |

### Conditions Often Associated with Failure to Develop Intelligible Speech

There is a close relationship between severity of mental retardation and difficulty in communicating. Many children with cerebral palsy have defective speech. Difficulty in oral expression is often associated with childhood aphasia, apraxia, suprabulbar palsy, and hearing impairments.

## TREATMENT OF THE CHILD AT RISK FOR DEVELOPMENT OF INTELLIGIBLE SPEECH

### Role of Parents

When the history, developmental lags, and examination findings suggest that a child might have difficulty developing intelligible speech, it is essential that parents be alerted to this possibility without alarming them. For infants who exhibit problems with a speech breathing pattern, hypertonus of laryngeal musculature, and poor oromotor control, treatment should be initiated to normalize tone and facilitate acquisition of normal movement. This, however, should not be considered enough. Parents, especially the mother, should know that their child might not make sounds like other children. They should be taught to respond positively to any sounds made by the child and to listen for differentiated sounds so they can respond differently to them.

With children who exhibit difficulties with prespeech functions, the importance of teaching the child to respond in a nonspeech mode by looking appropriately in response to questions like "Where is Daddy?", "Where is Mommy?", or "Where is the light?" should be stressed. The child may also need to develop attending skills. The parent must be sure that the child is looking at, focusing on, and being aware of what is going on. With some children it takes a long time to develop these early but essential behaviors (Kent, 1974).

### Providing Opportunities for Expression

After the child has learned to look at or point to a number of objects, his parents can present him with choice situations to help him learn that he can affect his environment by expressive action. For instance, the mother might ask, while she is holding the child's pajamas and toothbrush where he can see them, "Do you want to put your pajamas on first or do you want to have your teeth brushed first?" She would try to get the child to look at his pajamas or toothbrush to indicate which he wants first. This activity is within the child's experience and employs a mode of expression within his capacity. Too frequently what happens to the child who cannot express himself is that someone picks him up, puts his pajamas on, and then brushes his teeth, and the child gains no experience in using an expressive modality in a socially useful way—in a way that allows him to participate in decision making.

The child should be given opportunities to make choices in as many ways as possible. The question "Do you want milk or do you want juice?" gives him a chance to indicate which he wants. Later the child might indicate whether he wants juice or milk by looking selectively at pictures taped on the refrigerator door. In such simple ways the child can learn to indicate what is going on as he receives and processes language. The professional worker and mother should work together to provide the child with opportunities for language expression and to avoid making the child merely the recipient of some action. In other words, parents and professional workers should concentrate on helping the child become a *communicator*.

It has often been said that the older, multihandicapped child seems to lack motivation. Perhaps this results from the child's never having the satisfaction of gaining control over his environment. Communicatively handicapped children develop as passive, dependent individuals, content to have someone feed them, dress them, toilet them, and so on. If they are to learn to want to do things for themselves, they must be given techniques and opportunities early for indicating what they want to do or at least what they want others to do for them.

Small objects or doll furniture might be used instead of pictures. For example, we might take the child into the bathroom, point out the toilet, then call attention to the toilet from the doll furniture, and in this way get across the idea that the small toilet is a symbol for the large toilet. Polaroid camera photographs help children associate pictures with experiences. A picture of a toilet taken and developed while the child watches facilitates teaching the skill of pointing to that picture when the child needs to go to the toilet instead of waiting around until someone comes and asks, "Do you need to go to the bathroom?" Going to the toilet is a very personal affair. The inability of some handicapped persons to achieve independence in toileting is detrimental to their self-image. It is even more devastating to one's feeling of personal worth to be unable to indicate a need for toileting. Not all children with neuromuscular dysfunction will achieve independence, but we can help most of them develop a way to indicate when they need to go instead of suffering the indignity of waiting until someone tells them that it is time to go. Most non-oral persons want a symbol on their communication boards to indicate the *need to go to the toilet.*

Another need is to express a desire for something to drink or something to eat. Just as with toileting, it is common for multiply handicapped children to get food and drink on schedule. A cerebral palsied child whose difficulty with sucking and swallowing might adversely affect fluid balance could need liquids at times other than when the clock tells his attendants to bring juice. If the child has some way of signaling the need for a drink, we are able to provide for this need. With their very serious oromotor malfunction many of these children also have problems getting sufficient food intake. It should not be surprising that they want a symbol to use for communicating *hunger or thirst.*

A third need is for *activity*—to do something such as watch TV, hear a story, or have someone read to or play with them.

Early communication boards usually contain three line drawings: a cup to represent something to eat or drink, a toilet to represent a desire to go to the bathroom, and a TV set to express a wish to do something interesting (see Figure 3). From the simple three-picture communication board, one can go on to develop aids that include not only cognitive material but some affective material as well. To get across the idea of happiness or feeling good, a Polaroid picture of the child's speech clinician (it could be his mother) smiling as she played and had a good time with him can be taken and developed while the child watches so that this facial expression will be associated with the feeling of being happy. When the child feels good or happy, this feeling can be communicated by pointing to this picture. One might, of course, take a picture of the child

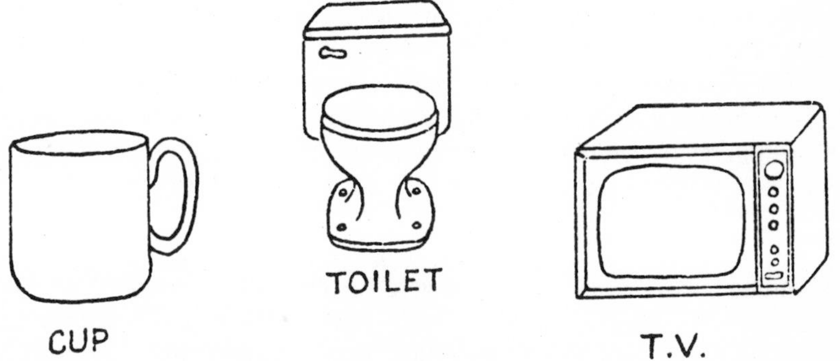


Figure 3. An early communication board.

rather than the clinician. However, children are usually not aware of how *they* look when they are happy or sad. Similarly, to convey feelings of unhappiness, a picture of the clinician frowning while she expressed disapproval of what the child was doing can be used. A picture of the nurse, taken while the child observes, provides a symbol to which the child can point when feeling ill.

**Developing Communication Boards**

In deciding what to put on a communication board it is essential to have the child communicate in any possible way (e.g., by pointing or rejecting things that are suggested) what elements should be on the board. Review of the situations in which the child might want to talk helps identify appropriate items. To facilitate creation of communicating environments, parents should participate in developing the board. We recommend that the boards be individually constructed using simple drawings or photographs made by the child's therapist. The use of commercially prepared boards is discouraged because of the strong belief that language has to grow out of the interaction of the child with his environment. It is now possible to draw on the experiences of many professional workers for help in developing communication boards (Goldberg and Fenton, 1960; Davies, 1973; Dixon and Curry, 1973; McDonald and Schultz, 1973; Vicker, Schurman, and Kladde, 1974; Vanderheiden and Grilley, 1976).

The first communication boards contain only a few lexical items (e.g., see Figure 3). By pointing to the cup the child indicates a need for a drink. Later this picture takes on other meanings such as "I'm hungry," "I want a cookie." Originally, pointing to the picture of a TV indicates that the child wants to watch TV. However, pointing to this picture may soon express a desire to hear a story, listen to music, or participate in other recreational activity.

As the child's vocabulary expands, new pictures are added (Figure 4) to keep pace with the growth of receptive and expressive language and the increased opportunities for communication that arise in his environment. The child's communication board must be viewed as a dynamic medium that can be changed and enlarged rapidly as the child advances in learning and socialization. This is another reason to discourage the use of commercially prepared communication boards. Notice in Figure 4 that the child is learning that Daddy is a man, Mommy is a woman, and the nurse and doctor take care of sick children. The individuality of the board can be seen in the drawing of a fish, an uncommon element of communication boards. It was needed in this display because the child had received a goldfish as a birthday present and naturally wanted to communicate about it. On the other hand, most boards will display

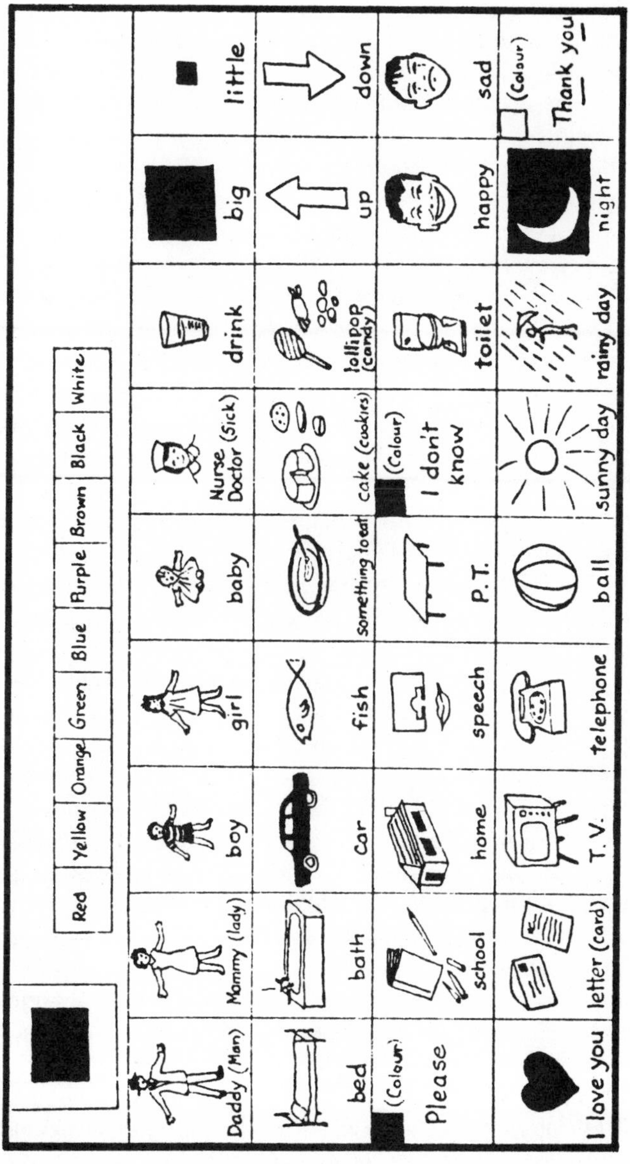

| Red | Yellow | Orange | Green | Blue | Purple | Brown | Black | White |
|---|---|---|---|---|---|---|---|---|

| | | | | | | | | |
|---|---|---|---|---|---|---|---|---|
| Daddy (Man) | Mommy (lady) | boy | girl | baby | Nurse Doctor (Sick) | drink | big | little |
| bed | bath | car | fish | something to eat | cake (cookies) | lollipop (candy) | up | down |
| (Colour) Please | school | home | speech | P.T. | (Colour) I don't know | toilet | happy | sad |
| I love you | letter (card) | T.V. | telephone | ball | sunny day | rainy day | night | (Colour) Thank you |

Figure 4. Picture-word communication board.

symbols to represent happiness, sadness, love, and other feelings. We must provide children with symbols to express affective as well as cognitive materials. Some older children have even requested expletives for expressing strong negative feelings.

The boy whose communication board is illustrated in Figure 5 was beginning to learn to spell. Since he was also learning to type with one finger, the alphabet was displayed in the form of a typewriter keyboard. Note that Kenny was learning the personal pronouns *I* and *me*. He liked to "talk" about his brother Steve and his new baby sister Christine. He was using the prepositions *in*, *out*, *up*, *down*, *under*, *beside*, and *on*.

The symbols displayed on the communication boards in Figure 3, 4, and 5 were not arranged to facilitate sentence construction; however, even in the prereading stage the pictures are arranged in the format of the "key" developed by Fitzgerald (1937). The Fitzgerald Key was developed to teach language structure to deaf children. Its use of columns to represent the various parts of speech is easily adapted to displaying pictures or words on a communication board. Also, examination of the communication boards illustrated here reveals that a word (or words) is printed with each picture. As the child develops skill in communicating, the pictures are faded out and the child learns to read the words as "sight" words. A communication board constructed for a child who no longer needed picture cues is illustrated in Figure 6. Note that the child now has a display that facilitates the use of proper syntax in expressing simple ideas or feelings: "I have a little book"; "I am go(ing) home tomorrow"; "I am sick."

For children whose manual control permits sufficiently rapid and accurate pointing, a direct selection signal can be used. The child points to the appropriate symbol, and the observer names it. For children whose neuromuscular control makes it difficult to point in certain areas, it may be necessary to place the display where the child can make pointing movements with a minimum of involuntary movement or increased tension (see Figures 7 and 8). Direct selection using a headstick as a pointer (Figures 9 and 10) is effective with children who have poor control of the upper extremities but adequate head and neck control to position the tip of the pointer accurately.

For children with limited ability to control arms, hands, and fingers or head and neck, a simple linear encoding procedure makes it possible to indicate a selection from a large display of symbols. In linear encoding the symbols in the display are numbered in sequence beginning with 1. The digits 0 through 9 are displayed where the child can easily touch each digit with a finger, a headstick, or in some other way indicate a number. The child can indicate what words are to be assembled in the intended message by pointing to the numbers that correspond to the words.

Yes Orange Green Purple Yellow Pink White Blue Red Brown Black 1 2 3 4 5 6 7 8 9 0 ?
I me Kenny | man Daddy | woman Mommy | boy Steve | baby girl Christine | No | Q W E R T Y U I O P | A S D F G H J K L | Z X C V B N M $ ¢ ½
school | P.T. | bed | bath | housemother | telephone | car | letter card
toilet bathroom | drink | cake birthday | candy | book story | house home | T.V. playroom | Speech
Please | something to eat | cookies snack | I don't know | Ice cream banana is my favourite! | big | under | happy
ball | in | I feel sick | rainy | up | little | beside | sad
I love you | out | snow cold | Sunny hot | down | day night | on | Thank-you

Figure 5. Picture-word communication board with alphabet.

| 0 1 2 3 4 5 6 7 8 9 10 | | | | | | | |
|---|---|---|---|---|---|---|---|
| YES. HI. HOW ARE YOU? I DON'T KNOW. PLEASE. THANK-YOU. GOOD-BYE. NO. | | | | | | | |
| WHO | VERB | | | WHAT | WHERE | WHEN | |
| I | HAVE | A | BIG | BALL | HOME | NIGHT | RED |
| MOMMY | PLAY | NOT | MY | COOKIE | PLAYROOM | YESTERDAY | YELLOW |
| DADDY | GO | IN | LITTLE | PRESENT | BATHROOM | TOMORROW | ORANGE |
| SANDY | AM | FOR | SICK | FUN | UP | WEEKEND | GREEN |
| LINDA | READ | THE | GOOD | CAR | SCHOOL | SUMMER | BLUE |
| BOY | SEE | WITH | BAD | PUZZLE | OUTSIDE | EASTER | PINK |
| GIRL | MAY | AT | HAPPY | BED | ROOM | CHRIST-MAS | PURPLE |
| YOU | LOVE | TO | SAD | WORDS | P.T. | THANKS-GIVING | BROWN |
| TEACHER | LISTEN | AND | | STORY | STORE | TODAY | BLACK |
| THERAPIST | IS | | | LETTER | INSIDE | | WHITE |
| HOUSE-MOTHER | WANT | | | GAME | DOWN | | |
| | ARE | | | CAKE | SPEECH | | |
| | WILL | | | CANDY | DINING ROOM | | |
| | EAT | | | MAT | | | |
| | LIKE | | | BOOK | | | |
| | GET | | | DRINK | | | |

Figure 6. Word communication board arranged in format of Fitzgerald Key.

A two-step encoding procedure makes communication possible for some children whose poor control of head and upper extremity movements precludes use of the direct selection or linear encoding procedures. In this coding procedure, sometimes referred to as a "column-row" code or an "X-Y" code, the symbols are arranged in rows (X) and columns (Y). Each row is designated by a color and each column by a numeral. (The same effect could be achieved by using, for example, pictures of animals, instead of numerals, for children who do not know numbers). The numbers and colors are also placed around the perimeter of the display (see Figures 11 and 12) where the child can fixate well enough to allow the observer to identify the child's intent. The child is taught the following two-step signal sequence: First, specify the row in which the intended symbol appears by looking at the appropriate color. Second, specify the column by looking at the appropriate number. Some children have become so adept in using this system that multiple displays are needed to keep pace with their expanding expressive capabilities.

For nonambulatory children, the communication boards described above have been designed to be carried on trays attached to wheelchairs. For children who are ambulatory, either unaided or with the assistance of crutches or walkers, the same principles of development and design are followed, but the displays are put on materials the children can carry with them (Figure 13).

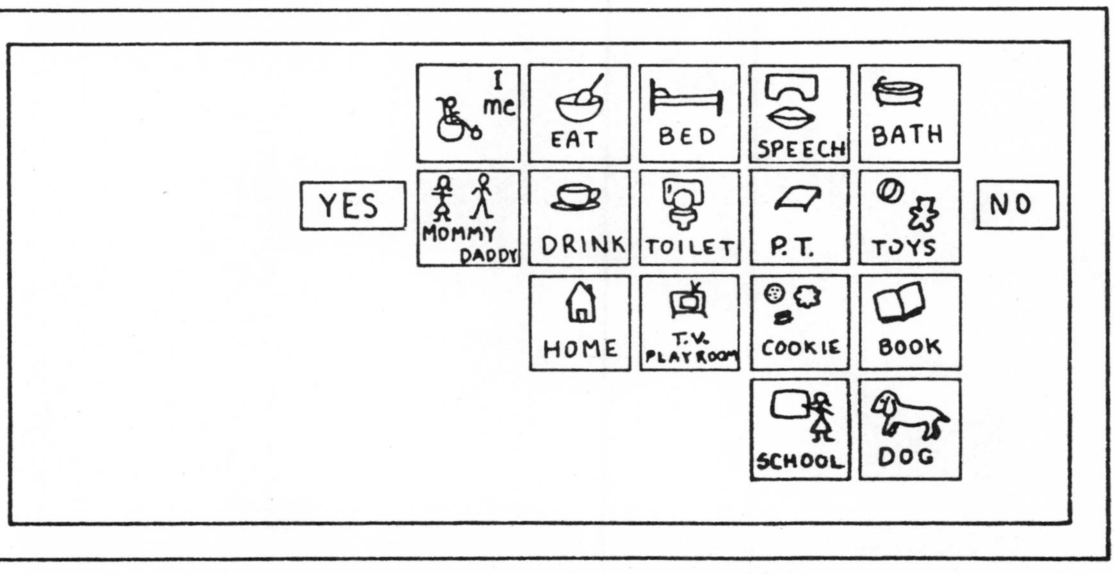


Figure 7. Communication board for child who has difficulty pointing to the left.

Figure 8. Communication board for child who has difficulty pointing to the right.

## Fostering Social, Emotional, and Cognitive Development

Just as with the handicapped individual it is not enough to work on language or speech to the neglect of developing communication skills, so, too, it must be emphasized that it is not enough to provide a child with a communication board. Our obligation extends to creating opportunities for the child to communicate in real-life situations. As noted in *Human Communication and Its Disorders* (1969), ". . . the function we call language involves a system of communication among persons who have grouped themselves together and therefore developed a community wherein certain symbols—both verbal and visual—possess arbitrary conventional meanings." The use of a communication board can help the child (whose speech is unintelligible) communicate, but he needs help in joining those persons "who have grouped themselves together." To reiterate, the word *communicate* has a Latin root that means "to share,

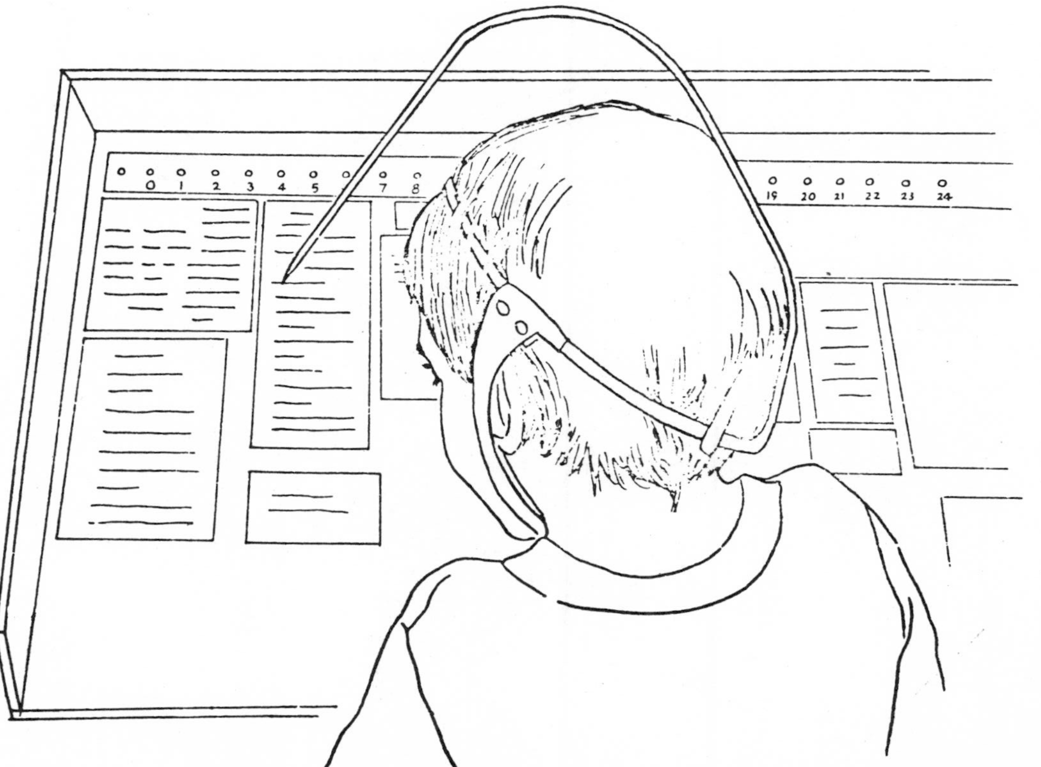


Figure 9. Use of headpointer for direct selection of words arranged in columns.

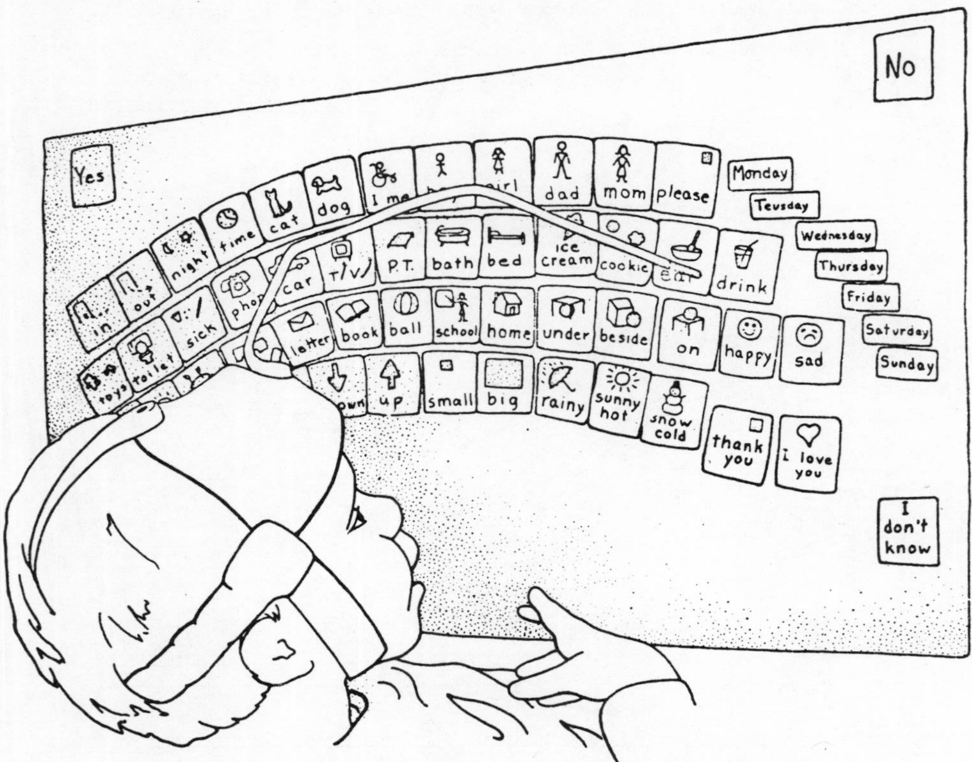


Figure 10. Use of headpointer for direct selection of pictures arranged in an arc to facilitate pointing.

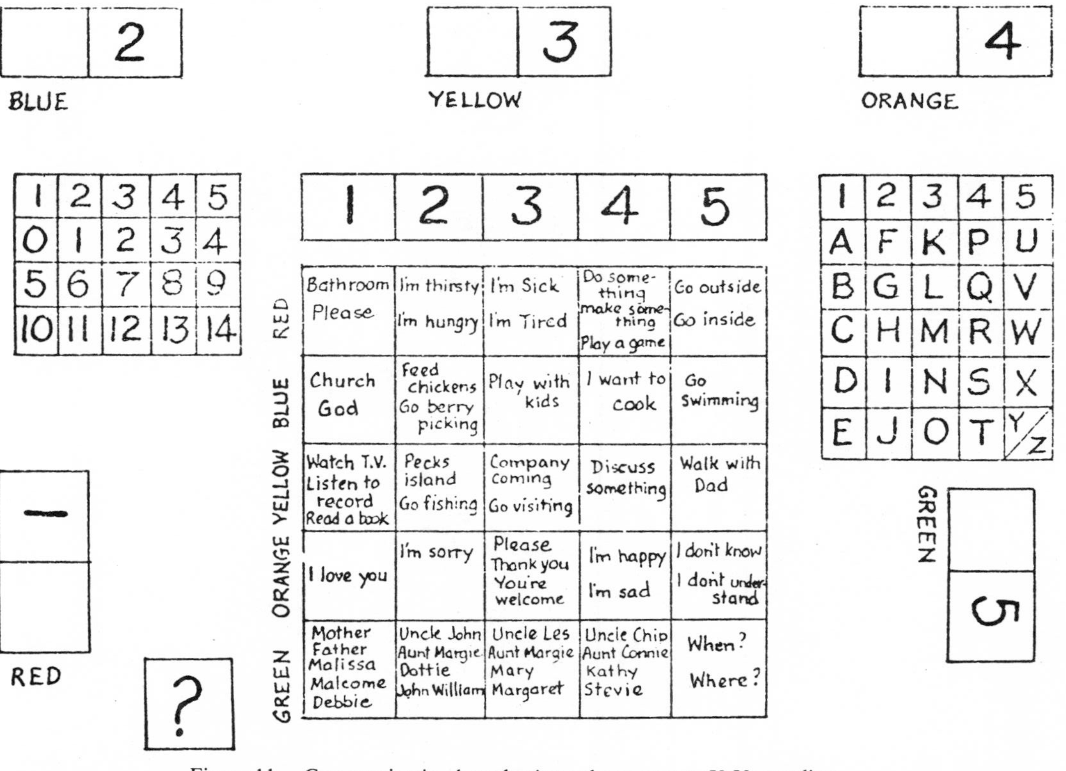


Figure 11. Communication board using column-row or X-Y encoding.

Figure 12. Using eye fixation to signal with an X-Y encoded communication board.

to make common." Even with a communication board a handicapped person cannot share ideas and feelings with himself. Professionals who undertake to help the child who cannot speak intelligibly must have a broader perspective than that of being merely a language teacher. Making language function to advance social, emotional, and cognitive development must be included in the professional's objective. It is not within the scope of this chapter to discuss ways to create real-life opportunities for the nonspeaking child to communicate; yet, it should be pointed out that failure to help the child become an active participant in his community will probably result in failure to develop communication skills.

## REFERENCES

Alderman, M. 1972. Cerebral palsy: "My baby is slow. . . ." Patient Care. January 14.

Berry, M. F. 1969. Language Disorders of Children. Appleton-Century-Crofts, New York.

Bobath, B. 1965. Abnormal Postural Reflex Activity Caused by Brain Lesions. William Heinemann Medical Books Limited, London.

Bosma, J. 1975. Anatomic and physiologic development of the speech apparatus. *In* D. B. Tower (ed.), The Nervous System, Vol. 3: Human Communication and Its Disorders. Raven Press, New York.

Figure 13. Communication board for an ambulatory child.

Bouhuys, A. 1974. Breathing: Physiology, Environment and Lung Disease. Grune & Stratton, New York.

Bram, J. 1955. Language and Society. Doubleday & Co., New York.

Darley, F. L., Aronson, A. E., and Brown, J. R. 1975. Motor Disorders of Speech. W. B. Saunders Co., Philadelphia.

Davies, G. A. 1973. Linguistics and language therapy: The sentence construction board. J. Speech Hear. Disord. 38:205–214.

Denes, P. B., and Pinson, E. N. 1963. The Speech Chain. Williams & Wilkins Company, Baltimore.

Denhoff, E., and Robinault, I. P. 1960. Cerebral Palsy and Related Disorders. McGraw-Hill Book Co., New York.

Dixon, C. C., and Curry B. 1973. Some thoughts on the communication board. J. Speech Hear. Disord. 38:73–88.

Finnie, N. R. 1968. Handling the Young Cerebral Palsied Child at Home. E. P. Dutton & Co., New York.

Fiorentino, M. R. 1963. Reflex Testing Methods for Evaluating C.N.S. Development. Charles C Thomas, Springfield, Ill.

Fitzgerald, E. 1937. Straight Language for the Deaf: A System of Instruction for Deaf Children. Steck & Co., Austin, Tex.

Gardiner, A. H. 1932. Speech and Language. Oxford University Press, London.
Gesell, A., and Amatruda, C. S. 1949. Developmental Diagnosis. Paul B. Hoeber, Inc., New York.
Goldberg, H. R., and Fenton, J. 1960. Aphonic Communication for Those with Cerebral Palsy: Guide for the Development and Use of a Communication Board. United Cerebral Palsy of New York State, New York.
Gray, G. W., and Wise, C. M. 1959. The Bases of Speech. Harper & Brothers, New York.
Hayakawa, S. I. 1948. Language in Action. Harcourt, Brace and Co., New York.
Human Communication and Its Disorders. 1969. U.S. Department of Health, Education, and Welfare, Bethesda, Md.
Kent, L. R. 1974. Language Acquisition Program for the Severely Retarded. Research Press, Champaign, Ill.
Korzybski, A. 1933. Science and Sanity. International Non-Aristotelian Library Publishing Company, Lakeville, Conn.
Lieberman, P., and Crelin, E. S. 1971. The speech of Neanderthal man. Linguist. Inquiry 2:203–222.
McDonald, E. T. 1964. Articulation Testing and Treatment: A Sensory-Motor Approach. Stanwix House, Pittsburgh.
McDonald, E. T., and Chance, B. 1964. Cerebral Palsy. Prentice-Hall, Englewood Cliffs, N.J.
McDonald, E. T., and Schultz, A. R. 1973. Communication boards for cerebral palsied children. J. Speech Hear. Disord. 38:73–88.
Mueller, H. A. 1972. Facilitating feeding and prespeech. *In* P. H. Pearson (ed.), Physical Therapy Services in the Developmental Disabilities. Charles C Thomas, Springfield, Ill.
Mysak, E. 1963. Principles of a Reflex Therapy Approach to Cerebral Palsy. Bureau of Publications, Teachers College, Columbia University, New York.
Mysak, E. 1968. Neuroevolutional Approach to Cerebral Palsy and Speech. Teachers College Press, Columbia University, New York.
Mysak, E. 1971. Cerebral palsy speech syndromes. *In* L. Travis (ed.), Handbook of Speech Pathology and Audiology. Appleton-Century-Crofts, New York.
Palmer, M. 1949. Laryngeal blocks in speech disorders of cerebral palsy. The Central States Speech J. 1.
Perkell, J. S. 1969. Physiology of Speech Production: Results and Implications of a Quantitative Cineradiographic Study. The MIT Press, Cambridge, Mass.
Piaget, J. 1926. The Language and Thought of the Child. Rutledge and Kegan Paul, London.
Seth, G., and Guthrie, D. 1935. Speech in Childhood. Oxford University Press, London.
Vanderheiden, G. C., and Grilley, K. (eds.). 1976. Non-Vocal Communication Techniques and Aids for the Severely Physically Handicapped. University Park Press, Baltimore.
Van Riper, C. 1939. Speech Correction Principles and Methods. Prentice-Hall, Englewood Cliffs, N.J.
Vicker, B., Schurman, J. A., and Kladde, A. G. (eds.). 1974. Non-oral Communication System Project. University of Iowa, Iowa City.

Vygotsky, L. S. 1962. Thought and Language. The MIT Press, Cambridge, Mass.

Westlake, H., and Rutherford, D. 1961. Speech Therapy for the Cerebral Palsied. National Easter Seal Society for Crippled Children and Adults, Chicago.

chapter

4

# Nonspeech Symbol Systems

## Summary Chapter

*Ronnie Bring Wilbur*

*School of Education*
*Division of Reading and*
*Language Development*
*Boston University*
*Boston, Massachusetts*

*contents*

Despite the distinct titles and focuses of the chapters in this section, both chapters share a common concern with *communication* rather than simply speech. They emphasize *what* to teach, not training procedures or teaching techniques for *how* to teach. They explore alternative communication modes that are tailor-made for the child in the educational setting and those that are commercially available. Signaling the need to determine the appropriate language intervention system for each child, they emphasize individuality. They stress the need to determine the child's capabilities and needs, to identify the relevant characteristics of the available systems, and to then try to match needs with solutions. Both chapters appeal for *caution* and stress the importance of avoiding incorrect assumptions that what works for one child will work for others.

## AVAILABLE NONSPEECH SYSTEMS

Moores surveys a variety of nonspeech systems: writing, typing, abstract plastic symbols to represent words (such as those used in Non-SLIP), rebuses, Blissymbols, pictures, and manual modes like fingerspelling and signs. McDonald's discussion of communication boards for severely handicapped children uses several of these approaches, and is concerned with determining which to use with which child. The input and output considerations are discussed separately below. Although the main purpose of Moores' chapter is to discuss manual modes, he provides background on alternative systems so the reader may better understand what manual communication is and what it is not. His discussion provides the reader with an overview of the nature of each system, the tasks involved in its use, indications of its effectiveness, and constraints on its use. For further bibliographic materials on these systems with nondeaf populations, the reader is referred to Fristoe, Lloyd, and Wilbur (1977) and the separate bibliographies on manual systems, graphic symbols systems (rebus and Bliss), and abstract plastic symbols. See also Fristoe and Lloyd (1977) and Lloyd (1979).

Moores separates American Sign Language (as used in the deaf community) from pedagogically modified signing systems (systems in the sense of Wilbur, 1976) used by educators. This separation is in keeping with the tone of caution throughout this section, in particular that one must understand the processing and response demands required by each of the nonspeech approaches. These systems use signed sentences with English-based syntax and morphology. This type of modification stems from: 1) simultaneous signing and speaking (as used in Total Communication), which is facilitated if the signing sequence matches the speaking sequence, and 2) a general increase in the use of manual modes with both deaf and nondeaf children. This requires that more and more adults learn to sign. Using English syntax (primarily English word order) eliminates the need for those adult learners to learn another syntax. There is also the assumption, as yet undocumented (Wilbur, 1976; Moores, 1977), that using English syntax and morphology facilitates transfer to written and spoken English.

Moores includes this separation in his discussion because there is a lack of understanding of the internal structure of the sign systems, of American Sign Language, and of the other symbol systems as well. For example, Fristoe found in her (1975) survey that many people who were using signs with severely and profoundly retarded individuals did not know whether they were using American Sign Language or signed English (signs from American Sign Language in English word order). This confusion is clearly indicated by those who said they were using American Sign Language and Total Communication. One can use signed English as part of Total Communication, but if simultaneous speaking and signing is used, then it is highly improbable that American Sign Language is being used (although the *signs* from American Sign Language can certainly be used). This nomenclature distinction is different from the other observed confusion in Fristoe's survey: that many interventionists did not understand the requirements their chosen system placed on the nonvocal individual with whom they were working. For example, full consideration was not given to the difficulties imposed by a choice of fingerspelling for use with severely and profoundly retarded persons.

## INPUT AND OUTPUT REQUIREMENTS

Nonspeech symbol systems are visual in presentation mode (although some also contain speech components in the presentation mode). Therefore, a primary concern regarding the input requirements is the type and degree of visual discrimination required. For purposes of discussion, these systems can be divided into those presented statically (e.g., Bliss, rebus, writing, pictures, abstract plastic symbols) and those presented dynamically (e.g., signs, fingerspelling).

Systems presented statically generally are placed in front of the student on a table, communication board, or slanted support, and remain visible until the message has been decoded. Written messages in English orthography require discrimination of 26 letters composed of straight, slanted, and curved lines. Pictures may be line drawings, black and white photographs, or even color photos. In these, the student is required to discern the main figures from the background (if any). The Blissymbols are line drawings, some of which are basic morphemic elements that combine with others to produce more complex forms. In all cases, the combined form preserves the basic shape so that it is still identifiable. Rebuses may be either line drawings or more complex pictures combined with English orthographic letters. For abstract plastic symbols, color, size, shape, and letters contribute to the identifiability of the plastic chip. Clark (1977) compared the ease of acquisition of traditional orthography, Bliss, rebus, and abstract plastic symbols, and found that the easiest was rebus, followed by Bliss, followed by abstract plastic symbols, followed by traditional orthography as the most difficult (all differences were significant at $p < 0.05$).

In the dynamically presented systems, fingerspelling includes 26 distinct finger configurations, one for each letter of traditional English orthography, while the signs of American Sign Language are complexes of handshapes, motions, orientation of the palm, and place of articulation (other elements may be involved as well, e.g., type of contact, base speed, and facial expression (Wilbur, 1976, 1979)).The rate both of signing and fingerspelling may be slowed without distortion considerably more than that of speech. Each configuration may be held in front of the student until recognition is ensured. However, for strings of input, the presentation of the second item requires removal of the first item, thereby placing requirements upon memory that may not be present with statically presented symbols.

This brings us to the other major consideration in terms of systems input: what are the processing demands? Aside from the visual discrimination processing and the recognition memory required, any system presented sequentially in which the first item is removed when the second is presented requires some short term memory to store the entire message until it can be processed linguistically. (This includes systems in which all of the items are present and are pointed to one at a time, e.g., communication boards, as well as signs and fingerspelling which are presented individually.) All systems require the ability to associate the symbol with its meaning by some direct object or action referent or more abstract concepts. For some of these systems, the task of making this association may be simplified by the nature of the relationship between the symbol and its meaning. For example, pictures, such as those used on the communication boards discussed by McDonald, are actual representations of their meanings; that is, they are completely iconic, and require no associative processing to move from recognition to meaning. At the other extreme, traditional orthography is completely unrelated to its meaning; therefore the ability to associate the recognized word with its meaning must be a stored retrieval process. Also falling into this latter category are the abstract plastic symbols, although the color and shape often provide grammatical and semantic clues. Fingerspelling is included here as well. If the student is familiar with traditional orthography, the possibility exists that the written form may serve as a mediator, although no experimental evidence currently exists to document this. Either way, however, the association between handshape and "letter," or between combinations of handshapes and words, is totally dependent on memory.

Between these two extremes, we find Bliss, rebus, and some American Sign Language signs. The basic Blissymbols are designed so meaning is apparent in their shape. Symbols for man, woman, house, water, and so on, iconically represent or depict aspects of their referents. The basic symbol HEART is used as a component of all symbols concerned with feelings. Thus, any of the symbols provide clues as to their meaning from their shapes or shapes of their components. Rebuses are, by definition, pictographic or logographic representations whose associated spoken names are single monosyllables. Thus, the rebus picture of an eye is used for the English words *I* and *eye* (and presumably *aye*). For the word *eye* the rebus of an eye serves as direct presentation and thus requires little processing or memory. For the word *I*, either the rebus of an eye must be memorized as also associated with *I* (along with the meaning of *I*, of course) or it must first be associated with its spoken syllable which presumably then mediates the association of the word *I* (also by memorization). Further processing may be required when rebuses appear as parts of words, combined with other rebuses or with letters. Thus there is a rebus for *in* which is indicated by a dot inside a square. For the word *in*, this rebus seems relatively direct. This same rebus, however, appears inside the word *pinch* (p–square with dot inside–c–h). This rebus does not give a clue to the meaning of *pinch*, only to its pronunciation. Notice also that a rebus for *inch* (if one exists, or a devised one) could also be used to form *pinch* (p–rebus of an inch). What this raises is a question of purpose. If the goal is to teach recognition for speech, then symbols that present easy clues to their spoken syllables are appropriate. If the goal is to teach recognition for purposes of communicating information, then it is the meaning that is important, and concentration of techniques to help the student identify the meaningful elements of a word or symbol is required (cf. Chomsky, 1970).

In our concern for association of symbol and meaning, another consideration is the difference between being able to make this association without information in addition to what is present in the symbol (as with pictures, some basic Blissymbols, and many uncombined rebuses) and being able to see a connection between the symbol and its meaning after someone has provided the additional clue (many users combine Bliss and rebus, and signs). The additional clue, once provided, can serve as a mediator between symbol and meaning. This is frequently encountered when hearing adults learn signs. Their teacher often provides a clue (e.g., "It means *man* because of the brim on the cap") to serve as a mnemonic device. Once they have learned this connection, hearing adults often assume that this "relationship" is equally apparent to all learners, that the signs are not interpretable without this extra clue, and that they are iconic. Investigations into sign iconicity by Bellugi and Klima (1975) revealed that subjects were very good at identifying a relationship (the additional clue) between a sign and its meaning, *if* they were given both the sign and its meaning. If they were given only the sign, they were unable to guess the meaning for 90% of the signs. For the remaining 10%, some of the subjects were able to guess the meaning, but no sign was identified by all of the subjects. Finally, in a multiple choice task, which included incorrect responses from the guessing task as foils, subjects did no better than chance (18.2% correct compared to 20% chance level), indicating that under the most constrained conditions these signs were uninterpretable without additional information. Lloyd and Fristoe (1978, 1979) are investigating the predominant presence of guessable signs in the vocabularies being used with severely and profoundly retarded individuals. The question of the effect of iconicity on learnability is still under investigation. Brown (1977) found that it helped hearing children learn some signs, while Baron, Isensee, and Davis (1977) have argued that iconicity is irrelevant for autisitic children. Bernstein (1979) has not found a facilitative effect of iconicity on sign learning in deaf children of deaf parents.

The final concern in this section is the output requirements of each of the systems. One of the most obvious considerations is motor coordination. Head nods and eye gaze are probably the simplest form of output. Pointing requires more control, especially if the symbols are close together. Thus pointing east for *yes* and west for *no* is simpler than pointing to one of five pictures on a communication board, which in turn is simpler than pointing to one of a hundred Blissymbols. Signs, particularly those made with very simple handshapes, with large movements, and from central locations require more coordination than pointing, but less than fingerspelling (extremely fine finger coordination), writing, typing, or more complex sign sequence. Actually, combinations of systems are possible. It may be desirable for the input to be signs, while the output may only be head nods or pointing. Another consideration, particularly with Bliss, rebus, and abstract plastic symbols, and communication boards in general, is their potential conflict with mobility, although some boards do fold up for ease of traveling. Last, but definitely not least, for writing, typing, fingerspelling, and pointing to letters of the alphabet on a communication board, the importance and sophistication of the ability to spell should not be underrated.

## ISSUES

Although some of the practical issues raised by these two chapters have been touched upon, two issues remain.

### Caution

Both chapters addressed the issue of caution—Moores from the perspective of the overexpectations sometimes placed on Total Communication, McDonald from the perceived lack of sensitivity to the needs of the child.

Jordan, Gustason, and Rosen (1976) have reported a rapid increase in Total Communication in programs for deaf children (in 1976, about 510 programs reported using Total Communication, some 333 of which—about 65%—had changed between 1968 and 1975). This change may be viewed as a "victory of the manualists," but the effectiveness of Total Communication has yet to be established. It is known that deaf children of deaf parents do considerably better academically and are four times more likely to go to college than deaf children of hearing parents. Presumably the early communication between deaf child and deaf parent contributes greatly to this difference, but this parent-child interaction is *not* Total Communication (simultaneous signs and speech). As Moores indicates, there is a lack of data on Total Communication, particularly when compared to the data available on the effectiveness of combined fingerspelling and speech. The problem remains, then, that the possibility exists that Total Communication may fail to provide the expected gains, which may then result in a backlash that would carry us toward total oralism again. The issues of simultaneous presentation of speech and signs (as opposed to delayed presentation, or totally separated presentation) remain to be investigated, as does the manner in which such combined messages are received and coded by the receiver. McDonald also emphasized this "false-hopes" problem with his concern that the system used with a particular child meet that particular child's needs. Not all children will reach full language potential, and one should not attempt to present more than the child can handle. The Introduction to the *Perkins Sign Language Dictionary* (Robbins et al., 1975) contains extensive discussion on assessing the child's linguistic capabilities before moving on to more complicated syntax. However, similar considerations must be made for the lower language ability of some individuals, and guidelines for moving from one-word communication to two words and more need to be developed. Discussion also centered on comparative benefits of progressing from one word to multiple word sequences as contrasted with the Non-SLIP (Carrier and Peak, 1975) approach of providing complete sentence frames within which the person must work, although the lack of data makes any decision impossible.

**Why Does It Work?**

The question of "Why does it work?" is probably the most interesting of all, and it generated considerable discussion at the Nonspeech Language Conference in Gulf Shores, Alabama, upon which this book is based. Evidence presented elsewhere (Hodges and Deich, 1979; McNaughton and Kates, Chapter 13, this volume; Schaeffer, Chapter 17, this volume) indicates that nonspeech communication includes signing, Blissymbols, and abstract plastic symbols, and that nonspeech communication is considered to work if increased or improved speech eventually results. As Moores indicates at the beginning of his chapter, there are numerous other reasons why nonspeech communication might be used, and for each of these functions the utility is observable.

But why should nonspeech language intervention lead to speech, especially when significant previous speech intervention has had little or no effect? Fristoe and Lloyd (1977) have summarized 16 points relating to the effectiveness of nonspeech intervention. The first two relate to all forms: 1) removal of pressure for speech, and 2) circumvention of problems of auditory short term memory and auditory processing.

The next four highlight what nonspeech approaches force the trainer to do: 1) limit vocabulary, particularly to functional forms, 2) simplify the language structure used, 3) reduce excess verbiage (noise), and 4) adjust the presentation rate to ensure comprehension.

Nonspeech approaches: 1) make it easier to determine student's attention, 2) enhance figure-ground differential, 3) facilitate physical manipulation (molding) if needed, and 4) facilitate observations of shaping to assess progress.

The final six relate to stimulus and processing factors inherent in nonspeech approaches: 1) stimulus consistency is optimized, 2) both paired associated learning and match-to-sample learning are facilitated, 3) intramodal symbol meaning associations are simplified, 4) multimodal representation is possible, 5) duration of stimuli is adjustable, and 6) visual representation (iconicity, spatial modifications) is possible. Undoubtedly there are others at work, since none of these can explain why nonspeech approaches can lead to speech. Another suggestion made during the conference discussion was that the rhythm of signs helps to provide a framework into which the segments of spoken speech can be integrated. The success of other forms of symbols suggests that it is not the characteristics of the signs themselves that determine their effectiveness. The search for the answer to this question should lead to exciting research.

## REFERENCES

Baron, N., Isensee, L., and Davis, A. 1977. Iconicity and learnability: Teaching sign language to autistic children. Paper presented at the Second Annual Boston University Conference on Language Development, Boston.

Bellugi, U., and Klima, E. 1975. Two faces of sign: Iconic and abstract. *In* S. Harnad (ed.), Origins and Evolution of Language and Speech. New York Academy of Sciences, New York.

Bernstein, M. 1979. The acquisition of locative expressions by deaf children learning American Sign Language. Unpublished doctoral dissertation. Boston University, Boston.

Brown, R. 1977. Why are sign languages easier to learn than spoken language? Paper presented at the National Symposium on Sign Language Research and Teaching, Chicago.

Carrier, J. K., Jr., and Peak, T. 1975. Non-speech Language Initiation Program. H & H Enterprises, Lawrence, Kan.

Chomsky, C. 1970. Reading, writing, and phonology. Har. Educ. Rev. 40:305, 307–308.

Clark, C. 1977. A comparative study of young children's ease of learning words represented in the graphic systems of rebus, Bliss, Carrier-Peak and traditional orthography. Unpublished doctoral dissertation, University of Minnesota, Minneapolis.

Fristoe, M. 1975. Language Intervention Systems for the Retarded. L. B. Wallace Development Center, Decatur, Ala.

Fristoe, M., and Lloyd, L. L. 1977. Manual communication for the retarded and others with severe communication impairment: A resource list. Ment. Retard. October: 18–21.

Fristoe, M., and Lloyd, L. L. 1978. A survey of the use of non-speech communication systems with the severely communication impaired. Ment. Retard. In press.

Fristoe, M., Lloyd, L. L., and Wilbur, R. B. 1977. Nonspeech communication: Systems and symbols. Short course presented at the American Speech and Hearing Association Conference, November, Chicago.

Hodges, P., and Deich, R. F. 1979. Language intervention strategies with manipulable symbols. *In* R. L. Schiefelbusch and J. H. Hollis (eds.), Language Intervention from Ape to Child, pp. 419–440. University Park Press, Baltimore.

Jordan, I. K., Gustason, G., and Rosen, R. 1976. Current communication trends at programs for the deaf. American Ann. Deaf 121:527–532.

Lloyd, L. L. 1979. Unaided nonspeech communication for severely handicapped individuals: An extensive bibliography. Unpublished manuscript, Purdue University, Lafayette, Ind.

Lloyd, L. L., and Fristoe, M. 1978. Iconicity of signs: Evidence for its predominance in vocabularies used with severely impaired individuals in contrast with American Sign Language vocabulary in general. Paper presented at the 11th Annual Gatlinburg Conference on Research in Mental Retardation, Gatlinburg, Tenn.

Lloyd, L. L., and Fristoe, M. 1979. Iconicity of signs in the functional vocabularies used with retarded individuals in contrast with American Sign Language vocabulary in general. Paper presented at the 103rd Annual Meeting of the American Association on Mental Deficiency, May, Miami.

Moores, D. 1977. Issues in the utilization of manual communication. Keynote address at National Symposium on Sign Language Research and Teaching, Chicago.

Robbins, N., Cagan, J., Johnson, C., Kelleher, H., Record, J., and Vernacchio, J. 1975. Perkins Sign Language Dictionary: A Sign Dictionary for Use with Multi-Handicapped Deaf Children in School. Perkins School for the Blind, Watertown, Mass.

Wilbur, R. B. 1976. The linguistics of manual languages and manual systems. *In* L. L. Lloyd (ed.), Communication Assessment and Intervention Strategies, pp. 423–500. University Park Press, Baltimore.

Wilbur, R. B. 1979. American Sign Language and Sign Systems: Research and Applications. University Park Press, Baltimore.

# Section III

# Perspectives on American Sign Language

chapter

5

# American Sign Language

## Historical Perspectives and Current Issues

*Donald F. Moores*

*Division of Special Education and Communication Disorders*
*The Pennsylvania State University*
*University Park, Pennsylvania*

## contents

Although it has been in existence for more than 160 years, American Sign Language (ASL), a system of communication used by the majority of deaf adults in the United States and Canada, is a source of mystery, confusion, and controversy to educators, psychologists, and linguists. Despite its continued use over most of the nineteenth and twentieth centuries, we know less about ASL, which has existed in the midst of our society, than about a variety of exotic non–Indo-European languages spoken by isolated populations. The reasons for this ignorance of ASL have changed over time. However, two themes consistently appear and reappear. First has been the "methods" controversy that has raged among educators over the issue of whether the use of manual communication detracts from the development of speech and "language," that is, spoken language and skills. Second, until recently linguists had made speech a *sine qua non* for language (Battison, 1978). Under this criterion ASL or any other nonvocal system could not be considered a legitimate language system, either in its own right or as a mechanism for expressing English in a different mode.

A third factor in the late nineteenth century and early twentieth century, oddly enough, was the impact of the eugenics movements. In 1883 Alexander Graham Bell, who was closely involved, among other ventures, with the American Breeders Association and various eugenics societies (Bruce, 1973), produced a treatise "On the Formation of a Deaf Variety of the Human Race." Bell argued that the apparent success of education of the deaf in America constituted in effect a deleterious effect on society by bringing together deaf people who then would intermarry and increase the incidence of deafness. Acknowledging the difficulty of passing laws restricting freedom of marriage choice for deaf individuals, Bell recommended the following steps to prevent his feared formation of a deaf variety of the human race:

1. Integrate deaf and hearing children in public school
2. Discourage organizations, conventions, and publications for deaf people
3. Eliminate deaf teachers
4. Abolish American Sign Language

Bell devoted his considerable financial and intellectual resources to achieving these goals and achieved a measure of success. Even though his basic fears were refuted by a careful analysis of the marriage patterns and hearing status of the offspring of deaf individuals (Fay, 1898), the legacy of Bell's misguided crusade has come down to the present time. Deaf individuals provided much of the intellectual leadership in education of the deaf in the nineteenth century. They were responsible for the establishment and administration of many schools, and they contributed to the development of a sizable proportion of the special curricula used in schools for the deaf. They also represented a significant proportion of the teaching staffs. All of that was reversed beginning in the late nineteenth century. With few exceptions deaf people were never hired in public school programs. In residential schools, they were restricted to secondary and vocational departments and prohibited from teaching elementary school–age children for fear they would contaminate the children with signs. For generations deaf individuals suffered from a dehumanizing system. There was a general fear among supporters of ASL that the sign language would disappear in a short period of time.

American Sign Language did not disappear; it went underground. Beginning in the early 1960s it has received attention and support from a growing number of educators and linguists. Not coincidentally, deaf educators have begun to assume rightful roles of leadership in the field.

The resurgence of interest in the use of sign language in educational settings and by clearly defined populations in our society has raised a number of issues regarding American Sign Language, its properties, and its relation to spoken English. Perhaps these can be approached best through a historical perspective.

## ROOTS OF AMERICAN SIGN LANGUAGE

### French Sign Language

The roots of American Sign Language may be traced to French Sign Language and the Spanish Manual Alphabet, both of which were brought to the United States by Laurent Clerc, a deaf teacher at the Paris School for the Deaf. In 1817 Clerc became the first teacher at the American School for the Deaf in Hartford, Connecticut. He established the French, or manual, method at the school and over the next 40 years was responsible for training a large number of teachers and administrators in the first schools for the deaf in the United States.

Little is known definitely about French Sign Language itself. The greatest documented influence came from the Abbé de l'Epée, who established a school for the deaf in Paris in 1755. Utilizing a base of signs employed by deaf individuals in Paris, de l'Epée attempted to develop a sign language that would convey all aspects of spoken French. He modified many existing signs and invented others to express aspects of French grammar such as number, gender, case, and tense. In his efforts he relied heavily on the work of Bonet who published in 1620 the first book still in existence on education of the deaf, which included an illustration of the Spanish Manual Alphabet. Many of the invented or modified signs were cued by alphabetic handshapes. Thus, the right hand assumed the *B* handshape for BON (good), *V* for VERDE (green) and *A* for AUTRE (other).

Another possible influence on French Sign Language may have been the sign systems used by Spanish Benedictine monks. The evidence strongly suggests (Chaves and Solar, 1974; Moores, 1978) that Bonet was influenced by the work of a sixteenth century Benedictine monk, Ponce de León, who apparently was the world's first teacher of the deaf. The Benedictines employed signs for everyday activities such as work and eating (Chaves and Solar, 1974). It is probable that Ponce used such signs with his deaf pupils and possible that these signs were known to de l'Epée (Solar, personal communication). Ponce did develop a manuscript on educating the deaf, which has either been lost or destroyed.

The system developed by de l'Epée was clumsy and arbitrary. It was modified over the years, with some of the elements eliminated. It was this modified, somewhat reduced, system that Clerc brought to America.

## American Sign Language

Clerc's educational approach was an extension of the French system with modifications developed by himself and others. To accomplish this, great reliance was placed again on the Spanish Manual Alphabet, now known in this country as the American Manual Alphabet. For example, the signs for Monday, Tuesday, Wednesday, Thursday, Friday, and Saturday are identical except for the shape of the right hand, which indicates the first letter of each word. For Thursday, the *H* handshape is used. Another example of initialization is the represenation of colors. Instead of a *V* for VERDE, ASL uses the *G* handshape for GREEN. Other signs have resisted change, probably for physiological, semantic, and linguistic reasons. The basic signs representing male and female gender are unchanged; OTHER is made with the right hand in the *A* handshape and GOOD with the *B* handshape. The author speculates that the *G* handshape was not adapted because the sign is made in such a manner that using *G* would tend to confuse it with the sign glossed as CORRECT or RIGHT in ASL.

Although variation existed across schools and over time, there seemed to be a consistent pattern in the presentation of lessons in the early schools. First, material would be presented in "natural"[1] sign language. Content was stressed and there would be little concern with word order or English grammar. Next, the same material would be presented in "methodical" signs, following English word order and utilizing elements of English grammar not commonly used in natural sign language, e.g., signs for different forms of the verb *to be* and tense markers for

[1] Descriptors varied. For the sake of consistency the terms "natural" and "methodical" are used here.

every verb. The final step would concentrate on written English expression.

As time went on differences developed between those who favored emphasized natural sign language and those who supported methodical signs. Natural sign language was criticized as not really being English and lacking its sophistication. Methodical sign language was criticized for being artificial and clumsy. The differences between the two camps were rendered academic with the triumph of the oral-only approach, which proscribed the use of *any* kind of manual communication. At the 1888 International Convention in Milan the following resolutions were passed:

1. Given the incontestable superiority of speech over signs in restoring deaf mutes to society and in giving them a more perfect knowledge of language, the oral method ought to be preferred to signs.
2. Considering that the simultaneous use of speech and signs has the disadvantage of injuring speech, lipreading and precision of ideas, that the pure oral method ought to be preferred (Moores, 1978, p. 72).

The first resolution dealt a blow to the advocates of the "natural" sign language approach. The second resolution rejected the efforts of those advocating "methodical" signs in coordination with speech.

## THE TWENTIETH CENTURY

Although the impact of the Milan resolutions was not as immediate in the United States as in Europe, its influence was felt and the use of signs for instructional purposes was phased out with all except some secondary school–age residential students. Deaf adults, however, tended to use some form of American Sign Language in their interactions with deaf acquaintances, regardless of their in-school training.

The situation began to change in the early 1960s. A series of reports was published indicating that deaf children who used manual communication from birth—those with deaf parents—were superior to children who received no manual communication in academic achievement, reading, written expression, and social adjustment. The use of manual communication seemed to facilitate all aspects of English, including speechreading. The only area not affected appeared to be articulation, which the use of manual communication neither facilitated nor hindered. For extensive reviews of the literature the reader is referred to Moores (1974) and Wilbur (1976).

Since the late 1960s there has been a move away from oral-only classrooms toward the simultaneous use of speech and manual communication. Some form of manual communication combined with speech is used in a majority of programs for the deaf today (Jordan, Gustason, and Rosen, 1976). Concurrent with this have been a number of efforts to modify the system used by deaf adults, frequently called Ameslan, to accommodate exactly to spoken English for use in the classroom. The two most commonly used revisions were developed by deaf individuals, with Anthony (1971) developing the Seeing Essential English (SEE 1) system and Gustason taking the leadership in developing Signing Exact English (SEE 2) (Gustason, Pfetzing, and Zowalkow, 1972).

The unresolved nineteenth century issues regarding natural and methodical signs have been raised again concerning the relative merits of Ameslan and SEE 1 or SEE 2. Most investigators agree that there is a wide variation in American Sign Language. Moores (1974), Stokoe (1970), and Woodward (1973) have postulated a diglossic continuum ranging from a one-to-one representation of standard English to systems having little relationship to standard English. Stokoe and Woodward consider the end of the continuum that incorporates Ameslan to constitute a language separate from English. Moores has argued that such systems may in fact be nonstandard dialects of English and that many of the noted differences may be caused by modality constraints—language in a visual-motor mode—rather than based on purely linguistic considerations. Their different interpretations may be explained at least in part by the fact that Stokoe and Woodward have tended to concentrate on the communication of adults outside of educational settings, whereas Moores has dealt with the development of communication skills in educational settings and on parent-child interaction where deaf parents consciously try to help their children develop English skills.

Regardless of the orientations of individual linguists, educators, and psychologists, it is obvious that we are on the threshold of exciting times. Issues that have been dormant for generations are being raised and examined. The next several years promise to be stimulating as long-standing questions are resolved and new ones inevitably rise to take their place.

## HISTORICAL PERSPECTIVES

The following three selections that comprise the chapters of this section on historical perspectives were chosen out of literally hundreds available. The first, "On the Natural Language of Signs; and Its Value and Use in the Instruction of the Deaf and Dumb," by T. H. Gallaudet (1848), first principal of the American School for the Deaf, is a justification of the use of natural signs in the educational process. Gallaudet's basic argument held that adequate academic, intellectual, and moral development was impossible for deaf children without reliance on natural signs. The next selection, written by E. M. Gallaudet (T. H. Gallaudet's son) more than 50 years later, is entitled "Must the Sign-Language Go?" and strikes a different note. The same man who once had argued that the sign language was used to excess in education of the deaf (E. M. Gallaudet, 1871) was fighting for its survival by the turn of the century. The final selection, by Stokoe, is a much more scientific and comprehensive treatment than the other two. Stokoe has conducted pioneering research in the area of sign languages for more than 20 years, and his work has provided the impetus for a widening base of linguistic research in the area. Although he has several excellent publications on the topic of ASL, the paper selected, "The Study and Use of Sign Language," seems particularly appropriate for inclusion in a section dealing with historical perspectives on ASL.

## REFERENCES

Anthony, D. 1971. Seeing Essential English. Educational Services Division, Anaheim School District, Anaheim, Cal.

Battison, R. 1978. Lexical Borrowing in American Sign Language. Linstok Press, Silver Spring, Md.

Bell, A. G. 1883. Memoir upon the Formation of a Deaf Variety of the Human Race. National Academy of Science, Washington, D.C.

Bonet, J. 1620. Reducion de las Letras y Arte para Ensenar a Hablar los Mudos. Par Francisco Arbaco de Angelo, Madrid.

Bruce, R. 1973. Alexander Graham Bell and the Conquest of Silence. Little, Brown, & Co., Boston.

Chaves, T., and Solar, J. 1974. Pedro Ponce de León: First Teacher of the Deaf. Sign Language Studies 5:48–63.

Fay, E. 1898. Marriages of the Deaf in America. Volta Bureau, Gibson Brothers, Washington, D.C.

Gallaudet, E. M. 1871. Is the sign language used to excess in teaching deaf mutes? Am. Ann. Deaf 16:23–36.

Gallaudet, E. M. 1899. Must the sign language go? Am. Ann. Deaf 44:221–229.

Gallaudet, T. H. 1848. On the natural language of signs; and its value and uses in the instruction of the deaf and dumb. Am. Ann. Deaf 1:79–93.

Gustason, G., Pfetzing, D., and Zawolkow, E. 1972. Signing Exact English. Modern Signs Press, Roosmoor, Cal.

Jordan, I. K., Gustason, G., and Rosen, R. 1976. Correct communication trends at programs for the deaf. Am. Ann. Deaf 121:527–532.

Moores, D. 1974. Nonvocal systems of verbal behavior. *In* R. L. Schiefelbusch and L. L. Lloyd (eds.), Langauge Perspectives—Acquisition, Retardation, and Intervention, pp. 377–417. University Park Press, Baltimore.

Moores, D. 1978. Educating the Deaf: Psychology, Principles, and Practices. Houghton Mifflin Co., Boston.

Stokoe, W. C. 1970. Sign language diglossia. Stud. Linguist. 21:27–41.

Stokoe, W. C. 1976. The study and use of sign language. Sign Lang. Stud. 10:1–36.

Wilbur, R. 1976. The linguistics of manual languages and manual systems. *In* L. L. Lloyd (ed.), Communication Assessment and Intervention Strategies, pp. 443–500. University Park Press, Baltimore.

Woodward, W. 1973. Implicational lects on the deaf diglossic continuum. Unpublished doctoral dissertation, Georgetown University, Washington, D.C.

chapter 6

# On the Natural Language of Signs; and Its Value and Uses in the Instruction of the Deaf and Dumb

*Rev. T. H. Gallaudet**

*Former Principal of the American Asylum for the Deaf and Dumb*

We have considered, in the preceding number, the origin, universality, and some of the advantages of the natural language of signs originally employed by the deaf and dumb; expanded and improved by themselves and their teachers; and used, more or less, in their social intercourse at the institutions where they are assembled, and in the process of their education. The extent to which these natural signs should be encouraged and made use of in this process, is a question about which there exists considerable diversity of views, especially in Europe, among the various schools, and among teachers whose talents and experience entitle their respective opinions to much weight.

My object is not to discuss this question of *extent* (though I may touch upon it as I go along), but to show the intrinsic value, and, indeed, indispensable necessity of the use of natural signs in the education of the deaf and dumb,—to a great degree in the earlier stages of their education, and, in some degree, through the whole course of it. In attempting this, I wish I had time to go, somewhat at length, into the genius of this natural language of signs; to compare it with merely oral language; and to show, as I think I could, its decided superiority over the latter, so far as respects its peculiar adaptation to the mind of childhood and early youth, when objects addressed to the senses, and especially to the sight, have such sway over this mind,—when the expressions of the human countenance, with the general air and manners, attitudes and movements of the body, are so closely scrutinized by the young observer, while he receives, from these sources, some of the deepest and most lasting impressions that are ever made on his intellect and heart,—and when his first understanding of the meaning of words, singly, or in short colloquial phrases, which he hears uttered, depends so much on the unfolding of this meaning by objects, or combinations of objects and circumstances addressed solely to his eye. The natural language of signs is abundantly capable of either portraying or recalling these objects and circumstances. The life, picture-like delineation, pantomimic spirit, variety, and grace with which this may be done, with the transparent beaming forth of the soul of him who communicates, through the eye, the countenance, the attitudes, movements, and gestures of the body, to the youthful mind that receives the communication, constitute a *visual* language which has a charm for such a mind, and a perspicuity, too, for such a purpose, that merely *oral* language does not possess.

It is greatly to be regretted that much more of this visual language does not accompany the oral, in the domestic circle, and, indeed, in all our social intercourse. Our public speakers often show the want of it, in their unimpassioned looks, frigid, monotonous attitude, and quiescent

---

Reprinted from Gallaudet, T. H. 1848. On the natural language of signs; and its value and uses in the instruction of the deaf and dumb. American Annals of the Deaf 1:79–93.

* Affiliation given reflects the author's affiliation at time of writing.

limbs, even when they are uttering the most eloquent, and soul-stirring thoughts. Would they but *look out* and *act out* these thoughts, as well as speak them, how much greater power their eloquence would have. Why has the Creator furnished us with such an elaborate and wonderful apparatus of nerves and muscles, to subserve the purposes of this visual language; with such an eye and countenance, as variable in their expressions are all the internal workings of the soul and graphically indicative of them; and with such a versatility of attitude and gesture susceptible of being "known and read of all men,"—thus to supply the deficiencies of our oral intercourse, and to perfect the communion of one soul with another, if we are to make no more use of these things than if we were so many colorless and motionless statues! If this *visual language* were vastly more cultivated than it is, and employed in the early training of children and youth in our families, schools, and other seminaries of learning, we should find its happy results in all the processes of education; on all occasions where the persuasions of eloquence are employed; and in the higher zest which would be given to the enjoyments of social life. As a people, especially in New England, we ought to be sensible of our deficiency in this respect, and labor to remove it. We have latent enthusiasm enough to do this, but we have so long kept it under restraint, as if we were too fearful, or too cautious, to look, move, and act as we think and feel, that we need strong convictions of the judgment and a course of persevering effort, to break up the inveteracy of the habit. Let us begin in our intercourse with children and youth, and lead them, by our example, to have the soul speak out freely in their looks and movements, and more than half the work will be done.

Most happily for the deaf and dumb, the God of nature has laid a necessity upon them to employ, as soon as they have wants and desires to express, this visual language, and to enlarge and improve it as their wants and desires expand. It is an unwise attempt, which some have made, to endeavor to check their propensity to do this in their childhood, if, indeed, it is possible to check it. It is cruel to try to take from them this spontaneous and ready means of intelligible intercourse, to a great extent, with those around them,—of the development of their intellectual and moral faculties—and of the pleasure which they feel in this constant exercise of their inventive powers, and from the consciousness of being able to overcome, in no small degree, the difficulties of their peculiar condition, and to help raise themselves to the dignity and delight of social existence. I would as soon think of tying the wings of the young lark that is making its first, aspiring essays to fly upward, and soar in the ethereal expanse.

I know it has been maintained, that this natural language of signs, if cultivated in the childhood, and earlier instruction of the deaf-mute, will retard his acquisition of written and printed language; of useful knowledge; and, if he should prove to be capable of acquiring it (which is far from being the case in the most numerous instances), of the ability to articulate intelligibly for the purposes of promiscuous conversation, and to understand, by the eye, what is spoken to him by others. But, on the other hand, this visual language, absolutely essential, in some form or other, to taking successfully the first steps of his education, and needed, in a greater or less degree, through the whole course of it (if wisely used, and kept subordinate when it ought to be), is an important auxiliary in accomplishing these very objects. It will be used, more or less, by the deaf and dumb themselves, do what you may to prevent it. It *is used*, more or less, in the actual process of instruction, sometimes of design, and sometimes involuntarily, by those who, in theory, decry it the most. As I have already said, the only true question concerning its value and use, is that of the extent to which it ought to be employed.

The great value of this visual language of natural signs, manifested by the countenance, and the attitudes, movements, and gestures of the body, in the education of the deaf and dumb, will appear, if we consider, as I now propose to do, some of its other uses.

How can the deaf-mute in the family and the school be brought under a wholesome government and discipline without it? Moral influence is the great instrument to be used in this government and discipline. The conscience is to be addressed and enlightened; the right and the wrong to be unfolded and made clear to the mind; a knowledge of those simple truths which affect our character and conduct to be conveyed to him who is, as yet, so ignorant of them. The blessings that attend virtue, and the evils of vice, are to be portrayed. Motives are to be presented. An enlightened self-interest is to be awakened; a laudable ambition to be excited; hope to be enkindled; and, sometimes, fear to be aroused. Nay, the sanctions of religion must be employed to complete the work. For the deaf-mute has his religious susceptibilities, implanted in his moral constitution by the Author of it, as well as other children. To feel and act entirely right, so as to secure the efficacy of a settled principle, and the uniformity of a fixed habit, he must feel and act *religiously*, in view of his relation and responsibility to God, of the sanctions of the divine law, and of the encouragements of the covenant of grace. The Bible, the Saviour, and the retributions of the future world, must be lights to shine upon his soul. He must be taught to pray, to pray in secret to his Father in Heaven, and thus, sensible of his dependence and weakness, to look above for wisdom, strength, and grace to aid him in being and doing right. This moral influence, too, must reach him as a *social*, religious being. He must feel it in common with others of the community to which he belongs. Its effect on us all is greatly enhanced by thus feeling it. Family and social worship, and the services of the sanctuary, bear witness to this truth. What would become of the laws of God, and of the laws of man, of the good order, or even the very existence of society, if men did not come together to bow before their common Lord, and collectively to learn his will, their relations to him and to each other, and their duty? These principles should be recognized more distinctly, and carried into effect more faithfully than they are, in the education of all our children and youth. They apply with peculiar force to deaf-mutes, and to the schools in which they are gathered. When carried out judiciously, they render the management of such schools comparatively easy and delightful.

This aggregate, moral influence, which I have thus described, cannot be brought to bear upon the youthful mind *without language* and a language intelligible to such a mind. There must be teacher and learner, one who addresses, and one who is addressed. There must be a suitable medium of communication between these two minds, a common language which both understand. For, let it never be forgotten that, in order to exercise a successful moral influence over the child, in his government and discipline, so as to lead him to do right of choice, and with a hearty good will, his confidence in his guide and governor must be secured. In cultivating this confidence, he must often be *listened to* patiently by the parent and teacher. He will have his questions to ask, his inquiries to make, his doubts and difficulties to state, that he may fully understand and feel what his duty is, and sometimes his excuses and extenuations to give, that he may escape blame when he does not deserve it. Collisions of feeling and of interest will arise between him and his fellows. Rights, on the one side or on the other, have been assailed, or wrongs inflicted. Each of the parties claims the privilege of stating his own case. They must both be heard. Facts must be inquired into, perhaps witnesses called in. Else, impartial and strict justice cannot be done. And if it is not done, confidence is weakened, and sometimes lost, and authority by moral influence paralyzed, or destroyed.

For all these purposes the child must have a language at command, common to him and the teacher, by which to make his thoughts and feelings known. This is indispensable to the exercise of a wholesome government and discipline over him.

In the exercise of this government and discipline, by a moral influence, one other very important thing is to be taken into account. Moral and religious truths, as we have seen, have to be presented by the teacher to the pupil. But the latter is too young to receive and understand these truths under the forms of abstract propositions. Abstract terms, and those of generalization, are not now level to his capacity. He as yet thinks in particulars. The teacher must go into particulars. He must describe individuals as acting right or wrong; state special cases; draw out detailed circumstances; give facts graphically and minutely delineated, in order to bring out the truths he wishes to present and inculcate, and to offer the motives which will have pertinency and efficacy. By degrees, he can unfold the powers of abstraction and generalization in the child, and be doing his work in a more concise way. But, at first, and indeed for a considerable length of time, he must patiently take the slow, inductive process. It cannot be hurried. To conduct this process, the teacher needs a language, common to him and the child, having graphical, delineating, and descriptive powers, capable of particularizing thought, of giving to it a "local habitation and a name." One prominent defect in the moral and religious training of children and youth, consists in not regarding these very obvious and simple principles of their sucessful instruction, so as to bring them, intelligently and voluntarily, under an efficacious moral influence. It is, undoubtedly, to meet this case, existing, not only among children and youth, but among thousands of ignorant and undisciplined adult minds, that so much of the Bible abounds with the detailed facts of biography and history; with circumstantial descriptions; with the results for good or evil, of human conduct; with living examples; and with simple and touching parables.

We see, then, for these various and conclusive reasons, the necessity of a *common language*, adequate to the exigencies of the case, to be employed by the teacher, and the deaf-mute, in order that a wholesome government and discipline may be exercised over him, through a moral influence.

Where shall we find this language, or must we go to work and create one for the purpose? The deaf-mute cannot hear what you say to him. He can *see* the motions of your lips, and organs of speech, more or less distinctly, when you utter words. But it is a long and laborious process, even in the comparatively few cases of complete success, to teach him to discriminate accurately between the various motions of the organs of speech, and so to notice their combinations, as to know the words which are intended to be uttered,—words, too, which are useless for the purpose of intercommunication until their meaning has been explained to him. To do this, and to teach him the proper combinations of words, so as to be able to impart the most simple kind of moral and religious instruction, is, also, another long and laborious process,—while, at the same time, I do not hesitate to say, without fear of contradiction, that neither of these processes can be successfully carried on unless resort is had to natural signs.

Then to make this language of intercommunication complete, as we have already seen, for the purposes of government and discipline, the deaf-mute must be able to convey his thoughts and feelings to the teacher. Shall he be fitted to do this by being taught how to articulate intelligibly, without the ear to guide him? You have another long and laborious process to go through, before, even in the few successful cases, he can have a sufficient stock of words which he understands, and be able to form their proper combinations, in order to furnish him with an adequate medium for thus conveying his thoughts and feelings. Nor can *this* process be carried on, as it ought to be, without the use of natural signs.

Similar difficulties must arise in the use of the manual alphabet for spelling words on the fingers, or in presenting written or printed words to the eye of the deaf-mute; though it is true that these difficulties will principally consist in teaching him the meaning of these words, and their combinations, to such an extent as to furnish the means of a free intercommunication between him and the teacher. And here, again, natural signs have their great value and necessary uses.

Bear in mind, too, that this common language should be one by which, as has been shown, the deaf-mute can intelligibly conduct his private devotions, and join in social religious exercises with his fellow-pupils. Otherwise, one very important means of their proper government and discipline, is wanting.

Now even admitting, what I yet believe to be impracticable, that, after very long and laborious processes, a sufficient command of language can be obtained by the deaf-mute, in one or the other of these ways that have been mentioned, for the various purposes of his government and discipline by moral influence, and without the use at all of natural signs, still great and needless evils must accrue from such a course. A considerable time must elapse, two or three years,—in not a few cases more, before the object can, in a good degree, be accomplished. In the meanwhile, the teacher and pupil are, at first, quite destitute of, and, all along, sadly deficient in an adequate medium of intercommunication. Under such embarrassments, is there not a better way, seasonably, intelligibly, and effectually, to cultivate the moral faculties of the deaf-mute, bring him under a wholesome moral influence, and train him in the right way; to furnish a due preparation of his mind and heart to engage in his own private devotions, and to enjoy the privilege of social religious exercises and instruction with his fellow-pupils; and to secure a judicious government and discipline in the institutions intended for his benefit?

The God of Nature and of Providence has kindly furnished the means of doing this. The deaf-mute has already spontaneously used, in its elementary features, before he comes to the school, that natural language of signs, which, improved by the skill of teachers, and current, as a medium of social intercourse, among the pupils at such schools, is adequate to the exigency. As we have seen, in the preceding number, he easily and quickly becomes acquainted with this improved language by his constant, familiar intercommunication with the teachers and his fellow-pupils. By means of it his government and discipline, through a kind moral influence, can at once be begun: for he has a language common to him and his teacher. Every day he is improving in this language; and this medium of moral influence is rapidly enlarging. His mind becomes more and more enlightened; his conscience more and more easily addressed; his heart more and more prepared to be accessible to the simple truths and precepts of the Word of God. The affecting contents of that Word are gradually unfolded to him. He recognizes his relation to God and to his fellow men. He learns much of the divine character, and of his own obligations and duties. At length, he is made to understand, like a child, indeed, but yet to understand the way of salvation through Jesus Christ. If he has the disposition to pray, he has a simple, beautiful language of his own, in which to address his Father in Heaven. He comes, every morning and evening, with his associates, to be instructed from the Word of God, and to unite with this silent assembly, through the medium of natural signs, employed for both these purposes, by the teacher, in a most expressive and touching mode of worship before the throne of Grace. On the Sabbath, he enjoys its sacred privileges. The moral influence of the government and discipline of the institution over the objects of its care, is thus secured, and rendered permanently efficient, through the medium of the language of natural signs, much, *very much sooner*, and with vastly more success, than it could be obtained in any other way, if, indeed, it could be obtained at all, to any effectual purpose, without the use of this language.

Some, while reading these remarks, may hesitate, and have a shade of skepticism pass over their minds, with regard to the competency of the natural language of signs thus to accomplish the various objects which have been mentioned, in the moral and religious training of the deaf-mute, and in his government and discipline. This language may seem to them so simple; so limited, in its narrow range, to the delineation and description of merely *sensible* things; so barren of all modes of expressing what lies, beyond the province of sense, within the human mind and heart, and in the spiritual world, as to lead them to doubt very much what the writer has said about its efficacy in these respects, and to attribute his descriptions of its genius and power to the ardor of a professional enthusiasm.

He pleads guilty, if needs be, to the charge of this enthusiasm; —though, mellowed, as it is, by advancing years, and the lapse of a considerable portion of time since the vigor of his manhood was devoted to the instruction of the deaf and dumb, and writing, as he does, with the retrospective soberness of one who retraces, in a quiet resting place, the difficulties and perplexities, as well as facilities of a journey long ago taken, his convictions are as strong as they ever were, that the deaf and dumb are themselves the original sources of the fundamental processes, so far as language is concerned, of conducting their education, and that, in this case, as well as in all others which relate to education generally, it is the part of wisdom to find the path which nature points out, and to follow it. Experience, philosophy, and art may, often, do a great deal to remove some of the roughnesses of this path, to make it more smooth and straight, more easily and expeditiously to be trod, more pleasant and delightful, but it will not do to quit it, else those whom you would lead in the way of knowledge, of truth, and of duty, will follow in with irksome and reluctant steps, if, indeed, they follow at all, except as the blind do when they are led by the blind, to incur the risk, every moment, of some difficulty or danger.

But this natural language of signs, comprising the various modes which the God of Nature has provided for one soul to hold communion with another, through the eye and countenance, the attitudes, movements, and gestures of the body, is, by no means so limited in its powers and range, as it might appear to be to him who has given it only a cursory attention, and who has not watched its practical applications and results.

In what relates to the expression of passion and emotion, and of all the finer and stronger sentiments of the heart, this language is eminently appropriate and copious. Here, without it, oral language utterly fails; while *it* alone, without oral language, often overwhelms us with wonder by its mysterious power. In this province its power, probably, will be denied by none. But the expression of the passions, emotions, and sentiments, constitutes no small part of that *common language* which, as we have seen, both the deaf-mute and his teacher must possess, in order that his moral and religious training may be properly conducted, and a wholesome government and discipline over him, be secured. How can he be taught the necessity and the mode of controlling, directing, and, at times, subduing the risings and movements of *this sensitive part* of his moral constitution, unless his attention is turned to the varieties, character, and results of its operations? How shall he be taught, for instance, that anger, within certain limits, is sometimes justifiable, while, at other times, it has no redeeming quality, but is utterly unjustifiable and wrong, unless this feeling is brought before his cognizance, and its nature and effects described. In this, as in other similar cases, the natural language of signs furnishes the only thorough and successful mode of doing this. Its necessity and value will be fully manifest, if we consider what an important part of the moral and religious training of children and youth, consists in leading them to bring their passions, emotions, and sentiments under the sway of conscience, enlightened by the Word of

God. In one word, *the heart* is the principal thing which we must aim to reach in the education of the deaf-mute, as well as of other children; and the heart claims as its peculiar and appropriate language, that of the eye and countenance, of the attitudes, movements, and gestures of the body.

The teacher of the deaf and dumb must have the use of this language, not only to convey command and precept, but to enforce both, by the power of a living example. He wishes to train aright the passions, emotions, and sentiments of those entrusted to his care. He should strive to be their model. But this model must not be a statue. He must look, act, move, and demean himself, at all times, in such ways as to let it be seen that his is a soul of rectitude, purity, and benevolence, swayed by love to God, and love to man,—self-denying, patient, kind, and forbearing, and yet firm, not only in obeying himself the right, but, in the exercise of a lawful authority, requiring others to obey it. His eye, his countenance, his whole air and manner, should be the spontaneous *outward* manifestations of these *inward* feelings. The clearness and spirit of such manifestations, depend greatly on the naturalness, the ease, and vivacity with which his whole physical man responds to the inner man of the heart. If he does not appreciate the value of the natural language of signs, if he does not cherish and cultivate it to the highest degree of force, beauty, and grace which it is possible for him to reach, he has not before him the true standard of what a thoroughly qualified teacher of the deaf and dumb should aspire to be. He may speak to them on his lips or fingers, or address them on his black-board, or slate; helping himself out, perhaps, with some signs and gestures, lacking life, clearness, and grace, and with an unmoved and unmoving countenance, but he is not the one to succeed as a guide and example in conducting their moral and religious education, or in exercising a wholesome paternal government and discipline over them. Neither is he qualified to conduct, in any good degree as they ought to be conducted, the other processes of their education.

It would be interesting to inquire, how far these principles apply to the teachers of children and youth who are in possession of all their faculties. Did time permit, I would attempt to show that they do thus apply with peculiar force.

But something more, it will be said, is necessary, in the training and governing of the deaf-mute, than that the common language between him and his teacher should be sufficiently complete so far as the passions, emotions, and sentiments are concerned. We have been told, it will be added, that the teacher must go into particulars; that individuals must be described; cases stated; circumstances drawn out in detail; facts graphically and minutely delineated; the biography, history, and parables of the Scriptures, and even its simple doctrines, and practical precepts presented to the mind of the pupil, and that he must be prepared, too, to engage in private and social religious exercises. Is the natural language of signs sufficient for these things? Let us see.

So far as objects, motions, or actions addressed to the senses are concerned, this language, in its improved state, is superior in accuracy and force of delineation to that in which words spelt on the fingers, spoken, written, or printed, are employed. These words consist of arbitrary marks, or sounds, which when put together in a certain order, *it is agreed* shall have a certain meaning. How do children originally acquire the meaning of these words? Does the shape or sound of the word convey its meaning? Not at all. How, then, is its meaning acquired? By the presence of the object, motion, or action which the word denotes, addressed to some of the senses of the child, when the word is offered to his notice,—or by some occurring event in nature, or in common life; by some circumstance, some attitude, sign, or gesture, some expression of countenance, which singly or together, unfold the meaning. Here you must always go back as the starting point; though when the meanings of a certain number of words are thus acquired, they may be employed, doubtless, to recall objects which are not at the time addressed to the senses, or even to describe new ones. Yet the *elements* of these processes must always be found in things which have once been present to the senses of the child.

Now even if the natural language of signs were as arbitrary as that of words, there is no reason why it should not be as adequate as that is to the purposes under consideration. If a certain sign made with the hands is agreed upon, always to denote *a book*, why is not the sign as definite and as available, as the letters b o o k, uttered from the mouth, spelt on the fingers, or written or printed? But this language is far from being an arbitrary one. In its original features, the deaf-mute copies nature in forming it,—the shapes, sizes, properties, uses, motions, in fine, the characteristics, addressed to some one of his senses, or sensations, of the *external* objects around him. And, with regard to his *internal* thoughts, desires, passions, emotions, or sentiments, he just lets them show themselves out (in accordance with the mysterious laws of the union of mind and body, and of the action and re-action of the one upon the other), spontaneously and freely, through his eye and countenance, and the attitudes, movements, and gestures of his muscular system. As he uses it, it is a picture-like and symbolical language, calling up the objects and ideas which it is designed to denote, in a portraying and suggestive way, which no oral, written, or printed language can do. It admits of great accuracy and vividness of description, and its simple signs are susceptible of permutations and combinations, which give it a significancy, copiousness, and fluency admirably adapted to the purposes of narrative, and of moral and religious instruction, enlarged and improved as it has been by the efforts of genius and skill, and yet preserving, except in a degree scarcely worth being mentioned, its original picture-like and symbolical character.

It is true that the genius of this natural language of signs is most favorable to the presentation of truth by the gradual, inductive process, and admits, scarcely at all, of exhibiting it in its forms of abstraction and generalization. But so much the better for the purpose for which it is used, the instruction and moral training of minds that need to have abstract and general truths analyzed, reduced to their simple elements, and thus made clear to their intellect, and effective on their heart.

As the deaf-mute advances in knowledge, and in his acquaintance with written and printed language, it is, doubtless, important to employ terms of abstraction and generalization in his moral training, and to make less use of the natural language of signs; but even this should be done with care, while this very language, for the most part, furnishes the best means of explaining these terms. Simplicity and perspicuity of conception, even when compelled to express itself in particulars, and in the language of childhood, and of unlettered minds, is of vastly more value than the half-formed and vague notions which, clothed in elevated and imposing terms, sometimes, indeed, chime on the ear, and excite admiration by their pompous swell, but effect nothing in the way of making men wiser and better.

That the natural language of signs has these characteristics and capabilities; that it is the very language which the deaf-mute continually needs for the purposes of private and social devotion, and for the reception, certainly in all the earlier stages of his education, of moral and religious truth; and that it is indispensable in the government and discipline of persons in his condition, the experience of a long course of years in the Asylum at Hartford for their benefit, most abundantly testifies.

In conclusion, the writer would urge upon the parents and friends of the deaf and dumb, in view of the remarks which he has made, to encourage the child who suffers such a privation, to make his thoughts and feelings known, as early and as fully as possible, through the medium of natural signs,—and to acquire themselves, with the other members of the family, the use of this language, that the intercommunication between them and the child may be an intelligible and pleasant one. It will certainly be so to the deaf-mute, and will become more and more so to those who are thus learning it from him, as they perceive, from day to day, its power, its beauty, and its practical uses. Instead of throwing obstacles in the way of the future progress of his education at the institution to which he may be sent, it will prove, as we have seen, highly auxiliary to this progress; while, whether at home, or at the school, it is an indispensable means of his moral training, and his judicious government and discipline.

The instructors, too, of the deaf and dumb, if the principles and views that have been advanced are correct, should appreciate the great importance of being masters of the natural language of signs,—of excelling in this language; of being able to make delineating and descriptive signs with graphical and picture-like accuracy; of acquiring the power to have the inmost workings of their souls,—their various thoughts and feelings, with their fainter and stronger shades of distinctive character,—*beam out* through the eye, countenance, attitude, movement, and gesture; and of doing all this with spirit, grace, and fluency, and for the love of doing it.

The labor is not small, indeed, that must be undergone, in order to possess these indispensable qualifications of an accomplished instructor of the deaf and dumb. To acquire them, the new and inexperienced teacher must consent, carefully and perseveringly, to take lesson after lesson of the older teacher who is a proficient in this language; while the older teacher must have the patience to give these lessons. For, the language of natural signs is not to be learned from books. It cannot be delineated in pictures, or printed on paper. It must be learned, in a great degree, from the living, looking, acting model. Some of the finest models, for such a purpose, are found among the originators of this language, the deaf and dumb. The peculiarities of their mind and character, and the genius of that singularly beautiful and impressive language which nature has taught them, should be the constant study of those whose beneficent calling it is to elevate them in the scale of intellectual, social, and moral existence; to fit them for usefulness and respectability in this life, and for happiness in that which is to come.

chapter 7

# Must the Sign-Language Go?

*Edward M. Gallaudet**

*President of Gallaudet College*
*Washington, D.C.*

Language should be subordinate to thought, not thought to language.
*—Henry Drummond*

One evening last March I sat among the students of the College and enjoyed with them a lecture by one of my colleagues, on "Man's First Steps Towards Civilization." This lecture was one of a course given during the winter by the members of the College faculty, in turn, on subjects naturally suggested by the line of work followed by each professor in his teaching. These courses have been given to our students for twenty years and the subjects of a few of them will furnish an idea of the wide range of thought thus presented: The Indo-European Family of Languages; Oxygen and Certain Oxygen Compounds; The Monroe Doctrine and the Panama Canal; The Ocean Tides; Student Life in Ancient Athens; What I Saw in Alaska; The Disputed Ownership of Alsace and Lorraine.

All the lectures in these courses have been delivered in the languages of signs, with very little manual spelling, and but few words written on the black-board. What I know of the giving of lectures to the deaf through the use of the manual alphabet alone, or speech and lip-reading, leads me to express the opinion that these lectures could not have been enjoyed by assemblages of deaf persons through either of these means with one-half the pleasure and profit with which our students enjoyed them through the language of signs.

Many years ago, in the early days of the College, that master of the sign-language, Rev. Wm. W. Turner, Instructor and Principal of the American School for the Deaf at Hartford, gave several lectures to our students on Natural Science. In closing the course he took an evening to describe the life-work of the great botanist Linnæus. This description stands out clear and sharp in my memory as a masterpiece of sign-making. I do not think any lecture which has reached my mind through the ear has charmed or interested me more than this.

I believe I enjoy lectures given in signs as keenly and understand them as completely as any deaf person can. I feel that my familiarity with the spontaneous language of the deaf from my earliest childhood makes it possible for me to appreciate what lectures in signs are to the deaf, as few are able to do who have learned the language of signs in adult life, and certainly as those cannot who have no knowledge of that language.

I hope it is not assuming too much for me to say that my long-continued relation to the deaf of instructor to pupil has opened my mind, as fully as that of any instructor could be, to the possibility of injurious effects resulting from the use of signs in the effort to give the deaf a command of verbal language. As long ago as 1868, in a paper read before the

---

Reprinted from: Gallaudet, E. M. 1899. Must the Sign Language Go? American Annals of the Deaf 44:221–229.

* Affiliation given reflects author's affiliation at time of writing.

First Conference of Principals, I called attention to an evil which I felt was then existing in many of our schools, namely, the excessive use of signs in the schoolroom, and urged that manual spelling should be brought largely into use at as early a stage as possible, with a view of securing frequent practice in verbal language on the part of the pupil. Two years later, in 1870, at the Indianapolis Convention, I spoke of the sign-language as a "dangerous thing" in the education of the deaf, and urged that it ought to be used "as little as possible." In the efforts which have been made lately to abolish the use of the sign-language altogether in schools for the deaf, these declarations of mine have been quoted to give the impression that I supported this extreme policy. That this does me great injustice will be easily seen by any one who will take the pains to refer to the proceedings of those meetings.

I have always believed, with Hill and other leading German teachers, and with my father, the Doctors Peet, Dr. Noyes, Dr. MacIntire, Mr. Stone, and a host of other American teachers of eminence and success, that the language of signs has its uses at all points in the education of the deaf. It is because this conviction is so strong that I have noticed with sincere regret that some for whom I have a high regard have lately been disposed to do away altogether with the language of signs. That such a result, if it could be accomplished, would produce more harm than good I will attempt to show.

The exclusion of signs from schools for the deaf, if I mistake not, is urged on two grounds and no others. *First*, because their use is thought to interfere with the acquisition, on the part of the pupil, of the power to comprehend verbal language and to use it with a reasonable degree of correctness. *Secondly*, because their use is believed to stand in the way of the development in the pupil of the power of speech and the ability to read the speech of others.

That the excessive and injudicious employment of signs is open to these objections is what I have admitted and urged for twenty years and more. Is there no way of preventing this but by total exclusion? To answer this question in the negative would be equivalent to saying that teachers of the deaf, generally, have so little intelligence and judgment and are so lacking in self-control that they cannot be trusted with a means of instruction commended as indispensable by such teachers as Reich, the son-in-law and successor of Heinicke, Wagner, Saegert, Gronewald, and Hill, in Germany, because they may possibly abuse it. Would it be reasonable to say that no surgeon should be allowed to use a knife because death has sometimes followed the careless use of that instrument?

But he who would banish signs altogether will naturally demand to be told in what ways signs are useful. Before responding to this I would like to say that I have visited recently three prominent schools for the deaf in this country in which it is declared that signs are not used. In each of these I saw signs used in the classroom, good clear, forceful "de l'Epée signs." I have never had the pleasure of visiting the Rochester School, but I have the authority of a German teacher of eminence who was at this school last June, and who was, evidently at great pains, particularly informed as to the methods pursued, for saying that in the Rochester School "unrestricted use of natural gestures at all stages of the course of instruction" is allowed. (See the *Annals* for April, 1899, page 202.) I do not speak of these things with any purpose of relecting on the sincerity or consistency of the managers of the schools referred to, but only to show that the German teachers I have just named, whom some might be disposed to speak of as belonging to a past age, would find, could they shuffle on their mortal coils and step into our schools to-day, ample justification for their claim that signs were indispensable in the education of the deaf.

But I was going to try to show, not that signs are necessary and inevitable, but that they are useful. I think the sentiment quoted from Henry Drummond at the head of this article is worthy of serious consideration by teachers of the deaf. The youngest instructor has had it impressed upon him most vigorously and persistently that his greatest work, from a pedagogic point of view, is to teach his pupils language. I do not think Drummond's declaration, the justice of which cannot be questioned, that "language should be subordinate to thought, not thought to language," has been so often urged. As a means of developing and stimulating thought, and of explaining the meaning of words and phrases new to a pupil, signs often serve a purpose that nothing else can.

I will ask the reader to observe that I say "often," and not "always," for I am quite ready to admit that in some cases finger-spelled or spoken words, the meaning of which is fully understood, may serve the purpose above indicated. When the teacher can be *sure* that they will, no one would be more ready than I to commend their use. But I am equally certain that in instances almost beyond number the worthy zeal of a teacher to be loyal to a "method" or a "theory" leads to a persistence in the effort to "build language upon language," to "explain words by words," that is barren of good results. The bewildered and wearied pupil declares he understands when he does not, and the teacher is often too tired to apply further tests.

I say in one of the leading so-called pure oral schools of Germany, in 1897, an exercise that surprised and pleased me. A class of young pupils was being taught a number of new words. Each pupil was required to write, speak, and make the sign for each word. I asked why the sign was demanded, and was told that it was to make sure the child understood the meaning of the word, ample evidence having been had in that school that, when no sign was asked for, the word was to the pupil often nothing more than a meaningless utterance.

Teachers in schools where signs are not allowed in the classroom have told me that they have repeatedly found themselves unable to explain the meaning of a word or phrase, which could readily have been made clear by the use of signs. This not only involves a series of distinct losses to the pupils, but it forms a habit of not understanding, which is injurious.

Serious as is the disadvantage of the complete abolition of signs from the classroom, an equally great, if not greater, deprivation, in my judgment, is imposed on the deaf by the giving up of the assemblage of the pupils in chapel or lecture-room for the purpose of religious instruction and devotion, and for entertaining and profitable lectures *in the sign-language*. Perhaps some reader may say, "No doubt the lectures given to your college students are all very well, but such things go over the heads of children." My reply is that in our Kendall School we have for years had courses of lectures suited to the capacity of the children, and these have been eagerly attended by them, and have been a great source of profit and pleasure.

I remember, as though it were yesterday, my first attempt to address a company of deaf persons. It was when I was a teacher in the Hartford School, a youth of nineteen, and my subject was Joan of Arc. My heart thumped and my knees shook as I began, but the interested, eager faces of the children gave me courage, and I succeeded in holding their attention for an hour. I cannot believe that the entertainment and instruction afforded by that lecture could have been imparted to as large a proportion of the two hundred present by means of the manual alphabet or speech as was given by signs, even though the children had been all good readers of finger-spelling or lip-movement.

I hope every reader of the *Annals* has read, or will read, Mr. J. L. Smith's article in the April number for this year on "The Questions of Chapel Services in Schools for the Deaf." Mr. Smith has said much I had in mind to say when I thought of writing this article soon after seeing the lecture alluded to at the beginning. He writes as one who knows, and I am sure his views will be sustained by great numbers of highly educated deaf persons who have enjoyed the advantage of seeing chapel services and lectures from real masters of the sign-language.

But I am loath to continue to undue length the discussion of a subject some may think too well worn already. The pages of the *Annals* are full of the experiences and opinions of leaders in our profession on the uses and abuses of "signs," as one will readily see by consulting the Index. In this it will be found that the use of signs is approved in varying degree and manner by such authorities as Arnold of England, Marchio of

Italy, Walther of Germany, and Greene and Gordon of our own country. The testimony of the last named is so pointed and so in accord with my own views that I shall ask the Editor to allow me to make a brief quotation from an article originally prepared for and read to the "parents' class" in Professor Alexander Graham Bell's Experimental School in Washington in 1885, and printed in the *Annals* for October in that year. Dr. Gordon says (*Annals*, xxx, 243):

> In my opinion, the sign-language, in the hands of its masters, is an invaluable means of instruction. By it the skilful teacher annihilates obstacles of time and space, and history becomes a living panorama, every quarter of the globe is transported to his school-room and becomes a present reality to his pupils, the stories so delightful to infancy become a part of their heritage, and the long line of Bible stories, with their sublime lessons, is woven in fadeless colors into their very being. To arouse dormant powers, to convey facts, to interpret relations, to stimulate the imagination, to appeal to the emotions, to regulate the passions, I know of no satisfactory substitute for the gesture-language; and thrice fortunate do I count those deaf children whose youthful minds are developed under the inspiration of the able master whose hands pluck the stars from their courses, who bring the rolling sea to his feet, whose arms become trees, and in whose fingers the budding flowers burst into bloom.

I trust the generous reader will not attribute an allusion to my father's opinions as due merely to filial partiality. For I think it is matter of settled history that, as a successful teacher of the deaf, he stands among the foremost. A large proportion of his pupils acquired that facility in verbal English which is the desideratum and has often been the despair of later instructors.

In the first volume of the *Annals* will be found an article by my father on "The Natural Language of Signs," which is worth, I think, the reading of the progressive teacher of to-day. In this article (page 90) he makes bold to claim that, "so far as motions or actions addressed to the senses are concerned, this language, in its improved state, is superior in accuracy and forceful delineation to that in which words spelt on the fingers, spoken, written, or printed, are employed." This claim of the superior accuracy and precision of sign-language, as compared with words, may, perhaps, excite surprise at first thought. But it is believed that its reasonableness will appear when it is remembered that the meanings attached to words are almost wholly arbitrary, very few giving the slightest hint to their signification in their shape or sound, while nearly every gesture used in sign-language carries with it a plain suggestion of its meaning, and in very many instances gives a vivid and easily recognized portrayal of the idea to be conveyed.

I believe I have said enough to establish the claim that through the use of signs the education of deaf children may be helped forward in many ways, that their mental development may be stimulated, and that useful and entertaining ideas and suggestions may be communicated in the form of lectures. I hope I have convinced most of my readers that every school which banishes the sign-language from its classrooms and chapel robs its pupils of a valuable means of education, thought development and stimulation, for which there are no adequate compensations in increased power to use and understand verbal language or speech. I say *adequate* compensation because even if it were proved, which it has not been to my knowledge, that the abolition of signs has secured a somewhat improved average standard of verbal accuracy and oral fluency, I have yet to be shown that this gain has not been purchased at a price out of all proportion to its value. My observations in American and European schools where signs are used with moderation and good judgment have satisfied me that in such schools the best "all-round" development of the pupils is secured. So, in answering finally the question presented in the title to this article, I should urge that if there ever was a problem for the solution of which the adoption of the golden mean, rather than either extreme, might be urged, the sign problem should be so solved. Shall men abolish free government and re-enthrone despotism because liberty may run into license? Shall Christians embrace atheism because religion may grow into fanaticism? Shall we all dismiss our doctors and call in the medicine-men of the aborigines because the practice of physic may be perverted to charlatanism and quackery?

chapter 8

# The Study and Use of Sign Language

*William C. Stokoe*

*Gallaudet College*
*Washington, D.C.*

contents

## HISTORICAL PERSPECTIVE

At its outset in 1817, education of the deaf in America was synonymous with sign language. The method of teaching in signs of the natural sign language of the deaf, augmented with signs invented to represent grammatical signals, was easily adapted to the American scene. As in France and many other countries to which it had spread, this method produced in a few school generations an educated deaf elite that strongly urged its continuance (see Markowicz, 1976).

However, for reasons that would require a good-sized history to explain, the educational use of sign language in the United States and in most countries declined. During most of the twentieth century, signing has been strictly prohibited in some schools, discouraged and neglected in many, and even if permitted to pupils in their out-of-class time, has been studiously ignored by teachers and staff in most schools for the deaf.

Recently linguists and sociolinguists have joined the deaf—who of course never stopped using sign language—to insist that the natural language for interaction among human beings who cannot hear be given once again a central role in their education. A growing discontent with the low achievement of the average deaf child in school has also turned attention to sign language and to other forms of manual communication (see O'Rourke, 1972).

As in any large movement (there are now almost 70,000 pupils in schools reporting to the Annual Survey of Hearing Impaired Children and Youth (Office of Demographic Studies, Gallaudet College, n.d.)), some of the issues may be confusing as well as confused, and even those engaged in the movement toward "total communication" may need a new perspective.

## PURPOSE

It is the purpose here to present sign language as a central fact in the life of deaf individuals and groups, and therefore as a focus for educational efforts. This will require looking at the relation of Sign to English—another central fact in the lives of American deaf persons. *Sign* is used here as a short and pronounceable abbreviation for the proper name, American Sign Language, otherwise abbreviated ASL. Ameslan, with its half-dozen observed pronunciations, is a special socio-economic, class dialect of Sign which Fant (1974–75) has described.

---

From: Stokoe, W. C. 1976. The study of sign language. *Sign Language Studies* 10:1–36. Reprinted by permission.

This paper is a revision of a document commissioned by and published by the ERIC Clearinghouse for Linguistics in 1970. Entered by the Center for Applied Linguistics in the ERIC Document Reproduction Service, the original version is in microfiche: ED 070 719. It was revised in 1972 for publication by the National Association of the Deaf but has been out of print for several years. Research cited in its present revision has received support from NSF Grants GS-31349 and SOC 741 4724 and NIH Grant NS-10302.

While sign languages generally and Sign in particular make excellent objects for scientific study—e.g., by anthropologists, linguists, and psychologists; the present intent is to treat Sign as a prime educational medium and as a language which in a true sense can make a deaf person both a sharer in general American culture and also a member of a special group with its own self-awareness and pride. To treat Sign in this way requires, first, to look at some of the different ways that languages are presented to the eye instead of to the ear. Second, we will examine bilingualism and its special place in the life and education of deaf persons. Third, we will look at ways for concerned teachers to apply research findings directly in their own work. And finally, teachers will be shown ways to ask and answer questions of importance about Sign, i.e., to do practical research in the study of sign language for themselves.

## 1. Sight, Language, and Speech

Education for the deaf confronts a central fact: Sight instead of hearing is the sense which conveys language symbols to the person who cannot hear. In the history of systematic education of the deaf this fact has not always been faced squarely. The French pioneers, de l'Epée and Sicard, in harmony with the empirical and scientific spirit of the Enlightenment, founded their teaching on this fact. Visibly distinct signals for French grammatical features were built into their programs of instruction. But even in de l'Epée's lifetime, Heinicke challenged the French approach, insisting that words and the ideas they stood for could never be presented inside the mind without sounds. The controversy, in letters between de l'Epée and Heinicke, began in 1780, and Paris, Leipzig, Vienna—the whole intellectual world of Europe became involved. The decision of the Rector and Fellows of the Academy of Zurich in de l'Epée's favor in 1783 did not end this controversy.[1] The fact remains, nevertheless, that eyes, not ears, are the deaf person's prime symbol receivers.

Modern heirs of Heinicke follow a train of reasoning that turns away from this central fact. He began by teaching "deaf-mutes" to make sounds, thence "to read and speak clearly and with understanding." Like all readers, his pupils had to use their eyes, but he contended that the written symbols had meaning for them only through association with the sounds that they had been taught to produce. He and teachers of the deaf before and since his time also try to have their pupils associate the sounds that they make (and that they must suppose others are making) with visible facial movements—in a word, to lipread.

---

[1] An account of the early controversy is given in Garnett, 1968; see also Seigel, 1969.

Language taught by these procedures is expressed in speech, but speech with a difference: Receptively, it is seeing the facial activity of persons speaking; expressively, it is making the sounds one has been taught to make. This way of teaching language is not marked by its success, as many eloquent reports are pointing out.[2] Yet various ways of using these procedures dominate American education of the deaf. Users of the "pure oral" method would postpone instruction in reading and writing until lipreading and voice production have been in use for several years. Proponents of the "natural method" do not teach language either analytically nor synthetically but as situations arise for its use in a classroom of deaf pupils with a hearing teacher, not notably a natural environment. "The oral method" differs from these first two chiefly in that reading and writing instruction accompany lipreading and speaking instruction. In theory, when any of these procedures is in use, there is nothing for the deaf child to see except for the lip and face movements of the teacher and the other pupils. In fact, there is a wealth of information presented to the eyes. Besides the inevitable gesturing of the teacher, there are the teacher's other actions, the room itself, and all the objects in it, not to mention the activity of a handful or a double handful of bright-eyed children. American educators of the deaf have gambled that all this and more information of a linguistic kind can be integrated and understood by means of spoken English as it is interpreted from visual inspection of a speaker's face. For a hearer spoken language does perform this function. Many will have had some contact with a three- or four-year-old's "Why?" and the countless repetitions and variations on the theme of that question. But the oral methods concentrate on getting a few syllables produced and lipread in the pre-school stage; and even after the child is in school, the expectation holds that in one full year the average deaf child will have gained a lipreading and speaking vocabulary of fifty words—fifty against the average five-year-old's five thousand!

The question then arises whether, used in this way, the deaf child's eyes and mind are being put to anything like efficient use. It is this question above all other considerations which has turned attention back to the sign language of the deaf. Sign, American Sign Language, is directly derived from the language of signs used by the generations of deaf people de l'Epée and Sicard instructed in French. It is the language of deaf adults in North America and has been their language for more than a century and a half. It has been put to special uses recently by hearing

[2] For example, in England, where an oral method was everywhere used, only 11.6% of children surveyed in 1963 were found to have clear intelligible speech and good lipreading ability—quoted by Denmark (1973) from a Medical Offices survey.

persons where speech will not work: in noisy locations, under water, in airless space, and in communication between humans and chimpanzees. Used simultaneously with spoken English, it is also the language in which deaf persons achieve higher education.[3]

## 2. The Nature of a Sign Language

A sign language uses sight, as lipreading speech does, but uses it in a radically different way. Sounds—vowels and consonants along with differences in speed and intonation—are the elements of language received by the normal ear. What is "read" by a deaf person who has learned to do so is the positions of the lips, teeth, and tongue producing the sounds. But the elements of a sign language are things seen exactly as they are done. They do not divide into vowels and consonants, but into four kinds of elements: these are places, or *tabs*, different from each other but all recognizable as the place where a sign starts or acts or ends; designators, *dez*, the distinctive look of the hand or hands which makes the sign; *sigs*, the action itself; and the orientation (since 1960 shown in written notation by subscripts to the *dez* symbol).[4]

Just as vowels and consonants in some sequences but not in others make syllables of English, and one or more syllables form words, so the elements of Sign combine in some ways and not in others as *signs*. Signs are considered to "have meanings" just as words are; but here some of the common misunderstandings of sign language have their beginning. The usual notion, fostered by English-to-Sign handbooks, is that a sign represents a word of English and conversely that each English word listed "has a sign." The facts are different. The study of languages as systems complete in themselves, has shown that no word-for-word translation of one language into another will result in grammatical output. A sign may have some of the meanings and uses of an English word but not others. Likewise, a word may translate a sign occurring in some contexts but not in others. This being so, the phrases and sentences of English and Sign may be even more different than the words and signs of these two languages.

Here it is necessary to stop a moment and look more closely at the notion of "languages as systems complete in themselves." This idea is really a convenient fiction of linguists. Far from being complete in themselves, languages mingle with other systems at either end. At the

---

[3] Actually, signs used simultaneously with spoken English by native speakers of English will tend to be code equivalents of words in English sentence structures, but higher education is more than the words of speaking teachers and includes to a degree usually unsuspected the signing of deaf collegemates and deaf teachers.

[4] The notational conventions and terms referred to briefly here were first described in Stokoe, 1960.

meaning end, language connects to everything in the world that its users do and say and think. In other words, at this end there is an interface between language and the language user's whole culture. At the other end, the physical world of sights and sounds, the structures of language in order to get expressed must connect with some bodily mechanisms to produce an output that sight or hearing can receive. For most of mankind, the primary output is speech sound. For the deaf, a minority whose size may have been underestimated (Schein and Delk, 1974), the primary output is bodily activity sometimes called gestural, motor, nonverbal, mimic, or Sign activity.[5]

The notion of languages as "systems complete in themselves" also fails to describe languages in real life, when people individually or in groups use more than one language. Both in the larger, social sphere and inside the language habits of an individual, two or more language systems can mingle with each other and so lose absolute completeness.

However, the possibilities of competing or combining of two languages are different when one is English and the other is Sign. Signing activity and speaking activity can be carried on at the same time, but when that happens the signing is not usually the output of Sign as a language system. Instead, the signing speaker, or the interpreter following a speaker, is using signs as code symbols for the words being spoken.

Much of what is called sign language, and indeed most of what is taught in sign language courses is this kind of signing. It is not in such uses a language but a word-encoding system. Nor is it a perfect code such as fingerspelling, in which one hand sign and only one represents one letter of the alphabet. In word-encoding signing, instead of one-for-one matching, some word-and-sign pairs are very familiar to all (the deaf and hearing people) who use the encoding system; but other words do not have familiar sign representations. When saying one of these less familiar words, the speaker or interpreter may fingerspell the word or may perform a sign usually paired with some word similar in meaning to the one spoken.

This way of using signs as an encoding device is of course the entry point for most hearing people who learn sign language to converse with, work with, or teach the deaf. It has the advantage of being easily learned, *as an expressive medium*, for the learner does not have a whole new language to learn. This sign-for-word code can be memorized in a relatively short time and with practice enables the learner to make normal spoken utterances visible to deaf persons—actually to those who have a reasonably good command of English at the encoder's level and who also have practice in using this double output system.

---

[5] For a discussion of terminology and treatment of this kind of behavior, see Stokoe, 1974.

Like Morse telegraphy and fingerspelling, this process of sign-encoding spoken words allows its learner to gain skill and speed in transmitting before receptive skill develops. Unfortunately, many hearers who have learned it thus never do learn to receive signing with facility. All this is quite characteristic of secondary language codes. Learning a true language works the other way around: the learner gains real ability to produce output in the new language only after some genuine receptive ability is gained.

The latter process, learning Sign as a language, follows normal language learning patterns. Those hearing persons who do succeed in learning how to sign in a way approaching that of deaf native signers reach that level only after a long period of watching and understanding signers. Deaf people too who report first encountering numbers of other deaf signers say that before venturing any signs of their own they spent much time watching and figuring out what the others were saying. Also interpreters who very fluently encode the words of a speaker they are listening to often find it very difficult and anything but fluent to watch a signer and put his Sign output into spoken English. The latter task is genuine translating, the former is secondary encoding. Much of the difference in difficulty arises in this system difference.

## 3. System Differences

When the two systems, English and Sign, are considered, the possibilities of difference in structure between something said in standard English and the same idea expressed in Sign have been exaggerated and misrepresented (see, for example, Tervoort, 1968). It is quite possible for an expression in Sign to be exactly parallel to an expression in English, as we shall see. It is also possible for the constructions expressing the same idea to be quite different in structure or order in the two languages. This has led some users of Sign as well as some of its detractors to claim that sign is "ungrammatical" or has "no syntactical rules." Unfortunately this false notion, uncorrected by any real knowledge about language, is repeated in many textbooks used in training teachers of the deaf and is widely believed.

The signs in a Sign sentence may occur in the same order as the words in an English sentence, or they may occur in different order. A Sign sentence may seem to omit signs for words that are essential in the English sentence. Again the Sign sentence may have signs for which the English sentence has no equivalent word. Sign language grammar has its own rules as well as its own lexicon, or vocabulary of signs; and rules and lexicon of Sign differ from the rules and lexicon of English.

Seen as a whole system, then, Sign is quite like English or any other language. Its elements contrast with each other—but visibly instead of audibly. They combine in certain ways and not in others. These combinations, the signs, "have meaning" as words or morphemes in other languages do. Constructions combining signs, like constructions combining words, express meanings more completely and complexly than single signs or words can. These constructions or syntactic structures are systematic rule-governed structures. There is a unique set of rules for making sign language constructions just as there is for making standard English constructions, non-standard English constructions, or the constructions of any language.

Before looking at the extreme differences between Sign constructions and constructions in English, we will look more fully into the possibility of similarity. One thing that makes parallel constructions in the two languages possible is the general agreement that many signs and words form for practical purposes equivalent pairs. Another reason that constructions in Sign can be made to duplicate the order of English is really incidental to Sign. There is a third way for language to be presented to sight—different both from the changing appearance of a speaker's face and from the combinations of the elements making up signs. This third way is usually known as fingerspelling, but it has also been called manual English, dactylology, the manual alphabet, and chirology. It is usually very closely associated with Sign, but may of course also be used as a way of encoding English (or any language) without using Sign at all.

Fingerspelling works by virtue of the pre-existence of alphabetic writing. There is some evidence that its use—perhaps more for secret communication than for serving the deaf—is as old as the practice of scratching, carving, and writing letters (Abernathy, 1959; also Stokoe, 1975). When it is combined with sign language, the differences between Sign and English grammar and vocabulary may disappear. Words that have no counterpart in sign language, like *the*, *a*, *an*, *of*, and all the forms of *be*, are fingerspelled when the encoder wants to have the manual expression follow English rules.

Fingerspelling also serves as an important link between the two languages for the bilingual American deaf person. New signs are coined, and many old ones have been, by using the manual alphabet "hand" as *dez* and moving it in a certain way in a certain place. Thus the first letter of the borrowed English word becomes the dez aspect of the new sign. Signs for days of the week, color names (except *red*, *white*, and *black* (Stokoe, in press)), personal name signs, and many other signs are made in this way.

To the linguist interested in grammars, English and Sign may seem to differ enormously; but with the link which fingerspelling provides, the deaf American shifts from one language to the other without conscious notice. But two sociolinguistic distinctions need to be made. First, the deaf signer who is seen sometimes to use a sign, sometimes to fingerspell an equivalent word, is likely to have reached a higher educational level than one who uses the sign only. Second, there are a whole group of signs which in form are derived from short, frequent fingerspelled words; however, these are *not* used by the deaf in conversation with the hearing (Battison, 1978).

The conditions then, under which a Sign sentence will preserve the order of an English sentence are (a) the free use of fingerspelling, (b) the signer's competence to use English structure, and (c) communication situations that call for the use of English-like signing instead of the colloquial or casual variety. Such a situation may be the signed interpretation for a deaf audience of a formal lecture, or it may be the natural tact of a deaf signer when conversing with a hearing partner who knows sign-encoded words but is unfamiliar with Sign structures. If the communication situation does not call for this kind of adjustment of the output to English-like structures, Sign sentences may show a wide departure from the patterns of standard English. Two examples of such divergence will be examined in detail.

**3.1. Surface Simplification in Sign** The first example comes from one possible way of signing a simple and basic sentence in English: *He saw me.* One reason for calling this simple and basic is that its syntax may be described by a small number of explicit rules. Leaving aside all explanation of meaning and the sound output, we may use three rules and a brief lexicon to generate the sentence:

| | Lexicon |
|---|---|
| 1. S → NP + VP | |
| 2. NP → Pro | Pro: *he*(1st time), *me*(2nd time) |
| 3. VP → VT + NP | VT: *saw* |

Below is a diagram of the structure these rules generate and the word-string which results from replacing the terminal symbols with lexical entries:

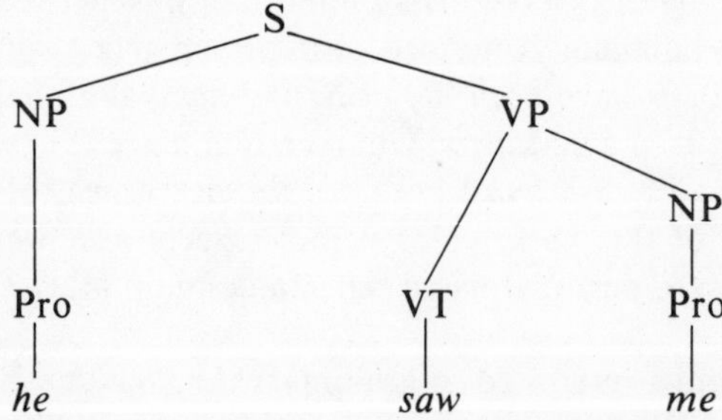


There should be no difficulty in relating this description by rule and diagram to the terminology traditionally used in parsing sentences. Rule 1

describes the structure as Subject followed by Predicate, and Rule 3 describes the predicate as Transitive Verb followed by Object.

The difficulty arises when the same sentence in Sign is put beside the English sentence or the English-like way of signing it. All that an observer will see is what manuals of sign language call one sign, but the sign is one this writer has not found in any of the manuals. The sign given for 'see' in the manuals is described approximately thus: "The V-hand, held up so that the fingertips are near the signer's eyes, back of hand outward, is moved away from the face a short distance." But instead of this, the signer making *He saw me* in Sign holds the V-hand pointing obliquely out at about shoulder level and looking at it bends the hand at the wrist sharply so that the fingertips point at the signer's own face.

Using the same rules for the Sign sentence just described as for the English sentence, we are forced to observe that two of three symbols are not given lexical entries:

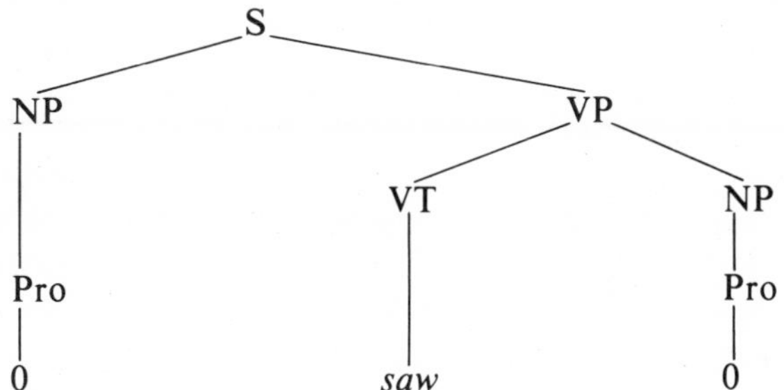


This does not seem satisfactory, although it seems to have a counterpart in English:

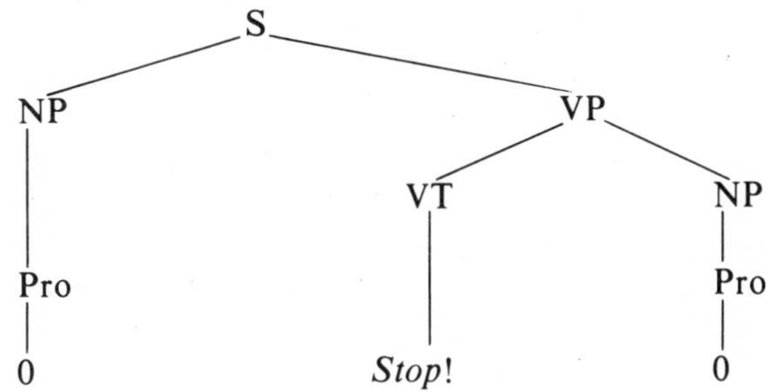


The speaker and hearer of English understand perfectly that *Stop*! may be expanded into *You stop* or *Stop that*! or *You stop that*!—any of which in fact may occur instead of *Stop*! Thus all four of these English sentences have the same structure and something like the same meaning.

In the case of *He saw me* signed, spoken, or written, the speaker and addressee understand: 'A masculine person, not the speaker or addressee (whom both could fully identify), saw the speaker.' In the English form (or the fully fingerspelled), there are two other bits of meaning which have surface representation. *Saw* has a form that indicates the seeing happened in the past; *me* redundantly indicates what its position in the string also tells, that it is the object. When an example like *He saw me* is used in a discussion such as this, we must suppose that the sentence was spoken where the speaker and hearer can both indicate and understand all the meaning of *he* through glances of their eyes. (Just how much sign language, actually gesticulation or kinesis (see Kendon, 1975), is necessary for efficient speech communication is another subject.) If we turn from speech to written English, we must suppose that *He saw me* is taken out of a series of sentences which more exactly identifies who *he* is.

In the Sign example, the same kinds of suppositions are needed. Since the Sign sentence translates 'He saw me,' the meaning 'past' must have come from some overt sign that occurred earlier in a sign language conversation or narrative. Although we can thus account for the element 'past' of the Sign sentence in the same way used to account for the reference of *he* in the English sentence, the problem remains how does the signer make his one sign sentence mean 'he saw me'? A signer does so (a) by a change in the way of making the sign SEE (which also means 'I see' or 'seeing' in general), (b) by starting the changed sign SEE with the hand held where it would be held to make the sign HE or HIM or HER, and (c) by moving the sign's salient feature, the spread fingers, to point toward the signer's self.

To sum up this comparison, or more properly this contrast, of the Sign and the English sentences more rules are needed. First, for the English sentence, *tense* and object-marking can be specified by rules:

1. S → NP + VP
2. NP → Pro (+Obj, in context of VP)
3. VP → VT + NP
4. VT → V + Past

The lexical choice and the verb-form change are now better managed by rule, as V: *see*, Past: vowel change, and Pro: *He*(*him*), *I*(*me*). But the structure changes very little:

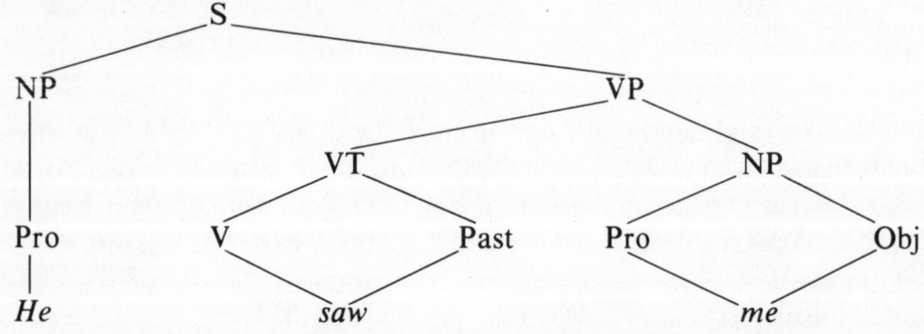

This is still a simple structure, but the one-sign sentence in Sign is not. To describe it requires more and different categories, as the diagram below shows:

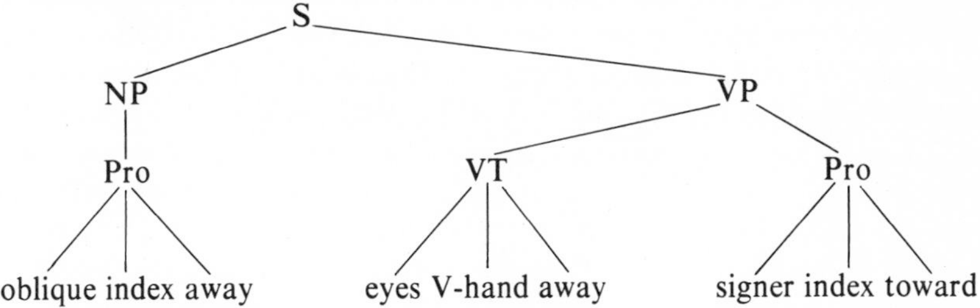


If these elements are put together in a Sign way, the result is a three-sign sentence with the same order as in English, but the one-sign sentence we have been considering can only be derived by transforming this structure. The elements, or features, of a sign actually occur simultaneously, as can be shown by writing them vertically, with the sign shown in caps underneath:

| | | | |
|---|---|---|---|
| *oblique* | near eyes | signer | ⟹ |
| index | *V-hand* | index | |
| away | away | *toward* | |
| HE | SEE | ME | |

The double arrow to the right above signifies that a transformation takes place; the italicized features are the ones preserved in the transformed structure shown below:

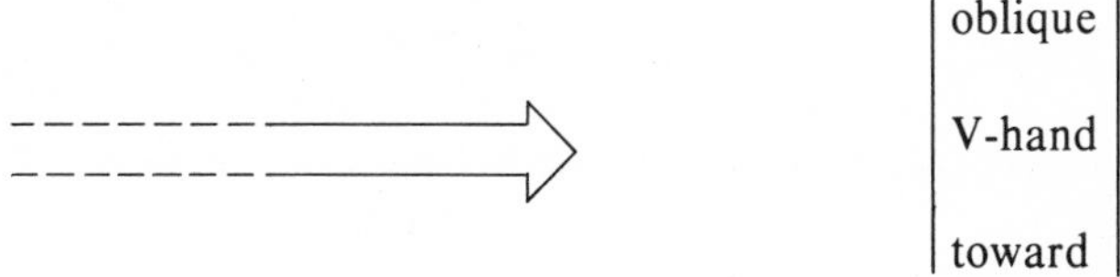


HE–SAW–ME

Other grammatical analyses of this one sentence of Sign may be made, but two points should be quite clear from the above: 1. Sign has just as much grammatical structure as English; and 2. Sign sentences convey exactly as much meaning to one who knows the language as do English sentences to a native speaker of English. And one point further: just as *He* saw me! and He *saw* me! and He saw *me*! and other possible intonations have different meanings for many speakers of English, so the Sign sentence can be varied with head and eye movements and modifications in the way the hand moves (Baker and Padden, 1978).

**3.2. Simultaneous Major Constituents in Sign Sentences** The second pair of sentences to be compared seems to show more complication on the English side. Grammarians who speak of generation by rules and transformations would say that there is a base structure underlying the sentence, *There's a man in there*, and point out that a transformation has made it what it is on the surface. They might write rules like the following to generate that base:

1. S → NP + VP
2. NP → Det + N
3. VP → Copula + Adv
4. Adv → Adv + Adv

The rules generate this structure for the base sentence:

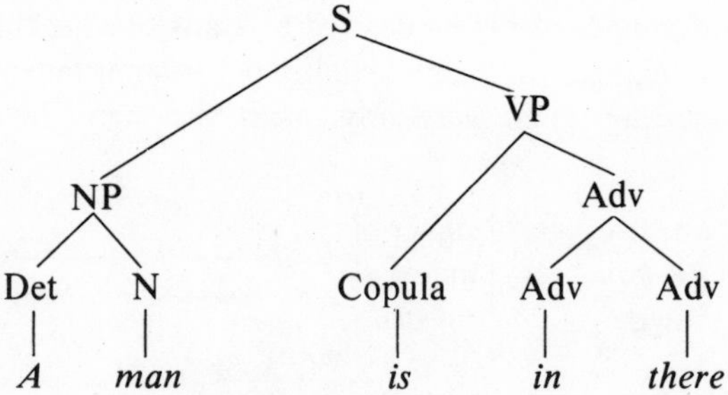


Various transformational rules to derive a *there*-sentence from a base like this have been proposed. (Part of the educational value of this kind of grammar is the practice it gives the proposer of rules.) One proposal is to consider that two bases are transformed by *embedding* one in the other. This requires the generation of another base: **There's something* (the * marks the sentence as non-occurring, suppositious). Then the part *something* is replaced by the whole original base sentence. The rule may be: something → S. The diagram below shows the first stage in this embedding transformation:

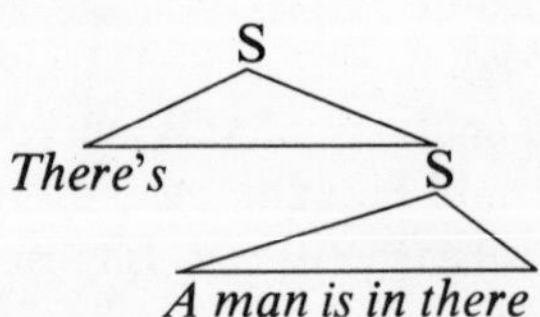


A deletion rule then allows removal of the extra *is*, to give: *There's a man in there*. The Sign sentence that "says" the same thing seems to be much simpler in structure. It uses only two signs, MAN and THERE. It has no determiner (i.e., no definite and indefinite article) exactly like those in English (see Chapter 5, "Syntax," in Stokoe, 1972) and no copula. Sign, like most of the world's languages does not translate *be* overtly, but in English-base to sign-encoded output all eight forms of *be* are fingerspelled, and in some new coding systems signs are invented for various forms of *be*. In this sentence—one actually observed as the output of an actual signer—the sign that equates with the English adverb *there*, means 'in there,' because the signer was pointing to a wall or a door in it; the man was not in sight. In English, *a man there* means 'where you can see him too.' Thus the actual situation in which it is used determines whether this sign means 'there' or 'in there.' This is not an unusual way for a language and its situational meanings to relate.

Despite the absence of articles and copula, despite its having just two signs, the Sign equivalent of 'There's a man in there' is a difficult structure to describe. What makes it so is that the system of rules we have been using specifies the *order* of the elements (whether like NP and Pro or like the words that replace them). But in the Sign sentence, both the signs composing it, its major constituents, appear at exactly the same time!

The rule, S → MAN + THERE, will not work, because any rule of the form, S → X + Y, means that X is followed by Y. Neither of the diagrams below can show the basic structure, because they also specify left-to-right order:

Order has meaning in Sign, of course, as in all languages. The difference between YOU FORGOT and FORGOT YOU signed may be just like the difference between these constructions in English. Sign, like English, has XY and YX as possible orders in its syntactical system, but nothing in our normal or special conventions of writing can show the third order Sign also has uniquely. If we write $\begin{smallmatrix}X\\Y\end{smallmatrix}$ or $\begin{smallmatrix}Y\\X\end{smallmatrix}$, we imply that one symbol, the upper, comes before the other. We might try what looks like a typist's error: **X**. But microscopic examination of a strikeover might reveal which key was hit first. Two signs performed at the same time contain no clues to help decide time priority. A speaker of English might cry, "In there! In there!" to which a listener might respond, "What?" and get the answer, "A man!" With this much to go on, grammarians will argue that beneath all this excitement lies the English language competence of speaker and listener, that their competence has quietly generated the base, *a man* (*is*) *in there*, and that two deletion rules have operated to produce the first outcry. But deletion, substitution, combination, and permutation transformations do not describe the sentence in Sign.

The point of this is not that generative-transformational grammars are inadequate. "All grammars leak." No theorist of language has yet adequately described the way languages work inside their own systems, let alone the way they work socially, in human groupings. The point, instead, is that Sign, far from having no grammar, has such interesting structure and so unusual a system that it challenges all theories of grammar (see Stokoe, 1972, Chapter 5). The difference seen in just two pairs of sentences should warn us that everything we know about English, right or wrong, must be questioned all over again before we apply it to a sign language and what its users do with it.

Equally important is the fact that languages are much easier to learn and use than to describe or explain. Every spoken language used (now or in the past) has been learned and learned thoroughly by every child, bright, normal, or dull, that is born among its users—provided of course that the child can hear. Children who cannot hear learn sign languages in the same way. Moreover, the elements of a sign language can with exposure and use become clear and understandable to anyone who can see. The combinations of these elements are signs that have meaning for all who use the particular language they occur in (see articles by Battison and Jordan (1976). Having meaning, the signs can also be used to translate English words,—but to translate them no better nor worse than the words of any language can translate the words of another. The combinations of these signs can make sentences in Sign, or with fingerspelling freely used, can be used to make a reasonable facsimile of an English sentence. Finally, it is possible then to encounter signing in which signs are arranged exactly like the words of a standard English sentence but also to encounter signing mildly or wildly different.

## 4. Social Implications of Sign Language

In the preceding section we saw that sign language structure in sentences is sometimes like, sometimes unlike the structure of English sentences. Education of the deaf is also both like and unlike American education in general. Of the latter, William Labov (1969) says, ". . . the fundamental role of the school is to teach reading and writing of standard English." But the schools which he looks at in the aggregate play their roles on the solid stage of language competence. An American child comes to school after four or five years of intensive language learning and use. As some would say, the child has the rules, i.e., the competence to generate and to understand countless sentences—in some standard or non-standard dialect of English, Labov might add. Others would put it somewhat differently: the child has completely learned the sound subsystem, is nearly done learning the inventory of grammatical forms and their combinations, but is only well started on learning the whole semantic system of the language spoken where he grew to school age.

Most deaf children probably will not have learned any of this. The school for the deaf child undertakes to teach literacy of course, but it assumes an additional role, to teach the child English, as if it were the child's native language. But hearing children learn naturally, do not have to be taught a native language. Language that is taught is either a second language or something as unrelated to real language as the *can/may* distinction drilled into every American boy with negligible results.

What surprises linguists like Labov when they learn of it, and shocks compassionate teachers like Herbert Kohl (1966), is that no school for the deaf uses sign language to perform either the role of teaching literacy or of teaching English.[6] It would take too much time away from the study of sign language to go into the language teaching methods in use and the rationalizations in vogue for not using Sign, and much of the educational literature about language is vague or worse. Time can be better spent in looking at the sociolinguistic facts of life in silence.

One of the most important uses of language is the formation and preservation of social groups. The term *group* can be given its widest meaning, for language has critical functions in the intimate group of two (though perhaps the smallest group is one person thinking), as well as in the widest groups: e.g., Western Civilization, The Free World, Socialist People's Republics. If these extremes are too remote to be convincing, one has only to recall the inclusive and divisive effect of just one word, *black*, as used in American society in the nineteen-sixties.

The most noticeable effect of Sign is to make deaf persons using it immediately visible and visibly different. Conversely, not using it hides the deaf person from detection as different by a casual observer. An unreasonably high valuation put upon this effect has worked along with outmoded language theories to keep Sign out of schools. Nevertheless, these facts remain: Those who cannot hear must use eyes instead of ears to receive information, and in this respect they are very different from hearing persons. Communication with others by lipreading and acquired speech is no more normal than communication by signing gesturally (see Sarles, 1974). Deaf persons, whether educated orally or left alone, do sign to each other.

The deaf constitute a social group both by the difference of not hearing but even more by the social working of language. But this is grouping

[6] Even in an era of "total communication" the usual school for the deaf allows a multitude of modes of expressing language—speech, signs, fingerspelling, cues, etc.—but only "straight" or "correct" English as that language.

by separation from hearing society, and deaf people form groups just as people generally do, in large part by the operation of language. Having a common language joins people with the strongest of bonds.

Using sign language, however, does not make a single and homogeneous group. Just as among users of any of the world's languages, there are all kinds of subgroupings determined also by language and its use. One of these is the subgrouping by age and language. Children, teenagers, adults who use sign language are in far more complete communication within these and smaller age groups than across them. The case of infants is somewhat different, as in any language community. The fortunate deaf ones—from a language standpoint—have deaf parents and perhaps deaf brothers and sisters with whom sign language puts them into perfectly natural communication at the earliest possible age. Once the sign language user joins a group of agemates—and those whose sign acquisition is not a family affair often first learn it then—this user's language is theirs too and stays for a lifetime.[7]

Another kind of language grouping, observed among speakers of all languages, is found among Sign users. Persons of the same age group sign alike, except that those of the same sex sign more alike. Obviously physiological causes in vocal tract size can be found for the difference between women's and men's voices; but when the focus is language, not speech, the differences in vocabulary, grammatical structures, and every other part of the system can be observed. Here the observer who comes new to signing is at an advantage. One of the first impressions will be of the difference between the signing of men and of women, a difference that may be described as angular or sharp *vs.* rounded, smooth, or graceful. The reader may doubt that there is a similar difference in male and female speakers of English unless he has heard and noticed this difference in other dialects than his own.

A third kind of grouping, a more precisely interpersonal relationship that language accomplishes, it does through style levels. Martin Joos in his book (1967) of the same name calls these "The Five Clocks." As five clocks can be set to tell different times, the style levels of language can be set—and are set—to tell different things of importance about the relationship of speaker to addressee. These levels Joos calls, "intimate, casual, consultative, formal, and frozen," with consultative as the central norm with opposite tendencies. Consultative style joins two people through language despite their differences, because "two heads are better than one" when consulting upon most subjects. The vocabulary, struc-

[7] A study of communication in a group of adult deaf signers shows this and other interesting features of deaf culture (Stokoe, Bernard, and Padden, 1976).

ture, manner of production, and information content of this style can be taken as standard for the language. In casual style, the language itself implies 'we're friends' and therefore much information may be left out that must be in place in consultative style. Also in casual style, slang is not only permitted but required. In the other direction, formal style treats the addressee as if he wasn't there—in fact he isn't able to reply now because he is one of an audience or other formal group. All the connections must be clear in this variety of language along with every bit of information; and since interruptions are not expected or allowed, *careful* is the obvious characterization of formal style. This is the speaking style, of course, that comes closest to written style of the kind which gets published.

Intimate style comes very close to being a contradiction to widely used definitions of language, because it is a social vehicle, a possession shared only by those who know the rules. For intimate style is *private* language. Husbands and wives, to take one kind of group, have a special vocabulary, including pet names for each other, as many observers have noted; but a clearing of the throat or a grunt or a word that would have little meaning in other circumstances—things like these have more force in an intimate group than whole paragraphs of formal language can have.

Frozen style is the imaginative label Joos gives to the style of (good) prose and poetry. He does not call it "literary" perhaps because in casual or consultative exchanges we may take the word *literary* to mean artificial, artsy-craftsy, or hoked up. "Frozen" seems a chilly label for language until we think of how our standard of eating has improved since the invention of frozen foods. From his discussion of this style level, Joos launches into a description of literature, its nature, uses, and production, by actually creating some. This is also pertinent to the study of sign language and is of the utmost importance to every person who has contact with a deaf child. Sign language is not written, but it has a literature. Careful language characterizes formal style, but artistic language, frozen style, has more than just care behind it. Many peoples whose culture does not include writing have songs, poems, dances, charms, histories, and liturgies that use frozen language style. Sign language users too have artistic forms of expression, and themes to express in them (see especially, Eastman, 1974). Two of the most intensively developed at the present time are fortunately widely accessible to non-signers. One is a union of Sign and interpretive dancing in which signs seem naturally—but really with consummate artisty—to merge into the total movement of the dance. The other is Theater of the Deaf—visible on television and in national and international tours as well as in local deaf communities. This too is a natural-seeming development, from pantomime and from the pioneering of the Gallaudet Dramatic Club in the fifties and sixties.[8]

All five of the styles Joos describes, then, are also found in the use signers make of Sign; and recognizing them has tremendous implications for the study of sign language. First of course is the conviction that recognition of them brings with it: if a sign language works intimately, casually, consultatively, formally, and artistically, even as it unites and divides its users by age, and as its structures come from its self-contained system—then surely it is a language of the depth and complexity that only languages have, a language well worth study. Second, when its "frozen style" embodies artistic achievements that make (hearing) critics of drama and dance jump to their feet in applauding, the parents and teachers of deaf children must come to realize that using signs does not cut off the heights but opens new ranges to be surmounted. And third, for the study of sign language itself, the five styles are indispensable instruments.

An attempt was made in 1965 by Elizabeth McCall to explain the syntax of Sign in "A Generative Grammar of Sign." She writes phrase-structure rules and transformational rules to generate some sentences of sign language she observed in use. One shortcoming is that the signs themselves, the physical elements of signing, are not described. Instead the sentences collected are recorded as sequences of English words used to translate the signs observed. But the use of "the five clocks" would have prevented a more serious flaw. The signing was observed at picnics and other social occasions. The persons signing were friends, fellow workers, immediate relatives, and intimates of each other, as is learned from the introduction and from the internal evidence of the sentences themselves. It is a safe bet, then, if not a certainty, that the signing observed was all on the casual and intimate level, never even rising to the consultative; since persons not on casual terms do not go to such gatherings with each other, or if they do, as Joos points out, they stay on strangers' footing for a few seconds at most—the time for a formal introduction and one response. Then, since the characteristics of casual style are *ellipsis* and *slang*, and those of intimate style are *extraction* (of information that the intimate already knows) and *jargon*, any attempt to write the grammar of Sign and its (partial) lexicon from this data is bound to describe something quite different from the standard (consultative or formal) sign language, the sign language that might be used to advantage in schools. Indeed, the first two rules of the McCall grammar

[8] See, for instance, the playbill for the Gallaudet College Theater's production of "hands," November 14, 15, 21, & 22, 1975, and the "Director's Note" by G. C. Eastman.

(page 22) show more things left out (in parentheses) than left in the base structures:

$$1.\quad S \rightarrow \left\{ \begin{matrix} G \\ (Adv_e) \end{matrix} + (NP) + Pred + (T) \right\}$$

$$2.\quad G \rightarrow \left\{ \begin{matrix} (Adv_e) \\ G_2 \end{matrix} \quad + \quad G_1 \right\}$$

Using this same procedure would result in a much elided and extracted English sentence structure. Suppose an overheard conversation between husband and wife goes like this:

"Dear?"
"Engh?"
"Checks."
"N't goin' that way."

After much study, a panel of experts on English as it is spoken might translate the passage as follows, with material in the parentheses to show what information has been left out because the person spoken to already knows it:

"*Dear*? (Are you listening, because I would like to remind you?)"
"*Engh*? (= Yes; I'm listening; what is it?)"
"(I am almost out of blank) *checks* (as you know, and I must do the accounts tonight. Would you please stop at the bank on your way to work and order some for me?)"
". . . (I have to drive Charlie to the airport this morning, and I wo)*n't* (be) *going that way*."

Then, if we were to write rules for English sentences like those actually spoken, with parentheses to show what elements were left out, we would possibly get a generative grammar of (intimate) English much like the first generative grammar of Sign.

Two other ranges that Joos relates to the range of five styles are those of *scope* and *responsibility*. A speaker or user of a language may be understood only by persons in a small locality, in a wider provincial region, or anywhere that the language is used. Scope widens from local, to provincial, to standard, then again it narrows to conservative or all the way to puristic. Education and variety of experience are usually the means of changing local and provincial ways of using language to standard, but personal preference usually accounts for the later narrowing if it occurs. There is frequent reference among sign users to other signers' "home signs" and much condescension in discussing these local and provincial manners of signing. "Ameslan" as Lou Fant (1974–75) describes it, appears to be provincial in scope. Ironically, the makers of handbooks and many teachers of sign language—to hearing adults mainly, since children are not supposed to use it—miss the standard scope and take a conservative or even purist attitude; their descriptions of "the right way" to make signs can depart as far from standard in one direction as home signers do in the other direction. Standard is of course not a matter of legislation but of currency. When leaders of the national deaf organizations discuss standardization of Sign as part of the work of, e.g., The National Association of the Deaf, The Communicative Skills Program (of the N.A.D.), or the Jewish Deaf Association, they are not trying to halt the tides of natural language change but only to recognize that there are local, provincial, standard, conservative, and puristic kinds of Sign, and to indicate that one who studies, practices, and uses standard Sign is on the surest ground.

The other range Joos treats is *responsibility*. Just as in a person's way of speaking we detect character, so it is in Sign use. The smooth operator, the promoter, the born loser, the show-off, and all the other types that we associate closely with a particular way of using language are all to be found in the sign-using community too. One does not have to be a native signer or expert in sign language to recognize the general indications of character in language use. This kind of language difference is what Joos calls responsibility. We judge it of course by the way a person talks, looks, and acts, so that it is a language difference closely linked to many other indications of character.

## 5. Bilingualism in Sign and English

The constant use of two languages, or bilingualism, may be looked at from either end of a sociolinguistic telescope. In the broad view, it is a complicated social and political problem with a linguistic center and a very explosive potential, if peoples of two language stocks must live under one government. It is also, if looked at closely, a valuable skill of an individual person. The study of sign language requires looking in both directions. The deaf population of the United States may suffer the same irritation, frustration, even loss of basic rights and privileges as do other minority language groups (Vernon, 1974). The deaf individual, however, faces a unique problem: one of the two languages he must use is not oral—the full definition partially quoted at the start of this paragraph reads, "Bilingualism is the constant *oral* use of two languages."

The broad social aspect of bilingualism has many facets when looked at worldwide. Canadian bilingualism involves two languages of high prestige, and the rivalry of French, British, and Canadian cultural values complicates the sociolinguistic situation. In other bilingual areas, only one of the languages may have the prestige of worldwide use, while the other remains little known and perhaps unwritten. In the past, obviously, the world language would become the language of the dominant group and the local language remain the tongue of the governed classes. In the present world, however, it is possible to find the language of the emerging nation made official, and English, French, Dutch, or Arabic reduced to secondary status.

These are but a few of the possibilities when languages are in contact, but for the deaf the pattern is still most like that of the colonial past. Sign language is not written, though now it may be. Sign is little known, either to the general public or to those whose study is language. It is excluded from school and religious instruction—though it should be said that several religious groups have been and continue to be its strongest supporters. For the deaf of other countries, the bilingual situation can be even less advantageous. Colonialism, imperialism, and racism—words that occur as often now in hot debate as in cool study—still summon up a social attitude that can be discerned in much official policy regarding Sign. Here for instance are the words of a British royal commission to examine "the place if any of 'manual communication' in the education of deaf children" (emphasis added):

> Clearly the *major risks* associated with the use of a combined method which includes signing would be eliminated if the signs were themselves chosen from a systematic language with normal grammatical structure (Lewis, 1968).

The chairman of this commission amplified his remarks in a later address to those concerned with teaching deaf children:

> Everybody knows what is commonly said about signing, that it may impede, may retard, the development of language. I think there is some misunderstanding about this, if I may give my personal opinion. The notion is that signing is more natural, that signing is easier than *the mother tongue* [whose?]. Up to a point this is true, but if signing is to be a means of educating the children, the question is whether it is in the hands of teachers who understand what they are doing and have the skill to put it into practice; and how far the signing itself is linguistic (Lewis, 1969).

The commonly held notion that "the mother tongue" is the sole repository of "normal grammatical structure" is a concept well known to anthropologists, who call it ethnocentrism. When it is used to deny that some other language is "systematic" and to impute to the out-group who use that other language a deficiency of mental functioning, this notion comes perilously near racism. The study of the grammatical system of sign languages as well as their semantic and symbolic systems is the best way to replace such superstition and prejudice with useful knowledge. To begin, one may with profit read the essays "The Linguistic Community" and "Sign Language Dialects" by Carl Croneberg (in Appendix C, 297-311, and Appendix D, 313-319, of *A Dictionary of American Sign Language on Linguistic Principles* (1976). More recently, several articles by James C. Woodward appearing in the quarterly journal *Sign Language Studies* have shown how all of these subsystems of language relate to the special social dimensions of the deaf community.

Social bilingualism is important to an understanding of American education of the deaf, but the bilingual development of the deaf individual is crucial—for an excellent case study of such development see *Sign Language Studies*, 1976,10:37–41. In fact, a deaf person faces more than the classic bilingual dilemma. The member of a minority language group has the choice of staying monolingual and so staying a second or third class citizen, socially and economically. If he tries to shift to the language of the dominant majority, he may either succeed and so shut himself off from his background and incur social and psychic costs, or fail and be rejected by the dominant group with equally serious consequences. Ideally, of course, he should grow up where he can learn and use both the languages with about equal frequency—a situation hard to realize.

But the person who cannot hear does not have even these hard choices. The chances are ten to one against his growing up in a family using sign language, and therefore he must come to school age without knowing any real use of spoken language or of standard, community governed sign language. Even with sign language learned at home or from association with older deaf children, the deaf person cannot receive any formal education in this language, because schools and teachers, if not his parents, reject signing. Instead, this person will be taught in school to make sounds and perhaps to lipread them, to recognize and to write letters, and even, in exceptional situations, to fingerspell. All of this activity has an English base, of course, and is designed to make out of this person a monolingual user of English. Early resistance, or failure, on his part to function like a native speaker of English—dropping out more than likely—consigns him not just to a depressed economic and social status but in some cases even to sheltered institutions.

Fortunately, the good sense and adjustment to reality of many members of the deaf linguistic minority exceeds that of well-meaning officialdom. None or very few of those whose native language is Sign suppose that a monolingual life in a sign-using deaf community is an open option—although there was a short-lived movement early in this century to set aside some of the Southwest Territory for a deaf state which would have the language of signs as its official language. While the authorities in school try to force deaf children to function monolingually in a vocal-symbol language, wiser heads in the deaf community strive for maximally effective bilingualism.[9] The higher the level of competence in reading and writing English the deaf signer can attain, the better his life chances in the bilingual situation. Acquired speech and lipreading skill are also valued assets that no deaf person despises. The deaf do object to a formal educational program which concentrates on the two "oralist" skills alone when all evidence shows that reasonable proficiency in them is attainable by very few individuals; while for most, even a dozen years of full-time effort brings only frustration and non-success. Meanwhile, the language competence in English that could have been fostered through use of the deaf pupil's Sign competence is lost.

From the point of view of one who cannot hear, bilingualism can be more a challenge than a dilemma. Direct personal communication with one's friends will naturally be in sign language. One does not have the same kind of relationship with foreigners; and all speakers of oral languages will always be in a sense foreign to one who must listen with eyes not ears. But consultative and formal participation with others is almost exclusively in English, the language of the general culture, which affords the only way into that culture and all its benefits. Therefore the person who cannot hear will learn just as much English just as well as circumstances allow. The real issue is not oralism *vs.* manualism, as much time has been wasted arguing; instead the issue is whether the true bilingual situation of the deaf—Sign *and* English—is to be recognized.

The question to be faced by all who have a hand in shaping the life circumstances of the deaf is this: will the deaf person reach maximum competence in English better if forced into apparent monolingual use of English or if the need for bilingual development is acknowledged and satisfied? This question is a somewhat different way of looking at the old controversy. Linguistics and sociolinguistics, that is, provide a way of saying not "one language or the other" but "both." Linguistics as an anthropological science starts from the view of language as central in total culture. From that it follows that differences in the way people communicate, in the things that they do, and in their languages are seen as data to be studied and not as deviation, error, deprivation, primitivism, or degeneracy. Again, sociolinguistic studies have shown repeatedly that bilingualism, diglossia, and other intimate combinations of languages in the individual and in social groups are facts of life. From a sociolinguistic viewpoint, the bilingual language competence of the deaf may be compound or complex; i.e., they may be more at home in Sign than in

---

[9] See especially reports from the Communicative Skills Program of the National Association of the Deaf, in the *Deaf American*.

English or may be equally competent in both. In contrast, the psychological model behind much current policy for the deaf treats the language of the deaf as a pathological condition.

Fortunately, some teachers' practice is better than their theory; but bad theory can corrupt practice. A teacher may understand a complicated statement, an explanation, or a request presented entirely in Sign and may respond appropriately. Yet this teacher is all too likely to tell an observer that the pupil who has just communicated in Sign "has no language"! What we are to understand from this amazing statement requires explanation:

1. By "language" the teacher means 'competence in English needed (a) to understand grammatical sentences presented in the teacher's voice or in writing, and (b) to produce grammatical sentences in the pupil's own voice or writing.'
2. By "no language" the teacher means: '(a) The pupil's responses to written or spoken sentences are inappropriate or are lacking; (b) the pupil's production is not grammatical; or (c) both of these.'
3. By "has no language" the teacher implies that the pupil is as much out of place in an ordinary elementary classroom as a two-year-old would be in second grade.
4. By using "language" as the token for 'correct English' and by not allowing *language* to stand for Sign or anything else than "correct" English, the teacher is guilty of falsely condemning the pupil to a subhuman, socially inferior status.
5. By implication this teacher is also unconsciously confessing and excusing failure—who could be blamed for not teaching anything to a child who "has no language"?

Such a teacher is still on the side of the angels. At least the pupil's communication in Sign has been responded to and understood adequately. What this teacher says and thinks about "language" are the residue of teacher-education and textbooks. That this teacher does not use Sign to address the pupil and to help pupils learn English is doubtless the policy of the school, and to run against such policy is as much as many teaching positions are worth. Yet the study of sign language could free this teacher from the fear and ignorance that equate all knowledge and thought with a single language or dialect.

Unfortunately the teacher who can understand the pupils' Sign utterances is not typical nor even part of a substantial minority. The usual teacher response to the first appearance of a deaf child's sign language is often such utter rejection that signing is ever afterward hidden from teachers. This does not keep the teachers from saying however that the pupil "has no language." Sociolinguistics could at least tell these teachers that even in a "one-hundred-percent American" community there are other languages than English in use and other varieties of English than that familiar to the teacher. Teachers and others in special education programs who will become teachers of the deaf can find other benefits too in the study of sign language and in the findings of linguistics.

The greatest obstacle to second language learning is lack of opportunity. There must be a great many persons, among them teachers, who would like to know another language if only they could find someone to teach it and use it with them. The good fortune of finding a person one spends minutes or hours with every day to learn from as a native speaker of an exotic language seems remote. Nevertheless, most teachers of the deaf are blessed with such riches to the point of embarrassment. An older deaf pupil knows far more sign language (both vocabulary and structure) than any teacher is likely to imagine. Indeed the pupil has probably become extremely skillful in hiding this knowledge because of the attitude of the school and its teachers.

So, if a teacher of the deaf has a genuine desire to learn Sign, the problem is not to find one who knows it but to persuade those who know it that using Sign is permissible and will not be punished overtly or covertly. A pupil who is at a loss, halting, inarticulate in English may be fluent, imaginative, even eloquent in Sign. Of course one who resolves to learn the pupil's language must first accept the fact that it is a language, must remain undisturbed by its differences from English, and must make the pupil-informant comfortable in the new situation. In some cases it may be easier to find an informant not in the pupil-teacher relationship. Many teachers in schools for the deaf can find a colleague (perhaps in the vocational department), a dormitory supervisor, or another staff member easier to approach and to learn Sign from. After all, learning the pupils' language requires a difficult reversal of roles. There are many references in the writing of deaf persons to the kind of response (often unconscious) from hearing persons that effectively and finally checks their attempts to speak. The looks on the faces of those standing near when they venture to produce their version of speech sounds are often mentioned in personal histories. Just as clearly, the deaf person is quick to perceive the kind of effect his use of signs has elicited in the strictly oral school environment. The classroom teacher who is at least open to being convinced that there is a case for the study of sign language has only to be attentive, sympathetic, encouraging. But this kind of attitude may go directly counter to the policy of the school and so needs to be carefully considered.

## 6. Classroom Research and Application

Once contact is made with a willing informant and a teacher is in a situation where the study of sign language can begin, progress can be rapid. Besides being in more direct communication with pupils, the teacher who learns to sign and to understand Sign is able to engage in fruitful research of a directly applicable kind. Contrastive study of Sign and English has barely begun as a formal research activity, so that any teacher with a classroom of deaf children is in a position to anticipate the professional researcher. The first kind of contrast noted by everyone who encounters a new language is vocabulary's contrasting pairs. "What is the sign for this word?" is a question asked hundreds of times by those who are starting to learn sign language. But the kind of information this question produces has only limited usefulness. If there were really a definite answer each time the question were asked, or if there were to be exactly one sign for each English word the asker already knows, there would be no sign language—only a simple one-for-one code of signs to represent all English words.

A more effective way to study contrasts may be put like this: Given sign A and word B, each translating the other, what are the differences in the way the word and the sign are used? This question is open-ended. A complete answer requires a full description of each of the two languages. Yet much useful information can be discovered by asking it. Take for example the word *to* and the sign TO: the third word in "from Chicago *to* New York" is equivalent to the third sign in, FROM CHICAGO TO NEW-YORK. The sign written as TO is made by touching one index fingertip with the other. However, in translating "he forgot *to* pay," no sign is used for the third word. HE FORGET PAY is perfectly grammatical Sign. This Sign sentence may be translated into English in various ways:

HE FORGET PAY

1. Him forget pay.
2. He forgot pay.
3. He forgot paid.
4. He forgot to pay.

The first is likely when a hearing translator has an open or a hidden animosity toward sign language and those who use it. The second and third are more likely to occur if the translator of the English sentence is more at home in Sign than in his second language—remember that the English speaker in a billion or so patterns similar to this has never failed to hear a [t′] between the two verbs and never failed to pronounce a [t′], but the deaf translator has *never* heard one. The fourth translation, the only one in grammatical English, is the one produced by the person seeing HE FORGET PAY in Sign and having the capability from studying sign language to make a full translation from one language to the other.

To return a moment from sentence translation: The inescapable contrast between mutually translating vocabulary items can be broken into more detailed questions, to which the teacher who studies sign language can apply answers immediately. One thing to look for is a one-to-two contrast. Some of the signs in Sign need two words to translate them; e.g., SEARCH (the cupped hand circles in front of the signer's face) equates with English *search for*. Conversely, some words of English need two signs for their translation; e.g., *discuss* goes into Sign as DISCUSS ABOUT.

No one has yet made a full study of these contrasting sets of singles and doubles, so that the teacher of deaf children with a real interest in sign language is in a better situation for studying them than are most graduate students in linguistics. The teacher may also be the most important user of this kind of research result, and that teacher's pupils are in line to receive the most benefit. Two-word to one sign and two-sign to one word pairs present obvious contrasts for anyone who is studying sign language; the bilingual deaf signer whose English proficiency is classed as "native" also finds these pairs clearly contrasting. But to deaf pupils in a classroom or doing homework, there is no such clear cut contrast between the patterns of one language and the patterns of the other. They will persist in writing "I searched the word in the dictionary" or "we discussed about Vietnam." Any experienced teacher of the deaf can list a great many more examples of these two kinds of mix-ups. The teacher who makes a study of sign language, however, will know how to take steps toward reducing the frequency of these pattern interferences and increasing the frequency of grammatical combinations that the pupils can produce. The algorithm here is a bilingual one: See here is the way that we sign it; but if we want to write it or say it in English, we put in this word for two signs (or put in two words for this sign).

How much and how fast the English production of pupils so taught will improve may be viewed optimistically or pessimistically, but there is good evidence that simply having a teacher who knows and makes known to the pupils that they are dealing with two language systems, not one, will pay educational as well as social dividends. Another approach is to look for pairs of English words that occur in the same order in habitual usage but when translated may take the opposite order in Sign (e.g., *plane reservation*: RESERVATION PLANE), and for word pairs that cannot be separated but are used apart in sign translations, and vice versa.

Besides these syntactic contrasts, which are relatively easy to discover and to deal with, there are other system differences between the two languages that need study. English has a unique tense system. Every finite verb in English must be marked for past tense or remain unmarked; sign language, however, does not use verbs as time indicators at all. Of course signers like everyone else must deal with time. Here too the classroom teacher is in a position to do front-line psycholinguistic research: How do children who use sign language deal with time while their understanding of time and sequence, their concepts for dealing with time, and their language symbols for the concepts are developing? The work of Piaget on children's growth in handling time, space, equivalence, proportion, and other matters is of use here, as is the application of it Furth (1966, 1973) has made in his Piagetian studies with deaf school children. Children must reach a certain stage in development to deal with such operations in language, and Furth has found that this stage occurs at about the same chronological age whether the children are native hearers-speakers of English or born deaf and so used to using visual instead of vocal signs for thought and communication.

To move from these syntactic contrasts to semantic differences, so common a matter as *degree* is treated in a quite different way in the two languages. The English speaker has command of resources of paralanguage and kinesics shared with other uses of the same dialect. Thus the speaker can say "good!", and use intonations and voice features and facial expression and gestures that will modify the effect of the word in several ways. But in addition to these modifications, the speaker has, usually, a wide range of similar words to choose among. Instead of *good*, the speaker might have said, fine, right, ok, excellent, wonderful, or first rate. A different choice of word, like the use of paralinguistic and kinesic modifications, will modify the effect—certainly it will indicate style, scope, and responsibility. Then too, all the users of English that the speaker frequently talks with are also in complete control (though it may be outside their awareness) of both of these scales of modification, the paralinguistic and the word choice. Like the speaker they know how to interpret the result of both ranges at once—e.g., to decide whether *wonderful* with lower than normal pitch, falling intonation, and a grimace of resignation indicates a more or less negative reaction than *good* spoken with false heartiness, speeded-up tempo, clipped resonance, and a frown.

In contrast with all of this is the sign language user's communication of similar ranges of meaning. The first and most striking difference is vocabulary size. Sign language generally has many semantic areas covered by a single sign, whereas the same or similar areas of meaning are covered by a number of different words in English. Everyone who first begins to study the communication of persons using sign language notes with surprise the subtlety and precision of their interchanges. Sign language has no need for large numbers of closely related separate items of vocabulary, because one sign can be easily modified to express many degrees of meaning. Sincerity, intensity, interest, and other nuances are part of the signer's performance of a sign. The size, speed, tension, precision, and duration of the actions involved in signing are all variable at will; and all are used and understood as message-bearing fractions of total communicative activity—but again most of this is outside the awareness of sign users just as speakers need not think about the tone of voice or gesticulations they are using.

But the way of looking at signing just described—as consisting of "signs" and different manners of "making signs"—is certainly under the influence of older ways of looking at languages generally. Looking at facial expressions, speed, size, and other things that occur as variable elements of "making a sign" in a different way may prove useful. In this way, a facial expression or eye movement or tempo change might not occur without an accompanying sign but might still have a definite and grammatical role in expressing meaning. Then the facial action or manner of performance would be very much like, for example, the *-s* of English, which does not occur except with a word, but which may make a noun plural or may mark a non-past verb with a singular subject.

This contrast between English and Sign vocabulary size and function finds a rough analogy in two mechanics' toolboxes. One has a complete set of wrenches, each of a fixed size to fit just one different size of nut or bolt head he expects to work with. The other has just one adjustable wrench, which will open wide enough for the largest and can be made to fit anything smaller. But this contrast of English and sign language needs more study. In fact it would be best to treat it as a hypothesis. The testing of its truth by observing sign language and English in operation is research which any teacher working with deaf pupils may undertake. Here too the opportunity to apply what one finds out is large. Those pupils who are adept at conveying to each other finely shaded meanings have real semantic skill and may prove apt learners, *if shown how to put the same message in standard English*. And this can be done once the teacher has worked out the full details of the contrasting patterns. For the teacher engaged in this contrastive study there are accessible materials of the most valuable kind in the classroom. What the pupils are saying to each other is by all odds the most interesting to them of all materials. What the lesson is about, what Dick said to Jane, what the teacher says—these things do not come near in pupil interest what the pupils sign to each other about. One real objective of the study of sign language is the ultimate ability of the teacher to participate in the real, intimate, vital communication of deaf pupils, then to impart all the knowledge and experience and understanding that a teacher has, and ultimately to show the pupils that what they have to say may be put in English appropriate also to the message.

Interesting as sign language is as a system, tantalizingly like other languages and fascinatingly different, the real value to be found in the study of sign language is a human, not an abstract scientific value. All language is unique; but the study of sign language reveals that *language* is both abstract, independent of speech and of gestural expression, and biologically concrete because of its expression. Language depends on the human brain, not on the naked or electronically assisted human ear.

## REFERENCES

Abernathy, E. R. 1959. An historical sketch of the manual alphabets. Am. Ann. Deaf 104:232–240.

Baker, C., and Padden, C. 1978. Focusing on the nonmanual components of American Sign Language. *In* Siple (ed.), Understanding Language Through Sign Language Research, pp. 27–58. Academic Press, New York.

Battison, R. M. 1978. Lexical borrowing in American Sign Language. Linstok Press, Silver Spring, Md.

Battison, R. M., and Jordan. 1976. *Articles in* Sign Lang. Stud. 10:53–80.

Croneberg, C. 1976. The linguistic community. *In* A Dictionary of American Sign Language on Linguistic Principles, Appendix C, pp. 297–311.

Croneberg, C. 1976. Sign language dialects. *In* A Dictionary of American Sign Language on Linguistic Principles, Appendix D, pp. 313–319.

Denmark, J. C. 1973. *In* Hearing 28.9:284–293.

Eastman, G. C. 1974. Sign Me Alice. (A play composed in sign language.) Gallaudet College, Washington, D.C.

Fant, L. 1974–75 (Winter). Ameslan. Gallaudet Today 5(2):1–3.

Furth, H. 1966. Thinking Without Language. The Free Press, New York.

Furth, H. 1973. Deafness & Hearing. Wadsworth, Belmont, Cal.

Garnett, C. B. 1968. Exchange of Letters between Samuel Heinicke and the Abbé Charles Michel de l'Epée. Vantage, New York.

Joos, M. 1967. The Five Clocks. Harcourt Brace, New York.

Kendon, A. 1975. Gesticulation, speech, and the gestural theory of language origins. Sign Language Studies 9:345–376.

Kohl, H. R. 1966. Language & Education of the Deaf. Center for Urban Education, New York.

Labov, W. 1969. The Study of Non-Standard Dialects. CAL/ERIC, Washington, D.C.

Lewis, M. M. 1968. The Education of Deaf Children. Her Majesty's Stationery Office, London.

Lewis, M. M. 1969. (From a speech at the Royal National Institute for the Deaf conference at Edinburgh.) *In* Hearing 24.4:102.

McCall, E. 1965. A generative grammar of Sign. Unpublished master's thesis, University of Iowa.

Markowicz, H. 1976. Methodology, educational objectives, and the deaf image. *In* Proceedings of the Third Gallaudet Research Symposium, January.

Office of Demographic Studies, Gallaudet College. Various articles and research monographs on hearing impaired students. Gallaudet College, Kendall Green, Washington, D.C.

O'Rourke, T. J. (ed.). 1972. Psycholinguistics and Total Communication: The State of the Art. American Annals of the Deaf, Washington, D.C.

Sarles, H. B. 1974. Could a non-H? *In* Wescott, Hewes, and Stokoe (eds.), Language Origins, pp. 219–238. Linstok Press, Silver Spring, Md.

Schein, J. D., and Delk, M. T. 1974. The Deaf Population of the United States. National Association of the Deaf, Silver Spring, Md.

Seigel, J. P. 1969. The enlightenment and the evolution of a language of signs in France and England. J. History Ideas 30:96–118.

Stokoe, W. C. 1960. Sign language structure: An outline of the visual communication systems of the American deaf. Studies in Linguistics: Occasional Papers 8. (Now available from Linstok Press, Silver Spring, Md.)

Stokoe, W. C. 1972. Syntax. *In* Stokoe, W. C., Semiotics & Human Sign Languages, pp. 74–107. Mouton, The Hague.

Stokoe, W. C. 1974. Motor signs as the first form of language. *In* Wescott, Hewes, and Stokoe (eds.), Language Origins, pp. 35–50. Linstok Press, Silver Spring, Md.

Stokoe, W. C. 1975. Classification and description of sign languages. *In* Current Trends in Linguistics 12:345–371.

Stokoe, W. C. Color terms in American Sign Language. Sign Lang. Stud. In press.

Stokoe, W. C., Bernard, C. and Padden, C. 1976. An elite group in deaf society. Sign Lang. Stud. 12:189–210.

Tervoort, B. Th. M. 1968. You me downtown movie fun? Lingua 21:455–465.

Vernon, M. 1974 (April). Deaf militancy. (Editorial.) Am. Ann. Deaf 119.1:15.

# Section IV

# Assessment of Nonspeech and Communication

chapter 9

# Analyzing Language and Communication in the Child

*Robin S. Chapman*

*Jon F. Miller*

*Department of Communicative Disorders*
*University of Wisconsin-Madison*
*Madison, Wisconsin*

## contents

How does the clinician decide that a child is a good candidate for a nonvocal mode of communication? Is the same program goal appropriate to every child? Which nonvocal symbol system is best suited to a child? These are difficult clinical questions. The purpose of this chapter is to discuss ways in which information on language development and communication may help the clinician in making decisions. Some progress in answering these questions for a child can be achieved by taking information about language development and communication into account.

## WHY USE NONVOCAL SYSTEMS?

Why should nonvocal systems be desirable alternatives for some children? Nonvocal communication systems are used for two primary reasons. First, they can *substitute* for verbal production for children who have failed to acquire productive speech. The failures of these children are usually due to severe auditory impairment or to severe neuromuscular involvement of the speech mechanism (for example, the impairment of children with dysarthria). Second, nonvocal systems can *augment* vocal production, either as an initial strategy for teaching language or as a means of facilitating productive vocal communication. Augmentative uses have been employed when the structure and function of the child's speech production mechanism is suspect or when eventual improvement in verbal communication is expected.

Augmentative uses of nonvocal systems presume that the alternative production mode will facilitate speech. This issue has been intensely debated for a century in deaf education, although there is little experimental evidence either way (Wilbur, 1976). In other populations, some evidence does exist that vocalization increases or improves following the introduction of a nonvocal communication system (Harris-Vanderheiden, 1975; Lebeis and Lebeis, 1975; Grimnel, Detamore, and Lippke, 1976; and Schaeffer, Chapter 17, this volume). The usual answers to "why," then, are that otherwise the child will not be able to talk, or so that the child can be helped to talk.

The usual answers to the question of which child is a candidate for a nonvocal system have similarly focused on talking. One major reason for considering the use of a nonvocal communication system is a child's failure to acquire productive speech commensurate with his chronological age. Other reasons have included unintelligible production (Grimnel, Detamore, and Lippke, 1976) or repeated failure in speech and language therapy with little or no functional verbalizations (Carrier, 1973, 1976; Kopchick, Rombach, and Smilowitz, 1975; Grimnel, Detamore, and Lippke, 1976).

There is little argument that these conditions constitute good reasons for considering a nonvocal communication system. These conditions are not in themselves sufficient, however, to decide whether a child is a candidate for a nonvocal system. Nor do they provide sufficient information to decide which system to use.

To use only chronological age and production criteria in deciding "for whom" and "which system" is to ignore: 1) the developmental status of a child's cognitive, language, and communicative behavior, 2) the language and communication characteristics of each nonvocal system, 3) the demands made on the child in learning and using a nonvocal system, and 4) the child's speech community and situation. Taking these topics into account will help us answer "why," "for whom," and "which system." Analysis of cognitive, language, and communication characteristics of the child, on the one hand, and nonvocal systems on the other, can lead us to more appropriate clinical decisions.

## DEVELOPMENTAL CHANGES IN CHILDREN'S COMMUNICATION

### The Cognition Hypothesis

Children whose language acquisition has been studied show a number of similarities in the way their language and communication skills develop (Brown, 1973). Similar sequences are found across language (Bowerman, 1973), across cultures (Mitchell-Kernan, 1971), in children learning to sign (Bellugi, 1972), and in developmentally delayed children (Lackner, 1968; Larson, 1974; Coggins, 1975). The rate at which individual children learn to communicate varies, but the ordering of major milestones in syntax, semantics, phonology, and pragmatics appears invariant.

How are we to explain both the individual differences in rate and the invariancy of sequence? A number of child language researchers (Bloom, 1970; Bowerman, 1974; Cromer, 1974, 1976) propose what is called the Cognition Hypothesis: the view that there are cognitive prerequisites to linguistic achievements that are necessary, but not sufficient, for these achievements. Cognitive development is seen as the major pacer of the development of communication skills. Experience, linguistic input, perceptual salience, already acquired forms, and reinforcing consequences all play their roles only within limits set by the child's cognitive status.

And what are the limits set by current cognitive status? Many students of child development believe that the ways in which children think, solve problems, interact, and understand the world change qualitatively as they grow (e.g., Piaget and Inhelder, 1969). Similar qualitative changes in thinking and problem solving have been demonstrated, at a slower pace, in developmentally delayed children (Woodward, 1959; Inhelder, 1976). What the child can say, the reasons and forms for communicating—these change with changes in the child's representation of his world and information-processing skills.

The correlations between cognitive and language development that the Cognition Hypothesis predicts are now being investigated by a number of researchers (Lezine, 1973; Beilin, 1975; Bates et al., 1976; Corrigan, 1976; Snyder, 1976; Dihoff and Chapman, 1977; Ingram, in press). The scattered early returns from this work suggest that semantic and pragmatic sequences are linked very closely to cognitive status, as well as to those aspects of syntactic development that are semantically based.

By making use of existing age-related data to supplement investigations of cognitive correlates to linguistic development, we can create pictures of the typical communication skills of the child functioning cognitively at eight months—or at eight years. In describing these skills, portraits of the child as listener and of the child as speaker are presented separately. This is done for two reasons. First, the facts about what children can understand are not easily predicted from what they say. Conversely, what they can say is only in part predicted by the linguistic cues they can understand (Chapman, 1978). Second, this approach allows the clinician to determine if the child is delayed in either or both processes relative to expectations based on cognitive level. *It is the child with production delay relative to cognitive level, rather than to chronological age, who is a candidate for a nonvocal system.*

The sketches are organized by cognitive level, providing a set of particular expectations for communication in the normal child and appropriate program goals in the language-disordered child. These communication goals are pointed out under the heading of "Programming" after each sketch. They reflect the communication needs and skills that are typical of the developmental level.

### The Preintentional Child (Birth to 8 Months)

From birth to about eight months, or sensorimotor Stages 1 through 3, infants give little evidence of carrying out goal-oriented actions (Piaget and Inhelder, 1969). Nor do they appear to carry out intentional communication (see Piaget and Inhelder, 1969, or Premack, 1976, for discussions of the ways in which intentionality can be inferred from behavior). They neither use nor understand words (Pierce, 1974).

**Programming for the Preintentional Child** Preintentional children should not be expected to use or understand nonvocal symbols (except perhaps as teething rings!). Communication programs appropriate for a child functioning preintentionally should focus on caregiver-child interactions prerequisite to the use of symbols. Social bonds must be established, so that the child will later wish to seek the company and conversation of others. Gestural interaction can be established through caregiver imitation of the child's own actions that are visible to himself, in a fashion analogous to turn-taking vocalizations for the child who has any usable hearing (Lewis and Freedle, 1973). Caregiver responsiveness to the child's cries in the preintentional period (three months) may lead to more frequent intentional use of other communicative means at one year (Bell and Ainsworth, 1972).

The significance of the chosen communication means—signing, button pushing, token display, talking—can be established through the caregiver's use of the mode in playful, repeated routines. During preintentional stages the only change in behavior sought from the child would be increased frequency of attending to the input and increased frequency of smiling recognition of the whole routine.

We can also attempt to accelerate the preintentional child's cognitive growth directly, as Bricker and Bricker (1974) tried for preintentional retarded children who were developing extremely slowly. Whether attempts to accelerate cognitive growth directly will work is still unclear. To the extent that maturation governs major changes during the sensorimotor period, it would seem that enrichment, rather than acceleration, should be the intervention goal of cognitive programming during this period.

### The Intentional Sensorimotor Child: Stage 4

Children at sensorimotor Stage 4 (typically 8 to 12 months) are like younger infants in that they do not yet use or understand words. They differ from younger infants in their capacity for intentional activity and their social experience. Although they are beginning to use familiar means to achieve novel ends, they are often sidetracked by the means themselves. Observations of nine-month-olds left in a room with toys show that they typically act on every new object in rapid succession, mouthing, banging, grasping and releasing, or looking (Lezine, 1973). When mother and child play together, they jointly attend to objects. The mother looks at and talks about what the child looks at, and the child follows the mother's line of regard to attend to what she is looking at (Bruner, 1975a, 1975b).

Sensorimotor Stage 4 children can imitate ongoing actions that are already in their repertoires, an achievement that allows them to participate in communication games with mothers (see Bruner, 1975a, 1975b). "Shake your head," says mother, shaking hers; "give me a kiss," as she smacks her lips; "clap your hands, pattycake," as she claps hers. The child complies. Although testing would usually reveal that Stage 4 children do not understand what mothers are saying, these games often give rise to parental belief that the children can now understand what is said to them. So, too, may children's predictable, simple actions on objects, or their ability to look where the mother looks, give rise to the appearance of word comprehension when the mother picks her request carefully. These nonlinguistic response strategies are listed in Table 1, which outlines the developmental sequence of comprehension skills in the intentional sensorimotor period.

Although Stage 4 children do not yet talk, their vocalizations are differentiated according to state. Mothers can identify the states from the cries (Ricks, 1975) and respond appropriately. Children begin syllabic babbling in Stage 4, which allows them to imitate the mother's models of their utterances. These events are listed as precursors to production in Table 2. It outlines the developmental sequence of production milestones in the intentional sensorimotor period.

**Programming for the Stage 4 Child** Caregiver-child play may be the crucible in which communicative intent and understanding are forged. It is in the context of communication games and joint attention to objects that the child has the opportunity to hear the simple, well formed, repetitious, expressive and referential speech with which mothers address their language-learning children (Snow, 1972, 1977; Nelson, 1973; Phillips, 1973). It is through familiar actions on objects that the child will later come to use novel means to achieve familiar ends. Signs, symbols, or spoken words used consistently in play routines by the caregiver now (*Peek-a-boo!*, *I'm gonna get you!*, and other tickling games; *Hi*!) may later appear among the child's early words (Bruner, 1975a, 1975b; Greenfield and Smith, 1976).

Appropriate intervention programs for the Stage 4 child, then, should also be focused on communicative interactions, rather than meaningful symbol use or comprehension. But programs for developmentally delayed Stage 4 children, should—as does the normal Stage 4 child's mother—give attention to modeling (with gesture, token, or word) the simple, short, well formed familiar language accompanying brief periods of games and object play: "Where's Joshua? Where's the baby? Peek-a-boo! Hi! Bye-bye! Lookit the block! Where's the block? There's the block. Lookit the cup! There's the cup! Uh-oh!"

### The Sensorimotor Stage 5 Child: First Performatives and Words

In sensorimotor Stage 5, 12 to 18 months, the child uses novel means to achieve familiar ends. Familiar, desired goals may include the adult's attention, a particular object, or an object's removal (Bates, 1976).

One set of novel means to these goals which Stage 5 children employ are communicative gestures accompanied by stereotyped vocalization (Halliday, 1975; Bates, 1976; Greenfield and Smith, 1976). The desired goals expressed by these communicative gestures in Stage 5 include requests for objects or attention and comments. For example, "Unhh!" says Joshua, pointing to the toy, then looking at his mother, then back to

Table 1. Comprehension in the intentional sensorimotor period (8 to 24 months)

| Cognitive level (approximate age range) | Development | Reference |
|---|---|---|
| Sensorimotor Stage 4 (8 to 12 months) | *No lexical comprehension.* | |
| | *Context-determined responses:* | |
| | 1. Look at objects that mother looks at. | Bruner (1975a, 1975b) |
| | 2. Act on objects that you notice. | Lezine (1973) |
| | 3. Imitate ongoing action or sound if it is already within your repertoire. | Uzgiris and Hunt (1975) |
| | 4. Laugh at familiar interaction sequences. | Bruner (1975a, 1975b) |
| Sensorimotor Stage 5 (12 to 18 months) | *Lexical comprenhension:* | |
| | 1. Understanding of one word in some sentences when referents are present. | Huttenlocher (1974)<br>Shipley, Smith, and Gleitman (1969)<br>Miller et al. (in press) |
| | *Comprehension strategies:* | Chapman (1978) |
| | 1. Attend to object mentioned. | |
| | 2. Give evidence of notice. | |
| | 3. Do what you usually do in the situation. | |
| Sensorimotor Stage 6 (18 to 24 months) | *Lexical comprehension:* | Miller et al. (in press) |
| | 1. Understanding of words when referent is not present. | Huttenlocher (1974)<br>Dihoff and Chapman (1977) |
| | 2. Understanding of action verbs out of routine context; carries out two-word commands, but often fails to understand three lexical elements. | Goldin-Meadow, Seligman, and Gelman (1976)<br>Sachs and Truswell (1976)<br>Smith (1972)<br>Larson (1974) |
| | 3. Understanding of routine forms of questions for agent, object, locative and action. | |
| | *Comprehension strategies:* | Chapman (1978) |
| | 1. Locate the objects mentioned. | |
| | 2. Give evidence of notice. | |
| | 3. Do what you usually do: | |
| | a. Objects into containers. | Clark (1973) |
| | b. Conventional use. | Lezine (1973) |
| | 4. Act on the objects in the way mentioned. | Shatz (1975) |
| | a. Child as Agent. | de Villiers and de Villiers (1973), Sinclair and Bronckart (1972) |

the toy, as if to say "Lookit that!" "Unhh-unhh-unhh" he says rapidly and insistently, with different intonation and open and closing of his pointing hand, when he wants the same object.

It should be pointed out that the vocal portion of these communicative gestures is often uninterpretable or unintelligible. If Joshua's conventionalized form had been "Da," or "Mama," rather than "unhh," he would have been credited with his first words as well as his first communicative functions. Tact and mand (Skinner, 1957), protodeclarative and protoimperative (Bates, 1976), indicative and volitional performative

Table 2. Production in the intentional sensorimotor period (8 to 24 months)

| Cognitive level (approximate age range) | Development | Reference |
|---|---|---|
| Sensorimotor Stage 4 (8 to 12 months) | *Precursors:* | |
| | 1. Differentiated cries. | Ricks (1975) |
| | 2. Syllabic babbling. | Menyuk (1974) |
| | 3. Communication games. | Bruner (1975a, 1975b) |
| | 4. Intentional action. | Uzgiris and Hunt (1975) |
| Sensorimotor Stage 5 (12 to 18 months) | *First words:* | |
| | 1. Performatives (gesture accompanies vocalization or word). | Bates (1976) |
| | a. *Hi, bye* routines. | Greenfield and Smith (1976) |
| | b. Comment. | Halliday (1975) |
| | c. Request object or attention. | Dore (1974) |
| | | Bloom, 1973 |
| | d. Reject. | |
| Sensorimotor Stage 6 (18 to 24 months) | *Transition to two-word* combinations: | Ingram (1974b, 1977) |
| | 1. New semantic roles: | Bloom (1973), Greenfield and Smith (1976), Goldin-Meadow, Seligman, and Gelman (1976) |
| Early | a. Action-object relations: agent, action, object, recurrence, disappearance. | |
| Later | b. Object-object relations: location, possession, nonexistence. | |
| | 2. Asks a *What's that* question. | |
| | 3. Answers some routine questions. | Dihoff and Chapman (1977) |
| | 4. Rapid acquisition of vocabulary. | Nelson (1973) |
| | 5. Successive one-word utterances. | Bloom (1973) |
| | 6. Increased frequency of talking. | |
| 20 months | 7. Onset of two-word utterances (MLU $< 1.5$) | |

(Greenfield and Smith, 1976), interactive and instrumental (Halliday, 1975), comment and request—whatever the labels for Joshua's two "unhh's," these functions typically arise in Stage 5 (Lezine, 1973; Bates, 1976; Dihoff and Chapman, 1977).

Other characteristics of the Stage 5 child's production are summarized in Table 2. Two facts about word or performative use are important to add. First, utterances are infrequent at the beginning of Stage 5. For example, rate of talking was approximately seven utterances per hour in Greenfield and Smith's (1976) early data. Second, the number of different words acquired is small, typically 10 to 30 (Nelson, 1973).

The first instances of true word comprehension also appear to arise in Stage 5 (see Table 1). Children typically begin to understand names of people, pets, or familiar objects, but with important limitations (Huttenlocher, 1974). They will look at, or point out, an object requested when it is present in the immediate vicinity, but they will not go search for it (Dihoff and Chapman, 1977; Miller et al., in press). Nor do they seem to understand action verb requests, if the only cue to action is the lexical one itself.

The fact that children begin to imitate and repeat novel actions in Stage 5 obscures their inability to bring objects or actions to mind on the basis of a symbol. A child brushes hair, cup, table, and doll with a hairbrush, before returning it to his mouth; pushes the broom around the floor and the table (Lezine, 1973). The mother has only to choose her command judiciously. Once her child's attention is directed to the object, he has only to do what he usually does with it to appear to carry out her request. Stage 5 comprehension strategies that give rise to the appearance of more complete understanding than the child possesses are discussed in Chapman (1978) and summarized in Table 1.

**Programming for the Stage 5 Child** It is in Stage 5, for the first time on the developmental ladder, that comprehension and use of symbols or signs become appropriate programming goals. Comprehension of signs will be limited to objects in the immediate referential context, just as words were. The use of pictures by the adult may actually enhance the child's comprehension, since the picture will evoke absent objects that the sign or word would not. The developmental facts suggest that the earliest signs or pictures to be introduced might usefully encode the pragmatic aspects: *Lookit*, *Want!*, and *Don't want*! Some means of accomplishing reference to objects in the environment must be found for the child: signing, token selection, looking, tapping, pointing, showing—whatever action the child can make. Communicative interaction is still the chief focus, but nonvocal symbols can now be used by the child to convey some communicative intents when referents are present.

## The Sensorimotor Stage 6 Child: Representational Thought

The onset of sensorimotor Stage 6 at approximately 18 months marks a "Great Divide" in the child's cognitive growth. The child's behavior gives evidence of internalized representations of actions and objects. The child can think symbolically.

With the capacity for representational thought comes a number of rapid changes in the child's language use (see Table 2). The list here is based on a summary by Ingram (1974b).

1. *Semantic roles:* Action words appear for the first time. The child uses his single words (later, his two-word utterances) to comment on or request agents acting on objects in the immediate context. Later, too, the child talks about relations between objects (possession, location, recurrence, nonexistence) in one and two words.
2. *What's that?* The child for the first time requests information, most typically the names of objects. The form, of course, may vary; for example, *Mama?* or *'Zat?*
3. *Speech-to-speech:* The child for the first time responds to speech verbally as well as with action. Answers to routine questions (*What's that?*, *Where's the ball?*, *What does the cow say?*) appear for the first time.
4. *Rapid vocabulary growth:* The rate of vocabulary acquisition increases sharply; the child may double his vocabulary the first month.
5. *Successive single-word utterances:* The child in the first part of Stage 6 still talks one word at a time, but now may have more than one thing to say about a single event. Joshua, seeing the dog bat the ball with its nose, says, "Ball! . . . Heidi!"
6. *Increased frequency of talking*
7. *Two-word combinations:* Midway through Stage 6 two-word combinations appear with fixed orders. Mean lengths of utterance (MLU) in morphemes typically associated with Stage 6 are 1.0 to 1.5.

Comprehension achievements are summarized in Table 1. Words no longer require the presence of the referent to be understood. Upon hearing the name of his dog, Joshua will go search for her. Asked if he needs a dry diaper, he goes and gets one. (Told that he now has on a dry diaper, he also goes and gets one!) Upon testing, comprehension is still limited to understanding of one or two words in a sentence rather than to the relationship among them cued by word order (Miller et al., in press). Asked, "Make the dog push the cat," the child may push the dog and cat himself. He has imposed a child-as-agent strategy upon the words he understood. Later, he may find other solutions (Chapman, 1978). The fact of his limited comprehension often poses no problems, for he can see the relationship among the objects mentioned; or he can do what he usually does, or what is possible to do, with frequent appearance of compliance.

**Programming for the Stage 6 Child** The child in sensorimotor Stage 6 is ready to use, understand, and combine symbols for meanings he understands, provided their identification or creation does not require complex spatial representation. Once the meaning of a symbol has been established, there is no longer the necessity that held in Stage 5 for the referent to be present if comprehension is to take place. Use of the symbol, however, may require the presence of the referent, at least for objects (Lezine, 1973).

Input, to judge by the data from comprehension studies (Smith, 1972; Larson, 1974) and mothers talking to their 18- and 24-month-olds (Snow, 1977), should be short, simple, well formed according to the nonvocal system's rules, and redundant in message. A mother's utterances are typically about two words longer than the child's (Nelson, 1973) for English. For systems in which a given symbol may carry more information (e.g., Ameslan) the difference might be smaller. Acceptance of whatever form the child manages to produce, together with a well formed repetition (or compliance), is typical of mothers. They wish to understand and be understood.

The meanings and communicative functions to be modeled in a nonvocal program for Stage 6 children are most probably those just described for normal children. Mothers of Stage 6 children talk about the same semantic roles their children talk about (Retherford, Schwartz, and Chapman, 1977; Snow, 1977). Two-year-olds learning Ameslan from their parents, for example, sign the same prevalent semantic roles and relations that their speaking counterparts talk about (Bellugi, 1972; Newport and Ashbrook, 1977). Miller and Yoder (1974) discuss the ways in which normal data can be augmented by data from the child's experience in selecting initial vocabulary and functions, and the specific techniques useful in establishing generalization for children, like the retarded, who are slow to generalize.

### Early Preoperations: 2 to 3½ Years

The period from two to approximately 3½ years is one in which children show striking changes in the structure of their sentences. Indeed, some investigators state that children acquire all the basic structures of their language by age three or four on the strength of the evidence from free-speech samples.

The ordering of the syntactic milestones for production are summarized in Table 3, adapted from Brown (1973). It is the ordering of the

Table 3. Production in the preoperational period (2 to 7 years): Syntactic processes

| Cognitive level | Brown's (1973) stage | New development | MLU (morphemes) |
|---|---|---|---|
| Early preoperations | | | |
| 2 years | I | Basic semantic relations | 1.75 |
| | II | Grammatical inflections | 2.25 |
| 2½ years | III | Differentiation of sentence modalities | 2.75 |
| 3 years | IV | Sentence embedding | 3.50 |
| Late preoperations | | | |
| 3½ years | V | Sentence conjoining | 4.00 |

Adapted from Brown (1973).

milestones that is similar across children. Typical ages are listed in Table 3, but some children make more rapid progress. Eve's speech, for example, progressed through all five stages between 20 and 27 months. The mean length of utterance in morphemes, which defines Brown's five stages, is a better predictor of the child's syntactic structures than chronological age.

Mental age may also predict certain syntactic achievements. A pilot study (Dihoff and Chapman, 1977) of 51 children ages nine months to eight years showed that 90% of children who were in early preoperations according to classification, seriation, and drawing tasks failed to conjoin sentences in free-speech samples. All of those functioning in the sensorimotor period failed. Conversely, 90% of the children in late preoperations according to these tasks produced conjoined sentences in free speech, and all those in the transitional (5½ to 7) or the concrete operations period (7 to 11) produced them.

Each development listed in Table 3 is best thought of as the process most clearly emerging at the time, but continuing to develop as other processes emerge. In Brown's Stages I through III the simple sentence develops. The one- and two-term basic semantic relations children talk about in Late Stage I, at two years, are the same basic semantic relations discussed by the three-year-old in three- and four-term combinations.

Some of the semantically simpler grammatical inflections are mastered in Stages II and III: plurals, progressive *-ing*, locatives expressing containment (*in*) and support (*on*), possessive. The longer utterances of Stage III make the formal differentiation of questions, declaratives, negatives, and imperatives more apparent. Definite and indefinite reference (*the* versus *a*) becomes established in Stage IV. In Stage IV, too, embedded sentences and auxiliary verb elements appear in the child's speech (Limber, 1973).

The changes in what children talk about in the early preoperational period are summarized in Table 4. Expressions of denial (e.g., *No bird* meaning *that's not a bird; it's a dog*) and number (one versus many) are new to the early preoperational period. More striking than any changes, however, are the similarities in content to sensorimotor Stages 5 and 6. The children talk about the same relations they began noting in the sensorimotor period, albeit more elaborately. They still talk, too, about the present, the immediate past, and the imminent future, although they have not yet mastered the inflections that encode these distinctions.

Comprehension testing (see Table 5) reveals lexical, but not word order, comprehension until about 3½ years, when children begin to use a word order strategy for understanding agent and object of action. This strategy results in correct performance on active sentences, but 100% incorrect performance on passives, for a time. Children at the beginning

Table 4. Production in the preoperational period (2 to 7 years): Semantics

| Cognitive level | Development | Reference |
|---|---|---|
| Early preoperations | | |
| 2 years | *Basic semantic relations:*<br>Agent-action<br>Action-object<br>Agent-object<br>Possessive<br>Entity-locative<br>Action-locative<br>Existence<br>Recurrence<br>Nonexistence<br>Rejection<br>Denial<br>Attributive | Brown (1973), Braine (1976), Bloom (1973) |
| 2½ years | Number (noun plural)<br>Locative containment and support (*in*, *on*)<br>Temporary duration (*-ing*) | Brown (1973) |
| 3 years | Immediate future (*gonna*) | Brown (1973) |
| Late preoperations | | Bates (1976) |
| 3½–7 years | *Event relations* (sequence of emergence):<br>a. *and* (coordinate and temporal)<br>b. *because*, *so* (causal)<br>c. *but* (contrastive)<br>d. *when* (conditional)<br>e. *while* (simultaneity)<br>f. *after*<br>g. *before* | Clancy, Jacobsen, and Silva (1976) |
| | Past time (*-ed*)<br>Possibility (*might*) | Brown (1973) |

Table 5. Comprehension in early preoperations (2 to 3⅓ years)

| Typical age | Development | Reference |
|---|---|---|
| | *Lexical comprehension:* Sequence for understanding of the meaning of Wh-questions in nonroutine forms | Ervin-Tripp (1970) |
| 2½ years | *What* for object<br>*What-do* for action<br>*Where* for location (place) | |
| 3 years | *Whose* for possessor<br>*Who* for person<br>*Why* for cause or reason<br>*How many* for number | |
| 3 years | Understanding of gender contrasts in third person pronouns. | Owings (1972), Miller and Yoder (1973) |
| 2 and 3 years | *Comprehension strategies:* | Clark (1974, 1975), Chapman (1978) |
| | 1. Do what is usually done. | |
| | a. Probable location strategy for *in*, *on*, *under*, *beside*. | Clark (1973), Wilcox and Palermo (1975), Hodun (1975) |
| | b. Probable event strategy for simple active reversible sentences. | Bever (1970), Strohner and Nelson (1974), Chapman and Miller (1975), Chapman and Kohn (1978) |
| | 2. Supply missing information (2 years). Supply explanation (3 years). | Ervin-Tripp (1970) |
| | 3. Infer most probable speech act in context. | Wetstone and Friedlander (1973), Shatz (1975) |

of the preoperational period, in contrast, respond to some (not all) sentences with the same interpretation regardless of word order, usually making the more probable (often the animate) toy the agent (Strohner and Nelson, 1974; Chapman and Kohn, 1978). They may also show consistent position biases. They do not show the child-as-agent strategies typical of the sensorimotor child.

These facts about comprehension are surprising in the light of free-speech data from the same period. Structural cues to meaning are emerging much more slowly in comprehension than one would expect from their productive control. Bloom (1974), Ingram (1974a), and Chapman (1974, 1978) all offer discussions of this issue. The data suggest that, for a given meaning, comprehension on the basis of lexical and contextual cues emerges earlier than production in (or out of) context, with comprehension on the basis of a word order cue the latest of the four events to emerge.

**Programming for the Early Preoperational Child** For a child in early preoperations, one may wish to focus on extending one- and two-word uses to simple sentence structures used to talk about ongoing action. In doing this, care must be taken that the meanings of the utterances modeled to the child are apparent from the context or predictable from his past experience, so that comprehension problems are not created for the child. Comprehension training for word order cues should consist of developing immediate context and probable event strategies in early preoperations—or delaying training to late preoperations.

The major limitations imposed on nonvocal program goals by the early preoperational level of development are semantic and formal. The meanings to be encoded should reflect the semantic limitations of normal children at these ages. If the nonvocal system relies on temporal or visual order to encode meaning, the child should not be expected to be able to use these devices as the only cue to meaning, although he may be able to order a few elements appropriately. The child's ability to discriminate or reproduce geometric shapes is quite limited in this period.

### Late Preoperations and Beyond

At 3½ to 4 years the child begins to apply systematic problem-solving strategies to classification and seriation tasks. At 3½ years, 50% will consistently sort a set of 22 blocks, varying in size, shape, and color, into two piles on the basis of a single attribute (Bingham-Newman, Saunders, and Hooper, 1976). At 4½ years, 50% will place seven blocks varying in height in order and place three missing blocks in the sequence. At four years, children will begin differentiating shapes within open and closed classes in their drawings. Squares may now have one corner to distinguish them from circles. The concomitant growth in production and comprehension of language is summarized in Tables 4, 5, and 6.

Briefly, the period from 3½ to 7 years witnesses the displacement of language use from the here-and-now. The language of time and Euclidean space develops (Boehm, 1971; Parisi and Antinucci, 1970; Johnston, 1973). Explicit encoding, through conjunctions, of relations between propositions emerges. Children learn more complex syntactic devices for making reference, now that the immediate situation is less often pertinent. Word order cues to basic semantic relations are now used.

We see children beginning to develop a sense of the pragmatic reasons governing syntactic and semantic choices (Bates, 1976), even if their ability to make themselves clear to the listener is still very limited (Glucksberg, Krauss, and Higgens, 1975). The mother's language is no longer a model of syntactic clarity. Language in the service of socialization—what the child is to do, think, say, and how—replaces language for learning, sometimes to the deterioration of mother-child relations (Gleason, 1973).

'able 6. Comprehension in late preoperations and concrete operations (4 to 11 ears)

| ypical age | Development | Reference |
|---|---|---|
| | *Lexical comprehension* | |
| ½ years | Understanding of contrasts for topological locatives (*in*, *on*, *under*, *beside*). | Owings (1972), Miller and Yoder (1973), Clark (1973), Hodun (1975) |
| | *How* questions for manner or instrument. | Ervin-Tripp (1970) |
| | Comprehension of word order cues to agent-object in active sentences (word order strategy). | Slobin (1966), Owings (1972), de Villiers and de Villiers (1973), Strohner and Nelson (1974), Chapman and Miller (1975), Chapman and Kohn (1978) |
| | Word order strategy overgeneralized to passive. | Bever (1970), Owings (1972), de Villiers and de Villiers (1973), Maratsos (1974), Beilin (1975), Maratsos and Abramovitch (1975), Horgan (1975) |
| years | Understanding of number contrasts in third-person pronouns. | Owings (1972), Miller and Yoder (1973) |
| | Comprehension strategy for *before* and *after*: Order of mention of clauses. | Ferreiro and Sinclair (1971), Clark (1971) |
| ½ years | *Wh-questions:*<br>*How long* for duration<br>*How far* for distance | Chapman (in preparation) |
| | Understanding of noun plural *s*. | Owings (1972), Miller and Yoder (1973) |
| years | *Wh-questions:*<br>*How often* for frequency<br>*When* for time | Chapman (in preparation) |
| | Understanding of tense inflections *-ing*, *-ed*. | Owings (1972), Miller and Yoder (1973) |

*continued*

Table 6. (*continued*)

| Typical age | Development | Reference |
|---|---|---|
| 5½ years | Understanding of possessive *'s*. | Owings (1972), Miller and Yoder (1973) |
| | Comprehension of word order cues to agent-object in passive sentences. | Owings (1972), Miller and Yoder (1973) |
| | Comprehension of word order cues to agent-object relations in relative clauses. | Brown (1971), Sheldon (1974), Lahey (1974) |
| 6 years | Understanding of temporal conjunction *before* and *after*. | Lovell and Slater (1960), Weil (1970), Hatch (1971), Clark (1971), Montroy, McManis and Bell (1971), Johnson (1975), Keller-Cohen, (1975), Barrie-Blackley (1973) |
| | Understanding of conditional conjunctions *if* and *when* (usual rather than logical sense). | Matalon (1962), O'Brien and Shapiro (1968), Peel (1967), Olds (1968), Roberge (1970), Shapiro and O'Brien (1970), Shine and Walsh (1971) |
| | Probable relation of events strategy for causal conjunctions. | Corrigan (1975), Kuhn and Phelps (1976), Johnson and Chapman (in press) |
| 8 years | Understanding of causal conjunctions *because* and *so*. | Katz and Brent (1968), Corrigan (1975), Kuhn and Phelps (1976), Johnson and Chapman (in press) |
| | Understanding of contrastive conjunctions *but* and *although* as though they mean *and*. | Hutson and Shub (1975) |
| 10 years | Contrastive conjunctions *but* and *although*. | Watts (1944), Hutson and Shub (1975 |

The major changes in development during the elementary school years, insofar as they have been studied, are the increasing complexity of children's utterances (Hass and Wepman, 1974) and the gradual unraveling of the propositional ordering force of different conjunctions in comprehension.

**Programming for Late Preoperational Children** Children functioning in late preoperations, or beyond, are ready for symbol systems that are productive and displaceable. They need to be able to create new messages and to talk about events remote in time and space from the conversational setting. They need to learn to recognize and use the presuppositions inherent in different speech acts and the expectations governing polite conversation.

If the nonvocal child's comprehension of syntax is on a par with his cognitive level, we would expect that he could easily use his syntactic knowledge in the service of production. Systems with productive syntax matching what he can understand are advised.

Pictures may be the most appropriate representative material for the 3½- to 5½-year-old. Arbitrary symbols or word cards taught by the whole-word method make cognitive demands that are more appropriate to the child functioning at age five and a half to seven. For a child functioning at seven years whose comprehension system is at cognitive level, phonic or letter-sound correspondence approaches to reading become appropriate (see Gibson and Levin, 1975).

## COMMUNICATION CHARACTERISTICS OF NONVOCAL SYSTEMS

We turn now from the communication characteristics of children at different ages to the communication characteristics of the representational codes. Slobin (1977) proposes four competing communicative requirements to which languages must be responsive:

1. Be clear.
2. Be humanly processible in ongoing time.
3. Be quick and easy.
4. Be semantically and rhetorically expressive.

These charges to language reflect the communicative needs of speakers to get messages across to listeners fully and easily, and the needs of listeners to retrieve messages accurately and easily. These same requirements apply to nonvocal symbol systems.

The codes used in nonvocal systems, and their cognitive and linguistic prerequisites, are summarized in Table 7. The first question asked about the codes was to what extent each symbol set was capable of meeting Slobin's charge for a wide range of meanings. Each symbol set was categorized as one of the following:

1. No limitation in expressing a broad set of meanings paralleling spoken English.
2. Limited by the symbol device. The symbol set cannot or does not allow for the expression of certain meanings. For example, pictures cannot express the full range of actions or of time and space notions precisely without an extremely large set of pictures.
3. Limited by program. The symbol set as currently used expressed "a small set of meanings," but could be extended. Non-SLIP (Carrier and Peak, 1975) is an example.

Table 7. Communication characteristics of nonvocal systems including prerequisite cognitive and linguistic entry behaviors

| Prerequisite | | Representational code | Limitations on meanings that can be expressed | Who can understand | Communication functions expressed |
|---|---|---|---|---|---|
| Cognitive | Linguistic | | | | |
| Sensorimotor Stage 5 or 6 intelligence | Communicative intentions | ASL<br>SEE<br>Signed English<br>Indian Sign Language | None | ASL signing community<br>SEE signing community<br>Signed English community<br>Indian signing community | All |
| | ↓ | Idiosyncratic signs | Limited to: objects/actions | Teacher/parents | Limited to: request, respond, comment |
| Complex representation of space (late preoperations or concrete operations) | ↓ | Blissymbols | None | English reading community or Bliss users | All |
| Sensorimotor Stage 5 or 6 | ↓ | Non-SLIP | Limited to: objects/actions | Anyone who can read | Limited to: comment |
| Sensorimotor Stage 5 | ↓ | Pictures | Difficulty expressing abstract events, time and space notions, movement | Everyone | Limited to: request, comment, respond |
| Sensorimotor Stage 5 | ↓ | Total Communication | None | Signing/speaking community | All |
| Early preoperations | Comprehension of yes/no questions | Code: eye blinks, foot taps | Limited by speaker and yes/no questions form | Teacher/parents | Limited to: respond |
| Late preoperations to concrete operations | Knowledge of English | Fingerspelling<br>Morse code<br>English orthography | None | Fingerspelling community<br>Must know code<br>Reading community | All |

Of the 12 representational codes reviewed, eight have no limitations on meanings expressed; four are limited to some extent. It appears that most nonvocal systems employ codes that can express a wide variety of meanings.

The second major characteristic examined in Table 7 is an interactive-environmental one: Who can understand the code? That the listener understand the code is a minimal condition for his finding the message clear. On this dimension, only pictures and Total Communication can be understood by everyone. Every other code excludes segments of the population. Since listening/speaking and reading/writing are the most commonly shared comprehension and production systems, those codes that offer reading as a potential comprehension mode provide interactive opportunities with the largest number of people. They do, however, exclude children under six years of mental age.

The last column on Table 7 is concerned with the range of communication functions that can be expressed by each system: To what extent is it rhetorically, as well as semantically, expressive? If the symbol set is constrained in the communication functions it can express, so too is the communicator. It is necessary to consider when choosing a system whether it is capable of expressing the communication functions available to the child as well as those required by his environment.

Slobin's requirements that the code by quick and easy to use and processible in ongoing time are not reflected in Table 7, but these are particularly important requirements for substitute systems. Good comparative discussion of the rate of information transmission in the different signing systems may be found in Mayberry (1978). The rate and ease of information transmission for the other codes depend critically on the motor response abilities of the individual child and the way in which the code's use is implemented.

For the severely motorically impaired child, none of the code choices permit quick and easy production of a wide range of messages, but the messages that the child wishes to send most frequently can be encoded in single units by automated means for some systems. More seriously, the long waiting times introduced for the listener as a motorically impaired child uses a nonvocal alternative may lead to impatience and unwillingness to engage in further communication.

Although Slobin's rate principle has long been taken into account from the speaker's point of view in designing communication devices, the listener's need for quick and easy communication is only beginning to be recognized, as sophisticated and automated language boards remain unused because no one comes to listen to the child (see Harris and Vanderheiden, Chapters 11 and 12, this volume).

## PREREQUISITE BEHAVIORS NECESSARY FOR LEARNING AND USING NONVOCAL SYSTEMS

Application of the communication characteristics of each system to the question of which system is appropriate for each child will be facilitated by considering the prerequisite behaviors necessary for each. Interestingly, little attention has been given to prerequisite behaviors in the literature with the exception of Harris-Vanderheiden (1975). She has suggested several basic skills that children may need in order to use Blissymbols: 1) eye contact, 2) object permanence, 3) attending to the task, 4) ability to follow oral directions, and 5) desire to communicate. (To this list may be added the complex representation of space necessary to establish differentiation of geometric figures and ground and skyline placements.) All these skills can be subsumed either directly or indirectly into two categories: 1) cognitive skills, and 2) linguistic skills. Basic prerequisite cognitive and linguistic behaviors necessary for learning and using each system are listed in the first two columns of Table 7.

Nonvocal systems use chips, graphic symbols, arm-hand-finger gestures to stand for objects, and events and relations in the environment. The use of these systems may require the child to supply the missing object, action, or relation with chips, graphic symbols, or gestures. Cognitively, this requires that the child be able to represent the object or event. It should be noted that the level of cognitive development required appears to be comparable to that required for the use and understanding of spoken language. The major question is to what extent more visual and tangible representational devices facilitate the acquisition of cognitive representational skills. This question is basic to the augmentative uses of nonvocal systems: Are nonvocal systems a means to teach representational skills, or do they themselves require representational skills in order to be learned?

Since all systems except pictures are representational by nature, they are similar in their cognitive requirements. Different cognitive stages will be necessary for different uses of the symbols, however. For example, at sensorimotor Stage 4 imitative routines involving the symbols can be expected. At Stage 5, limited productive use and comprehension can be expected if the objects are present. Stage 6 marks the beginning of representational thought and the first rapid acquisition of symbols. Symbols can now be understood in the absence of the referent. It is not until early preoperations, however, that children can be expected to use a symbol to invoke absent objects in play, marking symbolic uses in production as well as comprehension. Thus, teaching of symbol systems for appropriate meanings could be undertaken with the foregoing limitations throughout the intentional sensorimotor period. With this in mind,

Stages 5 and 6 are listed in Table 7 as the prerequisites to nonvocal symbol use.

The linguistic prerequisites for most nonvocal systems are minimal, usually requiring the learning of what Bates (1976) calls performatives. These are early expressive devices employed by children using motor gestures and vocal sounds to communicate basic intentions such as requests, demands, and comments. They can be considered a quantification of Harris-Vanderheiden's category "desire to communicate." The question arises (for children who lack the desire to communicate) whether nonvocal systems can be employed to teach those intentions.

## APPLYING DEVELOPMENTAL CRITERIA FOR NONVOCAL SYSTEMS: FIVE EXAMPLES

How may the developmental model be used to identify children who are candidates for nonvocal systems and to match them with the appropriate system? This aspect of the decision-making process appears to have been neglected. Only general considerations of the necessary child behaviors can be found in the literature. An example is the rule of thumb developed by Scheuerman et al. (1976): "If nonverbal students are well beyond the age at which verbal language should have appeared and verbal language training programs have failed, the student should be provided with some auxiliary form of communication." This rough guideline places a heavy emphasis on the dimensions of age and productive language development. Figure 1 shows the relationship between these two dimensions, plotted for five children evaluated at the Waisman Center, Madison, Wisconsin. Language production is evaluated for three characteristics: syntax, semantics, and articulation. Not all these characteristics were evaluated for all five children. Applying the Scheuerman et al. criteria to these five children would eliminate only child 5 as a candidate for an alternative communication system. Although all five display similar productive skills between 14 and 22 months, only child 5 has a chronological age within his range.

The Scheuerman et al. (1976) rule of thumb requires only language production data. A delay in language production is determined by relating language production performance to chronological age. Employing these criteria, all mentally retarded children would have delayed language development and would therefore be potential candidates for nonvocal systems. This, of course, is ridiculous. The example does point out, however, that age by language production data are insufficient for deciding who is a candidate and for what system.

In order to improve our decision-making ability, data on other dimensions of the child's behavior are necessary. These data can be

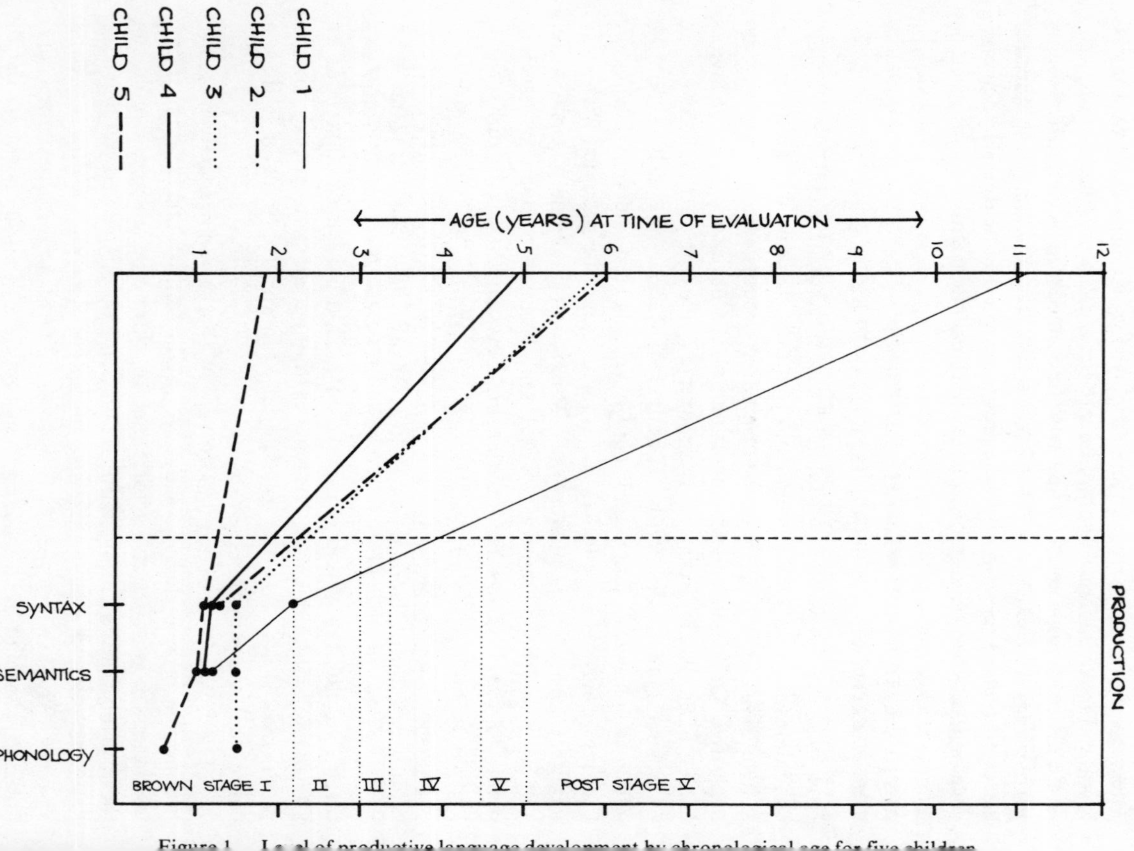


Figure 1. Level of productive language development by chronological age for five children

derived from evaluating the basic processes related to language acquisition and use: cognitive status, comprehension, production, and use of language (see Uzgiris and Hunt, 1975, and Miller, in preparation, for procedures). The data on these dimensions for the five children in Figure 1 can be found in Figure 2. Data on motor development can also be found in Figure 2, although they are not the focus of this discussion.

The importance of the cognitive dimension is demonstrated by comparing child 4 with child 5. Clearly child 4 is mentally retarded, but does he show a language delay? If age is considered relative to language development, the answer would be yes. If cognitive level is compared to language level, the answer would be no. This interpretation reflects the cognitive hypothesis expressed by Cromer (1974) that cognitive development is a necessary but not a sufficient condition in order for language to develop. With the addition of the cognitive data it can be determined that child 4 is not a candidate for a nonvocal system and, furthermore, that he does not have a language problem at all.

The decision that child 4 and child 5 are not candidates for a nonvocal system is based on the data resulting from assessing their cognitive and communicative performance. Their assessment data can be summarized as follows: cognitive development = comprehension = production = communication function. When development is equal across these four dimensions (and the speech production mechanism is normal), the child is not a candidate for nonvocal systems.

Children 1, 2, and 3 all show cognitive delays to some degree and have significant delays in language production. All three are candidates for nonvocal systems considering age, cognition, language production, and language use dimensions. Note that all three are expressing the early performatives of requesting and commenting.

The dimension most helpful in determining which system is appropriate for these children is comprehension. Note the variability of language comprehension relative to cognition and production. Child 1 demonstrates a comprehension delay relative to his cognitive status, with a further delay in production. Regardless of the productive system, this child will require eventual programming to bring comprehension up to cognitive capacity.

Child 1 is a Down's syndrome child with moderate hypotonia. In these cases it is difficult to determine the effect of the hypotonic condition on the speech production mechanism. The greatest involvement appears to be with respiratory control for speech. The decision for this child rests on determining to what extent this motoric condition has limited productive speech. Considering the child's age, 11.2 years, and the difference between his comprehension and his production, the possi-

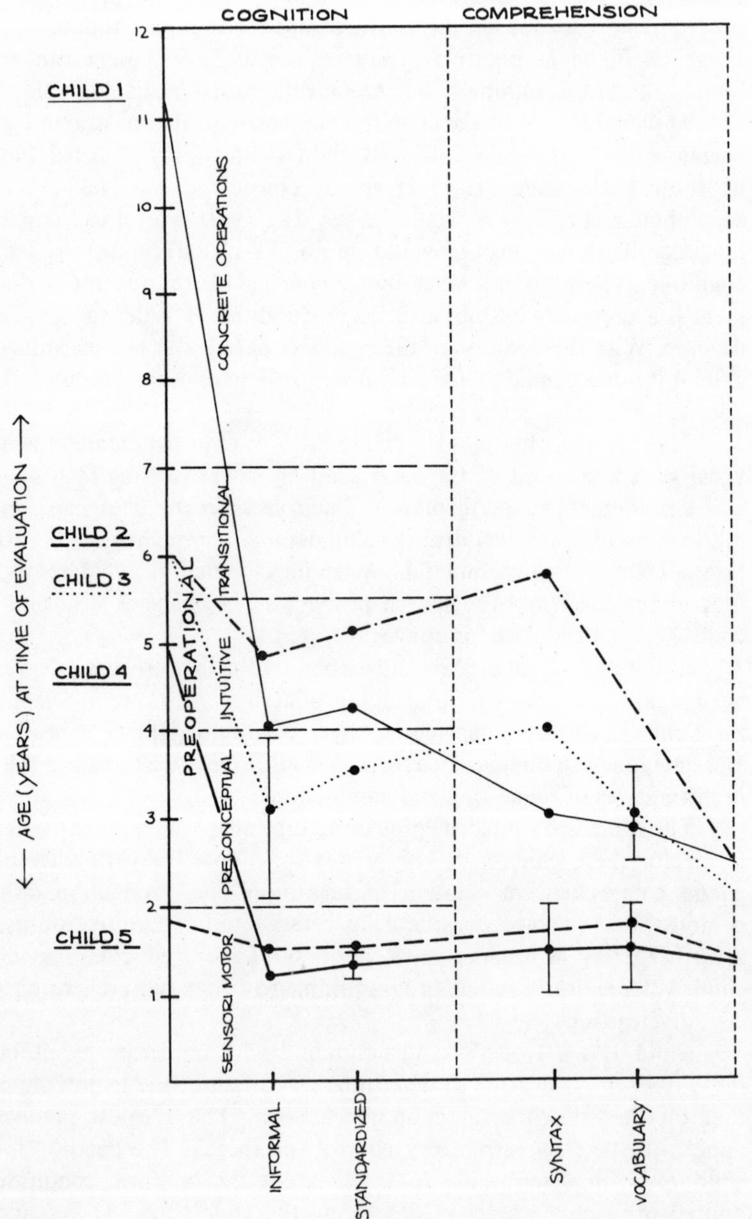
COGNITION
COMPREHENSION
CHILD 1
CHILD 2
CHILD 3
CHILD 4
CHILD 5
← AGE (YEARS) AT TIME OF EVALUATION →
12
11
10
9
8
7
6
5
4
3
2
1
CONCRETE OPERATIONS
TRANSITIONAL
INTUITIVE
PREOPERATIONAL
PRECONCEPTUAL
SENSORI MOTOR
INFORMAL
STANDARDIZED
SYNTAX
VOCABULARY

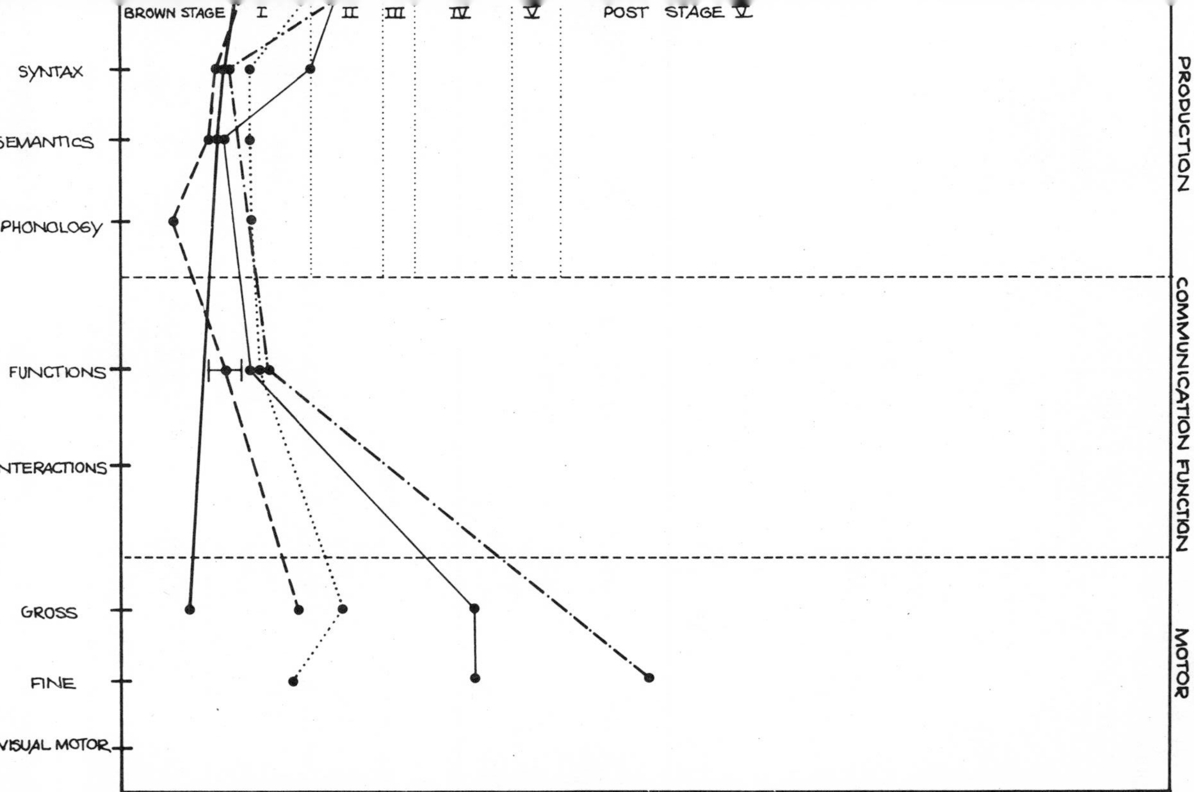


Figure 2. Developmental profiles of language and communication behaviors by chronological age for five children.

bility of motorically impaired speech is apparent. The nonvocal system that best fits this child's language or communication abilities is an augmentative approach with a symbol system capable of expressing the wide range of meanings available at the late preoperational period of conceptual development.

Several systems reviewed in Table 7 fit this description, including ASL, SEE, Indian Sign Language, Signed English, Total Communication, and Blissymbolics. Child 1 could be expected to learn any of these systems. The final decision requires that these systems be evaluated in light of the child's motor development and his home and school environment. Preferences should emerge depending on the available ongoing nonvocal school programs, parental preference, and the number of individuals the child usually interacts with who understand the system. For child 1, Total Communication was implemented because it could take advantage of his comprehension level of spoken English and provide an alternative productive means while ensuring verbal input and practice. Additionally, Total Communication was the system used by his school and his parents were highly supportive of the Total approach.

The data and the decisions for child 1 can be summarized as follows:

*Data:*

1. Cognition > comprehension > production = communication functions.
2. Questionable speech mechanism function.

*Decisions* (*see Table 8*):

1. Child is a candidate.
2. Nonvocal program should be augmentative to productive speech.
3. Late preoperational cognitive development requires a system that does not restrict the meanings that can be expressed (see Table 7).

Children 2 and 3 present somewhat different problems. Both children have severe speech mechanism problems in terms of structural and functional deviations. The level of language comprehension for both children parallels cognitive development, given the range of performance for informal Piagetian tasks at this stage. In both cases their lack of productive language appears related to severe speech mechanism involvement. Note that the fine motor development of child 2 is within normal limits. This child demonstrates the neuromuscular independence of the speech production mechanism from the upper extremities. Speech mechanism function cannot be predicted from the development of fine motor skills. For child 3 motor development is significantly delayed, but he is ambulatory and very hyperactive.

The cognitive and comprehension levels of these children require a system capable of expressing a wide range of meanings and communicative functions. This is particularly important for child 2 as we expect productive communicative capacity to develop rapidly along with continued comprehension and cognitive growth. The choices appear to be one of the signing systems or Blissymbols, with motor capacity, cognitive level, environmental constraints, and continued acquisition of the language decision points.

For children functioning within the late preoperational period of development, the parameter of time should be considered. How much time does it take to produce a message? This is particularly relevant when considering communication boards. It would appear that the more symbols available on a Blissymbol board, the longer it may take to produce a message. This, however, is dependent upon the delivery system (e.g., mechanical board versus symbols drawn on cardboard). The decision for child 2 comes down to a language board using Blissymbols or sign language; for child 3, sign language. Both children 2 and 3 could learn a signing system rather quickly. Child 3 learned and began to use three signs within a 2-hour evaluation. The final decision, of course, rests with the parents.

The data and decisions for children 2 and 3 can be summarized as follows:

*Data:*
1. Cognition = comprehension > production = communication functions.
2. Impaired speech mechanism, structure, and function.
3. Child 2 late preoperational period of conceptual development.
4. Child 3 early preoperational period of conceptual development.

*Decisions* (*see Table 8*)*:*
1. Both child 2 and child 3 are candidates for a nonvocal system.
2. Nonvocal system should serve as a substitute productive system.
3. Nonvocal system must be capable of coding a wide range of meanings.

In summary, the development of an appropriate data base for deciding who is a candidate and for which nonvocal system is dependent upon careful evaluation of the child's language, cognitive, and communication status (see Table 8). The child's status will determine: 1) if the child requires augmentative or a substitute productive system, 2) if the child has the necessary prerequisite skills, 3) the nature of the nonvocal system the child can learn and use, and 4) which system will meet his future needs.

Table 8 is a summary of the basic questions, with the criteria necessary to make the decisions regarding who is a candidate, for what type of program, and for which system.

Table 8. Nonvocal communication programs: Which one for which children?

*Decision 1:* Is the child a candidate for nonvocal communication?

Options: Yes if: / No if:

Criteria:

**Yes if:**

A. No intelligible single word utterances, and
B. Cognitive development at least sensorimotor Stage 6 level, and
C. Producing performative behaviors, and either D or E.
D. Deviant speech production mechanism, structurally and functionally, or
E. At least early preoperational cognitive development, e.g., cognitive development $\geq$ comprehension $>$ production $\leq$ communication function. If yes, continue.

**No if:**

A. Intelligible single- and two-word utterances.
B. Cognitive development = comprehension = production = communication function.

If no, stop.

*Decision 2:* What kind of nonvocal communication program is indicated?

Options: A. Substitute production mode

Criteria:

1. Deviant speech production mechanism, structure, and function.
2. Prognosis for improvement—poor or nonexistent.

B. Augmentative production mode

Criteria:

1. Deviant or questionable speech production mechanism, structure, and function.
2. Prognosis for improvement—unknown to good.
3. Cognitive development $>$ comprehension $\geq$ production $\leq$ communication function.
4. Cognitive development = comprehension $>$ production $\leq$ communication function.

*Decision 3:* Which nonvocal symbol system should be recommended?

Principle: Cognitive development provides the basis to answer this question in three ways.

1. Provides expectations of whether child can learn the system.
2. Provides expectations of what child is capable of communicating now.
3. In relation to chronological age it provides the basis for predicting future growth.

*continued*

Table 8. (*continued*)

| | |
|---|---|
| Application: | 1. For sensorimotor Stage 6 to early preoperational development, limited systems (see Table 7) are indicated unless there is a prognosis for growth to late preoperational level.<br>2. Mid to late preoperational level of development indicates an unlimited system is required to map the child's cognitive knowledge into a language-communication system. |

## SUMMARY

The purpose of this chapter has been to discuss ways in which analyzing language and communication can aid clinicians in the following activities:

1. Reviewing why nonvocal systems should be considered or used
2. Deciding who is a candidate for a nonvocal system and what goals for the system's use are developmentally appropriate
3. Deciding which nonvocal system should be used for each individual child

In order to do those three things, a developmental model was presented that emphasizes the qualitative changes occurring in language and communication behavior as a child grows intellectually. The application of the model was demonstrated for the child's language and communication characteristics and the nonvocal communication systems.

For the child, the developmental model provides a set of expectations for language and communication behaviors that are tied to cognitive level. It defines the behaviors to be assessed or taught in both production and comprehension. Assessment of these behaviors provides the necessary data for deciding whether the child is a candidate for a nonvocal system. This developmental focus on separate processes can reveal very different individual patterns of communication functioning, as we saw for the five children summarized in Figure 2. No single fact about the child, but the entire equation representing communication functioning, is necessary for decision making. The developmental model emphasizes the individuality of each child, stressing the careful, detailed, individualized assessment required to understand and solve individual problems.

The developmental model was used to specify what a child might be able to learn and use of each nonvocal system. It was also used to evaluate what each nonvocal communication system would allow the child to do, as similarities and differences were noted among systems in the messages that could be encoded, the degree to which the encoded message related to spoken English, and the language community that was available to understand the message. Such analyses provide the basis for an informed choice of nonvocal alternative: Will it let children say what they want to say, to the people they want to talk to, for the reasons they want to talk, now and in the future?

## REFERENCES

Amidon, A., and Carey, P. 1972. Why 5-year-olds cannot understand before and after. J. Verb. Learn. Verb. Behav. 11:417–423.

Barrie-Blackley, S. 1973. Six-year-old children's understanding of sentences adjoined with time adverbs. J. Psycholing. Res. 2:153–167.

Bates, E. 1976. Language and Context: The Acquisition of Pragmatics. Academic Press, New York.

Bates, E., Benigni, L., Bretherton, I., Camaioni, L., and Volterra, V. 1976. From gesture to the first word: On cognitive and social prerequisites. *In* M. Lewis and L. Rosenblum (eds.), Origins of Behavior: Language and Communication, pp. 247–308. John Wiley & Sons, New York.

Beilin, H. 1975. Studies in the Cognitive Basis of Language Development. Academic Press, New York.

Bell, S. M., and Ainsworth, M. D. S. 1972. Infant crying and maternal responsiveness. Child Dev. 43:1171–1190.

Bellugi, U. 1972. Development of language in the normal child. *In* J. E. McLean, D. E. Yoder, and R. L. Schiefelbusch (eds.), Language Intervention with the Retarded, pp. 33–51. University Park Press, Baltimore.

Bever, T. G. 1970. The cognitive basis for linguistic structures. *In* J. Hayes (ed.), Cognition and the Development of Language, pp. 279–352. John Wiley & Sons, New York.

Bingham-Newman, A. M., Saunders, R. A., and Hooper, F. H. 1976. Logical operations instruction in the preschool. Technical Report No. 354, Wisconsin Research and Development Center for Cognitive Learning, Madison.

Bloom, L. 1970. Language Development: Structure and Function in Emerging Grammars. The MIT Press, Cambridge, Mass.

Bloom, L. 1973. One Word at a Time: The Use of Single Word Utterances before Syntax. Mouton, The Hague.

Bloom, L. 1974. Talking, understanding, and thinking. *In* R. L. Schiefelbusch and L. L. Lloyd (eds.), Language Perspectives—Acquisition, Retardation, and Intervention, pp. 285–311. University Park Press, Baltimore.

Boehm, A. 1970. Boehm Test of Basic Concepts. The Psychological Corporation, New York.

Bowerman, M. 1973. Early Syntactic Development. Cambridge University Press, Cambridge, England.

Bowerman, M. 1974. Discussion summary—Development of concepts underlying language. *In* R. L. Schiefelbusch and L. L. Lloyd (eds.), Language Perspectives—Acquisition, Retardation and Intervention, pp. 191–201. University Park Press, Baltimore.

Braine, M. D. S. 1976. Monogr. Soc. Child Dev. 41(164).

Bricker, W. A., and Bricker, D. D. 1974. An early language training strategy. *In* R. L. Schiefelbusch and L. L. Lloyd (eds.), Language Perspectives—Acquisition, Retardation, and Intervention, pp. 431–468. University Park Press, Baltimore.

Brown, H. D. 1971. Children's comprehension of relativized English sentences. Child Dev. 42:1923–1936.

Brown, R. 1973. A First Language. Harvard University Press, Cambridge, Mass.

Bruner, J. S. 1975a. The ontongenesis of speech acts. J. Child Lang. 2:1–19.

Bruner, J. S. 1975b. From communication to language—A psychological perspective. Cognition 3:255–287.

Carrier, J. K., Jr. 1973. Application of functional analysis and nonspeech response mode to teaching language. Report No. 7, Kansas Center for Research in Mental Retardation and Human Development, Parsons, Kan.

Carrier, J. K., Jr. 1976. Application of a nonspeech language system with the severely language handicapped. *In* L. L. Lloyd (ed.), Communication Assessment and Intervention Strategies, pp. 523–547. University Park Press, Baltimore.

Carrier, J. K., Jr., and Peak, T. 1975. Non-speech Language Initiation Program. H & H Enterprises, Lawrence, Kan.

Chapman, R. S. 1974. Discussion summary: The developmental relationship between receptive and expressive language. *In* R. L. Schiefelbusch and L. L. Lloyd (eds.), Language Perspectives—Acquisition, Retardation, and Intervention, pp. 335–344. University Park Press, Baltimore.

Chapman, R. S. 1978. Comprehension strategies in children. *In* J. F. Kavanagh and W. Strange (eds.), Speech and Language in the Laboratory, School, and Clinic. The MIT Press, Cambridge, Mass.

Chapman, R. S. The development of question comprehension in preschool children. In preparation.

Chapman, R. S., and Kohn, L. L. 1978. Comprehension strategies in two- and three-year-olds: Animate agent or probable event? J. Speech Hear. Res. 21:746–761.

Chapman, R. S., and Miller, J. F. 1975. Word order in early two and three word utterances: Does production precede comprehension? J. Speech Hear. Res. 18:355–371.

Clancy, P., Jacobsen, T., and Silva, M. 1976. The acquisition of conjunction: A cross-linguistic study. Papers Reports Child Lang. Dev. 12:71–80.

Clark, E. V. 1971. On the acquisition of the meaning of "before" and "after." J. Verb. Learn. Verb. Behav. 10:266–275.

Clark, E. V. 1973. Non-linguistic strategies and the acquisition of word meaning. Cognition 2:161–182.

Clark, E. V. 1974. Normal states and evaluative viewpoints. Language 50:316–332.

Clark, E. V. 1975. Knowledge, context, and strategy in the acquisition of meaning. Paper presented at the 26th Annual Georgetown University Round Table: Developmental Psycholinguistics: Theory and Applications, Georgetown University, March, Washington, D.C.

Coggins, T. 1975. The classification of relational meanings expressed in the early two-word utterance of Down's syndrome children. Unpublished doctoral dissertation, University of Wisconsin, Madison.

Corrigan, R. 1975. A scalogram analysis of the development of the use and comprehension of "Because" in children. Child Dev. 46:195–201.

Corrigan, R. 1976. The relationship between object permanence and language development: How much and how strong? Paper presented at the Stanford Child Language Research Forum, Stanford University, April, Palo Alto, Cal.

Cromer, R. F. 1974. The development of language and cognition: The cognition hypothesis. *In* D. Foss (ed.), New Perspectives in Child Development, pp. 184–252. Penguin, Baltimore.

Cromer, R. F. 1976. The cognitive hypothesis of language acquisition and its implications for child language deficiency. *In* D. Morehead and A. Morehead (eds.), Normal and Deficient Child Language, pp. 283–333. University Park Press, Baltimore.

de Villiers, J., and de Villiers, P. 1973. Development of the use of word order in comprehension. J. Psycholing. Res. 2:331–342.

de Villiers, J., and de Villiers, P. 1974. Competence and performance in child language: Are children really competent to judge? J. Child Lang. 1:11–22.

Dihoff, R. E., and Chapman, R. S. 1977. First words: Their origins in action. Papers Reports Child Lang. Dev. 13:1–7.

Dore, J. 1974. A pragmatic description of early language development. J. Psycholing. Res. 4:343–350.

Ervin-Tripp, S. 1970. Discourse agreement: How children answer questions. *In* J. Hayes (ed.), Cognition and the Development of Language, pp. 79–108. John Wiley & Sons, New York.

Ferreiro, E., and Sinclair, H. 1971. Temporal relationships in language. Int. J. Psychol. 6:39–47.

Gibson, E., and Levin, H. 1975. The Psychology of Reading. The MIT Press, Cambridge, Mass.

Gleason, J. B. 1973. Code switching in children's language. *In* T. E. Moore (ed.), Cognitive Development and the Acquisition of Language, pp. 159–168. Academic Press, New York.

Glucksberg, S., Krauss, R., and Higgens, T. 1975. The development of referential communication skills. *In* F. Horowitz (ed.), Review of Child Development Research, Vol. 4. University of Chicago Press, Chicago.

Goldin-Meadow, S., Seligman, M., and Gelman, R. 1976. Language in the two-year-old. Cognition 4:189–202.

Greenfield, P., and Smith, J. 1976. The Structure of Communication in Early Language Development. Academic Press, New York.

Grimnel, M., Detamore, K., and Lippke, B. 1976. Sign it successful—Manual English encourages expressive communication. Teach. Except. Child. 8: 123–125.

Halliday, M. A. K. 1975. Learning How to Mean: Explorations in the Development of Language. Edward Arnold, London.

Harris-Vanderheiden, D. 1975. Blissymbols and the mentally retarded. *In* G. Vanderheiden and K. Grilley (eds.), Non-Vocal Communication Techniques and Aids for the Severely Physically Handicapped, pp. 120–131. University Park Press, Baltimore.

Hass, W. A., and Wepman, J. M. 1974. Dimensions of individual difference in the spoken syntax of school children. J. Speech Hear. Disord. 17:455–469.

Hatch, E. 1971. The young child's comprehension of time connectives. Child Dev. 42:2111–2113.

Hodun, A. 1975. Comprehension and the development of spatial and temporal sequence terms. Unpublished doctoral dissertation, University of Wisconsin, Madison.

Horgan, D. 1975. Language development: A cross-methodological approach. Unpublished doctoral dissertation, University of Michigan, Ann Arbor.

Hutson, B. A., and Shub, J. 1975. Developmental study of factors involved in choice of conjunction. Child Dev. 46:46–53.

Huttenlocher, J. 1974. The origins of language comprehension. *In* R. L. Solso (ed.), Theories of Cognitive Psychology, pp. 331–368. Lawrence Erlbaum Associates, Potomac, Md.

Ingram, D. 1974a. The relationship between comprehension and production. *In* R. L. Schiefelbusch and L. L. Lloyd (eds.), Language Perspectives—Acquisition, Retardation, and Intervention, pp. 313–334. University Park Press, Baltimore.

Ingram, D. 1974b. Stages in the development of one-word utterances. Paper presented to Stanford Child Language Research Forum, Stanford University, April, Palo Alto, Cal.

Ingram, D. 1977. Sensorimotor intelligence and language development. *In* A. Lock (ed.), Action, Gesture, and Symbol: The Emergence of Language. Academic Press, New York.

Inhelder, B. 1976. Some pathologic phenomena analyzed in the perspective of developmental psychology. *In* B. Inhelder and H. Chipman (eds.), Piaget and His School, pp. 221–227. Springer-Verlag, New York.

Johnson, H. L. 1975. The meaning of before and after for preschool children. J. Exp. Child Psychol. 19:88–89.

Johnson, H. L., and Chapman, R. S. Children's judgment and recall of causal statements. J. Psycholing. Res. In press.

Johnston, J. 1973. Spatial notions and the child's use of locatives in an elicitation task. Paper presented at the Stanford Child Language Research Forum, April, Stanford.

Katz, E., and Brent, S. 1968. Understanding connectives. J. Verb. Learn. Verb. Behav. 7:501–509.

Keller-Cohen, D. 1975. Children's verbal imitation, comprehension and production of temporal structures. Paper presented at the Biennial Meeting of the Society for Research in Child Development, April, Denver.

Kopchick, G., Rombach, D., and Smilowitz, R. A. 1975. Total communication environment in an institution. Ment. Retard. 13:22–23.

Kuhn, D., and Phelps, H. 1976. The development of children's comprehension of causal direction. Child Dev. 47:248–251.

Lackner, J. 1968. A developmental study of language behavior in retarded children. Neuropsychologia 6:301–320.

Lahey, M. 1974. Use of prosody and syntactic markers in children's comprehension of spoken sentences. J. Speech Hear. Res. 17:656–668.

Larson, V. L. 1974. Comprehension of telegraphic and expanded utterances by mentally retarded and normal children. Unpublished doctoral dissertation, University of Wisconsin, Madison.

Lebeis, S., and Lebeis, S. 1975. The use of signed communication with the normal-hearing, nonverbal mentally retarded. Bureau Memorandum, Wisconsin Department of Public Instruction, Fall 17:28–30.

Lewis, M., and Freedle, R. 1973. Mother-infant dyad: The cradle of meaning. *In* P. Pliner, L. Krames, and T. Alloway (eds.), Communication and Affect, pp. 127–156. Academic Press, New York.

Lezine, I. 1973. The transition from sensorimotor to earliest symbolic function in early development. Early Dev. 51:221–228.

Limber, J. 1973. The genesis of complex sentences. *In* T. Moore (ed.), Cognitive Development and the Acquisition of Language, pp. 169–185. Academic Press, New York.

Lovell, K., and Slater, A. 1960. The growth of the concept of time: A comparative study. J. Child Psychol. Psychiatry 1:179–190.

Maratsos, M. 1974. Children who get worse at understanding the passive: A replication of Bever. J. Psycholing. Res. 3:65–74.

Maratsos, M., and Abramovitch, P. 1975. How children understand full, truncated, and anomalous passives. J. Verb. Learn. Verb. Behav. 14:145–157.

Matalon, B. 1962. Etude genetique de l'implication. Etudes d'Epistemologie Genetique XVI, Implication, Formalisation et Logique Naturelle. 69–93.

Mayberry, R. 1978. Manual communication. *In* H. Davis and S. R. Silverman (eds.), Hearing and Deafness, pp. 400–420. Holt, Rinehart & Winston, Chicago.

Menyuk, P. 1974. Early development of receptive language: From babbling to words. *In* R. L. Schiefelbusch and L. L. Lloyd (eds.), Language Perspectives—Acquisition, Retardation, and Intervention, pp. 213–235. University Park Press, Baltimore.

Miller, J. F. (ed.). Assessing Children's Language Production: Experimental Procedures. University Park Press, Baltimore. In press.

Miller, J. F., Chapman, R. S., Branston, M. B., and Reichle, J. Language comprehension in sensorimotor stages 5 and 6. J. Speech Hear. Res. In press.

Miller, J. F., and Yoder, D. E. 1973. Miller-Yoder Test of Grammatical Comprehension. University Bookstore, Madison, Wis.

Miller, J. F., and Yoder, D. E. 1974. An ontogenetic language teaching strategy for retarded children. *In* R. L. Schiefelbusch and L. L. Lloyd (eds.), Language Perspectives—Acquisition, Retardation, and Intervention, pp. 505–528. University Park Press, Baltimore.

Mitchell-Kernan, C. 1971. Language behaviors in a black urban community. Monograph of the Language Behavior Research Laboratory No. 2. University of California, Berkeley.

Montroy, P., McManis, D., and Bell, D. 1971. Development of time concepts in normal and retarded children. Psycholog. Rep. 28:895–902.

Nelson, K. 1973. Structure and strategy in learning to talk. Monograph of the Society for Research in Child Development No. 149. University of Chicago Press, Chicago.

Newport, E., and Ashbrook, E. 1977. The emergence of semantic relations in ASL. Papers Reports Child Lang. Dev. 13:16–21.

O'Brien, T. C., and Shapiro, B. J. 1968. The development of logical thinking in children. Am. Educ. Res. J. 5:531–542.

Olds, H. F., Jr. 1968. An experimental study of syntactical factors influencing children's comprehension of certain complex relationships. Report No. 4, Harvard University Center for Research and Development on Educational Differences, Cambridge, Mass.

Owings, N. 1972. Internal reliability and item analysis of the Miller-Yoder Test of Grammatical comprehension. Unpublished master's thesis, University of Wisconsin, Madison.

Paris, S. G. 1973. Comprehension of language connectives and propositional logical relations. J. Exp. Child Psychol. 16:278–291.

Parisi, D., and Antinucci, F. 1970. Lexical competence. *In* G. B. Flores d'Arcais and W. J. M. Levelt (eds.), Advances in Psycholinguistics, pp. 197–210. North Holland, Amsterdam.

Peel, E. 1967. A method for investigating children's understanding of certain logical connectives used in binary propositional thinking. Brit. J. Math. Stat. Psychol. 20:81–92.

Phillips, J. R. 1973. Syntax and vocabulary of mother's speech to young children: Age and sex comparisons. Child Dev. 44:192–195.

Piaget, J., and Inhelder, B. 1969. The Psychology of the Child. Basic Books, New York.

Pierce, J. E. 1974. A study of 750 Portland, Oregon children during the first year. Papers Reports Child Lang. Dev. 8:19–25.

Premack, D. 1976. Language and intelligence in ape and man. Am. Sci. 64:674–683.

Retherford, K. S., Schwartz, B. L., and Chapman, R. S. 1977. The changing relation between semantic relations in mother and child speech. Paper presented at Second Annual Boston University Conference on Language Acquisition, October, Boston.

Ricks, D. M. 1975. Vocal communication in pre-verbal normal and autistic children. *In* N. O'Connor (ed.), Language, Cognitive Deficits, and Retardation, pp. 75–80. Butterworths, London.

Roberge, J. J. 1970. A study of children's abilities to reason with basic principles of deductive reasoning. Am. Educ. Res. J. 7:583–596.

Sachs, J., and Truswell, L. 1976. Comprehension of two-word instructions by children in the one-word stage. Papers Reports Child Lang. Dev. 12:212–220.

Scheuerman, N., Baumgart, D., Sipsma, K., and Brown, L. 1976. Toward the development of a curriculum for teaching nonverbal communication skills to severely handicapped students: Teaching basic tracking, scanning and selection skills. *In* N. Scheuerman, L. Brown, and T. Crowner (eds.), Toward an Integrated Therapy Model for Teaching Motor, Tracking and Scanning Skills to Severely Handicapped Students, Vol. VI, Part 3. Madison Public Schools, Madison, Wis.

Shapiro, B., and O'Brien, T. 1970. Logical thinking in children ages six through thirteen. Child Dev. 41:823–829.

Shatz, M. 1975. On understanding messages: A study in the comprehension of indirect directives. Unpublished doctoral dissertation, University of Pennsylvania, Philadelphia.

Sheldon, A. 1974. The role of parallel function in the acquisition of relative clauses in English. J. Verb. Learn. Verb. Behav. 13:272–281.

Shine, D., and Walsh, J. F. 1971. Developmental trends in the use of logical connectives. Psychonom. Sci. 23:171–172.

Shipley, E., Smith, C. S., and Gleitman, L. 1969. A study in the acquisition of syntax: Free responses to verbal commands. Language 45:332–342.

Sinclair, H., and Bronckart, J. 1972. SVO—A linguistic universal. J. Exp. Child Psychol. 14:329–348.

Skinner, B. F. 1957. Verbal Behavior. Appleton-Century-Crofts, New York.

Slobin, D. I. 1966. Grammatical transformations and sentence comprehension in childhood and adulthood. J. Verb. Learn. Verb. Behav. 5:219–227.

Slobin, D. I. 1977. Language change in childhood and in history. *In* J. Macnamara (ed.), Language Learning and Thought, pp. 185–214. Academic Press, New York.

Smith, L. L. 1972. Comprehension performance of oral deaf and normal hearing children at three stages of language development. Unpublished doctoral dissertation, University of Wisconsin, Madison.

Snow, C. E. 1972. Mothers' speech to children learning language. Child Dev. 43:549–565.

Snow, C. E. 1977. Mothers' speech research: From input to interaction. *In* C. E. Snow and C. A. Ferguson (eds.), Talking to Children, pp. 31–49. Cambridge University Press, Cambridge, England.

Snyder, L. 1976. The early presuppositions and performatives of normal and language disabled children. Papers Reports Child Lang. Dev. 12:221–229.

Strohner, H., and Nelson, K. 1974. The young child's development of sentence comprehension: Influence of event probability, nonverbal context, syntactic form, and strategies. Child Dev. 45:567–576.

Uzgiris, I., and Hunt, J. McV. 1975. Assessment in Infancy. University of Illinois Press, Urbana. 1975.

Watts, A. F. 1944. The Language and Mental Development of Children. George G. Harrap and Co., London.

Weil, J. 1970. The relationship between time conceptualization and time language in young children. Unpublished doctoral dissertation, City University of New York, New York.

Wetstone, K. S., and Friedlander, B. Z. 1973. The effect of word order on young children's responses to simple questions and commands. Child Dev. 44:734–740.

Wilbur, R. B. 1976. The linguistics of manual languages and manual systems. *In* L. L. Lloyd (ed.), Communication Assessment and Intervention Strategies, pp. 423–500. University Park Press, Baltimore.

Wilcox, S., and Palermo, D. 1975. "In," "On" and "Under" revisited. Cognition 3:245–254.

Woodward, M. 1959. The behavior of idiots interpreted by Piaget's theory of sensorimotor development. Brit. J. Educ. Psychol. 29:60–71.

chapter 10

# Approaches to Assessing the Communication of Non-Oral Persons

*Howard C. Shane*

*Developmental Evaluation Clinic*
*and*
*Hearing and Speech Division*
*Children's Hospital Medical Center*
*Boston, Massachusetts*

contents

My biggest problem isn't CP, its people's ignorance about the nonverbal person. (Sentiments expressed by Jim Viggiano, a severely handicapped, non-oral communicator who uses a communication board or electric typewriter.)

The importance of nonspeech communication systems has long been recognized by specialists working in the field of cerebral palsy and deafness. Manual approaches to communication give many hearing-impaired persons their primary means of developing a linguistic form of communication. Also, communication boards afford some individuals with cerebral palsy a graphic system of expressive language—that is, spelling in lieu of speaking.

In recent years, a growing number of professionals have come to the unsettling realization that inducing oral (speech) communication in all persons is an unrealistic objective. Consequently, considerable interest in nonspeech methods of communication for persons with extreme sensory, cognitive, emotional, linguistic, neuromuscular, or motor planning disabilities has arisen. Paralleling this rise in the number of persons within and across disability groups for whom nonspeech communication is being tried, is a precipitous rise both in electronic systems and devices (hardware) and in symbol systems and teaching strategies (software).

Despite recent advances, however, professionals having a traditional speech orientation to communication often encounter difficulty in determining and implementing a nonspeech communication system. This chapter presents some guidelines for approaching communication evaluation of individuals who are non-oral. It also develops a conceptualization of communication. Critical to the development of this model was the requirement that it provide a workable framework in which to view the evaluation process for the nonspeech communicator. Although this chapter reflects greater attention to communication problems having a congenital etiology, the model is applicable to adventitious communication deficits as well. In fact, the foundation of the model stems from the work of Wepman and what has come to be known as "Wepman's model."

## SPEECH AND NONSPEECH COMMUNICATION MODELS

Models . . . describe and help us understand complex systems (King, 1971).

### Background Model

In the mid 1950s and in the early 1960s, Wepman and his co-workers (Wepman and Van Pelt, 1955; Wepman et al. 1960) published a conceptualization of communication founded upon clinical information derived from adults with adventitious, neurologically based communication prob-

This chapter was supported in part through Project 928, Maternal and Child Health Service, U.S. Department of Health, Education, and Welfare.

lems. Their theoretical model was based on persons who were once normal communicators. It was intended to serve as a guide to oral rehabilitation, but several of its basic principles are applicable to communication problems of individuals who are non-oral.[1]

Figure 1 is a simplified version of the Wepman communication model. The integration component of this schematic, similar to what Darley, Aronson, and Brown (1975) have called the central language processor, is concerned with encoding and decoding vocal (that is, speaking and listening) and nonvocal (that is, writing and reading) linguistic information. Disturbance to this hypothetical mechanism results in the neurogenic language disorder know as aphasia. Persons with aphasia have impaired ability to speak, listen, read, and write, since all these functions require intact integrative capabilities.

The transmission component of Figure 1, unlike the integrative mechanism, is not concerned with symbolic or linguistic processing. Rather, it pertains to motor speech production or the structural mechanisms (for example, tongue, soft palate, larynx) and neurological structures (for example, cranial nerves) needed to express spoken language. In other words, transmission is the output mechanism for the symbolic, integration system. When neurological insult affects transmission, the clinical outcome will be dysarthria or apraxia of speech. Dysarthria is defined by Darley, Aronson, and Brown (1969) as:

> A collective name for a group of speech disorders resulting from disturbances in muscular control over the speech mechanism, due to damage of the central or peripheral nervous system. It designates problems in oral communication due to paralysis, weakness, or incoordination of the speech musculature (p. 246).

Apraxia of speech, on the other hand, is defined by Darley (1969) as:

> an articulatory disorder resulting from impairment, as the result of brain damage, of the capacity to program the positioning of speech musculature and the sequencing of muscle movements for the volitional production of phonemes. The speech musculature does not show significant weakness, slowness, or incoordination when used for reflex and automatic acts.

Dysarthria and apraxia of speech are distinctive motor speech problems separate from the more symbolic disorder of aphasia. An individual having either of these motor speech disorders in pure form will be able to understand spoken language and to read and write. Expression of spoken language, however, will be impaired, and this impairment will be related

---

[1] For the purposes of this chapter, non-oral designates persons whose primary means of expression is other than speech. Although the individual may produce limited speech, that output is basically unintelligible.

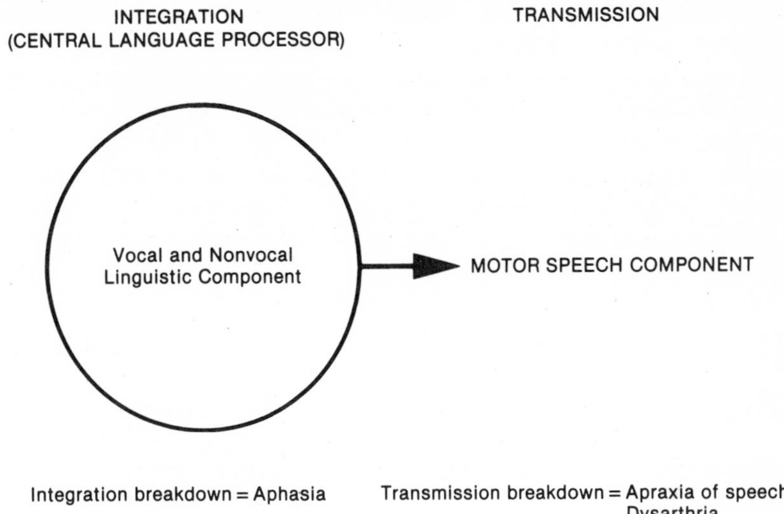


Figure 1. Simplified version of Wepman model based on adventitious neurogenic speech and language disorders.

to either a motor planning (apraxia of speech) or a neuromuscular (dysarthria) disturbance.

The simply stated, but clinically confusing (Darley, 1964) distinction between integration and transmission was of primary importance to Wepman in his conceptualization of communication. The question arises, however, whether that framework applies to persons with congenital communication problems. In other words, does a similar integration and transmission distinction apply to persons with severely delayed speech and language problems, and, more importantly, will knowing such information ultimately lead to effective intervention procedures?

One clinical investigation seems to shed some light on this subject. Lenneberg (1962) described the case of an eight-year-old boy born with anarthria (a severe from of dysarthria characterized by speechlessness). According to this noted language theorist, the child "had a normal and adequate understanding of spoken language" (p. 421). To investigate the boy's receptive language ability, Lenneberg tape recorded a number of oral commands that the child was expected to execute through motor behavior (for example, "Stand up," "Show me your right eye," "Pick up the ball and put it behind your back"). Analysis of the boy's performance indicated that his comprehension of language was "normal" for his age.

Lenneberg's paper has a number of theoretical and clinical implications. For our purposes, it lends support to the position that one can possess an intact integration system (as reflected by normal receptive language capabilities) despite an aberrant motor speech or transmission system. Furthermore, clinical experience with congenitally dysarthric persons (that is, children having some form of cerebral palsy) who communicate highly sophisticated linguistic messages with the assistance of communication boards lends further credence to making a transmission/integration distinction.

**Expanded Model of Communication**

To this point, only linguistic forms of communication have been discussed. The magnitude of communication breakdowns in persons who are non-oral or whose developmental picture suggests the possibility of remaining non-oral, however, requires that all potential forms of communication[2] be considered. Lloyd (1976) alludes to this point: "The more severely impaired the individual, the more likely the need for the clinician to supplement the aural-oral channel" (p. xi). In this section, an expanded model of communication is presented. The purpose of this conceptualization is threefold:

1. To provide a framework for classifying diverse forms of human communication
2. To provide a foundation for assessing communicative behavior in severely communicatively handicapped persons
3. To provide a foundation for the implementation of nonspeech communication

Figure 2 contains an expanded version of the simplified Wepman model. It attempts to represent all potential forms of expressive communicative behavior whether vocal or nonvocal, voluntary or reflexive. In this conceptualization, the feature of separate integration and transmission components has been maintained. However, the scope of these distinct components has been enlarged.

The integration component in the expanded model of communication represents major forms of expressive communicative behavior. The author recognizes that integration implies a level of cognitive and linguistic functioning in which certain forms of expression, such as reflexive behavior, are not included. However, to preserve the integrity of the integration/transmission dichotomy, the term *integration* (*forms of expression*) will be used.

[2] For the purposes of this chapter, *communication* is defined as a systematic exchange of information (not necessarily intentional) between a minimum of two persons.

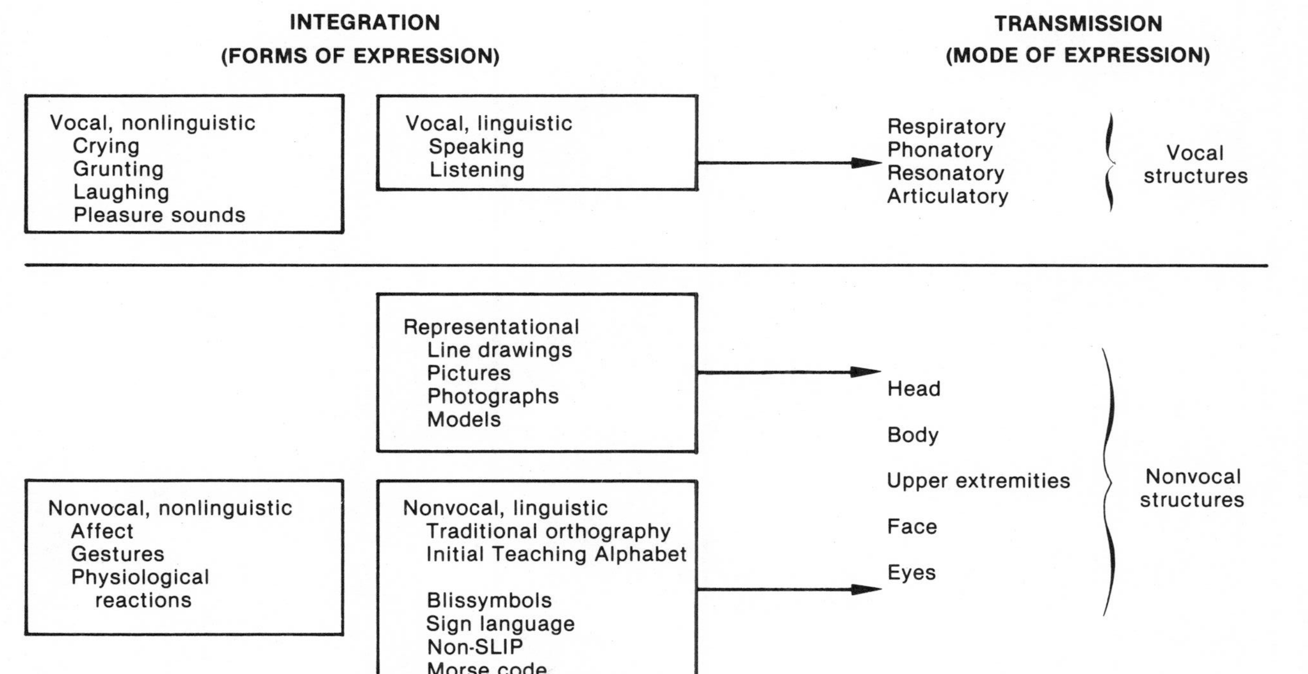


Figure 2. Expanded model of communication. The communicative information from the five integration components is expressed through either the vocal or nonvocal structures.

The integration component is divided into five subsections: vocal,[3] linguistic;[4] nonvocal,[5] linguistic; representational; vocal, nonlinguistic;[6] and nonvocal, nonlinguistic. Each component is discussed separately below.

### Vocal, Linguistic Component

The vocal, linguistic component is similar to the integration component in the Wepman model. In the expanded conceptualization, however, the nonvocal, linguistic function (for example, writing or reading) is under a separate subcomponent. Vocal, linguistic communication (discussed previously) is not to be elaborated on here except to suggest that it is generally considered the most obvious means of human information exchange. Despite the importance of spoken language, however, Birdwhistle (1970) points out that spoken language accounts for only 35% of human social interaction while 65% of language is nonverbal. According to Laver (1976):

> It is becoming more accepted that behavior in face-to-face conversation can profitably be viewed as an interwoven complex of many different communicative strands and that these strands have an important degree of mutual relevance. Language is still seen as a principal strand, but nevertheless, as only one among many strands contributing to the totality of communication. The view is taken that the communicative function of language can be better understood in the context of the operation of the other strands than in isolation. All the means of communication capable of conventionally coded, short-term manipulation—language, tone of voice, gesture, posture, body-movements, spatial orientation, physical proximity, eye contact, and facial expression—can be thought of as being woven together to form the fabric of a conversation, and we can understand the communicative texture of an interaction best by seeing the relationship of the different strands (pp. 346–347).

### Nonvocal, Linguistic Component

The nonvocal, linguistic component refers to the mechanism that processes varied forms of nonvocal linguistic information. This

---

[3] *Vocal* indicates that exteriorization (production) of information will be expressed through the vocal tract and will be heard by the listener/observer.

[4] Linguistic indicates that the system has convention-governed rules, productivity (Hockett, 1960, that is, the capacity to express and comprehend novel messages), and semanticity (Hockett, 1960, that is, there are fixed associations between elements in the message and features of situations in the world).

[5] *Nonvocal* indicates that exteriorization of the integrative information will be expressed through some physical structure (other than the vocal tract) and will be seen by the listener/observer. The term *paralinguistic* is a more widely used term to denote the nonverbal behaviors included in this category. However, many of the nonverbal behaviors included in this model are not included in a traditional definition of paralinguistic. Thus, *nonlinguistic*, a less common term, is used here.

[6] *Nonlinguistic* refers to diverse forms of communication that have no linguistic symbolic form (for example, phonemes, graphemes, or words).

mechanism is called upon to process orthographic information (for example, traditional orthography, or the Initial Teaching Alphabet) for reading and writing. The typical use of graphic information as a secondary linguistic sytem, however, is often markedly different for the non-oral person whose graphic system takes on a primary role as an expressive system of communication.

Furthermore, diverse handicapping conditions have stimulated the development of new, or the modification of existing, nonvocal, linguistic communication systems for handicapped persons. For example, sign language, initially developed for the deaf and hard of hearing, has recently been employed with some success with persons who are mentally retarded (Shaffer and Goehl, 1974; Richardson, 1975; Kotkin and Simpson, 1976; and Fristoe and Lloyd, 1977) and emotionally disturbed (Miller and Miller, 1973). Blissymbolics, originally intended as an international symbol communication system (Bliss, 1965), represent another nonvocal linguistic communication system that has widespread appeal with non-oral persons. Morse code has also been modified to meet the communicative needs of the communicatively handicapped. The author has witnessed tediously slow communication by a severely handicapped woman whose lateral gaze represented "dot" and vertical gaze "dash." Communication by this procedure requires an intact linguistic integrative component because a user must first have knowledge of traditional orthography and second be able to apply a code to the orthographic code. In a sense then, Morse code represents a tertiary linguistic system that is parasitic on written language.

Non-SLIP (Non-speech Language Initiation Program) is a nonpictographic communication program described by Carrier (1974a, 1974b, 1976). This approach is based on the work of Premack, who studied the ability of chimpanzees to manipulate various geometric shapes in order to communicate. The Non-SLIP format can be considered linguistic because all grammatical classes and all lexical items can be represented by a geometric chip.

**Representational Component**

The representational component refers to nonlinguistic material that represents persons, objects, or events from the environment. Included in Figure 2 are four levels within this component:

Line drawings—defined as two-dimensional drawings that outline the perimeter of objects they represent

Picture—defined as pictorial stimuli that are not actual photographs of an object

Photographs—defined as actual photographic representations of a real object, person, or event

Models—defined as miniature objects resembling actual objects (Items contained within a doll house exemplify the model level.)

Typically, representational material would not be included in a model of communication, even though normal children recognize that such depiction can stand for actual objects, persons, and events. However, since many communicatively handicapped children use such representations to express information, they are included in this conceptualization.

### Vocal, Nonlinguistic Component

During normal communication, much information has a vocal origin but is not linguistic. Vocal or audible, nonlinguistic information can be either independent or dependent (Abercrombie, 1969). The former classification designates audible information that can stand alone and convey meaning, while the latter signifies instances in which the conveyance of a message requires added information. An example of independent, audible, nonlinguistic communication is an interjection such as "uh-huh" or "shh," when the audible message communicates agreement or a request to be quiet, respectively. Another example, more germane to persons who have severe communicative handicaps, would be the vocal sounds associated with laughing or crying. The communicative importance of these independent behaviors was discussed by Chevigny and Braverman (1950):

> The child does not have to learn to laugh or cry—he does so naturally; and what might be termed the basic expressions indicating pain and grief are recognized, and have always been to all mankind (p. 69).

Vocal, dependent, nonlinguistic communication occurs frequently during normal communication and also represents an extremely important mode of expression for non-oral communicators. Tone of voice or loudness level, for example, can convey anger or compassion to a listener, and since the audible features depend on the linguistic content to specify actual intent, they are dependent. A communicatively handicapped person may produce a grunt-like noise while simultaneously looking toward a desired object. The grunt, in this case, is not sufficient by itself to communicate the intent. The author recently observed a six-year-old girl who had developed an elaborate audible, dependent, nonlinguistic communication system. The intensity level of her grunt accompanied by a pointing response indicated how strongly she desired the item.

### Nonvocal, Nonlinguistic Component

The nonvocal, nonlinguistic mode of communication includes such human expressive behavior as affect (that is, expression of information through facial postures) and gestures. To complete a model intended for persons who are severely handicapped, a number of physiological reactions not found in a traditional communication model are included here. For example, when an individual is cold, goosebumps may appear, teeth may chatter, fingertips may feel cold, and lips may appear blue. These physiological reactions, even though not emitted voluntarily, are responses that suggest an individual is cold.

For many severely handicapped persons, involuntary or physiologically based reactions, such as goosebumps, or the rubbing of eyes when tired, may be the only means of expression. The onus for interpreting the significance of these observable audible and/or visible, nonlinguistic behaviors is on those who know the person best.

With increased attention focused on nonspeech communication, new symbol systems will undoubtedly emerge that will have particular importance for the non-oral person. Those systems and others, currently available but not included here, should be classified according to the integration (forms of expansion) components listed here.[7]

**Expanded Transmission Component**

In the model proposed by Wepman, transmission was depicted as the output system responsible for exteriorizing linguistic information. The transmission section of Figure 2, labeled *transmission* (*mode of expression*), not only retains that function but also exteriorizes all expressive forms of communication. The entire body as well as combinations of its parts can be involved in transmitting integration (expressive forms) information. For example, affect is expressed by the face and gestures by upper extremity, trunk rotation, and head movement, whereas symbol, picture, or word selection (on a communication board) most often is expressed by upper extremity movement. All vocal integrative functions (that is, linguistic and nonlinguistic) are transmitted through the vocal tract. An audible message is produced by a complex interaction of respiratory, phonatory, resonatory, and articulatory structures. This interaction results in acoustic signals ranging from interpretable grunt-like noises to meaningful verbal speech.

The quality of a communicated message is directly related to the extent of structural, neuromuscular, and/or motor planning deficits. That is, a physical anomaly, such as a cleft palate, or a neurogenic one, such as a paralysis, weakness, or incoordination of vocal tract musculature,

---

[7] For a more comprehensive view of programming advantages and disadvantages of the different integration components (particularly for the linguistic and representational components) the interested reader is referred to: Shane, H. C. 1979. Approaches to communication training with people who are severely handicapped. *In* R. York and G. Edgar (eds.), Teaching the Severely Handicapped, Vol. IV. Special Press, Columbus, Oh.

will have a marked effect on the quality of vocalization. Likewise, the integrity of physical structures and musculature of the body as a whole will influence quality of movement and will ultimately have some bearing on assessment and management of the non-oral individual.

## COMMUNICATION EVALUATION PROCESS

> "Intelligence will out" . . . It is often amazing how a severely handicapped . . . child will demonstrate in some way his understanding and comprehension of what is expected of him (Denhoff, 1965, p. 69).

The expanded expressive communication model should serve as a guide in organizing subjective impressions and objective data concerning communicative functioning. Most important, the model's principle of separation between integration (forms of expression) and transmission (mode of expression) carries over to the evaluation stage and dictates investigation not only of integration (forms of expression) but also of the integrity of transmission structures that impart that integrative information. So, for example, a child's understanding that words stand for things as well as his ability to voluntarily control his oral musculature for speech will be assessed.

The primary objective of a communication evaluation for the non-oral individual is to delineate factors that facilitate communicative growth. In this evaluation section, diagnostic guidelines and procedures necessary to effect communication changes are reviewed. The section is divided into four parts. The first is concerned with establishing a basis (or underlying cause) for the oral expressive deficit. The second deals with guidelines for determining the range and type of expressive forms (integration) present, while the third evaluates the integrity of transmission structures. In the final section, clinical decision-making rules for selecting the most appropriate, alternative communication system are discussed.

### Underlying Cause

As noted previously, the goal of the diagnostic process is to gather information that leads to effective intervention. Knowing the basis of an individual's limited speech output is particularly relevant to this issue because varied underlying causes demand different intervention strategies.

There are six categories of disorders with which expressive speech deficits are most frequently associated. Two fall in the motor speech domain (apraxia of speech and dysarthria); one is cognitively based (mental retardation); one is emotional (emotional disturbance/autism); one is linguistic (specific language disorder); and the final is sensory (hearing impaired). A seventh category, "unknown," might be included because we are often unable to be precise.

The six disorders may occur in isolation and underlie limited speech output or may occur in combination. For example, the presence of a specific language (linguistic) disorder is often found in conjunction with a neuromuscular disorder (cerebral palsy). Either disorder in severe form can lead to a person being non-oral, while a combination of the two can result in a severe oral expressive deficit.

The type of intervention appropriate for an expressive deficit with a neuromusular basis would, of course, be different from that suggested for an emotionally or cognitively based disorder. Therefore, differential diagnosis of the etiology of the limited speech output is critical to the evaluation process and to management.

The determination of underlying cause usually requires the combined efforts of a number of professionals working closely with parents. The determination of hearing impairment, for example, may result from parental reports and professional observation that:

1. There is a cessation of infant vocalization (that is, babbling).
2. There is inconsistent reaction to, or reduced awareness of, the auditory environment.
3. There is a significant reduction in auditory sensitivity.
4. There is increased focus on visual stimuli.
5. There are behavioral or interpersonal difficulties (that is, overactivity, management problems, difficulty relating to peers or groups).

Or, alternatively, an emotional basis for the lack of expressive speech may be suspected in the presence of such factors as:

1. Flat affect
2. Minimal eye contact
3. Stereotypic behavior
4. Minimal affection
5. Minimal interest in the environment
6. Echolalia

### Integration (Expressive Forms) Evaluation

The reader will recall that five forms of expression were discussed in the expanded communication model. In this section guidelines for evaluating each are reviewed. Diagnostic information regarding two of these—vocal, linguistic (oral language) and nonvocal, linguistic (reading)—is more readily available because these forms have received both clinical and research attention. These linguistic forms are discussed below with emphasis on modification of existing receptive language tests as well as the importance of behavioral observation and nonstandardized testing. The vocal, nonlinguistic and the nonvocal, nonlinguistic, as well as the representational forms, have received virtually no attention in the exceptional child literature, and more specific guidelines for assessing these are provided below.

**Vocal, Linguistic** Gathering diagnostic information about the vocal, linguistic (oral language) capability of a non-oral person is seemingly a contradiction in terms because he does not speak. Since the intent of the evaluation is to determine the capability for linguistic expression, the determination of that ability or best estimate of that ability must, by necessity, be derived from the results of receptive language testing.

Typically, a language evaluation is concerned with determining whether a person's knowledge about his native language is developmentally appropriate and with isolating specific language deficits when and if they exist (for example, vocabulary deficits, morphological/ syntactic problems, and word retrieval deficiencies). In the "typical" language evaluation, the diagnostician goes about determining each of these factors through behavioral observation and through administration of formal receptive and expressive language tests.

The prediction of linguistic competence and the isolation of specific language disability are hindered in the evaluation of a non-oral person for several reasons. First, the lack of, or unintelligibility of, expressive language output makes standardized expressive language inventories inappropriate. Second, lack of oral expressive speech precludes the analysis of a spontaneous speech sample, which is usually a rich source of diagnostic information as to linguistic competence and the presence of specific language deficits. To further compound assessment difficulties, atypical motor movements resulting from neuromuscular or motor planning deficits can deter adequate assessment. That is, one may not be able to rely on gross motor behavior consequent to the presentation of verbal instruction as an indication of understanding of the linguistic code. Cooperation issues are also important. An emotionally disturbed child may understand the intent of an instruction and be physically capable of carrying it out, but will not do so for behavioral reasons.

Consequently, in the presence of severe expressive deficits with or without behavioral or motor complications, the diagnostician must rely on standardized receptive language measures,[8] and, more heavily than he may like, on clinical judgment. Formal evaluation procedures include

---

[8] As a rule of thumb, receptive language measures with modifications for motor involvement are applicable to the cooperative non-oral child. Modification may entail utilization of adaptive equipment (such as a head stick) to assist direct selection, scanning, or encoding procedures to help locate designated items on standardized tests.

receptive tests administered to the non-oral person, which may require modification. Typically a diagnostician administers tests to examine knowledge of vocabulary, morphology, syntax, a variety of language concepts, and memory. Similarly, with appropriate modifications, standard test procedures can yield substantial information about a non-oral person's language comprehension.

Systematic observation can provide a wealth of information concerning a person's understanding of his verbal environment, even when little overt oral expression is present. The reader will recall the child described by Lenneberg whose understanding of language was "normal" but whose expressive capability was severely depressed. To get at the child's level of comprehension, Lenneberg required the child to follow commands of differing linguistic complexity. In a similar fashion a number of tasks requiring gross motor movement (for example, "Come here," "Sit down," "Walk to the window") or, in extreme cases of neuromuscular involvement, eye gaze (for example, "Look up," "Look down") can be presented to the non-oral person. Such commands can be of varying degrees of linguistic complexity (for example, "Before blinking your eyes three times, look at the light," "If there is a donut on the table, look out the window," "After I touch your arm, you look at the floor"). The range of linguistic competence within the non-oral population extends from those persons with normal or near normal receptive language to those with extreme expressive language deficits. Thus, one can expect to find non-oral persons with comprehension skills ranging from no apparent comprehension (or ability to follow only simple one-step commands) to those who comprehend highly complex linguistic messages. Most persons who fall into the latter or upper end of this range have a neuromuscular or emotional basis for their limited expressive output. Those at the lower end may evidence the above but most likely will demonstrate marked cognitive deficits as well.

Another productive way to assess knowledge of such factors as vocabulary, syntax, and general information is to see how appropriately the individual responds to questions that require a yes/no response. Many non-oral persons depend on a "twenty questions" method to communicate. Effective communication by this procedure requires that the non-oral communicator first have distinguishable signals for yes and for no. After determining what those signals are, systematic questioning can be used. Again, the level of linguistic complexity may be varied in an attempt to determine levels of understanding. The non-oral person's success in responding to questions will reflect, in part, his receptive language ability.

In summary, the language evaluation of the non-oral person usually begins with a statement by a parent or person who knows the child well. A child is often described by a caregiver as one who "understands everything, but just can't talk." The task of the evaluator is to determine the accuracy of such a report. In other words, does the individual comprehend everything, and if not, where is communication breaking down? To help in that determination, a number of standard receptive language measures are useful. Additionally, close observation of the person's reactions to verbal information, the level of which can be controlled by the examiner, will be a rich source of information. And making an accurate assessment of language comprehension abilities is critical in designing an appropriate nonspeech communication program.

**Nonvocal, Linguistic** The individual who is non-oral may have the capacity to express language (because of adequate linguistic awareness (Mattingly, 1972)), but be unable to do so because of motor planning or neuromuscular involvement. In this case, knowledge and expressive use of nonvocal linguistic information can provide an alternative linguistic expressive system. Determining the capacity to use such a system is, in part, complete following adequate assessment of receptive language (see the preceding section, "Vocal, Linguistic"). In addition, information regarding the individual's readiness for reading and writing (such as left-right orientation, auditory analysis ability, sight vocabulary, visual memory, and perception) should be explored. Finally, visual acuity, a potential hindrance to any new reader, deserves consideration.

**Nonlinguistic—Vocal and Nonvocal** Typically, nonlinguistic information augments, substantiates, or contradicts a simultaneously occurring linguistic message. Birdwhistle (1970), a pioneer in nonverbal communication research, concludes that one cannot separate verbal and nonverbal forms of communication. Vanderheiden and Harris-Vanderheiden (1976) suggest that substitute communication systems are augmentative systems because they augment or add to other (usually nonlinguistic) forms of communication.

In this section, a method for examining nonlinguistic behavior (vocal and nonvocal) in severely handicapped, non-oral persons is described. This evaluative procedure was developed with two purposes in mind:

1. The evaluation would provide a functional assessment of communication abilities.
2. The communicative significance of involuntary or reflexive physiological responses would be included in the evaluation. Behavior need not be voluntary in order to provide usable communication data.

This functional communication assessment is divided into three sections: 1) basic needs, 2) affect, and 3) significant persons, objects, and events. The basic need category is concerned with activities necessary to sustain life (for example, hunger, thirst) and typical human biological functions (for example, toileting, physical comfort). The affect portion deals with information expressed through facial postures, while the significant environmental sections deal with objects, events, and people who are important to severely handicapped persons.

The assessment is conducted through an interview with a person who knows the person intimately (that is, parent, caregiver, friend). Table 1 contains a breakdown of the major categories covered during the interview. The basic need and affect categories are preceded by the question: "How does this person indicate that he or she is hungry, thirsty, needs to urinate, is happy, interested, etc.?" The significant environmental section is preceded by the question, "Which people, which events, and what objects are significant to this person?" Prior to the interview, the diagnostician should take the time to provide the informant with an orientation that emphasizes that communication is both a verbal and nonverbal phenomenon.

To test the efficacy of this functional communication tool, Shane (1977) interviewed 5 caregivers who served 11 institutionalized severely handicapped youngsters ranging in age from 3 to 11 years. All interviews were conducted individually in a quiet setting. The results revealed that all of the children, despite severe intellectual and neuromuscular involvement, emitted behaviors their primary caregivers could interpret as meaningful.

Second, the nature of the behaviors emitted were not atypical human responses. In other words, staring at objects for extended periods or reaching for objects are usual ways to indicate interest, just as laughing or making pleasurable vocalizations are typical ways of indicating happiness.

Table 1. Major areas investigated during the functional assessment of communication ability

| Basic needs | Affect | Significant environmental |
|---|---|---|
| Hunger | Happy | Objects |
| Thirst | Sad | People |
| Toileting | Interested | Events |
| Tired | Angry | |
| Cold | Afraid | |
| Hot | Frustrated | |
| Sick | | |
| Uncomfortable | | |
| Itchy | | |
| Pain | | |

*Note:* The reader may wish to add to the above items. The list should be considered suggestive, not definitive.

Table 2 contains a number of communicative behaviors reported by the parents of six non-oral children (Shane and Hendee, 1977). These data were gathered similarly to Shane (1977), but parents, not institutional caregivers, were informants. All of the students had severe neuromuscular as well as intellectual deficits.

During the interview, the examiner may find that the handicapped communicator is using spoken language or some representational system to indicate most of the categories in this assessment. In this event, the examiner should either 1) discontinue this particular assessment procedure, or 2) complete the evaluation to gather information about particular categories to assist in further educational planning (for example, if the person is not toilet trained, the instructor might explore vocal and nonvocal behaviors associated with onset and occurrence of elimination).

**Representational Component** No standardized tests are available for determining a person's ability to process and use what this author is classifying as representational information (that is models, photographs, pictures, and line drawings) for communicative purposes. However, this writer has had some success in ascertaining this information. The following suggestions overview those procedures:

1. *Interview:* Question persons who know the non-oral person intimately about whether or not he has made the association between real objects and line drawings, photographs, and the like. Family photographs are often particularly good eliciting stimuli for this information. One caution—do not assume that a report that a child "flips" through a book or magazine with recognition means that pictures in the book actually stand for an object or event.
2. *Direct training:* First, develop a set of test stimuli using familiar items from the student's environment. The stimuli should depict objects on several representational levels (for example, a photograph, line drawing, and miniature model of a chair or bed). Second, present the materials at the various levels to ascertain the level at which the student most consistently processes representational information.

   In other words, with what representational level is the student able to associate the verbal label for an object, person, or event or to match the object with some of its representations?

   For the nonvocal student who displays no apparent difficulty associating line drawing representations with familiar objects and events, the examiner should consider the student a potential candidate for a nonvocal, linguistic symbol system.

Table 2. A representative list of emitted behaviors interpreted by parents as reflecting vocal, nonlinguistic and nonvocal, nonlinguistic behavior

| Basic need item | Student behavior (based on parent response) | Affect item | Student behavior |
|---|---|---|---|
| Hungry/Desires food | Differentiated cry | Happy | Differentiated pleasure sounds |
| | Undifferentiated cry | | Smiles |
| | Moves toward food | | Kicks |
| Thirsty/Desires drink | Differentiated cry | Sad | Pouts |
| | Goes to sink or refrigerator | | Differentiated cry |
| | Salivates | Interested | Visual attention |
| | Reaches for glass | | Transfers hand-to-hand |
| Needs to defecate | Grunts | | Reaches for |
| Has defecated | Squirms | Significant people | Student behavior |
| Sick | Appears flushed | Father | Differentiated facial expression |
| | Sleeps more | Mother | Extends arms to be picked up |
| | Decreased activity | Grandparents | Puts hand out to shake |
| | Refuses food | Significant objects | |
| | Feels warm | Food | Eats |
| Hot | Perspires | TV (commercials) | Looks at consistently |
| | Pulls at clothes | Music box | Will not sleep without |
| | Differentiated cry | Significant events | |
| | | Car ride | Quiets and looks out |
| | | Being outdoors | Quiets, feels grass |
| | | Rocking | Differentiated smile |

From Shane and Hendee, 1977.

## Transmission (Mode of Expression) Evaluation

Assessing the transmission component requires a thorough evaluation of the structure and function of the motor and motor speech production systems. Regardless of whether integrative information (expressive forms) is expressed through the vocal tract or some other bodily structure, the quality of that response will be influenced by the degree of impairment to that transmission structure.

The discussion of transmission (mode of expression) is concerned with three topic areas:

1. Motor speech disorders
2. Manual dexterity and sign language
3. Voluntary motor control and communication board usage

**Motor Speech Disorders** The diagnosis of apraxia of speech or dysarthria is important to the overall management of the non-oral person. The diagnosis provides either totally, or in part, an underlying cause for the expressive deficit and leads to effective management. In addition to the diagnosis or identification, the evaluation is concerned with determining whether the degree of neuromuscular or motor planning deficits is significant enough to warrant a nonspeech alternative.

One goal of the diagnostic process is to isolate salient speech, behavioral and neurological features that help differentiate among disorders. It is only in recent years, however, that research has begun to provide the information necessary for differential diagnosis, not only between these distinct motor speech disorder categories but also among them. For example, Darley, Aronson, and Brown (1969) studied the speech errors of adult subjects having one of several known neurological disabilities. They found that different dysarthric types could be identified through error analysis of each neurological group's speech. A similar study of the salient acoustic characteristics across congenital cerebral palsy subtypes (for example, spastic, ataxic, athetoid) has not been conducted but is an important area for future research.

Critical aspects of speech production have also been identified for adults having apraxia of speech (Johns and Darley, 1970). Yoss and Darley (1974) have studied children with severe articulation disorders of unknown etiology and were able to isolate a definable group of children who had developmental apraxia of speech.

A review of research related to adventitious and congenital motor speech disorders suggests that salient clinical symptomatology can be used for differential diagnosis. A number of these features are listed in Table 3. Because this research, and consequently the clinical application, is in its infancy (particularly with childhood motor speech disorders), the table must be viewed as tentative and incomplete.

The diagnosis of motor speech disturbance as discussed above requires that some speech, whether intelligible or not, be available for analysis. However, many non-oral persons produce either no intelligible speech or such a limited amount that a diagnosis based on speaking behavior is impossible. In such a case, the motor speech impairment is sufficient to warrant the introduction of a nonspeech alternative (for additional considerations in making this decision see the following section, "Clinical Decisions"). Other clinical symptoms that suggest severe forms of motor speech involvement in the absence of extensive speech output include the following:

1. History of feeding problems
2. Persistent and obligatory primitive oral reflexes
3. Prevalence of vocalic speech sounds and lack of early developing consonant sounds
4. Extensive and persistent drooling
5. Diagnosis of some type of cerebral palsy
6. Gestures and affect as predominant mode of communication
7. Frustration associated with inability to speak

**Manual Dexterity and Sign Language** The complexity of information communicable through sign language will be affected by the extent of voluntary control over hand, arm, and finger movement, as well as by basic cognitive and linguistic abilities. In long term communication planning, the adopted nonspeech system should be capable of accommodating current and predicted linguistic abilities. With regard to motor ability and sign language, the decision to employ a manual communication approach should be made based on a consideration of current motor skills as well as predicted skills following prescribed physical therapy and maturation.

Therefore, the degree of neuromuscular involvement must be assessed in light of the manual dexterity required, for example, to articulate single signs (for example, EAT/TOILET) versus complex linguistic strings. Similarly, the presence of an apraxia or motor planning deficit involving manual movements can also influence the utility of signing as a nonspeech communication system (Wilbur, 1976). The author recently evaluated a five-year-old child with severe developmental apraxia of speech for whom signing had been attempted but discontinued because a significant motor planning problem emerged when two or more word sign combinations were attempted.

**Motor Control and Language Boards** Effective use of a communication board requires some method of indicating designated information. The transmission (mode of expression) evaluation for the potential communication board user involves the determination of an effective mode

Table 3. Differential diagnostic considerations for motor speech disorders

| Motor speech disorder | Clinical symptomotology | Nature of symptom[a] | Reference |
|---|---|---|---|
| Dysarthia | Type of articulation errors (in adventitious cases, distortion errors predominate); clinically seems applicable to cerebral palsy | S | Johns and Darley (1970) |
| | Voice quality deviations (nature of deviation related to type of dysarthia (e.g., strained, strangled voice quality in spastic dysarthia; breathy quality in flaccid dysarthia); clinically seems applicable to congenital cerebral palsy | S | Darley, Aronson, and Brown (1969, 1975) |
| | Speech rate deviations (nature of deviation related to type of dysarthia, e.g., slowness of rate characteristic of spastic dysarthia (adventitious)); clinically seems applicable to congenital cerebral palsy | S | Darley, Aronson, and Brown (1969) |
| | Greater intelligibility and articulatory proficiency in spastic versus athetoid type of cerebral palsy | S | Lencione (1965) |
| | Paralysis, weakness, or incoordination of speech musculature | N | Darley, Aronson, and Brown (1969) |
| | Greater respiratory problems in athetoid versus spastic type of cerebral palsy | NS | Lencione (1965) |

| | | | |
|---|---|---|---|
| Apraxia of speech | Reduced rate of oral diadochokinesis (congenital type only) | S | Yoss and Darley (1974) |
| | Increased articulatory difficulty as length of words increase | S | Yoss and Darley (1974), Johns and Darley (1970) |
| | Increased articulatory difficulty noted during sequencing of speech sounds | S | Yoss and Darley (1974), Johns and Darley (1974) |
| | Type of articulatory errors (in adventitious type, errors predominantly substitutions, additions, prolongations and repetitions; in congenital type, distortions are characteristic errors as well) | S | Yoss and Darley (1974), Johns and Darley (1970) |
| | Inconsistent error production | S | Johns and Darley (1970) |
| | Prosodic alterations (i.e., pauses, slowed rate, equalization of stress) | S | Darley, Aronson, and Brown (1969) |
| | High incidence of "soft" neurological signs (congenital type) | N | Yoss and Darley (1974) |
| | No muscle strength difficulty | N | Darley, Aronson, and Brown (1975) |
| | Accompanying oral apraxia (particularly with congenital type) | NS | Yoss and Darley (1974) |
| | Effortful groping for correct articulatory posture may occur | NS | Johns and Darley (1970), Yoss and Darley (1974) |

[a] S, Speech; NS, Nonspeech; N, Neurological considerations.

for this indication. Although the nature of a potential communication board (that is, electronic versus nonelectronic) often dictates the method for controlling the communication device, the reverse may also be the case. In other words, the severity of motor involvement may determine the type of board that a particular individual may be capable of controlling.

In approaching the motor evaluation of the potential communication board user, therefore, all controllable physical structures should be considered in light of available electronic and nonelectronic communication devices. The final decision about communication board type and method of indication (that is, direct selection, scanning, or encoding) will, in part, be based on usable motor control sights.

In summary, the assessment of transmission structure for the potential communication board user is extensive. Due to the severity of physical involvement of many communication board users, the transmission evaluation must involve examination of all bodily structures in order to isolate those functions most useful for operating a communication board. The type of communication board used and the method of designating information will be predicated on the available physical structures under voluntary control.

## Clinical Decisions

Once information is available about underlying causes of the expressive language deficit and the level of language comprehension, as well as the status of transmission structures and functions, decisions can be made about the most effective form of intervention. The diagnostician then becomes a program planner and attempts to take the results of the formal and informal assessments and design the most effective communication program. Informed decision making requires that the previous three sections be brought to bear on deciding whether a nonspeech system should be adopted for the non-oral person. If the decision is to adopt a nonspeech system, then which system? The decision will be based on discussions among a number of professionals involved in the habilitation program.

To assist the reader in the selection of the optimal nonspeech program for a given nonspeech communicator the following guidelines are offered. They need not necessarily be considered in the presented order.

1. Determine underlying cause.
2. Assess integrity of transmission (modes of expression). This should include information about manual dexterity and whole body movement, as well as the functioning of the vocal tract.
3. Investigate expressive forms. With the person having high receptive language skills, the need to use nonlinguistic avenues of expression,

such as interpretation of behavior, becomes less necessary. For persons showing little linguistic comprehension, on the other hand, these forms take on a more primary role.

4. Investigate environmental willingness to accept a nonspeech communication system. It has been this author's clinical experience that many well-thought-out nonspeech programs have failed because families or institutional caregivers would not accept an augmentative communication system or would accept one in theory but not in practice.
5. Determine length and quality of previous therapy. The intelligibility of some non-oral speakers can be greatly improved through speech therapy. Inappropriate or inconsistent therapy will not change behavior. The decision to adopt a nonspeech system should only be made after careful review of the nature and execution of the previous therapy. It is more desirable to make a person a vocal communicator! Nonspeech procedures should be attempted when other means have been thoroughly and appropriately tried. Another viable treatment option is to use a combined speech/nonspeech approach.
6. Consider the person's age. Although no definitive statement about when to introduce a nonspeech system can be made, as a general rule, the older the person and the longer speech has remained indistinct or nonexistent, the more likely it is that a nonspeech system should be adopted.
7. Determine cognitive level. Knowing a person's level of cognitive functioning should supplement the expressive forms of information and should be instrumental in designing effective intervention. The importance of knowing cognitive level for the establishment of manual sign language was discussed by Robbins (1976). She designates four language levels at which manual communication can be offered. These levels, presented in a hierarchical framework, range from the lowest (basic communication) to the highest (linguistic manipulations) level. She suggests that cognitive constraints will have a significant effect on the level at which language through expression in manual communication is possible.

   Kahn (1975) recommends that nonspeech intervention with persons who are "profoundly retarded" should take cognitive level into account. His research found that use of words in profoundly retarded subjects was related to performance at Stage 6 of Piaget's sensorimotor period.

## SUMMARY

As a result of the communication evaluation described here, considerable information regarding linguistic and nonlinguistic communication behavior should be available. For more severely handicapped non-oral persons, much will derive from involuntary behavior. The significance of such behavior necessitates considerable reliance on the interpretive skill of informed caregivers. The more cognitively and linguistically capable non-oral person, on the other hand, usually develops elaborate affective and gestural systems to communicate not only his basic wants and needs but also an understanding of his verbal environment. The task of the diagnostician is to ascertain the extent of those nonverbal systems and to determine the potential of that non-oral person to learn to use a symbolic expressive system.

It is the total of diagnostic information concerning all forms and modes of expression (integration and transmission) that ultimately and naturally leads to intervention.[9] Depending on the degree of handicapping condition, however, the intervention will range from a clarification or elaboration of the manner in which basic needs and wants are communicated, to a determination of whether manual sign, communication board, or oral speech program is the most promising speech/nonspeech intervention strategy. Also, any combination of signing, communication board, or speech in a kind of "total communication" approach can be considered.

Finally, the evaluation process does not terminate until the therapy process is complete. This statement suggests that one should not become complacent with one's initial impressions and preliminary diagnostic data. It suggests, also, that the severity of communication deficits of the severely handicapped communicator are such that an accurate evaluation may require long term diagnostic therapy. That is, additional ongoing observations may be necessary to help substantiate, refute, or add to initial diagnostic impressions.

## ACKNOWLEDGMENTS

The author wishes to thank Jon Lyon, Woodrow Leake, and Sarah Turpin for their comments on earlier drafts of this paper. Thanks, also, to Trudi Norman for her thoughtful criticisms.

## REFERENCES

Abercrombie, D. 1969. Paralanguage. Br. J. Disord. Comm. 3:55–59.

Birdwhistle, R. L. 1970. Kinesics and Context: Essays on Body Motion Communication. University of Pennsylvania Press, Philadelphia.

---

[9] For a full description of programming strategies that arise from the data generated by the above evaluative procedures, see: Shane, H. 1979. Approaches to communication training with people who are severely handicapped. *In* R. York and G. Edgar (eds.), Teaching the Severely Handicapped, Vol. IV. Special Press, Colombus, Oh.

Bliss, C. K. 1965. Semantography. Semantography Publications, Sydney, Australia.

Carrier, J. K., Jr. 1974a. Application of functional analysis and a nonspeech response mode to teaching language. *In* L. McReynolds (ed.), Developing Systematic Procedures for Training Children's Language. ASHA Monogr., Washington, D.C.

Carrier, J. K., Jr. 1974b. Nonspeech noun usage training with severely and profoundly retarded children. J. Speech Hear. Res. 17:510–517.

Carrier, J. K., Jr. 1976. Application of a nonspeech language system with the severely language handicapped. *In* L. L. Lloyd (ed.), Communication Assessment and Intervention Strategies, pp. 523–547. University Park Press, Baltimore.

Chevigny, H., and Braverman, S. 1950. The Adjustment of the Blind. Yale University Press, New Haven, Conn.

Darley, F. L. 1964. Diagnosis and Appraisal of Communication Disorders. Prentice-Hall, Englewood Cliffs, N.J.

Darley, F. L. 1969. Nomenclature of expressive speech-language disorders. Paper presented at the meeting of the Academy of Aphasia, September, Boston.

Darley, F. L., Aronson, A. E., and Brown, J. R. 1969. Differential diagnostic patterns of dysarthria. J. Speech Hear. Res. 12:246–269.

Darley, F. L., Aronson, A. E., and Brown, J. R. 1975. Motor Speech Disorders. W. B. Saunders & Company, Philadelphia.

Denhoff, E. 1965. Cerebral palsy: Medical aspects. *In* W. Cruickshank (ed.), Cerebral Palsy: Its Individual and Community Problems. Syracuse University Press, Syracuse, N.Y.

Fristoe, M., and Lloyd, L. 1977. The use of manual communication with the retarded. Paper presented at the Gatlinburg Conference on Mental Retardation, Gatlinburg, Tenn.

Hockett, C. 1960. The origin of speech. Sci. Am. 203:88–96.

Johns, D., and Darley, F. L. 1970. Phonemic variability in apraxia of speech. J. Speech Hear. Res. 13:556–583.

Kahn, J. V. 1975. Relationships of Piaget's sensorimotor period to language acquisition of profoundly retarded children. Am. J. Ment. Defic. 79:640–643.

King, M. 1971. Quest for synthesis. *In* R. B. Davis (ed.), The Literature of Research in Reading with Emphasis on Models. Iris Corporation, New Brunswick, N.J.

Kotkin, R., and Simpson, S. 1976. A sign in the right direction: Language development for the nonverbal child. AAESPH Rev. 1:75–81.

Laver, J. 1976. Language and nonverbal communication. *In* E. C. Carterette and M. P. Friedman (eds.), Handbook of Perception (7 vols.). Academic Press, New York.

Lencione, R. 1965. Speech problems in cerebral palsy. *In* W. Cruickshank (ed.), Cerebral Palsy: Its Individual and Community Problems. Syracuse University Press, Syracuse, N.Y.

Lenneberg, E. H. 1962. Understanding language without ability to speak: A case report. J. Abnorm. Soc. Psychol. 65:419–423.

Lloyd, L. L. 1976. Preface. *In* L. L. Lloyd (ed.), Communication Assessment and Intervention Strategies. University Park Press, Baltimore.

Mattingly, I. G. 1972. Reading, the linguistic process, and linguistic awareness. *In* J. F. Kavanagh and I. G. Mattingly (eds.), Language by Ear and by Eye. The MIT Press, Cambridge, Mass.

Miller, A., and Miller, E. E. 1973. Cognitive-developmental training with elevated boards and sign language. J. Aut. Child. Schizo. 3:65–85.

Richardson, T. 1975. Sign language for the SMR and PMR. Ment. Retard. 13:17.

Robbins, N. 1976. Selecting sign systems for multi-handicapped students. Paper presented at the annual meeting of the American Speech and Hearing Association, November, Houston.

Shaffer, T., and Goehl, H. 1974. The alinguistic child. Ment. Retard. 4:3–6.

Shane, H. C. 1977. Assessing the functional communication skills of the severely handicapped. Manuscript submitted for publication.

Shane, H. C., and Hendee, J. 1977. A description of functional communication skills of severely handicapped children. Unpublished manuscript.

Vanderheiden, G. C., and Harris-Vanderheiden, D. H. 1976. Communication techniques and aids for the nonvocal severely handicapped. *In* L. L. Lloyd (ed.), Communication Assessment and Intervention Strategies, University Park Press, pp. 607–652. University Park Press, Baltimore.

Wepman, J., and Van Pelt, D. 1955. A theory of cerebral language disorders based on therapy. Folia Phoniatrica 7:223–235.

Wepman, J., Jones, L. V., Bock, R. D., and Van Pelt, D. 1960. Studies in aphasia: Background and theoretical formulations. J. Speech Hear. Disord. 25:323–332.

Wilbur, R. 1976. The linguistics of manual languages and manual systems. *In* L. L. Lloyd (ed.), Communication Assessment and Intervention Strategies, pp. 423–500. University Park Press, Baltimore.

Yoss, K. A., and Darley, F. L. 1974. Developmental apraxia of speech in children with defective articulation. J. Speech Hear. Res. 17:399–416.

# Section V

# Nonspeech Strategies for Physically Handicapped Children

chapter 11

# Enhancing the Development of Communicative Interaction

*Deberah Harris*
*Gregg C. Vanderheiden*
*Trace Research and Development Center for the Severely Communicatively Handicapped University of Wisconsin-Madison Madison, Wisconsin*

contents

## NONVOCAL COMMUNICATION TECHNIQUES

During the past few years, clinicians, educators, researchers, and teachers have increased their use of nonvocal communication techniques with individuals who cannot speak. This increased attention results from many recent developments, including the manual sign language systems, communication boards and other aids, and the development of symbol and vocabulary systems for use with communication aids. One important motivation for the development of nonvocal communication systems has been an increased demand for appropriate education and related developmental experiences for severely handicapped children. Recent legislation has caused both professionals and parents to reformulate their views on educational processes for severely handicapped individuals.

The shift in education approaches for severely handicapped individuals has occurred so rapidly that educators and clinicians are faced with the responsibility of developing and implementing educational programs for these individuals while having little or no information on the effectiveness of various approaches or materials. Many children are severely motorically handicapped, confined to wheelchairs, and unable to speak, write, or manipulate traditional classroom utensils and learning aids. Many are entering the classroom with little or no previous educational programming.

The development of effective means to communicate and interact with educators, peers, parents, siblings, and others is of primary importance to the success of educational programs. This chapter presents a framework for the development of communication in nonvocal, severely physically handicapped children (NVSPH). The chapter illustrates the development of communication and interaction skills from a perspective of communication/interaction development programs for NVSPH children, with practical intervention suggestions and some current research issues. First, there are a few general issues related to nonvocal communication intervention that need to be placed in perspective.

### General Issues in Nonvocal Communication

The general issues in nonvocal communication include three basic areas of concern:

1. Generic application of terms like *nonvocal* or *nonspeaking* to any individual who does not speak and to any program that deals with developing communication skill through nonvocal or nonspeech modes
2. Reserved application of nonvocal techniques because of apprehension that such techniques may inhibit or deter speech development
3. Approaching nonvocal techniques as "alternatives" to speech

## Interpretation of Nonvocal and Nonspeech

There is currently both confusion and concern among educators, clinicians, and researchers resulting from the inappropriate use of the terms *nonvocal* or *nonspeaking* as generic labels for all persons who have not developed functional oral communication skills. Individuals may be nonvocal for a variety of reasons, each of which might require a different intervention program. Yet lengthy discussions are still held about which language program, teaching approach, or communication technique is most effective for the "nonvocal" individual, as if there were a single type of nonvocal individual. Generic use of the term implies that *nonvocal* (or *nonspeaking*) is a sufficient descriptor of conditions and is thus a meaningful label. However, teaching programs or communication techniques should be quite different for a nonvocal, hearing-impaired (NVHI) person, a nonvocal, mentally retarded (NVMR) person, a nonvocal, autistic (NVA) person, or a nonvocal, severely physically handicapped (NVSPH) person. The problem lies in the use of the descriptor *nonvocal* or *nonspeech* without elaboration of the individual's abilities (or, in the case of programs, without elaboration of target populations for whom they were designed and with whom they have been tested or successfully implemented). Titles such as "Communication Intervention for Nonvocal Individuals" or "Nonspeech Communication Program" imply that the research results or intervention procedures are applicable to all nonvocal persons, when, in fact, the research has been conducted or the program developed with a particular population.

One illustration of the need to clearly differentiate the *primary* cause for a nonspeaking condition is presented in Figure 1. The primary reason for a nonspeaking condition in child A may be impairment of the oral musculature, respiration, or fine motor coordination needed for speech and writing, resulting primarily in an expressive or productive deficit. The nonspeaking condition in child B may be the result of cognitive deficits or information-processing difficulties, and may not involve impairment in any of the child's physical production mechanisms. If one looks only at productive or expressive behavior (both persons are *nonvocal*), one may erroneously apply the same or similar communication intervention strategies for these persons. The need for researchers and clinicians to clearly describe both the individuals involved and the intervention program can therefore be seen. Also noted is the need for extra caution and attention when studying or applying techniques in this area. Some factors to bear in mind when comparing research results and/or intervention programs are:

What was the primary cause for the nonspeaking condition in the individual? (oral musculature impairment, cognitive/information-

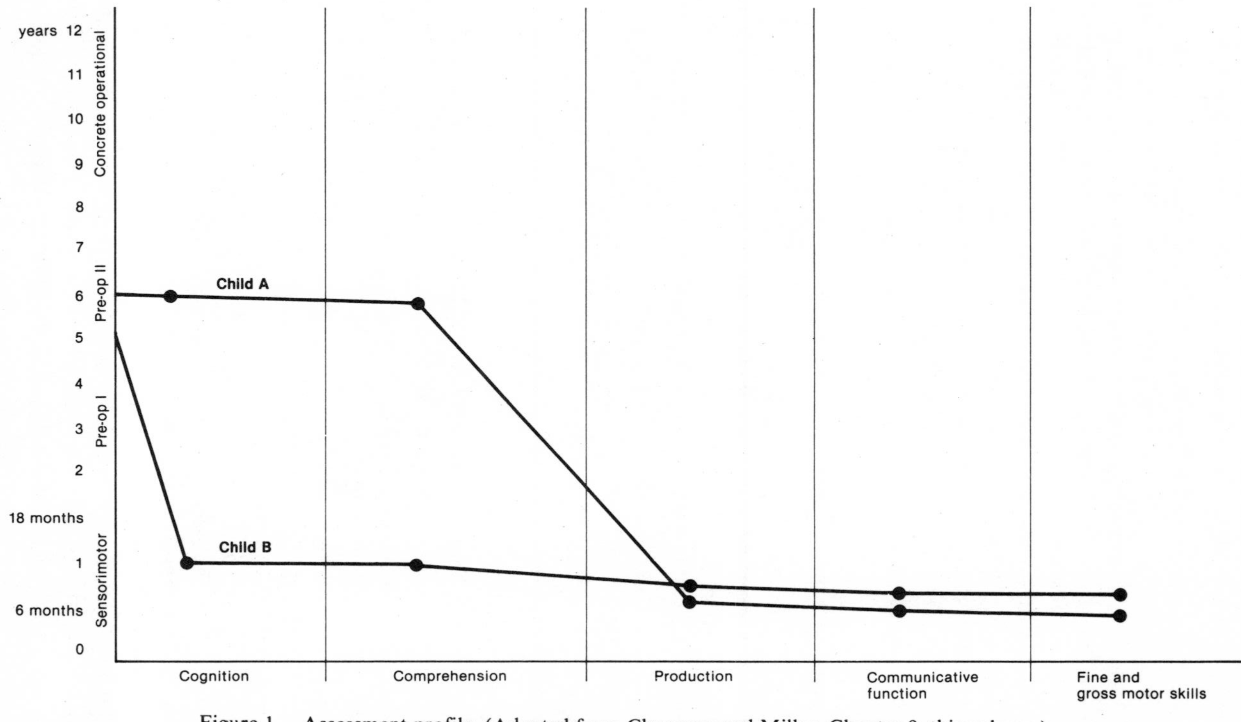


Figure 1. Assessment profile. (Adapted from Chapman and Miller, Chapter 9, this volume.)

processing deficit, hearing impairment, emotional/behavioral disorder, etc.)

To what extent were the persons able to functionally use their oral speech mechanisms for expressive communication?

To what extent were the persons able to control fine and gross motor movements for nonvocal communication purposes?

Researchers and clinicians should use general categories, such as NVMR, NVSPH, NVA, and NVHI, to roughly categorize different "nonvocal" programs for comparison and application. Nonspeaking individuals will not always fall neatly into one of the categories, and clinicians may need to look across categories to develop specific programming strategies. Labeling the primary intended population for specific programs, however, will help us understand and correctly apply programs (or research results).

## Nonspeech Techniques and Speech Development

A common concern in using nonspeech techniques is their potential effect upon the development of speech and oral communication. Many persons, parents in particular, have serious reservations about using nonspeech techniques unless all other techniques have failed. This reservation is unnecessary and may lead to delayed communication development and feelings of failure for both the child and the persons working with the child. It may also delay the development of intelligible speech for some children.

Clinical results to date indicate that nonvocal communication techniques do not impede or inhibit the development of speech or oral communication skill in NVSPH individuals. In some cases, nonvocal techniques enhance oral expression (McDonald and Schultz, 1973; Harris et al., 1977; McNaughton, Kates, and Silverman, 1978). Nonvocal communication techniques may enhance speech and oral expression by: 1) increasing motivation to speak or communicate as a result of more successful communication experiences, and 2) reducing tension or pressures related to oral expression by providing a nonvocal communication mode to fall back on should the spoken message be unintelligible. The studies cited above involved cerebral palsied individuals and included speech development programs as part of a general communication development effort. Since speech is the primary avenue of communication for most persons and is the most efficient means of communication, nonvocal techniques are not really "competition" for speech when it becomes functional for the individual. Early intervention with nonvocal techniques is not a deterrent to speech; rather, it may promote speech development for some children.

### "Alternative" versus "Augmentative" Communication

An issue related to the above discussion involves the perception of nonvocal communication techniques as "alternatives" to speech, or as techniques to implement when the possibility of speech has been ruled out. In many cases this has resulted in the application of nonvocal techniques only in defeat, and has reduced the importance of speech in partially vocal individuals.

Rather than being an alternative to speech, nonvocal communication techniques should be viewed as *augmentative* or supplementary techniques that enhance communication by complementing whatever vocal skills the individual may possess. Nonvocal techniques can supplement speech in partially vocal persons and can facilitate the development of language and communication in persons who cannot yet speak but who may later develop functional oral communication. If augmentative communication techniques are implemented early, delayed development in motor control necessary for speech and fine motor movement need not have such severe delaying effects upon the development of communication, language, social, and interaction skills.

Nonvocal communication techniques can be used with individuals who have varying degrees of physical involvement and speech abilities. They may be used:

1. As an initial communication system and a means for communication, interaction, language, and personal skill development with a child who is not yet vocal but who may later develop functional speech
2. As a supplementary mode of communication for an individual who has only limited intelligible speech comprising a small vocabulary that only a limited audience can understand
3. As a supplementary mode of communication for nonspeaking persons who can use other nonvocal techniques, such as manual sign, for communicating with message receivers who do not understand the system (e.g., signing)

In the above applications, the nonvocal technique supplements whatever other communication systems the individual has or may be able to develop (including speech, gesture, and facial expression). The goal is to develop effective communication *systems* for nonspeaking persons. These systems include the development and use of whatever modes of communication may be available to the individual.

## COMMUNICATION AND INTERACTION SKILLS IN NVSPH CHILDREN

### Barriers to Communication in the NVSPH Child

Severe physical and motor impairment can have many effects on the communication, cognitive, and motor development of NVSPH children. Potential barriers to the development of communication and interaction skills include:

1. Reduced or inconsistent ability to interact with and explore the environment
2. Reduced or inconsistent ability to play/interact with other persons motorically and vocally and to stimulate vocal feedback from caregivers and others
3. Inability to express emotions, needs, and thoughts and to exchange information with others in consistent, reliable, and effective manners
4. Inability to develop control of "normal" communication mechanisms (oral speech and fine motor mechanisms)

Severe physical handicaps can have profound effects upon the development of social, interpersonal, play, language, communication, and interaction skills. Severe impairment to fine and gross motor coordination can greatly handicap the NVSPH child's ability to explore, manipulate, and experience objects, persons, and events. In infancy and throughout the sensorimotor period (0–18 months), Piaget (1964) and others have postulated that motoric interaction and object manipulation are important for the development of symbolic representation and related cognitive skills that are prerequisite to the development of language. Reduced or inconsistent ability to play and interact with parents, peers, and others through "normal" motor movements, facial and vocal imitations, and verbal play may also affect the development of cognitive and linguistic skills. Yarrow et al. (1975) have found several variables that are related to cognitive development from as early as six months of age. These include level of social stimulation, intensity of expression of possitive affect, active kinesthetic stimulation, and variety in the inanimate environment.

Severely physically handicapped, nonspeaking children may be unable to stimulate positive attention from caregivers and others in their environments. Spastic or athetoid motor movement, persistence of infantile reflex patterns, involuntary facial grimaces, lack of a consistent social smile, inability to engage in typical infant games (e.g., cooing, patty cake, babbling, vocal imitation), necessity for continual extrasupportive care in feeding, toileting, and dressing, and necessity for a wide variety of assistive aids and devices may hinder or decrease social interacting with the child. Caregiver interactions involved in feeding, bathing, dressing, and playing with the infant and young child, actions that are normally warm and rewarding, may become situations of frustration and tension for caregivers who are uncomfortable in dealing with the physically handicapped child's erratic, involuntary, and spastic or athetoid reflexive movements. As a result, some NVSPH children spend a great deal of time in physical environments that change infrequently and in social environments that do not provide a great deal of touching, holding, hugging, or other kinesthetic support. Motor-related handicaps can thus result in social/emotional, interactional, motivational, and communicative handicaps.

In addition to motoric barriers to communication development, the NVSPH child may experience speech-related barriers to communication development. Inability to express happiness, sadness, pain, or discomfort, or to express ideas, desires, demands, and thoughts, through speech is a barrier to the development of communication. Most communities of speaking persons view language as speech. Nonspeaking children are seen as noncommunicative or nonlinguistic, and speech development programs are implemented to develop language. Insensitivity to the nonspeaking child's nonspeech communicative and interactive behavior, in conjunction with lack of positive reinforcement for other than speech-related communication, may seriously inhibit the development of communication and interaction.

Other factors may also present barriers to communication development. NVSPH children may experience cognitive and information-processing deficits in conjunction with deficits in motor and social skill development. Cognitive handicaps may range from mild or moderate mental retardation to severe or profound mental retardation. Mild or moderate information-processing or cognitive deficits may merely be a complicating factor that slows down but does not significantly alter the intervention program for the child. Severe or profound deficits in cognitive abilities in addition to severe motoric handicaps call for a combination of techniques and approaches in the development of communication. Cognitive and information-processing skills the child has acquired or can acquire are important determinants in the development of intervention programs (see Carrier, 1979; Chapman and Miller, Chapter 9, this volume; Schiefelbusch and Hollis, Chapter 1, this volume).

## Basic Components of a Communication Development Program

There are barriers to the communication development of NVSPH children that are not restricted to their oral speech mechanisms. In fact, all components of a symbolic communication system can be affected, including:

1. The development of interactive and communicative behaviors
2. The development of primary physical communication mechanisms (vocalization, gestures, facial expression, and speech)
3. Cognitive development and the evolution of symbolic representational skills
4. Exposure to, modeling of, and practice with a symbol system the child can use expressively (i.e., the NVSPH child is exposed to and interacts with persons who use vocalizations and spoken words as the symbolic system for communication, a symbol system that may be beyond the capabilities of the child)

As a result, when the NVSPH child reaches the stage when he would normally be communicating through referential speech, he may have poor interactive skills, limited social and physical interaction, limited control of social and physical interaction, limited control of social and physical aspects of the environment, no effective mechanism for producing symbols for communication (voice, gesture, or graphic), limited familiarity with a symbol system to communicate and interact, and deficits in cognitive, motoric, and social development. Intervention programs, therefore, should provide mechanisms and strategies to enable or enhance interaction and should not concentrate solely upon the provision of an augmentative physical means of expression. Moreover, intervention programs should encourage the development of interrelated skills in natural, self-motivating, and evolutionary manners, starting with basic forms of interaction and communicative exhange and slowly evolving to more advanced symbolic forms of communicating through referential language.

## AN EVOLUTIONARY PROGRAM APPROACH

A programmatic approach that adopts the above-described general approach to interaction development, and that is based upon the gradual, natural introduction of new skills based upon acquired skills, could be termed an evolutionary communication/interaction development program. The term *evolutionary* stresses the gradual, natural, evolving nature of the intervention program. The program would stress entering at the child's current skill level and developing new skills as elaborations or extensions of already acquired skills and activities. The term *communication/interaction* stresses the importance of interaction both as the ultimate goal of such a program and as the program's central focus of activity.

Table 1 presents six aspects that a program following the evolutionary approach would exhibit. The remainder of this section provides

Table 1. Six aspects of an evolutionary communication/interaction development program for nonvocal severely physically handicapped children

1 GOAL
The goal would be the development of *Interaction*. Communication, within this framework, would be considered one type of interactive skill. Therefore, language, speech, communication board competence, etc., would *not* be goals themselves but rather means to an end interaction.

2 A BASIC OPERATING PRINCIPLE
The communication/interaction development program would be a natural, evolving program, basing new skill development on existing skills and activities of the child/infant.

3 INTERVENTION ENTRY POINT
Communication/interaction development begins at birth, and many background skills are achieved before reaching the symbolic communication development program level. Very early intervention would therefore be essential for NVSPH children.

4 PROGRAM SCOPE
The program would involve more than the development of an augmentative physical mechanism. Also needed would be general interaction, communication, and language skill development components as well as facilitation of the individual's ability to move, explore, experience, act, and control.

5 PROGRAM IMPLEMENTATION
The program implementation team would be a closely cooperating group based upon the parents and other primary caregivers/interactors involved with the infant/child.

6 LIMITED USE OF NORMAL COMMUNICATION AS A PROGRAM MODEL
Although normal communication development (NCD) can serve as a useful comparative/contrastive model for intervention programs, there are some skills and experiences for which direct parallels are difficult to draw. The NCD model could lead to inappropriate expectations and possibly less effective program decisions. Care would be taken in design of the program to avoid blind use of any general model.

discussions of these aspects along with more specific programming guidelines and considerations related to each. These discussions are then followed by specific intervention program strategies and suggestions.

### Aspect 1: Interaction as the Program Goal

Interaction would be the ultimate goal of a program following the evolutionary communication/interaction development approach, not language, speech, or communication board competence. Although each of these would be an important and integral component of the program at various points, they are only means for achieving interaction competence and are not the program goals in and of themselves. Accordingly, no one particular form of communication or interaction would, of itself, be a goal (or even be desirable) unless it contributed to the individual's ability to communicate and interact. It is likely that the child's communication/interaction system would consist of several communication techniques that would be used at different times depending upon which is most functional at a given time, with a given audience, and under given circumstances. No a priori judgments regarding a particular mode should be made. The goal of all activities would be the development of effective interaction.

In addition to being the primary goal in this program approach, interaction would be the starting point and major activity of the program. The intervention program would start with more rudimentary forms of interaction and build upon these, gradually introducing techniques and developing skills to develop more effective interaction patterns. Thus, the program would initially focus on interaction for basic care and play activities and then gradually evolve toward more "advanced" levels of interaction, such as symbolic communication and the use of language. This program approach emphasizes that speech, communication boards, gestures, and the like, are *modes* through which interaction and symbolic communication can be expressed. Their development, therefore, would constitute only part of the intervention program. The program would focus on more than the development of *symbolic* communication skills and language. It would include activities and components related to the development of all levels and types of communication/interaction. A broadened program focus such as this should continue even after symbolic communication skills have been developed. The social/functional aspects of communication/interaction development would be emphasized in this type of program and would be equally as important as structural and physical mechanism aspects.

A strong program focus on interaction should be maintained in order to: 1) keep the emphasis of the program on the holistic process of developing interaction skills in the child, and 2) emphasize that the development of interaction starts before, continues beyond, and is more comprehensive than the development of language, speech, or communication board skills alone.

By focusing on interaction, the program helps avoid confusion regarding "prerequisite" skills needed for program entry, reduces the possibility of entering into program phases that are beyond the current level of the child, and avoids teaching language or communication skills the child cannot use effectively or functionally. Focusing on interaction also enhances factors that make language and communication skills functional for the individual.

Thus, developing and enhancing *interaction* in the NVSPH child would be both the goal of the intervention process and the major focus in the development and implementation of the program. The child's ability to interact effectively and meaningfully becomes the primary evaluative measure of the effectiveness and relevancy of the program.

## Aspect 2: A Basic Operating Principle

In developing intervention programs using the evolutionary program approach, it is helpful to look at communication development processes in vocal, nonhandicapped children. While direct parallels are often difficult to draw, certain basic principles and processes are useful to educators and clinicians in the development of communication/interaction programs for NVSPH infants/children. Of particular importance is the recognition that communication development is a gradual process in the vocal nonhandicapped child. Effective communication is not a sudden acquisition with immediate and final results. It would therefore follow that intervention processes for NVSPH infants and children (who experience a number of barriers to communication development that are not present for most vocal children) should also be gradual and evolutionary.

In vocal, nonhandicapped children, the development of interaction/communication begins with the reflexive cry at birth, a cry that develops into a tool to communicate different physical and emotional states (e.g., hunger, pain, anxiety). Reflexive behaviors other than the cry also make up part of the interaction between the infant and the social and physical environment. Initial interaction and communication centers around feeding, diaper changing, and other activities associated with caring for the infant. Interaction between the child and others during this time is through both physical and social contact during care and play. Vocal interactions contribute increasingly to play activities, and some play activities may involve only vocal (nonlinguistic) interaction.

Most important during this time is the development of the child's ability to communicate and to affect the environment through gestural, vocal, and other means (Bates, 1976). Around 9–11 months the child begins to use vocal mechanism to communicate and interact through vocal intonations, although word use is still not present. Around 12 months the child is interacting and communicating spontaneously, not only through physical and gestural means, but vocally as well, through sounds, word approximations, and intonation. As the cognitive skills necessary for symbolic representation are acquired, the child learns to use a new form (symbolic communication via vocalization and the use of words) to accomplish an already familiar function (communication through vocalization). Thus, the first use of *symbolic* speech is not a sudden acquisition but constitutes the next sequential (though very significant) advancement in the evolution of the child's communication/interaction skills. Many of the first communicative functions expressed via referential or symbolic speech are communicative functions the child is already capable of expressing through nonspeech modes.

Two features of the above discussion of normal communication development (NCD) processes are important features for communication/interaction development programs for NVSPH children.

The process is a slow, gradual, natural evolving process whereby more advanced skills emerge as extensions or elaborations of existing skills and activities rather than as "new" skills.

New skills/techniques/forms are initially expressed to accomplish functions with which the child is already familiar and new activities are developed with skills and capabilities that the child has already mastered (a developmental process in language acquisition that has been noted by Slobin, 1971.)

These observations lead to the basic operating principle for an evolutionary communication/interaction development program:

The program should be a gradual, evolutionary one that introduces advanced communicative and interactive skills as natural extensions of existing skills and activities; where new communicative forms or techniques are introduced to help the child better express already mastered or learned functions; and where new functions would initially be introduced within the context of already mastered physical and cognitive skills.

Another observation regarding the NCD process should also be noted:

The vocal, nonhandicapped infant/child develops many skills needed to communicate through speech as a part of other activities not initially associated with the specific purpose of learning to symbolically communicate via vocalizations (although many of the "other" activities are communicative/interactive in nature).

In the intervention program for the NVSPH infant/child, therefore, specific skills that will be needed later for symbolic communication should be similarly introduced and initially developed as nonlinguistic communication/interaction activities. The concept of a pointing communication board, for example, might first be introduced as an extension of a play activity where no symbols are used but where pointing results in direct action that the child previously elicited via another mechanism.

The intervention program should avoid the often occurring situation in which the NVSPH child's introduction to a communication system involves an introduction to a new physical system and a new visual-graphic symbol system as well as symbolic communication all at once. Except for children with good receptive communication skills, this approach usually meets with little success.

Summarizing aspect 2, then, the intervention program should start at whatever skill level the NVSPH infant/child has reached and with whatever activities the infant/child is currently physically and cognitively capable of (and interested in) doing. As with the vocal, nonhandicapped infant/child, early interaction and communication would initially center around basic needs, control, exploration, and play activities. Skills needed later for communication would not usually be taught in traditional or didactic manners, but would be introduced gradually as natural elaborations of the infant/child's interaction and play activities. It may sometimes be necessary to specifically teach a certain skill in order to ensure that it becomes a part of a child's interactive repertoire, but skills would usually be presented in meaningful contexts and introduced as extensions of existing skills and activities so they are more easily incorporated into the child's interactive skill repertoire.

The course of development would be slow at first, allowing time for the NVSPH infant/child to develop basic interaction skills. It is critically important to keep *interaction* in mind and focus upon providing the infant/child with efficient ways to interact using current skills (or with slight modifications to them) and to resist trying to jump ahead to the introduction of more advanced techniques or skills (e.g., symbolic communication via augmentative physical modes).

### Aspect 3: Intervention Entry Point

There is a threefold interest in early intervention for the NVSPH infant: 1) to develop basic interaction and communication skills from which more advanced or symbolic forms of communication will evolve, 2) to help develop physical and manipulative control skills needed to use techniques that will enable symbolic communication (e.g., augmentative techniques and aids), and 3) to help promote the development of cognitive skills by enhancing the NVSPH infant's ability to orient, explore, manipulate, and control.

Interaction development begins at birth. The communication/interaction development for nonvocal, handicapped children should therefore also start at birth. Symbolic forms of communication such as the use of augmentative nonvocal communication techniques should evolve concurrently with the development of cognitive and physical skills. Basic interaction and play activities, however, can be initiated and developed quite early and are necessary for the development of skills needed for more advanced communication/interaction systems leading to symbolic, representational communication.

A second area in which early intervention is important is the development of physical functioning. Since many NVSPH children are not able to communicate through speech, some form or forms of augmentative communication may be necessary. The child's ability to use one or more of these techniques, and the efficiency of the techniques the child will be capable of using, will depend on the child's physical capabilities and familiarity with the techniques. Early intervention to facilitate physical development and motor control is therefore very important to early acquisition of effective augmentative communication systems.

Early intervention should also include activities that help foster the development of cognitive function and physical/manipulative control of the physical and social environment. For the infant who experiences primarily motoric handicaps, early facilitation of manipulation, exploration, and orientation may reduce delays in cognitive development and, consequently, reduce delays in the development of advanced levels of communication. Although current research has not demonstrated a cause-effect relation between motoric function and early cognitive development, the attainment of early cognitive milestones may be facilitated by motor activities. The implications of this for intervention programs for severely physically handicapped children are great.

There are, therefore, three areas of concern regarding the early interaction skill development of NVSPH infants (as discussed above). Since all later aspects of communication development are based on one or another of these, early intervention is necessary to prevent unnecessary delays in the development of the child.

### Aspect 4: Program Scope

As suggested by previous discussions, the interaction development process is not confined to the development of language and communication skills. All of the NVSPH child's interactive activities and skills must be considered. In addition to the areas mentioned previously (which included interaction, manipulation, orientation, and exploration), the area of 1) mobility and control, 2) motivation, intent to communicate and communicative context, and 3) physical and social aspects of the environment should be included in intervention programs of this type.

Although mobility and control might at first seem tangential to interaction, clinical experience has demonstrated some interesting mobility phenomena. Not uncommon in clinical experience is the passive, unresponsive child who does not demonstrate progress or initiative in a communication program until he receives an electric wheelchair. Newly expressed aggression and mischievousness are often exhibited, followed by greater interaction, and communication advances. It is difficult to introduce, to an NVSPH child, the concept of control of the environment through communication when the child has never had (or been allowed) physical control of the environment. Early attempts by the child to control the environment and those in it are important first forms of communication and interaction. Facilitating those attempts is an important component of a communication/interaction program.

Motivation, intent to communicate, and communicative content are also important components of the child's interaction development, and should be an integral part of the intervention program. More energies are often expended on the development of communication skills than are spent in providing the child with experiences that provide something to communicate about. Two aspects related to this problem include: 1) the lack of input or control by the child with regard to everyday care activities, and 2) the lack of novel information that would be of interest to a listener.

A severely physically handicapped individual can be a physical burden for caregivers. As a result, there is a tendency to minimize the amount of care by regimenting daily routines. Caregivers are often unable to take the additional time to argue with the child about the difference between what the child would like to do (information they must take time to solicit) and their own ideas as to what is to be done with, to, or for the child. Thus, the time factor involved in nonvocal communication and the additional need for physical care may limit early opportunities for communication, interaction, and control by the young child. This may help to explain why clinicians are often faced with passive children who are uninterested in interaction with other persons.

Another problem stems from the fact that we seldom talk to others about things they already know. Yet, with the regimentation of much of the severely physically involved child's life, there is little that his parents and teachers do not already know. (The weekend is sometimes a good topic for Monday, but this can very quickly become a ritual.) For children whose basic needs are met via highly structured activities (including meals, recreation time, toileting), a pattern of noninteraction for self-care may be established early and effectively reinforced. A little less "tender loving care" and a little more demand for self-maintenance (even if this means making the child request it) help. (For example, tell the child to do something and let him direct you or others in the activity, such as getting ready for bed.) With this program approach, interventionists would work to broaden the individual's experiences and find ways to allow the child to move, act, control, and experience more independence so the child will have unique, unanticipated and nonstereotypic things to communicate about.

Finally, the program should be broad enough to include the whole environment. The child is only one component of, and participant in, the communicative situation and should not be the sole component of the intervention program. Some intervention may need to be directed toward the child's social and physical environment. A child with a severe physical handicap and a slow communication mode places a different interaction requirement on an environment and the persons in it than does a child with normal motor and communication capabilities. The NVSPH child's communication needs and functions may also be different. Thus, even if one could provide the child with an equivalent and effective means to communicate, interaction problems may not be solved without attending to the social and physical environment. All aspects (physical, social, personal, and environmental) of the interaction and communication process must be incorporated in the program to ensure its effectiveness.

### Aspect 5: Program Implementation

The primary implementors of the communication development program of this type would be the parents, caregivers, and others who spend time daily with the child in care, feeding, play, and other interactions. Because of the severity and multiplicity of the child's handicaps, the primary implementors of the program must have the support of other professionals for input and guidance in the intervention program. Work being directed by different specialties (occupational therapy, physical therapy, speech pathology) must be coordinated with and implemented by other professionals involved. For example, occupational therapy (OT) goals should be incorporated by the speech pathologist and teacher, among others, during their work with the child, just as communication skill development should be incorporated by the OT. The programs should also be designed with the schedule and constraints of the child's parents and caregivers in mind to facilitate the implementation of desired program activities. Cooperative implementation provides a more cohesive and natural intervention program for the child and helps prevent implementation of incompatible intervention programs by different professionals.

The makeup of the intervention team may involve any of the following: parents, parent trainers, physical therapists, occupational therapists, communication development specialists, communication aid specialists, adaptive seating/positioning specialists, regular teachers, special educators, rehabilitation counselors, social workers, rehabilitation engineers, medical personnel, siblings, peers, and friends.

### Aspect 6: Normal Communication as a Program Model

The process that a vocal, nonhandicapped child goes through as interaction and communication skills develop provides a valuable source of information for the development of similar or parallel skills in the NVSPH individual. Strict adherence to normal communication development processes, however, can result in overlooking communication and interaction problems that are specific to the communication development in the NVSPH individual and can lead clinicians to erroneous impressions about program design and expectations.

On a positive note, a close examination of normal communication/interaction development (NCD) points out components and principles that should be a part of intervention programs for the NVSPH individual. These include the need for consistent, positive feedback on the part of parents and caregivers, the need for modeling the communication systems to be used, and general skill acquisition expectations with which to mark program progress and to avoid rushing the child. An examination of NCD reveals that the communication/interaction development process is slow and builds on itself, that the vocal nonhandicapped child learns many skills that will be used later for symbolic communication in nonlinguistic play, or other activities, and that the child plays an active role in the communication development process.

Many of the problems that arise in trying to draw direct parallels between communication development in vocal, nonhandicapped children and NVSPH children stem from misconceptions surrounding the equivalency of components involved in the two similar but different processes. Nonvocal techniques are not a direct substitute for speech, and communication and interaction patterns as well as the overall communication development process may follow different courses for vocal and nonvocal children. First, the relatively slow speed of most augmentative communication techniques used by severely physically handicapped children negates direct substitution of the techniques into normal communicative routines and strategies. As an example, think of interacting with friends and colleagues for one day while talking at one word per second; then, one word per five seconds. Either way you will demonstrate that communicative interaction patterns are very specific to the *speed* of communication, much more so in fact than they are to the *mode* of communication. For example, you will be more successful at writing or typing at two words per second than speaking at one word per two seconds, especially if your typing is plainly visible. Thus, the most effective communication and interaction patterns or strategies for the vocal child may be inefficient or ineffective strategies for the NVSPH child.

Second, the rate of learning and acquiring competence with a communication system will probably be slower for the NVSPH child, even if the child experiences only motor (and no cognitive) handicaps. Inappropriate comparison of the NVSPH child's progress to "vocal" milestones may lead to erroneous judgments of the child's cognitive potential. In addition, expectations that the NVSPH child will develop on a cognitive and physical timeline similar to the vocal nonhandicapped child, and the ensuing anxiety if he does not, may reduce observations of progress being made by the child in other areas.

Since the NVSPH infant/child cannot develop the same skills as the vocal, nonhandicapped child in many areas, the NVSPH child will need to develop compensatory, alternative, or augmentative skills in these areas. It should also be kept in mind that the skills acquired that are the same as the vocal, nonhandicapped child's may be learned through different processes and strategies. In application, then, what works well as a teaching approach for vocal, nonhandicapped children may be very difficult to use or adapt for use with a nonvocal, nonmanipulative child. Although there has been little reported research in this area, skills acquired in a seemingly invariant order in vocal, nonhandicapped children may be best acquired through different mechanisms and in a different order for nonvocal, nonmanipulative children.

A final note regarding the use of NCD as a program model. Speech is such a primary and effective mode of communication for vocal children that interventionists often think along the lines of providing *one* major analogous communication technique for an NVSPH child. "If the child cannot speak, what will be his mode of communication?" Because speech is so powerful, efficient, flexible, and convenient, it can serve as essentially the only mode of communication in almost every communication environment for the vocal child. The nonvocal individual, however, does not usually have access to any one technique that can be as primary and powerful as speech is for the vocal child. As a result, the NVSPH child's communication system usually consists of many modes of communication that he alternately uses, depending upon which is the fastest, most flexible, and most effective in a particular situation. Thus, an NVSPH child might use vocalizations, manual signs, gestures, a communication board, and yes/no all at different times depending upon the listener's ability to understand the modes and his ability to produce the desired message via the modes available. The frequent use of the term *alternative* mode of communication is evidence to the "either/or" tendency that can result from over-reliance on NCD processes (the primacy of one mode—speech) as a model. The terms *augmentative* and *supplementary* modes of communication are more accurate for describing communication systems used by nonvocal individuals.

## DEVELOPING COMMUNICATION/INTERACTION SKILLS IN NVSPH CHILDREN

Because of the great degree of variation in NVSPH children (e.g., their individual handicaps, their environments, and the services available to them), communication/interaction development programs need to be individually designed. Based upon the above discussion, and an understanding of evolutionary communication development processes, however, several important common components of a communication/interaction development program for NVSPH can be delineated.

1. The development of communicative/interactive behavior, motivation, and interest in communication, and the desire to communicate and interact with others
2. The development of augmentative physical mechanisms for interaction, response, and expression
3. The provision of, and familiarization with, a compatible expressive symbol system before its comprehension or use in symbolic manners
4. The development of symbolic representation skills

These components, and some general procedures or strategies for incorporating them into a communication/interaction program for an NVSPH child, are discussed below.

### Developing/Enhancing Communication and Interaction

Communication development for NVSPH children should begin at birth. Primary emphasis should be placed upon providing ways for the NVSPH infant to affect his environment and to interact/communicate with others. To do this, early and continuous play and physical and social interaction should be encouraged, even if the responses to caregivers and others are poor, irregular, or unnatural. Effective procedures and techniques need to be developed in order to facilitate handling and interacting with the NVSPH child. Particular attention should be paid to (and a sensitivity developed for) other communication modes the child uses in addition to vocalizations or speech.

When "normal" interaction patterns or routines are not possible, new techniques should be developed. Adaptive play routines should be developed to be compatible with the child's motoric abilities. Special adaptations as well as special positioning may be necessary to compensate for severe physical handicaps.

The ability to make choices and control the actions of other persons is important in the child's early communication attempts. Allowing the child to select foods or toys via eye gaze or pointing is an example of this. The NVSPH child needs to be provided with ways to reject, refuse, accept, and choose. It is important to bear in mind that the objective of this process is to maximize interaction with the child at the cognitive or communicative level of the child, and with whatever physical skills the child possesses. In order to most closely approximate the natural evolutionary process and environment of the normal child, future cognitive and motoric milestones should be kept in mind, the adaptive tools the child will need should be on hand, and intervention tools and techniques should be introduced only as they facilitate interaction at the child's level.

A great deal of innovation and experimentation may be necessary to develop ways to facilitate successful, effective interaction strategies with the NVSPH child. Components meant to help accomplish future milestones (e.g., providing a means to indicate message elements) should be introduced *only* when it will be possible to incorporate them in a logical, developmental elaboration of the child's *current* interaction skills and activities.

### Developing an Augmentative Physical Mechanism for Indicating Communication Elements

Mechanisms (techniques or aids) will often be needed to enhance the NVSPH child's ability to choose or indicate communication (message) elements. There are several techniques that allow any child, no matter how severely physically handicapped, to effectively indicate communication elements to message receivers. (A complete review of techniques may be found in Vanderheiden and Grilley, 1976, and Vanderheiden and Harris-Vanderheiden, 1976. See also Harris and Vanderheiden, Chapter 12, this volume.)

Whichever augmentative techniques are chosen, however, they should be based upon evolutionary processes such as those described above. That is, the augmentative communication technique chosen should be introduced through existing play and interactive activities. For example, an NVSPH child who does not have pointing skills may be able to voluntarily control a light that scans across a matrix by utilizing a controllable gross motor movement such as moving the head, arm, foot, leg, or knee. This ability can eventually be used to communicate symbolically by having the child activate and stop a light that scans through a vocabulary matrix of words and pictures. Before referential communicative use, however, this technique can be applied in a variety of prelinguistic, interactive ways to allow the child to activate bells, pop-up toys, lights, and "light-picture" displays and to control environmental objects such as doors, radios, and television by starting and stopping the selector light on various squares in a matrix. The child could play with, interact, and control aspects of the motor and social environment with the same technique through which he will later express communicative intent. As the child develops, the mechanism should be adapted to allow the ability to interact in linguistic communicative manners as well as nonlinguistically. By developing mastery of the mechanism through prelinguistic communication, a physical mechanism for future expression will have already been mastered and will be available when the child reaches the level (cognitively and linguistically) where he will need it as a part of a symbolic communication system.

**Developing Familiarity with an Augmentative Symbol System**

Spoken words are natural symbol models for children who will develop speech, and children become familiar with them before achieving oral communication. Similarly, the symbols through which the nonvocal child will be communicating should be familiar to the child before their use in communication. The augmentative symbol system to be used by the child for communication (e.g., pictures, rebuses, or Blissymbols) should be visually available to the child prior to their use in communication. The symbols should be used (in conjunction with speech) in communicating with the child and with other persons in the child's presence. Pairing the symbols with spoken words, persons, physical objects, and locations will help the child learn their meaning by location and association with referents.

Many symbol systems are currently being used with augmentative communication techniques. For a discussion of these, the reader is referred to Clark and Woodcock (1976), Hollis, Carrier, and Spradlin (1976), Vanderheiden and Harris-Vanderheiden (1976), Harris et al. (1977), McNaughton, Kates, and Silverman (1978), and Carrier (1977).

**Developing/Enhancing Symbolic Representation Skill**

Another component of importance for inclusion in intervention programs is the development and enhancement of skills and behavior that lead to using symbolic representation. Providing the child with the means to interact with the environment motorically and socially helps the development of symbolic representational skills. (Research relevant to the development of cognitive prerequisites to linguistic communication may be found in Moore, 1973; Schiefelbusch and Lloyd, 1974; Uzgiris and Hunt, 1975; Lloyd, 1976; and Morehead and Morehead, 1976.)

Since the NVSPH infant is likely to have severe problems in moving about and acting upon the environment, special efforts may be needed to enhance the child's motoric exploration. Physical, manipulative, and perceptual difficulties may need to be accommodated in order to allow the child to effectively explore and interact with the physical environment.

Some of the delay in cognitive and linguistic development in NVSPH children may be alleviated by a greater variety of experiences for motoric and social interaction. Techniques used to provide a child physical mechanism for response, expression, and interaction could also be used to provide a means for motorically interacting with and controlling the physical environment (re previous example).

Objects and situations should be adapted to facilitate the child's observation and exploration of his action with or upon people and objects.

Attempts to communicate and interact in both speech and nonspeech manners should be reinforced by parents, siblings, and others who interact with the child. To enhance motoric and social interactions that help the child develop skills needed to communicate through nonspeech manners, parents, caregivers, and others should be made aware of motor movement, gestures, facial expressions, eye movements, and other behaviors that are being used by the child in communication.

## RESEARCH IN INTERVENTION PROGRAMS FOR NVSPH CHILDREN

Although nonspeech communication techniques are gaining acceptance in education and language fields and with the general public, there is little research in critical aspects of the development and application of these techniques. There are a number of research areas that can provide valuable information regarding cognitive, linguistic, and communication development in severely physically handicapped, nonspeaking children. Information generated through such research would be valuable as corroborative or contrastive information for theories of linguistic and cognitive development in the normal, vocal child. A discussion of some of these research areas follows.

### Comprehension and Production Strategies

There are many opinions regarding the role and contribution of comprehension and production processes to cognitive and linguistic development (Bloom, 1974; Chapman, 1974). Theories at issue are described elsewhere, but there are specific questions regarding comprehension and production processes in nonspeaking children that have important implications for sequencing and developing intervention strategies. There are numerous clinical experiences in which communication aids have been given to an older child or adolescent who has had severely limited production and who, upon mastery of the augmentative production mode, has demonstrated knowledge of the linguistic code that seems to have developed from primary reliance upon comprehension strategies. Some severely physically handicapped children seem to be able to develop linguistic knowledge and skill through a comprehension mode and "transfer" this knowledge to a production mode when provided with an appropriate and effective means of expression. Comprehension and production processes in NVSPH children should be explored to answer questions such as "Does the child really comprehend linguistic processes or only appear to comprehend more than he produces as a function of temporally and contextually relevant and cued verbal interaction that the child may be most frequently encountering?" More basic questions are: 1) How can we characterize comprehension development processes in NVSPH children? and 2) How do these processes relate to analogous comprehension processes in vocal children and to production processes in general?

**Role of Imitation**

Imitative skills have been described by Flavell (1963), Piaget (1964), Bates (1976), and others as the sensorimotor forerunners of symbolic functioning. Reviewing the development of imitative skills reveals that children initially imitate only those actions they can see or can perform themselves. Imitative skills usually require finely coordinated motor acts that may be difficult for the young physically handicapped child, whose motor movements are primarily reflexive and uncontrolled, to perform. As an accommodative act, imitation is an important process in cognitive and linguistic development. In view of the NVSPH child's problems, relevant research questions here include: Do severely physically handicapped children imitate others? If so, how consistent and reliable are their imitative skills, and what results do they produce? What can these children imitate, what do they imitate, and what feedback is provided them for imitating? What effect does a severe deficit of imitative behavior have on cognitive development? Can early imitative deficits be alleviated through providing the infant with reliable, biofeedback of his motor movement patterns?

**Role of Participation in Encoding Experiences**

Hymes (1974) and Halliday (1973) have commented that the vocal child is, through language and speech, able to code and organize perceptions, observations, and experiences, and thus to use speech as a socialization/interaction tool. Many nonspeaking children rely on message receivers and others to code, organize, and express their ideas and thoughts (e.g., to record messages communicated through communication boards). An interesting investigation would be the impact of limited participation in the organization and production of a communicative message upon the child's organization and encoding of his perceptions and observations. Related to this, a comparative analysis of the child's expressions formulated and organized through a message receiver, or by the child through an assistive aid, would also be of interest.

### Role of Written and Spoken Language and Communication

Most nonspeaking, severely physically handicapped children rely upon written, visual, or graphic output for communicative expression. A particularly critical research area concerns whether semantic, syntactic, and pragmatic development processes are analogous in oral and visual-graphic or written expressive modes. Vygotsky (1962) postulated a 6 to 7 year lag in linguistic age between speaking and writing for vocal children. He treats written expression as a separate linguistic function from speech production. If, in fact, there is a large gap in linguistic age related to acquisition of visual-graphic communicative competence, perhaps some "delayed" children are not as severely delayed as had been anticipated. An important question is whether there are significantly different cognitive and linguistic processing differences between speech and visual-graphic or visual-motor expressive modes.

Another issue is whether there are significant processing differences in different types of visual-graphic and visual-motor expressive modes (e.g., scanning, pointing, eye encoding, and manual signing). If so, what are they and how can we characterize the skills that constitute communicative competence through modes other than speech?

### Intention and Feedback Preceding Skill Development

Bruner (1975a) has theorized that an important factor in the development of intention and purposeful behavior is the comparison of the intended act with the resultant act and the use of the information for correcting the act. Intentional behavior may be prerequisite to symbolic representation. If so, it would be important to research the effects of aberrant or inconsistent feedback of motor pattern behavior upon the development of intentional acts in cerebral palsied children.

### Modularization and Information Processing

Along similar lines Bruner (1973) has discussed the notion of "modularization" or motor movement patterns by the infant. He refers to the observation that a normal child spends a great deal of his information-processing capacity in the execution of motor patterns. Gradually, as the child develops unconscious control of motor patterns, Bruner theorizes that information processing-capabilities are freed and can be used in the development of other skills. In this view, symbolic representation skills can develop once the child has "modularized" motor patterns and can begin to process and organize other types of information.

It would be interesting to investigate whether severely physically handicapped children ever attain modularization or unconscious control of motor patterns and, if not, to explore the amount of information-processing capacity devoted to regulating ongoing physical skills, and the amount available for cognitive symbolic processing.

Related to the above, Bruner (1973) has theorized that there are some major sources of awkwardness in infancy that the child must "grow out of" if cognitive development is to proceed effectively. These are: 1) primary reliance on gross motor movement patterns (the child needs to develop fine motor skill), 2) contradictory actions (the child needs to learn to control contradictory muscle action patterns), and 3) imperfect sequencing of component acts (the child needs to learn to smoothly execute component acts in motor movement patterns).

NVSPH individuals may never "grow out of" these behaviors. It is important to investigate what effect their persistence may have upon emerging cognitive and linguistic skills.

## Questions and Dialogue

Piaget (1964), Ginsberg and Opper (1969), and Halliday (1973) have discussed the role of dialogue and question answering in the development of communication. Piaget (1964) views dialogue and question answering as critical links between the child's expression of ideas that are dependent upon context and those that can be expressed in a displaced verbal context. An area to research here would involve investigation of the questions posed to and by NVSPH individuals and the amount of, and opportunity for, dialogue and communicative interaction. Related to intervention, it would be interesting to know if communication competence improved if the child was given more opportunity to pose and answer questions and participate in dialogue.

## Developing Increased Language/Communication Skill

Brown (1973) observed that a major factor in vocal children's improvement of communication skill and development of advanced syntactic skill is pressure from peers and persons outside the child's family or familiar environment. A related research area involves investigation of the impetus for the development of advanced linguistic skill in children who usually reside in a protective or sheltered environment or are consistently accompanied by someone who understands, interprets, and formulates the communication messages for the child.

## Early Labeling

Bowerman (1976) has observed that parents usually provide labels for objects and events that they assume the children will understand and that reflect the parents' assumption regarding the child's knowledge of the world. Parents' provision of labels for actions, objects, and events is important for the child's achievement of symbolic representations for the actions, objects, and events. Parents of NVSPH children may be unsure of their child's understanding or knowledge of the world, because the child may not have provided identifiable feedback to the parent. It is important to determine how this may affect the labeling behavior of parents and subsequent cognitive development of the child.

### Communicative Affect

A great deal of meaning is expressed through intonation and pause and stress patterns selected by the speaker. Vocal children express anger, frustration, happiness, and other emotions through these behaviors. Children who rely upon visual-graphic output modes will not be able to mark messages with intonation and stress. It would be interesting to investigate strategies used by nonspeaking children to express communicative affect, and the effect of these strategies upon the complexity of syntactic and semantic structures encoded by the child.

### Augmentative Response Interaction Modes

Nonspeaking children may communicate through visual-graphic or visual-motor expressive systems. There has been research in the area of investigating cognitive and linguistic development processes in vocal children who use aural-vocal communication channels, but there has been little research of the same processes that may be affected by reliance upon aural-motor communication channels. Research in this area will have implications for the augmentative expressive mechanisms and symbol systems that are chosen for a particular individual.

### Effects of Augmentative Symbol Systems

Until recent studies by Clark (1977), differential effects of particular augmentative symbols upon expression had not been researched. Relative advantages and disadvantages and appropriate application of various types of available symbol systems (rebuses, Blissymbols, pictures, and abstract plastic symbols such as those designed by Premack and Yerkes) need to be researched in order to help clinicians and educators choose and apply the most appropriate symbol system with a particular individual.

## SUMMARY

The development of communicative interaction skill in nonvocal severely physically handicapped children is currently being undertaken by educators, clinicians, and researchers. Although the task may be a difficult one, it is receiving the attention of a number of disciplines and the concern of a number of individuals who are developing communication intervention programs for nonspeaking individuals. This chapter has presented and discussed strategies related to the enhancement and development of communicative interaction in NVSPH children. Although children have been the focus of the discussion, procedures and strategies highlighted may be applicable to NVSPH adolescents and adults, and to other nonvocal populations as well.

The process of interaction/communication development has been presented from an evolutionary perspective, integrating interrelated processes of: 1) the development of physical mechanisms for the expression of communication and interaction with others, 2) the development of general interaction ability and of motivation and intent to communicate, and 3) the development of cognitive skills required for symbolic communication. A primary emphasis of the chapter involved the notion that the development of symbolic communication via vocalizations and the use of words is a gradually evolving process for the vocal child, and that many parts involved in the mastery of an expressive communication system are learned and used by the child prior to their employment specifically for the exchange of information with other persons. The discussion highlighted the importance of providing the same program so NVSPH children may develop effective communication systems.

Clinicians, educators, and researchers should be cautioned about the use of terms such as *nonvocal* and *nonspeaking* as sole descriptors of individuals or intervention programs. A similar caution applies to the importance of perceiving nonvocal communication techniques as augmentative, not as alternatives to speech to be employed only upon failure of the development of effective oral communication. More research is needed to help educators, clinicians, and parents in the application of nonvocal communication strategies. Some issues for further research have been presented here. These are far from exhaustive, and we hope further strategies will soon be developed and refined.

## REFERENCES

Bates, E. 1976. Language and Context—The Acquisition of Pragmatics. Academic Press, New York.

Bloom, L. 1974. Talking, understanding, and thinking. *In* R. L. Schiefelbusch and L. L. Lloyd (eds.), Language Perspectives—Acquisition, Retardation, and Intervention, pp. 285–311. University Park Press, Baltimore.

Bowerman, M. 1976. Semantic factors in the acquisition of rules for word use and sentence construction. *In* D. Morehead and A. Morehead (eds.), Normal and Deficient Child Language, pp. 99–179. University Park Press, Baltimore.

Brown, R. 1973. A First Language. Harvard University, Cambridge, Mass.

Bruner, J. S. 1973. Beyond the information given. *In* J. Anglin (ed.), W. W. Norton & Co., New York.

Bruner, J. S. 1975a. From communication to language: A psychological perspective. Cognition 3:255–287.

Bruner, J. S. 1975b. The ontogenesis of speech acts. J. Child Lang. 2:1–19.

Carrier, J. K., Jr. 1979. Perspectives on nonspeech symbol systems. *In* R. L. Schiefelbusch and J. H. Hollis (eds.), Language Intervention from Ape to Child, pp. 493–511. University Park Press, Baltimore.

Chapman, R. S. 1974. Discussion summary—Developmental relationship between receptive and expressive language. *In* R. L. Schiefelbusch and L. L. Lloyd (eds.), Language Perspectives—Acquisition, Retardation, and Intervention, pp. 335–344. University Park Press, Baltimore.

Clark, C. 1977. A comparative study of young children's ease of learning words represented in the graphic systems of rules, Bliss, Carrier-Peak and traditional orthography. Research Report 107, University of Minnesota Research, Development and Demonstration Center, Minneapolis.

Clark, C., and Woodcock, R. 1976. Graphic systems of communication. *In* L. L. Lloyd (ed.), Communication Assessment and Intervention Strategies, pp. 549–605. University Park Press, Baltimore.

Flavell, J. H. 1963. The Developmental Psychology of Jean Piaget. Van Nostrand Reinhold Co., Princeton, N.J.

Ginsburg, H., and Opper, S. 1969. Piaget's Theory of Intellectual Development. Prentice-Hall, Englewood Cliffs, N.J.

Halliday, M. A. K. 1973. Explorations in the Functions of Language. Edward Arnold Ltd., London.

Harris, D., Lippert, J., Yoder, D., and Vanderheiden, G. 1977. Blissymbols: An augmentative symbol communication system for non-vocal severely handicapped children. *In* R. York and E. Edgar (eds.), Teaching the Severely Handicapped, Vol. IV, pp. 238–262. Special Press, Seattle.

Hollis, J. H., Carrier, J. K., Jr., and Spradlin, J. E. 1976. An approach to remediation of communication and learning deficiencies. *In* L. L. Lloyd (ed.), Communication Assessment and Intervention Strategies, pp. 265–294. University Park Press, Baltimore.

Hymes, D. 1974. Foundations of Sociolinguistics. University of Pennsylvania Press, Philadelphia.

Lloyd, L. L. (ed.). 1976. Communication Assessment and Intervention Strategies. University Park Press, Baltimore.

McDonald, E., and Schultz, A. 1973. A communication board for cerebral palsied children. J. Speech Hear. Disord. 38:73–88.

McNaughton, S., Kates, B., and Silverman, H. 1978. Handbook of Blissymbolics. Blissymbolics Communication Institute, Toronto, Ontario, Canada.

Moore, T. (ed.). 1973. Cognitive Development and the Acquisition of Language. Academic Press, New York.

Morehead, D., and Morehead, A. (eds.). 1976. Normal and Deficient Child Language. University Park Press, Baltimore.

Piaget, J. 1964. The Origins of Intelligence in Children. W. W. Norton & Co., New York.

Schiefelbusch, R. L., and Lloyd, L. L. (eds.). 1974. Language Perspectives—Acquisition, Retardation, and Intervention. University Park Press, Baltimore.

Slobin, D. (Ed.). 1971. The Ontogenesis of Grammar. Academic Press, New York.

Uzgiris, I. C., and Hunt, J. M. V. 1975. Assessment in Infancy: Ordinal Scales of Psychological Development. University of Illinois Press, Urbana.

Vanderheiden, G., and Grilley, K. 1976. Non-Vocal Communication Techniques and Aids. University Park Press, Baltimore.

Vanderheiden, G., and Harris-Vanderheiden, D. 1976. Communication techniques and aids for the non-vocal severely handicapped. *In* L. L. Lloyd (ed.), Communication Assessment and Intervention Strategies, pp. 607–652. University Park Press, Baltimore.

Vygotsky, L. 1962. Thought and Language. The MIT Press, Cambridge, Mass.

Yarrow, L., Klein, R., Lomonaco, S., and Morgan, G. 1975. Cognitive and motivational development in early childhood. *In* B. Friedlander (ed.), Exceptional Infant, Vol. 3. Brunner/Mazel, New York.

chapter 12

# Augmentative Communication Techniques

*Deberah Harris*

*Gregg C. Vanderheiden*

*Trace Research and Development Center for the Severely Communicatively Handicapped University of Wisconsin-Madison Madison, Wisconsin*

contents

One of the first problems encountered in developing an effective communication system for nonvocal, severely physically handicapped (NVSPH) persons is one of establishing an effective mechanism through which the individual can interact, respond, and express himself. A person who is not able to speak, write, or manually sign, cannot be accurately evaluated for communicative competence or participate in an effective intervention program. Yes/no communication, which is within the capabilities of many physically limited individuals, is usually very restrictive. It is also prone to accidental cuing and is thus not helpful in assessment and in the general communication processes. Therefore, some reliable and consistent means of effective interaction must be established before effective intervention or remediation can begin.

NVSPH individuals who cannot use speech or sign language effectively (because of severe physical impairments) need some sort of visual-graphic communication system of pictures, symbols, words, and the like. This type of system usually consists of a chart or board with pictures, drawings, symbols, or printed words. The NVSPH person indicates, in some manner, the item(s) on the chart that he wants to use in order to convey a message. The person may initially use this method only respondently to select items cued by the message receiver. Later, if the chart or board also contains items about which the person wants to communicate, he may begin to use the chart spontaneously. By using the chart for interaction and expression, the person can initiate communication, express emotion, request something wanted, or request that something be done.

The process of developing effective communication and interaction skill in NVSPH individuals may be slow and painstaking or may move along rapidly, depending upon the person's age and the type and degree of disability. Programs for developing communication skills for these individuals also vary. One of the first components, however, of any program for communication development with an NVSPH person involves the development of an effective means to indicate message elements. Once the individual has a technique to indicate message choices, the teacher or clinician will have a mechanism for interaction. This, in turn, enables the teacher or clinician to initiate a program to develop functional communication capability.

One very important factor to bear in mind in program development is that the first technique chosen not be considered absolute. It should be considered as a starting point. From this, an individual's communication system should be modified to allow continuous growth and development. The communication system should eventually become flexible and comprehensive. This will most likely be achieved through gradual development and change. This may involve not only increasing the degree of complexity of a technique but also changing the technique or approach if warranted by the individual's physical and cognitive development.

Thus, the initial technique may be quite different from the system the individual will use later. For this reason, one should carefully assess the person's existing abilities when selecting an initial technique, rather than becoming concerned about what the communication system should look like in the long run. It is most important to get the individual *interacting* as soon as possible, and then to work on the development of skills to enable more effective and efficient communication.

## INITIAL TECHNIQUES

There are three basic approaches to communication systems for NVSPH persons: *direct selection*, *scanning*, and *encoding*. Direct selection and scanning are more fundamental approaches and are discussed here under "Initial Techniques." Encoding approaches are covered under secondary techniques. *Direct selection* requires that the user point directly to the elements of a message. This is a more straightforward, natural, and efficient approach than scanning. *Scanning*, however, requires only a minimum amount of physical control by a user, who signals when the desired element of a message is scanned. Scanning is generally (but not always) slower and more involved than direct selection, but it can be used with more severely physically disabled individuals. Each approach, therefore, has advantages in different situations. In general, the direct selection approach is tried first, although it is usually a good idea to work with both before deciding which initial approach is best for the individual.

### Direct Selection

Direct selection refers to techniques in which the message sender indicates elements of his message by directly pointing to them in some manner. Pointing to message elements on a communication board is a familiar example of this technique, as is a child pointing to a glass of milk or a cookie. Typing is an example of a direct selection approach because the typist directly selects the letters.

Although fingers and hands generally come to mind as pointers, other parts of the body can be used. Feet, toes, and elbows can be used in manners similar to hands. Headsticks (Figure 1) and mouthpieces are also useful for persons with good torso and head control.

With direct selection approaches, the nonvocal, physically handicapped person must be able to control some part of his body well enough to point to specified areas. Some persons can point with good accuracy to widely spaced message elements, but cannot point successfully to elements that are more closely spaced or smaller. Positioning, therefore, plays an important role in enhancing or impairing pointing abilities. Physical and occupational therapy input regarding seating and positioning for a nonvocal, physically handicapped individual is very important.

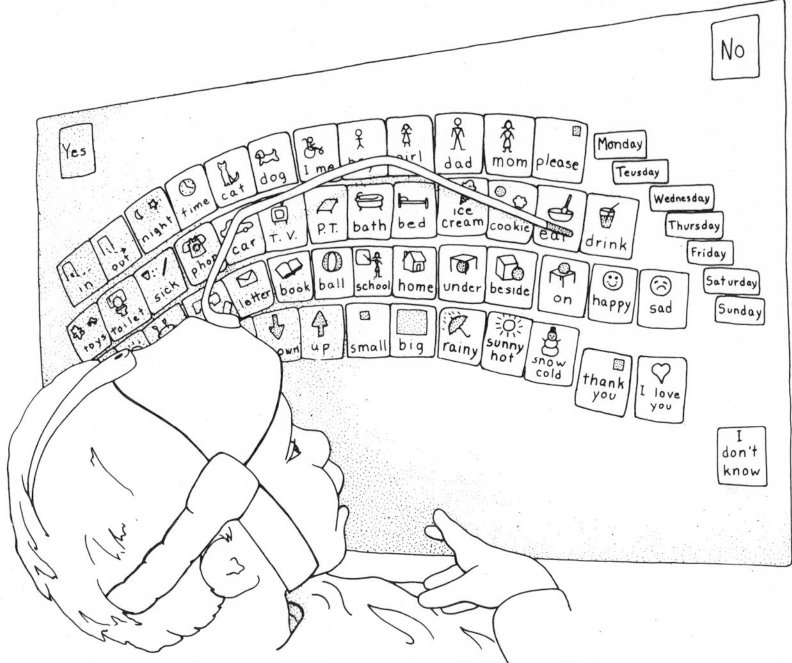


Figure 1. Headstick used for direct selection technique.

Persons who have sufficient control of some part of their body to be able to point accurately can use direct selection as a very simple, straightforward, and flexible channel for interaction and response. Some individuals, however, even with proper seating and positioning, may not be able to point well enough to use direct selection. For these individuals a scanning approach may be appropriate.

**Scanning**

Scanning techniques present message elements (e.g., pictures, words) or groups of elements one at a time to the handicapped person, who signals to select the desired element. In most cases, the individual merely indicates by a prearranged signal (e.g., movement of arm, leg, head, eyes) when the desired message element has been presented. With some techniques, it is also possible for the NVSPH person to direct the scanning process.

An example of scanning would be a "twenty questions" approach in which the message receiver asks a number of questions, such as "Are you hungry?", "Are you sick?", "Do you want to go to a show?", and so on, until the message sender indicates yes to one of the questions.

An example of "linear" (one at a time) scanning involves a com-

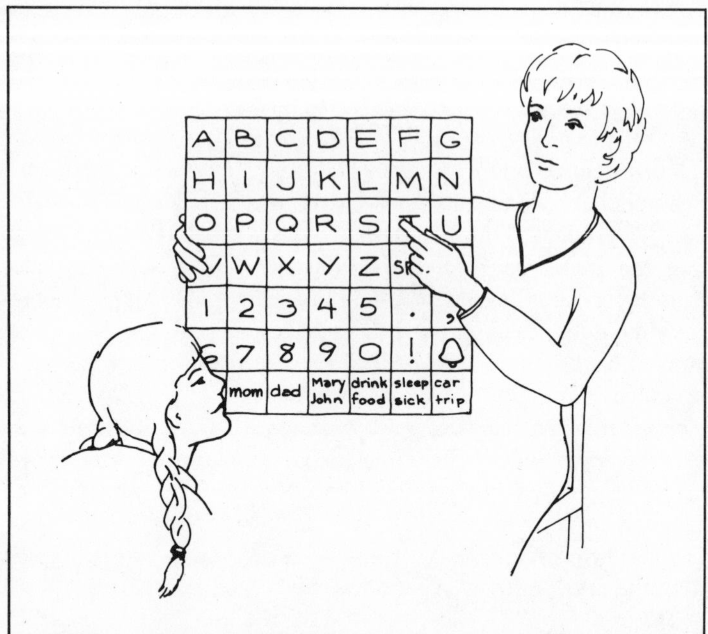


Figure 2. Linear scanning with second person.

munication board. Here, the message receiver manually points to each element until the message sender signals the correct element (Figure 2).

Scanning requires a minimum of physical control. The nonvocal physically handicapped person can use any consistent response, whether it is bending a finger, moving the head sideways, looking up, or the like. The scanning approach can be used with almost any individual, regardless of the type or degree of severity of the physical handicap.

The scanning process is usually slower than direct selection because the presenter must pause long enough at each element for the NVSPH individual to signal and respond. To help speed the scanning approach, several modifications to the basic technique have been developed by teachers and clinicians. One simple technique is "group-item" scanning.

In group-item scanning, the elements are arranged in groups or rows (Figure 3). Entire groups or rows of items are scanned until the NVSPH person signals. The elements in that group are then scanned, one at a time in order to find the correct element. Generally, the most time-efficient displays are squares (i.e., the same number of rows as columns), but other visual arrangements can be modified to fit individual needs. The time savings in a group-item approach are quite significant. For a 49-element display, the average selection time (number of steps to reach a desired selection) is 8 steps with group-item versus 24 steps with a linear (one at a time) scanning approach.

Scanning techniques should be introduced to the NVSPH person gradually. The individual should become familiar with the technique, as should all of the persons with whom the NVSPH person communicates. Once a consistent response or signal has been identified, it can be used to make choices between objects or pictures presented to the person. Selection can be gradually introduced with the message receiver manually scanning the items one by one. A pause at each item provides an opportunity for signaling by the message sender. A consistent scanning technique should be used, moving from left to right across the lap tray or communication board. As more items are introduced, additional rows can be added, maintaining the consistent scanning pattern. Some nonvocal, physically handicapped persons require little or no training to use the scanning technique. Others will require an orderly procedure with gradual additions to the vocabulary as they develop skill in attending, tracking, and communication.

The major advantage of the scanning approach is that it can be used with even the most severely physically handicapped individual. The tech-

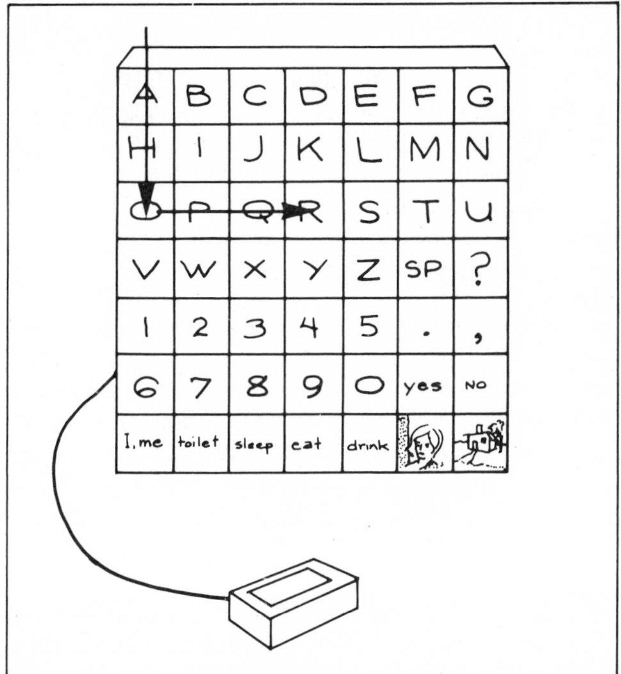


Figure 3. Row-column (group-item) scanning.

nique is slower and less obvious than direct selection, however, and may be more difficult to introduce and less motivating (because of speed and relative lack of activity) than direct selection, especially with very young or severely mentally retarded persons. For this reason, many clinicians try to develop direct selection skills in their nonpointing clients. For persons demonstrating poor pointing skills, a combination of direct selection and scanning techniques (point and scan) may be an effective communication technique.

### Point and Scan

If the individual has some pointing ability, but not enough to point to individual elements, a "point and scan" technique (also sometimes referred to as "indicated area scanning") may be used. With this technique, the child *tries* to indicate the desired element by pointing with the head, arm, a headstick, etc., or with the eyes. The message receiver notes the general area that the child is indicating, and then scans over the elements in that area one at a time in order to determine the desired element.

This technique has several advantages over the scanning approach (in addition to being faster), for those who cannot directly point to their message elements. Some of these advantages are:

1. The NVSPH person takes a more active role in the communication process.
2. The system compensates for good and bad days on the part of the person. On good days, the person may be able to almost directly select items, while on bad days, the person may need a slightly wider area to be scanned.
3. It provides good eye-hand coordination practice.
4. It has the potential for developing the pointing skills needed to use the faster and more flexible direct selection approach over time.

The greatest disadvantage of this system is that it is less straightforward for the message receiver than direct selection or scanning. This may cause confusion in nonhandicapped individuals who have seen communication boards but are not familiar with the technique being used by the person. (They may watch the pointing motions and think the person is trying to point to individual items rather than just indicating the general area of an item.) This problem can be partially overcome by placing a small card with directions for the system in prominent view on the communication board, facing away from the person and toward the message receiver.

### Developing and Applying Initial Techniques

It takes time to try the different techniques with an NVSPH individual and to determine which ones work. Not all nonvocal, physically handicapped persons will immediately utilize a technique. It may be necessary to spend time in training a particular technique in order to see if the person can develop effective control over the movements required. Selection of a technique is a process in which different systems are presented, tried, observed, modified, and changed, and observed again before another technique is considered. For some individuals, this intervention process will be the first time they have been successful in communicating specific messages to other persons. It may take time to learn to do what is being asked. For some, modifications in other aspects of their abilities or of their physical and social environment will be needed to allow them to take full advantage of the technique. Trials should continue until the best solution for each individual is found. Initially, of course, a technique that the person can control right away should be found and implemented so the individual has a means to interact and communicate while trying other techniques.

When working with various techniques, it is also important to keep in mind other potential problems the individual may have (e.g., poor vision or hearing) and to allow for their effects. Vision is particularly important when considering augmentative communication techniques, because good vision is necessary in visual-graphic communication systems. Visual memory is needed for direct selection, as is visual tracking. Visual tracking also plays a strong role in scanning, especially if an automated aid with backlighting is used. Figure-ground discrimination and visual acuity are also needed to identify message elements.

In addition, hearing and auditory comprehension play an important role in terms of input to the nonvocal, physically handicapped individual who learns through messages. The auditory signal of others serves as a feedback for the individual's messages. With severely physically involved people, a hearing loss can be easily misinterpreted as mental retardation.

**Summary of Initial Technique**

*Scanning* and *direct selection* are the two basic techniques to explore first in seeking an augmentative communication system. People with good range of motion and control of pointing usually use direct selection because it affords them the most straightforward approach, and usually the greatest speed. Scanning is a better choice for persons who are severely limited in movement and without an effective pointing skill.

In most cases, *direct selection*, *scanning*, or *point and scan* can be used as a preliminary or initial technique for a person just beginning to use an augmentative communication technique. The person then has a "basic means to indicate" and has a systematic way of interacting with other persons while expanding those approaches or exploring combination approaches or other new approaches to increase communication abilities.

## SECONDARY TECHNIQUES

Initial techniques meet the immediate communication needs of some nonvocal, physically handicapped individuals quite adequately. Over a period of time, however, communication needs and abilities usually expand. With this expansion, the individual may find initial techniques slow, inefficient, or too confining. This development may occur in a number of ways, and for a variety of reasons. For those individual using direct selection, there will be some who have only gross pointing skills that allow them to point accurately to only a small number of properly spaced items on their communication board. Other individuals have adequate pointing skills to meet their early communication needs, but as they expand their opportunities to communicate they may develop additional skills and vocabulary needs that go beyond the contraints imposed by the communication board. Making smaller individual elements may not be feasible when pointing skills or visual abilities are not well developed. Thus, new techniques may be needed.

Another example might be the person beginning with scanning. Vocabulary and communicative needs will grow as the individual interacts with other persons. Although the scanning approach can accommodate more message elements, the approach becomes unwieldy and slow as communication needs and vocabulary size increase. Communication experiences may become less frequent because message receivers are not as willing to interact with the nonvocal, physically handicapped person if the process is tedious and slow.

Unlike speech, which enables a person to gain access to a large and readily expanded vocabulary, a nonvocal person has access only to those message elements available through the techniques and aids he uses. Additional approaches must be designed to expand the utility and facility of the two basic initial approaches of direct selection and scanning.

### Encoding

One communication approach to consider for the individual with some control but poor range of motion is encoding. In encoding, a pattern or code of signals indicates the message elements. Generally, the code is memorized or displayed on a chart for both the message sender and message receiver to use as a reference during conversation.

An example of a two-movement encoding technique uses two-number combinations to designate message elements (Figure 4). Instead of pointing directly to the many possible message elements, the sender points to two numbers on a number line to indicate the code for each message element. In this way, the NVSPH person need only point to a possible maximum of 10 areas, one for each number. (For example, in Figure 4, pointing to "2" and then "4" would indicate the item next to

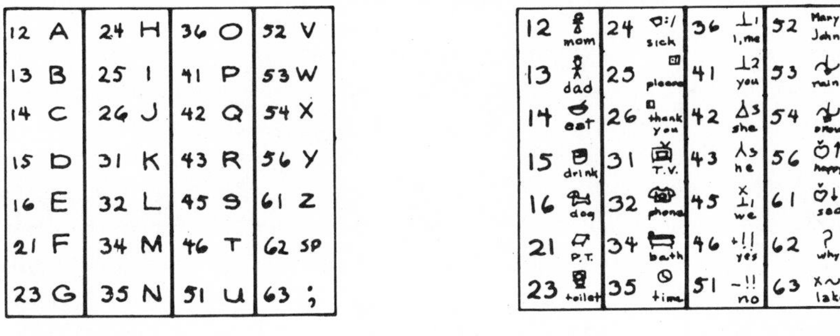

12 A
13 B
14 C
15 D
16 E
21 F
23 G
24 H
25 I
26 J
31 K
32 L
34 M
35 N
36 O
41 P
42 Q
43 R
45 S
46 T
51 U
52 V
53 W
54 X
56 Y
61 Z
62 SP
63 ;
12 mom
13 dad
14 eat
15 drink
16 dog
21 P.T.
23 toilet
24 sick
25 please
26 thank you
31 T.V.
32 phone
34 bath
35 time
36 I, me
41 you
42 she
43 he
45 we
46 yes
51 no
52 Mary John
53 rain
54 snow
56 happy
61 sad
62 why
63 lake


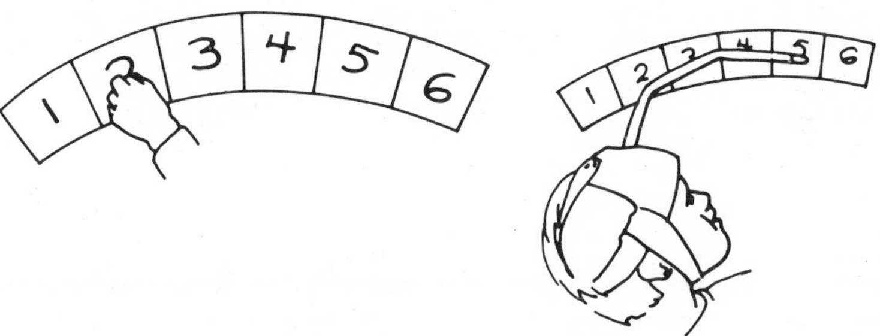


Figure 4. Two-movement encoding techniques.

24, or "sick.") It is possible to modify the code for more limiting pointing possibilities. For example, with only five numbers, and eliminating any double combinations (i.e., 11, 22, etc.), it is possible to code 20 message elements. Using a three-number code and only five possible numbers, it is possible to expand to 80 message elements. (Any double or triple numbers would be eliminated to avoid confusion in signaling.) Although encoding may require more movements per message, it can accommodate gross pointing skills and provide fast access to a large selection of possible message elements.

The encoding approach can be adapted for people who cannot remember number sequences accurately or who would reverse them. It is possible to use colors as coding signals, or combinations of colors and numbers. Using the system shown in Figure 5, a child could use an encoding system without knowing color or number concepts, as long as the child understood association and matching concepts. To indicate something, the message receiver could ask, "What color block is it in?" After the child had pointed to a matching color patch above the number line, the message receiver could ask, "And what number (or shape) is next to the word (picture, etc.) you want?"

If the person is not able to point by hand, arm, head, etc., any eye gaze chart such as the ETRAN-Number Chart shown in Figure 6 can

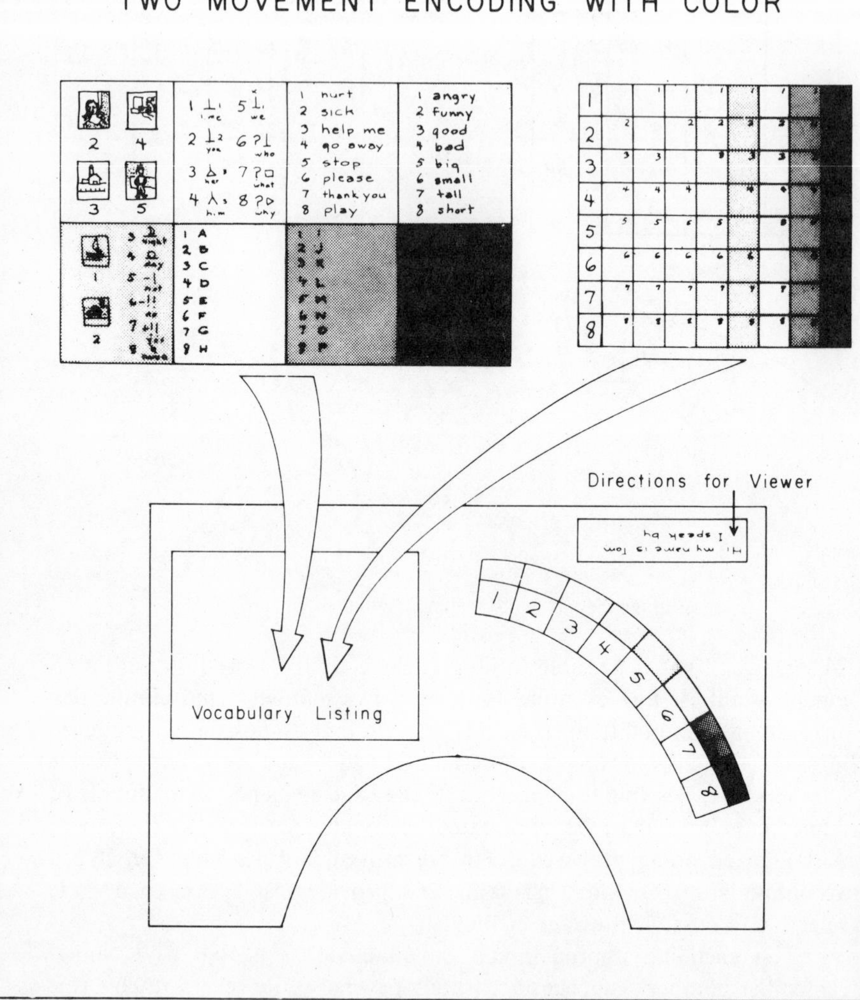


Figure 5. Two-movement encoding with color.

indicate the numbers of numbers/colors for encoding. Figure 7 shows a more advanced version of the ETRAN chart. With the ETRAN chart in Figure 7, the sender indicates (through eye pointing) the general group where the message element is found, and then its specific location in the group (Vanderheiden and Grilley, 1976).

The encoding approach allows an individual access to a large vocabulary, requiring only a limited range of motion. While these techniques

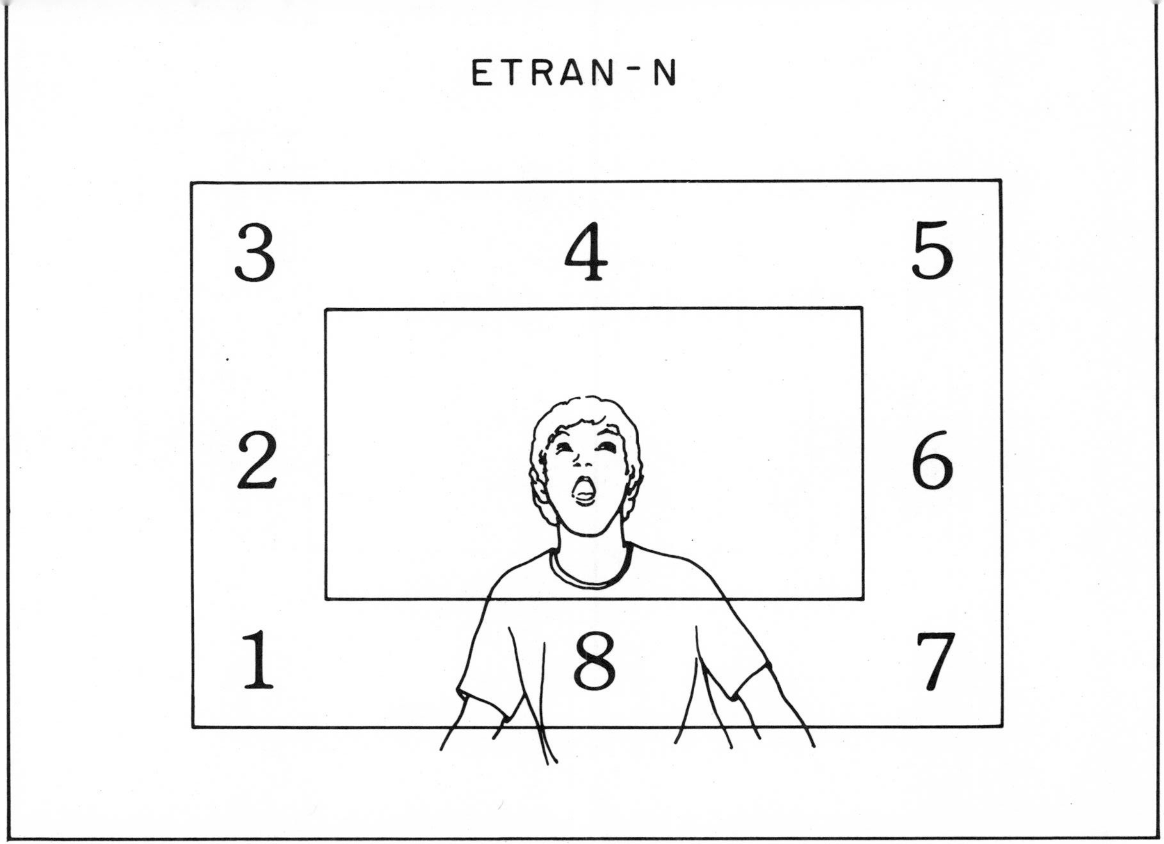

ETRAN-N

3 4 5

2 6

1 8 7

Figure 6. ETRAN-Number Chart, a two-movement eye gaze encoding technique.

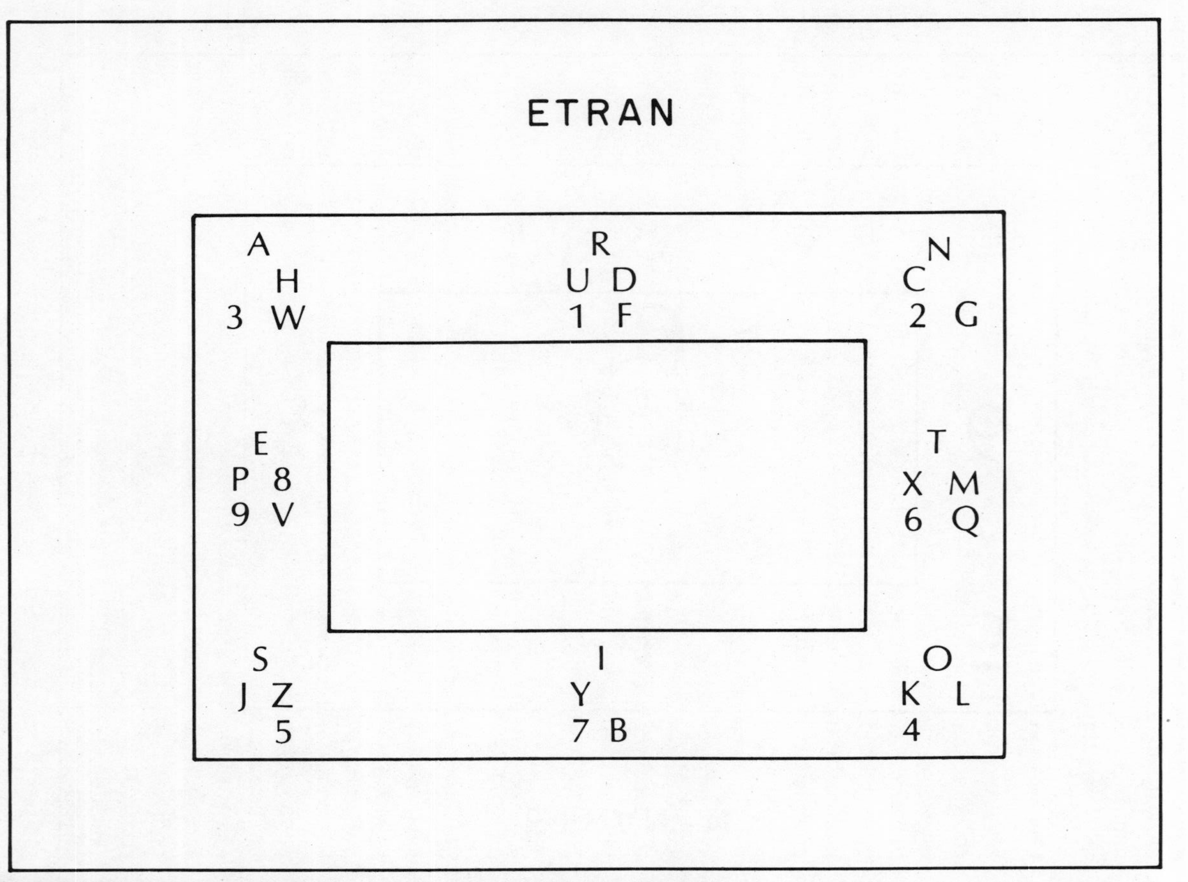
ETRAN
A
H
3 W
R
U D
1 F
N
C
2 G
E
P 8
9 V
T
X M
6 Q
S
J Z
5
I
Y
7 B
O
K L
4

are not appropriate for every individual, and are usually not appropriate as initial techniques (unless the individual is advanced), they do allow more efficient referencing of larger vocabularies than do direct selection or scanning approaches alone. It is common for individuals using scanning or direct selection to develop combination approaches in order to take advantage of the best aspects of each approach.

### Combination Techniques

As was true with the initial techniques, secondary techniques such as encoding can be combined with others to capitalize on the advantages of the various systems and meet the specific needs of an individual. Whereas the direct selection approach is the fastest and most straightforward, most persons who use it will eventually find that their vocabulary is limited by their ability to point. When this occurs, it is appropriate to provide the individual with a *combination direct selection and encoding* communication board. With such a board, the person points directly to the alphabet and the most frequently used words, but has a number line available to use in an encoding fashion to access a larger vocabulary (Figure 8). An individual using a scanning approach could similarly use the encoding approach in combination with scanning in order to increase the size of the vocabulary, without unrealistically increasing the time required to access the larger vocabulary.

## NEED FOR COMMUNICATION AIDS

We have discussed communication *techniques* but not communication aids. There are many communication aids for nonvocal, physically handicapped persons. Most are automated versions of the techniques already discussed. The function of the communication aid is to remove from the message receiver the burden of monitoring the sender's movement, determining the message elements, and assembling the final message. Communication aids of various types are available for some or all of the above tasks. The principal need for communication aids stems from the fact that the basic techniques described earlier require the constant and undivided attention of a message receiver. This complete attention from receivers is rarely available to physically handicapped individuals, and thus their communication is severely limited, occurring at the convenience of those in their environment. In the classroom, the teacher is physically unable to simultaneously direct a class and work one-to-one with an NVSPH child. The cost of having a teacher's aide working one-to-one with the individual to allow participation in classroom discussion, ask questions and make responses, and doing written assignments is prohibitively expensive. An educational placement without an effective way to

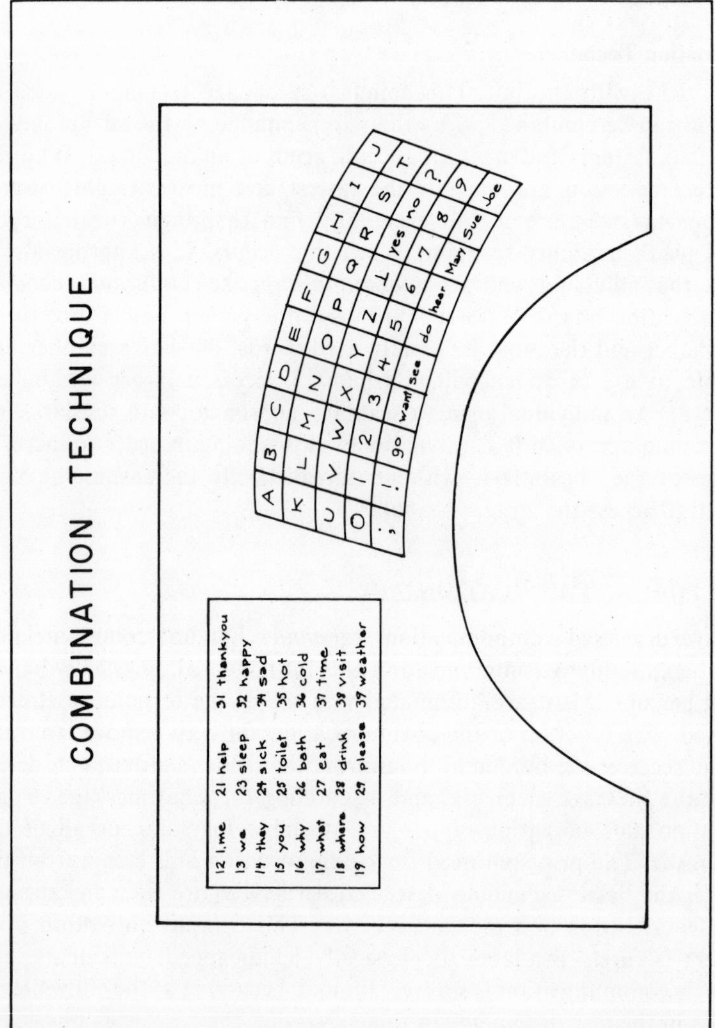


Figure 8. Combination encoding and direct selection techniques.

communicate or write is only of limited benefit to the individual. Moreover, without an effective means of communication, many NVSPH children can be misplaced in classroom situations because they are unable to function in more interactive, regular educational settings.

The need for effective independent communication is also necessary in other aspects of the individual's life. In any type of group interaction, it is difficult for a participant to remove himself from the conversation for the 3 to 5 minutes it may take for the nonvocal individual to assemble a message. For this reason, the nonvocal individual has very little opportunity to interact in anything but one-to-one communication unless there is a means of assembling messages on his own time. In addition, any creative or independent work is impossible without the constant attention of a second person. Since severely physically handicapped individuals are often unable to be creative in any manual sense, the ability to be creative through speech or writing is important.

## TYPES OF COMMUNICATION AIDS AVAILABLE

Aids range from simple communication boards to portable independent communication aids with LED displays (calculator-type displays), built-in strip printers, television displays (similar to those in airports), and typewriter controllers. In addition, most communication aids can be used as input modes to computers, opening the use of computers to handicapped persons.

In addition to various communication aids with printed output, there are currently a few aids with synthesized voice for their output, or as an output option. These aids are based upon VOTRAX, a voice synthesizer based upon a 64-phoneme set. With these aids, individual words can be stacked end to end to form sentences "spoken" by the aid. Individual words can also be created using the 64-phoneme set. Although there are shortcomings regarding voice quality and inflection, research is continuing.

Before discussing specific aids, it is useful to look at the different levels of complexity in aids, and to examine the advantages and limitations of each.

### Levels of Implementation

Techniques within each approach can vary from fundamental techniques to more sophisticated aids. Figure 9 shows various techniques, characterizing them by their degree of sophistication. Each of these levels has advantages and disadvantages for persons with differing abilities or in different situations. It is important to understand the significance of

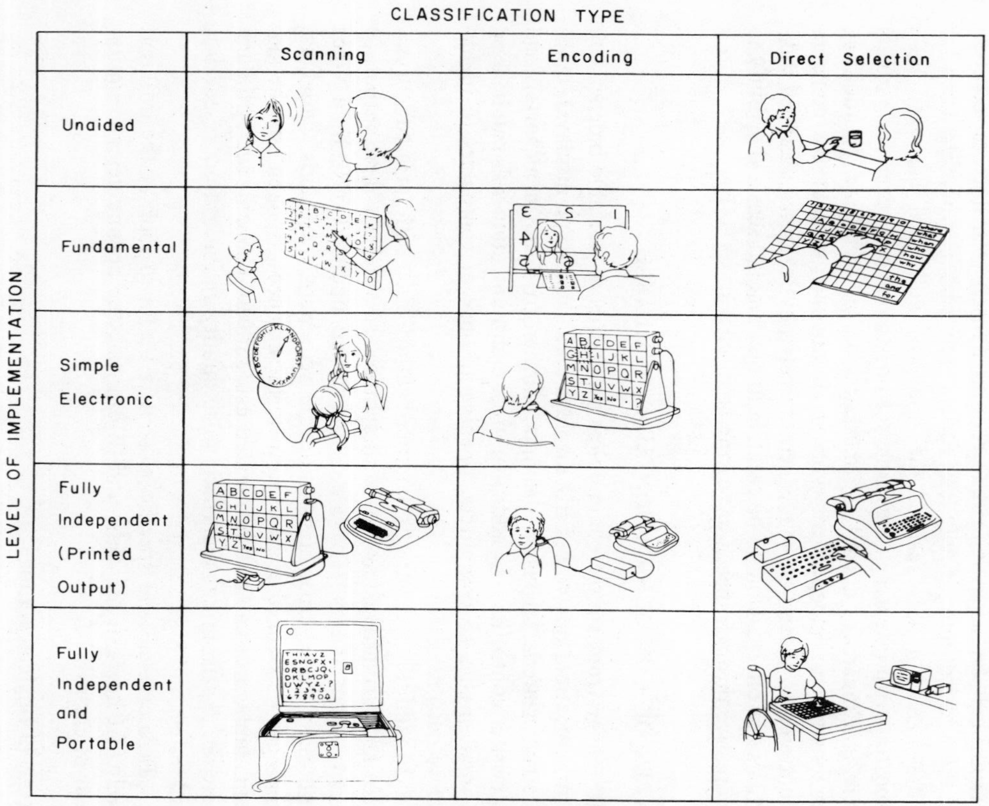

CLASSIFICATION TYPE

| LEVEL OF IMPLEMENTATION | Scanning | Encoding | Direct Selection |
|---|---|---|---|
| Unaided | | | |
| Fundamental | | | |
| Simple Electronic | | | |
| Fully Independent (Printed Output) | | | |
| Fully Independent and Portable | | | |

Figure 9. Levels of implementation.

these different levels, both when comparing one aid against another, and when selecting an aid for a particular individual.

In general, each successive category represents an increase in the complexity of the aid. It also generally represents an increase in the independence of communication for the handicapped individual, as well as a decrease in the amount of effort needed by the message receiver to interpret the handicapped person's message.

### Unaided Techniques

Unaided techniques are communication techniques that do not involve physical communication aids. These systems are limited because they are usually only viable between the NVSPH person and one or two persons who know him very well. The guessing game, or "intuition," is often effective between a mother and child for basic needs. It does not, however, provide the child with a means to ask questions or learn about the environment, nor does it provide the person with a viable means of expressing opinion or emotion or interacting with others.

### Fundamental Aids

Aids in this category represent basic methods of implementing scanning, encoding, or direct selection techniques. Any of the approaches, no matter how complex, could be implemented on the fundamental level, with the message being constructed and transcribed by the person working with the NVSPH person. For example, the fully independent, portable, encoding communication aid with printer could be implemented by an individual who would watch the child, interpret his movements, decode them to determine which letters the child was trying to indicate, and then write the letters to assemble the child's message. These techniques require a fair amount of effort on the part of the message receiver. Even when using a communication board, a second person is needed to interpret the child's movements, figure out which letters the child is pointing to, and assemble them to determine the message.

Fundamental techniques do have an advantage in that they are readily available to the teacher in the classroom. Most of the aids can be very easily fabricated by a teacher or by a local handyman. Their construction does not require any special expertise, since they generally do not incorporate any moving parts or electronics. These aids are also the most flexible and adaptable aids. They allow the greatest variation in symbol systems and are the easiest to modify to meet the changing needs of the individual. It is only the amount of time and effort on the part of the second person to use these aids for communication that keeps these aids from being used on a more widespread basis, and from fully meeting the communication needs of many NVSPH persons.

## Simple Electronic and Mechanical Aids

Aids in this category use an electronic or mechanical technique to interpret the person's motion and to transmit directly to the message receiver the letters, words, or pictures the person is trying to indicate. With these aids therefore, the message receiver does not interpret the NVSPH person's movement, but writes down or remembers the characters and assembles the message.

Because the person can (with the aid) directly produce the letters, pictures, etc., that make up the message, very little knowledge of the system is required by the message receiver. For this reason, the handicapped individual can generally communicate with a greater number of people by using this aid than by using simpler aids. Although the amount of work required by the message receiver is greatly reduced by these methods, the undivided attention of a second person is still necessary. This continues to be a problem if the NVSPH person's message is more than a few words long, or if the person wants to participate in group conversation or do independent work.

## Fully Independent Aids

The last two categories concern fully independent aids. An aid is fully independent if it has a printout or display (like a calculator's display). With these aids the NVSPH person has a means of assembling a message. The person can select letters that are assembled by the aid and printed out (or displayed) for the message receiver. The person needs no help in assembling a message and only needs the attention of the other person for a brief instant to read the completed message. With these aids, the person is able to participate in group conversations or classroom discussions and interrupts the class only for the brief amount of time it takes to read a completed message (rather than the entire time it takes to assemble it).

Many of these aids have some sort of printer, typewriter, or television display. With these aids, the person has a means of communication as well as a means of writing. This becomes very important if the NVSPH person is placed in an educational program. If the child is going to be held responsible for practicing lessons, doing homework, completing independent work, and taking tests, it will be necessary to have some means of writing without requiring the constant attention of a second person. This becomes even more evident when it is understood that a simple three-page book report can take between 7 and 12 hours to assemble, even if the child is using a letterboard (a relatively fast communication technique).

## Fully Independent, Portable Aids

Like the independent communication aids just discussed, portable aids allow the child to assemble a message completely independently. They also can move around with the user and function as the person's voice, rather than just a writing instrument.

In order to be considered portable, aids in this category need to incorporate some form of printout or readout other than a typewriter. For some of the aids, the typewriter is available as an accessory controlled by the aid. This provides the child with the ability to write longer messages in page form. This is very valuable in educational or vocational settings. Another form of page output is the television display. These displays, which resemble the TV displays in an airport (listing the flight schedules) have the advantage of being both highly visible and completely correctable. Because of these features, they are especially popular in educational settings. Their correctability is important because it allows the child to correct mistakes, and allows the teacher to separate inadvertent mistakes from mistakes made because the child truly does not understand something. The television display is also often less expensive than the specially adapted electric typewriters.

## Implications and Advantages of the Various Levels of Implementation

Looking at the various levels of implementation, it may appear that communication increases with complexity of the aid. While it is true that, as the aid becomes more complicated, less work needs to be done by the message receiver, it is not necessarily true that the *portable, independent* aids are the best aids for all NVSPH persons. There are many constraints that cause one aid to be more applicable to an individual than another. For instance, most of the independent aids cannot be used with pictures or symbols other than the alphabet. For this reason, these aids cannot be applied with children who are still on a picture level, children who cannot read, or children who will be communicating in only one- or two-symbol utterances. For these children, and for other persons just starting out, fundamental and simple aids are often more powerful because they can be used with letters, pictures, words, or special symbols. For developmental reasons, or for children who may not be able to read or spell, simpler aids may be more applicable.

Another restriction (which we hope is temporary) is that children are often not able to acquire the aid that is most appropriate for them because of financial restrictions. As the complexity of the aid increases, the cost of the aid goes up rapidly. Aids in the fundamental category generally cost between $5 and $50 if made at home, or between $10 and

$150 if purchased. The next level, simple electronic and mechanical aids, generally run from $50 or $100 to $1,000. Fully independent aids range in price from $1,000 to $7,000, depending upon how many accessories and different printouts are desired. Fully independent, portable aids cost about the same as the stationary aids. For aids that are portable and can also be used with a typewriter, the cost usually runs around $1,500 extra for a typewriter as an additional accessory.

Part of the reason for the high costs at the present time is the large amount of demonstration and information dissemination that must be done in connection with selling and distributing the aids. As these aids become more widely known, these "missionary" costs will decrease along with production costs. There should eventually be a decrease in the cost of the aids. Unfortunately, the cost to distribute and fit the aids will keep the prices higher than comparable mass-produced items. Although the cost of communication aids seems high when looked at alone, what is not seen is that it would cost from $4,000 to $8,000 a year to provide a child with a dedicated "second person" to interpret messages and allow independent work so the child could participate in an interactive classroom situation. When compared to the $400 cost of the more advanced aids ($3,000 divided by 10 years = $300 plus $100 maintenance = $400 per year) the cost of the aids does not seem so high. The cost of the aid can also be compared to the $1,500 to $2,500 per year (or even $24,000 per year in hospital school settings) being spent to keep many children in education programs (in which they cannot really successfully participate unless provided with an effective means to interact and communicate). Independent aids, therefore, seem to be not only necessary and appropriate, but also cost effective. It should be restated here as a reminder, though, that advanced aids are not appropriate for all children. It is often better to start a child on simpler aids until a need for more expensive and advanced aids has been established.

## PARTIAL SURVEY OF SCANNING AIDS

The survey that follows moves from simple aids to more complex aids. Only a few examples are given. There are many other aids, and readers are encouraged to check the bibliography at the end of this chapter for references (such as Vanderheiden and Grilley, 1976).

The first aid is a very simple rotating pointer aid, called the Roto-Com (Figure 10). This aid uses a linear scanning approach to provide the NVSPH person with a means of pointing. Because it uses a linear scanning approach, it is only useful with a limited number of pictures. It would be very slow if as many as 50 choices were displayed. Shown with

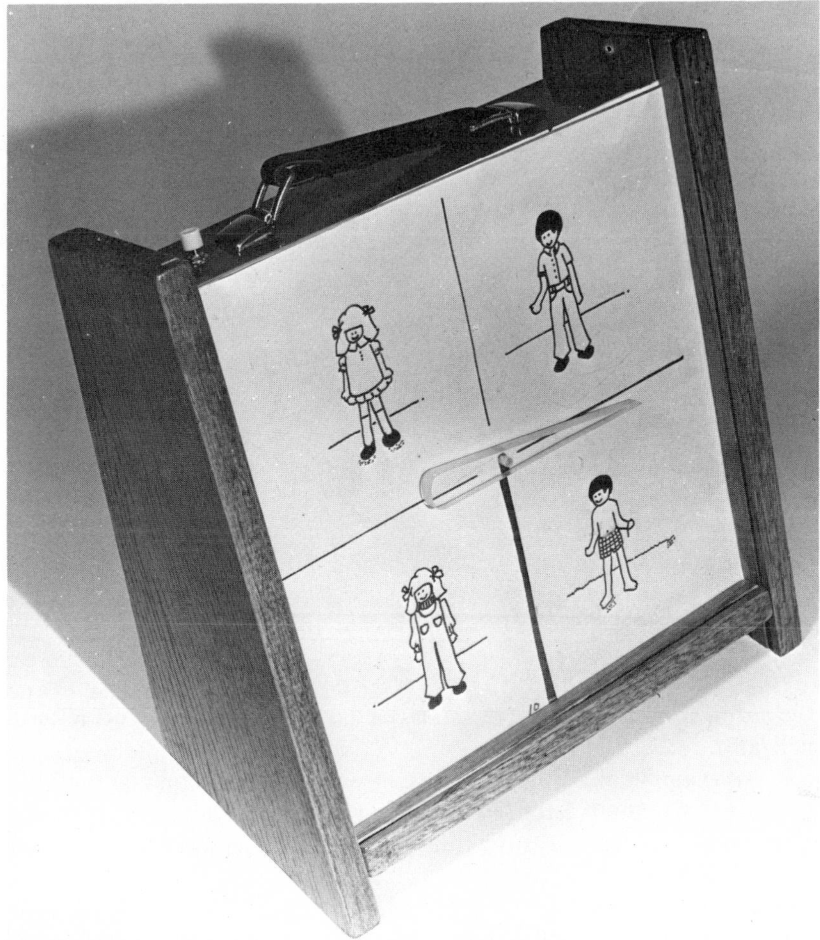

Figure 10. Roto-Com.

the aid are three of the many switches that may be used with it. As with all the aids in this category, there are many different switches that could be used by the NVSPH person, depending upon physical skills. The speed of all scanning aids is adjustable to meet the needs of specific individuals.

An "independent aid" using the linear scanning technique was developed by Palmstiernas Mekaniska Verkstad AB in Stockholm, Sweden (Figure 11). The aid, called the PMV Printer, helps alleviate the slower speed of the linear scanning process by introducing a two-speed scan. Two switches are used by the individual; one is held down to cause

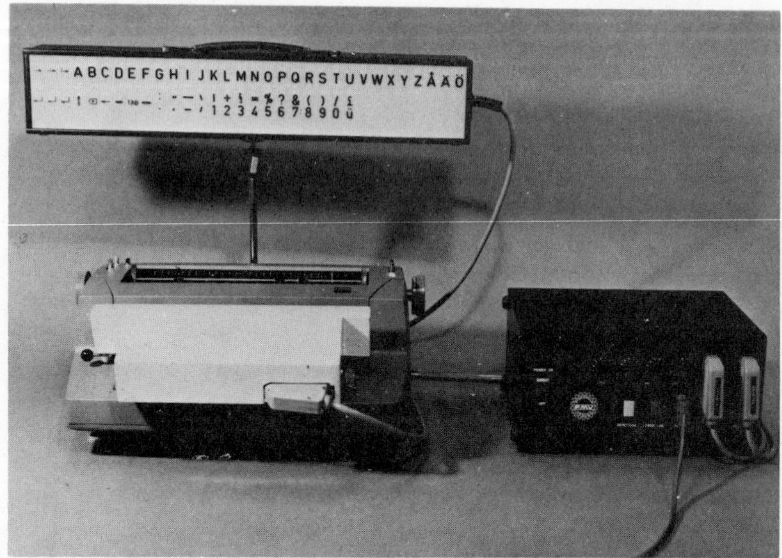


Figure 11. The PMV Printer, a two-speed, linear scanning, independent communication aid. (Developed by Palmstiernas Mekaniska Verkstad AB, Stockholm, Sweden.)

the aid to scan at the fast speed, and one is hit when the correct letter is indicated.

An example of a group-item (row-column) scanning aid is the Tufts Interactive Communicator (TIC) developed at Tufts University, Medford, Massachusetts (Figure 12). This aid is available in several versions, one of which incorporates an "anticipatory scanning" technique. The anticipatory scanning model, which is in final development, will use a limited set of rules to look at the last three letters printed when determining the next letters to be presented. A smaller, portable version of the TIC is also under development.

The first fully portable scanning aid to become available was the Portaprinter by Portacom, Inc., New York, New York (Figure 13). This aid uses a row-column scanning technique, which differs from other scanning techniques. Instead of returning to the upper right-hand corner after each selection, the aid continues its scanning pattern. The letters are arranged to form very commonly used patterns, and frequently used letters are repeated on the face of the display. The aid is normally battery operated, but can control two 110 volt outlets for environmental control when it is plugged into the wall. The output of the aid is on a ¼″-wide thermal strip-printer tape displayed at the very front edge of the aid. (A similar aid, using the conventional row-column scanning approach, has also been developed by Prentke-Romich, Shreve, Ohio.)

### Summary Remarks on Scanning Aids

It is important to remember that aids in this category can be controlled by almost anyone, no matter how severe the physical handicaps, if the receiver knows that the person is trying to communicate. There should be a switch to activate the scanning device. Once the person has a switch to operate, he has the physical means to use any of the scanning approaches or aids described. The disadvantage of the scanning approach is that it is slow for some types of handicaps. Other approaches may be faster. Those approaches, however, require increased physical skills. It is not always true that the scanning approach is the slowest technique for a given individual. If the individual has very restricted motion, but is fairly quick with it, the scanning approach may indeed be faster and less fatiguing than other approaches.

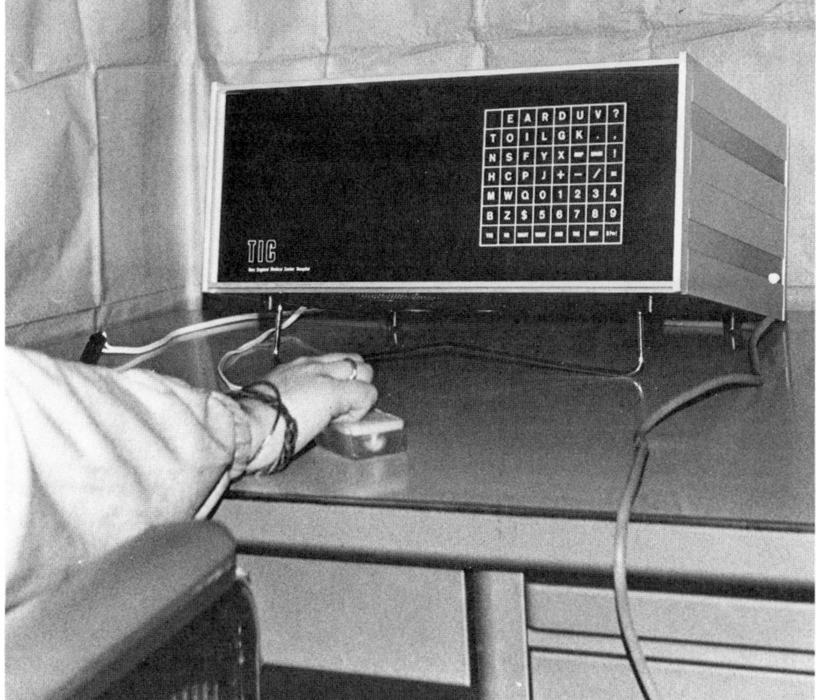


Figure 12. The TIC, a row-column scanning independent aid with electronic display and strip printer. Available with anticipatory scanning option. (Developed at Tufts University, Medford, Massachusetts.)

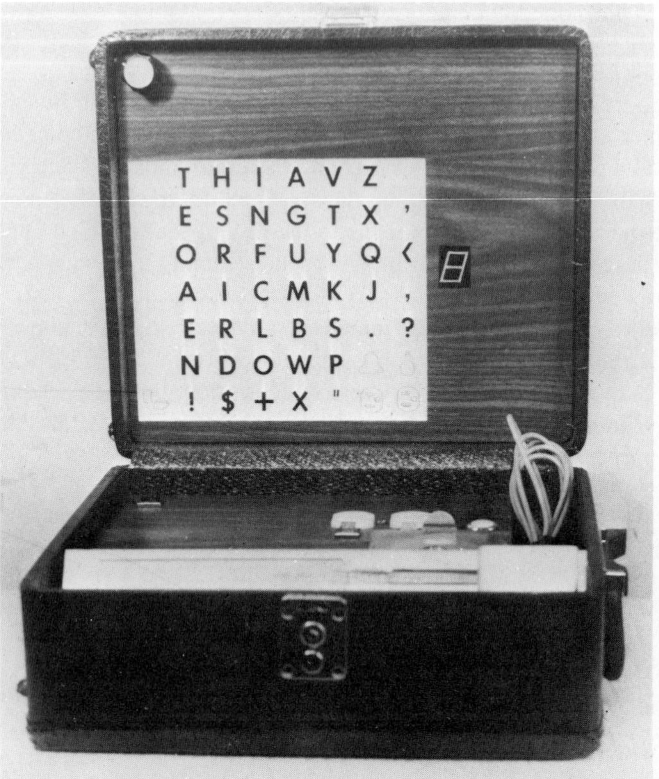


Figure 13. The Portaprinter, a portable independent aid that operates in a modified row-column scanning pattern, with strip-printer output. (Developed by Portacom, Inc., New York, New York.

## PARTIAL SURVEY OF ENCODING AIDS

Again, starting with simple aids, we begin with an encoding communication board developed by Karen Culhane at the Home de Rehabilitation, Huemoz, Switzerland (Figure 14). This board combines a color-number encoding technique similar to the one developed by McDonald and Schultz (1973). The vertical columns are numbered, whereas the horizontal columns are each a different color. The child uses the numbers and color patches around the outside of the board to communicate.

Figure 15 shows Jack Eichler with the original ETRAN chart he developed with Hugh C. Neale, Ridgefield, Connecticut. Figure 16 shows a version of the ETRAN-N which, when not in use, folds flat, providing a Plexiglas cover lap tray. A piece of Plexiglas is permanently screwed to

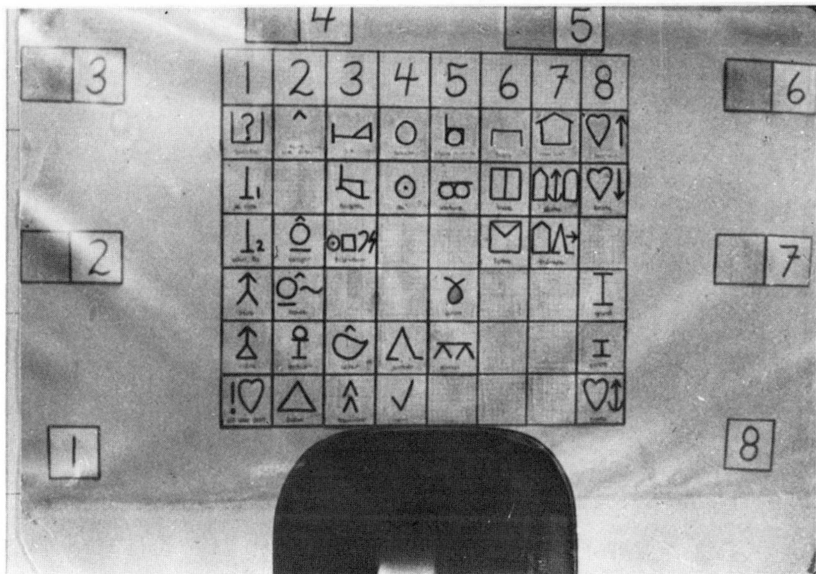


Figure 14. Two-movement encoding communication board. (Developed by Karen Culhane at the Home de Rehabilitation, Huemoz, Switzerland.)

Figure 15. The ETRAN eye gaze communication chart, a fundamental encoding aid. (Developed by Jack Eichler with Hugh C. Neale, Ridgefield, Connecticut.)

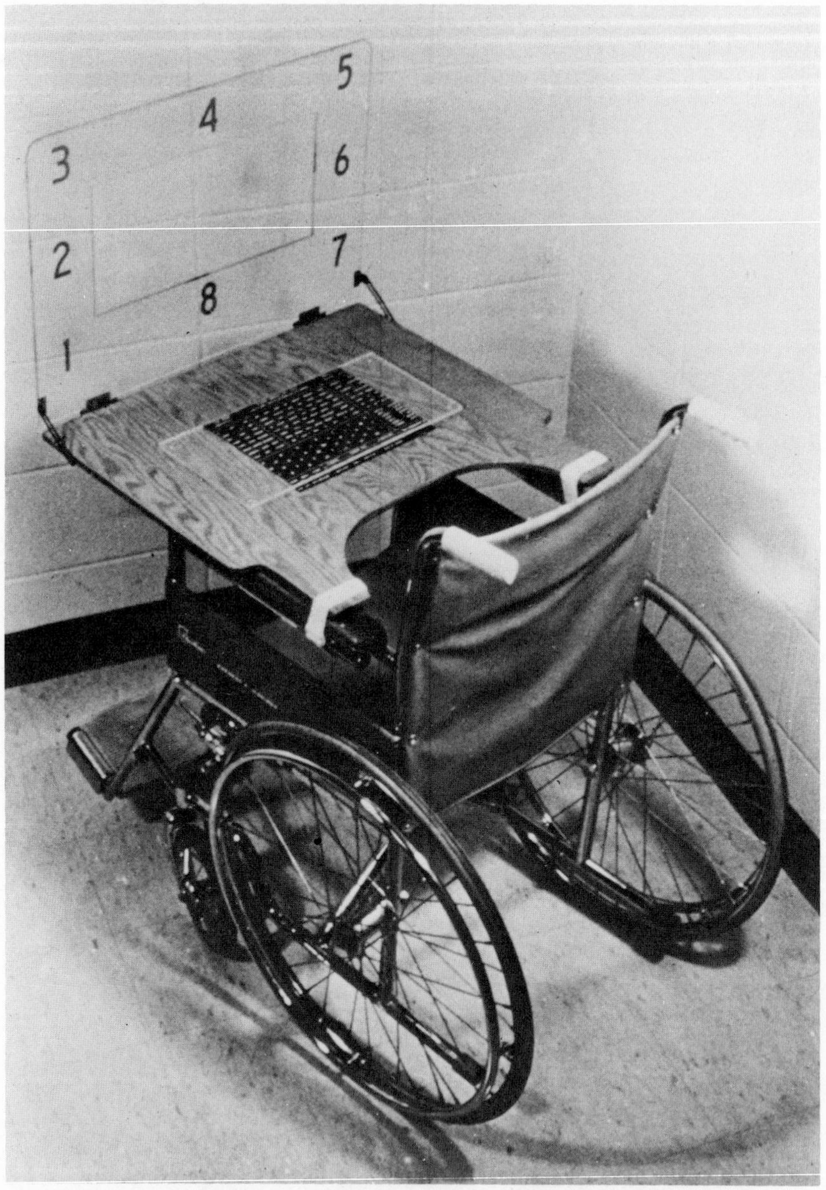


Figure 16. The ETRAN-N, a two-movement eye gaze encoding technique.

the tray. This fills the center hole in the ETRAN and makes a flat tray when it is folded down, and acts as a protective cover over the child's vocabulary.

The MC6400 communicator is a compact electronic communication aid developed by Medicel, Inc., Burlington, Vermont (Figure 17). The aid, which is entirely enclosed within the small package to the right, can decode Morse code from a variety of switch forms and display the results on the television screen. The unit provides high visibility and correctability, and has a printer option if typewritten copy is desired. The Medicel unit also takes a keyboard for input and can be used as a direct selection unit.

POSSUM Controls, Ltd., Aylesbury, England, has several encoding typewriter controllers. The one shown in Figure 18 is a unit originally developed by Hengrove. It uses a four-level sip and puff encoding system. Other models offered by POSSUM can be operated by chin and foot switches in addition to the sip and puff technique.

Figure 17. The MC6400, a Morse code–based independent communication aid. (Developed by Medicel, Inc., Burlington, Vermont.)

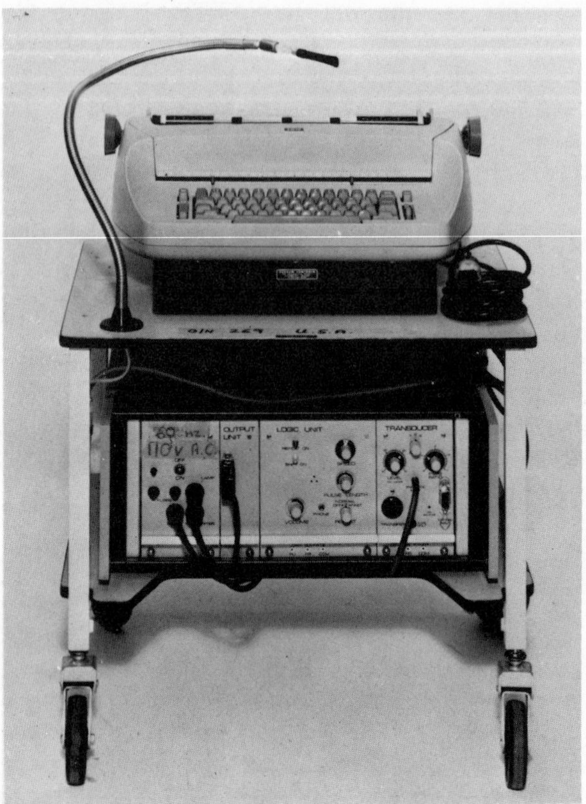


Figure 18. The Hengrove-POSSUM sip and puff typewriter system, an independent encoding aid. (Available from POSSUM Controls, Ltd., Aylesbury, England.)

## Summary Remarks on Encoding Aids

The basic advantage of encoding techniques over the scanning approach is the potential for greater speed for some individuals. Encoding techniques may require a greater degree of control on the part of the user. More complex movements, or more responses per message element, are usually required. In addition, some encoding schemes must be learned before a person is able to use the aid or technique. Clinicians who have used the encoding technique with children have indicated that the process of learning the simple encoding systems was much faster and easier for the children than they had at first expected.

A second advantage of the encoding system is the efficient accessibility of large vocabularies. Using only the numerals 1 through 10, and a three-movement encoding scheme, a person can have access to over 700 vocabulary elements in just a few seconds. This requires very fine motor control for direct pointing and is slow when used with the scanning techniques. Thus, encoding techniques may provide a faster means of communication and a means of gaining access to relatively large vocabularies, but they also require greater physical control and higher cognitive abilities than either the scanning or direct selection techniques.

## PARTIAL SURVEY OF DIRECT SELECTION AIDS

The most common direct selection aid is, of course, the communication board (Figure 19). As can be seen from these examples, communication boards take a variety of different forms. Even within the same setting or school (as is the case in Figures 20 to 25) communication boards for different children may have vastly different forms. It is interesting to note the different forms that a communication board used for a single child can take. Figure 22 was the first formal communication board for the child who is now using the communication board in Figure 23.

The communication board shown in Figure 26 is the thirteenth edition of a board designed by F. Hall Roe, a cerebral palsied individual who has been using communication boards since he was 12 years old. This last board was designed by him when he was in his 50s. These pre-

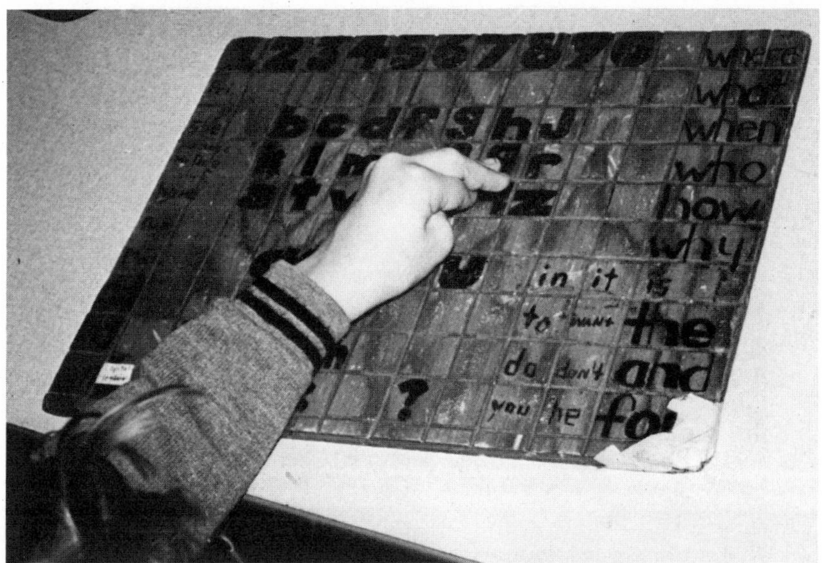


Figure 19. Manual communication board, a fundamental direct selection aid.

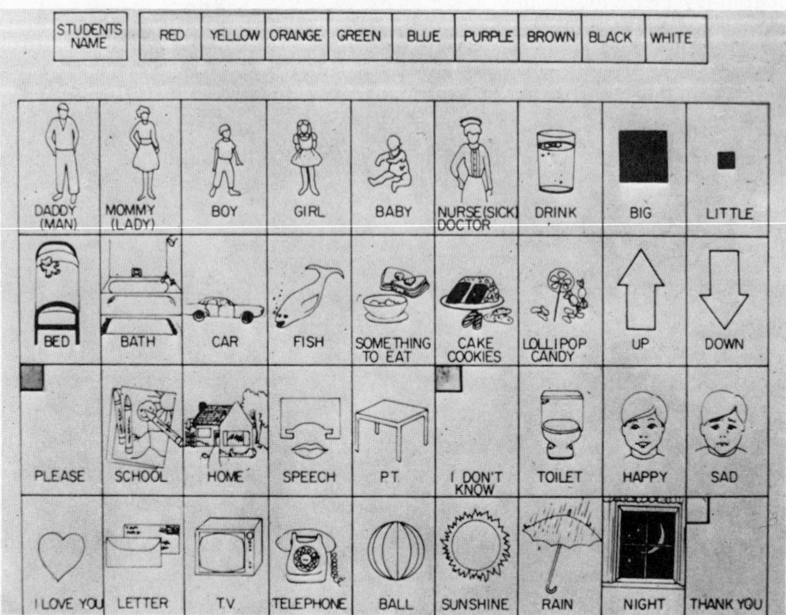


Figure 20. Picture/word board, University of Iowa Hospital School Nonoral Communication Project.

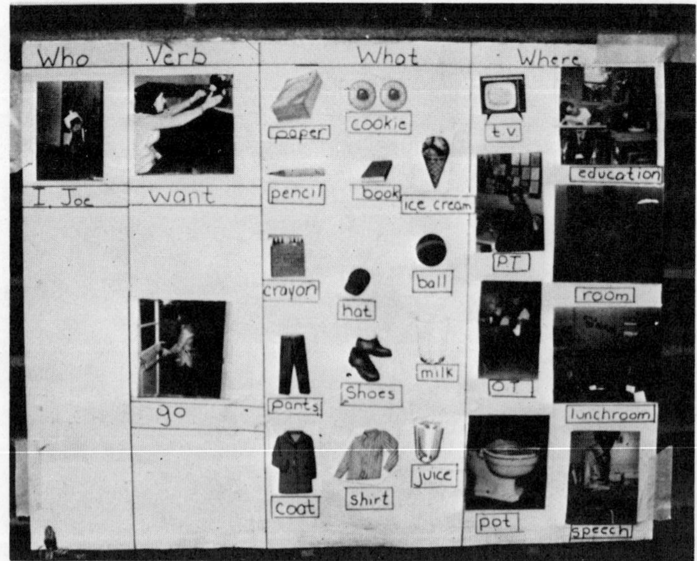


Figure 21. Picture/word board with alphabet, University of Iowa Hospital School Nonoral Communication Project.

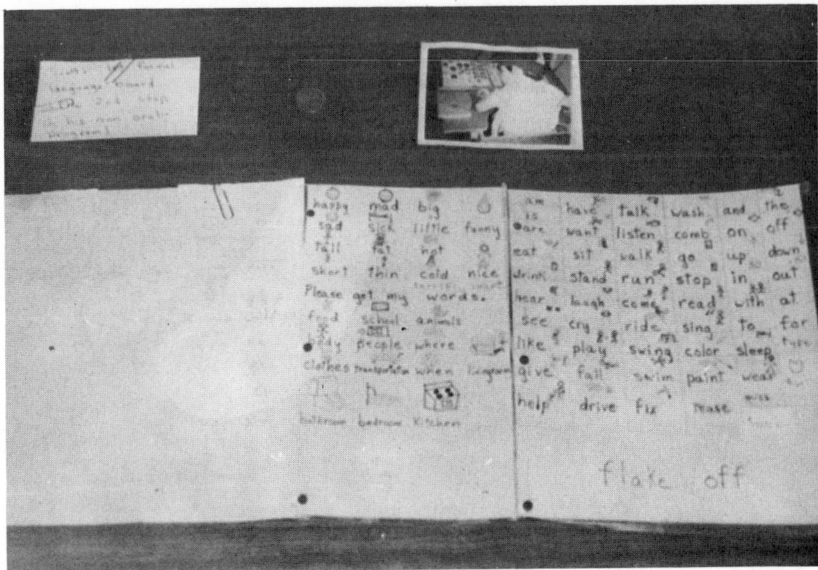


Figure 22. First formal communication board (second step of program) for one boy using headstick, University of Iowa Hospital School Nonoral Communication Project.

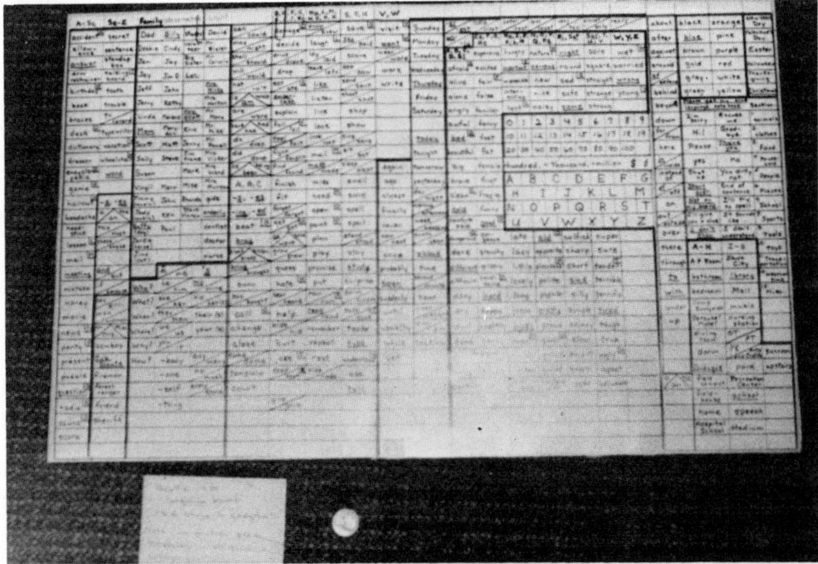


Figure 23. Later communication board (fifth stage) for the same boy as in Figure 22.

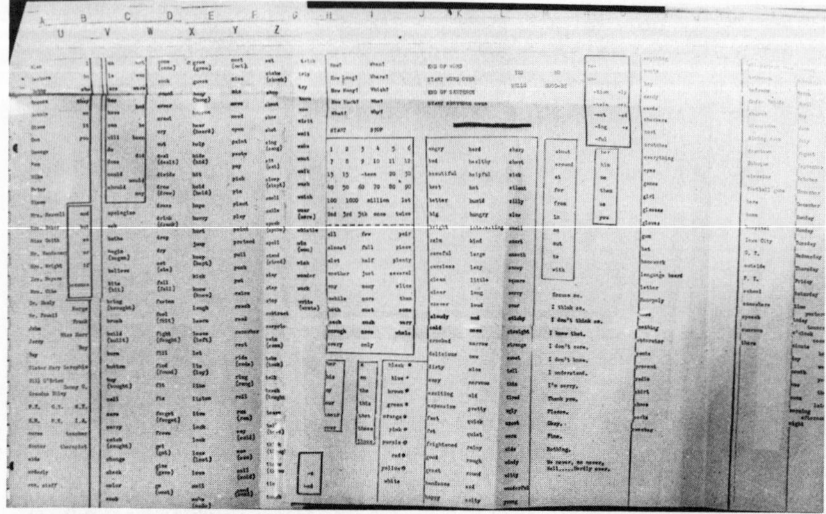

Figure 24. Communication book with foldout pages, University of Iowa Hospital School Nonoral Communication Project.

made boards are distributed as a service to the handicapped by Ghora Khan Grotto (a Masonic organization), St. Paul, Minnesota.

The communication board shown in Figure 27 was produced by the Ontario Crippled Children's Centre as part of its Symbol Communication Research Program. (Blissymbols are discussed in greater detail elsewhere in this book; see, particularly, McNaughton and Kates, Chapter 13).

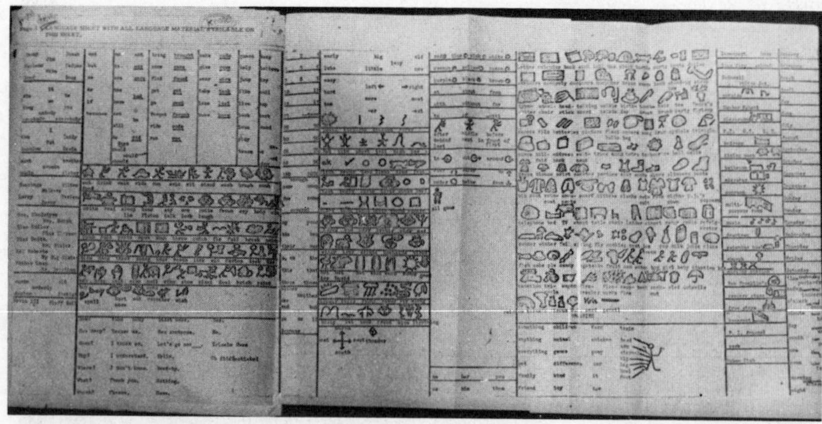

Figure 25. A communication board prepared on a typewriter, University of Iowa Hospital School Nonoral Communication Project.

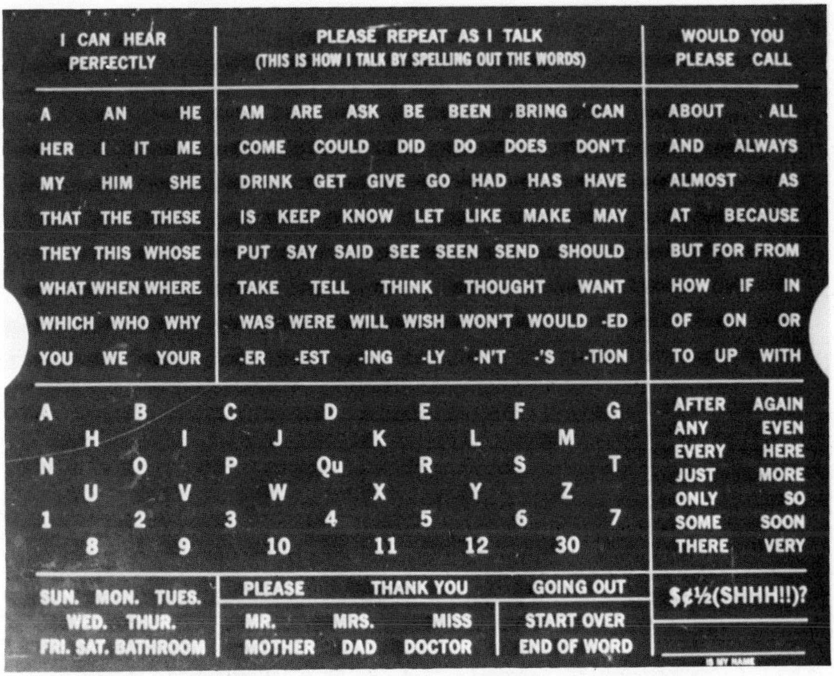

Figure 26. The F. Hall Roe communication board (notches are for hanging board between wheelchair hand push handles).

Moving to the independent aids, Figure 28 is a picture of an IBM typewriter with keyguard, armrests, and paper roll. IBM makes all these items available at low cost (the keyguard costs $10). IBM also has a special program whereby it sells used typewriters at the trade-in cost to handicapped individuals. With this procedure, handicapped individuals can secure the IBM typewriters for as little as $100 or $150, depending upon the condition of the machine.

Palmstiernas Mekaniska Verkstad AB, in Stockholm, Sweden, has produced several expanded and miniaturized keyboards for controlling typewriters. Figure 29 shows a collage of four of their expanded keyboards that are operated by different parts of the body.

Several aids specifically designed for the deaf are also used by severely physically handicapped persons. One is a portable communication aid developed for deaf persons in the United States. This unit, called the MCM, is distributed by Micon Industries, in Oakland, California. (Figure 30). The unit is completely self-contained and has a special low-power 32-character display. In addition, the aid has a telephone cradle so it can be used to communicate to other similar aids over a phone line.

| 0 | 1 | 2 | 3 | 4 | 5 | 6 | 7 | 8 | 9 |
|---|---|---|---|---|---|---|---|---|---|
| hello, goodbye | question | I,me,my | like | happy | do,make action | food | pen,pencil | friend | animal |
| please | why | you,your | want | angry | mouth | drink | paper, page | GOD | bird |
| thanks | how | man | come | afraid | eye | sleep | book | home | flower |
| I'm sorry | who | lady | give | funny | legs | toilet | table | school | water |
| opposite | what | father | make | good | hand | pain | television | hospital | sun |
| much, many | which | mother | help | big | ear | clothing | news | store | weather |
| music | where | brother | think | young,new | nose | outing | word | show | day |
|  | when | sister | know | difficult | head | car | light | room | week-end |
|  | how many | teacher | wash | hot | name | wheelchair | game,toy | street | birthday |

ONTARIO CRIPPLED CHILDREN'S CENTRE
SYMBOL COMMUNICATION RESEARCH PROJECT
100 VOCABULARY MARCH 1974

Figure 27. A Blissymbolics communication board, one of available preprinted formats. (Produced by Ontario Crippled Children's Centre, Ontario, Canada.)

This aid could be fitted with a keyguard to facilitate its use by more severely physically handicapped persons.

Probably the most compact and portable of all the independent aids is the Canon Communicator developed as a joint effort between Canon Incorporated in Japan and Drs. von Uden and von Mierlo in The Netherlands (Figure 31). The Canon Communicator straps to the wrist and has a small strip-printer output. In order to facilitate use by persons with muscular problems, special keyguards have been designed. They are shown in the background. Canon has also experimented with a slightly larger version with a built-in battery supply and a typewriter arrangement for the keyboard.

A recent development in the field has been the introduction of voice synthesis aids. Figure 32 shows a 128-square direct selection voice synthesis aid marketed by HC Electronics, Palo Alto, California. The aid is able to function in either a word or phoneme mode.

The Auto-Com (Figure 33) is a portable communication aid that utilizes an "auto-monitoring" technique which enables it to operate by even very erratic pointing motions (see Vanderheiden and Grilley, 1976). The aid has an optional 32-character LED display, in addition to its built-in 28-column printer output, making the aid completely correctable and portable. The aid is capable of printing single letters or whole words, phrases, or sentences with a single pointing motion. One of the unique features of this aid is that the vocabulary as well as the arrangement of the words and letters on the surface of the aid can be selected and changed by the user to meet specific needs. A text-to-speech voice output is also under development for the aid.

### Summary Remarks on Direct Selection Approach

The direct selection approach is straightforward and does not require the user to learn a special technique. This approach also provides good direct feedback and can be used with persons experiencing cognitive handicaps. In addition, the potential speed of this approach is quite high, limited only by the pointing speed of the NVSPH person.

A major limitation of these aids is that they generally require a large range of motion and fine motor skills. Nevertheless, the direct selection approach provides a relatively fast, fairly simple, and straightforward means of communication for the person who can develop the range of motion and the control necessary to use a letterboard or keyboard.

Figure 28. IBM typewriter with standard modifications available, a direct selection independent aid.

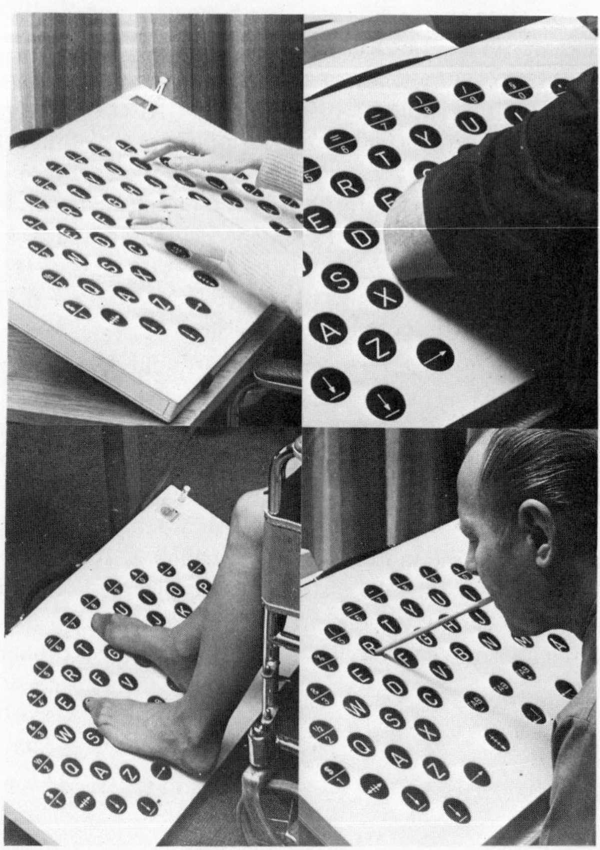

Figure 29. PMV expanded keyboards for typewriter control, direct selection independent aids. (Developed by Palmstiernas Mekaniska Verkstad AB, Stockholm, Sweden.)

## SUMMARY AND CONCLUSIONS

There are numerous techniques, each with its own advantages and disadvantages, and no easy guidelines to selecting particular approaches for a particular individual can be set forth. One might start with the direct selection approach if the person has those abilities, because it seems to offer the greatest potential, speed, and simplicity. Furthermore, if the person is able to develop enough skill to use a typewriter, a very inexpensive and powerful means for expression is provided. Even for persons who cannot learn to spell, the straightforward, direct selection approach may be very important in enhancing the early acquisition of communicative skill.

Figure 30. The MCM, a portable independent direct selection aid primarily designed as a telephone communication aid for the deaf. Modification for the physically handicapped available. (Distributed by Micon Industries, Oakland, California.)

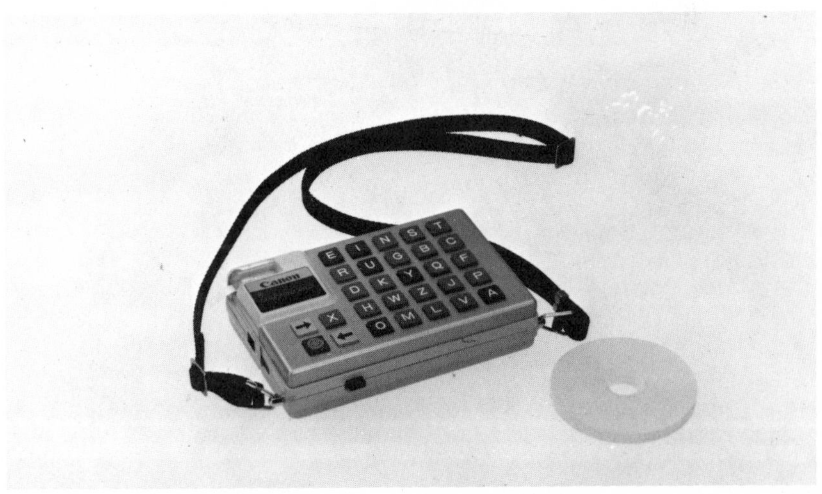


Figure 31. The Canon Communicator, a portable independent communication aid using auto-monitoring techniques. (Developed jointly by Canon Incorporated in Japan and Drs. von Uden and von Mierlo in The Netherlands.)

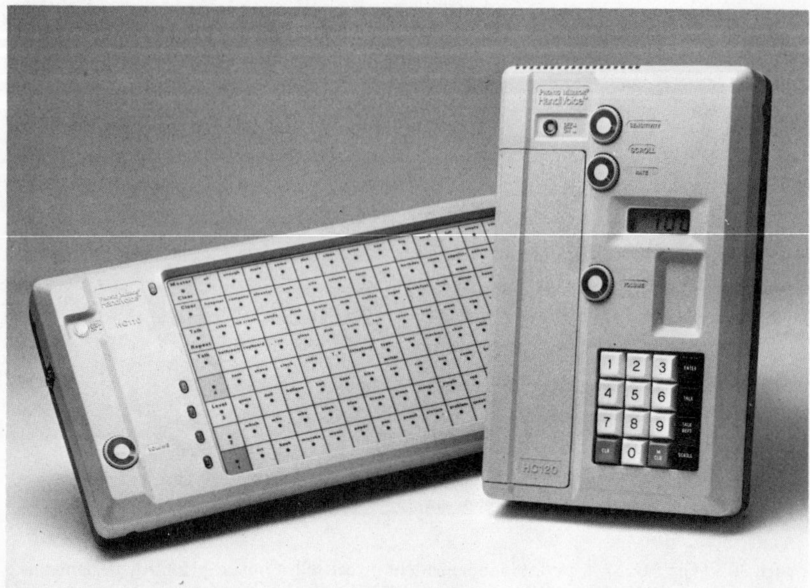


Figure 32. The Handivoice, a portable voice synthesis communication aid. (Marketed by HC Electronics, California.)

Figure 33. The Auto-Com, a flexible user-programmable portable communication and control aid (Telesensory Systems Incoporated, Palo Alto, California.)

Many severely handicapped individuals, however, will not be able to use any of the direct selection approaches, particularly in initial program steps. It is important to provide these individuals with an appropriate communication/interaction system even while working on other skills such as pointing. Some communication system should be established immediately so the individual has a viable means of interaction while work proceeds on the development of additional skills.

It is apparent that more work is needed on the development of very simple techniques for children, including young children, and for persons with severe cognitive deficits. Through the techniques discussed here, perhaps some ideas have been generated about how severely handicapped persons may be provided with "a means to indicate" pictures, words, or symbols that they can then use to communicate and interact with other persons.

## ACKNOWLEDGMENTS

The authors would like to acknowledge the input of Donna J. DePape in the preparation of the application section of this chapter.

## REFERENCES

McDonald, E. T., and Schultz, A. R. 1973. Communication boards for cerebral palsied children. J. Speech Hear. Disord. 38:73–88.

Vanderheiden, G. C., and Grilley, K. (eds.). 1976. Non-Vocal Communication Techniques and Aids for the Severely Physically Handicapped. University Park Press, Baltimore.

## ADDITIONAL READINGS

Anderson, K. 1978. An eye position controlled typewriter. *In* P. Nelson (ed.), Proceedings of Workshop on Communication Aids, June, Ottawa. Canadian Medical and Biological Engineering Society, c/o National Research Council, Ottawa, Ontario, Canada K1A 0R8.

Beesley, M. 1978. The importance of positioning and seating for the cerebral palsied child. *In* P. Nelson (ed.), Proceedings of Workshop on Communication Aids, June, 1977. Canadian Medical and Biological Engineering Society, c/o National Research Council, Ottawa, Ontario, Canada K1A 0R8.

Brulisaur, P. 1974. Making rehabilitation systems. *In* Proceedings of the Seminar on Electronic Controls for the Severely Disabled, pp. 37–39. Vancouver, British Columbia, Canada.

Calculator, S. N. Design and revision of non-oral systems of communication for the mentally retarded physically handicapped: A discussion of the uni-color binary visual encoding board with general implications for communication. Working Paper 101, Department of Communicative Disorders, University of Wisconsin-Madison, Madison.

Crochetiere, J. W., Foulds, R. A., and Sterne, R. G. 1974. Computer-aided motor communication. *In* Proceedings of the 1974 Conference on Engineering Devices in Rehabilitation, pp. 1–5, Boston.

Foulds, R. A., and Gaddis, E. 1975. The practical application of an electronic communication device in the special needs classroom. *In* Proceedings of the Seminar on Devices and Systems for the Disabled, pp. 77–80. Philadelphia.

Henkel, J. E. 1977. A micro-processor-based gesture entry non-vocal communication system. *In* Proceedings of the Fourth Annual Conference on Systems and Devices for the Disabled, Seattle, June, 1977. Sponsored by Department of Rehabilitation Medicine, University of Washington. Available from Continuing Medicine Education, University of Washington, School of Medicine, E303 HSB SC50, Seattle, Wash. 98195.

Holt, C. S., Buelow, D., and Vanderheiden, G. 1978. Interface switch profile and annotated list of commercial switches (1976). *In* G. C. Vanderheiden (ed.), Non-Vocal Communication Resource Book. University Park Press, Baltimore. (Also available separately from the Trace Center, University of Wisconsin-Madison, Madison, Wis. 53706.)

Holt, C. S., Raitzer, G. A., Harris, D., and Vanderheiden, G. Formative evaluation/design of a low cost scanning aid. The Trace Center, University of Wisconsin-Madison, Madison.

Kafafian, H. 1970–1973. Study of Man-Machine Communication Systems for the Handicapped (3 vols.). Cybernetics Research Institute, Inc., Washington, D.C.

Lloyd, L. L. (ed.). 1976. Communication Assessment and Intervention Strategies. University Park Press, Baltimore.

Maling, R. G., and Clarkson, D. C. 1963. Electronic controls for the tetraplegic. (POSSUM). Paraplegia 1:161–174.

Newell, A. F. 1974. The talking brooch, a communication aid. *In* K. Copeland (ed.), Aids for the Severely Handicapped. Sector Publishing, Ltd., London.

POSSUM Introductory Description and POSSUM-Control System for Severely Disabled, General Description. 1967. P.O.S.M. Research Project, Aylesbury, England.

Rinard, G. 1978. An ocular-controlled video terminal. *In* P. Nelson (ed.), Proceedings of Workshop on Communication Aids, Ottawa, June, 1977. Canadian Medical and Biological Engineering Society, c/o National Research Council, Ottawa, Ontario, Canada, K1A 0R8.

Ring, N. 1978. Specification of interfaces for communication aids. *In* P. Nelson (ed.), Proceedings of Workshop on Communication Aids, Ottawa, June, 1977. Canadian Medical and Biological Society, c/o National Research Council, Ottawa, Ontario, Canada K1A 0R8.

Ross, A., and Flanagan, K. 1977. Communication system using Morse code to printed English translation. *In* Proceedings of the Fourth Annual Conference on Systems and Devices for the Disabled, Seattle, June, 1977. Sponsored by Department of Rehabilitation Medicine, University of Washington. Available from Continuing Medical Education, University of Washington, School of Medicine, E303 HSB SC50, Seattle, Wash. 98195.

Roy, O. Z. 1965. Technical note: A communication system for the handicapped. Medical Electronic and Biological Engineering, Vol. 3, pp. 427–429. Pergamon Press, Oxford, England.

Vanderheiden, G. C. (ed.). 1978. Non-Vocal Communication Resource Book. University Park Press, Baltimore.

Vanderheiden, G., and Grilley, K. 1976. Non-Vocal Communication Techniques and Aids. University Park Press, Baltimore.

Vanderheiden. G. C., and Luster, M. J. 1975. Non-vocal communication techniques and aids as aids to the education of the severely physically handicapped: A state of the art review. The Trace Center, University of Wisconsin-Madison, Madison.

Vanderheiden, G. C., Volk, A. M., and Geisler, C. D. An alternate interface to computers for the physically handicapped. AFIPS Conference Proceedings of the 1974 National Computer Conference 43:115–121.

Vicker, B. (ed.). 1974. Non-Oral Communication System Project 1964/1973. Campus Stores, Iowa City.

chapter 13

# The Application of Blissymbolics

*Shirley McNaughton*

*Blissymbolics Communication Institute*
*Toronto, Ontario*
*Canada*
*Ontario Crippled Children's*
*Treatment Centre*
*Toronto, Ontario*
*Canada*

*Barbara Kates*

*Blissymbolics Communication Institute*
*Toronto, Ontario*
*Canada*
*Ottawa Crippled Children's*
*Treatment Centre*
*Ottawa, Ontario*
*Canada*

contents

Blissymbolics[1] is a graphic nonalphabet communication system. The original intention of its creator, Charles K. Bliss, was the construction of a "simple system of 100 logical pictorial symbols which can be operated and read like 1 + 2 = 3 in all languages" (Bliss, 1965). From 1942 to 1965, Bliss expanded and developed his system, which he dreamed would be used in international communication and commerce, industry and science. He also envisioned its "simple semantics, logic and ethics" assisting "even children" in solving their problems. The system was first applied as an augmentative aid to speech when it was introduced to physically handicapped, nonspeaking children at the Ontario Crippled Children's Centre, Toronto, Canada, in October, 1971.

Blissymbolics is a semantically based system. Most components relate directly or indirectly to meaning; for a few configurations, meaning has been assigned arbitrarily. Thus, Blissymbols contain pictographic, ideographic, and/or arbitary components which are organized in different combinations. The meaning represented by each symbol is derived through interpretation of the meanings of its component parts. When symbols are sequenced in Blissymbol sentences, they provide a comprehensive communication medium capable of covering every aspect of human experience. Because Bliss's intention was to create a system for use between different language groups, the rebus principle in which one symbol can represent words that *sound* the same but that have different *meanings* (e.g., *sea* and *see*) is never used. The homonyms of spoken language, such as *present* tense and *present* as gift, are depicted by two different Blissymbols according to the meaning represented by each word.

Blissymbols are constructed from a small number of basic geometric shapes:

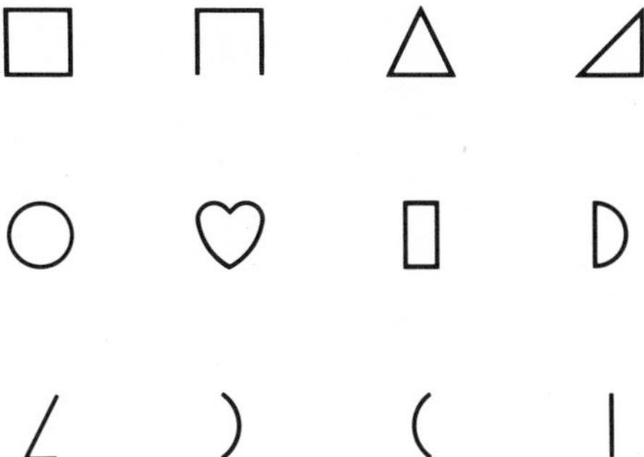

[1] For a more detailed description of the application of Blissymbolics, see Silverman, McNaughton, and Kates (1978); for an explanation of individual symbols for use within an applied context, see Hehner (1979); and for full exposition of the system and the rationale for each Blissymbol, see Bliss (1965).

Blissymbols can be categorized into four types:

1. *Pictographic Blissymbols*

building tree man woman chair container

2. *Ideographic Blissymbols*

happy (heart for feeling; arrow pointing up) protection (roof of building) (to) come (arrow depicting movement toward) over between (dot denoting position)

3. *Arbitrary Blissymbols*

the a this that what

4. *Mixed Blissymbols* (composed of pictographic [P], ideographic [I] and/or arbitrary [A] components)

question (open enclosure [I] and question mark [A]) answer (closed enclosure [I] and question mark [A]) father (man [P, I] who protects [I]) when (what [A] time [I])

Meaning is determined by:

1. *Size*

enclosure thing

2. *Position*

earth sky

3. *Direction/orientation*

room door opening

4. *Spacing*

far near

5. *Pointers*

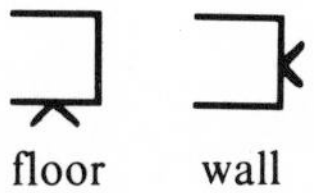

floor wall

6. *Positional reference*

a. For example, position of arrow with regard to referent line

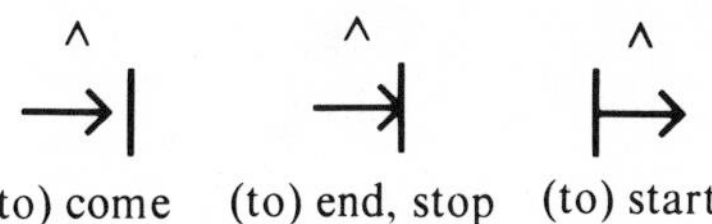

(to) come (to) end, stop (to) start

b. For example, position of dot with regard to referent enclosure

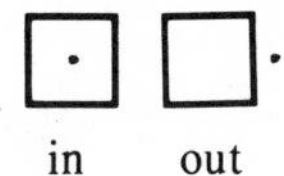

in out

The meaning represented by each component contributes to the meaning of the complete symbol:

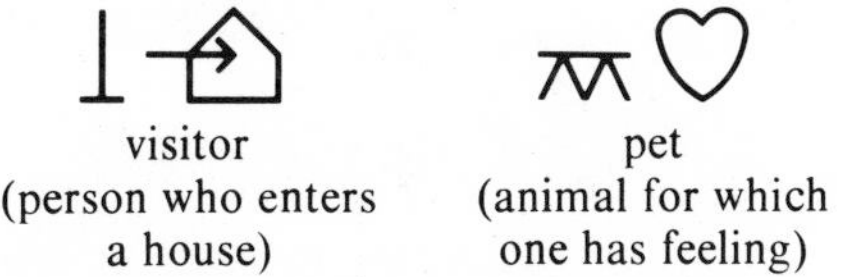

visitor (person who enters a house) — pet (animal for which one has feeling)

Blissymbols can have several translations, always relating to the meaning or concept represented by the symbol within the situational context:

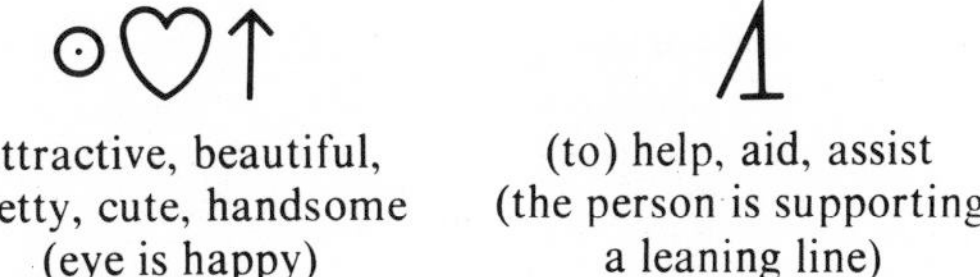

attractive, beautiful, pretty, cute, handsome (eye is happy) — (to) help, aid, assist (the person is supporting a leaning line)

Indicators further extend the meaning to be derived from each symbol:

1. *Plural indicator*

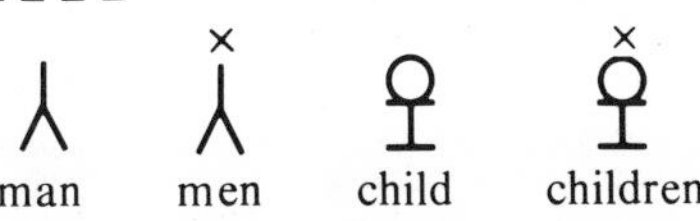

man men child children

2. *Thing indicator*

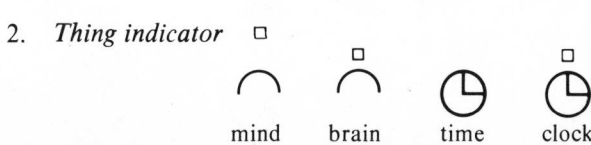

mind brain time clock

3. *Action (verb) indicator* ∧

(to) rain

4. *Description (evaluation) indicator* ∨

rainy

5. *Tense indicators* ) (

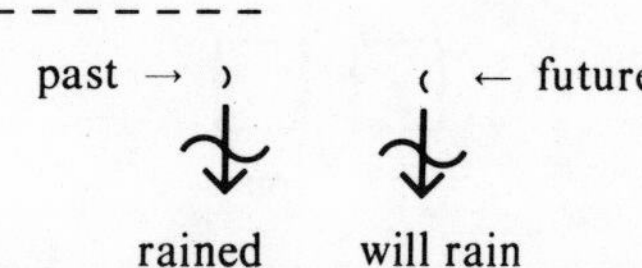


rained will rain

Tense indicators are derived from time symbols (present tense is unmarked):

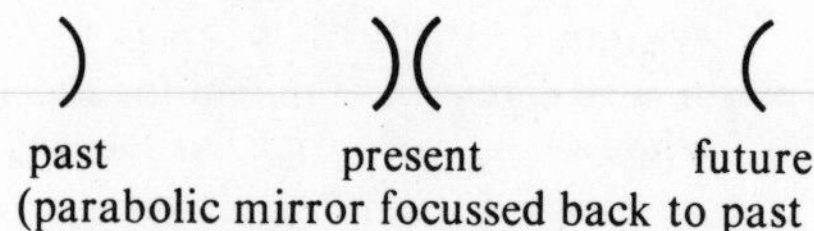

past present future
(parabolic mirror focussed back to past and ahead to future)

The indicators currently utilized by Blissymbol users are given below:

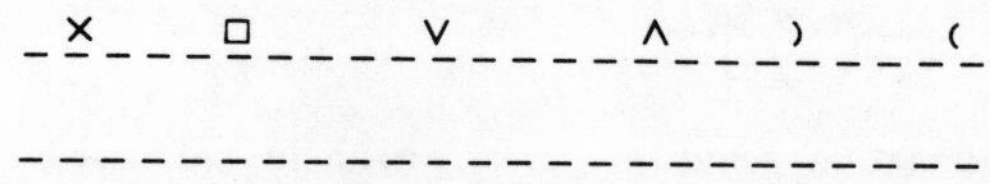

plural thing description (evaluation) action past future

Numbers are used with Blissymbols, to create new meanings.

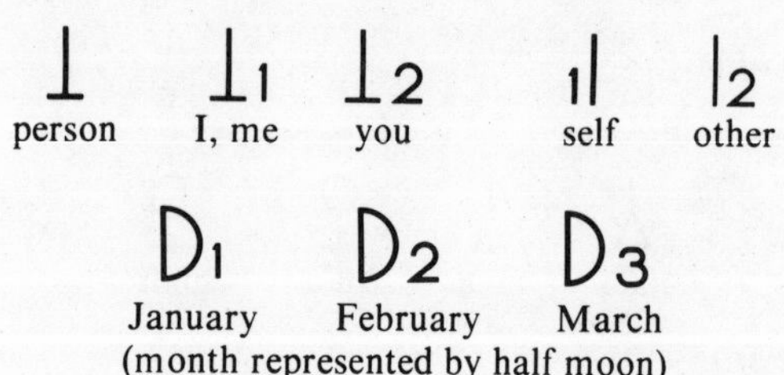

person I, me you self other

January February March
(month represented by half moon)

Strategies have been identified and used to enlarge the limited Blissymbol vocabulary that is accessible to the physically handicapped user. For example:

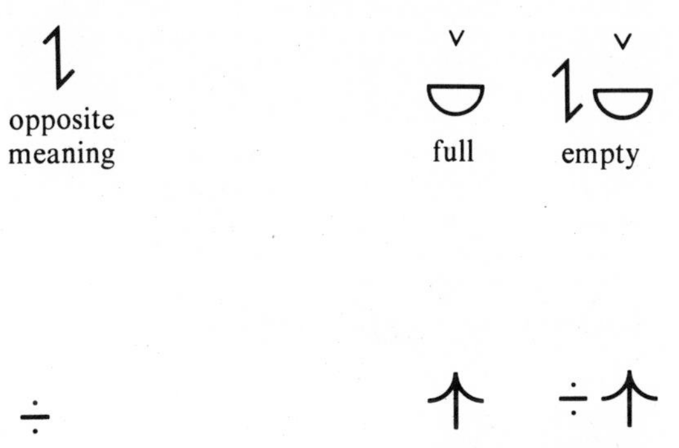


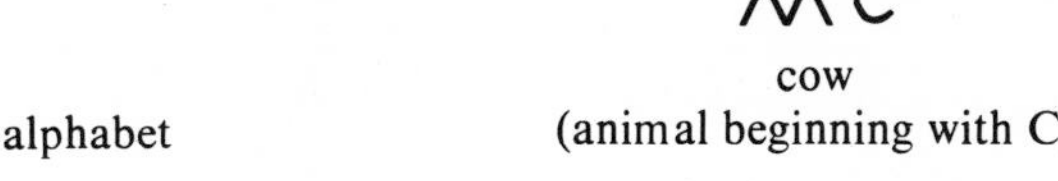


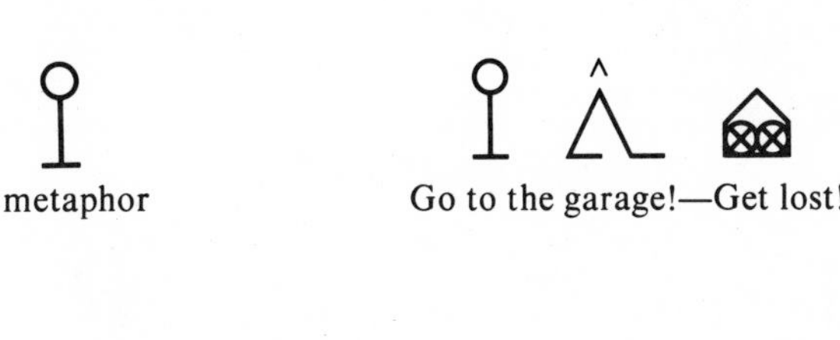

Symbols recur in many combinations:

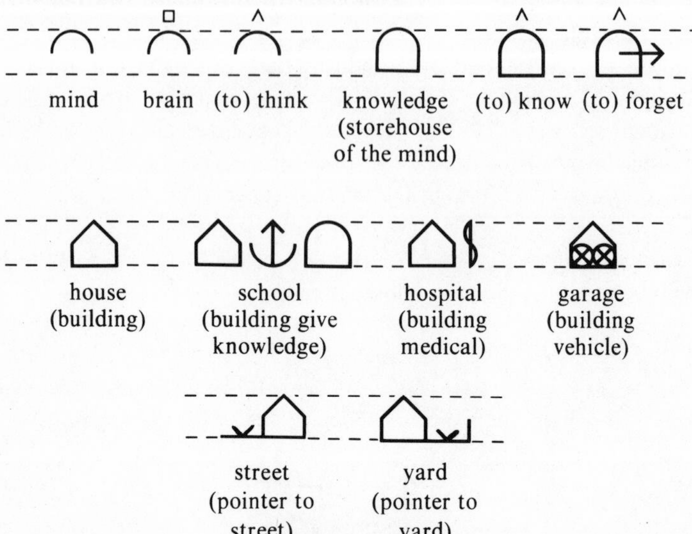


Some examples of Blissymbol sentences follow:

1. *Statement*

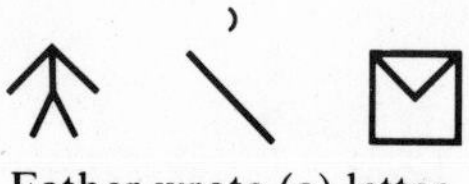

Father wrote (a) letter.

2. *Question*

When did father write (the) letter?

3. *Polite command*

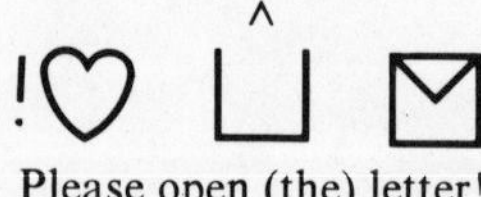

Please open (the) letter!

To preserve the standard form of all Blissymbols included in Blissymbolics and to recognize symbols created by individual symbol users, the *combine* strategy has been devised. Use of this strategy provides a means for independently and spontaneously creating new symbols for personal use, and of identifying these symbols as separate from the standard Blissymbols. Through marking newly created symbols as provisional by using the *combine* symbol, the user can explore and evaluate the effectiveness of symbols before proposing them to the Blissymbolics Communication Institute (BCI) for inclusion in the standard Blissymbol vocabulary. All users are encouraged to maintain the international standard form of the symbols contained in Blissymbolics by creating new symbols using the *combine* strategy and to contribute to the system's ongoing development by sending suggestions for new symbols to the BCI.

Examples of created symbols that have been submitted to the BCI are given below:

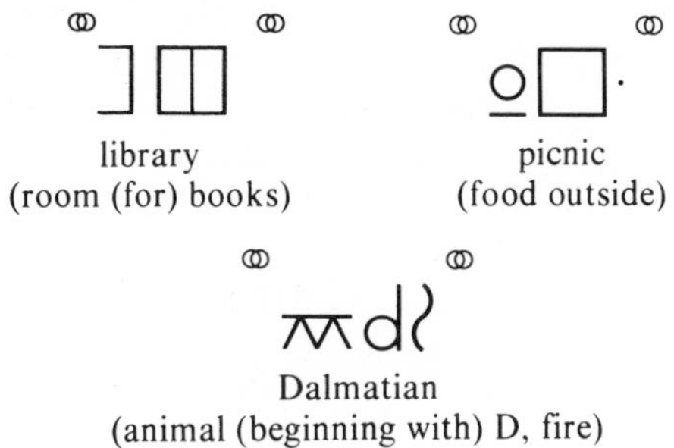


## APPLICATION OF BLISSYMBOLICS

Blissymbolics has been demonstrated as particularly valuable to physically handicapped persons whose physical limitations restrict them to a specific number of symbols. A limited number of Blissymbols arranged on a display can provide extensive communication potential.

The first successful users were children with cerebral palsy who had developed receptive language at age level or slightly below, and for whom an augmentative expressive communication system was required (Kates and McNaughton, 1975). The comprehensive and easily acquired communication capability provided by the Blissymbol display allowed the children to quickly move to a communication level well beyond the limited scope of a picture board, without requiring the developmental competencies and the time investment for the acquisition of the reading and spelling skills prerequisite to using a word board.

The clinical observations of early Blissymbol instructors have been supported by the findings of a Formative Evaluation of the Ontario Crippled Children's Centre, Symbol Communication Programme, contracted by the Ontario Ministry of Education. Results of the study, involving 130 symbol users within 21 settings, are reported in *Handbook of Blissymbolics*, by Silverman, McNaughton, and Kates (1978) and describe in detail the effects of an instructional program in Blissymbolics upon communicative capability. The study findings demonstrate the applicability of Blissymbols within a broad age and intellectual range for users with moderate and severe physical disabilities. Many positive changes were reported, as students developed skill in Blissymbol communication. In addition to general improvement in communication abilities, some degree of improvement was reported in physical areas of functioning, such as speech, hand control, head control, and general body relaxation.

Widespread observations of changes in the social and psychological development of the symbol users were made. Improvements in overall level of motivation and personal growth were reported, with changes affecting the emotional, behavioral, and social areas of development. Reports cited that students were happier, emotionally more stable, more independent, less frustrated, more stimulated and motivated, showed more pride in accomplishments, showed more initiative, were better able to accept failure, and were better able to express feelings and questions. Improved personal adjustment, increased maturity and self-confidence, and improved self-image were also noted.

Behaviorally, children were reported to be showing less hyperactivity and aggression, greater attentiveness, reduced behavior problems, and increased spontaneity and participation.

Socially, the children were described as having greater contact with adults and general increased social interaction with both adults and peers. Social integration seemed to be facilitated by the uniqueness, scope, and creative potential of the system—all of which seemed to generate interest on the part of many people.

In many cases, the symbol users were reported to be presenting such an improved image that higher expectations needed to be set as their potential abilities were revealed.

Results of the Blissymbol Program at Central Wisconsin Center (Harris-Vanderheiden et al., 1977) support these findings and, in addition, report that, as a direct result of increased communication skill, some of the children have been enrolled in more intensive educational programs.

The successful Blissymbol user can best be described as "an active, participating, contributing human being" (Silverman, McNaughton, and Kates, 1978). Having said this, it is important to exercise caution before implementing symbol programs. Because of the enthusiasm generated by an effective and appropriate Blissymbol instructional program, there is danger that Blissymbolics will be viewed as a panacea for all communication difficulties. Potential users must be cognizant that the application of Blissymbolics is in its infancy and requires much further study and refinement. As a communication medium it has been introduced with some encouraging results to other areas of exceptionality: adults with cerebral palsy, children and adults within a broad range of mental retardation, aphasic children and adults, and deaf children and adults. Blissymbolics is being explored as an educational tool for blind, deaf, and autistic students; for prereading activities; for remedial reading programs; for visual-perceptual remediation; for second language teaching; for concept and language development; as an enrichment activity; and for communicating with students with severe behavioral and emotional problems.

Although some of the newer applications of Blissymbolics show promise, there is need at this early stage of application for an approach that includes an ongoing, cooperative relationship among researchers with a theoretical perspective, clinicians with an awareness of the nonspeaking person's needs, and symbol users and their families. An important function of the Blissymbolics Communication Institute is the facilitation of Blissymbol programs through establishing a liaison between the BCI and different professionals, as well as the provision of information and training.

**Application Issues**

For those considering introducing Blissymbolics as an augmentative communication system for nonspeaking persons, the following approach is suggested as a guide:

**1. Establish that the student has the capability for communication.** Observe whether or not the individual is capable of interacting purposefully within his environment, i.e., that he is capable of functional communication. With individuals functioning at lower intellectual levels for whom a decision regarding this capability is difficult, Hollis and Carrier (1978) offer prerequisites to functional communication that must be either inherent in the individual or amenable to development with training.

**2. Define the communication objectives.**

a. *Assess* the individual with regard to his needs and abilities and those of his family (Silverman, McNaughton, and Kates, 1978).

b. *Consider* his future educational and vocational opportunities.

c. *Establish* for the individual the requirements of the nonspeech system in order that it be effective and accepted:

Is the nonspeech system intended for short or long term usage?

Is the nonspeech system intended as a primary or secondary means of communication?

Is the long term objective for use of the nonspeech system a sophisticated complex level of communication, or a simple limited level of communication?

What are the student's stronger and weaker learning modalities? What characteristics must the nonspeech system have in order to facilitate learning?

What are the family's requirements and expectations with regard to the nonspeech system in order that they will accept and support its use?

**3. Analyze the characteristics, capabilities, and limitations of the nonspeech systems being considered.** Examine the nonspeech system with regard to:

*Original purpose for the system:* Does this strengthen or weaken its capability in being applied as an augmentative communication technique for the nonspeaking person?

*Skills required by the learner (learning skills and physical skills):* Degree of stimulus permanence; degree of stimulus complexity; sensory requisites; and cognitive requisites

*Communication capabilities of the system:* (strengths)

*Disadvantages of the system:* (weaknesses)

*Community of users:* Persons who use the system and who can communicate with the user.

*Effects of the system's usage upon user:* Detrimental; positive

**4. Match the system with the individual.** After the nonspeech system has been analyzed, its appropriateness can be evaluated within the context of the individual's identified needs, abilities, and objectives, and a judgment can be made as to its suitability for the individual and his family.

If Blissymbolics is decided upon as the appropriate nonspeech system for the individual (see following section for examination of Blissymbolics), programming should be planned and implemented by a professional who is knowledgeable about the system. Information regarding training and materials is available from the Blissymbolics Communication Institute.[2]

## Implementation of a Blissymbolics Instructional Program

Once the decision has been made that Blissymbolics is the appropriate nonspeech system for an individual, the instructor faces a rewarding yet demanding endeavor. Originating, as it did, within the classroom and clinical setting and being potentially applicable to a broad range of age, intellectual, and disability levels, no formal teaching methodology has been developed. Rather, the system has been applied in a variety of ways, always requiring the instructor to plan an individualized teaching

[2] Blissymbolics Communication Institute, 350 Rumsey Road, Toronto, Ontario, Canada M4G 1R8.

program that relates to the student, the immediate instructional environment, the setting in which the program is located, the family, and the community. For instructors who enjoy the challenge of diagnostic teaching and for those who are prepared to use a teaching approach and develop a curriculum based on the student's developmental and communication needs, Blissymbolics offers a rich and stimulating experience for instructor as well as student.

To assist instructors in decisions regarding specific program content and procedures, three models for the application of Blissymbolics have been presented and discussed in the *Handbook of Blissymbolics* (Silverman, McNaughton, and Kates, 1978):

Model 1: Using Blissymbolics as an expressive language augmenting a developed receptive native language
Model 2: Using Blissymbolics as an expressive language paralleling and contributing to the development of native language
Model 3: Using Blissymbolics as a surface communication system

At this early stage in the application of Blissymbolics, such models offer, at best, a provisional framework to assist in planning an instructional program. Nevertheless, through identifying the model that best describes the purpose for which symbols are being used, the instructor can proceed in defining the instructional approach appropriate to the student.

Regardless of the model being applied, two program considerations are essential:

1. Instruction in the system of Blissymbolics should be concurrent with experiences in communicating with symbols. Immediate opportunities should always be provided to demonstrate and *purposefully* use newly learned symbols.
2. Total immersion, or as much immersion as possible, is recommended if Blissymbol users are to integrate Blissymbols into their way of relating with their world. This requires the involvement of family, friends, and all persons who interact with the student, in as many communication situations as possible with the symbol user. Within institutional settings, ways must be found to motivate the staff to use communication boards and to insist that the board regularly accompany the user. The words, which always appear with the symbol, can be used by all persons lacking knowledge of the symbol system. Provision must be made for symbol use at all times of the day, and in all environments and social situations. For the student in a wheelchair, continuous access to a symbol display is more easily arranged than for the mobile student. For symbol users who are not confined to a

wheelchair, ingenuity is required by the instructor to provide some form of portable symbol display, be it apron, kerchief, wallet, or folding board.

Blissymbol instruction usually begins with the gradual introduction of the most meaningful and relevant symbols for the particular user. These first symbols are usually displayed on 3″ × 3″ cards. The rate and manner of introduction is contingent upon the student's age and his physical and learning capabilities. Whenever appropriate, the meaning components of the symbols are explained. Often the symbols are color coded using the same coding as appears on the symbol displays. From a collection of cards, the student moves to a vocabulary of as many as 100 symbols. These are usually presented in 1″ × 1″ squares and organized on a grid using a format derived from the Fitzgerald key. At a later stage, the size of the symbols is further reduced and the number of spaces on the grid is expanded. Stick-on stamps produced by the Blissymbolics Communication Institute have been introduced in order to respond to the individual communication needs of the user. Using a grid of appropriate size, a customized display that contains a personal selection and arrangement of symbols can be constructed. The student points in sequence to the symbols that will convey his message; his meaning is "read" aloud and/or a written record is made by the person with whom he is communicating. For severely physically handicapped individuals who are unable to point accurately, a range of technical aids have been developed to enable them to use Blissymbols (see Harris and Vanderheiden, Chapter 12, this volume). Many experiences are provided that demonstrate to the student that communication *is possible* for him and that it is satisfying, interesting, and valuable. The *Handbook of Blissymbolics* provides suggestions for successful Blissymbol communication and outlines levels of communication for both the user and the person with whom he is interacting. The degree to which the strategies or techniques available with the system of Blissymbolics are introduced is contingent upon the total communication objectives for the individual. Blissymbolics offers a rich and creative communication potential to users who have the capability and the desire to explore the system's potential. It can be used as a second language, offering many exciting discoveries and making communication fun.

Blissymbolics also offers to both instructor and student an added dimension to all academic activities. One experienced symbol instructor has aptly described her approach to Blissymbol instruction: "I don't think of Blissymbols as being a separate part of my program. Even for Buddy, who uses them to communicate, they are an integral part of everything that is being learned. I like to think that symbols help me to do a better job of teaching everything that I would be teaching anyhow" (Mann, 1978).

To fulfil their professional responsibility to the individual learning Blissymbolics as his communication system, instructors must give high priority to obtaining accredited training in Blissymbolics. Established in 1975, the Blissymbolics Communication Institute has implemented a widespread instructor-training program throughout North America, Great Britain, and Scandinavia.

Blissymbolics is being used by an ever-expanding number and range of persons. The challenges and problems are being met by the system's users, their instructors, and the Blissymbolics Communication Institute. The excitement and motivation generated through discovering the potential of this highly sophisticated yet easily applied system holds high promise for further development.

## BLISSYMBOLICS: A DISCUSSION

### Original Purpose of the System

The original purpose of Blissymbolics was that of international communication. C. K. Bliss designed the symbols and provided a vocabulary with the objective of facilitating a better understanding between persons with different language backgrounds. As a secondary objective, he hoped his ethical system which underlies the organization of Blissymbolics could be learned by young children.

Blissymbolics was not designed as a speech augmentative for nonspeaking persons. It contains a structure of its own that, although compatible in some instances with patterns in some other languages, does not totally parallel any language. For this reason, its use to assist in the development of native language patterns is quite limited and requires distortion of the original structure recommended by C. K. Bliss.

On the other hand, the original international intention of Blissymbolics gives the system a worldwide community of users and opens many avenues of communication to the skillful Blissymbol communicator. It also offers a concise form of communication which is particularly valuable to the severely physically handicapped person, for whom every movement can be very demanding in both effort and time, and for whom a limited number of symbols can be accessed.

### Skills Required by the Learner

Blissymbols provide a permanent visual stimulus that allows for review and rehearsal. They can be presented individually, gradually expanding to a small array, or they can be presented through symbol displays composed of 100 to 512 or more symbols. The individual symbols vary in degree of complexity but are composed of a limited number of simple geometric shapes which can be readily learned by most symbol users. To initiate his own symbol messages using a wide symbol vocabulary, the student must be able to visually distinguish between differences in size, position, orientation, and arrangement of shapes and must be able to select a symbol within an array of symbols. To respond to symbol messages, he must be able to visually relate to a sequence of symbols.

Cognitively, the student must be able to comprehend that a visual symbolic representation can serve as a communication signal. Studies are needed to investigate the earliest cognitive level for which Blissymbolics can serve in this capacity. Attention has been directed toward the cognitive level at which lexical comprehension occurs, relating to the early understanding of spoken words when the referent is present, and later, when the referent is not present (see Chapman and Miller, Chapter 9, this volume). Similar information with regard to visual processing of Blissymbols could contribute to ascertaining the capacity of this system to be comprehended at an early cognitive stage.

The physical skills to use Blissymbols involve being capable of some means of indicating a symbol position. The severely involved child must learn to control some augmentative physical mechanism that can be used to directly or indirectly select a symbol (see Vanderheiden and Harris-Vanderheiden, 1976).

### Communication Capabilities of the System

The communication capabilities, or strengths, of Blissymbolics can be outlined as follows:

Blissymbolics is semantically based and therefore capable of expansion through the addition of new symbols and new strategies.

Blissymbolics is a totally visual-graphic system, and the simplicity of the symbol elements makes it easily recognized and retained. In its recorded form it allows review and rehearsal.

Blissymbols can represent extended and related meanings.

Blissymbolics provides for the generation of sentences and offers a complete language capability that can be utilized according to the user's ability.

Blissymbolics includes strategies and indicators that can extend the communication capability of individual Blissymbols.

New symbols can be created by the user for immediate application through the *combine strategy*.

Blissymbolics can be complemented and refined through combining it with traditional orthography.

Blissymbols can be translated according to the context of the given statement and situation, providing a broad communication potential.

### Disadvantages of the System

The weaknesses of Blissymbolics should also be noted.

Although Blissymbolics is potentially applicable to a broad age and intellectual range, the system can more appropriately be employed when the user is capable of understanding its logic and meaning-based symbols, rather than responding by rote to meaningless visual configurations.

Many of the symbols can only be explained meaningfully to the adult. Arriving at explanations for the young child can be difficult.

The initial reaction of some persons to Blissymbolics can be a feeling that it is complicated and difficult to learn. This early attitude may preclude their willingness to give attention and time to learning the basic structure of the system.

Blissymbolics, although initially conceived by Bliss in the 1940s, is still very new in its application and is still evolving through use. The changes to individual symbols as the BCI improves and arrives at the standard form of many symbols can be irritating to young users, their instructors, and families.

Blissymbols require that a display always be with the user. This can be bothersome to the active, mobile child and inconvenient in some locations, such as swimming pool, beach, and bed. Further development toward light, durable, portable, easily visible displays is urgently needed.

Blissymbols do not portray specific items in a manner suitable to the young user. Animals, vegetables, seasons, and so on, are symbolized through a number assignment within their classification (animal one, animal two, etc.,). There is a need for development of meaning-based symbols for individual members of classes.

The vocabulary devised by C. K. Bliss and contained in *Semantography-Blissymbolics* was directed toward the needs of the adult. A wider children's vocabulary is needed. Conversely, the symbol displays developed by the Ontario Crippled Children's Centre were designed for use by children. Displays containing adult vocabularies remain to be developed.

In response to the growing demand for Blissymbols, early attention focused upon producing symbol displays, evaluating the effectiveness of symbol usage, and training instructors. There is now need for further vocabulary development and supportive instructional materials.

**Community of Users**

Blissymbolics can be functional for a broad range of users. It can be used in a restricted way by persons at lower intellectual levels. It can also be studied and used at as sophisticated a level as the user's intellectual capability allows. Communicating with Blissymbols can be a creative, dynamic, enjoyable activity.

Because words that correspond to a common interpretation of the symbol's meaning always appear under the Blissymbol, anyone can communicate with the symbol user. Those unfamiliar with the symbols read the words; those proficient in Blissymbolics read the symbols. The uniqueness and scope of Blissymbolics make it an attractive, appealing medium to many persons, thus facilitating the social integration of the symbol user.

**Effects of the System's Use upon the User**

When considering the benefits of Blissymbolics to its users, the detrimental effects must not be overlooked:

The additional time and attention required for learning Blissymbolics can delay the allocation of instructional time to the learning of traditional orthography.

There is never total acceptance.

In some situations, the feeling of being different can have negative effects.

Blissymbolics has severe communication limitations when compared with speech, as does any nonspeech system.

It is necessary to always have a symbol display in order to communicate, frequently an inconvenient restriction in some situations.

The positive effects expand the user's communicative, developmental and social capabilities.

The use of Blissymbols facilitates expanded capabilities at various developmental levels; the user is better able to express his personality and realize his abilities. His self-esteem grows, as others realize his potential and help him achieve higher performance levels.

Communicating with Blissymbolics provides experience in the processing of visual information. Its value as a prereading activity warrants study.

The logical structure of Blissymbolics provides the user with a framework for organizing and presenting information.

Proficient use of Blissymbolics opens the possibility of more reliable assessment of nonspeaking, multihandicapped, and physically handicapped persons.

Both number and range of persons using Blissymbolics are expanding. The challenges and problems are being met by the system's users and their instructors. Their excitement and motivation as they discover the potential of this highly sophisticated yet easily applied system hold high promise for further development.

## REFERENCES


Bliss, C. K. 1965. Semantography-Blissymbolics. Semantography Publications, Sydney, Australia. (Distributed by C. K. Bliss, P. O. Box 222, Coogee 2034, Sydney, Australia.)

Bliss, C. K., and McNaughton, S. 1975. The Book to the Film: "Mr. Symbol Man." Semantography Publications, Sydney, Australia. (Distributed by C. K. Bliss, P.O. Box 222, Coogee 2034, Sydney, Australia.)

Fitzgerald, E. 1954. Straight Language for the Deaf. Volta Bureau, Washington, D.C.

Harris-Vanderheiden, D., Lippert, J., Yoder, D. E., and Vanderheiden, G. C. 1977. Blissymbols: An augmentative/symbol communication system for nonvocal severely handicapped children. *In* R. York and E. Edgar (eds.), Teaching the Severely Handicapped, Vol. IV. American Association for the Education of the Severely and Profoundly Handicapped, Seattle.

Hehner, B. (ed.). 1979. Blissymbols for Use. Blissymbolics Communication Institute, Toronto, Canada.

Hollis, J. H., and Carrier, J. K., Jr. 1978. Intervention strategies for nonspeech children. *In* R. L. Schiefelbusch (ed.), Language Intervention Strategies, pp. 57–100. University Park Press, Baltimore.

Kates, B., and McNaughton, S. 1975. The first application of Blissymbolics as a communication medium for non-speaking children, 1971–1974. Blissymbolics Communication Institute, Toronto. (Distributed by Blissymbolics Communication Institute, 350 Rumsey Road, Toronto, Ontario, Canada M4G 1R8.)

Lloyd, L. L. (ed.). 1976. Communication Assessment and Intervention Strategies. University Park Press, Baltimore.

Mann, G. 1978. Communication goals in the primary special class. Blissymbolics Communication Foundation Newsletter, Spring, 4(3):17–19.

Schiefelbusch, R. L., and Lloyd, L. L. (eds.). 1974. Language Perspectives—Acquistion, Retardation, and Intervention. University Park Press, Baltimore.

Silverman, H., McNaughton, S., and Kates, B. 1978. Handbook of Blissymbolics. Blissymbolics Communication Institute, Toronto. (Distributed by Blissymbolics Communication Institute, 350 Rumsey Road, Toronto, Ontario, Canada M4G 1R8.)

Vanderheiden, G. C., and Harris-Vanderheiden, D. 1976. Communication techniques and aids for the nonvocal severely handicapped. *In* L. L. Lloyd (ed.), Communication Assessment and Intervention Strategies. University Park Press, Baltimore.

# Section VI

# Strategies for Autistic and Severely Retarded Children

chapter 14

# A Presymbolic Training Program

*Diann Hahn Woolman*

*Los Angeles County Superintendent of Schools*
*Los Angeles, California*

## contents

In her initial evaluations of the language levels and abilities of trainable mentally retarded children, the author discovered that there was a small group of children in her school population who were essentially nonverbal. These children used no verbalization at all, a limited number of unintelligible phonemes, or made echolalic responses that had little meaning. The nonverbal behaviors of these children marked them as atypical among an already deviant population because the majority of their peers had at least a small amount of expressive language.

The author also discovered that these nonverbal children had attended school for at least three years and some for as long as 10 years. They had been exposed to classroom language training and most had received training from a credentialed language specialist. Why were these children still nonverbal while their peers had acquired the ability to communicate? Possibly the training had not begun at the child's level of functioning, or the training steps had not been broken into small enough increments to allow the child to complete a meaningful series of tasks.

Further evaluation of the behaviors they exhibited in specific training situations pointed out that they were often unable to attend physically and visually to a task without a great deal of physical manipulation and prompting by the trainer. Even though they had been exposed to hours of classroom training in sorting and matching by color and shape, they were not able to scan and discriminate the physical attributes of objects. They also lacked the ability to recognize or recall a stimulus. These children seemed to need a highly structured and systematic approach, broken into very small increments of learning, specifically designed for the remediation of these deviant behaviors. However, after researching the intervention strategies and programs for facilitating language acquisition in the mentally retarded, the author could find no program that began at the appropriate level for this group. Furthermore, she could find no program that offered specific training procedures for the needed prelinguistic behaviors. Since the author felt that this group lacked the prelinguistic skills required by existing programs, the alternative was to write a program that would train this group in prelinguistic skills required for language acquisition.

The following review of the literature provides a careful analysis of existing programs designed for low functioning children.

## REVIEW OF THE LITERATURE

The 1970s have seen a general shift in the direction of research with the mentally retarded. Before 1970 it was generally accepted that the retarded child acquired language in the same general manner and sequence as the normal child but at a much slower rate (Miller and Yoder, 1974). Therefore, the intervention strategies used for language remediation with the mentally retarded employed similar techniques and followed the same training sequences as those used with normal children experiencing language difficulties.

In the 1970s this logic was questioned (Hollis and Carrier, 1973; Bricker and Bricker, 1974; Cromer, 1974; Guess, Sailor, and Baer, 1974; Premack and Premack, 1974; Ruder and Smith, 1974; Schiefelbusch, 1974). These authorities noted that the severely retarded child did not acquire language comparable to the normal child with the same mental age. They therefore suggested that intervention strategies had to be developed to deal with the uniqueness of the severely retarded child's language acquisition problems.

Bricker and Bricker (1974) found that the severely retarded child needed training almost from birth in order to develop language comparable to that of a normal child. They also found that the ability to learn language depended on the development of cognitive skills they called "prelinguistic forms of behavior." Among these are the functional classification of objects, the interrelationships between child and object, motor and verbal imitation, development of attending behaviors, and the elimination of interfering behaviors. They discovered that most normal children developed these prelinguistic behaviors in their two or three years of life without any remediation. The severely retarded child, however, required specific training procedures to acquire these behaviors.

Miller and Yoder (1974) listed three "extra-linguistic behaviors" that restrict language learning by the severely retarded. They asserted that attending behavior, motivation, and cognitive behavior must be dealt with at the onset of any language acquisition training.

Ruder and Smith (1974) found that prerequisite to entering a language-training program, the severely retarded child must develop attending behavior, chair-sitting behavior, and motor imitation.

Premack and Premack (1974) stated that language acquisition is a " . . . mapping of an already existing conceptual structure" (p. 368). Although they admit that the conceptual structures underlying language are largely unknown, they were able to pinpoint three from their own research: 1) the ability to match on the basis of object similarity, 2) the ability to match pictures to objects, and 3) the ability to match pictures to pictures.

The reinforcement techniques used for shaping appropriate behaviors in the training of the severely retarded were reevaluated in the 1970s. Guess, Sailor, and Baer (1974) provided an excellent review of the successful history of language development as a reinforcement-based process. They pointed out that reinforcement techniques have been used successfully with nonverbal retarded children to develop language, correct inappropriate speech patterns, and to shape echolalic verbalizations into referent-controlled labels.

However, a new dimension in reinforcement was proposed by Estes (1972). He suggested that, in human learning, reinforcement can provide information about the correctness of a response. The learner uses the information to select subsequent responses, and reinforcement then becomes more than a stimulus-response association. Reinforcement techniques used for shaping appropriate behaviors in the severely retarded have now become a dual process. Not only do they encourage the child to repeat a response but they also give feedback about the appropriateness of the response.

In conjunction with this new awareness of prerequisite behaviors for language acquisition and the broadening of reinforcement techniques, researchers also discovered that new intervention strategies had to be developed. These new strategies often used methods that had not yet been accepted for training the severely retarded (Guess, Sailor, and Baer, 1974). A review of these new intervention strategies follows.

## INTERVENTION STRATEGIES CURRENTLY USED FOR FACILITATING LANGUAGE ACQUISITION WITH THE MENTALLY RETARDED

There is unanimous support for the use of a structured systematic approach for the training of mentally retarded children. By structured systematic approach is meant that a specific approach is used consistently by the trainer while the subject moves through a developmental sequence to the terminal objective. However, these authorities disagree about the areas of language that should be remediated and the type of intervention strategy that should be used.

In this review, the strategies used for facilitating language acquisition with the mentally retarded are divided into five major categories: 1) core vocabulary strategies, 2) vocal imitation strategies, 3) receptive language strategies, 4) Total Communication strategies, and 5) abstract symbol system strategies.

### Core Vocabulary Strategies

Core vocabulary strategy is based on the Brown (1973) and Bloom (1970) theories of semantic relations. The retarded person is taught the meaning and the verbal symbol for a limited number of function words that Brown and Bloom list as the ones first acquired by a normal child. Function words are divided into relational functions (recurrence, nonexistence, disappearance, rejection, cessation, and existence) and substantive functions (agent, object, action, and possession). At the one-word stage, the child learns one word for each function (the same word can be learned for several functions, like "no" for nonexistence and rejection and "Mama" for agent, object or possession). As the child moves to the two-word level, he uses a variety of combinations of the previously learned relational and substantial functions (e.g., "no" plus a substantive function or agent plus either action or object). This strategy allows the child to make maximum use of a minimum number of verbal symbols.

In 1974 Miller and Yoder presented their "Ontogenetic Language Teaching Strategy for Retarded Children." This program uses the core vocabulary format. Training is begun at the one-word level, and Miller and Yoder have stated their basic format as follows:

> Select a single frequently occurring experience demonstrating a particular semantic function. Pair with the appropriate marker and after the child demonstrates mastery, move to multiple experiences expressing the same function (p. 521).

They recommend that one function be taught at a time and that training begin with a relational function like "more" for recurrence or "no" for nonexistence.

Outlined below is the procedure used for teaching the verbal symbol for the relational function:

1. The trainer demonstrates the function and uses the verbal symbol simultaneously. (The trainer might pour small amounts of juice into a glass, each time saying "more" until the glass is full.)
2. The retarded child indicates a comprehension of the verbal symbol in relation to the function. (The child is allowed to drink the juice, and the trainer says "more"; the child must demonstrate that he understands by either nodding his head yes or holding out the glass.)
3. The child is required to imitate the verbal symbol. (He must say "more" to get more juice.)
4. The trainer begins to fade the child's imitation responses in favor of spontaneous responses by introducing different familiar experiences expressing the same function, but the trainer gives the verbal symbol for the child. (The trainer offers more candy, cookie, etc., each time saying "more.")
5. The trainer fades the verbal symbol, allowing the child to respond spontaneously until the function has been generalized.

Miller and Yoder concluded that with their program, regardless of when the child ceases to learn, he will be able to communicate to some extent. They listed the minimal requirements for entry to their program as: an intact speech mechanism, a cognitive awareness of one or more relational or substantive functions, and production of approximations of single words.

The core vocabulary strategy requires the child to verbalize. This obviously precludes the nonverbal child from participation in a core vocabulary remediation strategy.

### Vocal Imitation Strategies

This intervention strategy is used in training the nonverbal child to vocalize. Most programs of this type begin with gross motor imitation and move to vocal imitation (Sloane, Johnson, and Harris, 1968; Marshall and Hegrenes, 1972; Bricker and Bricker, 1974; Guess, Sailor, and Baer, 1974; Kent, 1974). This strategy may be necessary for the nonverbal, retarded child to acquire vocalization; however, there is some question about when this procedure should be instigated and what prerequisite behaviors are necessary.

Ruder and Smith (1974) indicate that training based on comprehension alone (receptive language training) is more effective in eliciting verbal production than training based on vocal imitation.

Schiefelbusch (1974) states that "receptive speech training should precede early speech production training. The receptive processes are simpler to acquire, more varied in content, and lead to productive rehearsal strategies which may be antecedent to spoken language" (p. 659). As a prerequisite to vocal imitation, the nonverbal retarded child needs to acquire a comprehension of the verbal symbols to be imitated (receptive language training).

### Receptive Language Strategies

The word *receptive*, as it is used here, means the comprehension of spoken words, commands, statements, or questions. The receptive language strategies specifically designed for use with nonverbal children require the comprehension of the spoken word (Chalfant, Kirk, and Jensen, 1968; Marshall and Hegrenes, 1972; Guess, Sailor, and Baer, 1974; Kent, 1974).

Chalfant, Kirk, and Jensen (1968) provided initial training steps for comprehension of the oral commands used in their program. However, they listed the following problems in assessing the retarded child's receptive abilities:

1. The child may not be able to sit in a chair and respond to directions.
2. The child may not understand the concepts that are presented in verbal directions.
3. The child may not be able to respond to specific questions.
4. The child may be unfamiliar with the words used in the directions.
5. The child may be unwilling to respond even when he knows the correct response.

The authors listed five criteria to be used in selecting language concepts to be taught and the order in which they should be presented. These criteria are: 1) relevancy, 2) physical proximity, 3) sequence and frequency of encounter, 4) concrete concepts, and 5) ease of auditory discrimination. Each child in the program has his own specific receptive vocabulary determined by the trainer using the above criteria. This technique is used because it is important for the child to learn a receptive vocabulary pertinent to his environment.

The training begins with the child learning to touch or point on verbal command from the trainer. Training continues until the child can distinguish among a variety of stimuli and demonstrate comprehension of verbal symbols by touching or pointing to the appropriate stimulus.

Receptive language is certainly a critical training area for the nonverbal child. With the normal child, or even the retarded child who is able to verbalize, it is a logical place to begin training. However, if the retarded child has not acquired verbalization, there is some question about his receptive language capacities (Ruder and Smith, 1974). He may not be successful if the program overestimates the child's receptive potential.

**Total Communication Strategies**

Total Communication includes three modalities (visual, auditory, and motor) to facilitate language acquisition in the nonverbal retarded child.

The Total Communication strategies suggested by Berger (1972) and Moores (1974) utilize the motoric system of signing simultaneously with auditory and visual cues suggested for use with the deaf.

Bricker and Bricker (1974) experimented with 22 severely retarded children to explore the possibility of using motor movements to facilitate the acquisition of receptive language. These motor movements were not sign language but gestural representations for the functions of the 30 objects presented (for example, running the hand over the hair for comb, cupping the hand and drinking from it for cup). The motor movements were presented in conjunction with the actual objects and the verbal symbols for the objects. The results indicated that the motor movements did facilitate the learning of word-object associations.

Kent (1974) has adapted her "Language Acquisition Program for the Severely Retarded" so that the entire program can be presented in a Total Communication format. This provides the nonverbal child with a temporary expressive language which reduces his "social retardation" by allowing him to communicate with his environment. Kent has found that signing facilitates receptive language skills and lays a foundation for later vocal expression.

The program is divided into three major sections: preverbal, verbal-receptive, and verbal-expressive. When the program is to be used with a nonverbal child, Kent recommends that training be initiated in the regular program format using an oral approach. If, at any point in the program, the child does not respond adequately to the expressive aspects of oral training, the Total Communication system should be instigated (at the receptive level this could be an inability to understand the trainer's oral commands or at the expressive level an inability to vocalize).

Kent's program offers the best format of all the Total Communication programs reviewed for the following reasons:

1. It uses a highly structured systematic approach.
2. Its content, sequencing of the content, and procedures are carefully detailed to ensure each child's success as a learner.
3. It begins training with attending and gives specific procedures for the elimination of interfering behaviors.
4. The signs are specified for each training area and illustrations given. The meaning of each sign is stated so the trainer need have no prior training in signing to utilize the techniques.
5. The oral command that accompanies the sign is also specified.
6. All natural reinforcements are given orally and signed by the trainer.
7. The program is designed to encourage the child to verbalize, but he can complete the entire program without verbalizing, emerging with a functional communication system.

The Total Communication strategy may be an effective training procedure with some retarded children. It is too new to be supported by extensive research. However, the ability to sign or to understand signing still requires the ability to symbolize (Dever, 1974; Moores, 1974; Schiefelbusch, 1974). If the nonverbal retarded child has not reached the level of symbolic language development, he will have no more success with signing than with auditory symbols.

**Abstract Symbol System Strategies**

This language intervention strategy uses abstract plastic symbols as a substitute for verbal symbols (Premack, 1971). Premack developed this strategy from research with his chimpanzee Sarah. He first devised a set of abstract plastic symbols that arbitrarily represented verbal symbols. The training began by presenting Sarah one plastic symbol with the actual object it represented. By the end of training, Sarah had acquired a vocabulary of 130 words, including nouns, verbs, adjectives, quantifiers, prepositions, and logical connectives. She was able to produce and comprehend simple sentences and question forms. The trainer presented one unknown at a time, and Sarah did not have to learn motor movements (like signing) other than placing the abstract plastic symbols on a board.

As a result of their research with Sarah, Premack and Premack (1974) found that the use of abstract plastic symbols, rather than signing or verbalization, did not require short term memory capability. The stimulus (abstract plastic symbol) was always visually present so Sarah did not have to hold it in her short term memory while formulating a response.

Following Premack's research with Sarah, Carrier and Peak (1975) devised a language program for the nonverbal child. Their program, the "Non-speech Language Initiation Program," bypasses the normal procedure of using verbal symbols by substituting abstract plastic symbols. From his own research, Carrier (1973) found that many severely retarded children could learn a symbolic communication system when offered Premack's nonspeech-response model.

In the Carrier and Peak program, 60 abstract plastic symbols are presented. Each symbol is a different shape, and each is color coded as to its syntactic class (all nouns are one color, all verbs another color, and so forth). The retarded child first learns to recognize and discriminate among the different symbols. He then learns to match symbols to construct sentences in a rote fashion (N + V + N). The various segments of the program then train the child to select appropriate symbols and to sequence these symbols according to grammatical rules and to use the available symbols and rules to generate new responses.

The subprograms are step-by-step procedures for teaching the semantic (names and meaning of symbols) and syntactic (correct word order in sentences) aspects of language without requiring the child to emit verbal responses. Carrier designed the program to circumvent the need for the child to learn to speak while he is learning the semantic and syntactic properties of language. The trainer presents a picture stimulus card and asks the child to name it by placing the appropriate symbol on the tray in front of him. The child learns to use the symbols as words and morphemes and to select and arrange these forms on the tray as if he were writing a sentence.

The purpose of the program is to give severely retarded children some form of basic communication skill. It takes three months to one year to complete the program. At the end of that time, training should extend into the use of signing or verbalization. However, the skills of some nonverbal retarded children may be limited to abstract plastic symbols.

Following the research of Premack and Carrier, McLean and McLean (1974) published "A Language Training Program for Nonverbal Autistic Children." They used the abstract symbol system strategy with three autistic children. From their own research, they concluded that for children who show a depressed ability for verbal language acquisition, the use of an abstract symbol system may be the only means of developing expressive language.

The one drawback to an abstract symbol system is the limiting factor of its usefulness. If it can indeed be used as a stepping stone to the acquisition of spoken language or even signing, it has great potential. It is too early for data to support this theory. However, if the nonverbal child cannot move on to spoken language or signing, he is left with a communication system that can be used only within the confines of the training situation. Whatever develops, Carrier has shown that the nonverbal retarded child is capable of acquiring a symbolic system of communication.

## UTILITY OF CURRENT STRATEGIES: CONCLUSION

No single intervention strategy offers remediation techniques for all severely retarded children. However, each of the five strategies offers valuable training procedures for unique individual needs. The trainer must assess the individual needs of each child and then use the strategy that is appropriate for that child.

This author has successfully used all five strategies with her retarded population. However, this author also found a small group of nonverbal retarded children who appeared to be deficient in the prelinguistic skills required for them to function in any of these strategies.

The inability to attend, physically or visually, to a task was a general characteristic of this group. The majority of the authors reviewed mentioned attention as a primary prerequisite to any learning situation. However, only one program of those reviewed (Kent, 1974) offers specific training procedures for attending.

The author found that two problems arose when she placed this nonverbal group on the Kent program. First, the training steps for physical attending were not specific enough. Physical attending in the program is divided into two sections: sitting still and elimination of interfering behaviors. The training for sitting still is included in one paragraph. Final criterion is met when the child sits quietly with his hands in his lap for 30 seconds before being reinforced. When the author attempted this training, she found that a great deal of physical manipulation of the child was required. Also, sitting still for 30 seconds was not enough. *How* the child was sitting became very important. If the child is to be able to attend physically and visually to a task, he needs to be sitting squarely on the chair, with his shoulders back and his head erect. He also needs to maintain this attention when placed in a chair at a table. Since there were no training procedures offered for any of these behaviors, the author developed her own.

The second section of physical attending in Kent's program was the elimination of interfering behaviors. This is certainly another critical area of training with these children. Kent used a training technique she called "reversal behavior." When a child exhibited an interfering behavior during a training session, he was first told, "Don't do that." If the behavior continued or reoccurred, he was removed to another part of the room and required to engage in the reversal behavior for set periods of time (beginning with 20 minutes). The reversal behaviors were specified for head movements, body movements, hand movements, and finger and thumb movements. They involved requiring the child to hold positions opposite to the interfering behavior. For example, a child who is holding his hands in front of his face and staring at them would be required to hold his hands up over his head, straight out to the side, and then down at his side. Each of these three positions would be held for 30 seconds in rotation for 20 minutes. This is a very time-consuming procedure when the training is not focused on the desired behavior of hands at rest in the child's lap. Kent cautions that 1-hour sessions may be required for this stage of training. However, this author felt that training should focus on the desired behavior while eliminating an interfering behavior. She also felt that 1-hour sessions were too time consuming; therefore, she developed other training procedures.

The second problem that arose with the Kent program was the use of oral commands. Another general characteristic of this nonverbal group was that they seemed to have little, if any, receptive language. With physical attending, this program did not become obvious because the author was engaging in so much actual physical manipulation of the child's body that the child was physically aware of the desired behaviors. However, when training began for visual attending this was no longer true and the group could not comprehend the desired behaviors from the oral instructions. In fact, the author felt that the oral instructions were compounding the learning experience by requiring the child to develop a comprehension of oral commands while the target behavior was to attend visually to a task. A question arose; Why not present training for attending in the visual-motor modalities exclusively? This approach had been used effectively by Premack and Carrier to teach a symbolic language system. Why could it not be used to teach the prelinguistic skills required for symbolic language learning?

From this research came the basis for the visual-motor program presented in this chapter. It is this author's contention that before some nonverbal children can be introduced to the language intervention strategies presented in this review, they need specific training in certain prelinguistic skills. This training can be done effectively through the visual-motor modalities.

## *VISUAL ATTENDING/MATCHING/MEMORY PROGRAM*

### OBJECTIVES OF THE PROGRAM

The primary objective of the visual attending/matching/memory program is to facilitate the acquisition of the abilities to:

1. Physically and visually attend to a task
2. Scan and discriminate visual stimuli
3. Use short term memory for recognition and recall

The program is divided into three levels: attending, matching, and visual memory. The objectives and an explanation of each level are given below.

### Level One: Attending

The nonverbal retarded child often exhibits an inability to attend to a task, either physically or visually. Since attending is paramount to any learning situation, training the child to attend is a necessary first step in any program. Attending is a twofold operation. The child must first attend physically to the trainer and the task, and then he must attend visually. Level One is divided into two training areas: physical attending and visual attending.

**Physical Attending** The objective of this aspect of Level One is to train the child to sit properly, in a chair, at a table, without interfering behaviors, for 30 seconds. (Thirty seconds is the maximum amount of time required to complete any task in the program.) The required physical attention is obtained by familiarizing the child with *consistent* physical prompts, administered by the trainer, that immediately trigger the desired physical behavior from the child, without interfering with the completion of the task.

**Visual Attending** The objective of this section of Level One is to train the child to establish eye contact with the trainer and to attend visually to specific objects pointed at by the trainer. This step also introduces the child to the objects and cards that will be used throughout the rest of the program.

### Level Two: Matching

The objective of Level Two is to train the child to match concrete and abstract objects.

Before a child can attach a verbal symbol to an object, he must be able to look at that object, scan it, and pick out certain features of that object that will enable him to recognize it the next time it is presented (Clark, 1973). The child must also be able to discriminate that object from another when two or more objects are presented.

Match-to-sample is a technique long used to teach and test a child's ability to identify two objects that are the same. The basic value of this technique is the trainer's ability to control the amount of "sameness" that must be identified. For example, the trainer might want a child to match by color, size, or shape. In this program, the matching is simplified by presenting three distinctly different objects (i.e., they differ in size, shape, and color), thus offering the child more features to discriminate.

Only three different objects are introduced for matching. In the development of the program, it was found tht once a child had mastered the task of matching he could transfer the training to a multitude of objects. Premack and Premack (1974) support this finding from their own research with retarded children. Since the objective of this level is for the child to be able to scan and discriminate at an abstract level of stimulus presentation, it serves no purpose to introduce more than three stimulus objects.

### Level Three: Visual Memory

The objective of Level Three is to train the child to recognize an abstract object and recall where the matching object is located.

Level Three initiates the long and difficult task of building short term memory. The most basic auditory-verbal language program requires the child to engage in a successive task. The auditory stimulus is given by the trainer (e.g., "Give me shoe," "Point to car," "Where is your nose?"). The child must hold that stimulus in his short term memory until he responds. Level Three provides training in the development of short term memory by presenting simultaneous tasks. The visual stimulus, presented by the trainer, is present until the completion of the task. The child is required to recognize the stimulus card as matching one of the three cards placed facedown in front of him and recalling where that card is located.

Levels Two and Three were specifically designed for the child functioning at a presymbolic level of language learning. However, Level One, attending, can be used with any child whose lack of attending behaviors is interfering with learning. At whatever level of language acquisition a child is functioning, attention to the task is still critical to learning.

### Terminal Objectives

The three levels of the program have been divided into six terminal objectives. The objectives have been arranged sequentially with a pretest to be administered at the beginning of each. In this manner, training begins at the proper level for the child.

The six terminal objectives are listed below.

**Level One Terminal Objective for Physically Attending** The child will sit in a chair, at a table across from the trainer, with his shoulders back, head erect, hands at rest, and with no interfering behaviors for 10 consecutive 30-second trials with 100% accuracy.

**Level One Terminal Objective for Visual Attending** The child will establish eye contact with the trainer and attend visually to three objects, when pointed to by the trainer, for 10 consecutive trials with 100% accuracy.

**Level Two Terminal Objective for Matching Concrete Objects** The child will match three presentation objects to three sample concrete objects with a random presentation order from the trainer on each trial for 20 consecutive trials with 90% accuracy.

**Level Two Terminal Objective for Matching Concrete to Abstract Objects** The child will match three presentation concrete objects to three sample abstract objects with a random presentation order and a reversal of the sampling order from the trainer on each trial for 20 consecutive trials with 90% accuracy.

**Level Two Terminal Objective for Matching Abstract Objects** The child will match three presentation abstract objects to three sample abstract objects with a random presentation order and a reversal of the sampling order from the trainer on each trial for 20 consecutive trials with 90% accuracy.

**Level Three Terminal Objective for Visual Memory** The child will match, from memory, three presentation abstract objects to three sample abstract objects with a random presentation order and a reversal of the sample order from the trainer on each trial for 20 consecutive trials with 90% accuracy.

## Intermediate Objectives

Each of the six terminal objectives is divided into two or more intermediate objectives. Given below are the 17 intermediate objectives of the program. Note that the last intermediate objective in each category is a restatement of the terminal objective for that area.

**Level One Intermediate Objectives for Physical Attending**

*A-1 Sitting in a Chair* The child will sit in a chair, shoulders back, head erect, and hands at rest for 10 consecutive 30-second trials with 100% accuracy.

*A-2 Elimination of Interfering Behaviors* The child will sit in a chair with no interfering behaviors for 10 consecutive 30-second trials with 100% accuracy.

*A-3 Sitting at a Table* The child will sit in a chair, at a table across from the trainer, with his shoulders back, head erect, hands at rest, and with no interfering behaviors for 10 consecutive 30-second trials with 100% accuracy.

**Level One Intermediate Objectives for Visual Attending**

*A-4 Eye Contact* The child will establish eye contact with the trainer, when the trainer points to his eyes, for 10 consecutive trials with 100% accuracy.

*A-5 Attending to Three Objects* The child will establish eye contact with the trainer and attend visually to three objects, when pointed to by the trainer, for 10 consecutive trials with 100% accuracy.

**Level Two Intermediate Ojectives for Matching Concrete Objects**

*M-1 Matching One Pair* The child will match one presentation concrete object to one sample concrete object for 10 consecutive trials with 100% accuracy.

*M-2 Matching Two Pairs* The child will match two presentation concrete objects to two sample concrete objects with a random presentation order from the trainer on each trial for 20 consecutive trials with 90% accuracy.

*M-3 Matching Three Pairs* The child will match three presentation concrete objects to three sample concrete objects with a random presentation order from the trainer on each trial for 20 consecutive trials with 90% accuracy.

**Level Two Intermediate Objectives for Matching Concrete to Abstract Objects**

*M-4 Matching One Pair* The child will match one presentation concrete object to one sample abstract object for 10 consecutive trials with 100% accuracy.

*M-5 Matching Two Pairs* The child will match two presentation concrete objects to two sample abstract objects with a random presentation order and a reversal of the sampling order from the trainer on each trial for 10 consecutive trials with 90% accuracy.

*M-6 Matching Three Pairs* The child will match three presentation concrete objects to three sample abstract objects with a random presentation order and a reversal of the sampling order from the trainer on each trial for 20 consecutive trials with 90% accuracy.

**Level Two Intermediate Objectives for Matching Abstract Objects**

*M-7 Matching One Pair* The child will match one presentation abstract object to one sample abstract object for 10 consecutive trials with 100% accuracy.

*M-8 Matching Two Pairs* The child will match two presentation abstract objects to two sample abstract objects with a random presentation order and a reversal of the sampling order from the trainer on each trial for 10 consecutive trials with 90% accuracy.

*M-9 Matching Three Pairs* The child will match three presentation abstract objects to three sample abstract objects with a random presentation order and a reversal of the sampling order from the trainer on each trial for 20 consecutive trials with 90% accuracy.

**Level Three Intermediate Objectives for Visual Memory**

*VM-1 Introduction to the Task* The child will attend visually to one sample abstract object, when pointed to by the trainer, and will match one presentation abstract object to a sample abstract object, which has been turned facedown by the trainer, in 10 consecutive trials with 100% accuracy.

*VM-2 Matching Two Pairs from Memory* The child will match, from memory, two presentation abstract objects to two sample abstract objects with a random presentation order and a reversal of the sampling order from the trainer on each trial for 20 consecutive trials with 90% accuracy.

*VM-3 Matching Three Pairs from Memory* The child will match, from memory, three presentation abstract objects to three sample abstract objects with a random presentation order and a reversal of the sampling order from the trainer on each trial for 20 consecutive trials with 90% accuracy.

The intermediate objectives have been broken down into specific training steps. Each training step contains the exact procedures to be used by the trainer, the materials to be used, the reinforcement and scoring procedures, the criterion required for completion of the step, and the specific objective of that step. (See appendix to the chapter for an example of the training steps.)

At the beginning of each level are listed:

1. The terminal objective for that level
2. The intermediate objectives for that level
3. A definition of the terms used in that level
4. The materials needed for that level
5. The reinforcement procedures for that level
6. The scoring procedures for that level
7. The criterion requirements for that level
8. The pretest for that level

## STRUCTURE OF THE PROGRAM

The structure of the program is based on the concepts of simplicity and consistency.

The program is simple in design and easy to administer. Each task has been carefully analyzed and broken down into small increments so that a child can move successfully through each task. The materials required are minimal and inexpensive. The scoring does not require graphing, computing, or analyzing.

The success of the program rests with the consistent use of materials and techniques. This allows the child to begin training at each new session without having to spend time familiarizing himself with the situation, materials presented, or the techniques used by the trainer. From the onset of training, it is imperative that materials remain constant. Every training session should take place in the same room with the same table and chairs. This gives the child a familiar setting. When objects are introduced in Level One, they must be the same three objects that will be used in Levels Two and Three. The three picture cards used in Levels Two and Three are introduced in Level One by being placed facedown in front of the child. For Level One, they are used to designate sites of visual attention for the objects that are placed on them. They are also building into the child a familiarity with the cards' sizes and locations. When they are turned faceup in Level Two, the child has already learned to attend to their positions. The techniques acquired by the trainer in Level One to maintain physical and visual attention are used consistently throughout the program.

## ADMINISTRATION OF THE PROGRAM

### Procedures

Any person deciding to use the program should first read the entire program and become familiar with the specific objectives of each level. The next step is to carefully assess the child with whom the program is to be used. *Every* child is different. Even though severely retarded, a child will present specific needs for remediation. The trainer must be prepared to adapt the program to each child's specific needs. The author never intended this program to be run verbatim with any child. It was written to be adapted to any situation that could arise. What is offered are guidelines; the *trainer* must determine the child's specific needs.

The program is designed to be administered without auditory cues from the trainer. The tasks are visually presented by the trainer and motorically executed by the child. This does not mean that every session must be void of any verbalization. The child should be greeted at each session by name and made to feel welcome and comfortable by the trainer. When the actual training begins, it is important to curtail all verbalization that might interfere with the administration of the program.

## Reinforcements

This is a difficult area to mandate in any program because successful reinforcement depends on the expertise of the trainer to evaluate the needs of the individual child. The trainer must decide what is required to motivate a child to exhibit a desired behavior and how much feedback the child requires to know his behavior is correct. The decision to use primary (edible) or secondary (e.g., verbal praise) reinforcements to facilitate behavior shaping must be made by the trainer. This decision should be based on the trainer's evaluation of the child after observing him in other training situations and talking to the people involved with the child. Any trainer running a program such as this one should always remember that any reinforcement procedures used by him must eventually be withdrawn before the training can be accepted as successful. This does not mean reinforcement procedures should be eliminated; they are often necessary and useful at this low level stage of training. This author is only suggesting that a trainer needs to be constantly alert that he is not supplying reinforcement when it is no longer necessary.

At Level One of training, primary reinforcements are often vital to establishing good attending behaviors. It is the trainer's responsibility to find the primary reinforcement that will motivate the child to repeat a desired behavior. The child who does not respond to edible reinforcements may take some detailed research on the trainer's part. At Levels Two and Three of the program, primary reinforcements should be continued only if the trainer feels they are absolutely necessary. The reinforcement schedule for the entire program has been carefully specified so it does not interfere with the execution of a task.

Verbal reinforcements may be used at the completion of a task and should be used at the end of each session, but never during an actual response or series of responses. In this particular program, the primary objectives are physical and visual attention to a task, scanning and discriminating of visual stimuli, and use of short term memory for recognition and recall. Verbal reinforcement during the training of any of these objectives can be an interference or an overload.

## Materials

The materials needed are basic items, easily obtained.

1. Two chairs
2. Table
3. Three pairs of concrete objects
4. Three pairs of pictures of these objects
5. Edible reinforcements

6. Daily score sheet and a notation sheet
7. Pencil or pen

The chairs should be identical and suitable to the child's size. The table should be narrow enough so the trainer can reach across it easily to touch the child, and it should be a comfortable height for the chairs.

The objects should be selected carefully, using the following criteria:

1. They should be familiar to the child, something he encounters daily like a cup, shoe, car, comb, or toothbrush.
2. They should be small enough for the child to manipulate with one hand.
3. Each pair should be easily distinguished from the other by color, size, and shape.

The trainer should have an extra pair of objects and pictures in reserve in case the child cannot handle one of the first three, but it should be substituted early and any previous object training readministered.

The three pairs of matching pictures should be mounted on identical cards (same color, size, and shape), no smaller than 3 by 5 inches. This allows room for the object to be placed on the card with the picture still visible. The pictures can be taken from magazines or drawn by hand, but black and white pictures or drawings are not acceptable because they add another dimension of difficulty for the child. Pictures should be selected that are similar in size and color so when the child reaches Level Two he will discriminate other relevant features.

**Daily Scoring and Notations**

Before each session, the date, task (by number of the training step), criterion (percent correct per number of trials), and stimulus used are recorded on the score sheet (see chapter appendix). After each trial is completed, the response or responses are marked in the response squares, moving from left to right. Ten squares are provided on each line because criterion is based on either 10 or 20 trials. At the completion of the required number of trials, the percent correct *for each response* is calculated. If criterion is 100% every response in every trial must be correct. If criterion is 90%, *each response* must have a final total of 90% correct for the required number of trials. For 10 trials, the number of correct responses is multiplied by 10; for 20 trials, the number of correct responses is multiplied by 5. These figures are entered in the percent column, and if any total is under criterion the step must be readministered.

The scoring procedure for the entire program is consistent:

1. (+) response correct
2. (+VP) response correct with a visual prompt from the trainer
3. (+P) response correct with a physical prompt from the trainer
4. (−) response incorrect
5. (NR) no response

Some training steps instruct the trainer to write down certain behaviors observed during a trial. The trainer should also make notations at the end of each session, recording the date, task, and any behaviors the child exhibited that would not be obvious from looking at the score sheet.

### Session Length

At the beginning of the program, no session should exceed 15 minutes. It is unnecessarily exhausting to the child and trainer to require more than 15 minutes of physical attending behavior. A second 15-minute session may be administered effectively later in the same day. More than two sessions in one day should not be attempted because the child needs time to assimilate and adapt to the training.

## EXTENSIONS OF THE PROGRAM

At the conclusion of this program, the trainer must decide what the next set of objectives will be for the child in his language acquisition training. The author has spent the past year developing a total communication program utilizing verbalizing, signing, and word recognition in a core vocabulary format designed to follow the completion of the presymbolic program presented here. Some other possibilities open to the trainer are:

1. A noun-naming or labeling program, starting at the receptive level (The trainer should begin with the three objects used in this program.)
2. Administering further training in visual memory that includes sequencing tasks (Again, training should begin with the objects used in this program.)
3. Training for the same and different concepts by continuing the use of the child's matching skills (Correct matching would be used to teach *same*, and the oddity factor would be introduced to teach *different*.)
4. Signing introduced as an intermediate step to verbalization
5. A vocal imitation program introduced to stimulate verbalization (signing and vocal imitation can be combined very effectively.)
6. Placement on one of the existing language programs that begins at a receptive level
7. Placement on an abstract symbol system program

## REFERENCES

Berger, S. L. 1972. A clinical program for developing multimodal language responses with atypical deaf children. *In* J. E. McLean, D. E. Yoder, and R. L. Schiefelbusch (eds.), Language Intervention with the Retarded, pp. 212–235. University Park Press, Baltimore.

Bloom, L. 1970. Language Development: Form and Function of Emerging Grammars. The MIT Press, Cambridge, Mass.

Bricker, W. A., and Bricker, D. D. 1974. An early language training strategy. *In* R. L. Schiefelbusch and L. L. Lloyd (eds.), Language Perspectives—Acquisition, Retardation, and Intervention, pp. 431–468. University Park Press, Baltimore.

Brown, R. 1973. A First Language: The Early Stages. Harvard University Press, Cambridge, Mass.

Carrier, J. K., Jr. 1973. Application of functional analysis and nonspeech mode to teaching language. Report 7, Kansas Center for Research in Mental Retardation and Human Development, Parsons.

Carrier, J. K., Jr., and Peak, T. 1975. Non-speech Language Initiation Program. H & H Enterprises, Inc., Lawrence, Kan.

Chalfant, J., Kirk, G., and Jensen, K. 1968. Systematic language instruction: An approach for teaching preceptive language to young trainable children. Teach. Except. Child. 1:1–13.

Clark, E. 1973. What's in a word? On the child's acquisition of semantics in his first language. *In* T. Moore (ed.), Cognitive Development and the Aquisition of Language. Academic Press, New York.

Cromer, R. F. 1974. Receptive language in the mentally retarded: Processes and diagnostic distinctions. *In* R. L. Schiefelbusch and L. L. Lloyd (eds.), Language Perspectives—Acquisition, Retardation, and Intervention, pp. 237–267. University Park Press, Baltimore.

Dever, R. B. 1974. Discussion summary—Nonspeech communication. *In* R. L. Schiefelbusch and L. L. Lloyd (eds.), Language Perspectives—Acquisition, Retardation, and Intervention, pp. 419–427. University Park Press, Baltimore.

Estes, W. 1972. Reinforcement in human behavior. Am. Sci. 60:723–729.

Guess, D., Sailor, W., and Baer, D. M. 1974. To teach language to retarded children. *In* R. L. Schiefelbusch and L. L. Lloyd (eds.), Language Perspectives—Acquisition, Retardation, and Intervention, pp. 529–563. University Park Press, Baltimore.

Hollis, J., and Carrier, J. K., Jr. 1973. Prosthesis of communication deficiencies: Implications for training the retarded and deaf. Working Paper 298, Parsons Research Center, Parsons State Hospital and Training Center, Parsons, Kan.

Kent, L. 1974. Language Acquisition Program for the Severely Retarded. Research Press, Champaign, Ill.

McLean, L., and McLean, J. 1974. A language training program for nonverbal autistic children. J. Speech Hear. Disord. 39:186–193.

Marshall, N. R., and Hegrenes, J. R. 1972. A communication therapy model for cognitively disorganized children. *In* J. E. McLean, D. E. Yoder, and R. L. Schiefelbusch (eds.), Language Intervention with the Retarded, pp. 130–150. University Park Press, Baltimore.

Miller, J. F. and Yoder, D. E. 1974. An ontogenetic language teaching strategy for retarded children. *In* R. L. Schiefelbusch and L. L. Lloyd (eds), Language

Perspectives—Acquistion, Retardation, and Intervention, pp. 505–528. University Park Press, Baltimore.

Moores, D. F. 1974. Nonvocal systems of verbal behavior. *In* R. L. Schiefelbusch and L. L. Lloyd (eds.), Language Perspectives—Acquisition, Retardation, and Intervention, pp. 377–417. University Park Press, Baltimore.

Premack, D. 1971. Language in chimpanzee? Science 172:808–822.

Premack, D., and Premack, A. J. 1974. Teaching visual language to apes and language-deficient persons. *In* R. L. Schiefelbusch and L. L. Lloyd (eds.), Language Perspectives—Acquisition, Retardation, and Intervention, pp. 347–376. University Park Press, Baltimore.

Ruder, K. F., and Smith, M. D. 1974. Issues in language training. *In* R. L. Schiefelbusch and L. L. Lloyd (eds.), Language Perspectives—Acquisition, Retardation, and Intervention, pp. 565–605. University Park Press, Baltimore.

Schiefelbusch, R. L. 1974. Summary. *In* R. L. Schiefelbusch and L. L. Lloyd (eds.), Language Perspectives—Acquisition, Retardation, and Intervention, pp. 647–660. University Park Press, Baltimore.

Schiefelbusch, R. L. and Lloyd, L. L. 1974. Language Perspectives: Acquisition, Retardation, and Intervention. University Park Press, Baltimore.

Sloane, H., Johnson, M., and Harris, F. 1968. Remedial procedures for teaching verbal behavior to speech deficient or defective young children. *In* H. Sloane and B. MacAuley (eds.), Operant Procedures in Remedial Speech and Language Training. Houghton Mifflin Co., Boston.

Yoder, D. E. and Miller, J. F. 1972. What we may know and what we can do: Input toward a system. *In* J. E. McLean, D. E. Yoder, and R. L. Schiefelbusch (eds.), Language Intervention with the Retarded, pp. 89–107. University Park Press, Baltimore.

## APPENDIX: *VISUAL ATTENDING/MATCHING/MEMORY PROGRAM*

**Level One: Attending**

***Physical Attending***

A-1 Sitting in a chair
A-2 Elimination of interfering behaviors
A-3 Sitting at a table

***Visual Attending***

A-4 Eye contact
A-5 Attending to three objects

**Level Two: Matching**

***Matching Concrete Objects***

M-1 Matching one pair
M-2 Matching two pairs
M-3 Matching three pairs

***Matching Concrete to Abstract Objects***

M-4 Matching one pair
M-5 Matching two pairs
M-6 Matching three pairs

***Matching Abstract Objects***

M-7 Matching one pair
M-8 Matching two pairs
M-9 Matching three pairs

**Level Three: Visual Memory**

VM-1 Introduction to the task
VM-2 Matching two pairs from memory
VM-3 Matching three pairs from memory

### LEVEL ONE: ATTENDING

**Level One Terminal Objective for Physical Attending**

The child will sit in a chair, at a table across from the trainer, with his shoulders back, head erect, hands at rest, and with no interfering behaviors for 10 consecutive 30-second trials with 100% accuracy.

**Level One Intermediate Objectives for Physical Attending**

*A-1 Sitting in a chair*

The child will sit in a chair, shoulders back, head erect, and hands at rest for 10 consecutive 30-second trials with 100% accuracy.

*A-2 Elimination of interfering behaviors*

The child will sit in a chair with no interfering behaviors for 10 consecutive 30-second trials with 100% accuracy.

*A-3 Sitting at a table*

The child will sit in a chair, at a table across from the trainer, with his shoulders back, head erect, hands at rest, and with no interfering behaviors for 10 consecutive 30-second trials with 100% accuracy.

**Level One Definition of Terms for Physical Attending**

***Proper Sitting Positions***

*Sitting in a chair:* The child sits squarely on his chair with his back touching the back of the chair (he cannot be sitting on the edge or side of his chair with his back curved). He has his knees together and his feet flat on the floor (he cannot have his knees wide open or at the side of his chair and he cannot have his legs extended, feet upright, resting on his heels).

*Shoulders back:* The child sits with his torso erect and his shoulders back (he cannot have his shoulders in a rounded or slumped position).

*Head erect:* The child sits, his head erect, facing straight ahead (he cannot have his head turned to the side or hanging down).

*Hands at rest:* The child sits with his hands relaxed and open, either resting in his lap or on the table (he cannot have his hands clenched in a fist, clasped together, or grasping his body or clothing).

***Interfering Behaviors***

*Leg movements:* Unnecessary movements of the knees, legs, or feet.

*Torso movements:* Unnecessary rocking or swaying of the torso.

*Head movements:* Unnecessary nodding; tongue chewing; protruding tongue; or mouth open.

*Arm movements:* Unnecessary arm waving; moving of the fingers in front of the face; plucking or touching with the fingers; or wringing the hands.

**Level One Materials Needed for Physical Attending**

*Two chairs:* The two chairs should be the same size and small enough so the child's feet touch the floor.

*Table:* The table should be narrow enough so the trainer can reach across it and touch the child. It should be a compatible height for the chairs.

*Daily score sheet and a notation sheet*

*Pencil or pen*

*Edible reinforcements*

**Level One Reinforcement Procedures for Physical Attending**

All reinforcements for physical attending are placed directly in the child's mouth by the trainer. Each step specifies when to reinforce.

**Level One Pretest for Physical Attending**

***Procedures:***

1. The trainer reads all training steps for A-1, A-2, and A-3.
2. The trainer administers step A-3.
3. If the child does not reach criterion in 20 trials, the trainer terminates the pretest, checks the notation sheet, and does one of the following:
   a. If *any* sitting positions were noted as being incorrect, the trainer begins training with step A-1.1.
   b. If the sitting positions were correct but interfering behaviors were noted, the trainer begins training with step A-2. Only the training steps for the specific behaviors noted are administered. If more than one behavior requires training, the trainer should follow the A-2 sequence. For example, if the trainer notes that the child is rocking and chewing his tongue during a trial, he would first administer A-2.2 and then A-2.3.
4. If the child reaches criterion in 20 (or less) trials, the trainer administers the pretest for Level One: Visual Attending.
5. The trainer should be very stringent when evaluating the child's physical attention. Visual attention is built into the next two levels of the program, but physical attention is not. The purpose of this program is not to require the child to sit immobile for the duration of a training session. It is required that the child physically attend, without interfering behaviors, to the matching tasks presented in Levels Two and Three. If the trainer sees a behavior starting to interfere with the execution of a task and the child does not respond to the physical prompt, the trainer must stop the program and readminister attending training until the behavior is back on criterion.

## TRAINING FOR LEVEL ONE: ATTENDING

**Level One: Physical Attending A-1**

*A-1 Sitting in a chair*

The child will sit in a chair, shoulders back, head erect, and hands at rest for 10 consecutive 30-second trials with 100% accuracy.

**Objectives of Training Steps for A-1**

*A-1.1 Sitting in a chair with knees touching the trainer's knees*

The child will sit in a chair with his knees touching the trainer's knees for 30 seconds.

*A-1.2 Shoulders back*

The child will sit in a chair, knees touching the trainer's knees, and shoulders back for 30 seconds.

*A-1.3* *Head erect*
The child will sit in a chair, knees touching the trainer's knees, and head erect for 30 seconds.

*A-1.4* *Hands at rest*
The child will sit in a chair, knees touching the trainer's knees, and hands at rest for 30 seconds.

*A-1.5* *Sitting in a chair without knees touching the trainer's knees*
The child will sit in a chair without his knees touching the trainer's knees for 30 seconds.

*A-1.6* *Posttest for A-1*
The child will sit in a chair, knees no longer touching the trainer's knees, shoulders back, head erect, and hands at rest for ten consecutive 30-second trials with 100% accuracy.

**Criterion Test for A-1**

Each sitting position in A-1 is learned individually. The 30-second trial required at the end of each step is for that step's position only. The child is not required to hold all the sitting positions for 30 seconds until the A-1 posttest (A-1.6). It becomes necessary, therefore, to review each previously learned sitting position at the beginning of each new training step.

***Procedures:***

1. The trainer evaluates the child's sitting positions.
2. If *all previously learned positions* are correct, the trainer reinforces and begins the new training step.
3. If *any previously learned positions* are not correct, the trainer must administer a 30-second trial for *each* position.
4. For each 30-second trial required, the trainer gives the physical prompt for that position and reinforces if the child holds the position for 30 seconds. If the child does not hold the position for 30 seconds, the trainer must readminister training until the position is back on criterion.
5. When *all previously learned positions* are back on criterion, the trainer begins the new training step.

**Training Steps for A-1**

*A-1.1* *Sitting in a chair with knees touching the trainer's knees*
Procedures:

1. Place the child in a chair. (Reinforce.)
2. Place the other chair directly across from the child, close enough to the child so the trainer's knees will touch the child's knees.
3. The trainer sits and proceeds to position the child squarely in the chair, with knees together, feet flat on the floor, and back touching the back of the chair.

4. The trainer places his knees outside the child's knees and exerts as much pressure as needed for the child to maintain the sitting position for 30 seconds. (Reinforce.)
5. The trainer gradually decreases the amount of pressure exerted until the child can maintain the sitting position for 30 seconds with his knees touching the trainer's knees.
6. The trainer reinforces each trial that is as long or longer than the previous one.
7. The objective of this step is to stabilize the child in the sitting position by the trainer keeping his knees touching the child's knees. This technique will be used until step A-1.5 is reached because it also stabilizes the child in the following training steps.
8. Go to step A-1.2.

*A-1.2* *Shoulders back*

Procedures:

1. Place the child in a chair. (Reinforce.)
2. The trainer sits directly across from the child, with his knees touching the child's knees.
3. The trainer administers the A-1 criterion test.
4. The trainer pushes the child's shoulders back with both hands and exerts as much pressure as needed for the child to maintain the shoulders back position for 30-seconds. (Reinforce.)
5. The trainer gradually decreases the amount of pressure exerted until the child can maintain the shoulders back position for 30 seconds when initiated by the trainer with a light push on the child's shoulders (this is the physical prompt for the shoulders back position).
6. The trainer reinforces each trial that is as long or longer than the previous one.
7. The objective of this step is to train the child to assume the shoulders back position, when initiated by the physical prompt from the trainer, and to hold it for 30 seconds.

*A-1.3* *Head erect*

Procedures:

1. Place the child in a chair. (Reinforce.)
2. The trainer sits directly across from the child, with his knees touching the child's knees.
3. The trainer administers the A-1 criterion test.
4. The trainer cups his hand under the child's chin and moves the child's head into an erect, straight forward position. The trainer holds the child's head in this position and exerts as

much pressure as needed for the child to maintain the head erect position for 30 seconds. (Reinforce.)

5. The trainer gradually decreases the amount of pressure exerted until the child can maintain the head erect position for 30 seconds when initiated by the trainer with a light tap under the child's chin (this is the physical prompt for the head erect position).
6. The trainer reinforces each trial that is as long or longer than the previous one.
7. The objective of this step is to train the child to assume the head erect position, when initiated by the physical prompt from the trainer, and to hold it for 30 seconds.
8. Go to step A-1.4.

*A-1.4* *Hands at rest*

Procedures:

1. Place the child in a chair. (Reinforce.)
2. The trainer sits directly across from the child, with his knees touching the child's knees.
3. The trainer administers the A-1 criterion test.
4. The trainer places the child's hands, palms open and down, on the child's thighs and covers the child's hands with his. The trainer holds the child's hands in this position and exerts as much pressure as needed for the child to maintain the hands at rest position for 30 seconds. (Reinforce.)
5. The trainer gradually decreases the amount of pressure exerted until the child can maintain the hands at rest position for 30 seconds when initiated by a light tap on the back of the child's hands (this is the physical prompt for the hands at rest position).
6. The trainer reinforces each trial that is as long or longer than the previous one.
7. The objective of this step is to train the child to assume the hands at rest position, when initiated by the physical prompt from the trainer, and to hold it for 30 seconds.
8. Go to step A-1.5.

*A-1.5* *Sitting in a chair without knees touching the trainer's knees*

Procedures:

1. Place the child in a chair. (Reinforce.)
2. The trainer sits directly opposite the child, with his knees touching the child's knees.
3. The trainer administers the A-1 criterion test.
4. The trainer moves his chair back a few inches, so his knees are no longer touching the child's knees. The trainer places

his hands on the child's knees and exerts as much pressure as is needed for the child to maintain the sitting in a chair position for thirty seconds. (Reinforce.)

5. The trainer gradually decreases the amount of pressure exerted until the child can maintain the sitting in a chair position for 30 seconds when initiated by a light push on the knees (this is the physical prompt for the sitting in a chair position).
6. The trainer reinforces each trial that is as long or longer than the previous one.
7. The objective of this step is to train the child to assume the sitting position, when initiated by the physical prompt from the trainer, and hold it for 30 seconds without his knees touching the trainer's knees.
8. Go to A-1.6.

*A-1.6 Posttest for A-1*

Procedures:

1. Place the child in a chair. (Reinforce.)
2. Place the other chair directly across from the child and the table's width away.
3. The trainer evaluates the child's sitting positions and initiates any necessary corrections using the following physical prompts:
   a. Sitting—a push on the knees
   b. Shoulders back—a push on the shoulders
   c. Head erect—a tap under the chin
   d. Hands at rest—a tap on the back of the hands
4. After all necessary prompts have been given, the trainer administers the first 30-second trial.
5. If the proper sitting positions are maintained for 30 seconds, the trainer reinforces and marks the trial with a (+).
6. If the proper sitting positions are not maintained for 30 seconds, the trainer does not reinforce and marks the trial with a (–). The trainer makes a notation of which position the child was not able to hold after every (–) response.
7. The trainer readministers steps 3 and 4 until the criterion of 10 consecutive 30-second trials with 100% accuracy is attained.
8. If the child has not reached criterion by the end of the session, the trainer checks the notation sheet and at the next session readministers the training steps for the positions the child was not able to maintain.

9. The objective of the posttest is to train the child to hold all the sitting positions for 30 seconds. The tasks in Levels Two and Three can all be completed in thirty seconds so A-1 was designed to train the child to hold the sitting positions for that length of time.
10. If interfering behaviors have been noted by the trainer during the administration of A-1, go to step A-2.
11. If no interfering behaviors have been noted by the trainer during the administration of A-1, go to step A-3.

## SCORE SHEET

Name________________________________________

Scoring code: (+) response correct; (+VP) response correct with visual prompt from trainer; (+P) response correct with physical prompt from trainer; (−) response incorrect; (NR) no response

| Date | Task | Criterion | Stimulus used | Responses | % Correct |
|---|---|---|---|---|---|
| | | | | | |
| | | | | | |
| | | | | | |
| | | | | | |
| | | | | | |
| | | | | | |
| | | | | | |
| | | | | | |
| | | | | | |
| | | | | | |
| | | | | | |
| | | | | | |
| | | | | | |
| | | | | | |
| | | | | | |

chapter 15

# Word Identification and Comprehension Training for Exceptional Children

S. Vanost Wulz
John H. Hollis
Bureau of Child Research
University of Kansas
Lawrence, Kansas
and
Kansas Neurological Institute
Topeka, Kansas

contents

Recently there has been a proliferation of recommendations for using nonspeech response modes for communicatively handicapped persons. While the benefits of nonspeech systems are clearly established, research has neglected the role of the dominant system (usually spoken) in teaching nonspeech communication.

Nonspeech language systems are used predominantly with handicapped children who can hear (Fristoe and Lloyd, 1978). Thus, in addition to the nonspeech response mode, these children may comprehend spoken words. For the nonspeech system to be of maximum benefit to such a child, the relationship between the nonspeech system and speech should be clearly established.

There is little research on the best way to teach this relationship. Fristoe and Lloyd (1978) found that most teachers employ simultaneous presentations of spoken and nonspeech systems. However, they also report that descriptions of these procedures are generally vague and unsystematic.

Two types of basic nonspeech systems are available for language training. Manual signs are most commonly used (Fristoe and Lloyd, 1978). In manual signs, the movement, configuration, and placement of the communicator's hand distinguishes the lexical items from each other. This permits rapid and flexible communication, but may not be practical for some children because of memory or physical deficits (see Hollis and Carrier, 1978).

Communication boards are often used with children who cannot be taught manual signs (Vanderheiden and Grilley, 1976). Communication boards have a finite number of symbols, pictures, or words. The child must only indicate which symbol, picture, or word he wishes to employ. That is, the child is required only to select the response, rather than produce fine motor movements that are necessary for signing.

The goal of these nonspeech modes is to provide the individual with a communication method. It is difficult to evaluate the success of nonspeech training. The primary deterrent to evaluation of the effectiveness of nonspeech training is the poor definition of the skill. Goodman, Wilson, and Bornstein (1978) conclude that there is a need for a clarification of terminology and standardization of procedures in nonspeech language training.

In this chapter, single-word comprehension is defined for nonspeech training in terms of previous research on reading. Nonspeech communication involves many of the same skills that are necessary in reading. For example, a literate person can associate a printed word with spoken

---

This investigation was conducted at the Kansas Neurological Institute, Topeka, Kansas. It was supported by grant HD-00870 from the National Institute of Child Health and Human Development and by grant G007802087 from the U.S. Office of Education (BEH) to the Bureau of Child Research, University of Kansas, Lawrence, Kansas.

words and both of these symbols with their meaning. This is the goal of nonspeech training when used with hearing children. This aspect of reading and nonspeech training is studied in the remainder of this chapter in three experiments with severely and profoundly retarded children.

## TASK ANALYSIS OF WORD RECOGNITION

There are many definitions of reading. Some concentrate on the meaningful interpretation of printed material, while others deal primarily with the process of recoding from the printed symbol to the spoken word (Weiner and Cromer, 1967). It is evident that reading involves both of these processes. Mackworth (1972) has defined successful reading performance as "the achievement of a three-way synthesis among meaning, . . . the spoken word, and the written word" (p. 511). While this definition accounts for the relationship between printed and spoken words and their meanings, it does not specify how this should be measured.

The ideal definition of a behavior includes a description of the process by which it is measured (Wulz and Hollis, 1979b). There are several practical advantages to this approach. First, the definition provides a clearly specified criterion measurement. The child performs the task to some degree of proficiency that can be quantitatively reported. Second, if the child does not perform the task correctly, the skill is already defined for teaching; that is, the task is taught directly. Third, the question of *how* the child performs the task (i.e., the mental processes involved) is separated from *what* is done (i.e., the task performed).

Sidman (1971b) defined reading in a manner similar to Mackworth (1972). He specified four types of stimuli involved in the reading performance: (A) the spoken word pronounced by the teacher (auditory label), (B) the referent, (C) the printed word, and (D) the spoken word produced by the student (oral label). Successful reading performance requires that the child be able to associate these four stimuli for any particular word. Thus, the child should know that the oral label "cat" means the same thing as the printed word *cat*, and be able to match both to a picture of a cat.

### Discrimination Testing

In order to learn to associate these four different stimuli, the child must be able to discriminate among stimulus classes (e.g., between printed words and pictures) and among members of the same class (Premack, 1973). Obviously, if a child cannot see the difference between the signs for "toilet" and "candy," training will have little effect. Therefore, discrimination must be tested. Imitative match-to-sample procedures are useful for this purpose.

In the imitative match-to-sample procedure, two or more stimuli (e.g., pictures of a cat and a car) are placed in front of the child. The child will choose one of these pictures, so they are called the *response choices*. The teacher then shows the child another stimulus identical to one of the response choices (e.g., a picture of a car). This is the *sample stimulus*. The child's task is to select the response choice that exactly matches the sample stimulus. In this example, the child should select the picture of the car.

Match-to-sample has several positive characteristics. The number of response choices can be manipulated, which controls the possibility of the child getting a correct response simply by chance. For example, when there is only one response choice, the child will be 100% correct; when two response choices are available, the child will be 50% correct by chance; and so on. Second, the child need not produce a complex motor response (see Hollis and Carrier, 1978). Third, specific discriminations can be tested by varying the attributes of the response choices. For example, if two symbols are commonly confused, the teacher can teach the children the discrimination by presenting them together as response choices.

Three imitation tasks should be tested prior to word recognition training. If the referents are pictures, then the *picture-to-picture* match should be tested. If objects are used, then the *object-to-object* match should be tested. In either case, two or more referents should be placed on the table. When the teacher presents the sample stimulus, the child selects the referent identical to it.

The *symbol-to-symbol* match is tested in the same manner. If the child has a communication board, it would be best to use the board. When the teacher holds up a symbol, the child selects the symbol on the board that is identical to the sample stimulus.

Many children may not successfully perform the *auditory-oral imitation task*. In this task, the teacher says a word and the child repeats it. A child who is able to perform this task probably should not be taught a nonspeech communication system except in the context of reading.

Discrimination of spoken words might also be tested by *direction following*. Even some severely handicapped children understand instructions, such as "Sit down" and "Come here." If these are presented without accompanying gestures and children respond, they can be credited with some hearing and speech discrimination.

Children who can discriminate the relevant stimuli may still have trouble with reading. It appears to be the relationship among nonidentical stimuli, rather than intramodal discrimination and matching, that causes many language-related problems (cf. Sidman, 1971a).

### Word Recognition Testing

Weiner and Cromer (1967) point out that definitions of the reading process differ in their emphasis on "identification" (producing the oral label for a word) and "comprehension" (understanding the word). These two processes can be independent. Harris and Sipay (1977) report that when a child does not know a word there are three possibilities: 1) he does not know how to pronounce the word, 2) he does not know the meaning of the word, or 3) he knows neither the meaning nor the pronunciation of the word. Sidman's six tasks defining reading recognition will determine which, if any, of these aspects of word recognition the child is able to perform with a particular word. These observations also apply to nonspeech language training.

There are six tasks defining identification and comprehension of single words (Sidman, 1971b). These tasks test the matches among (A) auditory labels, (B) pictures (or referents), (C) printed words, and (D) oral labels. The first four tasks can be taught by the match-to-sample procedure described earlier, but tasks 5 and 6 require the child to produce oral responses (see Table 1).

All words must be presented on each task. It cannot be assumed that a child who can perform task 2 with, for example, the word "cat" can perform the same task with the word "car," nor can it be assumed that the child who can perform task 2 with one word can perform the other tasks, such as tasks 3 and 4, with the same word (see Table 1).

**Task 1: Receptive Comprehension** This task measures the child's ability to select the referent (object or picture) when given the auditory label. When verbs are tested, the teacher can "act out" the behavior and ask the students, "What am I doing?" (see Bellugi-Klima, 1971).

**Task 2: Receptive Reading** Task 2 tests the child's ability to select the printed word or nonspeech symbol when given the auditory label (spoken word). That is, successful performance of this task demonstrates that the child can match the dominant verbal labels (speech) with the nonspeech symbols that are being trained.

**Task 3: Reading Comprehension–1** This determines if the child knows the meaning of the word, or that particular meaning indicated by the referent. Again, if verbs are being tested, the teacher may act out the verb.

**Task 4: Reading Comprehension–2** This is identical to task 3 except that pictures or objects are the response stimuli and symbols are sample stimuli.

**Task 5: Referent Naming** A child who cannot perform the auditory-oral imitation task will be unable to perform this task correctly. Therefore, task 1 (auditory comprehension) is a better indication of the nonvocal child's knowledge of a particular referent. However, a child who can speak some words should definitely be tested on this task. It provides useful information about the degree of generalization that would be occurring were the child able to say more words.

Table 1. Functional analysis of reading

| Component name | Notation | Stimulus | Response |
|---|---|---|---|
| | | Receptive Tasks | |
| 1. Receptive comprehension | A–B | Auditory label | Picture |
| 2. Receptive reading | A–C | Auditory label | Symbol or printed word |
| | | Associative Tasks | |
| 3. Reading comprehension–1 | B–C | Picture | Symbol or printed word |
| 4. Reading comprehension–2 | C–B | Symbol or printed word | Picture |
| | | Expressive Tasks | |
| 5. Referent naming | B–D | Picture | Oral label |
| 6. Oral reading | C–D | Symbol or printed word | Oral label |

Adapted from Sidman and Cresson (1973).

**Task 6: Oral Reading** As with task 5, this task is less applicable to a totally nonvocal child than a child with some spoken words. However, it should be tested whenever possible.

## UNTRAINED EQUIVALENCES

Sidman and his colleagues demonstrated that specific training on each of the above discussed tasks is unnecessary. When children can perform task 1 (auditory comprehension, spoken word-picture) on the initial test, they should be able to perform all six tasks after training on task 3 (reading comprehension–1, picture–printed word) as a result of mediated transfer (Sidman, Cresson, and Willson-Morris, 1974). That is, task 1 (auditory comprehension, spoken word–picture) and task 3 (reading comprehension–1, picture–printed word) were sufficient to establish transfer to the remaining tasks. Similarly, children who could perform task 1 (auditory comprehension, spoken word–picture) and were trained on task 2 (auditory receptive reading, spoken word–printed word) could subsequently perform all six tasks (Sidman, 1971a, 1971b; Sidman and Cresson, 1973). Thus, tasks 1 and 2 *or* tasks 1 and 3 were sufficient to establish correct responses to all six tasks. These studies are impressive because they indicate that teaching is not necessary on each aspect of word recognition and that there are at least two ways to establish the same behavior.

Wulz and Hollis (1979a) compared three different ways of teaching word recognition using manual signs. In the *stimulus equivalence* procedure, the students were taught tasks 1 (receptive comprehension, gesture–picture) and task 3 (reading comprehension–1, picture–printed word) in either order and correct responses were established to the remaining four tasks. In the *response equivalence* procedure, task 1 (receptive comprehension, gesture–picture) and task 3 (reading comprehension–1, gesture–printed word) were taught in either order. Again, the students responded correctly to the remaining six tasks. The contiguity procedure involved the simultaneous presentation of two stimuli (speech and signs) with task 1 (receptive comprehension, speech and sign–picture) and task 2 (receptive reading, speech and sign–symbol). Contiguity was also tested by the simultaneous presentation of tasks 2 and 3 (gesture and picture-symbol). In all four of these procedures, the two trained tasks established correct responses to all six tasks. The authors concluded that generalization to untrained tasks will occur if students reach the proficiency criterion on the training tasks and if the training tasks involve each of the critical stimuli.

## READING EXPERIMENTS

Three experiments were designed to study the acquisition of integrated single-word reading performance as defined by Sidman (1971a, 1971b).

In the first experiment, a nonspeech language system was employed with severely retarded children to replicate the research done in reading and to compare the acquisition and transfer of three training tasks. Experiment 2 was designed to determine if severely retarded children who learned to use nonspeech symbols could also learn to read using printed words. In experiment 3, abstract stimuli were employed in training to determine the effectiveness of the three training tasks when subjects were unfamiliar with all of the stimuli.

## Method

**Subjects** Table 2 presents a summary of subject characteristics. Four young adult residents of Kansas Neurological Institute, Topeka, Kansas, were subjects in these studies. All of the subjects except S. C. could imitate speech, although the spontaneous speech of subjects S. M. and C. H. consisted primarily of stereotyped, repetitive phrases. All subjects successfully performed the imitative matches (tasks A, B, and C). V. G. had some sight words, and S. C. was being trained on a communication board using pictures. No subject had previous contact with Non-SLIP (Non-speech Language Initiation Program) symbols or the stimuli used for these experiments.

**Materials** Two sets of 15 stimuli were each divided into three lists of five words. List A, B, and C each consisted of five pictures of common objects, five Non-SLIP symbols (Carrier and Peak, 1975), five printed words, and five spoken labels (see Figure 1). The printed and spoken words were the common names for the pictured objects.

Lists D, E, and F each consisted of five consonant-vowel-consonant syllables (Hilgard, 1951), Non-SLIP symbols (Carrier and Peak, 1975), and abstract pictures (see Figure 1). The symbols, syllables, and pictures were randomly matched to one another and randomly assigned to the three lists D, E, and F.

## Procedure

A single-subject successive and simultaneous treatment design with multiple probes was employed in all three experiments. Each subject was probed or trained on three stimulus lists in each session. The order of the lists within the session was counterbalanced so that each list was trained first, second, and third across sessions.

**Probes** In all three experiments, the probes consisted of the six tasks shown in Table 1. Fifteen trials were presented on each task with each of the three stimulus lists. Except the expressive tasks (task 5, referent naming, picture–oral label, and task 6, oral reading, symbol–oral label) all testing involved the two-choice match-to-sample procedure described earlier.

Table 2. Characteristics of the subjects used in the experiments[a]

| Subject | Age (in years) | Years in institution | Measured intelligence[b] | PPVT[c] MA[d] (in years) | Sensory deficits | | Speech |
|---|---|---|---|---|---|---|---|
| | | | | | Visual | Auditory | |
| S.C. | 23 | 16 | –5 | 3–7 | Normal | Normal | Bilabials and vowels |
| V.G. | 19 | 14 | –4 | 3–5 | 20/100 | Normal | Conversational |
| S.M. | 26 | 16 | –5 | 2–3 | Normal | Normal | Stereotyped |
| C.H. | 28 | 11 | –5 | 2–5 | Normal | Normal | Stereotyped |

[a] At start of experiment.
[b] Heber (1961).
[c] Peabody Picture Vocabulary Test.
[d] Mental age.

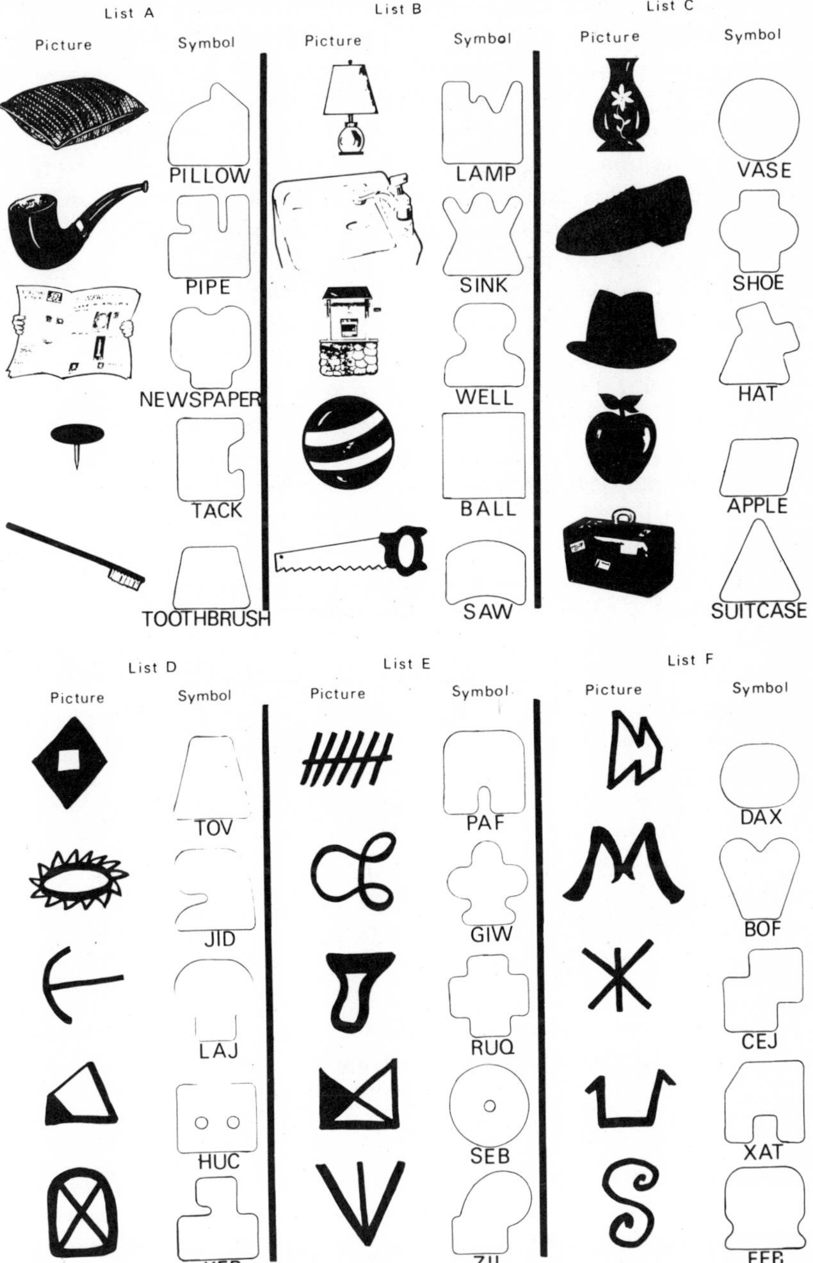


Figure 1. *Top*: The stimuli used in Experiments 1 and 2. *Bottom*: The abstract stimuli used in Experiment 3. (The pictures (top) are from Goldman-Lynch, American Guidance Service, 1979.)

**Training** Three training conditions were run in each experiment.

*Condition I* consisted of training on task 3 (reading comprehension–1, picture-symbol) in experiments 1 and 2. In experiment 3, task 3 (reading comprehension–1, picture–symbol) was repeated followed by task 2 (receptive reading, auditory label–printed word) in training phase 2.

In *Condition II*, task 2 (receptive reading, auditory label–printed word) and task 3 (reading comprehension–1, picture–printed word) were taught simultaneously. That is, the experimenter held up a picture and said the name of the picture at the same time. The subject selected the printed word or symbol that matched the picture and spoken word. In experiment 3, these tasks were repeated in training phase 2.

*Condition III* consisted of training on task 2 (receptive reading auditory label–picture) in experiments 1 and 2. In experiment 3, task 2 training was followed by task 3 (reading comprehension–1, picture–symbol) training.

All training involved the two-choice, match-to-sample procedure described earlier. Ten trials of each condition were presented in each session. When a subject performed 90% correct in two conditions for two consecutive sessions, probes were repeated.

**Feedback** All correct responses during training and probes were followed by praise and edibles. S. M. and C. H. received a piece of a cookie or cereal for each correct response. The other subjects (S. C. and V. G.) received a cookie at the end of the session, providing their performance was as good as or better than that in the previous session. Stimuli were removed following incorrect responses.

**Reliability** Reliability was assessed by an independent observer present in the room. Observers were instructed to disregard the experimenter's feedback to the subjects when judging the responses as correct or incorrect.

## EXPERIMENT 1

The purposes of experiment 1 were to apply Sidman's functional analysis of reading to nonspeech language training using Non-SLIP symbols (Carrier and Peak, 1975) to compare three training tasks in establishing the behavior, and to compare the transfer obtained from each task.

### Method

Subjects V. G., S. C., S. M., and C. H. participated in this experiment (see Table 2). Lists A, B, and C were employed with Non-SLIP symbols rather than printed words.

Initial probes were not presented to subjects V. G. and S. C. It was assumed they could not match the Non-SLIP symbol to the picture or spoken word, since they had no previous training with the symbols. After training, V. G. and S. C. were presented the probe tasks with two and then five response choices.

Three sets of probes were given S. M. and C. H. before training probes were given to confirm their inability to match Non-SLIP symbols to the stimuli. After 300 training trials, probes were presented to see if there was any change in behavior. Then training was continued for an additional 300 trials before probing again.

A correction procedure was instituted for the last 300 trials for subjects S. M. and C. H. During the correction procedure, the stimuli were removed and the same stimuli were presented again for two trials or until the correct response was made. These trials were not included in the percent correct.

**Results and Discussion**

Figures 2 and 3 indicate that there was a clear difference in the acquisition of the three training tasks by subjects S. C. and V. G. Both subjects consistently responded correctly to condition II (tasks 2 and 3, combined) and condition III (task 2, auditory label–printed word), but failed to learn task 3 (picture–printed word, condition I).

There was a less dramatic difference on the probes (see Tables 3 and

Table 3. Percent correct on probes for subject S.C. in experiment 1

| | | Posttests | | | | | |
|---|---|---|---|---|---|---|---|
| | | Experimental conditions | | | | | |
| | | I | | II | | III | |
| Reading components | Notation | 2-Choice | 5-Choice | 2-Choice | 5-Choice | 2-Choice | 5-Choice |
| | | Receptive Tasks | | | | | |
| Receptive comprehension | A–B | 93 | 100 | 100 | 100 | 100 | 100 |
| Receptive reading | A–C | 73 | 53 | 100[a] | 100 | 100[a] | 100 |
| | | Associative Tasks | | | | | |
| Reading comprehension–1 | B–C | 93[a] | 67 | 100[a] | 100 | 93 | 100 |
| Reading comprehension–2 | C–B | 100 | 80 | 100 | 100 | 100 | 93 |
| | | Expressive Tasks[b] | | | | | |
| Referent naming | B–D | 0 | 0 | 20 | 20 | 0 | 0 |
| Oral reading | C–D | 0 | 0 | 20 | 20 | 0 | 0 |

[a] Task trained prior to posttest.

[b] This subject's vocal repertoire was limited to bilabials and vowels.

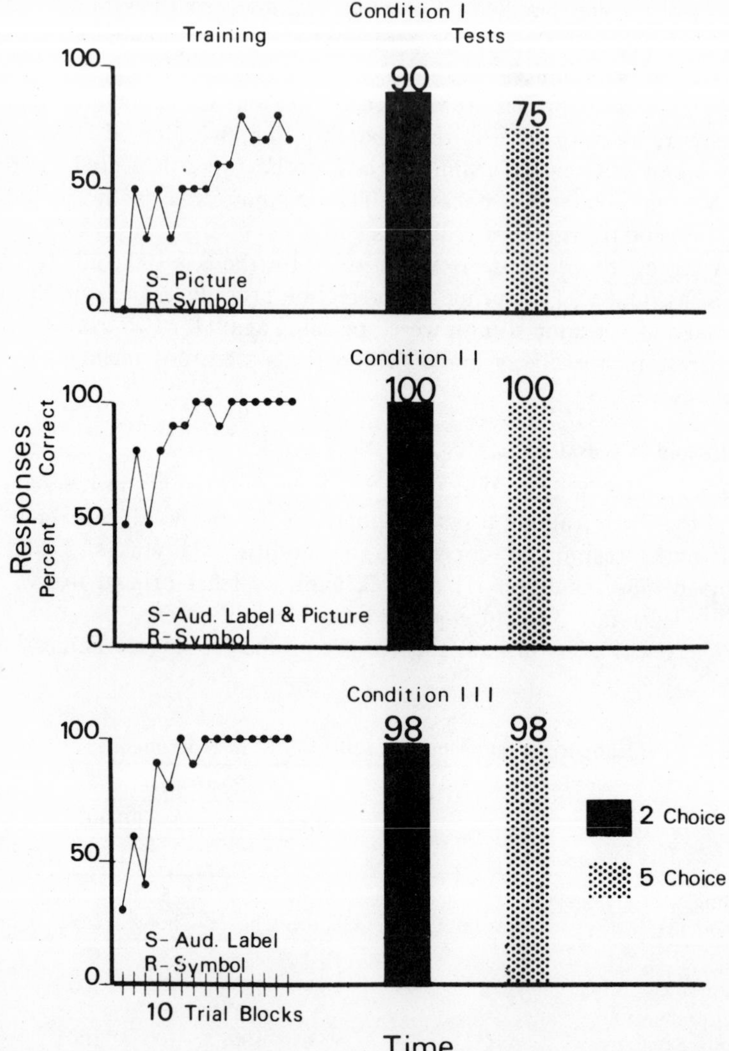


Figure 2. A comparison of three training conditions and receptive and associative reading probes for subject S. C. in experiment 1. Training conditions: I, associative B–C; II, simultaneous receptive and associative (A + B) – C; and III, receptive A–C.

4). Both S. C. and V. G. performed the six tasks in conditions II and III more accurately than those in condition I. However, it appears that they learned the equivalences among condition I stimuli during the probes.

There is an apparent improvement in V. G.'s performance on condition I probes when presented five response choices instead of two. This

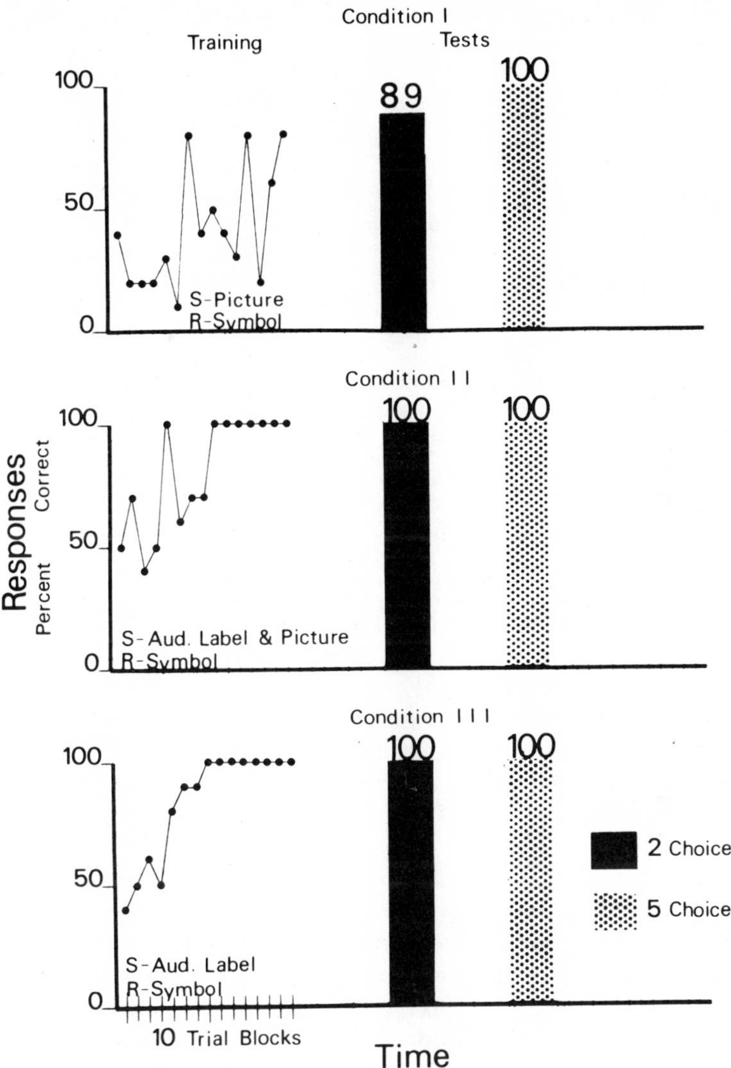


Figure 3. A comparison of the three training conditions and six reading probes for subject V. G. in experiment 1.

improvement is probably due to the learning that occurred on the previous two-choice probes, rather than an effect of increasing the number of response choices. S. C. also appeared to learn the equivalences in condition I during the two-choice probes; however, her performance was disrupted by increasing the number of response choices to five.

Table 4. Percent correct on probes for subject V.G. in experiment 1

| Reading components | Notation | Posttests — Experimental conditions I 2-Choice | I 5-Choice | II 2-Choice | II 5-Choice | III 2-Choice | III 5-Choice |
|---|---|---|---|---|---|---|---|
| | | Receptive Tasks | | | | | |
| Auditory comprehension | A–B | 100 | 100 | 100 | 100 | 100 | 100 |
| Auditory receptive reading | A–C | 60 | 100 | 100[a] | 100 | 100[a] | 100 |
| | | Associative Tasks | | | | | |
| Reading comprehension–1 | B–C | 87[a] | 100 | 100[a] | 100 | 100 | 100 |
| Reading comprehension–2 | C–B | 87 | 100 | 100 | 100 | 100 | 100 |
| | | Expressive Tasks | | | | | |
| Referent naming | B–D | 100 | 100 | 100 | 100 | 100 | 100 |
| Oral reading | C–D | 100 | 100 | 100 | 100 | 100 | 100 |

[a] Task trained prior to posttest.

As Figures 4 and 5 show, neither S. M. nor C. H. met criterion in any training condition in 300 training trials. However, the intermediate probes indicated that both subjects could perform task 1 (auditory label–picture) with 100% accuracy in all conditions (see Tables 5 and 6). Increases on task 5 (picture–oral label) were more variable.

Training task 2 was conducted with a correction procedure for 300 trials. Two two-choice posttests were given. This training showed little effect on S. M.'s probe results (see Figure 4 and Table 5).

C. H. met the training criterion in condition II (see Figure 5). Condition I (Task 3, picture-symbol) probe results did not reliably increase in posttest A or B. However, in condition II, C. H. performed task 2 (auditory label–printed word) with 93% and 80% accuracy in posttests A and B, respectively. Increases were also evident on task 5 (symbol–oral label). Responses to task 3 (picture-symbol) and task 4 (symbol-picture) were only 47% correct in posttest A, but increased to 87% correct in posttest B. C. H. also appeared to have learned task 2 (auditory label–printed word) in condition III, when she responded with 87% accuracy on Task 2 in posttest A. However, retesting in posttest B led to a drop to 67% correct.

Reliability was 100% for 150 training trials and 240 probe trials.

This study demonstrated that the research conducted by Sidman and his colleagues (Sidman, 1971a, 1971b; Sidman and Cresson, 1973, and

Sidman, Cresson, and Willson-Morris, 1974) on single-word reading is also applicable to single-word nonspeech training. If learning nonspeech symbol systems involves the same process as learning to read, it is logical to ask if these children could learn to identify printed words. Printed words have the obvious value of widespread use and availability.

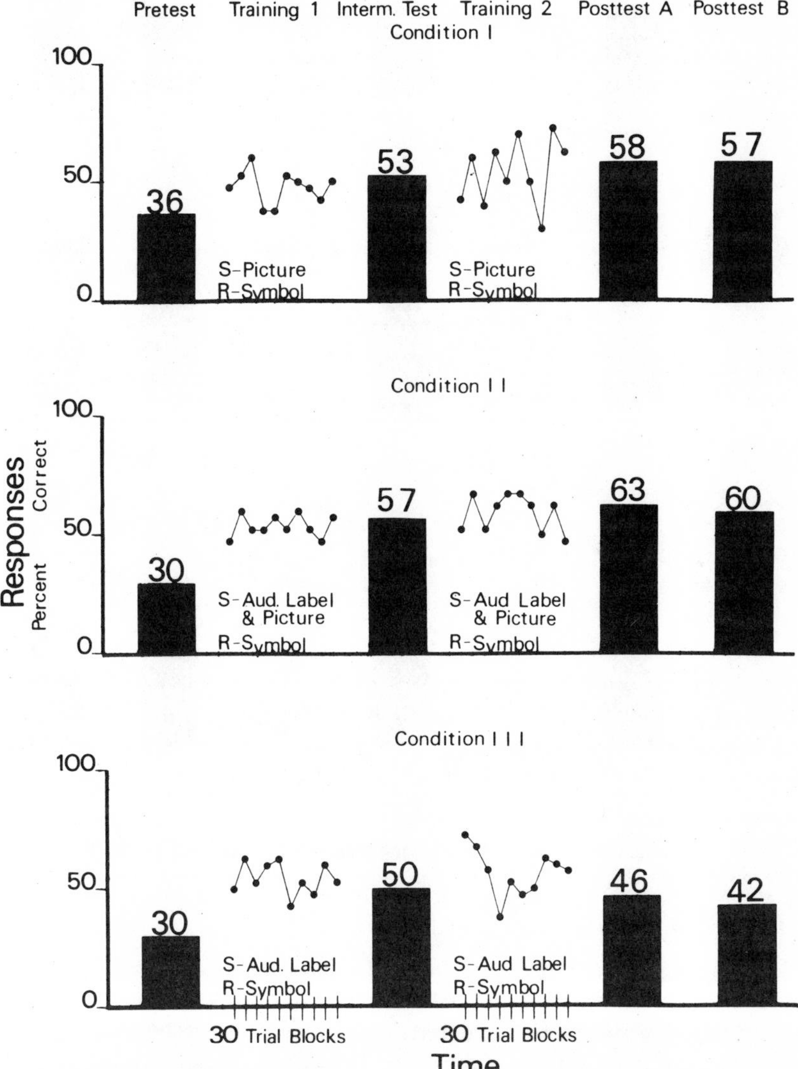


Figure 4. A comparison of three training conditions and six reading probes for subject S. M. in experiment 1.

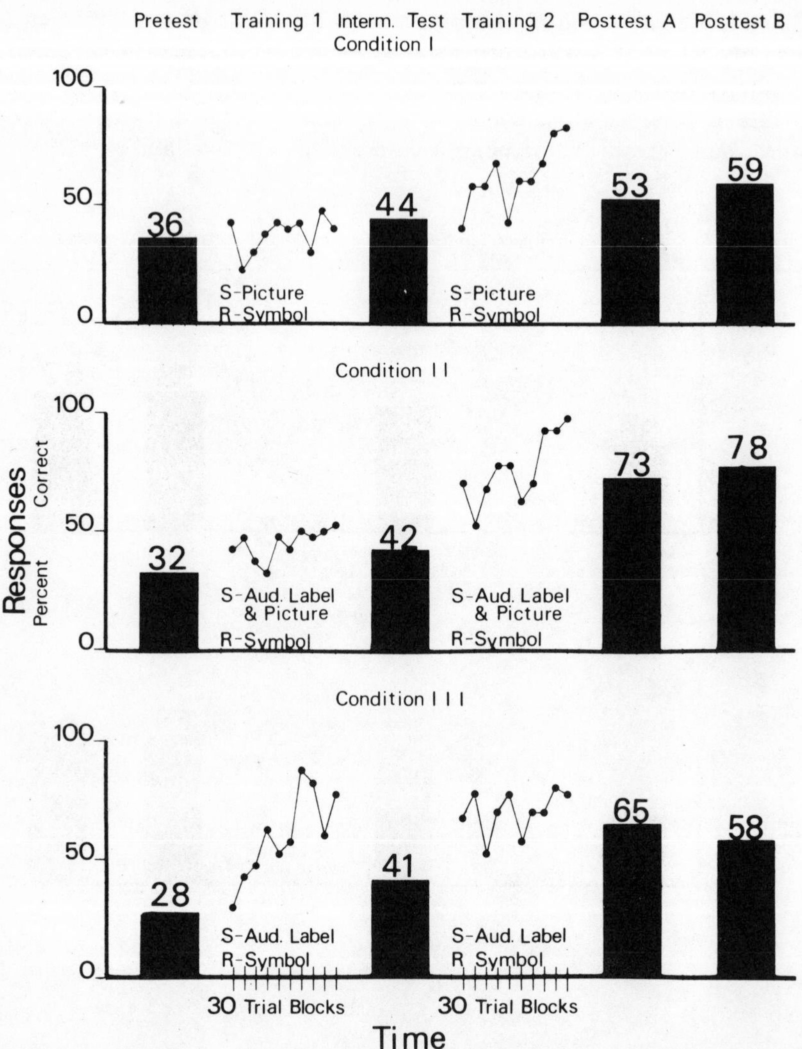


Figure 5. A comparison of three training conditions and six reading probes for subject C. H. in experiment 1.

## EXPERIMENT 2

Experiment 2 was designed to determine if severely retarded children who were capable of learning a nonspeech language system could learn to read printed words, and to compare the acquisition and transfer of three training tasks using printed words.

Table 5. Percent correct on probes for subject S.M. in experiment 1

| | | Tests | | | | | | | | | | | |
|---|---|---|---|---|---|---|---|---|---|---|---|---|---|
| | | Experimental conditions | | | | | | | | | | | |
| | | I | | | | II | | | | III | | | |
| Reading components | Notation | Pre | Int. | Post A | Post B | Pre | Int. | Post A | Post B | Pre | Int. | Post A | Post B |
| Receptive Tasks | | | | | | | | | | | | | |
| Receptive comprehension | A–B | 87 | 100 | 100 | 100 | 73 | 100 | 100 | 100 | 87 | 100 | 93 | 87 |
| Receptive reading | A–C | 20 | 33 | 47 | 47 | 13 | 27[a] | 47[a] | 47 | 20 | 33[a] | 27[a] | 40 |
| Associative Tasks | | | | | | | | | | | | | |
| Reading comprehension–1 | B–C | 13 | 60[a] | 67[a] | 67 | 20 | 60[a] | 73[a] | 60 | 7 | 93 | 47 | 27 |
| Reading comprehension–2 | C–B | 27 | 47 | 53 | 47 | 27 | 40 | 33 | 40 | 27 | 27 | 47 | 47 |
| Expressive Tasks | | | | | | | | | | | | | |
| Referent naming | B–D | 73 | 80 | 80 | 73 | 47 | 80 | 100 | 87 | 40 | 47 | 60 | 53 |
| Oral reading | C–D | 0 | 0 | 0 | 7 | 0 | 33 | 27 | 27 | 0 | 0 | 0 | 0 |

[a] Task trained prior to test.

Table 6. Percent correct on probes for subject C.H. in experiment 1

| Reading components | Notation | Tests | | | | | | | | | | | |
|---|---|---|---|---|---|---|---|---|---|---|---|---|---|
| | | Experimental conditions | | | | | | | | | | | |
| | | I | | | | II | | | | III | | | |
| | | Pre | Int. | Post A | Post B | Pre | Int. | Post A | Post B | Pre | Int. | Post A | Post B |
| Receptive Tasks | | | | | | | | | | | | | |
| Receptive comprehension | A–B | 87 | 100 | 100 | 80 | 80 | 100 | 100 | 93 | 67 | 100 | 93 | 93 |
| Receptive reading | A–C | 13 | 0 | 47 | 53 | 13 | 0[a] | 93[a] | 80 | 7 | 27[a] | 87[a] | 67 |
| Associative Tasks | | | | | | | | | | | | | |
| Reading comprehension–1 | B–C | 20 | 7[a] | 40[a] | 60 | 0 | 40[a] | 47[a] | 87 | 7 | 40 | 53 | 47 |
| Reading comprehension–2 | C–B | 13 | 53 | 60 | 60 | 0 | 40 | 47 | 87 | 7 | 40 | 53 | 47 |
| Expressive Tasks | | | | | | | | | | | | | |
| Referent naming | B–D | 80 | 93 | 73 | 73 | 80 | 100 | 93 | 93 | 80 | 60 | 67 | 60 |
| Oral reading | C–D | 0 | 13 | 0 | 27 | 7 | 0 | 33 | 47 | 0 | 7 | 27 | 20 |

[a] Task trained prior to testing.

## Method

Experiment 2 was conducted in the same manner as experiment 1. Lists A, B, and C were employed with printed words substituted for symbols. The printed words were 96-point standard capital letters mounted on wooden blocks for easy handling.

Subjects V. G. and S. C. participated in this experiment (see Table 2). Both subjects were presented pre- and posttests. The posttest included another probe, testing the match between the symbol trained in experiment 1 and the printed word trained in experiment 2. This task employed a two-choice match-to-sample procedure, as did the other probes. In the printed word–symbol task, two symbols were placed on the table, and then the experimenter held up a printed word. The subject selected the symbol that matched the printed word. This was also reversed to test symbol–printed word.

## Results and Discussion

Both subjects performed task 1 (auditory label–picture) with 100% accuracy on the initial probes in all three conditions. V. G. also named all of the pictures (task 5, picture–oral label). (S. C. was incapable of naming the pictures because of her speech disorder.) Neither subject exceeded 60% correct on any other task in the initial probes.

Both subjects met criterion in all three conditions within 200 training trials (see Figures 6 and 7). The percent correct was more variable across sessions than in experiment 1 (cf. Figures 2 and 3).

The posttests demonstrated that training was successful in producing transfer to untrained tasks (Figures 6 and 7). Both subjects performed the match between the symbol trained in experiment 1 and the printed word in experiment 2 with an average of 75%, 95%, and 65% accuracy in conditions I, II, and III, respectively.

Although the training results were slightly more variable than training with symbols, both subjects were successful in learning the task and transferring to other untrained tasks.

The next question is whether these results would hold true for subjects who did not already have some knowledge about the referents. That is, what would happen if these tasks were taught to children who did not know the meaning of the word?

## EXPERIMENT 3

The previous studies demonstrated that acquisition of task 2 (auditory label–printed word) and task 3 (picture–printed word), presented simultaneously or successively, would establish correct responses to the remaining tasks in Sidman's functional analysis of reading. This is true

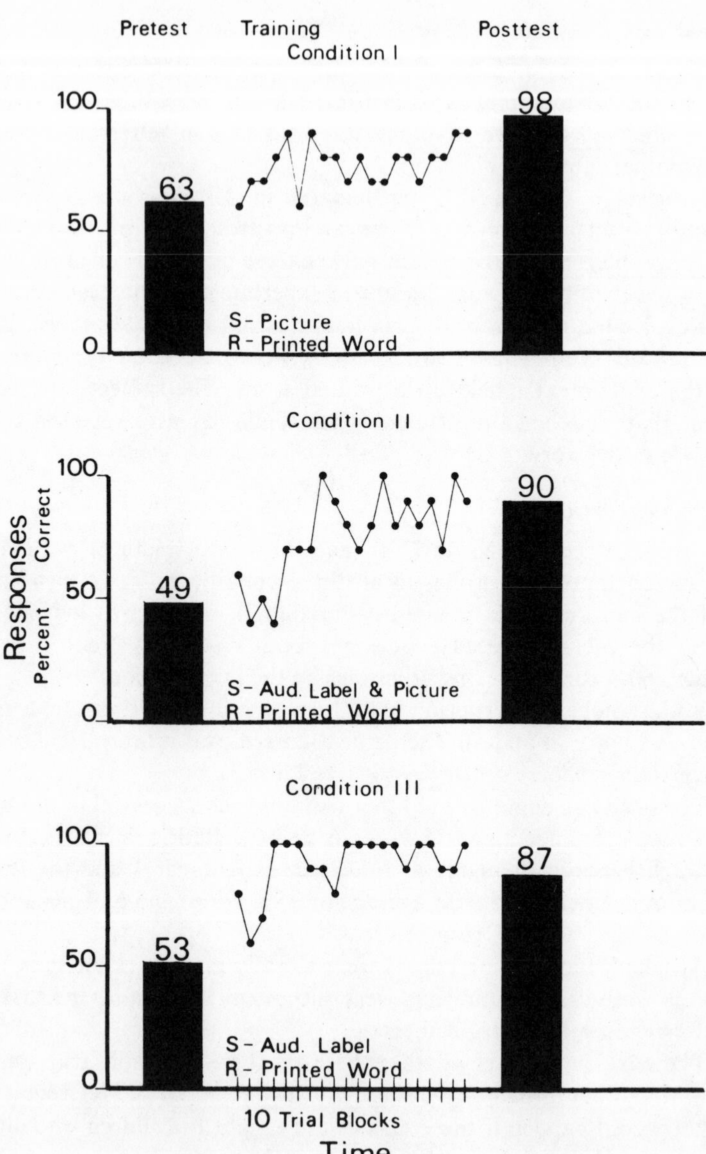


Figure 6. A comparison of three training conditions and the receptive and associative probes for subject S. C. in experiment 2.

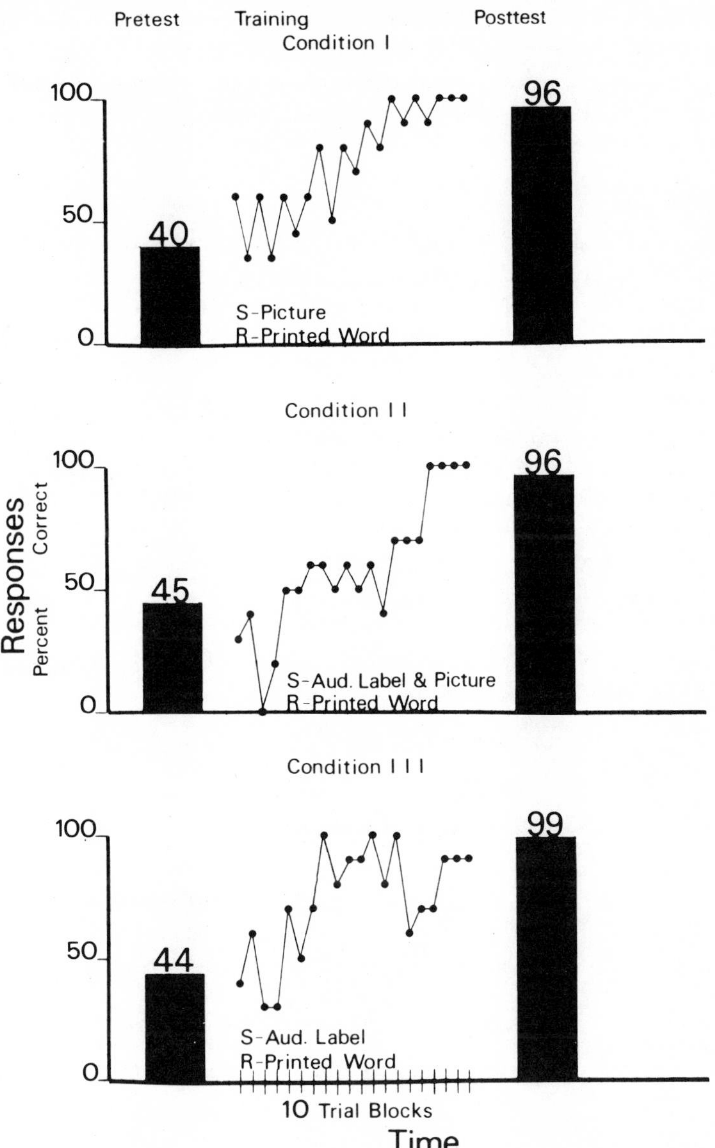


Figure 7. A comparison of three training conditions and six reading probes for subject V. G. in experiment 2.

for nonspeech, as well as printed stimuli. However, in each case the subjects could perform task 1 (auditory label–picture) before training. Experiment 3 was designed to eliminate correct responses to task 1 on the initial probes by using abstract stimuli, and then to study the effect of the three training tasks.

## Method

Experiment 3 differed from the previous studies in that two training phases were presented. *Condition I* training involved task 3 (picture-symbol) in phase 1 followed by task 2 (auditory label–symbol) in phase 2. As before, *condition II* involved the simultaneous presentation of task 2 (auditory label–symbol) and task 3 (picture-symbol). This training was the same in phase 2. *Condition III* was task 2 (auditory label–symbol) in phase 1 and task 3 (picture-symbol) in phase 2.

All four subjects participated in this experiment. Stimulus lists and training order were counterbalanced to eliminate order differences.

Probes were presented before and after each training phase. The six probes described in Table 1 were tested.

## Results

As Tables 7 and 8 indicate, neither S. C. nor V. G. could perform any of the probe tasks prior to training.

Table 7. Percent correct on probes for subject S.C. in experiment 3

| Reading components | Notation | Tests | | | | | | | | |
|---|---|---|---|---|---|---|---|---|---|---|
| | | Experimental conditions | | | | | | | | |
| | | I | | | II | | | III | | |
| | | Pre | Int. | Post | Pre | Int. | Post | Pre | Int. | Post |
| | | Receptive Tasks | | | | | | | | |
| Receptive comprehension | A–B | 20 | 20 | 73 | 20 | 93 | 100 | 20 | 7 | 73 |
| Receptive reading | A–C | 13 | 40 | 93[a] | 13 | 100[a] | 80[a] | 13 | 100[a] | 100 |
| | | Associative Tasks | | | | | | | | |
| Reading comprehension-1 | B–C | 33 | 60[a] | 87 | 27 | 93[a] | 100[a] | 27 | 40 | 100[a] |
| Reading comprehension-2 | C–B | 20 | 67 | 47 | 13 | 93 | 100 | 20 | 27 | 87 |
| | | Expressive Tasks[b] | | | | | | | | |
| Referent naming | B–D | 0 | 0 | 0 | 0 | 20 | 14 | 0 | 0 | 0 |
| Oral reading | C–D | 0 | 0 | 0 | 0 | 20 | 20 | 0 | 0 | 0 |

[a] Task trained prior to probe.

[b] This subject's vocal repertoire was limited to bilabials and vowels.

Table 8. Percent correct on probes for subject V.G. in experiment 3

| Reading components | Notation | Tests: Experimental conditions I Pre | I Int. | I Post | II Pre | II Int. | II Post | III Pre | III Int. | III Post |
|---|---|---|---|---|---|---|---|---|---|---|
| | | Receptive Tasks | | | | | | | | |
| Receptive comprehension | A–B | 13 | 33 | 100 | 13 | 100 | 100 | 20 | 20 | 87 |
| Receptive reading | A–C | 13 | 33 | 100[a] | 13 | 93[a] | 100[a] | 13 | 67[a] | 93 |
| | | Associative Tasks | | | | | | | | |
| Reading comprehension–1 | B–C | 30 | 100[a] | 100 | 7 | 100[a] | 100[a] | 13 | 13 | 100[a] |
| Reading comprehension–2 | C–B | 7 | 100 | 100 | 13 | 100 | 100 | 13 | 20 | 100 |
| | | Expressive Tasks | | | | | | | | |
| Referent naming | B–D | 0 | 20 | 73 | 0 | 40 | 80 | 0 | 13 | 80 |
| Oral reading | C–D | 0 | 0 | 73 | 0 | 67 | 73 | 0 | 80 | 100 |

[a] Task trained prior to probe.

As Figure 8 shows, S. C. failed to meet criterion in condition I, task 3 (picture-symbol) after 100 trials. Table 7 indicates that only a slight increase was evident in tasks 3 and 4 (symbol-picture). Training phase 2 (task 2, auditory label–symbol) resulted in correct responses to the receptive and associative tasks, with the exception of task 4 (symbol-picture).

As Figure 8 shows, S. C. failed to meet the training criterion in condition II (simultaneous training of task 2, auditory label–symbol, and task 3, picture-symbol). However, she performed all of the receptive and associative probe tasks correctly (see Table 7).

As Figure 8 shows, S. C. met criterion in condition III (task 2, auditory label–symbol). However, only task 2 showed subsequent improvement (see Table 7). Training task 3 (picture-symbol) in phase 2 resulted in correct responses to the remaining probes (see Table 7).

V. G. met criterion on task 3 (picture-symbol) in condition I, phase 1, after 100 trials (see Figure 9). Subsequent improvements on tasks 3 and 4 (symbol-picture) were observed on the probes (see Table 8). Training task 2 (auditory label–symbol) in phase 2 resulted in correct responses to all the probes (see Table 8).

V. G. met criterion in condition II (task 2, auditory label and picture–symbol) in 100 trials (see Figure 9). All tasks improved on the probes (see Table 8).

Condition III responses (task 2, auditory label–symbol) failed to meet criterion in 100 trials. Although only a slight improvement was observed in task 2, responses to task 6 (symbol–oral label) increased to 80% cor-

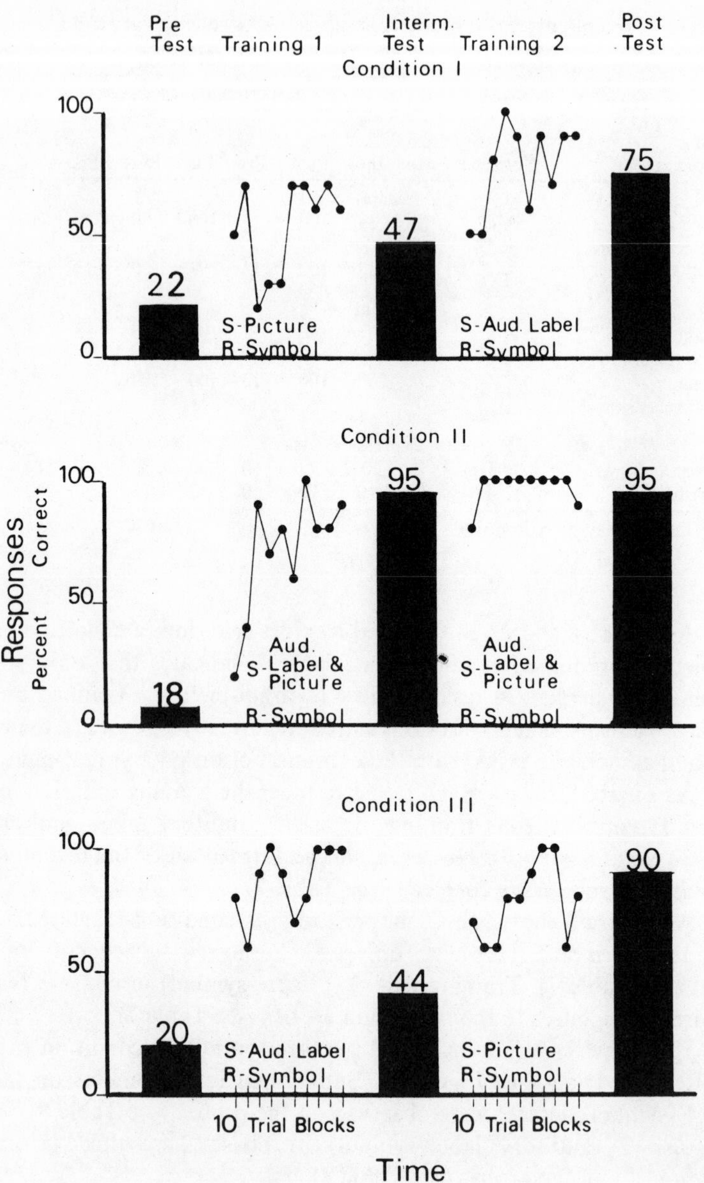


Figure 8. A comparison of the three training conditions and the receptive and associative reading probes for subject S. C. in experiment 3.

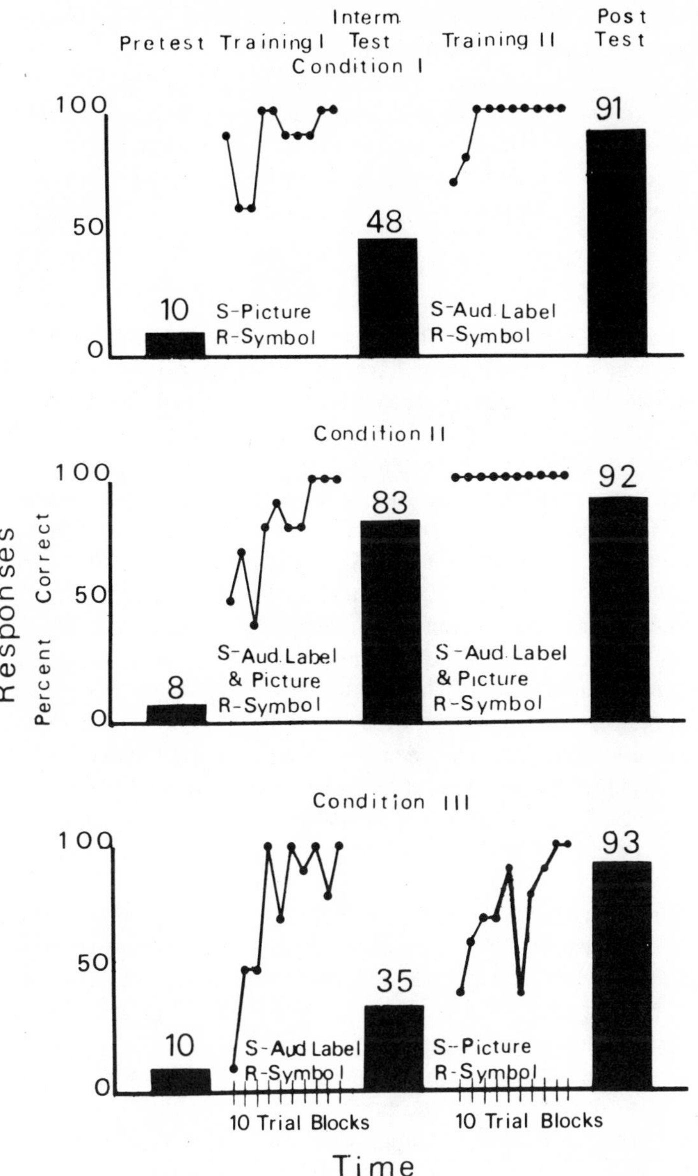


Figure 9. A comparison of the three training conditions and the six reading probes for subject V. G. in experiment 3.

rect (see Table 8). Phase 2 training, on task 3 (picture–symbol) resulted in accurate responses to all probe tasks.

S. M. and C. H. were presented 100 trials during training task 1 with no consistent increase in correct responses. Since no improvements were observed on the probes, no further training was given.

Reliability for 315 training trials and 195 probe trials was 100% interobserver agreement.

## DISCUSSION

These studies suggest that the learning involved in nonspeech language systems may not be different from the learning involved in reading. In experiment I nonspeech symbols were used. When the children could already select pictures of the referents given their oral name (task 1, receptive comprehension), teaching task 2 (receptive reading) or task 3 (reading comprehension) resulted in correct responses to all six reading tasks. These results are the same as obtained by Sidman (1971a, 1971b), Sidman and Cresson (1973) and Sidman, Cresson, and Willson-Morris (1974) with printed words. Experiment 2 provided further evidence of the relationship between reading and nonspeech language training. The two children who learned the matches in experiment 1 were taught the same tasks with printed words. The results with printed words were the same as with Non-SLIP symbols in experiment 1.

These experiments also demonstrated that the behavior of children in the baseline probes determines what needs to be taught. In experiments 1 and 2 the children performed task 1 (receptive comprehension, auditory label–picture) correctly on the baseline. Thus, training either task 2 (receptive reading, auditory label–printed word) or task 3 (reading comprehension, picture-symbol) established correct responses to all six tasks in the posttests. On the other hand, the subjects were not able to match any of the stimuli used in experiment 3 prior to training. As a result, training on both tasks 2 and 3 was required in order to establish correct responses on the six probes in the posttest.

This is critical information to teachers of reading or nonspeech communication. A child whose receptive vocabulary includes the words to be taught will require fewer training tasks than the child who is not already familiar with the word. However, by the simultaneous presentation of two tasks (as in condition II in these experiments), the amount of time required for training may be reduced. Simultaneous presentation of two tasks may also be more effective than training involving single tasks. However, additional research needs to be done to establish the generality of these findings.

The data obtained from S. C. indicate that children who cannot speak can still learn to read and to use nonspeech symbols. Furthermore, the inability to produce verbal stimuli does not disrupt generalization from trained to untrained tasks. S. C. learned the initial tasks rapidly and transferred to other untrained tasks as well as V. G., who could speak. Again, these findings need to be replicated with other individuals.

The results may have been affected by the individual's mental age. The two subjects who failed to learn these tasks had mental ages below 3.0 years. Other research with the same population has suggested that 3.0 may be a critical level for the type of symbolic learning described in these studies (Hollis, 1979). However, this appears to indicate the probability of learning, rather than a clear impossibility. For example, C. H. did learn the associations among the five words trained in condition II and showed some transfer to untrained tasks as well. However, it took 600 trials as opposed to the 150 trials required for S. C. and V. G. Thus, the mental age may suggest that training will be difficult, rather than an outcome of training.

The training procedures used in this experimental study were not optimal. Fifteen matches were trained in each session, and only reinforcement procedures were used in training. It would have been more effective educationally if the number of items trained was reduced and fading or shaping procedures were used instead of trial and error.

Nonetheless, the subjects who learned the tasks demonstrated mediated transfer to untrained tasks. The use of mediated transfer in teaching has important implications. First, the teaching can be programmed to maximize its benefits. For example, if a child could perform task 1 (receptive comprehension, auditory label–picture), teaching task 5 (referent naming, picture–oral label) would produce only limited benefits, since it would increase with any training (see C. H. and S. C.'s data). On the other hand, task 2 (receptive reading, auditory label–printed word) or task 3 (reading comprehension, picture–printed word) would lead to complete proficiency with all the tasks.

A second benefit to the application of mediated transfer in teaching is that children's optimal learning modalities can be utilized. Jones (1972) reports that there may be individual differences in modality preference. One advantage to Sidman's analysis of reading is that a child who is failing on one task can be taught another task instead, without changing the terminal behavior. For example, in experiment 1 (see Figures 2 and 3), when V. G. and S. C. failed to learn task 3 (reading comprehension–1, picture–printed word), probing task 2 (receptive reading, auditory label–printed word) established all six reading behaviors including task 3. Mediated transfer allows a great deal of flexibility in teaching word recognition.

On the other hand, it cannot be assumed that mediated transfer will occur. C. H. in experiment 1 learned the task in condition II and showed some transfer. However, additional training would have been required to obtain the broad transfer evidenced by S. C. and V. G. This is only evident from the results of the posttest. Thus, testing is essential to measure the success of teaching, just as pretesting is essential to determine what to teach.

More research is needed on mediated transfer. The results need to be generalized to other populations, especially those with difficulties learning to read and normal children who are capable of reading. For example, would deaf children show the same forms of transfer using signs and printed words? Mediated transfer research also has to extend its scope to other types of behaviors, both academic and social. Research with other children who fail to learn the tasks needs to be done to determine how to teach the task to them.

## SUMMARY

This chapter has attempted to delineate the role of receptive language (speech) in the development of a nonspeech language system. It has also discussed the relationship between learning nonspeech language and reading. The second part of the chapter has presented data on the establishment of these relationships.

The word identification and comprehension training was based on a task analysis of word recognition (functional analysis of reading) and mediated transfer (acquisition of untrained equivalences). The functional analysis of reading provides for the breakdown of reading into the following tasks: 1) receptive comprehension, 2) receptive reading, 3) reading comprehension–1, 4) reading comprehension–2, 5) referent naming, and 6) oral reading.

It has been demonstrated that specific training on each of the six tasks is generally unnecessary. That is, training on some of the tasks (e.g., task 1 and task 3) should enable the child to perform all six tasks as a result of mediated transfer.

In general, the results from the experiments show that the functional analysis of reading and mediated transfer paradigm are applicable to nonspeech language training. The results have also shown that children who have learned a nonspeech language system were capable of learning to read printed words. However, in this case the children had previous knowledge about the referents. In order to eliminate the referent problem, the final experiment employed abstract stimuli as referents. In general, the results showed that the subjects were able to perform the reading tasks after training on two tasks. It was concluded that the role of receptive language (speech) in the development of a nonspeech language system is an important one and that in many cases printed words may be substituted for plastic word stimuli.

## REFERENCES

Bellugi-Klima, V. 1971. Some language comprehension tests. *In* C. Lavatelli (ed.), Language Training in Early Childhood Education. University of Illinois Press, Urbana.

Carrier, J. K., Jr., and Peak, T. 1975. Non-speech Language Initiation Program. H & H Enterprises, Inc., Lawrence, Kan.

Fristoe, M., and Lloyd, L. L. 1978. A survey of the use of non-speech systems with the severely communication impaired. Ment. Retard. 16:98–102.

Goodman, L., Wilson, P. S., and Bornstein, H. 1978. Results of a national survey of sign language programs in special education. Ment. Retard. 16:104–106.

Harris, A. J., and Sipay, E. R. 1977. How to Increase Reading Ability. David McKay Co., New York.

Heber. 1961. A manual on terminology and classification in mental retardation. Am. J. Ment. Defic. Monogr. Suppl.

Hilgard, E. R. 1951. Methods and procedures in the study of learning. *In* S. S. Stevens (ed.), Handbook on Experimental Psychology. John Wiley & Sons, New York.

Hollis, J. H. 1979. Use of nonspeech responses to teach communication. (Final progress report.) NICHD Grant No. HD07339, Kansas Neurological Institute, Topeka.

Hollis, J. H., and Carrier, J. K., Jr. 1978. Intervention strategies for nonspeech children. *In* R. L. Schiefelbusch (ed.), Language Intervention Strategies, pp. 57–100. University Park Press, Baltimore.

Jones, J. P. 1972. Intersensory Transfer, Perceptual Shifting, Model Preference and Reading. International Reading Association, Newark, Del.

Mackworth, J. F. 1972. Some models of the reading process: Learners and skilled readers. Read. Res. Q. 7:701–733.

Premack, D. 1973. Cognitive principles. *In* J. McGuigan and G. Lumsden (eds.), Contemporary Approaches to Conditioning and Learning. V. H. Winston & Sons, Washington, D.C.

Sidman, M. 1971a. The behavioral analysis of aphasia. J. Psychiatr. Res. 8:413–422.

Sidman, M. 1971b. Reading and auditory-visual equivalence. J. Speech Hear. Res. 14:5–13.

Sidman, M., and Cresson, O. 1973. Reading and crossmodal transfer of stimulus equivalence in severe retardation. Am. J. Ment. Defic. 77:515–523.

Sidman, M., Cresson, O., and Willson-Morris, M. 1974. Acquisition of matching to sample via mediated transfer. J. Exp. Anal. Behav. 22:261–273.

Vanderheiden, G. C., and Grilley, K. (eds.). 1976. Non-vocal Communication Techniques and Aids for the Severely Physically Handicapped. University Park Press, Baltimore.

Weiner, M., and Cromer, W. 1967. Reading and reading difficulty: A conceptual analysis. Harv. Educ. Rev. 37:620–643.

Wulz, S. V., and Hollis, J. H. 1979a. Application of manual signing to the development of reading skills. *In* R. L. Schiefelbusch and J. H. Hollis (eds.), Language Intervention from Ape to Child, pp. 465–489. University Park Press, Baltimore.

Wulz, S. V., and Hollis, J. H. 1979b. Word recognition: A task-based definition for testing and teaching. Read. Teach. 32:779–786.

chapter 16

# Procedures for Determining the Optimal Nonspeech Mode with the Autistic Child

*Cathy Alpert*

*Bureau of Child Research*
*University of Kansas*
*Lawrence, Kansas*

contents

## PROBLEMS IN SELECTING A NONSPEECH MODE FOR TRAINING

Two major factors have contributed to the use of nonspeech language intervention procedures with autistic children. First, research investigations (e.g., Hingtgen and Churchill, 1969) have provided strong evidence that speech therapy is often very time consuming for the clinician and relatively unproductive for the child. Moreover, as noted by Baker et al. (1976), the language problems of autistic children are intimately related to other features of the syndrome (e.g., establishing relationships with people), as well as to eventual outcome. Since greater chances for improvement in social development have been associated with the presence of useful speech by age 5 (Eisenberg, 1956; Rutter, 1970), emphasis has been placed on introducing language-training procedures as soon as possible. Thus, due to a growing awareness of the limitations of traditional speech-training procedures plus a realization of the importance of instituting effective early language intervention procedures, an increasing number of interventionists are using alternative, nonvocal means for teaching autistic children. Various nonspeech modes have been tried with this population in the hope that they would facilitate or supplement the acquisition of a more natural spoken language. In addition, if, for whatever reason, a child does not learn to talk, the nonvocal mode provides a functional means of communicating with others.

The potential benefits of employing a nonspeech intervention approach with some autistic children have been indicated in the literature. For example, Premack and Premack (1974), McLean and McLean (1974), and de Villiers and Naughton (1974) taught autistic children to make communicative responses with abstract symbols. Other nonspeech modes tried with this population have included sign (Creedon, 1973; Miller and Miller, 1973; Webster et al., 1973; Fulwiler and Fouts, 1976; Schaeffer, Chapter 17, this volume) and the written word (Hewett, 1964; Marshall and Hegrenes, 1972; LaVigna, 1977). While the advantages of nonspeech training for some autistic children have greatly expanded the range of language intervention approaches available to the clinician, several new problems have been created. These problems include: 1) when to introduce the nonspeech procedures (e.g., as an initial means of intervention or after speech training has proved to be generally ineffective), and 2) which nonspeech mode to select for training. This chapter addresses the latter issue.

A number of nonspeech symbol systems exist, including at least four systems of signing (fingerspelling, Signing Exact English (Gustason, Pfetzing, and Zawolkow, 1972); Seeing Essential English (Anthony, 1971); and American Sign Language), iconic symbol systems (e.g., Blissymbols (Bliss, 1965) and rebus (Woodcock, Clark, and Davies, 1968)), abstract symbol systems (e.g., Non-SLIP (Carrier and Peak,

1975)), and the phonetic or whole-word approach to reading written words. Other nonspeech modes such as an electronic talking machine or a tactile system similar to braille could also be considered for training. In programming for intervention, the interventionist will inevitably be faced with the task of determining which mode to teach each child. The interventionist must specify those criteria in which the decision to teach, for example, sign over abstract symbol or the written word over sign, are based.

Hollis, Carrier, and Spradlin (1976) and Hollis and Carrier (1978) have suggested that a functional communication channel must be established before intervention techniques can be applied. This process involves identification of a sensory input mode (visual, auditory, tactile, or olfactory), an integrative process or conceptual level (imitative, nonimitative, constructive, or transformative), and a response output mode (gross motor movements, signing, writing, or speech). As stated by Hollis and Carrier (1978):

> . . . it is the clinician's or the teacher's task to assess the child's handicapping condition(s) and select the communication channel that has the highest probability of being functional for that child. For example, if the child is retarded and has an auditory impairment, it might be possible to establish a functional communication channel as follows: 1) *input*–visual, 2) *mediation/function level*–imitation, and 3) *output*–gross motor. The selection of input, process, and response levels will depend on the type and degree of handicapping condition(s) exhibited by the child (p. 64).

The necessity of determining a functional communication channel as a first step in planning language therapy is evident. The process, however, is more difficult for some children than for others. When planning intervention for a visually handicapped or deaf child, for example, restrictions are immediately placed on functional input and output modes. In contrast, because of the ambiguity of the sensory impairment(s) of autistic children, the difficulty of locating a functional communication channel may be increased.

Rimland (1964) and Schopler (1965) agree that the autistic child shows a preference for the proximal sense of touch, taste, and smell over the distal senses of vision and hearing. According to Ornitz and Ritvo (1968), "while auditory changes are most often noted, unusual perceptual aberrations may be seen in the visual, tactile, gustatory, olfactory, proprioceptive and vestibular senses" (p. 81). More recently, Ornitz and Ritvo (1976) have stated that the failure of adequate modulation of sensory input appears behaviorally as hypo- or hyperresponsive states that alternate in the same child. Furthermore, hypo- and hyperreactivity may be observed in all sensory modalities. With regard to the auditory channel, they note that the autistic child may either be very sensitive to, or may not respond to, speech or nonspeech noises. Hypersensitivity to sounds has been noted when, for example, the child induces auditory input by grinding his teeth, flicking or banging his ears, or by placing his ear close to a sound source. Many autistic children cover their ears and show signs of distress with environmental sounds such as a dog's barking, a vacuum cleaner, or a siren. In contrast, a loud, sudden noise may fail to evoke a visible reaction in the child. Condon (1975) reported that at least some autistic children show a delayed or multiple response to sounds. With respect to the visual modality, Ornitz and Ritvo (1976) note that hyporesponsiveness occurs when the child walks into or past objects as if he did not see them. On the other hand, the child may become very upset over slight changes in the home environment, such as the relocation of an ash tray from one coffee table to another. The child may scrutinize the details of surfaces and attend to marks, tears, discolorations, and the like in furniture and clothing. Autistic children are also said to stimulate the visual modality by producing hand and finger movements at the sides of their heads or by intensely viewing their hands from various perspectives. Similar unusual unresponsiveness to tactile, gustatory, and olfactory senses have also been described. The children may show no reaction to painful stimuli, but they may create tactile input by carefully feeling the surfaces of objects. Autistic children have been known to put such unedibles as dirt, wood, and stones in their mouths. Strong food preferences, sometimes for unusual foods, have also been noted. In regard to the olfactory sensory modality, a heightened sensitivity to smell is characteristic of many autistic children.

The range of sensory deficits in any one autistic child may be broad and varied. Assessing the type and degree of these impairments may be a difficult, if not an impossible task for the clinician. Furthermore, different nonspeech communication systems may have overlapping qualities that cause confusion about which mode to teach. Additional information may be necessary to determine which nonspeech symbol system a child is most likely to learn. This chapter describes one potential method for determining the optimal nonspeech mode for training a language-impaired child. The procedures were developed at the Judevine Center for Autistic Children in St. Louis, Missouri, with children exhibiting autistic-like behaviors. Although the procedures will be discussed in terms of their applicability to this population, they may also be used with other language-disordered children. Before presenting the training/assessment model, a brief overview of autism is appropriate, with special attention directed to the speech and language characteristics associated with the disorder.

## VOCAL AND NONVOCAL ASPECTS OF COMMUNICATION IN THE AUTISTIC CHILD

Unusual speech development is the most common indicator to parents that something may be wrong with their child. Parental reports, often given in retrospect, indicate that atypical nonvocal development also occurs during the first 30 months. Briefly, behavioral characteristics associated with the autistic infant include: little response to the mother's voice (Ricks and Wing, 1976), lack of an anticipatory response to being picked up (Rimland, 1964), inconsistent responses to environmental sounds, causing the child to appear to be either deaf or extremely sensitive to noises (Ruttenberg and Wolf, 1967; Rutter, 1974), deficient or deviant babbling (Bartak, Rutter, and Cox, 1975; Ricks, 1975), and failure to adapt body posture to that of the person carrying the child (Rimland, 1964; Wing, 1966).

Nonvocal deficits usually persist as the child gets older. Unlike deaf children who are also severely impaired in the ability to express themselves vocally, autistic children do not use gestures to communicate. Although a child might pull an adult by the hand and place the hand on a desired object or push the hand through a movement (e.g., opening the refrigerator door), the child typically does not look into the adult's face and appears to use the hand ". . . in isolation from any affective relationship with the adult" (Rutter, 1966, p. 61). The gesture of pointing may occur spontaneously, although it often requires specific training. Similarly, nodding and shaking the head to signal yes and no are seldom used as substitutes or supplements for speech. Thus, these communicative gestures must also be specially trained. Rutter (1978) recently pointed out that autistic children frequently fail to show social imitation typified by such activities as waving "bye-bye," playing games like "pat-a-cake," or imitating their parents (e.g., ironing, dusting, raking leaves). In addition, young autistic children lack imaginative play and are unlikely to play the pretend games (e.g., cowboys, Superman) in which normal children engage.

Attempts to understand the intentions of the autistic child by noting his facial expressions may be of little value. Ricks and Wing (1976) have noted that, although autistic children are usually able to smile, laugh, cry, etc., they tend to show the extremes of emotions. They may exhibit stoical appearances or laugh or cry uncontrollably for no apparent reason. The more subtle emotions such as doubt or embarrassment are rarely expressed. The emotional displays are oftentimes quite inappropriate to the child's age and environment. Ricks and Wing (1976) further note that clinical impressions suggest that the expression of emotion in older autistic individuals, including persons with speech, is just as idiosyncratic as in young autistic children without vocal skills. Comprehension of nonvocal aspects of communication also seems to be lacking. Perhaps because the autistic child does not appear to cue into the facial expressions and symbolic gestures of others, or because the meanings behind them are elusive, special efforts must be taken to teach comprehension of different nonvocal behaviors.

Half of all autistic children never acquire oral language, and most who do speak typically show abnormal speech patterns (Rimland, 1964; Rutter, 1965; Bartak, Rutter, and Cox, 1975). According to Baker et al. (1976), relatively few details have been added to Kanner's (1946) early descriptions of the speech of autistic children. Characterizing features include immediate and delayed echolalia, pronoun reversal of *you* and *I* (now generally recognized to be a function of echolalia; Rutter, 1968), affirmation by repetition (indicating *yes* by repeating the question asked), extreme literalness, metaphorical use of language in which words and phrases are used with idiosyncratic references, and an absence of original remarks. Hingtgen and Bryson (1972) have reported that autistic children rarely ask questions or produce informative statements. Their speech tends not to be used for social communication. Semantic and syntactic errors are also common (Hermelin and O'Connor, 1970; Rutter, 1972) and include the omission of prepositions, conjunctions, and pronouns and the use of neologisms. Deviations in articulation, pitch, volume, and stress may also exist. Some autistic children speak in a monotonous manner that lacks rhythm and inflection. Others speak in a sing-song or whispering manner. Ricks and Wing (1976) have described a small proportion of autistic children who are able to use the rules of grammar correctly. These authors note, however, that the content of the speech shows signs of abnormality. Topics of conversation are often restricted to individually favored, factual subjects. Frequently the children perseverate on a particular topic, using stereotyped phrases to relate concrete bits of information or to ask routine questions. These individuals have difficulty with more abstract concepts and are unable to give their opinions or discuss subjects from different perspectives.

## OVERVIEW OF THE TRAINING/ASSESSMENT MODEL

The remainder of this chapter concerns strategies of program design, maintenance, and evaluation. Special attention is directed toward the program's potential as a tool for language interventionists to identify factors that indicate which nonspeech mode to prescribe for training. The procedures are based on a study involving a sample of only three children. Thus, while the design lends itself to further experimentation,

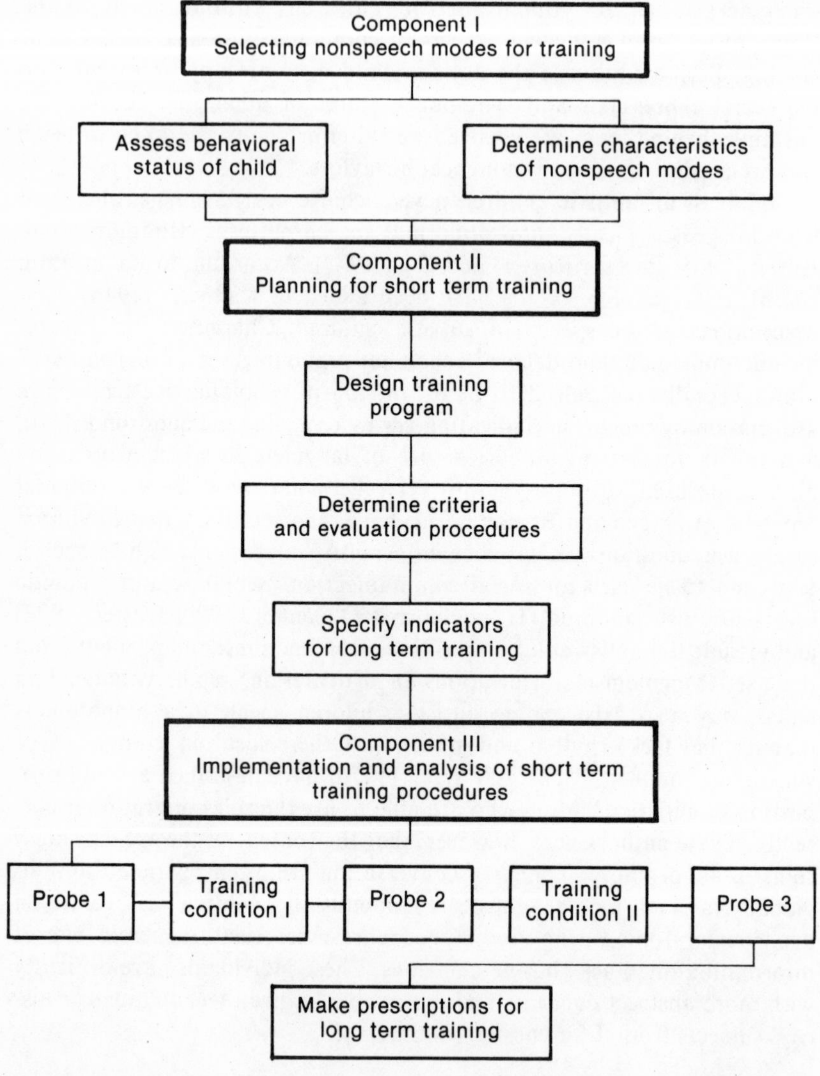


Figure 1. Flowchart of training/assessment model for determining the preferred nonspeech mode.

applications of the basic methodology may be considered when programming for communication therapy.

The basic training/assessment model presented in the form of a flowchart in Figure 1 is comprised of three major components. Component I deals with issues involved in determining nonspeech modes for subsequent training. The process of selecting two nonspeech modes for which the child shows the most potential for learning is based primarily upon consideration of two variables: 1) an assessment of the child's pretraining behavioral status, and 2) characteristics of the individual nonspeech modes.

Component II focuses on planning the procedural aspects of the training/assessment paradigm. That is, the language interventionist must determine the target language structure for training, the sequence of training tasks, and the strategies to employ in teaching the goal behaviors. In addition, procedures for assessing the effects of training must be devised. Finally, specific variables must be identified to indicate which of the two nonspeech modes to prescribe for future training.

Component III deals with the application of evaluation and training procedures to individual language-disordered children. The interventionist using these tactics is free to structure the training format and schedule to meet the needs of the students and the limitations of the training environment. In the pilot study, for example, each child was seen for approximately 30 minutes per day, in from one to four individual training sessions. The entire program was completed in 7 weeks. It is important to keep in mind that the methodology was not designed to be a comprehensive intervention program to establish functional communication behaviors in the language-impaired child. The deliberately brief nature of the program is essential to its main objective of identifying the nonspeech language mode, which, when taught in the context of a comprehensive language intervention program, has the highest probability of success.

Upon completion of the training and probe conditions, the interventionist must refer to the previously identified "indicators" for determining the nonspeech mode to prescribe for additional training. Although the flowchart depicted in Figure 1 ends here with "Make prescriptions for long term training," intervention with the child is in its initial stages. Issues for long term nonspeech training are detailed elsewhere in this volume, and are addressed only briefly in the latter part of this chapter.

In order to provide the reader with a more complete understanding of the training and assessment strategies adopted in the present program, procedural perspectives related to the basic issues involved in the program model are described. Following each discussion of procedural perspectives, the issues are illustrated by describing their application in the pilot study.

## A PLAN FOR DETERMINING THE PREFERRED NONSPEECH MODE

### Assessing the Behavioral Status of the Child

**Procedural Perspectives** Although the proposed training/assessment paradigm may be applied to any nonspeech child, its practicality is greater for some children than for others. When a child exhibits a particular impairment of sensory input (e.g., a visual or auditory deficit) or response output (e.g., motoric difficulties), automatic limitations will be set on the nonspeech modes that can be trained. As noted earlier, when the nature of the disorder is less easy to determine, as is frequently

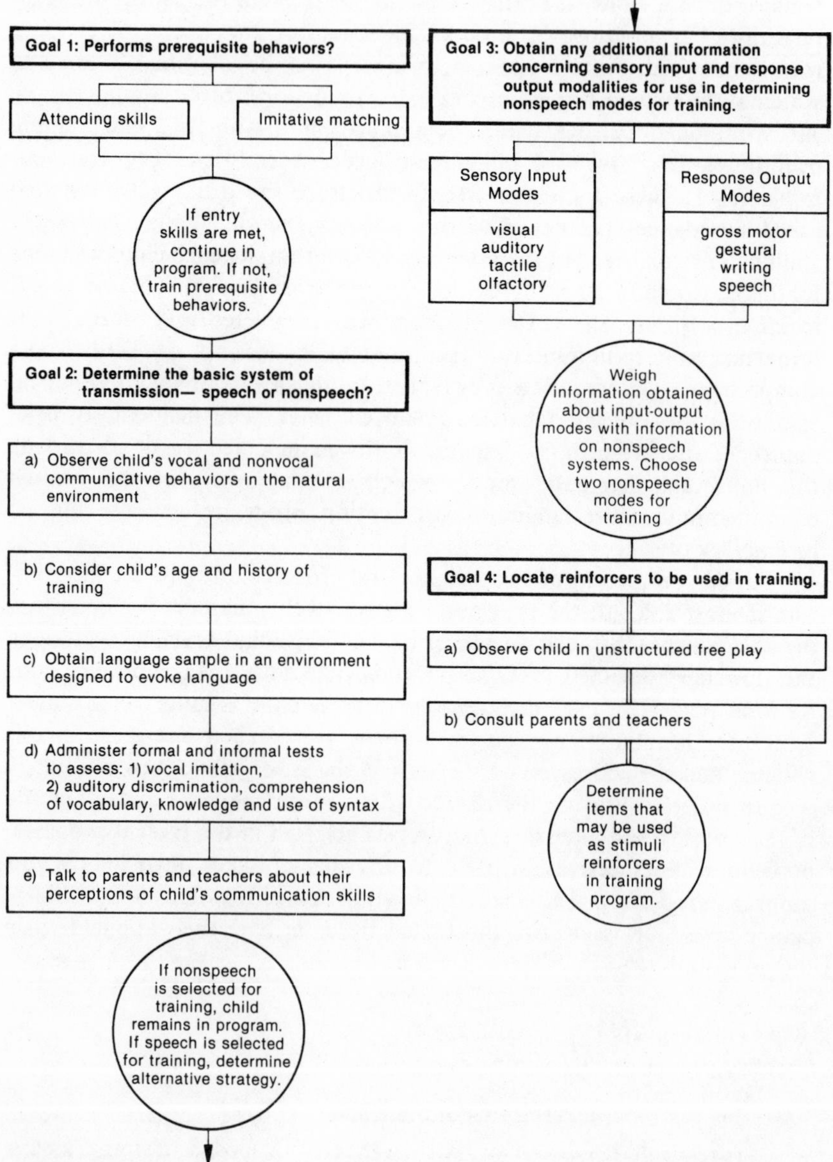


Figure 2. Flowchart showing procedures for assessing behavioral status of the child.

the case with autistic children, more than one nonspeech mode may qualify as potential training systems. In order to predict with some certainty which mode to adopt for intervention purposes, the modes most likely to be learned by a child can be taught, and the effects of learning subsequently compared.

The question still remains, however, of *how* to determine the nonspeech modes for training. Reasonable predictions can be made by relating information obtained from a behavioral assessment of the child with information about the characteristics of available nonspeech symbol systems. As Figure 1 indicates, the first step in program planning deals with this issue. In addition to providing information for choosing the training modes, the assessment procedure should serve several other functions. These are outlined in the flowchart in Figure 2.

First, the assessment period should be used to evaluate the child's ability to perform prerequisite behaviors. Two entry skills established for participation in the program require the child to sit in a chair and attend to the task at hand, and to perform imitative matching with objects, gestures, and abstract symbols. If the child proves unable to complete the imitative tasks, he is assigned to a training program designed to develop discrimination skills. The rationale underlying this procedures has been detailed elsewhere (Hollis, Carrier, and Spradlin, 1976; Hollis and Carrier, 1978) and implies that a child will be unsuccessful in learning the nonimitative matches required in using symbols for language purposes if he cannot perform less complex within-modality matching tasks.

A second, very important goal of pretraining assessment is to determine if nonspeech training is the best form of language intervention for the child. It is conceivable that some children who are better candidates for speech therapy might be mistakenly referred to the program. Administration of a variety of carefully selected assessment measurements should indicate when vocal training is the more desirable training system. Several assessment tactics deemed to be useful for the present program are outlined in Figure 2. They include: a) observation of the child's vocal and nonvocal communicative behaviors in the natural environment; b) consideration of factors such as the child's age and history of training experiences; c) language sampling conducted in an environment that is structured to evoke language; and d) the administration of formal and informal tests to assess: vocal imitation, auditory discrimination, comprehension of vocabulary, and knowledge and use of syntax. Additional information about the child's communication skills may be obtained by consulting the child's parents and teachers.

When analysis of the data suggests that the nonspeech approach is desirable, efforts to obtain any additional information related to sensory input and response output functioning should be attempted. These findings should then be weighed with information obtained from the assessment measures listed above, plus information about the natures of available nonspeech systems, so that reasonable predictions concerning the modes to select for training can be made.

Finally, a fourth objective of the assessment period is determining reinforcers for the child that can be used in training. Reinforcers may be identified by observing the child in an unstructured situation where he has access to various toys, foods, etc., and noting things to which he is attracted. Parents and teachers should also be consulted.

**Application** The pilot study was conducted at the Judevine Center for Autistic Children, St. Louis, Missouri. After explaining the purpose of the study to the teachers there, they were asked to submit names of students who could benefit from participation in the program. Five children, four boys and one girl, who ranged in age from five to eight years, were selected for inclusion in the study. None of these children used spoken language for communicative purposes. Their attempts to communicate through gestures were also extremely limited.

Intervention strategies employed by the teachers at the Judevine Center were successful in teaching the children basic attending and sitting behaviors. Thus, all of the children entered the program with the first prerequisite behavior. Assessment measures indicated, however, that two of the children were unable to perform imitative matching with objects or abstract symbols. Furthermore, they did not imitate gross motor movements with any degree of consistency. These children, then, were assigned to a separate program that emphasized training of discrimination abilities.

Continued assessment of the three remaining children, Marlon (chronological age, 5.5), Shane (CA, 8.0), and Tony (CA, 5.7), indicated that all would benefit from nonspeech language training. As judged by their performance on standardized tests and their abilities to follow directions, the receptive language skills of each child exceeded expressive language skills. In brief, Marlon rarely produced speech spontaneously, although he could imitate a one-word model when instructed to do so; Shane made infrequent attempts to communicate vocally. When he did, his utterances were no longer than one or two words. Moreover, his extremely poor articulation caused much of his productive speech to be unintelligible. Tony displayed echolalic speech and a spontaneous repertoire that consisted primarily of "Okay," "Stay here," and "Don't want it." He produced these utterances both appropriately and inappropriately in a variety of situations. "Okay," for example, was sometimes used to signify "No."

Little useful information could be obtained regarding possible sensory deficits of the boys. Audiological examinations indicated that their hearing was within normal limits. No particular visual problems could be determined. Response output assessment revealed that the boys were free of gross and fine motor involvement. While they could use a writing instrument for scribbling, they were unable to trace or copy letters.

Items to be used as stimuli and reinforcers in the training program were chosen by questioning parents and teachers about things each child liked to do, play with, or eat. Additional information regarding the reinforcing value of the items was determined by making them available to the child and noting his response.

## Determining Characteristics of Nonspeech Symbol Systems

**Procedural Perspectives** The increasing acceptance of nonvocal systems as viable means for building communication skills has led to their earlier application with children displaying impairment of the auditory-vocal channel. Early intervention of any kind, however, speech or nonspeech, is less likely initiated when the type and degree of the child's impairment are neither directly observable nor easily assessed. Because medical examinations often reveal that autistic children have normal hearing and the physiological capability to produce speech, initial and sometimes prolonged therapeutic efforts usually take the form of speech training. Typically, alternative nonspeech intervention will be attempted only after the child has persistently failed to learn functional vocal behavior. This is unfortunate, for not only does the child remain without a means of communicating during the entire training period, but as the child gets older, the probability that he will acquire functional communication skills may be reduced. Ideally, future research will increase the sophistication of our knowledge concerning the correspondence between patterns of behavioral characteristics of language-disordered children and the optimal form early intervention measures should take.

As mentioned above, the implementation of a nonspeech-training program often occurs only after attempts to train vocal skills have met with repeated failure. In such cases, decisions regarding which nonspeech mode to select for training must be based upon an assessment of the behavioral characteristics of the child and upon an analysis of possible nonspeech modes. A discussion of the first issue was just presented. A thorough review of the second issue was reported by Hollis and Carrier (1978), who presented several of the more common symbol systems in terms of "iconicity versus arbitrariness, the input and output modes used, permanence versus transitivity, complexity versus simplicity, time required for transmission, and degree to which presentation can be automated" (p. 96). The authors also categorized the various nonspeech modes according to three types of symbol systems. These included: 1) orthographic, 2) word-unit, and 3) mixed or concept-based symbols. Printed letters, braille, and fingerspelling are classified as orthographic symbol systems; word-unit systems include printed words, Signing Exact

English, and Non-SLIP (abstract plastic symbols); and rebuses, Blissymbols, and American Sign Language are listed as compound systems. Which mode is selected for training depends in part on whether the intervention is viewed as a tool to help the child attain more natural linguistic skills or as a long term communication system. If the nonspeech intervention is viewed as a facilitator to vocal behavior, to be discarded once the latter has been firmly established, then it would be wise to select a word-unit method of training, which is the type of symbol system most "compatible with English phrase-structure grammar and should provide generalization within the English language" (Hollis and Carrier, 1978, p. 88).

**Application** The decision to teach a nonspeech communication system to the children participating in the pilot study was based primarily on the following considerations: The children ranged from five to eight years of age; they had individually received between two to five years of intensive speech therapy; and, at the time the study was instigated, none of the boys had effective methods for communicating functionally with others in the environment. A nonspeech intervention plan was adopted in hope that the procedures would facilitate spoken language, or serve as a substitute system if speech never developed. In order to encourage generalization from the nonspeech mode to speech, a word-based approach was selected as the system for learning. Consequently, possible nonspeech modes were narrowed down to printed words, Signing Exact English, and abstract plastic symbols. To further increase the probability that the children would use the nonvocal symbol as a tool to attain speech, the trainer paired speech with nonspeech stimulus presentation.

Assessment of the children's sensory input and response output modalities provided few clues as to which of the three word-unit approaches would be most readily learned and used. Medical reports indicated that all of the children had adequate visual and hearing capabilities. With regard to output modalities, all of the boys were free of neurophysiological impairment affecting gross motor movements; all were capable of imitating manual signs; and none were able to print, copy, or trace letters of the alphabet. Based on these findings, then, all three of the nonspeech modes qualified as systems that could be used by all of the subjects (given that responses made with printed words consisted of the manipulation of word blocks or word cards, rather than printing).

To meet the requirements of the pilot study, which involved training two nonspeech modes as a means of determining which is used most efficiently by the child, potential advantages and disadvantages of the three word-unit systems were specified (see Table 1). Then, based primarily on

Table 1. Potential advantages and disadvantages of nonspeech word-unit systems

| Printed word | | Signing Exact English | | Abstract plastic symbols | |
|---|---|---|---|---|---|
| + | – | + | – | + | – |
| 1. May be shared with majority of the population | 1. Complexity of stimulus input (which may be difficult for very young and/or severely retarded children to learn) | 1. Attempts to maintain English morphology, semantics, and syntax, which may facilitate learning of speech | 1. Response output requires motor movements (which may prove to be difficult for some children) | 1. Can be designed to maintain English morphology, semantics, and syntax, which may facilitate learning of speech | 1. Symbols must always be accessible to the child |
| 2. Circumvents difficulty of learning phonetic rules | 2. Response output requires: a) complex fine motor response (i.e., printing), or b) child to carry word cards with him | 2. Circumvents difficulty of learning phonetic rules | 2. Limited number of people will be able to communicate with the child | 2. Circumvents difficulty of learning phonetic rules | 2. Unless printed word is written on plastic symbol, majority of people will not be able to communicate with the child |
| 3. Corresponds in a one-to-one relationship with English, improving the possibility of generalization to writing and speech | | 3. Does not require child to carry any extra materials | 3. Stimulus permanency: Fleeting | 3. Child may use symbols without producing them | |
| 4. Stimulus permanency: Semi-permanent | | 4. Physical movement paired with verbal stimulus may stimulate speech production | | 4. Stimulus permanency: Semi-permanent | |
| 5. The number of available choice symbols may be controlled by the trainer | | | | 5. The number of available choice symbols may be controlled by the trainer | |

the possibility that the children would have difficulty making the fine visual discriminations required in reading printed words, Signing Exact English and abstract plastic symbols were chosen as the nonspeech modes for training.

## PLANNING FOR SHORT TERM TRAINING

### Designing the Training Program

**Procedural Perspectives** It may go without saying that the first step in designing a language-training program is a clear and objective specification of the program's purpose. With regard to the proposed training/assessment model, the purpose is to empirically identify the nonspeech symbol system that an individual language-disordered child has the highest probability of learning for communicative purposes. This objective contains obvious differences from most language intervention programs, which share the ultimate goal of teaching functional communication skills to children with language problems. Issues concerning the content and procedural methodology of language therapy, however, which have been discussed in terms of programs for training communicative behavior (e.g., Miller and Yoder, 1974; Ruder and Smith, 1974; Holland, 1975; Lahey and Bloom, 1977), are also relevant to the training/assessment paradigm discussed here. Basically, these issues include: 1) what to train (training content), 2) the order in which to present the content material (sequence of training), 3) how to teach the target behaviors (instructional strategy), and 4) determining the effectiveness of the total intervention program (assessment).

In the following pages, attention is focused upon several factors relevant to these four issues that hold special significance for procedures involved in determining the "preferred" nonspeech modes.

**Training—Content, Sequence, and Instructional Strategies** The term *training/assessment model* has been applied to the current procedures because the language interventionist teaches specific linguistic responses through the application of a nonspeech mode, while simultaneously assessing the rate and quality of the child's learning. The process is then repeated with another nonspeech system. Because the interventionist will want to move as quickly as possible to a more comprehensive intervention program using the preferred mode, the training/assessment procedures will ideally be completed as rapidly as possible. Logically, learning may best be expedited by training lexical items that represent persons, objects, or actions in which the child shows an interest (perhaps, for example, "candy" or "tickle") and that he will consequently be motivated to label or "ask for." The first step in planning program content, then, is identifying what is reinforcing to the child. This may be completed by asking parents and teachers about what the child likes, or by observing the child in a free-play situation.

The following step involves determining the target language structure. Since the expressive linguistic abilities of children participating in nonspeech language intervention would characteristically be low, the selected semantic relations for training should be of limited complexity. In addition, the targeted language structure should ideally be one upon which more complex linguistic behaviors can be built, and, insofar as it is feasible, should be of some functional use in the natural environment. While the latter issue is a "must" for long term language training, for purposes of determining the preferred nonspeech mode in the shortest possible amount of time, it is of primary importance that the structure be functional within the reciprocal exchange context of the teaching situation.

Ruder and Smith (1974) and Miller and Yoder (1974) have discussed the advantages of teaching agent-action-object relations early in training. When carefully selected lexical items are applied to the corresponding S–V–O structure, it fulfills all of the requirements listed above and, therefore, qualifies as an appropriate program goal in the training/assessment model.

Clearly, the steps of the training program should be sequenced to facilitate learning. Therefore, the child should be given the opportunity early in training to learn that attending and producing the desired responses will in some way "pay off." It logically follows that the first lexical item to be trained should be the one representing the most reinforcing component of the agent-action-object string. The subsequent two-word combination to be trained (expressing agent-action, action-object, or agent-object relations) should be selected according to the ease with which the concept may be demonstrated and the related issue of the child's interest level in the concept being conveyed. The last step of the program involves teaching the entire three-word expression.

The term *reciprocal exchange* was used above in reference to the context in which training occurs. The term reflects the nature of the trainer-child interactions, in which the trainer presents something he knows the child likes and then offers it, contingent upon the latter's production of the desired response (in this case, the sign or plastic symbol representing the stimulus). The reinforcing object (or action, as the case may be) therefore serves the dual role of both training stimulus and reinforcer. Building skills in this manner has the practical advantage of teaching the communicative function of language from the beginning of therapy. The procedures are similar to the simple social transaction that

Premack (1970) adopted in teaching Sarah to linguistically map perceptual classes.

**Application** During the pretraining assessment procedures, reinforcers for the three children in the pilot study were determined by questioning their parents and teachers about things each child especially seemed to enjoy. Without exception, the most frequently listed "likes" were food items. Therefore, several food reinforcers, which the parents agreed could be used in training, were ascertained at that time.

Next came the more difficult task of determining the agent-action-object expression to be targeted as the ultimate training goal. Lexical items representing foods would obviously fill the object position, but several possible alternatives existed for the agent and action functions. Options included, for example, "Marlon want candy," "I like pretzel," and "Tony see cookie." The expression "I see (noun)" was selected as the target language structure, primarily because less was inferred in teaching the child to answer a question about what he sees rather than what he wants or likes.[1] In other words, although the training foods were selected because they had reinforcing value to the child, on some occasions he may not "want" or "like" the particular item about which the interventionist trains the response "I want ______" or "I like ______." In this context, the likelihood of teaching the meaning of "want" and "like" is considerably reduced. There is less risk of distorting the meaning involved in the response "I see cookie," for example, when the trainer shows the child a cookie and asks, "What do you see?" The child may or may not want the cookie, but in all probability, he does see it. If the cookie is not reinforcing on a particular trial or day, the basic question and answer pattern can be retained with correct responses followed by a more reinforcing consequence.

It became necessary to adopt such a strategy with one of the boys in the pilot study. During the symbol-training phase, Tony demonstrated that he could discriminate the plastic symbols and sequence them to form two-element phrases. During the course of training, however, when criterion on the "see donut" step had nearly been met, he seemed to lose interest in that food. Instead of making the appropriate response to obtain the donut, Tony engaged in disruptive behavior when it was presented. Rather than dropping the "see donut" step from the training program, by changing the contingency of reinforcement, i.e., when in addition to being offered a piece of donut, Tony was also offered a stamp and ink pad and the back of a data sheet, criterion on the "see donut" step was soon achieved.

---

[1] In retrospect, an S–V–O string such as S(trainer's name)-give-O is likely to hold more functional utility for the child's everyday communicative needs than does the chosen structure, S(child's name)-see-O.

As implied earlier, a decision was also required concerning the form to teach for coding the agent category. Recent research in language development (Nelson, 1975) has revealed important individual differences in the extent to which normal children use pronouns. Before they attain a mean length of utterance (MLU) of 2.5 morphemes, some children apparently use predominantly pronominal forms to code agents, location, and objects. Other children use predominantly nominal forms to code the same semantic relations. By the time an MLU of 2.5 morphemes is reached, both nominal and pronominal references may be found in the child's spontaneous speech.

For several reasons, the decision was made to teach Marlon, Shane, and Tony to use the lexical item "I" in the three-word goal expression. First, since the related data did not give clear evidence that one or the other form is typically learned earlier by most normal children, it was not assumed that either the nominal or pronominal form would be easier for the boys to learn. Furthermore, the more grammatically correct language structure was "I see ______," not, for example, "Shane see ______." Therefore, rather than teaching a behavior that must eventually be unlearned, the lexical item "I" was chosen for training. If a child could be taught the appropriate use of "I" in the initial position of the agent-action-object string, then he was that much closer to accurate communicative behavior; if problems arose in teaching "I," then modifications could be made in the training program, so that another symbol (plastic symbol or sign) representing the child's name would be taught.

Insofar as the sign and plastic symbol systems would allow, training programs in both nonspeech modes were controlled for content and complexity of stimulus presentation. The basic reciprocal exchange pattern was:

<u>Initiation</u>

Trainer: Shows child a food item and asks, "What do you see?"

<u>Response</u>

Child:
a. Makes correct response in nonspeech mode
b. Makes incorrect response in nonspeech mode
c. Does not respond

<u>Reciprocation</u>

Trainer:
a. Praises child and gives him a bit of the food he has correctly labeled
b.&c. Repeats initiation procedure and immediately prompts and then reinforces the child (Prompts are gradually faded and food reinforcement is contingent upon the child's attempts to perform the correct response unassisted.)

Although the trainer used spoken language in the interactions with the child, the child was never required to produce vocalizations in conjunction with nonspeech responses. In addition to scoring his nonspeech responses as correct or incorrect, however, data were also recorded on vocal responses emitted following stimulus presentation (i.e., a correct vocal response was defined as one that corresponded to the response to be made in the nonspeech mode). In this way, the data could later be analyzed to determine if either sign or abstract plastic symbols worked more effectively to facilitate the production of speech by a given child. The content and training sequence of sample programs used in the pilot study to teach sign and plastic symbol language responses are presented as flowcharts in Figures 3 and 4.

### Determining Criteria and Evaluation Procedures

**Procedural Perspectives** In addition to designing program strategies, methods must be developed to evaluate how efficiently the child is learning the target behaviors taught in each nonspeech mode. There are several ways learning may be assessed. First, ongoing assessment can be carried out by monitoring the child's progress as he moves from one step of training to the next. Persisting difficulties that prevent the child from achieving the established criterion levels should serve as a cue to structure program modifications such as branching steps. In addition, ongoing assessment may similarly be completed by noting the extent to which learning responses in the nonspeech mode facilitate appropriate vocal responses. (It is important to note that changes in the child's speech production should reflect his learning of the nonspeech mode. Learning of the nonspeech mode should be maximized by making appropriate procedural adjustments in the training program. Therefore, program modifications should not be based on performance of the dependent measure, speech.)

Another method of evaluation, which also reflects learning of program content, involves the periodic administration of structured probes. Thus, the difference between the child's pretraining and post-training nonspeech skills may be assessed by administering specific probes before training of the nonspeech mode has been initiated and then again after training has been completed.

**Application** The three assessment procedures described above were adopted in the pilot study. The criterion level for moving from one step of training to the next was set at 80% correct in two consecutive sessions. In addition, the number of correct vocalizations (i.e., those that corresponded to the nonspeech response being trained) was also recorded, so

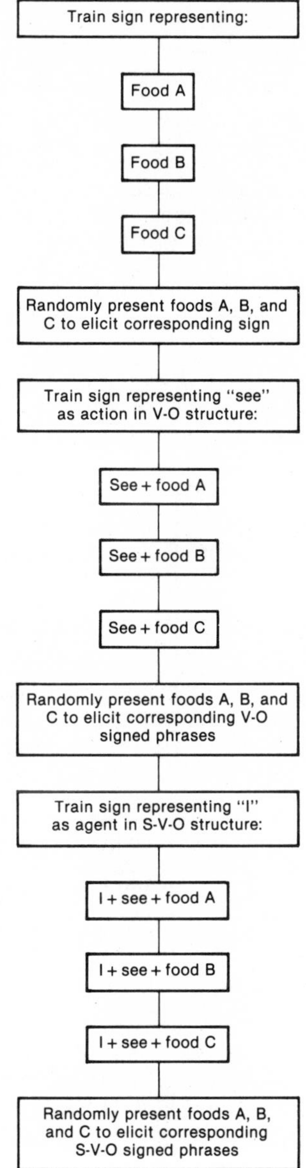


Figure 3. Flowchart of sample training program for teaching language responses in sign.

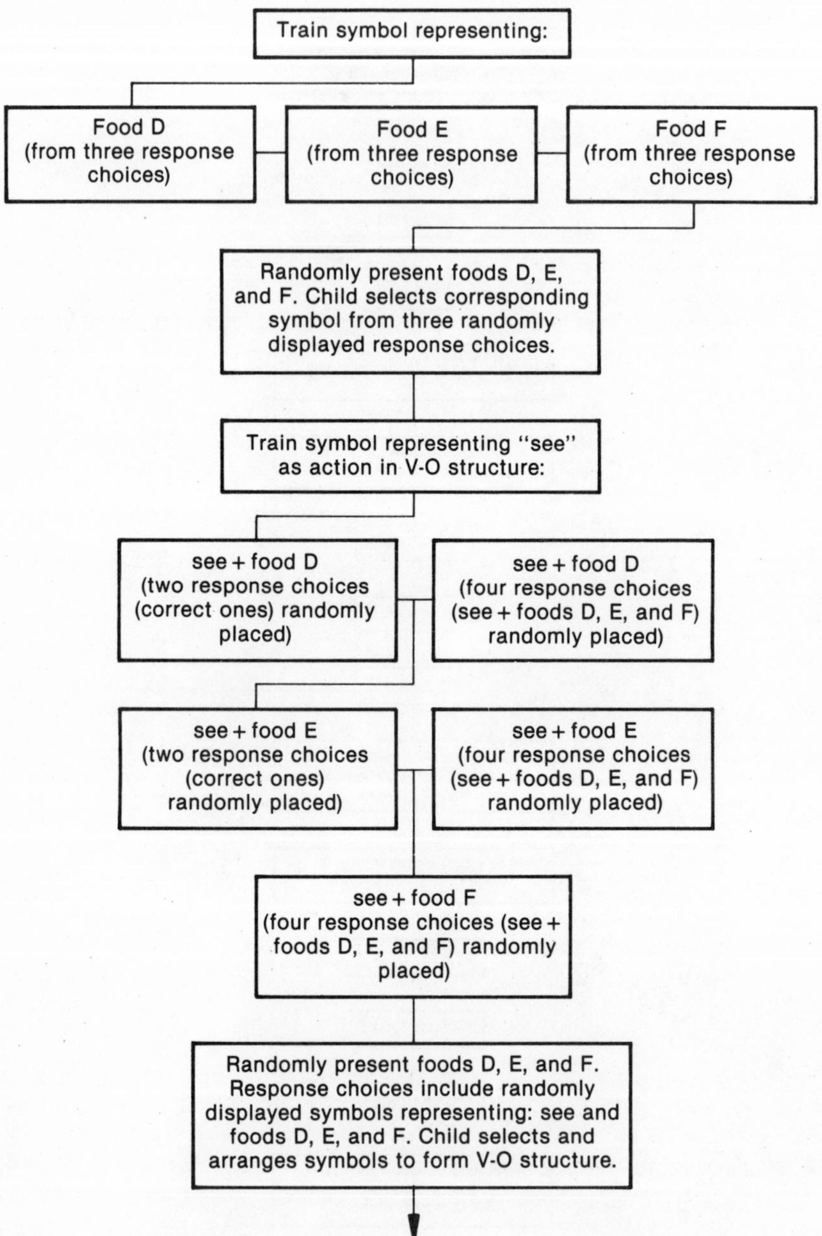
Train symbol representing:
Food D
(from three response choices)
Food E
(from three response choices)
Food F
(from three response choices)
Randomly present foods D, E, and F. Child selects corresponding symbol from three randomly displayed response choices.
Train symbol representing "see" as action in V-O structure:
see + food D
(two response choices (correct ones) randomly placed)
see + food D
(four response choices (see + foods D, E, and F) randomly placed)
see + food E
(two response choices (correct ones) randomly placed)
see + food E
(four response choices (see + foods D, E, and F) randomly placed)
see + food F
(four response choices (see + foods D, E, and F) randomly placed)
Randomly present foods D, E, and F. Response choices include randomly displayed symbols representing: see and foods D, E, and F. Child selects and arranges symbols to form V-O structure.

Figure 4. Flowchart of sample training program for teaching language responses with abstract plastic symbols.

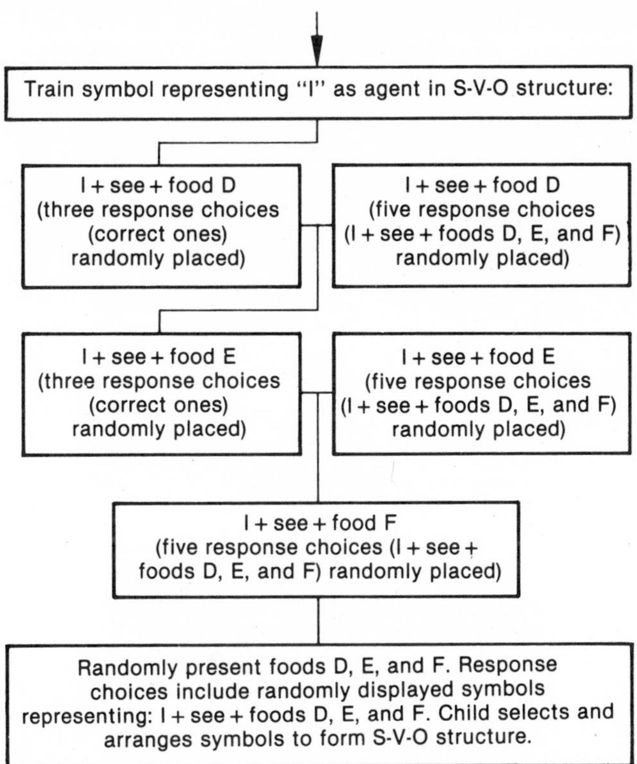
Train symbol representing "I" as agent in S-V-O structure:
I + see + food D (three response choices (correct ones) randomly placed)
I + see + food D (five response choices (I + see + foods D, E, and F) randomly placed)
I + see + food E (three response choices (correct ones) randomly placed)
I + see + food E (five response choices (I + see + foods D, E, and F) randomly placed)
I + see + food F (five response choices (I + see + foods D, E, and F) randomly placed)
Randomly present foods D, E, and F. Response choices include randomly displayed symbols representing: I + see + foods D, E, and F. Child selects and arranges symbols to form S-V-O structure.

that the average number of appropriate vocalizations per training session (15 trials) could be determined.

Finally, structured probes were administered before and after each nonspeech-training condition. The probes were designed to assess knowledge of stimulus equivalences which were directly and indirectly taught during the training conditions. They included assessment of receptive and productive skills in sign, associative abilities using abstract plastic symbols, receptive and productive skills in speech, and cross-modal transfer between speech and the nonspeech modes. The stimulus input and response output involved in the total 10 probes are listed in Table 2, and presented diagrammatically in Figure 5.

## Specifying Indicators for Long Term Training

**Procedural Perspectives** Before initiating the actual implementation of the training and probe conditions, one last methodological issue must be resolved. Recall for a moment the main purpose of the train-

Table 2. Probes: Stimulus input and response output

| Probe | Stimulus input | Response output |
|---|---|---|
| 1. Production | Object | Sign |
| 2. Comprehension | Sign | Object |
| 3. Association | Object | Symbol |
| 4. Association | Symbol | Object |
| 5. Production | Object | Speech |
| 6. Comprehension | Speech | Object |
| 7. Cross-modal transfer | Sign | Speech |
| 8. Cross-modal transfer | Speech | Sign |
| 9. Cross-modal transfer | Symbol | Speech |
| 10. Cross-modal transfer | Speech | Symbol |

ing/assessment model—to provide empirical evidence testifying to the potential advantages of prescribing a particular nonspeech mode for the future training of a language-impaired child. The remaining methodological issue involves the specification of those measures that will yield the required evidence. Put another way, there remains a need to specify

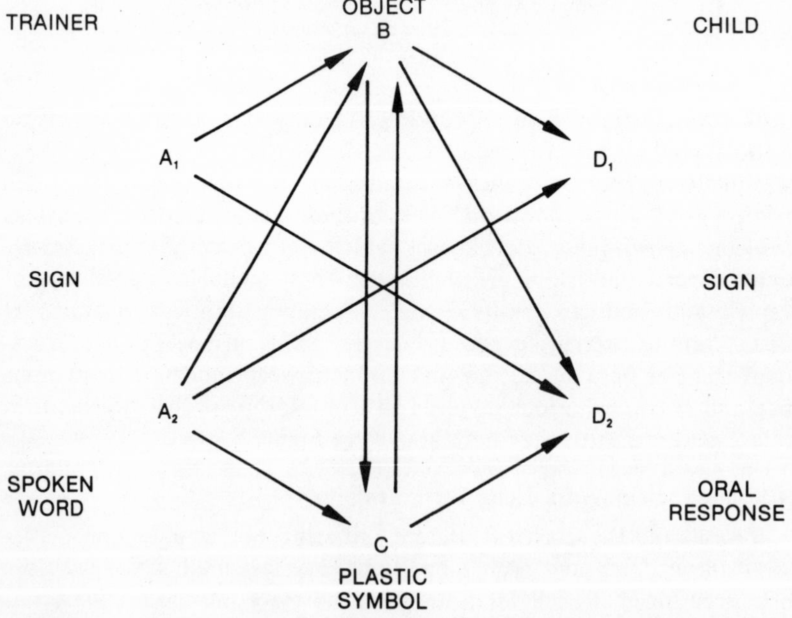


Figure 5. Schematic summary of 10 probe items. (Adapted from Sidman, 1971.)

factors to serve as "indicators" of the "preferred" nonspeech mode. This task should be a relatively simple one, for the selected measures should be those that provide the most significant information about the speech and nonspeech behaviors the child has acquired during the training process. Thus, one needs only to refer back to previously outlined evaluation procedures to determine the measures that will function most effectively as *indicators* of the mode to *prescribe* for long term training.

**Application** As previously stated, three types of evaluation procedures were scheduled in the pilot study. These three measures, which would later serve as "indicators," included:

1. Learning of nonspeech responses taught in each training condition
2. Percentage of correct vocalizations produced during each training condition
3. Performance on the probes

## IMPLEMENTATION AND ANALYSIS OF SHORT TERM TRAINING PROCEDURES

Referring back to Figure 1, attention has been given to the prerequisite tasks that must be completed by the interventionist prior to the implementation of the probe and training conditions. While most of the relevant notions pertaining to training and evaluation procedures have been discussed, several organizational aspects of the pilot study can serve as guidelines for persons planning to use the paradigm with other language-disordered children.

The three boys in the pilot study were randomly assigned to either sign or symbol training during the first training condition. Marlon and Shane, for example, were individually taught to make several language responses using abstract plastic symbols, and Tony received training in sign. In the next training condition, the boys were individually instructed in the nonspeech mode that had not been previously trained. The trainer met with each child from one to four times per day, with each day's training totaling approximately 30 minutes. Each training condition lasted for 3 weeks, and the three sets of probes were administered on 3 separate days (before and after each training condition). Thus, the entire training/assessment model was completed in about 7 weeks.

Decisions about the organizational strategies to adopt in future studies must be based upon factors such as the child's rate of learning, and the prevailing conditions in the training environment. If, for example, a child progresses very slowly through the training program or may be seen for only 10 minutes per day, the length of the training conditions may need to be extended. In contrast, there will undoubtedly be some cases when the training conditions can be shortened. The latter, of course, is the more ideal situation, since one would ultimately strive to make reliable prescriptions in the shortest time.

## MAKING PRESCRIPTIONS FOR LONG TERM TRAINING

The process of prescribing a nonspeech mode for long term training can probably best be conveyed by discussing the general outcome of the pilot study. The performance of each child is presented in terms of indicators and prescriptions.

**Marlon**

*Indicators:*

1. Learning of nonspeech responses taught in each training condition:

| Sign training | versus | Symbol training |
|---|---|---|
| Marlon learned to make the signs representing 3 foods. He also learned to sign the phrase SEE COOKIE. | | Marlon learned to associate two symbols with two corresponding foods. |

Conclusion: Marlon learned more nonspeech responses in the sign training condition.

2. Percentage of correct vocalizations produced during each training condition:

| Sign training | versus | Symbol training |
|---|---|---|
| 70% | | 51% |

Conclusion: Marlon made more appropriate vocal responses during the sign training condition.

3. Performance on the probes:

| Sign training | versus | Symbol training |
|---|---|---|
| Criterion was met on the probes assessing expressive and receptive skills: object-sign and sign-object. Criterion was also met on the probes assessing cross-modal transfer: spoken word–sign and sign–spoken word. | | Criterion was met on the probes assessing association between symbols and objects: object-symbol and symbol-object. Criterion was not met on the probes assessing cross-modal transfer: spoken word–symbol and symbol–spoken word. |

Conclusion: Marlon attained a higher performance level on the sign probes.

*Prescription:*

Sign training

**Shane**

*Indicators:*

1. Learning of nonspeech responses taught in each training condition:

| Sign training | versus | Symbol training |
|---|---|---|
| Shane learned to make the signs representing three foods. He also learned to sign the phrase SEE (NOUN), using each of the food signs. | | Shane learned to associate three symbols with three corresponding foods. |

Conclusion: Shane learned more nonspeech responses in the sign training condition.

2. Percentage of correct vocalizations produced during each training condition:

| Sign training | versus | Symbol training |
|---|---|---|
| 65% | | 84% |

Conclusion: Shane made more appropriate vocal responses during the symbol training condition.

3. Performance on the probes:

| Sign training | versus | Symbol training |
|---|---|---|
| Criterion was met on the probes assessing expressive and receptive skills: object-sign and sign-object. Criterion was also met on the probes assessing cross-modal transfer: spoken word–Sign and sign–spoken word. | | Criterion was not met on any of the probes involving symbols. |

Conclusion: Shane attained a higher performance level on the sign probes.

*Prescription:*

Sign training

**Tony**

*Indicators:*

1. Learning of nonspeech responses taught in each training condition:

| Sign training | versus | Symbol training |
|---|---|---|
| Tony learned to make the signs representing three foods. He also learned to sign the phrase SEE (NOUN), using each of the food signs. By the end of 3 weeks, he was able to sign I SEE (NOUN), using two of the food signs. | | Tony learned to discriminate nine symbols, and could arrange them to construct the sentence I SEE THE (NOUN). The noun class included symbols representing four foods, boy, and girl.* |

* Because Tony learned so rapidly, additional steps were added to the training program outlined in Figure 4.

Conclusion: Tony learned more nonspeech responses in the symbol training condition.

2. Percentage of correct vocalizations produced during each training condition:

| Sign training | versus | Symbol training |
|---|---|---|
| 59% | | 74% |

Conclusion: Tony made more appropriate vocal responses during the symbol training condition.

3. Performance on the probes:

| Sign training | versus | Symbol training |
|---|---|---|
| Criterion was met on all probes involving signs. | | Criterion was met on all probes involving symbols. |

Conclusion: Performance was equivalent on the sign and symbol probes.

*Prescription:*

Symbol with emphasis on developing reading. (Based on the accuracy of Tony's responses in the symbol-training condition, and the rate at which learning occurred, it was recommended that a reading program be implemented. Printed words, like abstract plastic symbols, involve stimuli that are both visual-spatial and permanent. Reading, however, involves the discrimination of more complex stimuli. Reading is considered to be the more functional mode of communication because it can be shared with a greater proportion of the population.)

## ISSUES FOR LONG TERM TRAINING

The primary concerns underlying systematic planning and programming of nonspeech intervention correspond to those variables with which all language intervention programs must contend. Because of the nature of nonspeech systems and their limitations, several issues specific to nonspeech programming can be raised. Three of the four issues discussed below entail unresolved issues to which future research should be directed. However, one issue, parent involvement, can be discussed with more certainty.

Several recent papers discuss training parents as interventionists for their own children (Baker, 1976; Schumaker and Sherman, 1978). When the intervention mode is a nonspeech system, there is no doubt that parents *must* be included in the therapy process. For that matter, all relevant persons in the child's life, teachers, siblings, grandparents, babysitters, and so on, must be trained to use the system if it is to become truly functional for the child.

Several other issues, to which answers are not as readily available, should also be mentioned. Given that a nonspeech child's articulation system appears to be intact, should speech training be conducted in addition to training in the nonspeech mode? Moreover, if the answer to this question is yes, what form should the two intervention programs assume? They could, for example, train similar verbal behaviors, albeit in different modes. In other words, if the nonspeech target behavior involves using abstract plastic symbols to construct the phrase, "want doll," should the same lexical items be trained in a concurrent speech therapy session? Or, would it be more realistic to focus speech training on less complex vocalizations, such as imitative CV and VC combinations?

Another problem in nonspeech training is knowing when to change from one nonvocal system to a more functional nonvocal system. An ongoing assessment strategy should be adopted to help the interventionist determine when a child is capable of learning a more useful (and probably more complex) symbol system. As a hypothetical example, consider that at some point after a signing program has been instituted, a child's behavior indicates that teaching him to read has become a higher probability. The interventionist is faced with: 1) eliminating sign intervention in order to focus training efforts on the more practical symbol system—the printed word; 2) training the use of printed words as a functional communication system, without discontinuing training in sign, and thereby providing the child with two potential avenues for communication; or 3) using the child's signing abilities to teach stimulus equivalences with the printed words.

In a related vein, questions may be posed concerning the optimal strategies to adopt when, concurrent with nonspeech training, vocal behaviors emerge in the child. Should all immediate efforts be aimed at strengthening the child's speech skills through more conventional approaches to speech and language intervention, or, should the teaching strategy continue to incorporate nonspeech tactics as a means of augmenting conceptual and linguistic knowledge?

## SUMMARY

This chapter provides language interventionists with a potential means of determining the optimal nonspeech language mode for individual language-impaired children. The procedure holds special merit in that its application may prevent the loss of valuable time spent searching for a viable communication mode. Basically, the procedure involves teaching specific language responses in two successively trained nonspeech modes. In order to maximize the possibility for learning to occur, selection of training modes should be based on the relation between the nature of the child's problem and the characteristics of available nonspeech modes. Specific probes are administered at critical points so that the effects of training can be analyzed in a number of different tasks. The pragmatic aspects of this training/assessment model may be found primarily in its function of providing *indicators* to use in determining which mode to *prescribe* for training.

Although the study described in this chapter involved children exhibiting autistic-like characteristics, the methods used are noncategorical in nature. Thus, the procedures have potential value for determining an optimal nonspeech language mode for any language-impaired child, regardless of diagnostic classification.

The benefits that nonvocal language training may have for facilitating the development of oral communication, or in serving as a substitute for speech, have received increased attention in recent years. Determining an efficient means of identifying the *optimal* nonvocal system for training is an essential component of the nonspeech approach to language building. The training/assessment paradigm discussed in this chapter is a means of dealing with that issue.

## REFERENCES

Anthony, D. 1971. Seeing Essential English. Educational Services Division, Anaheim School District, Anaheim, Cal.

Baker, B. L. 1976. Parent involvement in programming for developmentally disabled children. *In* L. L. Lloyd (ed.), Communication Assessment and Intervention Strategies, pp. 691–733. University Park Press, Baltimore.

Baker, L., Cantwell, D. P., Rutter, M., and Bartak, L. 1976. Language and autism. *In* E. R. Ritvo (ed.), Autism: Diagnosis, Current Research and Management, pp. 121–149. Spectrum Publications, Inc., New York.

Bartak, L., Rutter, M., and Cox, A. 1975. A comparative study of infantile autism and specific developmental receptive language disorder. I. The children. Br. J. Psychiatry 126:127–145.

Bliss, C. K. 1965. Semantography-Blissymbolics. Semantography Publications, Sydney, Australia.

Carrier, J. K., Jr., and Peak, T. 1975. Non-speech Language Initiation Program. H & H Enterprises, Lawrence, Kan.

Condon, W. S. 1975. Multiple response to sound in dysfunctional children. J. Aut. Child. Schizo. 5:37–56.

Creedon, M. P. 1973. Language development in nonverbal autistic children using a simultaneous communication system. Paper presented at the Research in Child Development Meeting, March, Philadelpha. (Available from EDRS, Leasco Information Products, 4827 Rugby Avenue, Bethesda, Md. 20014. Reprint No. ED-78624 in microfiche and hard copy.)

de Villiers, J. G., and Naughton, J. M. 1974. Teaching a symbol language to autistic children. J. Consult. Clin. Psychol. 42:111–117.

Eisenberg, L. 1956. The autistic child in adolescence. Am. J. Psychiatry 112:607–612.

Fulwiler, R. L., and Fouts, R. S. 1976. Acquisition of American Sign Language by a noncommunicating autistic child. J. Aut. Child. Schizo. 6:43–51.

Gustason, G., Pfetzing, D., and Zawolkow, E. 1972. Signing Exact English. Modern Signs Press, Rossmoor, Cal.

Hermelin, B., and O'Connor, N. 1970. Psychological Experiments with Autistic Children. Pergamon, London.

Hewett, F. M. 1964, Teaching reading to an autistic boy through operant conditioning. Read. Teach. 17:613–618.

Hingtgen, J. N., and Bryson, C. Q. 1972. Recent developments in the study of early childhood psychoses: Infantile autism, childhood schizophrenia and related disorders. Schizo. Bull. 5:8–53.

Hingtgen, J. N., and Churchill, D. W. 1969. Identification of perceptual limitations in mute autistic children: Identification by the use of behavior modification. Arch. Gen. Psychiatry 21:68–71.

Holland, A. L. 1975. Language therapy for children: Some thoughts on context and content. J. Speech Hear. Disord. 40:514–523.

Hollis, J. H., and Carrier, J. K., Jr. 1978. Intervention strategies for nonspeech children. *In* R. L. Schiefelbusch (ed.), Language Intervention Strategies, pp. 57–100. University Park Press, Baltimore.

Hollis, J. H., Carrier, J. K., Jr., and Spradlin, J. E. 1976. An approach to remediation of communication and learning deficiencies. *In* L. L. Lloyd (ed.), Communication Assessment and Intervention Strategies, pp. 265–294. University Park Press, Baltimore.

Kanner, L. 1946. Irrelevant and metaphorical language in early infantile autism. Am. J. Psychiatry 103:242–246.

Lahey, M., and Bloom, L. 1977. Planning a first lexicon: Which words to teach first. 42:340–350.

LaVigna, G. W. 1977. Communication training in mute autistic adolescents using the written word. J. Aut. Child. Schizo. 7:135–149.

McLean, L. P., and McLean, J. E. 1974. A language training program for nonverbal autistic children. J. Speech Hear. Disord. 39:186–193.

Marshall, N. R., and Hegrenes, J. R. 1972. The use of written language as a communication system for an autistic child. J. Speech Hear. Disord. 2:258–261.

Miller, A., and Miller, E. E. 1973. Cognitive-developmental training with elevated boards and sign language. J. Aut. Child. Schizo. 3:65–85.

Miller, J. F., and Yoder, D. E. 1974. An ontogenetic language teaching strategy for retarded children. *In* R. L. Schiefelbusch and L. L. Lloyd (eds.), Language Perspectives—Acquisition, Retardation, and Intervention, pp. 505–528. University Park Press, Baltimore.

Nelson, K. 1975. Individual differences in early semantic and syntactic development. *In* D. Aaronson and R. Rieger (eds.), Developmental Psycholinguistics and Communication Disorders. New York Academy of Sciences, New York.

Ornitz, E. M., and Ritvo, E. R. 1968. Perceptual inconstancy in early infantile autism. Arch. Gen. Psychiatry 18:76–98.

Ornitz, E. M., and Ritvo, E. R. 1976. Medical assessment. *In* E. R. Ritvo (ed.), Autism: Diagnostic, Current Research and Management, pp. 7–23. Spectrum Publications, Inc., New York.

Premack, D. 1970. A functional analysis of language. J. Exp. Anal. Behav. 14:107–125.

Premack, D., and Premack, A. J. 1974. Teaching visual language to apes and language-deficient persons. *In* R. L. Schiefelbusch and L. L. Lloyd (eds.), Language Perspectives—Acquisition, Retardation, and Intervention, pp. 347–376. University Park Press, Baltimore.

Ricks, D. M. 1975. Vocal communication in pre-verbal normal and autistic children. *In* N. O'Connor (ed.), Language, Cognitive Deficits and Retardation. Butterworth, London.

Ricks, D. M., and Wing, L. 1976. Language, communication and the use of symbols. *In* L. Wing (ed.), Early Childhood Autism: Clinical, Educational and Social Aspects, pp. 93–134. Pergamon Press, New York.

Rimland, B. 1964. Infantile Autism: The Syndrome and Its Implications for a Neural Theory of Behavior. Prentice-Hall, Englewood Cliffs, N.J.

Ruder, K. F., and Smith, M. D. 1974. Issues in language training. *In* R. L. Schiefelbusch and L. L. Lloyd (eds.), Language Perspectives—Acquisition, Retardation, and Intervention, pp. 565–605. University Park Press, Baltimore.

Ruttenberg, B., and Wolf, E. 1967. Evaluating the communication of the autistic child. J. Speech Hearing Disord. 32:314–324.

Rutter, M. 1965. Speech disorders in a series of autistic children. *In* A. W. Franklin (ed.), Children with Communication Problems. Pitman, London.

Rutter, M. 1966. Behavioural and cognitive characteristics. *In* J. K. Wing (ed.), Early Childhood Autism: Clinical, Educational and Social Aspects, pp. 51–81. Pergamon Press, New York.

Rutter, M. 1968. Concepts of autism: A review of research. J. Child Psychol. Psychiatry 9:1–25.

Rutter, M. 1970. Autistic children: Infancy to adulthood. Sem. Psychiatry 2:435–450.

Rutter, J. 1972. Psychiatric causes of language retardation. *In* M. Rutter and J. A. M. Martin (eds.), The Child with Delayed Speech, pp. 147–160. J. B. Lippincott Co., Philadelphia.

Rutter, M. 1974. The development of infantile autism. Psychol. Med. 4:147–163.

Rutter, M. 1978. Diagnosis and definition. *In* M. Rutter and E. Schopler (eds.), Autism: A Reappraisal of Concepts and Treatment, pp. 1–25. Plenum Press, New York.

Schopler, E. 1965. Early infantile autism and receptor processes. Arch. Gen. Psychiatry 13:327–335.

Schumaker, J. B., and Sherman, J. A. 1978. Parent as intervention agent: From birth onward. *In* R. L. Schiefelbusch (ed.), Language Intervention Strategies, pp. 237–315. University Park Press, Baltimore.

Sidman, M. 1971. Reading and auditory-visual equivalences. J. Speech Hear. Res. 14:5–13.

Webster, C. D., McPherson, H., Sloman, L., Evans, M. A., and Kuchar, E. 1973. Communicating with an autistic boy by gestures. J. Aut. Child. Schizo. 3:337–346.

Wing, J. K. 1966. Diagnosis, epidemiology, and aetiology. *In* J. K. Wing (ed.), Early Childhood Autism: Clinical, Educational and Social Aspects, pp. 3–49. Pergamon Press, New York.

Woodcock, R. W., Clark, C. R., and Davies, C. O. 1968. Peabody Rebus Reading Program. American Guidance Service, Circle Pines, Minn.

chapter 17

# Spontaneous Language through Signed Speech

*Benson Schaeffer*

*Department of Psychology*
*University of Oregon*
*Eugene, Oregon*

contents

"George hugging," says Jimmy as he spontaneously walks over to George (his therapist) and hugs him. Jimmy is a seven-year-old autistic boy who originally neither spoke nor responded to speech. He was taught to describe his own or others' actions with the phrase, "(Actor) X-ing," during signed speech treatment, but was not taught to specify the object of an action. Jimmy's unprompted replacement in an egocentric utterance of his name, as the actor, with his therapist's name, as the object, is but one example of his creative use of language. Signed speech is a treatment that can help language-deficient children like Jimmy develop spontaneous speech.

The phrase *signed speech* refers to the simultaneous production of signs and words, as does the term *Total Communication*. Teachers of the deaf developed Total Communication for teaching sign language, and consequently Total Communication has come to refer only to what teachers do, not to what their pupils do (O'Rouke, 1972). Teachers of autistic and mentally retarded children adopted Total Communication when they began teaching their pupils sign language (Larson, 1971; Creedon, 1973b). My colleagues (George Kollinzas, Arlene Musil, and Peter McDowell) and I taught three nonverbal autistic boys (Jimmy is one of them) to sign and speak simultaneously, and we signed and spoke simultaneously ourselves as we taught. We therefore needed a label with which we could refer to both their and our simultaneous signs and speech: hence, *signed speech*.

We began signed speech treatment by teaching the three autistic boys sign language and verbal imitation as independent skills, during different lesson periods. When they began integrating the two skills on their own, we taught them to use signed speech, that is, to sign and speak at the same time. The mastery of two independent language systems by autistic children is an astonishing feat, yet the boys we treated accomplished the task. They learned to communicate spontaneously in signed speech. After they had used signed speech for about 5 months they began occasionally speaking without signing. At this point we systematically faded the signs from their utterances; that is, we taught them to speak without signing. The children progressed from spontaneous sign language, to spontaneous signed speech, to spontaneous verbal language. The sign language fostered spontaneity, and the spontaneity transferred to speech as the children simultaneously signed and spoke. When the signs were faded, the spontaneity remained an integral part of the children's verbal language. This chapter outlines our signed speech treatment and presents and analyzes a number of examples of the children's spontaneous utterances. (For a fuller account, see Schaeffer et al., 1978). Four propositions are suggested by the data:

1. Instruction in sign fosters spontaneous communication by children with severe language deficits.

2. Signing facilitates speech initiation by children with severe language deficits.
3. Sign language and speech can be integrated as signed speech.
4. The relation between sign language and goal attainment suggests a functional-developmental structure for language acquisition programs for the language handicapped.

## SIGNED SPEECH TREATMENT

### Spontaneous Sign Language

At the start of treatment our three pupils, Tommy (five years old and nonverbal), Jimmy (five and a half years old and nonverbal), and Kurt (four and a half years old and minimally echolalic) neither spoke nor responded to speech; their previous participation in educational programs had apparently taught them little. We taught them sign language and verbal imitation as two independent skills in different lesson sessions. We taught them a version of sign language called Signed English (which has the same syntax as spoken English), but, as did Bornstein et al. (1975) and Kopchick and Lloyd (1976), we left out inflectional markers at first. The result was that the children learned to sign spontaneously and to imitate sounds on command. They signed in new situations and for their own purposes; they signed to themselves, egocentrically (see Vygotsky, 1962); they invented new linguistic constructions and generalized concepts beyond their taught meanings; and they learned signs incidentally, without being explicitly taught them. Below are six examples of the boys' spontaneous sign language.

| Spontaneous sign language | Context |
|---|---|
| TOMMY WANT KISS. MAMA BYE-BYE. (Tommy, October, 1974) | Produced at home during a simple game Tommy invented himself. In this game, he would first ask his mother for a kiss, then sign MAMA BYE-BYE when he wanted her to move away after she had kissed him. He usually repeated the game several times in succession. He had previously learned to sign TOMMY WANT X, THIS MAMA, and BYE-BYE. Here he combined the three sign constructions in a playful request-command. His two-utterance sequence is almost conversational. |

| | |
|---|---|
| TOMMY WANT LOOK-AT-ME. (Tommy, September, 1974) | Produced when he desired Arlene's (his therapist's) attention. He had previously been taught in separate situations to request foods and to sign LOOK-AT-ME for attention. Here he inserted LOOK-AT-ME in his TOMMY WANT X construction. |
| JIMMY WANT HELP. (Jimmy, December, 1974) | Produced to request assistance after a coughing fit. Jimmy had previously been taught to sign HELP for aid in opening food jars and in buttoning his pants. Here he extended its use to a new situation. |
| JIMMY WANT HUG (Jimmy, February, 1975) | Produced to request a piggy-back ride. He was explicitly taught to request affection with JIMMY WANT HUG, and had many times been given piggy-back rides and shown the sign RIDE. Here he used a sign he knew, HUG, to request an activity, ride, whose sign he had not yet mastered. |
| KURT WANT JUMP DOWN (Kurt, December, 1974) | Produced during playtime as a request for Pete (his therapist) to catch him when he jumped down from a shelf. Here Kurt combined two constructions, KURT WANT X, which he was taught, and JUMP DOWN, which he learned incidentally. |
| TIME GO POTTY (Kurt, January, 1975) | Produced at home before he walked to the bathroom, sat down on the toilet, and defecated. Kurt had been taught to sign TIME GO POTTY before he was taken to the toilet at school to urinate. He had, however, not been taught to use the phrase to describe defecation and also had not previously used the toilet appropriately for bowel movements at home (he defecated on the floor beside it as he had |

once fallen in.) His use of signs to describe and possibly control a novel appropriate behavior at home is striking.

**Spontaneous Signed Speech**

Three to four months into treatment, Tommy, Jimmy and Kurt began on their own to produce verbal approximations to the words corresponding to their signs as they signed. (Why instruction in sign facilitates speech initiation is discussed later.) When the boys began adding verbal approximations to their signs, we began explicitly teaching them signed speech, that is, simultaneous signs and words, and they soon began communicating spontaneously in signed speech.

The major instructional reasons for their accomplishment may be listed briefly. First, they were constantly exposed to our signed speech and undoubtedly learned about the relation between signs and words from it. Second, during sign language lessons we spoke the corresponding word as they signed. As did our signed speech, this also helped them learn about the relation between signs and words, and, because they could imitate sounds, probably also stimulated their own speech. Third, we began teaching them to pronounce the words corresponding to the signs they knew as soon as they had the requisite sound production skills. Fourth, we systematically taught the boys to imitate our words *after* we spoke, rather than to shadow our voices *as* we spoke. This forced them to rely on remembered sounds for imitation and probably helped give them voluntary control over their voices. Fifth, once they began spontaneously producing word approximations along with their signs, we required them to continue doing so. And, finally, we taught them to coordinate their signs and speech precisely, that is, to utter the word at the same moment that they produced the sign and to coordinate each syllable with a hand movement. They soon were signing and speaking more spontaneously than they had previously signed. Below are six examples that illustrate the creative, generative nature of the boys' signed speech.

| Spontaneous signed speech | Context |
|---|---|
| "TOMMY IN UP." (Tommy, April, 1975) | Produced in response to the question "WHERE IS TOMMY?" when Tommy was up in a tree. He had previously been taught to describe his own location with "TOMMY IN BOX" (school, etc.), and to |

| | |
|---|---|
| | request that he be picked up with "TOMMY WANT UP." Here he combined the two constructions. |
| "ARLENE DOLL TICKLING." (Tommy, June, 1975) | Produced in response to the question "WHAT IS ARLENE DOING?" when Arlene was tickling the doll. Tommy had previously been taught to describe Arlene's action with the two-concept construction, "ARLENE X-ING." Here, on his own, he added the object of the action (he had not been taught to do so) in between the actor and the action. His construction seems almost transformational in structure. |
| "WANT NO DOLL...BOOK." (Jimmy, March, 1975) | Produced in response to the question "DO YOU WANT THE DOLL?" to indicate that he did not want the doll but did want the book. Here Jimmy combined a shortened request form (he had been taught "JIMMY WANT X"), the "NO" with which he was taught to reject undesired objects and activities, and an appended counter-proposal. The adjectival (possibly adverbial) insertion of "NO" suggests an underlying linguistic transformation. |
| "COOKIE...COOKIE...COOKIE." (Jimmy, July, 1975) | Produced egocentrically while searching among several objects for the cookie he was asked to touch. Jimmy seemed to be using his signed speech to help himself remember what it was that he had been asked to touch, and thus to guide his search. |

| | |
|---|---|
| "KURT WANT PUT COOKIE IN BOX." (Kurt, July, 1975) | Produced as a request for permission to put the jar of cookies in the storage box at the end of the lesson. Here Kurt combined a request, he incidentally learned "PUT," and the locative description "COOKIE IN BOX," in asking for permission to engage in a complicated (by his standards) anticipated activity. |
| "KURT WANT TIRE SWING." (Kurt, July, 1975) | Produced at home as a request for help getting into his tire swing. The incidentally learned word he inserted, "TIRE," was accompanied by his idiosyncratic flattened ball sign; he had not been taught or shown the sign for "tire." |

## SPONTANEOUS VERBAL LANGUAGE

The boys began occasionally speaking without signing after about five months of signed speech. At this juncture we began teaching them to communicate verbally, without signing. We told them not to sign, held their hands to keep them from signing, and, to help them remember what they were saying, taught them to speak more loudly and quickly than they had previously. Signs were first faded from their most overlearned construction ("Child want X"), and later from others. The result was that the boys learned to speak, without signing, as creatively as they had previously signed and spoken. (Discussed later is the internalization of signing that appeared to occur as they began to speak.) Below are several examples of their spontaneous verbal language.

| Spontaneous verbal language | Context |
|---|---|
| "Tractor...no more tractor here." (Tommy, September, 1975) | Produced when he was alone in the playroom; the toy tractor he sometimes played with was not present. Here Tommy combined "tractor" (taught), "no more" (learned incidentally), and "here" (learned incidentally) as he thought aloud to himself. |

| | |
|---|---|
| "What is this?" (Tommy, January, 1976) | Produced after being asked, "What time is it?" when he found himself unable to respond. Tommy's use of the question form to ask about time shows that he associated asking a question with a felt lack of information rather than with the object-labeling situation in which he was taught to ask the question. |
| "Happy yes candy." (Jimmy, January, 1976) | Produced as he watched George arrange candy reinforcers for a verbal imitation lesson. Jimmy had recently been taught to label his own and others' emotional states with "(Person's name) (state)," where (state) might be "happy," "sad," "sleepy," or "angry." Here he combined a state term with two others he knew to describe his feeling about, and desire for, candy. |
| "I want Pete nut in cup." (Jimmy, March, 1976) | Produced in response to "What do you want?" referring to a peanut in a cup Pete was holding. Jimmy had been taught the possessive request "I want Pete nut," and the locative description "Nut in cup." Here he combined the two constructions. |
| "Cowboy want hug." (Kurt, January, 1976) | Produced as a request for a hug; preceded by several minutes during which Pete called Kurt a cowboy because Kurt was wearing a cowboy hat. The utterance suggests a minimal awareness of role-playing possibilities. |
| "Pete belting pants." (Kurt, March, 1976) | Produced in response to the question "What is Pete doing?" when Pete was fastening his belt. Here Kurt transformed a noun he knew, "belt," into a verb and used it to describe an action he had not previously been taught to label. |

The boys used verbal language creatively just as they had previously used signed speech and, earlier, sign language. They spoke in new situations and for their own purposes; they talked to themselves, egocentrically; they invented new linguistic constructions and generalized concepts beyond their original meanings; and they learned words incidentally. Their progress from spontaneous sign language, to spontaneous signed speech, to spontaneous verbal language shows that simultaneously produced signs and words provide a natural intermediary between creative signing and creative talking. It appears that the spontaneity promoted by signing transferred to speech as the boys used signed speech. In the discussion that follows of the four propositions listed earlier, the relations between sign language and spontaneous communication are considered in more detail.

## PROPOSITION 1: INSTRUCTION IN SIGN FOSTERS SPONTANEOUS COMMUNICATION BY CHILDREN WITH SEVERE LANGUAGE DEFICITS

Terms as used here should first be defined. *Instruction in sign language* refers to the teaching of manual communication, but excludes both fingerspelling and the manipulation of concrete symbols other than hands (Carrier and Peak, 1975; Vanderheiden et al. 1975). The system of manual communication my colleagues and I chose to teach is called Signed English. We selected Signed English rather than Ameslan because the syntax of the former bears a one-to-one correspondence to that of spoken English, whereas the syntax of the latter does not. Kopchick and Lloyd (1976) made the same choice and, like us, also decided not to teach inflectional markers (see Bornstein et al., 1975). *Spontaneous communication* refers to utterances produced in new situations for the children's own purposes, to egocentric communication, to newly invented linguistic constructions, and to incidentally learned concepts (here, signs). Spontaneous utterances are either produced freely, that is, not in response to questions, or consist of new (untaught) responses to questions. *Children with severe language deficits* refers to nonverbal autistic, mentally retarded, or aphasic individuals, without overwhelming motor dysfunction. (The use of sign language with partially verbal individuals is discussed later.)

Many investigators have noted that nonverbal, severely handicapped individuals spontaneously employ the signs they are taught. Creedon (1973b), Miller and Miller (1973), Webster et al. (1973), Bonvillian and Nelson (1976), Fulwiler and Fouts (1976), and my colleagues and I have documented the spontaneous use of sign language by nonverbal, autistic children. Larson (1971), Kopchick, Rombach, and Smilovitz (1975), Topper (1975), and Stremel-Campbell, Cantrell, and Halle (1976) have recorded spontaneous signing by mentally retarded individuals. The data available thus strongly argue that instruction in sign promotes spontaneous communication by children with severe language deficits. These data are all the more striking because there is little or no evidence that analogous instruction in verbal language is systematically related to the acquisition of spontaneous speech. In the extreme, autistic children who are taught verbal language tend to use it only on demand in the treatment situations, or in similar ones, as they interact with therapists or people trained as therapists. They tend not to use their verbal language in new situations when interacting with untrained people, and they tend not to learn new words on their own.

## Signing as Goal-Directed Hand Movement

The question that arises at this point is: Why do severely language-deficient individuals use sign language spontaneously? The major suggestion proposed here is that sign spontaneity develops primarily out of the goal directedness of normal hand movements and secondarily as a result of motor fluency and the rich sign-teaching situation.

Signing is a method through which individuals with severe language deficits can achieve social goals mediated by others. A language-deficient individual can use signs to ask another person for something, or to reject what he is offered; likewise, he can obtain the attention of another person by describing some aspect of the world for the person, by asking the person a question, or by requesting that the person attend to a particular part of the environment.

Autistic and mentally retarded youngsters use their hands to attain physical goals, just as normal children do. They grasp objects, foods, and people they want and push away objects, foods, and people they do not want. Thus, despite their language deficits, they know the relation between hand movements and fulfillment of desires, and they know, furthermore, that hand movements must be adjusted to fit the desire. (A candy cannot be grasped in exactly the same fashion that a person can.) Before instruction in sign, however, nonverbal autistic and nonverbal mentally retarded youngsters do not seem to know how to achieve social goals via language. My hypothesis is that they learn to sign spontaneously by adapting the goal-directed hand movements they use for grasping to the social goals that are normally mediated by verbal language. An outline of how my colleagues and I taught the autistic boys we treated their first signs helps demonstrate the connection between signs and desires.

We taught each boy his first sign by converting his spontaneous reach for a desired food to the sign label for that food. We would hold the desired food out to him and wait. When he reached for the food we molded his reaching arm and hand into the proper position for signing, moved his hand through the sign, and then gave him the desired food (whose sign he had produced). We did this many times. Eventually, however, to help him begin signing on his own, intentionally, we started molding his arm and hand into the proper sign position *without* then moving his hand appropriately. Eventually his frustration at not obtaining the desired food that usually came his way prompted him to move his hand appropriately and intentionally on his own. After he had moved his hand voluntarily a number of times, we stopped molding his arm and hand into the proper sign position. His desire and frustration now prompted him, first, to put his arm and hand in the proper sign position and, next, to move his hand appropriately, that is, to complete the entire sign intentionally. Self-directed signing was thus established by frustrating a desire in a situation where intentional signing, in the form of a request, could alleviate that frustration. Even now, after more than 2 years of treatment, "I want (X)," where (X) may be more than one word, is still the primary utterance of the boys we trained. (It might be noted, in passing, that investigators of language acquisition by normal infants also point to the expression of desires as an important function, and motivator, of early language (Bates, Camaioni, and Volterra, 1973; Carter, 1975; Dore, 1975).)

The step from goal-directed hand movement to the spontaneous use of sign language, itself a form of hand movement, for the attainment of social goals is easier for language-deficient individuals than the step from goal-directed hand movement to the spontaneous use of words. This is not surprising. The gestural expression of desires by normal infants is regularly observed by parents. My reasons for arguing that sign spontaneity arises out of goal-directed grasping, however, are not only that desire-driven hand movements can be easily adapted to the attainment of social goals or that normal infants express desires gesturally. In addition, it appears that signing facilitates speech initiation in part by allowing the language-deficient child to learn that speech can be used in a goal-directed fashion, and that language acquisition programs would do well to begin by teaching children to make requests that express their desires. (These issues are discussed later.)

### Motor Fluency and the Rich Sign-Teaching Situation

Goal directedness is not the only source of sign spontaneity, however; motor fluency and the rich sign-teaching situation also play a role. Language-deficient individuals are not typically grossly deficient in terms of motor skills (severely palsied youngsters are an exception). The fluency and coordination of their hand movements, relative to their speech, probably make it easier for them to learn to sign than to learn to talk, and thus contribute to the development of spontaneity. Furthermore, therapists' use of Total Communication, that is, signed speech, during instruction in sign makes the sign-learning situation a richer one, informationally, than the word-learning situation. Because the therapist teaching sign speaks two languages at once, the language-deficient individual has two sources of information on which to rely. If he forgets the meaning of a sign, he can pay attention to the word that accompanies it, and if he forgets the meaning of the word, he can attend to the sign. In a related sense, because the language-deficient individual can learn about word meanings and about the relation between signs and words as this therapist simultaneously signs and speaks, instruction via signed speech can help him behave appropriately outside school, where people only speak. Simultaneous instruction in two modes also may stimulate the language-deficient individual to allot more of his limited attentional capacities to the task of communicating.

To summarize, then, instruction in sign prompts spontaneous communication, probably in the main because language-deficient individuals can adapt goal-directed hand movements to the task of communication in sign.

## PROPOSITION 2: SIGNING FACILITATES SPEECH INITIATION BY CHILDREN WITH SEVERE LANGUAGE DEFICITS

Speech initiation refers to voluntary, or spontaneous, sound production in a communication setting. Creedon (1976) has reported that approximately two-thirds of the autistic children she and her colleagues taught to sign, but not to speak, developed some speech on their own, in the form of single mouthed words, verbal approximations, or, for a small number, fluent speech. Miller and Miller (1973) have described the spontaneous acquisition of speech by two of 19 autistic children taught only sign. Fulwiler and Fouts (1976) have recorded the spontaneous production of concurrent speech by a nonverbal, autistic boy taught manual language. The three autistic boys to whom we taught signs and imitative speech began voluntarily voicing verbal approximations to the words corresponding to their signs 3 to 4 months into treatment. And Stremel-Campbell, Cantrell, and Halle (1976) report that six of nine trainable mentally retarded youngsters taught to sign began pairing verbal approximations with their words. These findings suggest a natural link between signing and speech.

If it is remembered that signs are consistently paired with words during signed speech instruction, the existence of a ready tie between manual and verbal language becomes comprehensible. The teacher's signs are paired with words as he consistently uses signed speech. The child's signs are paired with words as the teacher consistently utters the corresponding word when the child signs. The child learns the relation between signs and words and between words and objects as he attends to his teacher's signed speech, and to the words (his teacher's) that accompany his (the child's) signs. My colleagues and I did not test extensively for word comprehension prior to speech initiation. What little testing we did, however, showed that the boys we were treating understood most of our words even when they were not paired with signs. Bricker (1972) showed that severely retarded children learned word-object associations more quickly after they were taught the corresponding signs and sign-word associations. None of the available data, however, discriminates among the various possible facilitating roles sign might play in relation to the acquisition of receptive language: that of a redundant cue that aids learning, an intermediate term between word and object, or a director of attention to the word-object relation.

Receptive knowledge alone, however, does not solve the basic problem. Why do previously nonverbal children who know sign-word and word-object relations initiate speech? Undoubtedly, there is no single cause. Therefore, suggested here are what seem to be the most important factors in speech initiation:

1. *Untapped expressive language skills:* Most nonverbal children who are taught signs initiate speech with actual word approximations, rather than merely with grunts and mumbles. This shows that they have untapped expressive skills. If not, they would be unable to translate their receptive knowledge of sign-word and word-object relations into actual word approximations.
2. *Frustrated desires:* A child may begin speaking when he is frustrated in his attempts to get what he wants by signing. Suppose a child emits a frustration-prompted verbalization that causes his momentarily inattentive teacher to turn to him and notice his signed desire. The child might learn that signs accompanied by sounds are a more effective attention-getting and communicating tool than signs alone. Tommy, one of the boys we treated, uttered his first verbal approximation, "otsie," as he signed OUTSIDE. He wanted to play and was signing OUTSIDE repeatedly. His teacher had deliberately turned away from him because she did not want to take him outside. Out of frustration, he then simultaneously signed OUTSIDE and said "otsie," and his teacher, of course, took him outside to play.
3. *Goal-directed speech:* A child may begin to understand that speech can be used to attain goals as his teacher consistently utters the word(s) corresponding to the child's sign(s) as the child signs. The child may therefore try vocalizing, along with his signs, to attain his desires. (The assumption is made here that the child knows that he uses his signs to attain desires.)
4. *Generalized imitation:* The child's motor imitation of his teacher's signs, be it immediate and deliberate (in the case where signs are

taught by imitation) or deferred and accidental (in the case where signs are shaped), may stimulate attempts at concurrent verbal imitation. Stremel-Campbell, Cantrell, and Halle (1976) present a similar argument.

5. *Release from fear and frustration:* Sign language is an expressive mode with which the nonverbal child can be spontaneous and successful. This may increase his confidence to the point that he is willing to try using expressive language skills previously suppressed by fear and frustration.
6. *Language-facilitated speech:* The child's spontaneous and productive sign language may prime speech. That is, his generative, goal-directed use of manual symbols may, through some as yet unknown physiological mechanism, elicit concurrent vocalization.

## PROPOSITION 3: SIGN LANGUAGE AND SPEECH CAN BE INTEGRATED AS SIGNED SPEECH

The three originally nonverbal autistic boys we trained began spontaneously adding verbal approximations to their signs 3 to 4 months into treatment and eventually learned to communicate in signed speech, or simultaneously produced signs and words. In light of the link between signing and talking that is created when signs are taught by persons who speak as they sign, signed speech techniques may be viewed as a set of procedures for capitalizing on ties between signs and words that arise naturally. Signed speech did not overtax the limited attentional capacities of the children we instructed probably because its two components functioned as redundant languages. The children likely used remembered signs to cue forgotten words, and remembered words to cue forgotten signs. Nonverbal, mentally retarded and aphasic children should be able to master spontaneous signed speech much as did the autistic children my colleagues and I trained. In fact, I have recently taught an epileptic, aphasic, autistic-like child with severe memory deficits (due to recurrent seizures) to sign and speak at the same time, and he now does so spontaneously.

Spontaneous signed speech is important because it provides language-deficient children with the opportunity to acquire spontaneous verbal language: the handicapped youngster who uses signed speech spontaneously can move from it to verbal language when the signs are removed. What appears to occur as children sign and speak simultaneously is that the spontaneity promoted by signing transfers to the speech that accompanies it. The most important source of the transfer would seem to be the goal-directedness of signing. Children who attain social goals through signs, and who speak as they sign, learn that words can be used to attain social goals. (That goal-directedness is the only source of verbal spontaneity is not implied here, however. The motor fluency of language-deficient individuals and the rich sign-teaching situation make it easier for the handicapped to master sign language than to master speech, and the rhythmic, organized patterns of movement that underlie their fluent sign language may create a context for natural improvement in the rhythm and organization of the speech they subsequently learn.)

After approximately 5 months of signed speech, the autistic boys with whom we worked began occasionally speaking without signing. At this juncture we began deliberately fading the signs from their signed speech. We told them not to sign, and held their hands when they signed. To help them maintain their train of thought in speech alone, we taught them to speak more loudly and quickly than they had previously spoken. The result was that they spoke as, or more, spontaneously than they had previously signed and spoken, and continued to refine and expand their verbal language on their own. Goal-directedness had become an integral property of their speech.

During fading, it seemed that something like the internalization of signs was taking place. To begin with, the boys often signed in foreshortened fashion as they spoke. (Piaget, 1952, refers to foreshortened action as evidence of interiorization.) Second, two of the boys, Jimmy and Kurt, developed an action mnemonic which suggests internalization. When they began teaching the boys possessive concepts, the therapists signed close to the person (or object) the sign described, to aid the boys. Thus, in the utterance, "THIS IS ARLENE'S SHOE," THIS would be signed close to Arlene's shoe, IS would be signed in the air, ARLENE'S would be signed close to Arlene's face, and SHOE would be signed close to Arlene's shoe. Soon the boys themselves began spontaneously using close signing as a mnemonic. As signs were faded out they first foreshortened their close signs, then reduced them to perfunctory, indistinct pointing, and finally dropped them altogether. Even now, however, when new concepts are introduced, or old concepts are complicated, all three boys tend to revert to foreshortened signing or to close signing. A last example to suggest the internalization of signs: Tommy is now, in his new program, learning to read. As he reads aloud he often signs in foreshortened fashion. (It should be mentioned that, although the therapists presently speak to the boys without signing, they do introduce new concepts in signed speech, to provide the boys with redundant information.)

Although it appeared that the signs were internalized during fading, it is probably not the case that the speech that emerged derived its spontaneity from internalized signs alone. It seems more likely that its spontaneity flowed more from the children's knowledge that speech can be used to achieve desired ends. The goal directedness that appeared to mediate the acquisition of spontaneous speech can be capitalized on in the construction of language programs.

## PROPOSITION 4: THE RELATION BETWEEN SIGN LANGUAGE AND GOAL ATTAINMENT SUGGESTS A FUNCTIONAL-DEVELOPMENTAL STRUCTURE FOR LANGUAGE ACQUISITION PROGRAMS FOR THE LANGUAGE HANDICAPPED

Signing promotes spontaneity by providing nonverbal children with a nonverbal means for attaining social goals mediated by other persons. This suggests that nonverbal children should be taught the relation between social goals and communication at the start of language training and that further instruction should be based on this initial learning. (Creedon, 1973a, and Miller and Miller, 1973, also stress the importance of communication directly related to goals.) At the start of signed speech treatment we therefore taught our pupils to express their *desires;* we then taught them to use *person concepts*, *inquiry skills*, and *abstractions*. (Between desires and person concepts, inquiry skills, and abstractions, we taught *reference*, that is, how to label, or describe, objects. Reference was taught because labeling and description are a part of the use of person concepts, inquiry skills, and abstractions. The children eventually began to describe events spontaneously, apparently for the sake of using language and maintaining social interaction. However, their spontaneous descriptions have remained less frequent than their spontaneous requests. Reference is not discussed in detail here.) Figure 1 outlines the signed speech language program.

We started language instruction with the expression of desires. Person concepts and inquiry skills may be viewed as implicit components of the expression of desires. A child expressing a desire to another person must address that person and must solve the problem of getting that person to satisfy his (the child's) desire. Thus, the child must use a person concept, if only implicitly, and must make an inquiry, that is, try to find out if the person he addresses will help him. The more the child knows about the person he addresses and about people in general, the more likely he is to initiate a request, and the more precise and personal he can make his address. In other words, the more person concepts he knows, the more effective he is likely to be in expressing and satisfying his desires and the more likely he is to expand his patterns of appropriate social interaction. Similarly, the more inquiry skills he possesses, that is, the more capable he is of using his language to gain information and solve problems, the more likely he will be to get another person to help him satisfy his desires, that is, to achieve his social goals.

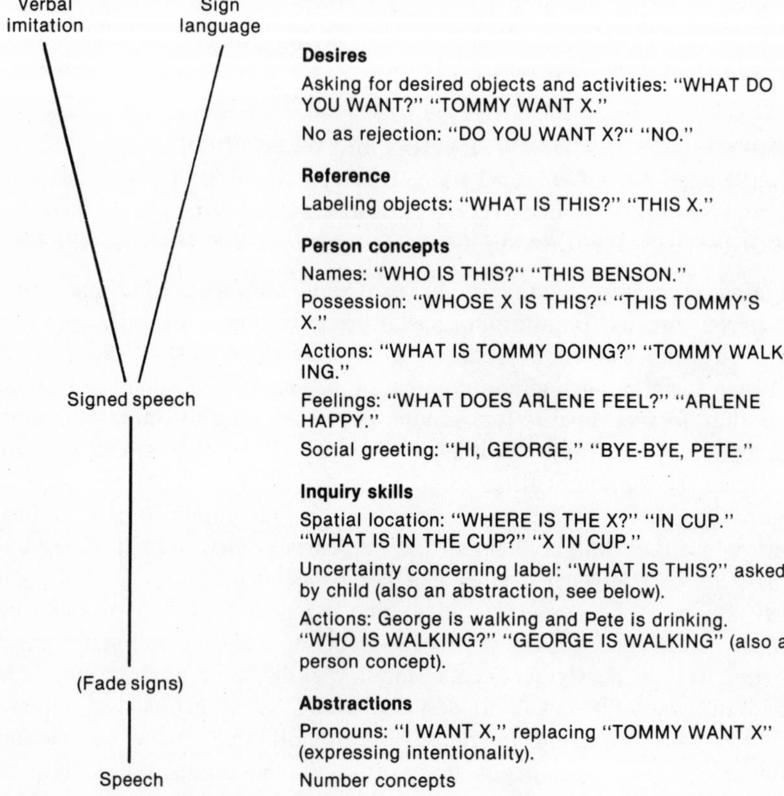


Figure 1. The chronology of the signed speech language program in terms of both utterance mode and conceptual content.

In signed speech treatment, the expression of desires was the second source of linguistic spontaneity after sign language, and person concepts and inquiry skills were, jointly, the third. Normal children learn language by interacting with, thinking about, and paying finely differentiated attention to people (Cazden, 1972). My colleagues and I felt that we could expand the social desires of autistic (and other language-deficient) children and facilitate the normal social learning of communicative skills by teaching person concepts. We also felt that by teaching person concepts we could help these children learn about and attend to similarities and differences between people. We, therefore, taught the autistic boys with whom we worked people's names, possessive terms, labels for emotional states (such as *sad*, *happy*, *angry*, and *tired*), labels for the actions people perform, and other linguistic forms relating to people.

Also, for the purpose of increasing their range of social desires and facilitating normal language acquisition, we taught the boys inquiry skills, that is, the use of language to gain information about the world. Luria (1961) and Vygotsky (1962) have shown that by the time normal children are six years old they use language coordinated with action to solve problems. Casual observation suggests they use language to gain information about the world even sooner. We explicitly taught the autistic children we treated language and search procedures appropriate for gaining information and solving problems. For example, we taught them: to "FIND THE CANDY," which might be in a cup, a box, a doll house, or a crumpled pair of pants; to find out "WHAT IS IN THE (X)?", where "WHAT" might be, for example, a toy dog, a car, a cookie, or a ball and (X) might be any object in which a "WHAT" could be hidden; and to ask "WHAT IS THIS?" when they did not know an object's label.

In other words, we taught them to search for hidden objects, to remember and describe the objects' locations, and to ask questions about objects' names and locations. Normal children master the object concept naturally (Piaget, 1952) and link it to veral language (Huttenlocher, 1974). Instruction in inquiry skills provided the boys we trained with an analogous language-related object concept which, if it generalizes beyond treatment, might help them develop independent, socially oriented problem-solving abilities.

A note: We began teaching person concepts and inquiry skills at about the time the boys began adding verbal approximations to their signs; they began occasionally speaking without signing at about the time, or a little after, they started using simple person concepts and inquiry skills. Perhaps these two new sources of linguistic spontaneity decreased their need to rely on sign language.

## DETERMINING COMMUNICATION MODE AND CONTENT

Considered thus far have been mode of communication (signs, signed speech, and words) and content of communication (desires, person concepts, and inquiry skills.) Discussed below are issues at the interface between mode and content: whether or not a child with some verbal language should be taught to sign; programming for children with some verbal language; instruction of mentally retarded (as opposed to autistic) youngsters; and the role of imitation in sign-based instruction.

### To Sign or Not to Sign

One of the boys we treated, Kurt, was minimally echolalic at the start of treatment. He occasionally echoed, in a garbled or incomplete fashion, one- and two-word utterances. Because his verbal skills were poorly developed, my colleagues and I decided to teach Kurt both signs and speech, and, as did the nonverbal boys, Tommy and Jimmy, Kurt progressed from spontaneous sign language, to spontaneous signed speech, to spontaneous verbal language. His echolalia did affect his progress, however. In addition to learning more language incidentally than did the two mute boys, he presented different learning problems. Because he was somewhat echolalic, he learned signs and words imitatively more quickly than he learned to associate them with their referents, as compared to the other boys. Consequently, he required more rigorous discrimination training than the others, to disambiguate the larger number of signs and words he could produce by rote. Because he was echolalically attracted to therapist cues he could imitate, negative information in the form of a "NO" was of little use to him (the mute boys did not have this difficulty). And because his imitative skills allowed him to sign and talk with such facility, relatively speaking, it was hard to keep him from rapidly repeating himself, that is, stuttering in both sign and speech. These echolalia-related problems were overcome only after much effort.

Children who know more language than did Kurt, but whose language is often echolalic, inappropriate, or uncoordinated, may benefit from instruction in sign. The decision as to whether or not to teach these children signs to promote appropriate spontaneity is a difficult one. An evaluation of the relation between a child's verbal language and his desires can be an aid in making the decision: the more closely a child's speech is related to his apparent goals, or desires, the less likely he is to require instruction in sign. Several examples are illustrative.

1. Ted is an autistic boy who needs to expand and refine his speech but probably would not benefit from instruction in signed speech, because the syntactic and semantic variations in his speech are appropriately related to his desires. I sat with Ted and showed him some candy.
   Benson: "What do you want?"
   Ted: (points to the candy)
   Benson: (waits)
   Ted: "Want it."
   Benson: "What do you want?"
   Ted: "Candy."
   Benson: (waits)
   Ted: "Want the candy."
   Benson: "What do you want?"
   Ted: "Ted wants that (pointing), please."
   Benson: (gives Ted some candy)
2. Bill is an autistic boy who would benefit from instruction in signed speech, even though he verbalizes frequently, because his speech

lacks a consistent rhythm and pitch and tends toward uncontrolled echolalia. Signed speech would help bridge the gap between his utterances and his desires by adding a measure of coordination to his speech. I showed Bill a Jack-in-the-box that his teachers said he enjoyed.

Benson: "What do you want?"

Bill: "Go p-o-t-t-y." (uttered with an inappropriate, half-whining, half-screaming, rising inflection)

Benson: "Not now. What else do you want?"

Bill: "Wanted to want it the . . . some . . . want to . . . (hands up in front of face, fingers moving rapidly in self-stimulatory fashion, eyes crossed) . . . some J-a-c-k–i-n–the–b-o-x." (high, rising inflection)

3. Fred is a trainable mentally retarded youngster who would benefit from instruction in signed speech. He answers questions related to his desires most often with wordless, but apparently inflected, babbling similar to that produced by some infants before they learn to talk. The act of producing sounds is an effort for him. As he verbalizes, his face usually reddens, and he usually clenches his fists and tightens his arms; very infrequently does he answer a simple request appropriately.
4. Melanie is not easily labeled as either mentally retarded or autistic. Signed speech is probably appropriate for her because she answers questions related to her desires in a variety of inappropriate ways. Sometimes she walks away after she is asked a question. Sometimes she produces wordless, but apparently inflected, babbling (as she tenses up and begins to self-stimulate). Sometimes she begins one of her ritual conversations about her pet pony, in the barn, needing hay, next to the tree, "Can I go there?" Very infrequently, she becomes almost rigid, blushes, and blurts out a simple, appropriate answer (which usually trails off into wordless babbling).

**Programming for Children with Some Verbal Language**

Children with limited language who do not need instruction in signed speech might benefit from learning the signs that correspond to psychological verbs that express desire (such as *want*, *give*, and *put*), people's names, labels for emotional states, labels for human actions, interrogative and possessive terms, and prepositions. For even more advanced children, children on the brink of appropriate language, instruction in verbal language (without signs) that emphasizes desires, person concepts, and inquiry skills would also be appropriate. An example can illustrate how the expressions of desires can be stressed with an advanced child. One of my colleagues, Arlene Musil, was working with a bright, echolalic boy named Jack. To enable Jack to begin talking coherently, Arlene created a situation in which he had to express his desires verbally in order to avoid social interaction.

Arlene: (took a chip out of its container)
Jack: "No! No!"
Arlene: "No what?"
Jack: "Put it back."
Arlene: "Put what back? What is this?"
Jack: "Chip. Put it back."
Arlene: "Put what back?"
Jack: "Put the chip back."
Arlene: "Back where? In the cup?"
Jack: "No. Put it back!"
Arlene: "Put it where? In the hat?"
Jack: "No!"
Arlene: "Put it where? In the dish?"
Jack: "In the dish."
Arlene: "Put the chip where?"
Jack: "Put the chip in the dish."

By extending the paradoxical talk-to-avoid-talk, Arlene was able to keep Jack conversing and gradually phase in more formal language instruction.

It should be noted that advanced children need to learn to use abstractions, as well as to express desires and use person concepts and inquiry skills. The previous discussion of these children's treatment is meant as an outline, rather than as a prescription, and therefore does not elaborate the how, what, and why of teaching abstractions.

### Instructing Mentally Retarded Children

Up to this point a distinction has not been made between autistic and mentally retarded youngsters in terms of treatment. There are differences between these children, however, and these differences necessitate variations in treatment. In particular, some nonverbal, mentally retarded children, unlike autistic children, are inquisitive and social and engage in imaginative play. These children need initial instruction in sign and signed speech, but their instruction should capitalize on their social and representational capacities. They should be taught to ask questions from the start, since they attempt to ask questions through pointing and quizzical facial expressions even without formal language. They should be taught to request that people look at what they are pointing to, since they attempt such requests on their own anyway. And they should be taught to describe the guns, toys, houses, fathers, mothers, and animals that populate their imaginative play. By linking signs and then signed speech to their high-level social and representational abilities, their teachers can help them use relatively inaccessible information in a truly social fashion, and thus help them integrate language more thoroughly into their lives.

### Role of Imitation

For many professionals who teach language-deficient individuals, the first step in sign language instruction is the establishment of motor imitation of signs. My colleagues and I rely primarily on direct shaping of signs and only secondarily on the use of imitative cues. Primary reliance on imitation in initial sign instruction can interfere with the establishment of voluntary, or spontaneous, signing because of its built-in stress on mimicry and compliance. Kurt, the echolalic boy we treated, imitated easily and for that very reason had difficulty giving up imitative cues and initiating spontaneous communication. Initial signs should therefore be directly shaped; imitative cues should be used as aids to proficient signing rather than as a starting point.

## CONCLUSION

Instruction in signed speech, with a focus on the expression of desires and the use of person concepts and inquiry skills, promotes speech in children with severe language deficits. The speech is spontaneous in that it is used in new situations and for the children's own purposes; it is employed egocentrically; it contains linguistic constructions the children invent on their own; its concepts are generalized beyond their original meanings; and some of its component words are acquired incidentally. Granted, the children speak spontaneously much less frequently than do normal children; their utterances are about as complex as those of normal two- and three-year-olds; and continued spontaneous communication probably requires a very supporting, yet at the same time demanding, environment. Nevertheless, the minimal spontaneous speech that signed speech treatment establishes is a great gain. Studies will be needed to determine whether or not the spontaneous verbal language fostered by signed speech is a more effective means of communication for language-deficient children than is sign language (see Creedon, 1973b). I believe speech will prove more effective than sign language because normal speakers are more responsive to speech than to sign and because the signing community has limited resources. Furthermore, it is easier to speak and act than to sign and act when actions involve the hands, and most language-deficient children have an ability to hear and produce sounds that can be developed. More importantly, the autistic boys my colleagues and I treated have continued speaking spontaneously and have continued to refine and extend their speech on their own. Finally, my experience suggests that signed speech is probably as appropriate for trainable and severely retarded youngsters, and for aphasics, as it is for autistic children. The aphasic, epileptic, autistic-like child I am presently teaching, who started without any language, is progressing, at a slower rate, through the same stages as the three autistic boys whose spontaneous verbal language has been described.

Sign language has been discussed as a tool for spontaneous language development and speech initiation. Hodges and Deich (1979), Parkel and Smith (1979), and Vanderheiden and Vanderheiden (Chapters 11 and 12, this volume) note that the use of manipulable lexical systems, such as Blissymbolics and the LANA system, and manipulable plastic prespeech programs, such as Non-SLIP, also promote spontaneous language and facilitate speech initiation. Of particular interest, nonverbal, retarded youngsters with severe motor deficits (due to cerebral palsy) can learn to communicate spontaneously with plastic symbols; they can learn to nod their heads, or move their eyes, to signal which Blissymbols convey their intended message.

Spontaneous sign language has been described as growing out of goal-directed hand movements adapted to the attainment of symbol-mediated social goals. The spontaneous communication by eye movements of nonverbal, retarded, palsied youngsters argues that neither hand movements nor symbols formed by the child (signs rather than plastic symbols) are crucial to the establishment of spontaneous communication. This suggests that the minimum conditions for the development of spontaneous communication include the use of 1) any movement under voluntary control to signal 2) an active choice 3) by way of a shared symbol 4) to another person. (I am indebted to Savage-Rumbaugh and Rumbaugh, 1979, for the basic argument.)

These minimum conditions notwithstanding, I believe that sign language will (in the absence of severe motor deficits) prove a more effective tool for fostering spontaneous language and facilitating speech initiation than will manipulable plastic systems. The primary reasons are:

1. The nonverbal child can sign when, where, and to whom he wishes, but cannot use plastic symbols in as unrestricted a fashion.
2. The nonverbal child can determine by himself the length and order of his sign utterances and the form of individual signs; he cannot do so with plastic symbols.
3. The precise coordination of symbol and word that mediates speech initiation appears easier to establish with signs (in signed speech) than with plastic symbols. Hence, instruction in sign will probably prove more effective for purposes of speech initiation than will instruction in the use of plastic symbols.

## REFERENCES


Bates, E., Camaioni, L., and Volterra, V. 1973. The Acquisition of Performatives Prior to Speech. Technical Report No. 129, Consiglio Nazionale delle Richerche, Rome.

Bonvillian, J. D., and Nelson, K. E. 1976. Sign language acquisition in a mute autistic boy. J. Speech Hear. Res. 41:339–347.

Bornstein, H., Saulniev, K. L., Hamilton, L. B., and Roy, H. L. 1975. The Signed English Dictionary for Preschool and Elementary Levels. Gallaudet College Press, Washington, D.C.

Bricker, D. D. 1972. Imitative sign training as a facilitator of word-object association with low-functioning children. Am. J. Ment. Defic. 76:509–516.

Carrier, J. K., Jr., and Peak, T. 1975. Non-speech Language Initiation Program. H & H Enterprises, Lawrence, Kan.

Carter, A. L. 1975. The transformation of sensorimotor morphemes into words. Papers and Reports on Child Language Development, No. 10, Department of Linguistics, Stanford University, Palo Alto, Cal.

Cazden, C. B. 1972. Child Language and Education. Holt, Rinehart & Winston, New York.

Creedon, M. P. (ed.). 1973a. Appropriate Behavior Through Communication: A New Program in Simultaneous Language. Dysfunctioning Child Center at Michael Reese Medical Center, Chicago.

Creedon, M. P. 1973b. Language development in nonverbal autistic children using a simultaneous communication system. Paper presented to the Society for Research in Child Development, March, Philadelphia.

Creedon, M. P. 1976. The David School: A simultaneous communication model. Paper presented at the National Society for Autistic Children Meeting, Oak Brook, Ill.

Dore, J. 1975. Holophrases, speech acts and language universals. J. Child Lang. 2:21–40.

Fulwiler, R. L., and Fouts, R. S. 1976. Acquisition of American Sign Language by a noncommunicating autistic child. J. Aut. Child. Schizo. 6:43–51.

Hodges, P., and Deich, R. F. 1979. Language intervention strategies with manipulable symbols. *In* R. L. Schiefelbusch and J. H. Hollis (eds.), Language Intervention from Ape to Child, pp. 419–440. University Park Press, Baltimore.

Huttenlocher, J. 1974. The origins of language comprehension. *In* R. L. Solso (ed.), Theories in Cognitive Psychology: The Loyola Symposium, pp. 331–368. John Wiley & Sons, New York.

Kopchick, G. A., Jr., and Lloyd, L. L. 1976. Total communication programming for the severely language impaired: A 24-hour approach. *In* L. L. Lloyd (ed.), Communication Assessment and Intervention Strategies, pp. 501–521. University Park Press, Baltimore.

Kopchick, G. A., Jr., Rombach, D., and Smilovitz, R. 1975. A total communication environment in an institution. Ment. Retard. 13:22–23.

Larson, T. 1971. Communication for the nonverbal child. Acad. Ther. 6:305–312.

Luria, A. R. 1961. The Role of Speech in the Regulation of Normal and Abnormal Behavior. Liverright, New York.

Miller, A., and Miller, E. 1973, Cognitive-developmental training with elevated boards and sign language. J. Aut. Child. Schizo. 3:65–85.

O'Rourke, T. J. (ed.). 1972. Psycholinguistics and total communication: The state of the art. Am. Ann. Deaf Washington, D.C.

Parkel, D. A., and Smith, S. T., Jr. 1979. Application of computer-assisted language devices. *In* R. L. Schiefelbusch and J. H. Hollis (eds.), Language Intervention from Ape to Child, pp. 441–464. University Park Press, Baltimore.

Piaget, J. 1952. The Origins of Intelligence in Children. International Universities Press, New York.

Piaget, J. 1954. The Construction of Reality in the Child. Basic Books, New York.

Savage-Rumbaugh, E. S., and Rumbaugh, D. M. 1979. Initial acquisition of symbolic skills via the Yerkes computerized language analog system. *In* R. L. Schiefelbusch and J. H. Hollis (eds.), Language Intervention from Ape to Child, pp. 277–294. University Park Press, Baltimore.

Schaeffer, B., Kollinzas, G., Musil, A., and McDowell, P. 1978. Spontaneous verbal language for autistic children through signed speech. Sign Lang. Stud. 21:317–352.

Stremel-Campbell, K., Cantrell, D., and Halle, J. 1976. Manual signing as a language system and a speech initiator for the nonverbal, severely handicapped student. Unpublished manuscript, Parsons State Hospital and Training Center, Parsons, Kan.

Topper, S. T. 1975. Gesture language for a nonverbal severely retarded male. Ment. Retard. 13:30–31.

Vanderheiden, D. H., Brown, W. P., MacKenzie, P., Reinen, S., and Schiebel, C. 1975. Symbol communication for the mentally handicapped. Ment. Retard. 13:34–37.

Vygotsky, L. S. 1962. Thought and Language. The MIT Press, Cambridge, Mass.

Webster, C. D., McPherson, H., Sloman, L., Evans, M. A., and Kuchar, E. 1973. Communicating with an autistic boy by gestures. J. Aut. Child. Schizo. 3:337–346.

# Section VII

# Interpretative Issues

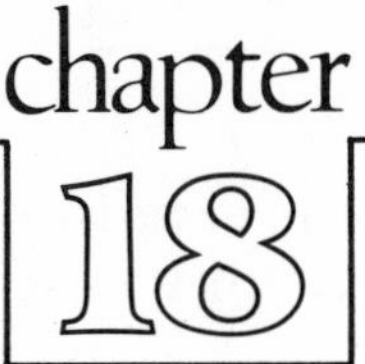

# Perceptual Requisites for Language

*Paula Tallal*

*Department of Psychiatry*
*University of California, San Diego*
*La Jolla, California*

*Children's Hospital and*
*Health Center*
*San Diego, California*

contents

Most work reported here concerns nonspeech language intervention strategies. Such strategies were developed specifically for individuals who have failed to develop or maintain normal speech or language. The precise etiology of their disabilities is known in some instances. Speech and language disabilities may result from a variety of causes, including inadequate hearing, intellect, or motor control of the speech musculature. In many other instances the exact cause of the speech or language disorder is not known. There is an underlying assumption that nonspeech language intervention should be directed toward individuals who are unable to adequately utilize the speech stream and hence require a nonacoustic means of implementing language.

An alternative approach to using nonspeech systems with individuals who are not adequately using the speech stream is to determine in more detail the precise nature of their difficulties in speech perception. The goal of such an approach would be to develop means of altering the acoustic input to aid in speech perception rather than bypassing the auditory modality altogether. This is what is done with amplification systems for the hearing impaired. The work reported in this chapter uses this approach with individuals who have demonstrated normal hearing thresholds and normal intellectual capabilities, but who have severe language disabilities. The status of their auditory-perceptual abilities has been of concern for many years (Efron, 1963; Benton, 1964; Hardy, 1965; McReynolds, 1966; Eisenson, 1972). The purpose of the work described here is to develop more precise methods for assessing auditory-perceptual abilities, and to investigate the possibility of developing improved auditory intervention strategies for individuals with auditory-perceptual dysfunction.

When a child who has failed to develop language at the expected age is brought to a clinic, evidence of the more obvious causes of such a disorder (e.g., hearing impairment, mental retardation, emotional disturbance, dysfunction of the vocal apparatus) is sought. When these more obvious factors have been ruled out, it is not uncommon for a diagnosis of "auditory-perceptual impairment" to be reached. The evidence for such a diagnosis is often difficult to find. It may be that the diagnosis was based on "clinical impression"; that the child seemed to have difficulty processing speech auditorially. In other instances, clinicians may cite the results of tests that indicate auditory-perceptual dysfunction. Many such results are obtained from isolated subtests taken from a broader test battery. For example, the digit span subtest of the Weschler Intelligence Scale for Children (Wechsler, WISC-R, 1974) is often cited. In this subtest a series of numbers are spoken to the child, and the child is

---

The American Association of University Women, the Grant Foundation of New York, The Medical Research Council of Great Britain (Grant No. 6973/144/C), and the National Institutes of Health (NINCDS Contract No. 75-09) have provided generous support of the research reported in this chapter.

required to repeat as many as can be remembered in the correct order. Progressively longer series of digits are given until the child fails to repeat them correctly. Difficulty on this task is often taken to indicate an auditory sequential memory deficit.

What are the major components of this test? In order to perform adequately on this test, the child must first comprehend the task problem, that is, what he is expected to do. Furthermore, the child must correctly perceive the spoken numbers and be able to sequence them, store them, and then retrieve them. Finally the child must be able to formulate and sequence the motor output and produce the series of numbers in the correct order. Difficulty with any one or more of these major components may be the basis of poor performance on this task.

Not all of these major components are related to auditory perception. If it is of clinical as well as theoretical interest to ask to what extent auditory misperception could be involved in certain language disabilities, then we must: 1) define better what it is that we mean by the term *auditory perception*, and 2) devise more precise means of testing it.

## DEFINITION OF AUDITORY PERCEPTION

There are many definitions and detailed models of auditory perception in the literature. It is not within the scope of this chapter to discuss all of them in detail. Rather, the broadest definition of auditory perception is considered and then refined through a presentation and discussion of data directly pertaining to it. In the broadest sense, auditory perception is everything that occurs between the detection of an acoustic signal and its transformation into form.

What might some of the basic steps in this process be? First, the organism must be able to detect the acoustic signal. Then it is necessary to determine if more than one signal has occurred. If so, one must be able to determine whether they were the same two signals or two different ones. In order to make such a judgment, analysis of the physical components of the signal (frequency, amplitude, and duration) must be made. If it is determined that the two signals were different, one then must be able to judge the order in which they occurred. The difference in frequency, amplitude, and duration of the signals, as well as the rate of presentation of these signals, may affect this ability. In addition, storage, memory, and retrieval processes are brought into play. Finally, these processes must be combined when more than two signals are presented.

This simplistic model of auditory perception is not a detailed description of all of the mechanisms involved in auditory perception. It is rather a skeletal model from which to begin an investigation and onto which we can later build as more data become available. Furthermore, this model is not an original one. It is taken from previous models and experimental results pertaining to simple auditory perception (Hirsh, 1959; Cutting and Pisoni, 1977).

## DESIGNING A TEST OF AUDITORY PERCEPTION

### Method

When designing a test of auditory perception there are some very basic (but extremely important) principles that must be taken into account. Because auditory perception is an integral part of speech perception, it is important to establish that the results obtained from auditory perceptual tests are not significantly affected by the subject's ability to understand the test instructions or by his capacity to produce a verbal response. Thus, when designing a perceptual test battery it is essential to eliminate the need for verbal instruction or verbal responses. Another important feature of a perceptual test design should be its flexibility and versatility. The method should allow the subject to report in detail exactly what he has perceived in each stimulus presented, in a nonverbal manner. It should also be flexible enough to allow several different aspects of perception to be investigated in a hierarchical manner, systematically moving from one subtest to another. The subtests should begin with the most basic functions of interest and, by changing only a single variable at a time, proceed to more complex functions. Furthermore, the same method should be adaptable to a variety of stimulus materials and should be appropriate for testing in several different sensory modalities.

### Stimuli

When selecting stimuli to be used in a test, many of the same issues that apply to designing the test method pertain. Because auditory perception is so intimately interrelated with speech perception, the use of verbal stimuli in an auditory-perceptual test will lead to confounded results unless careful controls are included. If verbal stimuli are to be included in the test, then it is necessary: 1) to use nonverbal stimuli as well, so that a direct comparison can be made between the two, or 2) to use the test only as a measure of speech perception, rather than auditory perception. This issue is particularly important when the test is used with patients with known or suspected language disabilities. If verbal stimuli alone are used as test items, then the results of the test can yield information *only* about speech perception. It will not be possible with such a test to acquire information specifically about auditory perception, because it is possible that these same patients might have responded quite differently had non-verbal rather than verbal stimuli been used. Thus, if we think back to the earlier example of the digit span test, it becomes clear that such a test should not be used (although it often is) as a measure of auditory sequential memory. It is quite possible that auditory sequential memory ability could be intact and yet language ability be such as to interfere with adequate performance on this task. This is a basic criticism of many of the "auditory perceptual tests" presently available for clinical use. They do not measure auditory perception per se.

Another issue of concern when choosing stimuli for an auditory perceptual test is to control as precisely as possible the stimulus parameters. For example, if the test is intended to measure auditory sequencing ability, performance on the test may be affected by temporal, spectral, or amplitude differences between the stimuli to be sequenced, or the rate of presentation of the stimuli. Changing any of these properties of the stimuli may result in significant changes in the sequencing performance purportedly being measured.

## THE REPETITION TEST

Our work has been directed toward establishing a better understanding of the perceptual prerequisites for normal language development. Of specific interest has been the development of new methods for assessing a variety of perceptual abilities of young children with and without delayed language development. In this pursuit, the concepts discussed in the previous section have been incorporated into a perceptual test battery. The resulting test is known as the Repetition Test. Because the test design is such a fundamental aspect of the experimental findings, it is discussed in detail below. When the method is understood, the results of the perceptual experiments with various subject populations become more meaningful.

In the Repetition Test, two different stimuli are used in combination. Subjects are trained with operant conditioning techniques to respond to these stimuli by pressing either of the two identical panels mounted side by side on a response box. This method was devised to enable a subject to nonverbally "repeat" in detail exactly what he perceives in each stimulus presentation by making an appropriate motor response. Any two stimulus items can be incorporated into the test method. The test can be given repeatedly with various stimulus pairs as long as the order of presentations of the various stimulus pairs is counterbalanced to control for learning or fatigue. Thus, the same test procedure can be used to test nonverbal and verbal perception in any sensory modality. Results obtained using nonverbal acoustic stimuli can be compared directly to those using nonverbal visual or tactile stimuli in order to test for modality differences in the same subject or group of subjects. Similarly, nonverbal perception can be compared directly to verbal perception using this method. Finally, by carefully selecting stimulus pairs to be used in the test, specific aspects of acoustic and phonetic processing can be investigated.

The Repetition Test is made up of a series of subtests. The subtests (described below) are arranged to investigate a hierarchical series of perceptual abilities. The subtests must always be given in the following order because each subsequent subtest relies on skills learned in the previous subtest.

**Detection**

Stimulus 1 is presented and the experimenter shows the subject that the bottom panel on the response box is to be pressed each time stimulus 1 occurs. Stimulus 1 is presented repeatedly until the subject has pressed the bottom panel in response to stimulus 1 ten times in succession. Next, stimulus 2 is presented and the experimenter indicates that the top panel of the response box is to be pressed each time stimulus 2 occurs. Stimulus 2 is presented repeatedly until the subject has pressed the top panel of the response box ten times in succession. Correct performance on this test indicates that the subjects can detect the presence of the stimulus and make the correct motor response.

**Association**

Stimulus 1 or stimulus 2 is presented individually in random order. Subjects are trained to respond to each of these stimuli by pushing the appropriate panel on the response box. Training continues until criterion is reached (20 out of 24 consecutive responses correct) or 48 trials have been given. Correct performance on this subtest indicates that a subject perceives the difference between stimulus 1 and stimulus 2 (when each is presented individually) and is able to associate each stimulus with the correct panel on the response box.

**Sequencing Training**

In this subtest for the first time two stimuli are presented sequentially. Subjects who reach criterion on the association task are trained to respond to each of the four possible two-element patterns (1-1, 1-2, 2-2, 2-1) with a 428-msec inter-sound-interval (ISI), by pushing the panels in the corresponding order. Correct responses are demonstrated for four trials by the experimenter, followed by eight training trials in which knowledge of results is given. Next, 24 two-element patterns are presented randomly, with no knowledge of results. Subjects who reach criterion on this task are able to detect that two stimuli were presented, to determine whether they were the same two stimuli or two different ones, and, if they were two different ones, indicate the order in which they occurred. Subjects who do not reach criterion on this subtest (make more than 14 errors) are given two additional subtests to determine at what point the difficulty arose. That is, did their difficulty result from an inability to perceive that two signals were presented, to discriminate between the two signals, or to perceive their temporal order?

**Same/Not Same**

The same/not same subtest is only to be given at this time to subjects who failed to reach criterion on sequencing training. The same two-element patterns presented in sequencing training are presented again in this subtest. The response box is turned by 90° to avoid confusion between the two tasks. Subjects initially are presented with two identical stimuli, separated by a 428-msec ISI, and trained to press the right panel to indicate that the two stimuli are the same as each other. Then subjects are presented with two different stimuli, separated by a 428-msec ISI, and trained to press the left panel to indicate that the two stimuli are not the same as each other. Visual examples are used in training to ensure that all subjects fully understand the response required on this task. Next subjects are presented with the same series of two-element sequences as that used in the sequencing training subtest. However, in this case subjects are required only to indicate whether the two elements in the sequence are the same or not the same as each other. If, after 48 trials a subject fails to reach the criterion, he is not continued further on this test using the same stimulus items. Once the subject reaches the criterion, a series of 24 two-element patterns with ISIs between 8 and 305 msec identical to those used in the sequencing with short ISIs subtest (described below) is presented. However, this time the subject is required only to indicate whether the two stimuli in each sequenced pattern were the same or not the same as each other.

The same stimuli are given in the sequencing and the same/not same subtest. However, in the sequencing subtest, knowledge of the order of the stimuli is required, whereas in the same/not same subtest, knowledge of temporal order is not required. If a subject fails to reach criterion on the sequencing subtest but does reach criterion on the same/not same subtest, then it can be determined that this subject is having difficulty in perceiving the temporal order in which the stimuli are presented. However, if a subject fails to reach criterion on both the sequencing and the same/not same subtest, then the subject is having difficulty perceiving the sound quality of the two stimuli, i.e., he cannot discriminate between them. If the subject cannot discriminate between two stimuli, he will also be unable to sequence them. However, it would be incorrect to say that this subject has difficulty sequencing. The sequencing ability may be adequate once the stimuli to be sequenced can be discriminated.

**Sequencing with Short ISIs**

This subtest is only to be given to subjects who reach criterion on the sequencing training subtest. The same series of 24 two-element stimulus patterns as were used in the sequencing training subtest is presented again. However, in this subtest, the duration of the interval between the offset of the first element and the onset of the second element in the stimulus pattern (ISI) is varied. ISIs of 8, 15, 30, 60, 150, and 305 msec are presented randomly, four trials at each ISI. For subjects who reached criterion on the sequencing training subtest, but have difficulty with this subtest, the rapid rate of presentation of the stimulus items is responsible for the breakdown of performance on this subtest.

**Sequencing with Long ISIs**

The same series of 24 two-element stimulus patterns as were used in the sequencing training subtest is presented again. However, in this subtest the duration of the ISI is varied between 947 and 4,062 msec (947, 1,466, 1,985, 3,023, 3,543, and 4,062 msec); four trials at each ISI are presented randomly. Subjects are trained to wait until both elements in the stimulus pattern have been presented before responding, placing additional demands on short term memory. Thus, for those subjects who reach criterion on the sequencing training subtest, but experience difficulty with this subtest, the increased demand on short term memory, which is specific to this subtest, is responsible for the deterioration of performance.

**Serial Memory**

In these tests the same two stimulus elements are used, and the procedures are the same as for the previous subtests, except that the ISI is constant at 428 msec and the number of elements in the stimulus pattern is increased. These stimulus patterns consist of three, four, and five elements composed of random combinations of the two stimulus elements. Subjects initially are given a stimulus pattern incorporating three stimulus elements (e.g., 1-1-2). The experimenter will demonstrate that the response panels are to be pressed three times in the corresponding order in which the stimulus elements occur. Subjects are trained to wait until the entire pattern has been presented and then make the appropriate response to the stimulus pattern. Each subject begins with the three-element patterns and proceeds to the next higher pattern length once criterion has been reached. If the criterion is not reached at any sequence length, subjects are not tested at any higher sequence length with that stimulus pair.

**Same/Not Same**

This subtest is given at this time to those subjects who reached criterion on the sequencing training subtest, but failed to reach criterion on the sequencing with short ISIs subtest. Because new associations for the response panels must be learned for this subtest, it is deferred until the end of the serial memory subtest. This test is given to determine whether difficulty experienced on the sequencing with short ISIs subtest was the result of an inability to perceive the temporal sequence of the stimulus pattern or an inability to discriminate between the stimulus items at rapid rates of presentation. The response box is turned by 90° to avoid confusion between the two methods.

The procedure for the same/not same subtest has already been described. It is mentioned here again because the order in which the test is given depends on the individual subject's performance. Subjects who fail sequencing training do not go to the more complex tasks involving the response panel associations to the individual stimuli. Thus, for these subjects, the new panel associations required for the same/not same test can be taught directly after the sequencing training subtest and given at that time. However, subjects who meet the criterion on sequencing training continue on to the other sequencing tasks and serial memory tasks using the same panel associations. It would cause undue confusion to teach the new associations necessary for the same/not same test directly after sequencing, and then have to retrain again for serial memory. Therefore, the same/not same test is deferred until after the serial memory subtests are completed.

It is important to note that although it is essential to give the subtests in the same order, it is not necessary to use the entire battery with each stimulus pair selected for study. The number of subtests to be given should depend on what questions one intends to answer with each stimulus pair. For example, if one merely wants to know if a subject can discriminate between two stimulus items presented in isolation, one need only give the test battery through the association subtest. If it is of interest, on the other hand, to find out whether a subject can discriminate between two stimulus items presented successively, it is possible to give the same/not same subtest alone. However, it is essential if the test is to be used to measure sequencing or serial memory performance that each subtest preceding these measures be given in the described order.

## EXPERIMENTAL RESULTS USING THE REPETITION TEST

The Repetition Test has, to date, been used with four different subject populations: language-impaired children, reading-impaired children, adults with acquired brain lesions, and normally developing children. Various nonverbal and verbal, auditory and visual stimuli have been used in these studies. Detailed descriptions of the stimuli, subjects, and the results of these studies have been published elsewhere (Tallal and Piercy, 1973, 1974, 1975; Tallal, 1976; Tallal and Newcombe, 1977). Therefore, the results of these studies are summarized only briefly here.

### Children with Language Disabilities (Dysphasics)

The Repetition Test was originally designed to investigate the perceptual abilities of children with delayed language development. Most of the research with this test battery has been done with this population. Studies have been done with various nonverbal acoustic stimulus pairs (Tallal and Piercy, 1973), nonverbal visual stimulus pairs (Tallal and Piercy, 1974), and a variety of verbal stimulus pairs (Tallal and Piercy, 1975).

These studies indicate that the language-impaired group (age seven to nine years) performed as well as a normal matched control group on all subtests of the Repetition Test using a nonverbal, visual stimulus pair. However, the performance of these language-impaired children on the same tests, but with auditory stimuli, was quite different. Using two different 75-msec complex tones as stimuli, it was found that there was no significant difference between the performance of the language-impaired and normal control groups on the detection, association, and sequencing training subtests. However, the language-impaired children were significantly impaired in their ability to respond correctly to rapidly presented two-element patterns. Furthermore, their performance was impaired on both the sequencing with short ISIs subtest and the same/not same with short ISIs subtest. Thus, although these children were impaired in their ability to report the temporal sequence of rapidly presented auditory signals, as had been reported previously (Lowe and Campbell, 1965), they showed equally inferior discrimination of sound quality of rapidly presented auditory stimuli, a dysfunction that must underlie their sequencing difficulty. Interestingly, when the duration of the interval between the two nonverbal tones was increased, placing additional demands on short term memory, the language-impaired children responded as well as the control children. Thus, once these language-impaired children were able to discriminate between the two stimulus items, they were able to hold them in short term memory and sequence them as well as normal children could.

Further studies showed that the rate of presentation of stimulus items also significantly affected the performance of language-impaired children on the serial memory tasks. The language-impaired children were able to remember significantly longer series of nonverbal tones when duration of the tones was 250 msec rather than 75 msec. However, even with these longer duration stimulus items, the language-impaired children were able to remember significantly fewer items in series than normal control children remembered. This result demonstrates that a lower level deficit can significantly affect the performance on a more complex task. Therefore, had the test begun by investigating higher level functions, such as sequencing or memory, the more primary deficit would have been overlooked and the disability misinterpreted.

How could a deficit in processing rapidly changing acoustic information affect the speech perception abilities of language-disordered persons? Recent basic research in speech synthesis and perception has demonstrated that certain consonants and vowels have different acoustic features and are processed differently by normal subjects. These basic differences in phoneme perception have been attributed to the differential duration of the critical formant information of these two classes of speech sounds, as well as their differently shaped formants. For the stop consonants there appears to be a relatively complex relationship between the phoneme and its auditory representations. The essential acoustic cue is a rapidly changing spectrum provided by the formant transition. These are transitional in character and of relatively short duration. On the other hand, the major cue for synthetic vowels used in perceptual experiments is the steady-state frequencies of the first three formants, which have a relatively long duration and remain constant over the entire length of the stimulus (Fry et al., 1962; Liberman et al., 1967).

On the hypothesis that impaired auditory processing of rapidly changing acoustic cues in speech is a primary disability of language-impaired children, it was predicted that merely changing from nonverbal to verbal stimuli would not significantly affect these children's performance, as long as the verbal stimuli did not require rapid acoustic analysis. On the other hand, it was hypothesized that these children would show significantly impaired performance with verbal stimuli that did require rapid acoustic analysis for their discrimination. Therefore, the Repetition Test of perceptual abilities was given to these children two additional times. In one instance, two steady-state vowels (/ɛ/ and /æ/) of the same duration (250 msec) as the nonverbal steady-state tones studied previously were used as the stimulus pair. In another instance, two synthesized stop consonants (/ba/ and /da/), which had the same total duration (250 msec), but with an initial transitional component of only approximately 40 msec in duration, were used as the stimulus pair. The order in which the Repetition tests, incorporating these two different stimulus pairs, were given was counterbalanced. The results of these experiments were striking. As predicted, merely changing from nonverbal to verbal stimuli did *not* significantly affect the performance of these children, as long as the verbal stimuli were steady-state in nature. However, these children's performance was significantly impaired on all subtests of the Repetition Test incorporating the stop consonant pair as stimuli.

Further experiments show that the limiting factor underlying the inferior performance of these language-disordered children on the consonant task was the short duration of the rapidly changing initial portion of the acoustic spectrum. In these experiments the initial formant transitions of the same stop consonants were extended (by use of a speech synthesizer) from 40 msec to 80 msec, while maintaining the total length of the stop consonant syllables at 250 msec. The ability of language-disordered children to discriminate between these consonant-vowel syllables, incorporating transitions of this longer duration, was found to be unimpaired.

## Developmental Reading Disabilities (Dyslexics)

Orton suggested as early as 1937 that children with developmental reading disorders may be perceptually impaired. Since Orton's time, reports have continued to stress the predominance of both auditory and visual processing impairments in children with reading disabilities (Bakker, 1967, 1971; Doehring, 1968). Myklebust (1965) has suggested that we think of dyslexic children as forming a heterogeneous rather than a homogeneous group, comprising both "visual dyslexics" as well as "auditory dyslexics." Other authors have also delineated these two subgroups of dyslexics and have reported that the difficulties of children within these groups reflect deficiencies of either central visual or central auditory processing (Quiros, 1964; Bateman, 1968; Boder, 1971). Boder (1971) concluded that reading may be a two-channel function requiring the integration of intact visual and auditory processes that are basic to the two standard methods of reading instruction. The whole-word, or look-and-say, technique requires the reader to experience the printed word globally as a visual gestalt, while the phonetic technique requires the reader to analyze words into phonetic elements. Hence, for the two subgroups of dyslexics these two methods of teaching reading would not be equally appropriate. Presumably the whole-word teaching method (which relies heavily on visual processing) is more appropriate for teaching auditorially impaired dyslexic children than the phonetic approach (which relies more on auditory processing), and vice versa for the visually impaired dyslexic child.

However, before this hypothesis can be investigated experimentally, it is important to establish whether within a group of children with specific reading disability there are those who have specific auditory-perceptual or specific visual-perceptual dysfunctions. The Repetition Test was used to assess the auditory perceptual abilities of a group of reading-impaired children (Tallal, 1976). As in the study with the language-impaired children, 75-msec complex tones were used as the stimulus pair. Twenty reading-impaired children participated as subjects.

The performance of all 20 reading-impaired children was virtually errorless on the detection, association, and sequencing training subtests of the Repetition Test. However, as the duration of the interval between the two stimulus tones was shortened, the performance of the reading-impaired children, as a group, deteriorated. Although the performance of the group of subjects as a whole was significantly poorer on this task, further analysis demonstrated that the performance of individual subjects varied considerably. Some of the reading-impaired subjects' performance remained virtually errorless on this subtest. The performance of others was significantly poorer than their own previous performance on the sequencing training subtest. Results showed that these subjects were equally poor at *discriminating* between the two nonverbal complex tones as they had been at sequencing them. All subjects' performance was virtually errorless on the remaining subtests of the Repetition Test.

The results of this study indicate that of the several auditory perceptual skills tested, only one, the ability to respond to rapidly presented information, proved to be difficult for some reading-impaired children. Furthermore, there was a wide range of performance between the 20 subjects tested on these tasks. Some achieved a nearly perfect score. Others had considerable difficulty. It was hypothesized that if a child was having difficulties with one or more aspects of auditory processing, this deficit would result in specific difficulty in learning phonics skills, and hence in learning to read. Therefore, a correlation coefficient between the number of errors made in responding to rapidly presented acoustic stimuli on the Repetition Test and the number of errors made reading nonsense words on a phonics reading test was computed. The results of this analysis showed that there was a high positive correlation between these two factors. Those children who had little or no difficulty on the auditory processing tests also had little or no difficulty reading nonsense words, and vice versa.

The results of this study indicate that the Repetition Test may be a useful method for determining the perceptual strengths and weaknesses of children with reading disabilities. The visual-perceptual abilities of the children have not, as yet, been tested. However, by using the Repetition Test with visual stimulus pairs, direct comparisons between precise auditory- and visual-perceptual abilities of individual children could be made. Teaching methods could therefore be selected to take the perceptual abilities of each child into account. These studies are in progress.

## Normally Developing Children

On the basis of the results with developmental dysphasic children, it was hypothesized that a rate-specific perceptual impairment may be sufficient to explain the failure of dysphasic children to develop normal language proficiency at or near the expected age. The dysphasic children's ability to respond to rapidly changing acoustic stimuli was found to be substantially poorer than that of their age-matched (approximately eight and a half years) controls. However, the ability of normally developing younger children to respond to similar rapidly changing acoustic stimuli had not been established. Thus, it was difficult to assess the magnitude of language-impaired children's perceptual disability in developmental terms. Therefore, a developmental study was undertaken to study rapid auditory processing in normal children and make a comparison between the development of rapid auditory processing in dysphasic and normal children (Tallal, 1976). Only the Repetition Test subtests, through the sequencing with short ISI subtest, were used in this developmental study.

Pilot studies with the Repetition Test indicated that reliable results could not be obtained with normally developing children less than four years of age. Therefore, children between the ages of 4.6 and 8.6 years old participated in these studies. The stimulus pair used in these studies was two 75-msec complex, nonverbal tones.

The results of this developmental study of nonverbal auditory-perceptual abilities showed that there were no significant differences between the age groups in the number of children reaching criterion on the detection or association subtest. Significant differences between groups occurred for the first time on the sequencing training subtest. Although there was no significant difference between the performance of the 8.6-year-old group and that of the adult controls, all groups younger than 8.6 years old showed significantly inferior performance on this task. Furthermore, when the interval between the two tones in the stimulus pattern was decreased in the sequencing with short ISIs subtest, the 8.6-year-old group continued to perform as well as the adult group, but all younger age groups showed inferior performance to that of the adult. When the interval between the two-element stimulus pattern was increased, placing additional demands on short term auditory memory, the performances of the 6.6-, 7.6-, and 8.6-year-old groups were not significantly different from that of the adult groups. Only the 4.6- and 5.6-year-old groups continued to show significantly inferior performance to that of the adults on this task.

Thus, by the age of 6.6 years, the normal children were performing as well as adult controls on the nonverbal, two-element auditory patterns with the longer ISIs. However, the ability to perform as well as adults on these same stimulus patterns, but with shorter intervals, was not achieved until the age of 8.6 years. On the basis of these results, it can be concluded that the ability to respond correctly to nonverbal auditory signals, presented rapidly in succession, develops progressively with age. The ability to respond as well as adults to nonverbal auditory stimulus patterns presented very rapidly in time lags behind (by as much as two years) the ability to respond correctly to the same auditory patterns when they are presented more slowly.

**Acquired Brain Damage in Adults**

It was of interest to investigate whether the very precise pattern of impairment in responding to rapidly presented acoustic information, previously demonstrated in children with developmental communication disorders, was also characteristic of some adults with well defined focal brain lesions (Tallal and Newcombe, 1977). Furthermore, by giving the Repetition Test to patients with various well defined brain lesions, it was hoped that it would be possible to determine which hemisphere of the brain was specifically involved in rapid acoustic analysis. Twenty ex-servicemen who had sustained missile wounds of the brain during World War II and the Korean War participated as subjects. Ten had lesions of the right hemisphere and ten of the left hemisphere. In addition, a control group matched for age and sex was included.

The results of the Repetition Test, incorporating 75-msec complex tones as the stimulus pair, showed that there was no significant difference between the performance of any of the groups on the detection, association, or sequencing training subtests. However, when the interval between the two tones was decreased in the sequencing with the short ISIs subtest, marked differences between the groups were found. Whereas decreasing the interval between the tones in this *nonverbal* task did not significantly affect the performance of the right hemisphere group or the control group, the performance of the left hemisphere group was significantly poorer than their own previous performance on the sequencing training task, and also significantly inferior to that of the two other groups on this task. There were no significant differences between the performance of the right hemisphere group and the control group on any of these nonverbal auditory perceptual tasks.

Further administrations of the Repetition Test using steady-state vowels, stop consonants incorporating rapidly changing formant transition, and stop consonants with extended duration formant transitions were given to these subjects. Subtests of the Repetition Test through sequencing training only were given.

The results of these studies showed that there were no significant differences between the performance of any of the groups studied on any of these subtests using the steady-state vowels as the stimulus pair. However, when the stop consonants, incorporating rapidly changing acoustic spectra critical to their discrimination were used, significant differences between groups were found. Whereas nine of the ten subjects with right hemisphere lesions and five of the six control subjects reached criterion on all subtests given with these stimuli, only four of the ten subjects with left hemisphere lesions reached this criterion on the association task and three on the sequencing training tasks with these stop consonant–vowel syllables.

Extending the duration of the critical acoustic information within the stop consonant–vowel syllables resulted in improved performance for some, but not all, of the patients with left hemisphere lesions. The performance of those patients who were the most severely impaired on this task (and were also the most severely aphasic) failed to improve with the extended stop consonants. However, three of the seven patients with left hemisphere lesions, who had been unable to discriminate between the stop consonants with 40-msec transitions, were able to discriminate between the same stop consonants with 80-msec transitions. All of the subjects with right hemisphere lesions and all of the control subjects reached criterion on all subtests using these extended consonant syllables as the stimulus pair.

The results of these experiments demonstrate that damage to the left, *not* the right, cerebral hemisphere of the brain results in impaired performance on rapid auditory temporal processing tasks, regardless of whether acoustic information is verbal or nonverbal. Thus, an intact left hemisphere seems to be critical for the accurate analysis of rapidly changing acoustic nonverbal as well as verbal information. These results indicate that the widely accepted hypothesis that nonverbal acoustic information is processed in the right hemisphere of the brain and verbal (phonetic) information in the left (or dominant) hemisphere appears to be grossly oversimplified. The data presented here demonstrate that the dominant hemisphere must play a primary role in the analysis of specific rapidly changing acoustic information, both verbal and nonverbal, and that such analysis is critically involved in both the development and maintenance of speech and language.

## CONCLUSIONS

This chapter has described the steps in going from clinical observation to the development of a test battery to investigate that observation experimentally. The concepts and considerations leading to the development of the test battery and the description of the test itself have been given in some detail. Emphasis has been placed on the description of the test design and procedures. Through this detailed description it is hoped that the pressing clinical needs for precise delineation of test questions and the formulation of measures that allow investigating functions in a systematic, heirarchical manner, changing only a single variable at a time has been demonstrated.

The results of several experiments using the Repetition Test battery with a variety of subject populations and several different test stimuli were given as examples of precise information that can be derived using such an approach. In designing this battery of perceptual tests, it was not our intention to develop a static battery of tests. Rather, this method was seen as flexible enough to allow additions and deletions in the test battery as further data become available. The results of these studies have led to the formulation of additional questions. In attempts to answer these questions, the Repetition Test has been modified in some instances and additional subtests included.

In summary, the Repetition Test of perceptual abilities is a useful means of evaluating some basic perceptual abilities in a hierarchical manner. The test is effective with children and adults with and without language disabilities. It can be adapted to investigate perceptual abilities in various sensory modalities, both nonverbal and verbal. Furthermore, it has been successful in isolating precise perceptual disabilities in various groups of patients with communication disorders. Comparative investigations of specific aspects of auditory perception may serve to increase our understanding of the role of auditory perception in the development and maintenance of language.

## REFERENCES

Bakker, D. J. 1967. Temporal order, meaningfulness, reading ability. Percept. Mot. Skills 24:1027–1030.

Bakker, D. J. 1971. Temporal Order in Disturbed Reading: Developmental and Neuropsychological Aspects in Normal and Reading Retarded Children. Rotterdam University Press, Rotterdam, The Netherlands.

Bateman, B. 1968. Interpretation of the 1961 Illinois Test of Psycholinguistic Abilities. Special Child Publications, Seattle.

Benton, A. 1964. Developmental aphasia and brain damage. Cortex 1:40–52.

Boder, E. 1971. Developmental dyslexia: A diagnostic screening procedure based on three characteristic patterns of reading and spelling. *In* B. Bateman, (ed.), Learning Disorders, Vol. 4, pp. 293–342. Special Child Publication, Seattle.

Cutting, J. E., and Pisoni, D. B. 1977. Speech perception. *In* J. Kavanaugh and J. Jenkins (eds.), Language Research in the Laboratory, Clinic and Classroom.

Doehring, D. O. 1968. Patterns of impairments in Specific Reading Disability. Indiana University Press, London.

Efron, R. 1963. Temporal perception, aphasia and deja vue. Brain 86:403–424.

Eisenson, J. 1972. Aphasia in Children. Harper & Row, London.

Fry, D. B., Abramson, A. S., Eimas, P. D., and Liberman, A. M. 1962. The identification and discrimination of synthetic vowels. Lang. Speech 5:171–189.
Hardy, W. G. 1965. On language disorders in young children: A reorganization of thinking. J. Speech Hear. Disturb. 8:3–16.
Hirsh, I. J. 1959. Auditory perception of temporal order. J. Acoust. Soc. Am. 31:759–767.
Liberman, A. M., Cooper, F. S., Shankweiler, D. P., and Studdert-Kennedy, M. 1967. Perception of the speech code. Psychol. Rev. 74:431–461.
Lowe, A. D., and Campbell, R. A. 1965. Temporal discrimination in aphasoid and normal children. J. Speech Hear. Res. 8:313–314.
McReynolds, L. V. 1966. Operant conditioning for investigating speech sound discrimination in aphasic children. J. Speech Hear. Res. 9:519–528.
Myklebust, H. 1965. Development and Disorders of Written Language: Picture Story Language Test. Grune & Stratton, New York.
Orton, S. 1937. Reading, Writing and Speech Problems in Children. Chapman & Hall, Ltd. London.
Quiros, J. de. 1964. Dysphasia and dyslexia in school children. Folia Phoniatrica 16:201–222.
Tallal, P. 1976. Rapid auditory processing in normal and disordered language development. J. Speech Hear. Res. 19:561–571.
Tallal, P., and Newcombe, F. 1977. Impairment of auditory perception and language comprehension in dysphasia. Brain Lang. 4(4).
Tallal, P., and Piercy, M. 1973. Developmental aphasia: Impaired rate of non-verbal processing as a function of sensory modality. Neuropsychologia 11:389–398.
Tallal, P., and Piercy, M. 1974. Developmental aphasia: Rate of auditory processing and selective impairment of consonant perception. Neuropsychologia 12:83–93.
Tallal, P., and Piercy, M. 1975. Developmental aphasia: The perception of brief vowels and extended stop consonants. Neuropsychologia 13:69–74.
Wechsler, D. 1974. Manual for the Wechsler Intelligence Scale for Children. The Psychological Corporation, New York.

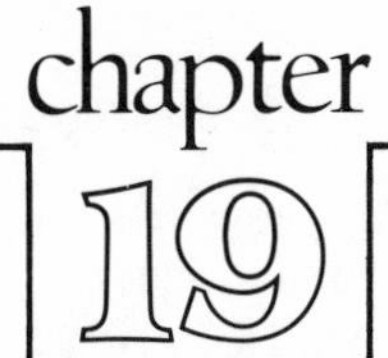

# A Performance Grammar Approach to Language Teaching

*John B. Carroll*

*Department of Psychology*
*University of North Carolina at Chapel Hill*
*Chapel Hill, North Carolina*

Any efforts to teach a language, or more generally, a communication system, should be based on an adequate theory of message production. The great preoccupation of recent work in psycholinguistics has been with the role of language structure in the *comprehension* of sentences and discourse. Until recently (Rosenberg, 1977b), there was very little work on the role of language structure in the *production* of messages. Because most research in psycholinguistics has been concerned with oral and printed language, there has been little work on either the production or the comprehension of messages in other types of communication systems, including the nonspeech systems considered in this volume. If we are to make progress in helping children, or even chimpanzees, produce messages (whatever the symbol system), we must at least have a theory about how the process of message production takes place.

There is a possibility that message *production* is something we do not have to teach, provided organisms can learn message *comprehension* (with or without teaching). It could be argued that an organism's capacity to produce messages, once it has learned enough about the structure of messages to comprehend them, is a natural consequence of general cognitive capacities, and that it is needless and perhaps futile to be concerned with how message production is learned or how it can be taught. There are several bases for this argument.

An obvious one is that, in acquiring the mother tongue, children do not normally have to be taught to produce messages. They begin to produce messages as soon as they have progressed far enough in their ability to comprehend messages. But we should be cautious in accepting such an argument as completely valid. Not all children start to produce messages when their comprehension level reaches a certain stage. Lenneberg (1962) reported the case of a child who had acquired advanced comprehension ability without starting to speak. Message production is not an automatic consequence of learning to comprehend. There are aspects of it that need to be taught, at least in the case of some children.

Another possible basis for arguing that language production does not have to be taught comes from second-language learning, where it is claimed (Postovsky, 1974, 1975) that better language production skills are attained (eventually) if in the earliest stages of second-language acquisition the student is encouraged *not* to attempt language production, but simply to listen and try to understand. At the Defense Language Institute in Monterey, California, some intensive foreign language courses for adults discourage language production for a number of weeks after the start of instruction. When these students are finally allowed to speak in the foreign language, they tend to be more fluent, with better pronunciation and grammatical control than they would have had otherwise. Although this evidence is impressive it is not a sufficient basis for arguing that production need not be taught, or that a theory of production is not needed. Second-language learners have already learned some message production skills in the process of acquiring their native language. Producing messages in a second language is partly a matter of transferring these skills. Even starting with this advantage, second-language learners still have much more to learn about how to produce messages in the second language. A theory of message production should help in guiding this process (Carroll, 1973).

There is, however, a more fundamental reason why we should turn our attention to language production, or more generally, to message production. It is likely that message production processes also participate in the act of message comprehension. When a listener or a message receiver engages in comprehending a message, he is in a sense sharing in the communicator's production of that message. We often know how a speaker is going to finish a sentence, and we sometimes finish the sentence for him. The so-called redundancy of language helps in comprehending messages. This indicates that messages contain cues for the receiver's implicit message productions—productions that play a role in the comprehension of the message. In this light, it can be claimed that a theory of message production processes is fundamental to the scientific understanding of comprehension processes. Since the ideal output of the comprehension process is the receiver's knowledge of the "intentions" of the speaker, and since that comprehension depends upon how those intentions are encoded by the message producer, an understanding of the comprehension process depends on an understanding of the message production process.

For the past several years I have been working on a theory of message production. In many ways the theory is not new. Some of its fundamental assumptions are similar to those attributed to Wundt (among others) in Rosenberg's (1977a, pp. 1–5) overview of theories of sentence production. What is new about the theory is its explicitness about the nature of speaker's meanings ("intentions") and the way these meanings are encoded in sentences of a particular language system.

The theory was outlined in a European journal (Carroll, 1974). A central part of the theory is embodied in a *performance grammar*, i.e., a grammar that proposes to account for the performance behavior of message senders in producing messages in a language. For illustration, a performance grammar was sketched for a limited subset of sentences in standard English, but in principle a performance grammar can be developed for the whole of any dialect of English, or, for that matter, the whole of any language system.

Since the publication of the 1974 article, a performance grammar of English has been expanded to account for, or "generate," a larger subset of sentences. Indicated later in this chapter is the scope of the performance grammar as it now exists in the form of a computer simulation algorithm. First, however, it is necessary to examine the plan and rationale of a performance grammar. The discussion is restricted, for the most part, to the limited performance grammar that was outlined in the 1974 paper.

In the conference that produced this volume, one of the speakers noted that Chomsky (1965) did a great disservice to linguistics by introducing a distinction between what he called competence and performance. There has been much discussion about what these terms mean. The distinction is most frequently regarded as one between the speaker's abstract knowledge of a language system or grammar and his use of that knowledge in communication situations. "Performance factors" are said to account for such phenomena as hesitations, slips of the tongue, "ungrammatical" utterances, and the like.

The term *performance*, as used here, simply means rule-governed *behavior*. A performance grammar is intended to specify the rules that govern speech behavior, hence message production. These rules, however, are psychological; that is, they are specifications of acquired habits.

The expression "performance" grammar emphasizes the contrast between this theory of language production and the formal analysis of language structure popular among linguists, particularly those who have espoused the transformational theories of Chomsky. Chomsky has asserted (1968) that linguistics is a branch of psychology. But if language is a system of rules of behavior, those rules need to be formulated and studied, in the context of psychological theories and methods, *qua* rules of behavior rather than as purely formal rules similar to those of mathematics or logic.

In a sense, a performance grammar is a psychological redefinition of what Chomsky means by competence, i.e., what the speaker knows about his language in order to produce "grammatical" sentences. A performance grammar is *not* a grammar that is intended to account for hesitations, slips of the tongue, and similar phenomena, although it might be a basis for studying such phenomena, in the sense that they represent deviations or aberrations from the norms of performance rules.

The basic purpose of this chapter is to present the outlines of a performance grammar and to consider the role of such a grammar in a general theory of message production. The chapter also considers the applications of such a performance grammar in problems of language intervention in children and in other organisms (e.g., chimpanzees) insofar as one may desire to teach such organisms how to produce messages in speech or in some other communication system.

## THE ROLE OF A PERFORMANCE GRAMMAR IN A THEORY OF MESSAGE PRODUCTION

Figure 1 shows, in schematic form, the basic components of a theory of message production. The middle two boxes constitute the performance

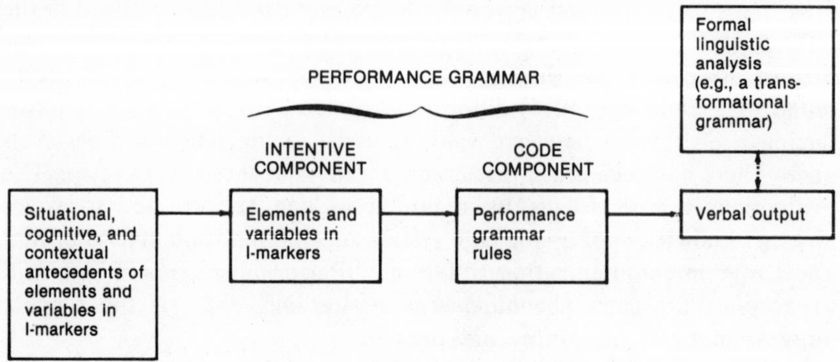


Figure 1. Components and relations of a message production theory.

grammar. The box at the left is the input to the grammar. The box at the right is its output, that is, a message.

The *input* to the performance grammar consists of situational, cognitive, and contextual factors that shape what a message sender might wish to communicate at a given time.

The performance grammar itself has two components: the *intentive* component or *I-marker*, and the *code* component.

Formal linguistic analysis has no necessary role in a theory of message production, except that certain findings in linguistics may guide the way one formulates the code component of the performance grammar. Figure 1, nevertheless, represents formal linguistic analysis as a supplementary mode of describing verbal output. There are several formal linguistic theories. Some of these, transformational generative grammar for example, do not consider verbal output, message, or texts as their data base, preferring to rely on the linguist's intuitions into his own language system. Each type of grammar, however, claims to give some account of observed messages, for example, by assigning "structural descriptions" to messages. But formal linguistic grammars do not claim to give an account of how messages are produced *in behavior*. In fact, transformational grammarians explicitly disavow any attempt to do so, even though they regard their analyses as representing the "competence" of the user of a language. Performance grammar gives an account of the essential behavioral processes in message production. In an analog of Chomskian rhetoric, we may say that performance grammar seeks to specify exactly what habits on the part of speakers make sentences "well formed" and grammatical.

As a performance grammarian, I am not particularly interested in formal linguistic analyses of language, or in exploring possible relations between the performance grammar (as I have formulated it) and selected formal analyses. Parenthetically, however, it may be noted here that Halliday's "systemic grammar," as presented by Huddleston (1971), Hudson (1971), and Muir (1972), is the type of grammatical analysis closest in spirit to my performance grammar theory. I follow the work in formal linguistics because it offers many examples of messages that need to be accounted for in a performance grammar. I should also comment that I am aware of developments in computational linguistics that may have a bearing on a performance grammar, for example the "augmented transition networks" proposed by Kaplan (1972) and others. But it would be distracting to consider these here.

## THE PERFORMANCE GRAMMAR MODEL

Performance grammar has two components, the intentive component and code component. This division is for convenience in analysis. From a psychological process viewpoint, these components may be inseparable because the creation of an "intention-marker," or "I-marker," by a speaker may automatically entail the activation of the appropriate sequence of operations in the code component. Recent research by Danks (1977) implies an intimate and automatic connection between the intentive and the code components of a performance grammar.

### The Intentive Component

In producing an utterance (or written text), the speaker (or writer) possesses an "intention," or assemblage of intentions, that he wishes to transmit to his audience. The speaker or writer may have many purposes in producing a message to influence hearers or readers in some way. The speaker or writer may even wish to lie or to deceive. The term *intention* represents only what the message sender intends to formulate in a message. The speaker's intentions or meanings have to be encoded according to certain linguistic conventions if they are to have the best chance of being transmitted and hence understood by the audience in the way "intended" by the message producer. The intentive component of a performance grammar specifies the nature of the intentions encoded into verbal output.

Intentions in terms of I-markers (intention-markers) are analogous to the P-markers (phrase-markers) of formal linguistic analysis. The term *I-marker* was proposed by Schlesinger (1971), but in recent writings Schlesinger (1977) puts an interpretation on the I-marker that is different from that proposed here. Schlesinger permits alternative "realizations" of a given I-marker. He assumes that different sentences with similar meanings, such as (1-3),

(1) *The logs were cut by the axe.*
(2) *It is the logs that were cut by the axe.*
(3) *The axe cut the logs.*

come from the same I-marker but stem from different "communicative considerations" that operate through "shunting markers" to produce different realizations. In contrast to Schlesinger's view, this author assumes that any difference in verbal output stems from a difference in I-markers. Bloomfield (1933, p. 145) notes that any difference in form implies a difference in meaning. Thus, the sentences just cited stem from different I-markers, and even very small differences between sentences, as in sentences (4) and (5), result from differences in the underlying I-markers.

(4) *John called up Mary.*
(5) *John called Mary up.*

These assumptions put a burden on the analysis of the I-marker. The I-marker, when formed, already contains the results of whatever communicative or sociolinguistic considerations dictate the difference between, for example, sentences (6) and (7):

(6) *Pass the salt!*
(7) *Would you mind passing the salt?*

The central interest of the performance grammar is in how speakers and writers are able, by applying the rules in the code component, to form sentences from I-markers. It is the task of psycholinguistics and sociolinguistics to develop knowledge concerning how the I-marker itself gets formed as a consequence of situational, cognitive, and contextual factors, and how such knowledge constitutes a part of a general theory of message production. Although it is not my immediate concern to develop this kind of knowledge, such knowledge cannot be developed soundly in the absence of an adequate theory of the I-marker.

To introduce the manner in which the notion of the I-marker may be formulated, let us consider a performance grammar for a small but important segment of English, namely, independent sentences in the declarative or interrogative modes involving two noun phrases and a transitive verb such that one of the noun phrases is the logical or "deep" subject of the verb and the other noun phrase is its logical or "deep" object. For the present, modal elements, agreement in concord, different tenses, and adverbial phrases of time, place, reason, or manner will not be considered, although such phenomena can easily be taken care of in an extended performance grammar. Note also that the limited grammar presented here does not provide for the construction of noun phrases from simpler constituents. Such phrases are assumed to be givens. The main interest here is in how noun phrases are incorporated as continuous units into sentences. Discontinuous noun phrases, as in sentence (8), are relatively rare in actual verbal output.

(8) *The man came who was going to fix your blinds.*

A complete performance grammar must specify how noun phrases are constructed and realized; that is, it must specify what entities in I-markers underlie noun phrases and what code-component rules govern their construction and realization.

The noun phrases are represented here by personal pronouns (*he*, *she*), partly because it must be demonstrated that the grammar properly selects the nominative and accusative cases of these pronouns, and partly because these particular noun-phrase representations are very short. Actually, the grammar will accept noun phrases of virtually any length and complexity (e.g., *the man who told me that you were coming*). The verb *choose* is used in the illustrations because it is a "strong" verb, having three different forms for the infinitive, simple past, and past participle (*choose*, *chose*, *chosen*).

The I-marker can be analyzed in terms of two types of entities: *elements*, and *variables*. The *elements* are the basic semantic contents of the I-marker, i.e., the nominals, verbals, adjectivals, and adverbials that can be "plugged into" various sentence types (depending on content), whereas *variables* determine the particular grammatical form a sentence will take, and they account for variations recognized in traditional grammar, such as active/passive, tense, mode, and aspect. Both elements and variables have semantic content, but their antecedents in the communicative situation have different characters. The antecedents of elements are objects, events, and qualities, whereas the antecedents of the variables have to do with relationships in time, order, space, etc., and with the nature of the speaker's interpretation of these relationships and his perception of the immediate communicative situation. It is beyond the scope of this chapter to discuss these antecedents further.

For simplicity, let us restrict our attention to an I-marker that has the following three elements:

DSB (deep subject) . . . . . . . . . . . . e.g., HE
DVB (deep verb) . . . . . . . . . . . . . . e.g., CHOOSE
DOB (deep object) . . . . . . . . . . . . . e.g., SHE

DSB, DVB, and DOB are mnemonics for entities in a computer program that are mentioned later. Other mnemonics with obvious derivations are introduced in the course of the discussion.

These three elements form a meaningful set of relations, whereby DSB "does" DVB to DOB. Each element could be instanced by a very large number of possible linguistic forms. DSB or DOB could be instanced by a very large number of noun phrases, and the DVB could be instanced by a large class of transitive verbs (possibly including compound verbs such as *call up* or *show off*, although such verbs involve variables that may determine how their constituents are ordered). The performance grammar does not consider possible semantic constraints upon the selection of elements. Any such constraints, for example the dubious constraint that the verb *build* cannot take a human object, are assumed to be imposed, if at all, by the input to the grammar. Thus, it is perfectly reasonable for an individual to select "the mad biologist" for the DSB and "a man that flies" for the DOB in order to utter the sentence "The mad biologist tried to build a man that flies."

The variables in an I-marker take one of several possible distinct values of a finite set. Among the more important variables are those listed in Table 1, shown with an indication of some possible values that they may take.

Table 1. Some of the possible variables in I-markers[a]

| Variable | Some possible values |
|---|---|
| THM (theme or grammatical subject) | DSB (deep subject)<br>DOB (deep object)<br>[DIO (deep indirect object)] |
| MDE (mode) | DEC (declarative)<br>INT (interrogative)<br>[IMP (imperative)] |
| PCN (positive, challenge, negative) | POS (positive)<br>NEG (negative)<br>CHA (challenge) |
| [TNS (tense)] | [present], past, [future] |
| [ASP (aspect)] | simple, [progressive] |
| [PRF (perfective)] | simple, [perfective] |
| QRY (query) | QOO (no query)<br>QDS (deep subject query)<br>QDO (deep object query)<br>QDV (deep verb query)<br>[QDI (deep indirect object query)] |
| EMP (emphasis) | EOO (no emphasis)<br>[EDS (emphasis on deep subject)]<br>[EDV (emphasis on deep verb)]<br>EDT (emphasis on truth value of deep verb)<br>[EDO (emphasis on deep object)] |
| [ECH (echo)] | [EC0 (no echo)]<br>[ECl (echo)] |

[a] Variables and values in square brackets [ ] are not implemented in the flow diagrams of Figures 2a and 2b.

A most important variable is the *theme*. In conventional terminology, it is the grammatical subject of a sentence. In the sample I-marker under consideration here, it is possible for the speaker to attach the theme to either DSB or DOB, depending upon certain antecedent circumstances linked to the prominence, salience, or "givenness" of the element in the speaker's cognitive construction of his message (Ertel, 1977). Depending upon the choice of the theme, sentences may appear in "active" or "passive" forms:

(9) (THM = DSB) *He chose her.*
(10) (THM = DOB) *She was chosen by him.*

It may be that the active versus passive construction of a sentence is determined by the choice of the theme, but the matter is rather complicated. For example, if we let DVB = *show* and DOB = *the baby*, we can also have an indirect object, DIO = *she*. Attaching the theme to DSB, DIO, and DOB, respectively, yields the following sentences:

(11) (THM = DSB) *He showed her the baby.*
(12) (THM = DIO) *She was shown the baby* [*by him*].
(13) (THM = DOB) *The baby was shown* [*to*] *her* [*by him*].

Furthermore, there are many verbs (e.g., *ask*, *order*, *cause*) that permit complement verb constructions whereby it is possible to speak of both a "principal theme" and a "secondary theme." In sentence (14),

(14) *I caused him to show her the baby.*

consider that *I* is DSB1, and *he* [*him*] is DOB1, functioning also as the DSB of the verb complement phrase. *She* [*her*] is the DIO2 for the verb complement phrase, and *the baby* is DOB2. It is now possible to attach the principal theme (PTM) to any one of the set DSB1, DOB1, DIO2, and DOB2. Furthermore, if PTM = DSB1, the secondary theme (STM) can be any of the three remaining in the set. If PTM is not DSB1, the secondary theme is attached to the same element as PTM. Thus, six possible conditions can occur.

| | PTM | STM | |
|---|---|---|---|
| (15) | DSB1 | DOB1 | *I caused him to show her the baby.* |
| (16) | DSB1 | DIO2 | *I caused her to be shown the baby* [*by him*]. |
| (17) | DSB1 | DOB2 | *I caused the baby to be shown* [*to*] *her* [*by him*]. |
| (18) | DOB1 | DOB1 | *He was caused* [*by me*] *to show her the baby.* |
| (19) | DIO2 | DIO2 | *She was caused* [*by me*] *to be shown the baby* [*by him*]. |
| (20) | DOB2 | DOB2 | *The baby was caused* [*by me*] *to be shown her* [*by him*]. |

In view of this variety, characterizing sentences simply as "active" or "passive" is not very informative. Characterization in terms of themes seems preferable.

A second variable is MDE (mode). In the simple grammar being considered here, it may be either declarative or interrogative. Other traditional modes are imperative and exclamatory. I shall not digress to review the very limited literature (Carroll, 1958) on the antecedents of MDE, i.e., the situational factors determining whether a speaker will cast the production in declarative, interrogative, or imperative mode—the factors, for example, that determine which of the following sentences will express a request:

(21) *Maybe you will pass the salt, please?*
(22) *Will you pass the salt?*
(23) *Pass the salt, please.*

Note that the first of these sentences is declarative *in form*. It is important to distinguish MDE from the variables QRY and ECH, discussed below.

A third important variable is PCN. There seems to be no simple word (*positivity?*) to label it. It can take three possible values. The distinction comes out most clearly in certain interrogative sentences, such as:

(24) (POS) *Did he choose her?*
(25) (CHA) *Didn't he choose her?*
(26) (NEG) *Did he not choose her?*

Sentence (24) is cast in positive form, indicating that the speaker simply wants to know whether *he chose her* or *he did not choose her*. Sentence (25) presents a challenge to the hearer to deny the speaker's apparent assumption that *he chose her*. In fact, the speaker could have said,

(27) *He chose her, didn't he?*

with the tag question in challenge form. Sentence (26) is a more neutral question, almost offering the presupposition that *he did not choose her*, and in fact the tag question form would be

(28) *He did not choose her, did he?*
or
(29) *He didn't choose her, did he?*

The exact status of the CHA value is still indeterminate. In the current version of my performance grammar, it determines whether the auxiliary is contracted into the form *didn't* as opposed to *did not*, even in sentences where MDE = DEC, as in

(30) (NEG) *He did not choose her.*
(31) (CHA) *He didn't choose her.*

The PCN variable must be assumed to have three values because it determines the post-position of *not* after a post-posed theme in interrogative sentences. An alternative analysis would simply say that CHA dictates an "informal" form of the negative, whereas NEG gives a formal form. Thus, in formal writing, we would more likely have:

(32) *Is it not true that....?*
rather than
(33) *Isn't it true....?*

even though there is clearly a "challenge" implied in sentence (32).

In the simple performance grammar under consideration, it is assumed that TNS has the value *past*. Complicated verb phrases can be produced if we assume that TNS can have other values (such as present and future) and if, in addition, we take account of ASP (aspect) and PRF (the perfective/non-perfective feature). For example, we can get

(34) *She will have been chosen by him.*

with future progressive perfective, and THM = DOB.

Another variable, QRY (query), can have any one or more of several values, including a zero value in which no element is queried. QRY has to do with the speaker's knowledge or lack of knowledge of the identity of a particular grammatical element, the DSB, DOB, or DVB. When a query occurs, that element is replaced by a *wh* form such as *who*, *whom*, *what*, *by whom*, or *by what*. The QRY variable is largely independent of MDE. For example, QRY = QDO can produce the following declarative sentences:

(35) *He chose whom?*

Nevertheless, when QRY is attached to the element that is also a (principal) theme, the sentence necessarily has MDE = INT, as in

(36) *Who was chosen by him?*

It seems reasonable to allow for query of the DVB. Suppose, for example, that the speaker knows that DSB "did something" to, or with respect to, DOB, but the nature of the action is not known. This will yield such sentences as

(37) *He did what to her?*
(38) *What did he do to her?*

Possibly "do something to" is not an appropriate substitution form for the verb *choose*, but it is clearly appropriate for a large class of verbs (*hit*, *kill*, *kick*, *drop*, etc.), and it may be assumed that QDV is incorporated into the I-marker only when the speaker perceives it as appropriate for the class of actions being queried. QRY can have several values at once. In sentences (39–44)

(39) *Who didn't do what to whom?*
(40) *By whom wasn't what done to whom?*
(41) *What didn't who do to whom?*
(42) *What wasn't done to whom by whom?*
(43) *To whom didn't who do what?*
(44) *To whom wasn't what done by whom?*

we have QRY = QDS, QDO, and QDV. The differences between these sentences, however, are differences among the priorities of special types of thematic selection in an underlying structure

(45) *Someone did something to someone.*

that is generated by a QDV query.

The variables EMP and ECH are postulated to operate in the I-marker primarily to account for subtleties of expression that are exhibited more prominently in spoken language than in written language. Consider sentences (46–55):

| | EMP | ECH | |
|---|---|---|---|
| (46) | EOO | EC0 | *He chose her.* |
| (47) | EOO | EC1 | *?He chose her?* |
| (48) | EDS | EC0 | ***He** chose her.* |
| (49) | EDS | EC1 | *?**He** chose her?* |
| (50) | EDO | EC0 | *He chose **her**.* |
| (51) | EDO | EC1 | *?He chose **her**?* |
| (52) | EDV | EC0 | *He **chose** her.* (rather than rejecting her) |
| (53) | EDV | EC1 | *?He **chose** her?* (and didn't reject her?) |
| (54) | EDT | EC0 | *He **did** choose her.* (despite your belief to the contrary) |
| (55) | EDT | EC1 | *?He **did** choose her?* (expressing disbelief) |

The variable ECH can be either neutral (EC0) or positive (EC1). With a positive value, the speaker asks for a confirmation or amplification of the utterance—either because a previous utterance may not have been heard or understood with confidence, or because the speaker wants to express doubt or disbelief. (Sentence 21, cited previously, shows the operation of EC1 in a request put in declarative form.) EC1 also occurs in rhetorical questions.

The variable EMP operates independently of ECH to place added stress in the utterance of particular elements in the sentence, usually DSB or DOB, EDV places emphasis on the particular lexical content of the DVB, i.e., its differentiation from verbs with other lexical contents. In contrast, EDT places emphasis on the "truth value" of the verb. This is one value of EMP that can show up in written discourse by the insertion of the form *did* or *does*. Other positive values of EMP can show up in print through underlining, italicization, or similar devices. Both EMP and ECH make for variations in the stress and intonation patterns of utterances in complex ways.

This analysis of I-marker variables is not final in any sense. This discussion is only an approximation, but it illustrates the way the intentive component of a performance grammar can be specified.

**The Code Component**

The code component of a performance grammar consists of a series of performance rules representing the habits the speaker has acquired in the course of learning to talk in grammatically acceptable sentences. They are rules that specify how to transform the contents of any given I-marker into verbal output that will satisfy the conventions of the language system. These conventions are built into performance rules that contain a complete and adequate description of the syntax of the language system. No other set of rules (e.g., phrase-structure and transformational rules) provided by a formal linguistic analysis are necessary, even if they do in fact "generate" the same verbal output as the performance rules. The rules that are necessary and sufficient in the code component of a performance grammar are quite different from the rules offered in typical linguistic analyses. A major difference between performance grammar rules and linguistic rules has to do with the order in which they are applied. In developing a set of performance rules to transform I-markers into well formed sentences, the production of a sentence is assumed to be a temporal, "left-to-right" process in which words are emitted one by one (or in groups) in an appropriate temporal order. Thus, the first decisions to be made in transforming an I-marker are *not* decisions concerning the major constituents of a sentence, such as the NP and the VP, as in a transformational analysis, but decisions concerning the first words to be emitted. These decisions may depend upon elements located near the terminals of tree structures in a transformational analysis.

The psychological assumptions that underlie the specification of performance grammar rules concern the actual generation, in real time, of *sentences*, one by one. It is assumed that I-markers are for sentences, rather than for more extended discourse, and that they represent what Schlesinger (1977) calls "coagulations" of communicative elements into groups or chunks suitable for expression in sentences. Successive sentences call on the coagulation of different successive I-markers, although certain elements often carry over from one I-marker to the next. For example, successive sentences may be comments about a certain "deep subject," with the same tense and aspect used in several sentences. Just how these coagulations occur, as a function of the total communicative situation and the changes that inevitably occur in the total communicative situation as successive sentences are "read out," is important in a theory of message production, but it is beyond the scope of this chapter.

Another assumption is that the I-marker is read into a short term memory buffer, in the focus of the speaker's more or less conscious attention, while its contents get expressed and actualized in verbal output. During the time it takes for a sentence to become actualized, *any* element or variable in an I-marker can function as a stimulus for the operation of a particular performance rule that depends on that stimulus. Furthermore, the very operation of the performance rules themselves can generate further stimuli, read into a short term memory buffer. These can function in the operation of successive performance rules. For example, some rules may require that, once elements are "used," i.e., actualized in verbal output, they are so tagged. This means that in speaking we retain in short term memory at least some of what we have said, and we do not normally repeat words already spoken.

The rules are always of a conditional type, in the general form "if $A = x$, then $B$; else $C$," where $A$ is generally a variable, $x$ is a particular value of that variable, and $B$ and $C$ are any outcomes of the decision. These outcomes may include the "writing out" of a particular linguistic form, the changing of the value of a variable, and the movement to another decision point which again takes the general form just described. Decisions thus may be regarded as entailed by, or dependent upon, the outcomes of previous decisions. The whole of the code component can be depicted as a flow diagram suitable for a computer program. Our work has been much aided in the development of the rules by testing their operation in a computer program that will write out the sentence implied by a given I-marker.

The realization of the performance grammar rules in a computer introduces a certain artificiality about the way such rules operate in a living organism. This is because typical digital computers are serial rather than parallel processors. Thus, for example, if a certain outcome is dependent upon the presence of *any one* of a certain set of conditions, the computer must test the presence of each of these conditions, one after the other, whereas a living organism is presumably able to detect the relevant conditions by "parallel processing," without the necessity of a serial search. This is illustrated in the opening phases of the performance grammar, in which one of the early decisions in sentence production depends upon the presence of any query, i.e., QDS, QDO, or QDV, in order to output the appropriate *wh*-word or phrases (*who, whom, by whom, what,* etc.). The computer program must show a sequential search of these possibilities. This artificiality is not critical, however, because it is legitimate to simulate parallel processing with serial processing as long as we recognize that the processes might not be serial at all. Furthermore, it is possible to formulate the performance grammar rules on the assumption of parallel processing. This can also be done with high-level computer languages that permit the (apparent) simultaneous testing of multiple conditions.

There are other artificialities in a computer program, the principal one being that the computer program must constitute an algorithm for producing *any* sentence within a defined set, and thus may appear to be more complicated than it needs to be for any given sentence. In actual sentence production, there may be a relatively limited number of routines or subprograms (chosen in early phases) that are running off without the complications that must be included in a complete flow diagram.

Figure 2a shows the first half of a flow diagram for generating sentences within the limited set defined previously, i.e., sentences with the elements DSB, DVB, and DOB (the DSB and DOB having the "feature" third-person singular), and variables and values indicated in Table 1. The second half of the flow diagram is in Figure 2b. Considering the flow diagram as a whole, we see that the program is divided into seven phases: opener, auxiliary, postposed theme, main verb, object, to (DAT), and by (DSB). Not every sentence within the defined set that has been programmed actually uses all three phases. A phase is often skipped or omitted. Nevertheless, this is the basic order observed in every sentence. Some of the communication boards exhibited at the Gulf Shores, Alabama, conference upon which this book is based (for use by children who lack capacity to articulate speech) were set up in columns whereby the child could communicate a message by pointing to options in each of a series of successive columns. A complete performance grammar could indicate what optimal set of phases of sentence generation might be embodied in the columns of these communication boards.

The flow diagram is entered with a "preprocessing" state (not shown in the flow diagram) wherein the values THM or NTHM (non-theme), and any queries present, are attached to the elements DSB, DOB, and DVB. Such associations are specified in the I-marker prior to generation of a sentence. Desired lexical insertions for DSB, DOB, (hence for THM and NTHM), and DVB are made in the I-marker.

The flow diagram shows a series of programmed decisions. Each decision point is represented by a circle. The conditions affecting a given decision point are shown as labels for lines emanating from the circle. If

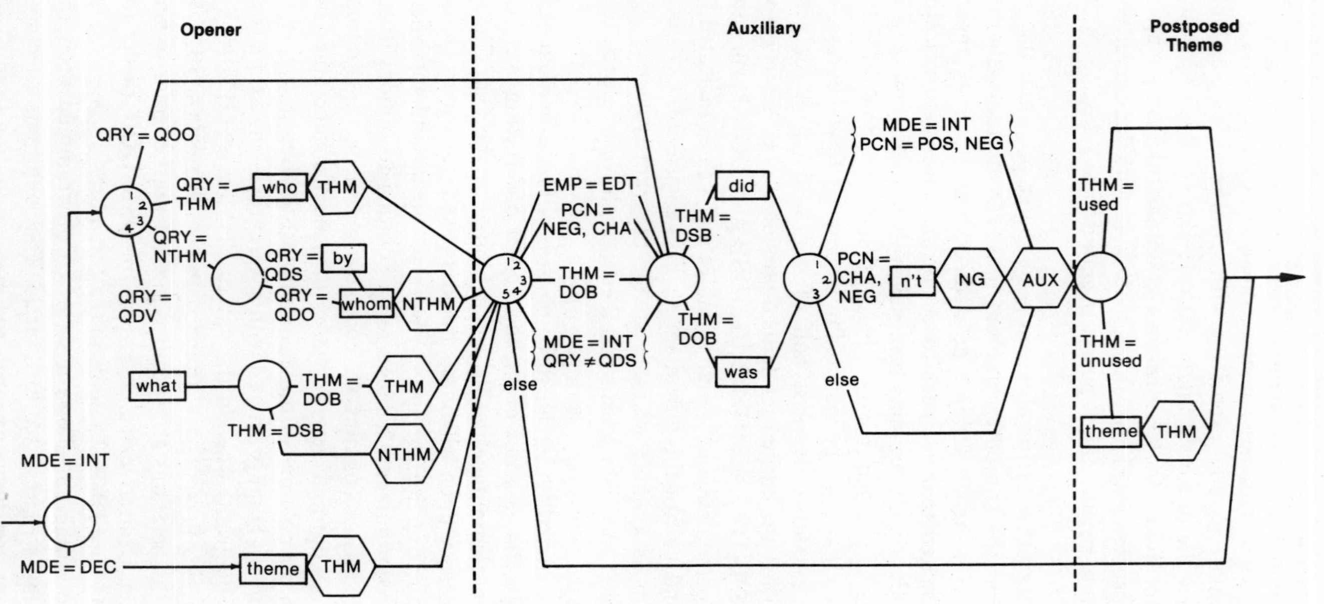


Figure 2a. Performance grammar for core sentences.

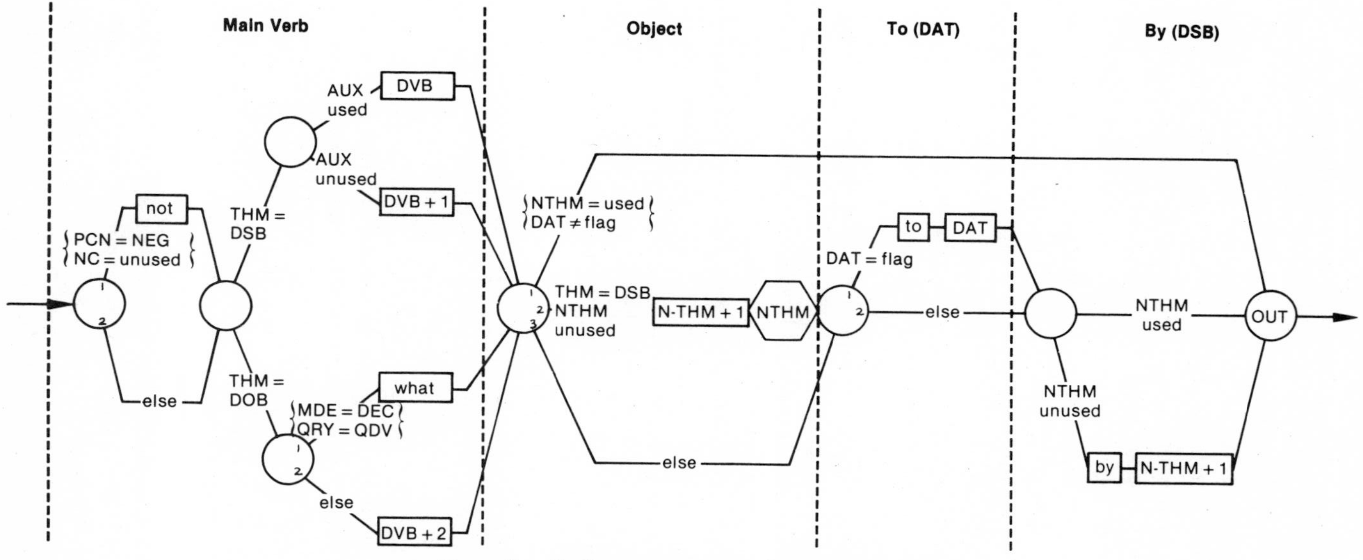


Figure 2b. Performance grammar for core sentences.

we start at point S (start of sentence), the first decision is whether the mode is declarative or interrogative. If MDE = DEC, the first word or phrase that is output or "written" is the *theme*, whether it be the DSB or the DOB. Any word or element that is output in this way is shown in a rectangle. As soon as an element is output, it may be necessary to make a record of this fact in a special counter, represented by a hexagon. Thus, a special counter holds the information that the theme has been "used." Later in the flowchart, decisions may be based upon whether the theme has or has not been "used" up to that point.

If the first decision point yields the fact that MDE = INT (interrogative), further decisions are necessary before there can be any output. If there is no query, i.e., if QRY = QOO, the program can proceed directly to a decision point where it is necessary to decide whether to start the sentence with *did* or *was*, depending upon whether the theme is DSB or DOB. If there is a query, however, the progression through the program depends upon what that query is. Here the program must test each of several possibilities in order (because a serial processor is assumed). The order in which the possibilities are tested is generally immaterial, but this is not always the case. Where the order is relevant, the possibilities are numbered in sequence within the decision point. Testing whether there is a query of the theme in this case takes priority over other tests. If the theme is queried, the word *who* is written (assuming that the theme has the feature +human). If, however, the NTHM (non-theme, i.e., DOB if THM = DSB, and DSB if THM = DOB) is queried, the outcome leads to a decision point where the program decides whether to write *by whom* or simply *whom*. Failing these tests, the program assumes that there is a query of the deep verb, in which case the word *what* is written, followed by notations as to whether *what* is considered a "use" of THM or NTHM. Whatever happens, all these outcomes lead to the next decision point where selection of the *did/was* decision point or a move to a later phase of the program takes place.

The reader may now proceed to examine the remainder of the flow diagram, with the guidance given above. The only additional explanation needed is the following: DVB alone represents the infinitive form, DVB + 1 represents the past tense and DVB + 2 represents the past participle. DAT in the penultimate phase represents a writing of the DOB after the preposition, *to*, encountered when QRY = DVB, and a "flag" has been set that the "dative" is to be used.

Even if DSB, DOB, and DVB have fixed lexical insertions, the program will generate a variety of sentences, depending upon the combination of values of variables assumed in the I-marker. If different lexical insertions for elements are assumed, and particularly if complex NPs are inserted for DOB and DSB, the possible variety of sentences produced by this program becomes much greater, but this is essentially a trivial fact. The real interest and value of the code component resides in its capacity to handle a variety of conditions associated with the variables assumed in the I-marker, and to produce or generate only "grammatical" sentences when there is a valid structure in the I-marker. (An invalid structure would occur, for example, if the I-marker did not contain a DOB for a transitive DVB without a further complement.)

## AN EXPANDED PERFORMANCE GRAMMAR FOR ENGLISH

Work is now nearly complete on an expanded performance grammar for English sentences that will accept I-markers containing copulative and intransitive verbs, along with the transitive verbs assumed in the illustrative grammar described above. Also, it allows transitive verbs that take indirect objects, and transitive verbs that take complement verbs (that in turn may be copulative, intransitive, or transitive, with or without indirect objects), as in the verb phrases *try to be*, *want* (*someone*) *to go*, *cause* (*someone*) *to show* (*something*) *to* (*someone*), and the like. With appropriate selection of principal and secondary themes, it will generate sentences such as (15–20). Other expansions include allowing for the full range of values of the variables indicated in Table 1, and allowing for the concord agreements needed when nominal elements like DSB, DIO, and DOB are permitted to take features of person, number, and humanness. Copulative verbs are permitted to take nominal and adjectival complements, and verbs may take adverbial complements and modifiers.

Further work will permit the use of verbs with *that* and *wh*-complementation, as *know* (*that* . . . . , *where* . . . .), etc., and the production of variants such as *It was known that* . . . . , and the like. Work can also be started on performance grammar rules for construction of noun phrases, including noun phrases that contain relative clauses.

Throughout this endeavor, it has not as yet been necessary to depart from the general plan of a performance grammar as illustrated above, and no essential departures are foreseen in work that is contemplated. It is, of course, necessary to add complications to the elements and variables specified in the I-marker, but there has been no need to modify the basic conditional rule employed thus far. There are no limitations, except those of time and patience, to the expansion of a performance grammar to encompass any syntactic construction that one might desire to produce.

Furthermore, the development of an expanded performance grammar reveals cognitive processes in I-marker formation and sentence construction. For example, it is apparent that constructions involving copulative auxiliaries (forms of the verb *to be*), yielding either passive and/or progressive clauses, form a psychological unity in that they express perception of *state*. The performance rules generating these constructions are either identical or very similar, and parallel.

The current version of the performance grammar requires a greater number of phases than was allowed for above in the sequencing of sentence components. These phases, all of which (except for 3) are optional in any given sentence, but whose order is generally invariant, may be described as follows:

1. Query opener: insertion of necessary *wh*-words or phrases for queries in the interrogative mode
2. Principal theme
3. First (and sometimes only) word of the principal verb phrase, with optional negative elements
4. Postponed principal theme
5. Remainder of principal verb phrase, with optional negative elements
6. Informal dative
7. Object/secondary theme/complement noun/complement adjective
8. Formal dative (with *to*)
9. *By* DSB
10. Complement verb phrase, with any negative elements
11. Informal dative for complement verb phrase
12. Second object/complement noun/complement adjective
13. Formal dative for complement verb phrase
14. *By* DSB2

These 14 phases could, for example, define the successive columns of a communication board for generating sentences.

Table 2 gives sentences whose successive phases are in accord with this order. In the table, the sentences are to be read from top to bottom. It may be instructive for the reader to attempt to specify the I-markers that underlie each sentence.

## IMPLICATIONS FOR PSYCHOLINGUISTICS AND LANGUAGE INTERVENTION

Numerous questions will have arisen in the reader's mind: What is the significance of a performance grammar for a theory of message production? How well do the rules represented in flowcharts and computer simulation programs correspond to the psychological processes actually involved in sentence production? Can these rules be taught, or, at least, would knowledge of these rules help a teacher? Would a performance grammar such as this assist in language intervention efforts?

Table 2. Sentences illustrating ordering of component phases

| Phase | (56) | (57) | (58) | (59) | (60) | (61) | (62) | (63) |
|---|---|---|---|---|---|---|---|---|
| 1. QRY | | | | *Who* | *To whom* | | *By whom* | |
| 2. Principal THM | *He* | *He* | *He* | | | *He* | | |
| 3. First Vb word | *was* | *showed* | *had not* | *didn't* | *has* | *wanted* | *was* | *Will* |
| 4. Postposed THM | | | | | *the baby* | | *the baby* | *he* |
| 5. Remainder VP | | | *been showing* | *show* | *not been shown* | | *caused* | *be caused* |
| 6. Informal dative | | | *her* | | | | | |
| 7. DOB/CN/CA | *sick* | *the baby* | *the baby.* | *the baby* | | *me* | | |
| 8. Formal dative | | *to her.* | | *to her?* | | | | |
| 9. *By* DSB | | | | | *by him?* | | | *by you* |
| 10. Complement VP | | | | | | *to show* | *to have been shown* | *not to show* |
| 11. Informal dative 2 | | | | | | *her* | | *her* |
| 12. DOB2 | | | | | | *the baby.* | | *the baby?* |
| 13. Formal dative 2 | | | | | | | *to her* | |
| 14. *By* DSB2 | | | | | | | *by him?* | |

As yet, these questions can be answered only speculatively. However, some major virtues of a performance grammar model like that presented here are the following:

1. It makes explicit what classes of linguistic elements and variables can be involved in the process of sentence (and message) production, and thus offers a basis on which one can study the transition from antecedent conditions (situational, cognitive, and contextual variables) to actual message production.
2. It offers a model of how these elements and variables are processed, sequentially, in a sentence production event.
3. The model is suitable for interpretation in terms of a causal analysis of language behavior, including language learning.
4. The model can be expanded to be as comprehensive as one might desire in order to account for, or "generate," the full range of grammatical sentences (and longer productions) in a language. Even in its current form, the model can generate a very large number of grammatical sentences in standard English. Comparable models could be developed for other languages.
5. "Degenerate" forms of the model can be used to account for successive stages in the acquisition of a language system by a child or other language learner. Similarly, degenerate or partial forms of the model can provide guidance in the development of materials and procedures in the teaching of language production.
6. The model provides a basis for the interpretation of various phenomena of interest, such as syntactic ambiguity or speech hesitations.

Each of these claims is discussed briefly. One additional claim, that the model has pertinence to the study of language comprehension, is not within the scope of this chapter.

## Explicitness of the Model

If one is concerned with how speakers formulate utterances in response to situational, cognitive, and contextual antecedents of message production, one must have an explicit specification of the categories offered by the particular language in which messages are to be formulated. (There are obvious "Whorfian" overtones in this assertion.) The elements and variables postulated for this performance grammar represent the categories for sentence production in standard English. Furthermore, each element and variable has a unique psychological significance that must be addressed in studies of message production. The "deep subject" element would have a totally different significance, for example, from that of the PCN variable.

Likewise, the model is explicit concerning the rules by which elements and variables in an I-marker are processed to produce messages. Explicitness of rule formulation is necessary to test hypotheses about whether these rules are indeed acquired habits that can be taught or otherwise modified.

### The Production Process

The obvious question here is whether the rules of the performance grammar correspond to actual psychological processes. The performance grammar outlined here is "generative" in a Chomskian sense. Given elements and variables, it can generate any one of a very large set of "grammatical" sentences, and no ungrammatical ones. The rules are functional because they can generate sentences that would be acceptable as grammatical by native speakers of English, and no ungrammatical ones. This is not a guarantee that they properly simulate message producers' behavior. Identical results could be produced by entirely different sets of rules. Indeed, the sentences produced by the performance grammar could also be generated by a transformational grammar. Yet the rules employed in a transformational grammar are quite different from those employed in a performance grammar. The argument for the validity of a performance grammar therefore centers around the type of rule it employs.

The most persuasive argument for the validity of the rules of a performance grammar is that their structure conforms to a reasonable model of the emission or activation of behavior. In the simplest terms, these rules conform to a stimulus-response model. These stimuli are, in the first instance, the elements and variables specified in an I-marker. As the construction of a message proceeds, the units of the message output themselves can become further stimuli. The responses are the words or other linguistic units appearing in the message being constructed. Since the rules of a performance grammar are stated as contingencies, in the general form "If $A = x$, then *B;* else *C,*" we can view the responses as discriminated operants.

An earlier paper (Carroll, 1974) characterized the rules of a performance grammar as similar to the rules of a finite-state grammar that specify the conditions under which the output moves from one state to another. This characterization may have been confusing because the performance grammar is not by any means a strict finite-state grammar. A strict finite-state grammar does not assume a memory. The transitions from state X to state Y are probabilistic, and are governed solely by conditions existing at state X. The performance grammer, in contrast, assumes that during sentence production a speaker has a memory for all the elements and variables existing in the I-marker at the start of the production. Furthermore, the rules are determinate, not probabilistic.

For some years, now, it has been claimed that stimulus-response models cannot account for language behavior. This claim is sometimes based on a wholesale rejection of the stimulus-response model itself. I am not prepared to consider such a stance here. It has been customary to make the claim that language behavior is too complex to be accommodated within stimulus-response models. While there may indeed be aspects of language behavior for which this is true, the power of a performance grammar based on stimulus-response principles to generate complex productions refutes the claim that sentence production is too complex to be accounted for in this way.

One other theoretical objection to a performance grammar (this one likely to come from radical behaviorism) could arise from rejection of the notion that conditions in an I-marker can constitute stimuli. It could be argued that the existence or operation of such conditions is gratuitous and unnecessary. To meet this objection, the entities postulated as existing in the I-marker should be viewed simply as convenient intervening variables that operate as antecedents for the code component of the grammar, but have their source in prior conditions in the context of message production.

It would be possible to verify the rule structure of a performance grammar by experimental means. One such experimental procedure would be an attempt to teach performance grammar rules to some appropriate organism. The most available organism in my laboratory is a college student of psychology. One could try to teach some foreign or artificial language to such a student by writing an appropriate performance grammar for the language and employing some form of computer-assisted instruction. There would be no attempt to teach the rules as such. Rather, one would try to teach behavior *based on the rules*.

It would perhaps be more interesting and revealing to select a chimpanzee or other primate as the organism to be taught a language prescribed by a set of performance grammar rules. It is understandable why the Yerkes Regional Primate Research Center group chose to teach Lana the simple language called Yerkish (Rumbaugh, 1977), but it would seem possible to teach a chimpanzee a language much closer to regular English. The performance grammar outlined here can generate a sentence like *Wasn't a banana eaten by Tim?* and many others of this sort. From what we now know about the capabilities of chimpanzees, and about the efficacy of the procedures that have been used to teach Yerkish, there is no reason why one could not teach a chimpanzee to communicate in an analog or subset of full English. The transition from such an experiment to use of a performance grammar in various types of language intervention efforts with language-disabled children should be relatively easy.

Other experimental investigations of a performance grammar model could be suggested. Various laboratory experiments with mature native speakers, involving the measurement of reaction times (latencies) to produce sentences based on given I-marker elements and variables, or to complete sentences on the basis of limited cues, might reveal the relative potency or validity of the postulated performance grammar rules.

A possible difficulty in accepting a performance grammar as a model of language production is that such a grammar quickly becomes complex as it is expanded to account for any reasonably large and diverse subset of sentences. It is absurd to suppose that a speaker consciously applies such rules in sentence production, and it may be difficult to accept the notion that such a complex rule structure is capable of being learned. To meet the objection that the rule structure is too complex to be learned, it should be pointed out that the rules do not have to be learned all at once. Child language acquisition takes place over a sufficiently long period of time to permit the acquisition of a very large number of rules, along with a very large vocabulary. Furthermore, human behavior provides many examples of highly complex learning. A skilled pianist, for example, in performing a musical selection of even moderate length, can exhibit memorization of literally thousands of responses. This behavior illustrates the functioning of the rather mysterious process known as automatization, that is, the process whereby rule-governed habits can come to operate very quickly and facilely, with minimal conscious attention on the part of the behaver. It is not unreasonable to think that processes of automatization occur in the learning and use of performance grammar rules to produce fluent, nearly effortless speech. Goldman-Eisler (1968) has offered evidence showing that syntactic processes operate with minimal cognitive activity, whereas word and content selection processes are much less automatic and require relatively complex and difficult cognitive activity.

## Appropriateness of the Model for Causal Analysis

A basic tenet of scientific inquiry is that events have causes, whether simple or complex. One goal of scientific inquiry is to discover the laws or regularities governing the causal nexus between prior and consequent events. It is also assumed that in no case do temporally later events determine prior events. Lashley (1951; see also discussion in Fodor, Bever, and Garrett, 1974, pp. 25 ff.) noted that speech provides many examples where the character of an earlier portion of a sentence appears to be determined by later portions. For example, in sentence (64), the plural form *are* seems to be governed by the later constituent *John and*

(64) *Are John and Mary coming?*

*Mary*, apparently in contradiction to the normal assumption of temporal sequence in causation. This evidence led Lashley to reject an associationistic interpretation of language behavior. But the kind of associationism that Lashley objected to is the oversimplified view that words themselves are stimuli for the following words. The evidence from sentences like (64) does not rule out the possibility that the determination of an earlier event by a later one is the outcome of a process in which *both* are determined through associationistic connections with a still earlier event. If we assume that the utterance of a sentence like (64) is a result of conditions in an I-marker that are held in a short term memory buffer during sentence production, there should be no problem in applying the usual canons of scientific thinking to this case. Sentence (64) is one that can easily be generated by the performance grammar model. The element *John and Mary* is a DSB that is assigned the feature plurality in the I-marker, and selection of the plural form *are* is determined by this plurality feature very early in the sentence production process, since the conditions in the I-marker (interrogative mode with no query) dictate that the sentence begin with an auxiliary verb form. The performance grammar model lends itself to a causal analysis. Indeed, it *constitutes* a causal analysis of language behavior.

Having this causal analysis available, one is in a better position to interpret language learning in terms of the general principles of learning pertinent to the learning of responses to stimuli. What is needed now is an analysis of how conditions in the I-marker are determined by still earlier events. In the relatively simple case of the plurality feature exhibited in sentence (64), plurality is determined by the fact that *John* and *Mary* are perceived as more than one entity acting or moving together. (Otherwise, two questions might be asked: *Is John coming?* and *Is Mary coming?*)

Current linguistic theories often address the problem of how sentences are "related," e.g., active sentences as related to passive sentences, and declarative sentences as related to interrogative sentences. At one point in the history of transformational grammar (Chomsky, 1957), it was assumed that relations between such sentences could be accounted for by transformations from base-form or "kernel" sentences. More recent transformational models assume that related sentences, even "kernel" sentences, are derived from "deep structure" by different transformational rules. It should be noted that these formulations are within the context of formal linguistic analysis, with no necessary implications for how sentences are actually produced. A causal analysis, such as that provided by a performance grammar, is more relevant in accounting for actual sentence production in behavior. According to this analysis, "related" sentences are produced from I-markers that have different values of variables such as THM, PCN, MDE, etc., while the elements (DSB, DVB, etc.) remain the same. The values of variables are assumed to be actual "causes" of different sentence productions which also differ in meaning to the extent that the I-marker values are different. (In transformational theory, passive sentences are sometimes claimed to have the same "meaning" as the active sentences to which they are related. In my view, such a claim is based upon an entirely too liberal interpretation of what is meant by *meaning*.)

**Comprehensiveness of the Model**

The performance grammar model is in principle expandable to encompass any syntactic construction in English, or any language. This is a large and bold claim whose confirmation can come only with the accumulation of evidence. The computer program in which the current version of the performance grammar for English has been implemented is, in effect, a "grammar tester" analogous to computerized grammar-testing programs based on transformational grammar (e.g., Friedman, 1971). Through successive amplifications of this program it should be possible to refine the analysis to discover and test performance grammar rules for production of any type of sentence. Some work has been done on performance grammar rules for German and Mandarin Chinese. It will be of interest to explore the performance grammar rules required in languages that, unlike English, use the basic order SOV (subject, object, verb) rather than SVO (Greenberg, 1966).

Thus far, in the construction of a performance grammar, there has been no concern with the functioning of so-called subcategorial constraints, e.g., those that specify what kinds of subjects or objects can be associated with particular verbs, mainly because such constraints do not operate within the grammar. Rather, they operate in the formation of the I-marker. As far as the performance grammar is concerned, a verb like *build*, for example, can take an object with a +human feature, as in sentence (65), which seems a perfectly reasonable one.

(65) *The mad biologist tried to build a man that flies.*

In general, the subcategorial constraints observed by linguists appear to be produced by semantic rather than syntactic factors. Also, contrary examples exist for many of the constraints. For example, it has been claimed (Stockwell, Schachter, and Partee, 1973, p. 56) that the verb *have* cannot be passivized. Yet, sentence (66) is often heard, and sentence (67) seems not entirely unacceptable.

(66) *A good time was had by everyone.*
(67) *An extensive discussion was had of the merits of the plan.*

## Application of the Model in Studying Language Acquisition

It is possible to use the performance grammar model in the analysis of child grammars. In early stages of language acquisition, a child has learned only some of the rules specified by a performance grammar, with the result that speech appears to be "telegraphic" (Brown and Bellugi, 1964). At the same time, some of the regularities found in a child's speech at early stages can be quite different from those of adult speech, as, for example, the placing of negative elements prior to verb elements. Such regularities can be incorporated in a "child performance grammar," and developmental changes toward adult speech can be described in terms of changes in the rule structure of such grammars. For illustration, developmental changes of this type have been implemented in a computer program (Stanley, 1976).

It has been observed (e.g., Bowerman, 1973) that language acquisition in the child seems to be motivated more by semantic than by syntactic considerations. Upon analysis, many of the rules of a performance grammar are semantically motivated, in that they depend upon semantic categorizations of the elements and variables in the I-marker as "deep subject," "theme," "copulative verb," and the like. There is, at any rate, no essential contradiction between a performance grammar analysis of child speech and the notion that development is semantically motivated. The performance grammar analysis does, however, provide a framework for describing the rules of word order that are the outcomes of learning that may be based on semantic factors.

## Interpretation of Various Phenomena of Interest

A grammar of language should provide an account of syntactic ambiguity in verbal output. The performance grammar does this by showing that identical outputs can be produced from different I-markers. Thus, the famous example, sentence (68), could be produced either from an

(68) *They are flying planes.*

I-marker that contains the copulative verb *be* and the complement noun-phrase *flying planes*, or from an I-marker containing the transitive verb *fly*, *planes* as DOB, and the progressive value of the variable ASP (aspect).

A performance grammar should, in addition, provide a framework for the analysis of speech hesitations and other phenomena having to do with the production of sentences in a live communication situation (Maclay and Osgood, 1959; Boomer, 1965; Goldman-Eisler, 1968). Performance grammar may be of particular value in describing points at which hesitations are most likely to occur, and in interpreting the sources of such hesitations.

## SUMMARY AND FINAL REMARKS

This chapter has outlined a performance grammar model for the syntactic aspects of message production. Such a performance grammar model constitutes an essential part of a larger theory of message production. Except insofar as the performance grammar makes certain assumptions about the nature of the elements and variables that are postulated to exist in I-markers that antecede message production, the chapter has little to say about the semantic aspects of message production. A comprehensive account of how situational, cognitive, and contextual variables activate the formation of I-markers has yet to be developed.

The rules of the performance grammar are couched in a form to make them applicable to the interpretation of language production in causal, behavioral terms, and hence to the teaching of language production in cases where the capabilities of language learners are not in themselves sufficient to permit the untutored acquisition of language competence. In such cases, the meanings to be expressed are present and available. What is lacking is the means to express those meanings. The performance grammar model will provide the means.

## REFERENCES

Bloomfield, L. 1933. Language. Holt, Rinehart & Winston, New York.

Boomer, D. D. 1965. Hesitation and grammatical encoding. Lang. Speech 8:148–158.

Bowerman, M. 1973. Early Syntactic Development: A Cross-Linguistic Study with Special Reference to Finnish. Cambridge University Press, Cambridge, England.

Brown, R., and Bellugi, U. 1964, Three processes in the child's acquisition of syntax. Harv. Educ. Rev. 34:133–151.

Carroll, J. B. 1958. Process and content in psycholinguistics. *In* R. A. Patton (ed.), Current Trends in the Description and Analysis of Behavior. University of Pittsburgh, Pittsburgh.

Carroll, J. B. 1973. Some suggestions from a psycholinguist. TESOL Q. 7:355–367.

Carroll, J. B. 1974. Towards a performance grammar of core sentences in spoken and written English. Intl. Rev. Appl. Ling. 12:29–49. (Special Festschrift issue in honor of B. Malmberg; G. Nickel,, ed.)

Chomsky, N. 1957. Syntactic Structures. Mouton, The Hague.

Chomsky, N. 1965. Aspects of the Theory of Syntax. The MIT Press, Cambridge, Mass.

Chomsky, N. 1968. Language and Mind. Harcourt, Brace & World, New York.

Danks, J. H. 1977. Producing ideas and sentences. *In* S. Rosenberg (ed.), Sentence Production: Developments in Research and Theory. Lawrence Erlbaum Associates, Hillsdale, N.J.

Ertel, S. 1977. Where do the subjects of sentences come from? *In* S. Rosenberg (ed.), Sentence Production: Developments in Research and Theory. Lawrence Erlbaum Associates, Hillsdale, N.J.

Fodor, J. A., Bever, T. G. and Garrett, M. F. 1974. The Psychology of Language. McGraw-Hill Book Co., New York.

Friedman, J. 1971. A Computer Model of Transformational Grammar. American Elsevier Publication Company, New York.

Goldman-Eisler, F. 1968. Psycholinguistics: Experiments in Spontaneous Speech. Academic Press, New York.

Greenberg, J. H. 1966. Some universals of grammar with particular reference to the order of meaningful elements. *In* J. H. Greenberg (ed.), Universals of Language. 2nd ed. The MIT Press, Cambridge, Mass.

Huddleston, R. D. 1971. The Sentence in Written English: A Syntactic Study Based on an Analysis of Scientific Texts. Cambridge University Press, Cambridge, England.

Hudson, R. A. 1971. English Complex Sentences: An Introduction to Systemic Grammar. North-Holland Publishing Co., Amsterdam.

Kaplan, R. M. 1972. Augmented transition networks as psychological models of sentence comprehension. Artific. Intell. 3:77–100.

Lashley, K. S. 1951. The problem of serial order in behavior. *In* L. A. Jeffress (ed.), Cerebral Mechanisms in Behavior. Hafner, New York.

Lenneberg, E. 1962. Understanding language without ability to speak: A case report. J. Abnorm. Soc. Psychol. 65:419–425.

Maclay, H., and Osgood, C. E. 1959. Hesitation phenomena in spontaneous English speech. Word 15:19–44.

Muir, J. 1972. A Modern Approach to English Grammar: An Introduction to Systemic Grammar. B. T. Batsford, Ltd., London.

Postovsky, V. A. 1974. Effects of delay in oral practice at the beginning of second language learning. Mod. Lang. J. 58:229–239.

Postovsky, V. A. 1975. On paradoxes in foreign language teaching. Mod. Lang. J. 59:18–21.

Rosenberg, S. 1977a. Introduction and overview. *In* S. Rosenberg (ed.), Sentence Production: Developments in Research and Theory. Lawrence Erlbaum Associates, Hillsdale, N.J.

Rosenberg, S. (ed.). 1977b. Sentence Production: Developments in Research and Theory. Lawrence Erlbaum Associates, Hillsdale, N.J.

Rumbaugh, D. M. (ed.). 1977. Language Learning by a Chimpanzee: The LANA Project. Academic Press, New York.

Schlesinger, I. M. 1971. Production of utterances and language acquisition. *In* D. I. Slobin (ed.). The Ontogenesis of Grammar: A Theoretical Symposium. Academic Press, New York.

Schlesinger, I. M. 1977. Components of a production model. *In* S. Rosenberg (ed.), Sentence Production: Developments in Research and Theory. Lawrence Erlbaum Associates, Hillsdale, N.J.

Stanley, S. C. 1976. Computer simulation of language acquisition: A developmental study. Unpublished undergraduate honors thesis, Department of Psychology, University of North Carolina at Chapel Hill, Chapel Hill.

Stockwell, R. P., Schachter, P., and Partee, B. H. 1973. The Major Syntactic Structures of English. Holt, Rinehart & Winston, New York.

# A Discussion of Special Issues

Richard L. Schiefelbusch

*Bureau of Child Research*
*University of Kansas*
*Lawrence, Kansas*

contents

This interpretative summary has four themes that concern both this volume and the preceding volume in this series, *Language Intervention from Ape to Child*. The themes will require discussion beyond the scope of these two publications, but the themes are important to language intervention programs in general, and to nonspeech language in particular.

In order of presentation the themes are: 1) *language designs*, 2) *language functions*, 3) *language interventions*, and 4) *special topics*.

## LANGUAGE DESIGNS

At the beginning of the Nonspeech Language Conference project, held in Gulf Shores, Alabama (which resulted in *Language Intervention from Ape to Child* as well as this book), the planners were concerned about language models and designs. The possible models we considered were focused on the output and input features of nonspeech communication. We were especially interested in a general design to describe alternative forms of nonspeech language. (See Schiefelbusch and Hollis, Chapter 1, this volume, and Hollis and Schiefelbusch, 1979.) Viewed in the perspective of both publications, we can claim success even though the comparisons and distinctions that we have highlighted are limited to referential functions of communication. Krauss (1979) and Glucksberg (1979) have clearly highlighted additional issues of communicative competence in social contexts. The codes of communicative behavior clearly are not embedded in the processing levels of language usage, that is, the rules of grammar, the perception of form, and the meaning of word strings. As Krauss points out, a psycholinguistic model of communication leaves out the context that gives the event its intended meaning. While analyzing the issues of nonspeech language in communication, the planners were concerned with the more obvious functions of receptive and expressive features and the ways messages are mediated. We were looking for ways to design equivalences for nonspeech systems that would be as functional as possible in comparison with spoken language. What has emerged, however, is a picture of the limitations of language models (both speech and nonspeech) for displaying the pragmatic functions that determine the success of a communication event. This indicates a need for further research on the social competence features of language and communication.

In the meantime, however, let us teach a system of equivalences (language alternatives) to children who cannot speak so that they can have a functional system to use as they grow and develop. In this way they will gain social experience and learn the pragmatic skills of influence and social hyperbole required in effective discourse. On the way to this advanced objective, they are likely to acquire cognitive skills that will serve them well in many contexts.

## LANGUAGE FUNCTIONS

This volume and the preceding volume indicate that the really functional test of a language system is in how well it serves an individual's communication needs. The presumption is that some language systems are better than others, i.e., more flexible, more complete, and more generalized to the society in which the individual lives. In this respect we could readily assume that speech-oriented language should always serve individual communication needs. However, this issue has already been addressed, and we have seen that some individuals have great difficulty acquiring speech.

This leads to the consideration of alternative systems. We must be concerned with the utility of the nonspeech system that the user develops and with how well the individual uses the language systems. Does the individual actually convey his intentions, secure cooperation, solve problems, describe events, or indicate a readiness for further communication? In short, is the individual's language functional?

Krauss (1979) points out that competence in the functional utilization of language exists apart from the mastery of the grammar or other specific features of the system. As an individual acquires and uses some system of symbolic behavior, he develops sensitive, effective ways of interacting with others. The pragmatic codes that derive from these experiences are essential to the individual's efforts to communicate. As Krauss (1979) has pointed out, there are almost no limits to the ways language can be used contextually to convey meaning.

But before a child can set about developing these communicative competencies, there must be a language system to serve the functions of these transactions. That system and its related experience should begin early in the child's life and should fill many of the child's waking hours. Long delays in acquiring a functional language system are detrimental to the acquisition of cognitive and social skills.

## LANGUAGE INTERVENTIONS

Harris and Vanderheiden (Chapter 11, this volume) discuss four barriers to symbolic communication. Although their discussion concerns physically handicapped children, the issues can be extrapolated to children with other primary disabilities. The barriers are: 1) the development of interactive and communication behaviors, 2) the development of primary physical communication mechanisms, 3) the development of symbolic representational skills, and 4) experience and practice with a symbol system.

A few words about each of these possible barriers should be enough to highlight their significance for language-impaired children. First, *interactive (communication) behavior* begins during infancy for normal children. Mahoney (1975), in discussing an ethological emphasis, speculates that language acquisition results from the synchronization of two behavioral systems, the communication system of the adult and the communication system of the child.

If a behavioral system is to be synchronous it must be shared. The infant and the adult must be able to respond to each other in kind. If they do not have a common communication mode and a common symbol system, interactive symbolic behaviors are not likely to develop. In the absence of such early experience there must be a design for such reciprocal practice at a later time.

*Physical communication mechanisms*, such as vocalizations, gestures, facial expressions, and other forms of cuing, instruct the adult(s) about the child's communicative intentions. These cues are especially apparent in the behavior of normal infants after the first six months. Richards (1974) discusses such cuing activity in communicative contexts and posits that the refinements of such cuing behavior lead to early forms of communicative competence.

Physically, intellectually, sensorially and emotionally handicapped children have more difficulty cuing and transacting with adult models. They also experience difficulty in imitating and responding to adult symbolic behavior.

*Cognitive development* and *symbolic representational skills* are promoted by experiences. Just as communicative behaviors emerge from adult and child transactions, so do symbolic skills. However, the latter emerge during a period of extensive exploration and in relation to a later period of the perceptual-motor period, probably during sensorimotor Stages 5 and 6. It is important to consider that symbolic skills are modeled and monitored for children during numerous activities within homes prior to similar efforts by professional teachers.

*Modeling* and *practice* can be made more effective in the home and in the formal training program if the modes and channels are matched to the child's developmental status. This matching of the topography of the symbol system with the capabilities of the developmentally handicapped child is an important feature of all five intervention programs in this book.

The procedures proposed by McDonald (Chapter 3), Harris and Vanderheiden (Chapters 11 and 12), and McNaughton and Kates (Chapter 13) are designed to help physically handicapped children overcome barriers to language. McDonald's system is excellent for small children in the home and in early educational settings. It provides for individualization and direct mapping of the child's environment, and the purposes of daily communication are considered and natural contexts are used extensively.

Harris and Vanderheiden plan competently and demonstrate skills in human engineering. They select the natural, intact mode of the child, no matter how limited, and provide a functional system for transactional experience. Their combined skills clearly enhance the field of augmentative communication. The combination of engineering and clinical planning allows them to design, adjust, and facilitate solutions and to overcome the obstacles that have traditionally limited the communication range of severely physically impaired children and adults.

McNaughton and Kates are also major contributors to the language and communication needs of physically impaired individuals. The success of the ingenious system of Blissymbolics is credited primarily to the developer of Blissymbols, Charles K. Bliss. Nevertheless, the clinical acumen and the creative foresight of McNaughton have led to adaptations of productive variations of the system. The practical impact of this system is observed in a number of critical aspects. Its iconicity makes it interesting and easy to learn. It is a system that can be shared with peers and adults. It bridges to reading. It lends itself to the limited response capabilities of severely physically impaired persons.

Woolman (Chapter 14) Wulz and Hollis (Chapter 15) Alpert (Chapter 16) and Schaeffer (Chapter 17) have developed special, adaptive programs for severely retarded, autistic, or multiply handicapped children.

Woolman's program of presymbolic instruction is for severely limited, nonverbal children. Her program may be unique. She has designed a communication program for children who do not speak or gesture and who do not attend to the speech and gestures of others. Her visual attending/matching/memory program advances children's capabilities for responding to their social environment. Her analysis of other nonspeech systems suggests that she is providing an antecedent program for subsequent language training. The skills she is teaching are usually learned during infancy by normal children. The approach she describes can lead to language programs, with speech, signing, or other systems. However, the specific procedures for such bridging are not provided.

Wulz and Hollis have used nonspeech modes of language instruction to teach word identification and comprehension. Their objectives are geared toward teaching reading skills. Their designs include the association of a printed word and a spoken word with their meaning. They were able to validate experimentally that reading skills can generalize to nonspeech language use.

Alpert and Schaeffer have each designed nonspeech intervention tactics with autistic children. Alpert is concerned with procedures for selecting the appropriate system for each child, whereas Schaeffer is concerned with the language and communication issues of the autistic. Alpert's procedures are instrumental in matching children and systems. On the other hand, Schaeffer's are designed to move the child from signs to speech. Both authors acknowledge the initial difficulty that autistic children have with speech, and each seeks to facilitate the development of a functional system. Schaeffer sees signs as a possible speech initiation system, and Alpert is interested in signs as an alternative language system.

In this book and the preceding volume there is the presumption that a language system (as well as the intervention designs used to teach the system) has functional components that can be analyzed and modified to serve individual needs and objectives. There is the presumption that language systems are subject to data analysis. This means that the operational acts of clinicians and the environmental designs used for instruction can be modified to refine and strengthen intervention features. If these presumptions are correct, the experimental validity of the procedures should lead us toward more powerful and more elegant intervention efforts.

Although the system of science, as applied to humans and nonhuman primates, has limitations, researchers can identify and refine important variables. We also derive experimental designs from a range of research fields, and we use automated data-handling systems and operational designs for planning and analyzing masses of data. We draw on sophisticated fields of study, including linguistics, anthropology, psychology, systems analysis, computer science, and neurophysiology. Yet we are handicapped by incomplete theories of language, human development, learning, and cognition. At times, our progress is spectacular. Nevertheless, one sees great areas of needed work and comes to the realization that the effort has just begun. We are still near the beginning of the journey. Even so it is good to know that additional groups of clinicians and researchers have extended their efforts to natural environments, including the home, while at the same time they have brought the problems of incomplete language and communication into the laboratories and the interdisciplinary clinical centers. It should be consoling to know that once a difficult problem gets the attention of society and is given a high priority by special segments of the research community, progress is made. In this perspective the *Nonspeech Language* theme is now on our agenda. Let's keep it there while we search for answers to the implied questions of both speakers and nonspeakers.

## SPECIAL TOPICS

Several special issues are considered in this section. The issues are highlighted because they have special relevance for nonspeech language and communication.

### The Issue of Perception

Tallal (Chapter 18) makes the point that children with language deficiencies often have auditory-perceptual problems. Although Tallal does not specifically study nonspeaking children, her research is pertinent for professionals in the nonspeech area of symbolization tasks to fit the child's processing capacities. Tallal's work highlights the importance of checking the possible auditory-perceptual deficits of children who have otherwise unexplained difficulty with language acquisition. One issue that might have special meaning is brought out by Woolman (Chapter 14). Her visual-motor procedures are based on the assumption that the severely limited children in her program can attend to visual stimuli more effectively than to auditory stimuli and that, indeed, a visual attending/matching/memory program can establish the basis for a more complex symbol system. This issue illustrates the importance of designing the mode and the topography of symbolization tasks to fit the child's processing capacities.

### The Issue of Signing

The historical analysis of American Sign Language presented in Section III highlights our persistent efforts to teach speech to children at all costs. By implication, at least, the "costs" may sometimes be very high. Moores (Chapter 5) and Stokoe (Chapter 8), together with the venerable Gallaudets (Chapters 6 and 7), make a strong case for sign language as a legitimate, prominent language system. They also give perspective to the controversies that have retarded the acceptance of various forms of signing as alternative communication systems and have impaired the potential uses of signing in teaching symbol functions to deaf children.

From this perspective the case for signing is clear. Nevertheless, the change will not take place for many years. New forms of training, new programs, new research, and even new generations may be required to bring about widespread uses of flexible sign systems in language training.

Although deaf education, in all its facets, provides the richest opportunity to study functional, nonspeech language, other areas should also be considered in similar detail. Lloyd (1976), Harris and Vanderheiden (Chapters 11 and 12), McDonald (Chapter 3) and McNaughton and Kates (Chapter 13) have given considerable attention to the language and communication problems of cerebral palsied individuals. Their capabilities are no longer measured exclusively by their abilities to speak. Similar efforts in behalf of the severely retarded and the autistic appear in this volume (Woolman, Chapter 14; Wulz and Hollis, Chapter 15; Alpert, Chapter 16; Schaeffer, Chapter 17).

There is some similarity among the issues that emerge in each area of work. Speech is preferred, but we should not perseverate beyond a point of futility in teaching speech to children who may already demonstrate that (for them) an alternative system is feasible, preferred, and functional. For other children who cannot make such declarations, we as professionals have a heavy responsibility.

**The Issue of Assessment**

Three chapters (3, 9, and 10) provide information about developmental problems that may result in a nonspeech status for children. In addition, two chapters (9 and 16) provide some indications about which nonspeech system to prescribe. Together, these chapters provide a state of the art report on nonspeech evaluation techniques. The issues presented are intriguing and insightful but incomplete. A great deal of new research is needed.

McDonald (Chapter 3) is concerned with respiratory irregularities that result in inadequate support for speech functions, especially phonation and loudness changes. The *at risk for speech* concept should become a prominent feature of birth-defect clinics and other infant and early childhood clinics. If speech probabilities can be assessed at an early age, alternative language systems can be initiated as a part of early acquisition phases. The emerging symbolization functions of the child can then be normalized.

Chapman and Miller (Chapter 9) look closely at the infant's emerging cognitive functions. They plot the cognitive stages of the child and determine the expectations for language/speech at each stage. Production delays can be expected if the cognitive level lags seriously. After creating an evaluation strategy based on developmental criteria they are able to identify children who are candidates for nonvocal systems.

Shane (Chapter 10) is concerned about the individual with impaired integration functions. He divides the functions into five subsections: vocal, linguistic; nonvocal, linguistic; representational; vocal, nonlinguistic; and nonvocal, nonlinguistic. Shane's evaluative system delineates factors that facilitate communicative growth. A key feature of this effect is to determine the integrity of transmission structures. Impairments in structures of speech may, of necessity, lead to an alternative symbolic expressive system.

In Chapter 16, Alpert presents a plan for assessing the behavioral status of the child and a plan for determining the preferred nonspeech mode. Although the plan was tested experimentally on a small number of autistic children and was limited to only three nonspeech systems, her training/assessment model should be useful for a broad set of clinical contexts and designs. This work may be the first to test the validity of such experimental efforts, but it surely will not be the last.

## The Issue of Grammar

Carroll's (Chapter 19) emphasis upon performance grammar presents another special intervention issue. Regardless of the topography of the symbols under consideration, they must be presented in a sequence. The order of the sequence has a great effect on meaning. In order to produce certain desired meanings the user may be called upon to create a novel string or to generate a different string from one already learned. Although Carroll is concerned primarily with the syntactic aspects of language, he does attempt to analyze the intention-markers (I-markers) that are apparently antecedent to message production. His system can serve as a starting point for research or for clinical experience designed to create a fully functional system of language. He points out that a "comprehensive account of how situational, cognitive, and contextual variables activate the formation of I-markers has yet to be developed" (page 499). This insightful and candid comment highlights much of the information that is needed but is, as yet, unavailable to the language interventionist.

The lack of knowledge about how a child learns or uses cognitive functions and how situational and contextual events influence subsequent language behavior produces a dilemma for the interventionist. The dilemma can be expressed as a question: Is it better to use what we know about language to design and teach a formal language system or is it better to simply expand a child's experiences in natural contexts which allow the child to abstract and synthesize a natural language?

There is much to be said for each possibility. What clinicians may tend to do, because they are resourceful and because they are forced to innovate beyond the teaching procedures provided for them, is to use as formal a system as they can within as natural a context as they can devise. In short, they attempt to combine elements of both. As they do that, however, they will need to think along with Carroll and design some performance features to give the child a response repertoire to use in functional contexts. However, it is also likely that the contexts will progressively determine the generative and the pragmatic variations that the child uses. The more the clinician knows about the communication of the child the easier will be the transition from a formal performance grammar to an informal, functional grammar that meets the child's needs in the natural environment. This principle is likely to apply equally well to language learned through speaking or language learned in some alternative form that also can be shared within the child's environment.

## SUMMARY

This is a book about nonspeaking children. It is not a book about how to teach them speech. Instead it is about alternative and augmentative modes of communication using manual, lexical, or physically manipulable symbols. The children who are the subject of this book could be designated "nonspeaking" and could be classified as severely physically handicapped, or deaf-handicapped, or cognitively handicapped, or autistically handicapped. This simple classification system suggests that among *nonverbal children* there are four sets of problems—motor problems, sensory problems, cognitive problems, and autistic problems.

These distinctions are especially useful in delineations made by clinicians and others who work with children who have been referred for services. However, the classification categories are also useful for researchers. For instance, severely physically impaired children may have difficulty making expressive responses (forming words), while a deaf child may be impaired for both receptive and expressive speech. Although the problem of speaking is radically different for each of these disability groups, each has difficulty learning standard modes of linguistic expression. Consequently, the alternatives to standard speech for each group is different. For instance, the deaf child may use a manual system of language expression that combines hand and other body language movements of great subtlety and dexterity which the physically impaired child cannot manage. In contrast, the severely physically impaired child may have normal sensitivity to speech inputs and may require only an alternative response mode in order to transact language. Consequently, the physically impaired child listens normally and responds by indicating visual symbols on a communication board. Thus, both deaf and severely physically handicapped children become functional language users by adapting a language system congruent with their functional modes. The physically handicapped child uses a communication board, and a deaf child uses signs. The simplicity of this analysis is deceiving, but it clarifies alternative language interventions.

Nonspeaking severely retarded and autistic children may be more difficult to analyze. Their problem(s) focuses on transmission. For instance, each may have echolalic speech and each may selectively respond to speech instructions. Nevertheless, there may be little consistent functional language and communication. Individual children from either group may learn sign language or other physical representations of language more readily than they learn speech. This observation holds even under conditions of expert instruction.

This discussion is not a comprehensive analysis of nonspeech language issues. It is intended to emphasize the need for careful planning in language programs for differentially impaired children. Several points should be made in summarizing the content of this book:

1. Meaningful individual differences can be identified and used in planning language intervention programs.
2. Among the individual differences are physical, sensory, cognitive, and affective features that may indicate which nonspeech mode of language the child may use the most advantageously.
3. The individual differences and the options (alternative modes) can be matched to produce a functional language system.
4. Although the alternative modes are functional, at this stage of nonspeech language intervention they are not optimal. Further research is needed.
5. Nonspeech language modes may (under certain conditions) facilitate or augment speech and produce better communication.

## REFERENCES

Glucksberg, S. 1979. Language and communication models: Summary discussion. *In* R. L. Schiefelbusch and J. H. Hollis (eds.), Language Intervention from Ape to Child, pp. 107–117. University Park Press, Baltimore.

Hollis, J. H., and Schiefelbusch, R. L. 1979. A general system for language analysis: Ape and child. *In* R. L. Schiefelbusch and J. H. Hollis (eds.), Language Intervention from Ape to Child, pp. 3–42. University Park Press, Baltimore.

Krauss, R. M. 1979. Communication models and communicative behavior. *In* R. L. Schiefelbusch and J. H. Hollis (eds.), Language Intervention from Ape to Child, pp. 49–72. University Park Press, Baltimore.

Lloyd, L. L. (ed.). 1976. Communication Assessment and Intervention Strategies. University Park Press, Baltimore.

Mahoney, G. J. 1975. Ethological approach to delayed language acquisition. Am. J. Ment. Defic. 80.

ichards, M. P. M. 1974. The development of psychological communication in first year of life. *In* K. Connolly and J. Bruner (eds.), The Growth of etence. Academic Press, New York.

# index